LATE
VICTORIAN
POETRY
1880–1899

CATHERINE W. REILLY

LATE VICTORIAN POETRY

1880–1899

AN ANNOTATED
BIOBIBLIOGRAPHY

First published 1994 by
Mansell Publishing Limited, *A Cassell imprint*
Villiers House, 41/47 Strand, London WC2N 5JE, England
387 Park Avenue South, New York, New York 10016–8810, USA

British Library Cataloguing in Publication Data
Reilly, Catherine W.
　　Late Victorian Poetry, 1880–99:Annotated
　　Biobibliography
　　I. Title
　　016.8218

　　ISBN 0–7201–2001–2

Library of Congress Cataloging-in-Publication Data
Reilly, Catherine W.
　　Late Victorian poetry, 1880–1899 : an annotated biobibliography
Catherine W. Reilly.
　　　　p. cm.
　　Includes bibliographical references and index.
　　ISBN 0–7201–2001–2 : $140.00
　　　1. English poetry–19th century–Bio-bibliography. I. Title.
　　Z2014.P7R453　1994
　　[PR581]
　　016.821′808–dc20　　　　　　　　　　　　　　　　　94–4657
　　　　　　　　　　　　　　　　　　　　　　　　　　　　　　CIP

Typeset by York House Typographic Ltd.
Printed and bound in Great Britain by Biddles Ltd, Guildford and King's Lynn

CONTENTS

To the memory of my father,
Frederick Cornelius Reilly

ACKNOWLEDGEMENTS

I am extremely grateful to those who have helped me, in various ways, with the preparation of this book. My thanks are due to the following: the librarians and staffs of all the libraries visited in the course of my research, especially the staffs of the libraries where most of my work was carried out, i.e. the Department of Printed Books, Bodleian Library, Oxford; The British Library, London; Manchester Central Library; and the Department of Special Collections, University of California, Davis; to Joan Unsworth of The North West Regional Library System, Manchester; Alice Lock of Tameside Libraries & Arts; Michael Redhead of Trafford Library Service; John Thorn of Hampshire County Libraries; and Geoffrey Wright of Leicestershire Libraries and Information Service; to Patricia Doran, Lorna Fergusson, Anne Harvey, Catherine and Fergus Lee, Ann MacEwan, R. Julian Roberts, Barbara and Richard Small, Barbara Tostevin, Edna Walmsley, Elon and Elizabeth Wells, and the President and Fellows of Lucy Cavendish College, Cambridge; and finally to The British Academy for the award of a personal research grant, without which the work could not have been completed.

INTRODUCTION

The national libraries, university libraries, and older-established public reference libraries in the United Kingdom are filled with volumes of poetry and verse published in the Victorian period. Yet the vast majority of the authors of these volumes are completely unknown as no comprehensive bibliography of Victorian poetry exists, a situation I have attempted to remedy with this first volume, covering publications from 1880 to 1899, of what is planned to be a three-volume work.

In this book 2,964 authors of the United Kingdom (England, Ireland, Scotland, Wales) are identified, although some only by initials or pseudonym. In addition there are 101 titles for which no author could be found. Of the authors 579 were women but there may be many more as sometimes only initials rather than forenames were used. Included are a small number of writers from abroad who had settled in the United Kingdom and so were familiar with Victorian life. Also included are some writers born in the United Kingdom who emigrated or worked abroad for long periods. Many Britons spent most of their working lives in 'far-flung outposts', helping to maintain the British Empire across the globe. A great number, largely from the working class, emigrated to find a better way of life, the preferred countries being Australia, Canada and the United States of America. Not included are works by authors who had died before 1880, even though editions of their works were published after that date. It is intended to record these editions in another volume of this bibliography alongside the original editions published within the period of an author's life.

The amount of material is so large that certain specialist categories have had to be omitted from this study to make it viable. These are volumes consisting *exclusively* of: verse drama; dialect; hymns with music; songs with music; native languages other than English, i.e. Gaelic, Irish and Welsh; literal translations from foreign languages; pamphlets, defined as items having fewer than eight leaves, i.e. fifteen or sixteen pages; children's verse, although an occasional important item in the latter category is included, e.g. Robert Louis Stevenson's *A Child's Garden of Verses*. However, elements of all these categories do appear within the volumes listed.

The whole panorama of Victorian life at the end of the nineteenth century is represented. The poets came from all strata of society. Then, as now, writing poetry was not a full-time job, and even the most popular poets earned a living by other means, often by other forms of writing. A cursory examination of the biographical notes reveals some of the occupations followed, and there are many others: accountant; actor; archaeologist; architect; artist; auctioneer; banker; barrister; blacksmith; botanist; carpenter; civil servant; clergyman (of all denominations, and ranking from curate to archbishop); clerk; company director; composer; cowherd; diplomat; draper; engraver; estate agent; farmer; flax dresser; glazier; governess; house painter; ironmonger; journalist; lace maker; landowner; librarian; local government officer; maidservant; manufacturer (of cotton, jewellery, metal, silk, wool, etc.); merchant seaman; mineralogist; musician; newspaper proprietor; pattern maker; physician; policeman; postman; railway worker; school inspector; shepherd; shipowner; soldier (of all ranks from private to general); solicitor; spinner; stockbroker; stonedyker; storekeeper; surgeon; teacher (parish school to university level); warp dresser; watchmaker; weaver. Many names not usually associated with the writing of verse emerged, e.g. William Friese-Greene, pioneer of cinematography, and Thomas Henry Huxley, distinguished scientist.

The Victorian age was not only a period of exciting scientific and technical discovery leading to a huge expansion of industry and trade, it also brought progress in free education for all provided by the state. In 1850 it was reported that fewer than eight per cent of the nation's children attended school but the Education Acts of 1870 and 1872 ensured literacy of the masses. The educated upper and middle classes had always had the means to appear in print but for members of the working class a new-found pride in the ability to read and write often led to a wish to publish, and poetry seems to have been a favourite medium. Publication was comparatively easy as there were many printing houses in even the smallest provincial town. Quite often printers were also publishers and booksellers; some had access to established London publishers who were willing to share the cost of publication. Sometimes would-be authors were able to raise the necessary money by subscription. One wonders how many of these volumes of verse were successful in business terms. Comparatively few of the publishing houses have survived to the present day; some of the exceptional names are W.H. Allen, Blackwell, The Bodley Head, Burns & Oates, Cassell, Chapman & Hall, Chatto & Windus, Eyre & Spottiswoode, Heinemann, Longman, Macmillan, and Murray, though not all still publish poetry. Several firms, such as Grant Richards, Jarrolds, Elkin Mathews, Simpkin, Marshall, Hamilton, Kent, and Elliot Stock, survived until well into the twentieth century, while others were absorbed into larger publishing companies or went into other kinds of business, often into printing or retail trade.

The poets themselves appear to have been conscious of the vagaries of poetry publication. George Henry Wilson, a factory worker of Ossett, Yorkshire, was under no delusion when he wrote in the preface to his volume *Miscellaneous Poems*, published in 1896: 'I am perfectly aware that the country is almost flooded with books of poems, and that the general reader has not much taste for this class of literature. Yet I hope, notwithstanding the adverse criticism which I know this small volume will receive, that nevertheless it may do some little good to those who peruse its contents.'

The major Victorian poets, those whose work forms the accepted canon of nineteenth-century British poetry, are well documented and intensively studied. Their publications are already covered by existing bibliographies and so, to avoid unnecessary listing, in each case I have given details of the most authoritative bibliography available.

There are many minor and lesser poets whose work, although interesting and of some merit, is virtually unknown. These minor poets certainly deserve further investigation from a late-twentieth-century perspective. I am reminded of T.S. Eliot's words on 'Minor Poetry', December 1944: 'Has this poet something to say, a little different from what anyone has said before, and has he found, not only a different way of saying it, but *the* different way of saying it which expresses the difference in what he is saying? When you read poetry by someone whose name is not yet widely known, someone whom the reviewers have not yet passed, you are exercising, or should be exercising, your own taste. *There is nothing else to go by* . . . I need time in order to know what I really felt at the moment. And that feeling is not a judgement of greatness or importance: it is an awareness of *genuineness*'. Of course Eliot was referring to new and emerging poets of the mid-twentieth century but the same test could be applied to unknown poets of any period. Poetry can be a clever and sensitive form of writing. Even those poets whose work is of modest literary merit should attract more attention; their verses reflect on life in their time, often saying in a few telling lines what would otherwise take a chapter of prose.

The research for this biobibliography has been carried out in a variety of libraries. The major national libraries, now 'copyright libraries', based at the British Library, London, the Bodleian Library, Oxford, Cambridge University Library, the National Library of Scotland in Edinburgh, the National Library of Wales at Aberystwyth, and Trinity College, Dublin, were obviously the prime locations in which to seek Victorian poetry. The holdings of these libraries are large but not comprehensive. The Copyright Act entitling them to receive free copies of books published in the United Kingdom did not come into force until 1911. As educational institutions obliged to cater for formal academic courses of study they would have been unlikely to purchase items perceived as ephemeral. Today these libraries are all endeavouring to fill the gaps by purchase when possible.

I was fortunate at the beginning of my research to be made aware of a remarkable collection of Minor British Poets, 1789–1918, in the Library at the University of California, Davis, housed in the Department of Special Collections. This collection was assembled by the bookseller C.C. Kohler over a period of twelve years. The two principles guiding his selection of titles were – that all be poetry and all be minor. A printed catalogue to the collection was published, and I was able to examine the volumes pertaining to the Victorian period before visiting the collection; these are *Part Two The Early Victorian Period 1840–1869* and *Part Three The Later Victorian Period, 1870-1899*. In his introduction to Part II Professor G.B. Tennyson, of the University of California, Los Angeles, describes it as 'a collection of extraordinary rarity and value that has enormous potential for enriching our understanding of the

Victorian age in literature'. As a bibliographer I must agree with his verdict wholeheartedly.

It was well worth travelling to use this collection and to find the books so easily accessible in one place. The fact is that it is surprisingly difficult to trace poetry by an individual author unless one knows the author's name. Library catalogues almost always give only one entry i.e. under the author. This is fine in the case of prominent authors already popular but present a real problem with unknown authors. To maintain a subject catalogue covering individual authors would create duplication and take up scarce space; therefore one finds that entries under the subject heading VICTORIAN POETRY tend to refer only to anthologies, histories, and general critical studies of Victorian poetry. Computerized catalogues go some way to solving this problem but in most cases they reveal only items where such key words as 'poems', 'verses', 'sonnets', etc. form part of a work's title. Sometimes a library's 'shelf list' (a vital record of library holdings not usually available for public scrutiny) will reveal new names but this cannot occur unless the shelf list is arranged by subject classification. Occasionally items of poetry have been classified under subject matter rather than form; this happens most usually with works on particular public figures or works on particular topographical locations. The result could be that these works may never be found.

Many items not found in the copyright libraries were located in the older public libraries established before the end of the nineteenth century, e.g. Birmingham, Liverpool, Manchester, Newcastle upon Tyne. All have expanded their local history collections from the time when 'local studies' was first accepted as a suitable subject for academic research. The private sub-scription libraries e.g. The Leeds Library, The Portico Library in Manchester, The Devon & Exeter Institution in Exeter, were also a good source of material with emphasis on the local area.

On some occasions I was unable to locate a copy of a volume of poems known to exist from evidence in catalogues or bibliographies. Such a case is indicated by the addition of an asterisk at the end of the entry. My time at the University of California, Davis, was limited; consequently I was unable to examine a number of volumes listed in its printed catalogues.

There is an immense variety of style and theme in the volumes that comprise this biobibliography. Much of the verse is of a religious nature, typical of an age when religious faith was widespread. Contemplative, meditative and philo-sophical poems are often sub-titled 'musings' or 'lays' or 'lyrics' or even 'breathings'. Narrative poems based on fictional or factual incidents are common and often very lengthy; Greek, Roman, Norse and Arthurian legend were often the inspiration. Nature poems abound, no doubt an inheritance from the Romantic period. The social conditions of the poor are portrayed in sympathetic fashion although some poets appeared to believe that the great inequalities were in the natural order of things. Many poets chose to write about their own localities, and there is a wealth of poems about holiday places at home and abroad. Members of the royal family were a constant source of poetic attention which increased markedly on such occasions as the jubilees of Queen

Victoria in 1887 and 1897 and the wedding of the Duke of York and Princess Mary of Teck, later King George V and Queen Mary, in 1893. Political figures such as Gladstone and Disraeli, and popular heroes like General Gordon of Khartoum, are also commonly featured, as are general political matters, the question of Home Rule for Ireland being one of the regular themes. However, the most popular theme of all was love, easily surpassing the 'in memoriam' poems which were a feature of an age when infant mortality was high and life expectancy was short.

This biobibliography will fill a long-existing gap in the history of English literature; it will provide the 'seed cord' for scholars of nineteenth-century poetry; it will become a working tool for librarians, social historians, bibliographers, antiquarian booksellers, and others.

ARRANGEMENT OF THE MATERIAL

The biobibliography is arranged in a single alphabetical sequence in author order, then title order of individual works. Anonymous works are listed under the title. A separate title index lists all distinctive titles. Volumes with contributions by more than two poets are not included. When two poets share a volume, working either in collaboration or separately, the entry is given twice, i.e. under each poet's name.

A version of a standard library catalogue entry is used, the data given being sufficient to identify any item easily. The information in each entry is given in the following sequence: title, sub-title; editor, compiler, etc.; edition if other than the first; place of publication; publisher, or printer in the absence of a publisher's name; date of publication; pagination; illustrations; series; annotations; library location.

The system of alphabetization used is 'word by word' or 'nothing before something' except for the 'Key to Library Locations', 'Abbreviations' and lists which are 'letter by letter'. For filing purposes the definite or indefinite article at the beginning of a title is ignored. Surnames with the prefix 'Saint' are filed in one single sequence, no matter whether the prefix is in the form 'Saint' or 'St'. Scottish surnames with the prefix 'Mac' are filed in one single sequence, no matter whether the prefix is in the form 'Mac', 'Mc', or 'M''.

The form of publisher's name given on the title-page is preferred, although this can be inconsistent and vary from book to book. For the sake of brevity in company names the following abbreviations are employed: '&' replaces 'and'; 'Co.' replaces 'Company'; 'Ltd' replaces 'Limited'.

When the date of publication is not printed inside the book, the supposed publication date is given, in square brackets, from allusions in the text or from outside sources such as bibliographies and library catalogues. If there is some doubt about the supposed date this is indicated by a question mark (e.g. [1887?]).

The number of pages in single-volume works is given in arabic numerals, counting the colophon page, if any. Preliminary matter is usually separately paged by means of roman numerals. The pagination is thus recorded (e.g. xviii, 195 pp.) Unnumbered pages are given in square brackets with certain exceptions: when there are blank pages between the preliminary matter and the text, these pages are counted in the pagination of the preliminary matter; when the final page of text, sometimes a colophon page, is unnumbered, as is often the case, it is counted in the pagination of the text.

When a book belongs to a series, the name of the series is given in curved brackets at the end of the entry, followed by the serial number, if any e.g. (Garland of new poetry, I).

Authors' names are given in their most complete form as found in the bibliographical sources consulted, followed by any other forms of names used. Cross-references are given from all alternative forms of name to the form of name selected here, the author's real name being preferred.

Noblemen are listed under their family name with a cross-reference from their title, no matter which form of name appears on the title-page, e.g. CAMPBELL, George Douglas, Duke of Argyll (author wrote as Duke of Argyll).

Pseudonymous authors are listed under their real name, when this can be ascertained, e.g. HANSON, Samuel, (Halifax Cheesemonger, pseud.), with a cross-reference made from HALIFAX CHEESEMONGER, pseud.

Married women are listed under either their maiden name or their married name, depending on which form of name was used most consistently in their publications, with appropriate cross-references given.

Double-barrelled hyphenated names (e.g. QUILLER-COUCH, Sir Arthur Thomas) are listed under the first part of the name with a cross-reference from the second part. Double-barrelled names without a hyphen (e.g. MARRIOTT WATSON, Rosamund) are listed under the first part of the name with a cross reference from the second part.

Brief biographical notes are given on each poet where possible, the details coming from the standard biographical and reference works listed in the Select Bibliography of Biographical Sources and from many other works. A foreword or introduction to a poet's work can often provide good and reliable information. In some cases only a poet's dates or the place where he lived was forthcoming; in several hundred cases no biographical details of any kind could be found. The amount of information given in the notes bears no relationship to the importance of a particular author. Data were compiled from so many different sources that the notes are of uneven quality and occasionally bizarre. County names used prior to the local government re-organization of 1974 are retained; locations now forming part of city suburbia were country hamlets at the end of the nineteenth century.

All titles are those of first editions unless otherwise stated. The statement of other editions than the first follows the title in each entry. The pagination of later 'editions' is often identical to that of the first edition, implying no substantial change in the text, in which case a note follows the entry for the first edition (e.g. Also 2nd ed. 1888; 3rd ed. 1891). When a later edition is obviously different, i.e. enlarged or revised or illustrated or produced by a different publisher, then a full new entry is given. Occasionally only later editions of a work are recorded. In this situation either the first edition was published prior to 1880 in a shorter version or it was impossible to find any copy of the first edition.

When a title-page is missing from the particular copy of a work examined or where there is no proper title-page, as is sometimes the case in privately printed items, the title is taken from the cover of the book and this is indicated by the phrase 'Title from cover' as an annotation.

On the occasions when two publishing houses have collaborated in the publication of a book, the names of both publishers are given in the entry, separated by a semi-colon, (e.g. Paisley; J. & R. Parlane; London: Houlston & Sons).

Many works were not handled by commercial publishers but were privately printed. When a publisher's name does not appear inside the book, the implication usually is that the book has been privately printed for the author, or another private individual, at his own expense. In these cases, when the printer's name appears anywhere in the book, it is included as part of the entry in lieu of a publisher and is prefixed by the word 'Printed' (e.g. Printed Aberdeen: G. Cornwall & Sons). This information is particularly useful as it often denotes the area where a poet lived. More often than not he would be inclined to use a local printer. When a title-page bears the information the fact is recorded at the end of the entry as an annotation (e.g. Privately printed for the author).

Privately printed books in this sense should not be confused with books that emanate from private presses. A private press is usually a small establishment using hand presses or small letterpress machines, producing well-printed books often on hand-made paper and often in limited editions. The owner prints solely what he chooses, often his own work or the work of a particular circle of friends, or perhaps some other work (usually previously printed) that he finds attractive.

The annotations to the entries give supplemental information of many kinds, gleaned from the books themselves in some cases. An annotation is placed within single inverted commas if it is reproduced verbatim from the book concerned and/or if it is not in the wording or style which would have been ideally chosen.

The following examples represent the kind of annotation most commonly encountered:

a. Title from cover.
b. Printed for private circulation.
c. Printed on one side of leaf only.
d. Printed on card.
e. Parallel English and French texts.
f. A limited ed. of 250 copies signed by the author.
g. 'The profits will be given to St. Lucy's Free Hospital for Sick Children at Kingsholme, Gloucester'.
h. Cover-title is *Little poems*. [In this case the cover-title differs from the title printed on the title-page].

At the end of each main entry a symbol denotes the library where the book was seen but does not imply that this is the only library holding a copy. An asterisk denotes that it was not possible for a copy of the book to be examined.

KEY TO LIBRARY LOCATIONS

BIP	Birmingham Central Library
BL	British Library
BLD	British Library Document Supply Centre, Boston Spa
BOP	Bolton Central Library
BUP	Bury Central Library
CHE	Chetham's Library, Manchester
CPL	Chester Central Library
CU	Cambridge University Library
DEI	Devon & Exeter Institution, Exeter
EC	English Catalogue
EPL	Edinburgh Central Library
GPR	Priaulx Library, Guernsey
HPL	Heywood Public Library
JRL	John Rylands University Library of Manchester
LEP	Leeds Central Library
LL	The Leeds Library
MPL	Manchester Central Library
MPO	The Portico Library, Manchester
NLI	National Library of Ireland, Dublin
NLP	Newcastle upon Tyne Literary & Philosophical Society
NLS	National Library of Scotland, Edinburgh
NLW	National Library of Wales, Aberystwyth
NPL	Newcastle upon Tyne Central Library
NUC	National Union Catalog, Pre-1956 Imprints
OPL	Oldham Central Library
OXB	Bodleian Library, Oxford
RPL	Rochdale Central Library
TAU	Local History Library, The Castle, Taunton
TCD	Trinity College, Dublin
TPL	Stalybridge Public Library, Tameside
UCD	University of California, Davis
WCM	Working Class Movement Library, Salford
WPL	Birkenhead Public Library, Wirral

ABBREVIATIONS

★	No copy seen
anon.	anonymous
ARIBA	Associate of the Royal Institute of British Architects
b.	born
BA	Bachelor of Arts
Bart	Baronet
BBC	British Broadcasting Corporation
BCL	Bachelor of Civil Law
BD	Bachelor of Divinity
Bros	Brothers
BS	Bachelor of Surgery
CIE	Companion of the Indian Empire
Co.	Company
col.	coloured
CSI	Companion of the Star of India
DBE	Dame Commander of the British Empire
DCL	Doctor of Civil Law
DD	Doctor of Divinity
D.Litt.	Doctor of Letters
Dr	Doctor
DSc	Doctor of Science
ed./eds	edition/s
facsim./s	facsimile/s
FCS	Fellow of the Chemical Society
FEIS	Fellow of the Educational Institute of Scotland
FGS	Fellow of the Geological Society
FLS	Fellow of the Linnean Society
FRCP	Fellow of the Royal College of Physicians
FRCS	Fellow of the Royal College of Surgeons
FRGS	Fellow of the Royal Geographical Society
FRHS	Fellow of the Royal Horticultural Society
FRIBA	Fellow of the Royal Institute of British Architects
FRMet.S	Fellow of the Royal Meteorological Society
FRS	Fellow of the Royal Society
FRSL	Fellow of the Royal Society of Literature
FSA	Fellow of the Society of Antiquaries/Arts
FSS	Fellow of the Statistical Society

FZS	Fellow of the Zoological Society
GHQ	General Headquarters
HM	Her/His Majesty's
HMS	Her/His Majesty's Ship
Hon.	Honorary/Honourable
il.	illustrated/illustration/s
JP	Justice of the Peace
Jun.	Junior
Ld	Limited
Lim.	Limited
LL.B	Bachelor of Laws
LL.D	Doctor of Laws
LL.M	Master of Laws
LRCP	Licentiate of the Royal College of Physicians
LRCS	Licentiate of the Royal College of Surgeons
Ltd	Limited
MA	Master of Arts
MB	Bachelor of Medicine
M.Ch	Master of Surgery
MD	Doctor of Medicine
MP	Member of Parliament
MRAS	Member of the Royal Academy of Science/Royal Asiatic Society
MRCP	Member of the Royal College of Physicians
MRCS	Member of the Royal College of Surgeons
ms/mss	manuscript/s
PEN	(International Association of) Poets, Playwrights, Writers, Essayists and Novelists
Ph.D	Doctor of Philosophy
por.	portrait/s
pp.	pages
pseud.	pseudonym
QC	Queen's Counsel
Rev.	Reverend
RN	Royal Navy
RNVR	Royal Naval Volunteer Reserve
St	Saint
vol./vols	volume/s
WEA	Workers' Educational Association
YMCA	Young Men's Christian Association
YWCA	Young Women's Christian Association

SELECT BIBLIOGRAPHY OF
BIOGRAPHICAL SOURCES

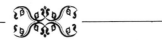

ALLIBONE, S. Austin. *A critical dictionary of English literature, and British and American authors, living and deceased* . . . Philadelphia: Childs & Peterson; J.B. Lippincott & Co. 1859–73. 3 vols.
Also *Supplement*; by John Foster Kirk, Philadelphia: J.B. Lippincott Co. 1891. 2 vols.

ANDREWS, William. *Modern Yorkshire poets*. Hull: A Brown & Sons; London: Simpkin, Marshall, & Co. 1885.

BATESON, F.W., editor. *The Cambridge bibliography of English literature*. Cambridge: University Press. 1940–57. 5 vols.

BOASE, Frederic. *Modern English biography* . . . Truro: Netherton & Welsh. 1892. 6 vols.

BRADY, Anne M., & Cleeve, Brian. *A bibliographical dictionary of Irish Writers*. Mullingar: Lilliput Press. 1985.

The CAMBRIDGE HISTORY OF ENGLISH LITERATURE. Cambridge: University Press. 1918–21. 4 vols.

CRONE, John S. *A concise dictionary of Irish biography*. Revised & enlarged ed. Dublin: Talbot Press. 1937.

DAVIS, Gwenn, & JOYCE, Beverly A. *Poetry by women to 1900: a bibliography of American and British Writers*. London: Mansell Publishing Ltd. 1991.

The DICTIONARY OF NATIONAL BIOGRAPHY . . . FROM THE EARLIEST TIMES TO 1900. London: Oxford University Press. 1885–1901. 22 vols. Also *Supplements*, 1901–11 – 1941–50. London: Oxford University Press. 1912–59

EDWARDS, D.H. *Modern Scottish poets with biographical and critical notes*. Brechin: Edwards. 1880–97. 16 vols.

FOSTER, Joseph. *Oxford men and their colleges illustrated with portraits and views*. Oxford: James Parker & Co. 1893. 2 vols.

HALKETT, Samuel, & LAING, John. *Dictionary of anonymous and pseudonymous English literature*. London: Oliver & Boyd. 1934.

KUNITZ, Stanley J., & HAYCRAFT, Howard. *British authors of the nineteenth century*. New York: H.W. Wilson Co. 1936.

MURDOCH, Alexander G. *The Scottish poets, recent and living*. Glasgow: Thomas D. Morison; London: Hamilton, Adams & Co. 1883.

MYERS, Robin, editor. *A dictionary of literature in the English language from Chaucer to 1940*. Compiled for the National Book League. Oxford: Pergamon Press. 1970. 2 vols.

O'DONOGHUE, D.J. *The poets of Ireland: a biographical and bibliographical dictionary of Irish writers of English verse*. Dublin: Hodges Figgis & Co., Ltd; London: Oxford University Press. 1912.

SHARP, R. Farquharson. *A dictionary of English authors: biographical and bibliographical*. New ed. London: Kegan Paul, Trench, Trübner & Co., Ltd. 1904.

VENN, J.A., compiler. *Alumni cantabrigienses: a biographical list of all known students, graduates and holders of office at the University of Cambridge from the earliest times to 1900*. Part II. From 1752 to 1900. Cambridge: University Press. 1940.

VINSON, James, & KIRKPATRICK, D.L., editors. *Poets*. London: Macmillan Press Ltd. 1979. (Great Writers of the English Language Series).

WHO WAS WHO Vol. I. 1897–1915 – Vol. V. 1951–1960. London: Adam & Charles Black. 1920–61.

The recent publication of two biographical archives on microfiche, between them covering 1,524 biographical reference works, have proved a helpful and time-saving aid to research. They are *British & Irish Biographies, 1840–1940*, published by Chadwyck-Healey with a partial index, and *British Biographical Archive* published by K.G. Saur in a single-alphabet cumulation.

THE BIOBIBLIOGRAPHY

A

A. *see* **ADAMS, Alfred Wallace**, (A.)

A. *see* **SHORE, Arabella**, (A.)

A., A.W. *see* **AULD, Agnes Wellwood**, (A.W.A.)

A., E. *see* **RUSSELL, George William**, (A.E.)

A., F.S. Of Cheltenham, Gloucestershire.
A legend of Saint Kew, in three parts: being a sheet omitted in the ancient annals of Kewstoke. Printed Cheltenham. 1888. 16 pp. il.
Printed for the author. *★UCD*

A., G.J.
A summer day beneath the cliffs, and other poems; by G.J.A. Printed Bournemouth: W. Mate & Sons, Ltd. [1898]. [iv], 45 pp.
Printed for private circulation. *OXB*

A., J. *see* **ANDREWS, John**, (J.A.)

A., J. *see* **ASHTON, J.**, (J.A.)

A., O.B. Lived at 1 Hornsey Rise Gardens, and afterwards at 5 Station Parade, Hornsey Rise, London N.
Fashion our master: a satirical review; by O.B.A. London: Beveridge & Co. [1883]. 16 pp. *OXB*
Hope, Life's treasurer; by O.B.A. Hornsey Rise, London: Hamor House. 1884. [23] pp.
Printed on one side of leaf only. *OXB*
Sentiment, or salvation?, and other short poems; by O.B.A. Hornsey Rise, London: Hamor Press. 1898. 20 pp. *OXB*
The tankard in grief: a warning; by O.B.A. London: Beveridge & Co. [1883]. 16 pp. *OXB*
Twin-love; by O.B.A. London: H.B. Miller. [1883]. 15 pp. *OXB*

A., R.M.E. *see* **ASHE, Robert Martyn** with **ASHE, Emily**, (R.M.E.A.)

A., T.B.
The praises of heroes: [poems]; by T.B.A. London: Burns & Oates, Ld; New York: Catholic Publication Society Co. [1888]. viii, 117 pp. *BL*

A-Y-D, S. *see* **APPLEYARD, S.**

ABBAY, Richard (1844–1924). Son of Thomas Abbay of Hunday Field near
Aldborough, Yorkshire. Educated at St Peter's School, York, and Exeter
College, Oxford. Lecturer in natural science, King's College, London, 1868;
Fellow of Wadham College, Oxford, 1869. He carried out scientific research
in Ceylon, Australia, Java, New Caledonia, New Zealand and California;
contributed papers to learned societies on botany, geology, astronomy, etc.
Rector, Little Bromley, Essex, 1878; rural dean, Loes, 1893. County
councillor, East Suffolk, 1900; alderman, 1911. Lived latterly at Earl Soham,
Framlingham, Suffolk.
  The Castle of Knaresborough: a tale in verse of the Civil War in Yorkshire, 1644;
and, The white mare of Whitestonecliff: a Yorkshire legend of the fifteenth century; by
Richard Abbay. London: Kegan Paul, Trench & Co. 1887. xiv, 337 pp.
map. *OXB*

ABBOTT, Sir James (1807–96). Educated at the East India Co.'s College.
Commissioned in Bengal Artillery, 1823-76, promoted major-general, 1866;
general and colonel-commandant, Royal Artillery, 1877; served on the march
to Kandahar, 1838, the mission to Herat, 1839, and in the Sikh War, 1848.
Commissioner of Hazara, 1845-53. In retirement he lived at Ryde, Isle of
Wight.
  The legend of Maandoo; by [James Abbott]. 2nd ed. London: Kegan Paul,
Trench, Trübner, & Co. Ltd. 1893. xx, 188 pp. il. *OXB*

ABBOTT, Wilfrid Horace, (Oxford Undergraduate, pseud.) (1867–19).
b. Bermondsey, Surrey, son of George I. Abbott. Educated at St Mark's
College, Chelsea, and Trinity College, Oxford.
  Songs for the People; by an Oxford undergraduate. Oxford: F.H. Plummer.
1891. 15 pp. *OXB*

ABEL, George
  Gordon, and other poems; by George Abel. [London]: 376 Strand. [1885]. xx,
236 pp. *OXB*

ABERCROMBIE, Beatrice, (Jane Young, pseud.)
  Songs and verses; by Jane Young (Beatrice Abercrombie). London: H.R.
Allenson. 1896. 96 pp. *OXB*

ABINGER RHYMES. London: Mitchell & Hughes. 1893. 60 pp.
  Privately printed.*

ABRAM, William John. Eldest son of William Abram, law stationer of
Middle Temple Lane, London. Barrister, Middle Temple; called to the Bar,
1855; member of the South-Eastern circuit. Historian and topical writer, he
lived at 22 Devonshire Road, Holloway, London N.
  An old man's love, and other poems; by W.J. Abram. London: Henry J. Drane.
[1890]. 83 pp. *UCD*

ABRAMS, John. Lived at 2 Park Villas, Grove Road, New Southgate, London.
The songs of Devon; by John Abrams. Printed Tottenham: Fisk Bros. [1880]. [ii], 63 pp. por. *OXB*

ACKROYD, Laura G.
Homer's wine, and other poems; by Laura G. Ackroyd. Westminster: Roxburghe Press. [1896]. 119 pp. *BL*

ACTON, Philip, pseud. *see* **HOLME, James Wilson**, (Philip Acton, pseud.)

ADAMS, Alfred Wallace, (A.) Of Penarth, Glamorgan.
[Poems]; by A. London. 1891. ★

ADAMS, Mrs Clayton *see* **CLAYTON ADAMS, Mary Frances**

ADAMS, Edith C.
Idyls of love and life; by Edith C. Adams. London: Kegan Paul, Trench, Trübner, & Co. Ltd. 1893. xii, 148 pp. *OXB*

ADAMS, Francis *see* **ADAMS, Francis William**

ADAMS, Francis William (1862–93). b. Malta, son of Andrew Leith Adams, zoologist and military surgeon. Educated at Shrewsbury School, and in Paris. Anti-capitalist and a champion of the working class, he emigrated to Australia in 1882 after an unsuccessful attempt at schoolteaching. A novelist, dramatist and essayist, he worked on the staff of the *Sydney Bulletin*, returning to England in 1889. Seriously ill with consumption he shot himself dead at Alexandria.
Henry, and other tales: [poems]; by Francis William Adams. London: Elliot Stock. [1884]. 152 pp.
  Cover-title is *Poems. OXB*
Lines on special occasions; by Francis Adams. 1883. iv, 67 pp. *BL*
The mass of Christ; by the late Francis Adams. Printed Manchester: Labour Press Society Ltd. [1894?]. 15 pp. *BL*
Songs of the army of the night; by Francis Adams. London: Vizetelly & Co. 1890. 119 pp. *BL*
Songs of the army of the night; by Francis Adams. 2nd ed. London: William Reeves. [1892]. 119 pp. *TCD*
Songs of the army of the night; by Francis Adams. [New ed.]. London: William Reeves. 1894. 132 pp. por. (Bellamy library, 19). *OXB*

ADAMS, Mary Frances Clayton *see* **CLAYTON ADAMS, Mary Frances**

ADAMS, R.D., (Alpha Crucis, pseud.)
Songs of the stars, and other poems; by Alpha Crucis. London. [1882]. ★

ADAMS, Thomas
The tercentury [sic] of the defeat of the Spanish Armada; by Thomas Adams.
Printed London: J.W. Weatherstone. 1888. [15] pp.   *OXB*

ADDLESHAW, William Percy, (Percy Hemingway, pseud.) (1867–19).
b. Bowdon, Cheshire, son of John W. Addleshaw, solicitor of Old Trafford,
Lancashire. Educated at Shrewsbury School, and Christ Church, Oxford.
President of the Palmerston Club at Oxford. Barrister, Inner Temple;
practised on the Northern circuit. Travelled in Europe, Africa, India and
Australia. JP for Sussex. Contributed to the *Academy* and the *Manchester
Guardian*. Lived latterly at The Hill Side, Hassocks, Sussex.
The happy wanderer, & other verse; by Percy Hemingway. London: Elkin
Mathews; Chicago: Way & Williams. 1896. x, 76 pp.
A limited ed. of 500 copies printed for England and America.   *OXB*

ADELINE, pseud. *see* **SERGEANT, Jane**, (Adeline, pseud.)

ADEN, J. Redfearn, pseud. *see* **WILLIAMSON, Joshua Redfearn**, (J.
Redfearn Aden, pseud.)

ADLEY, C. Of Lapford, Devon.
Lovely homes, and other poems; by C. Adley. London: Remington & Co. 1889.
[xii], 98 pp.   *OXB*
The victorious hero (The Einherjar): or, the imperial hall; by C. Adley. London:
Simpkin, Marshall, Hamilton, Kent & Co., Ltd. [1893]. 123 pp.   *OXB*

ADON, pseud *see* **TRAILL, William Frederick**, (Adon, pseud.)

ADRA, pseud.
Legends of lakeland: [poems]; by Adra. Scarborough: S.W. Theakston. 1881.
[x], 168 pp.   *OXB*

AE *see* **RUSSELL, George William**, (A.E.)

AGED PILGRIM, pseud. *see* **BISHOP, John B.**, (B.) (Aged Pilgrim, pseud.)

AGNOSTIC, pseud. Member of the British Secular Union, the leading
organization of British agnosticism.
Songs by the wayside of an agnostic's life; by himself. London: W. Stewart &
Co.; Edinburgh; J. Menzies & Co. [1883]. 67 pp.   *OXB*

AGRA, pseud.
Poems and ballads for penny readings: original and translated from the German; by
Agra. London: Wyman & Sons. 1883. [iv] 125 pp.   *OXB*

AGRIKLER, pseud. *see* **EDWARDS, Joseph**, (Agrikler, pseud.)

AIDE, Hamilton (1826–1906). b. Paris, son of an Armenian merchant; his mother was the daughter of Sir George Collier. Educated privately, and at Bonn University. He joined the British army, taking a commission and serving until 1853. On selling out he travelled widely before settling in London in 1875. A prolific musical composer and accomplished amateur artist, he occasionally wrote for the stage, and was a lavish host in his London home.

Songs without music: rhymes and recitations; by Hamilton Aide. London: David Bogue. 1882. x, 183 pp. *OXB*

    Also 2nd ed. 1882.

Songs without music: rhymes and recitations; by Hamilton Aide. 3rd ed. enlarged. London: George Bell & Sons. 1889. xiv, 255 pp. *OXB*

AINSLIE, Douglas (1865–19). Lived at Dalgety Castle, Turriff, Aberdeenshire.

Escarlamonde, and other poems; by Douglas Ainslie. London: George Bell & Sons. 1893. viii, 140 pp. *OXB*

AINSLIE, Ralph St John (1861–1908). b. Corfe, Somerset, son of Archdeacon Ainslie. Educated at Sherborne School, and Oriel College, Oxford (scholar); BA 1885. Master at Sedbergh School, Yorkshire; headmaster, Greenbank School, Liverpool, 1900–03. He retired to Sherborne, Dorset.

Sedbergh School songs; written and illustrated by R. St John Ainslie. Leeds: Richard Jackson. 1896. 104 pp. il. *OXB*

AITCHISON, James (1846–). b. Glasgow, son of a potter. Educated at St Matthew's parish school and at the sessional school. Apprenticed to a watchmaker before entering Glasgow University; his health broke down and he was unable to continue his studies. He eventually enrolled at the Divinity Hall of the United Presbyterian Church. Licensed to preach in 1873, he was successively pastor at Orkney, Eaglesham and Falkirk.

The chronicle of mites: a satire politico-philisophico-theological, and other pieces: [poems]; by James Aitchison. London: Kegan Paul, Trench & Co. 1887. viii, 195 pp. *OXB*

AITKEN, Inspector *see* **AITKEN, William**

AITKEN, William (1851–). b. Sorn, Ayrshire. A few years later the family moved to the village of Bridge-End of Montgarswood. He attended school but at the age of ten was apprenticed to a shoemaker. Aged twenty he entered the service of the Glasgow & South Western Railway Co., eventually becoming a traffic inspector on the line between Glasgow and Greenock.

Echoes from the iron road, and other poems; by Inspector Aitken. Glasgow: John Menzies & Co.; Ardrossan: Arthur Guthrie. 1893. 310 pp. por. *OXB*

Lays of the line, and other poems; by Inspector Aitken. Edinburgh: John Menzies & Co. 1883. [vi], 141 pp. *OXB*

Rhymes and readings; by William Aitken. With an introductory notice by John Rankine. Printed Glasgow: Horn and Connell. 1880. 184 pp. *NLS*

AITKEN, William Shearer (1856–). b. Edinburgh. Employed in a commercial office in Aberdeen.
Maximus in minibus: or, sketches and poems; by William S. Aitken. Printed Aberdeen: Free Press Office. 1890. 144 pp. *UCD*
Star-dust: or, poems, songs, and sonnets; by William S. Aitken. Aberdeen: William Walker. 1883. xii, 136 pp. *NLS*

AIZLEWOOD, John William. Barrister of Inner Temple. Lived at Sheffield, Yorkshire.
Echo and Narcissus, [and other poems]; by John William Aizlewood. London: Kegan Paul, Trench, Trübner & Co., Ltd. 1893. viii, 84 pp. *OXB*

AKERMAN, William. LL.B. Dramatist, and writer of operas.
Rip Van Winkle, and other poems; by William Akerman. London: George Bell & Sons. 1897. viii, 184 pp. *OXB*

AL-SO, pseud. *see* **SOMERS, Alexander**, (Al-So, pseud.)

ALDRIDGE, Edward G. FGS, FRMet.S.
Mendreva: (a dream); by Edward G. Aldridge. London: Simpkin, Marshall, Hamilton, Kent, & Co., Ltd. 1890. 33 pp. *OXB*

ALERE FLAMMAN, pseud.
Parodies & satires: [poems]; by Alere Flamman. London: Simpkin, Marshall, Hamilton, Kent & Co., Ltd; New York: Charles Scribner's Sons. [1894]. 84 pp. *OXB*

ALEXANDER, Cecil Frances (1818–95). b. County Wicklow, daughter of Major John Humphreys, Royal Marines. Best known as a hymn writer, she came under the influence of the Oxford Movement, publishing a series of tracts that first appeared in 1842. In 1850 she married the Rev. William Alexander, rector of Termonamongam in Tyrone, who later became Bishop of Derry and subsequently Archbishop of Armagh.
Moral songs; by Mrs. CF Alexander. Illustrated. London: Masters & Co. 1880. viii, 158 pp. il. (by various artists). *OXB*
Poems; by Cecil Frances Alexander, (C.F.A.). Edited, with a preface, by William Alexander. London: Macmillan & Co., Ltd. 1896. xliv, 463 pp. por. *BL*

ALEXANDER, Sidney Arthur (1866–19). b. Hampstead, Middlesex, son of Frederick Alexander, gentleman. Educated at St Paul's School, London, and Trinity College, Oxford (scholar); BA 1889. Tutor, Keble College, 1892. Curate, St Michael's, Oxford, 1889-93; reader at the Temple, 1893-1902; canon of Gloucester and head of Gloucester College of Missionary Clergy, 1902–09.
Sakya-Muni: the story of Buddha: Newdigate Prize poem, 1887; by Sidney Arthur Alexander. Oxford: A. Thomas Shrimpton & Son; London: Simpkin, Marshall, & Co.; Hamilton, Adams, & Co. 1887. 19 pp. *OXB*

ALEXANDER, William (1824–1911). b. Londonderry. Educated at Ton-bridge School, and Exeter and Brasenose Colleges, Oxford; BA, MA; DD 1867. Ordained minister in the Church of Ireland, 1847. Appointed Bishop of Derry and Raphoe, 1867; Archbishop of Armagh and Primate of all Ireland from 1893. Writer on theology, and an eloquent preacher and lecturer. His wife was the hymn writer Cecil Frances Alexander.

St. Augustine's holiday, and other poems; by William Alexander. London: Kegan Paul, Trench & Co. 1886. xiv, 300 pp. *OXB*

ALFORD, Daniel Pring (1838–). b. Taunton, Somerset, son of Rev. Henry Alford. Educated at Exeter College, Oxford; BA, MA. Curate, St John's, Taunton, 1862–64, Clayhidon, 1864, Scilly Isles, 1865–69; vicar, St Paul's, Tavistock, 1869-78; rector, Apsley-Guise, Bedfordshire, 1878-80; vicar, Houghton Regis, 1880-83, Tavistock, 1883-95. Writer on Devon and Somerset.

A tale of Tresco; The Tavistock chimes, and other poems, mostly of the West Country; by D.P. Alford. Tavistock: T.W. Greenfield; London: Simpkin & Marshall. 1894. [vi], 72 pp. *OXB*

'ALFRED THE GREAT: OR, ENGLAND'S DARLING' ON THE EGYPTIAN CAMPAIGN. Bristol: J.W. Arrowsmith; London: Simpkin, Marshall, Hamilton, Kent & Co. Ltd. [1898]. 24 pp. *OXB*

ALLAN, E. Heron- *see* **HERON-ALLAN, E.**, (Blasé Man, pseud.)

ALLAN, Robert (1848–). b. Jedburgh, Roxburghshire, son of a wool merchant. After a good education he became tenant of a farm on the Wolfelee estate. In his spare time he studied literature, eventually entering Edinburgh University. Lived at Redhouse, Gasstown, Dumfries, and at 18 Marchmont Road, Edinburgh.

Border and other poems; by Robert Allan. Kelso: J. & J.H. Rutherfurd. 1887. viii, 133 pp. *OXB*

Border lays, and other poems; by Robert Allan. Paisley: J. & R. Parlane. 1891. 269 pp. *OXB*

Poems, lyrical and descriptive, chiefly connected with Edinburgh, the Lothians, and the Scottish border; by Robert Allan. Edinburgh: W. Smith Elliot & Co. 1899. 248 pp. il. *NLS*

ALLAN, Sir William (1837–1903). b. Dundee, Angus. Served as an engineer in the Royal Navy and the merchant service. Chief engineer blockade runner in the American Civil War, taken prisoner at the capture of Charleston, 1861. Manager of North-Eastern Marine Engineering Co., 1868; founded Scotia Engine Works, Sunderland; director of the Albyn shipping line there. Liberal MP for Gateshead from 1893; deputy lieutenant, County Durham. Lived latterly at Scotland House, Sunderland. Knighted in 1902.

After-toil songs; by William Allan. London: Simpkin, Marshall, & Co. 1882. x, 246 pp. *OXB*

A book of poems, democratic chants, and songs, in English and Scottish; by William Allan. Sunderland: Hills & Co. 1891. [viii], 188 pp. il.   *OXB*

A book of songs in English and Scottish; by William Allan. Sunderland: Hills & Co. 1890. [viii], 162 pp. il., por.   *OXB*

Gordon: or, the rose of Methlic; by William Allan. Sunderland: Hills & Co. 1894. [viii], 240 pp. il.   *NLS*

Lays of leisure: poems and songs; by William Allan. London: Simpkin, Marshall, & Co. 1883. xii, 226 pp.   *OXB*

Northern lights: or, poems and songs; by William Allan. London: Simpkin, Marshall, & Co. 1889. viii, 203 pp.   *OXB*

Sunset songs; by William Allan. Sunderland: Hills & Co. 1897. 78 pp. por.   *★NUC*

ALLEN, George W.

Songs of thought and feeling; by George W. Allen. London: Edward Bumpus. 1888. viii, 91 pp.   *OXB*

ALLEN, Gertrude Frances (18 –93)

Sketches and poems; by Gertrude Frances Allen. Printed Westminster: Army & Navy Co-operative Society, Ltd. 1893. viii, 152 pp.   *OXB*

ALLEN, Grant (1848–99). b. Kingston, Canada, son of Rev. J.A. Allen of Holy Trinity Church, Wolfe Island. Educated in the United States, France, King Edward's School, Birmingham, and Merton College, Oxford. After four years at Queen's College, Jamaica, as professor of English, he returned to England in 1876 and adopted a literary career. A prolific novelist, he also wrote in the field of evolutionary science, and the philosophy of religion, and published a series of guide books to European cities.

The lower slopes: reminiscences of excursions round the base of Helicon, undertaken for the most part in early manhood: [poems]; by Grant Allen. London: Elkin Mathews & John Lane at the sign of The Bodley Head; Chicago: Stone & Kimball. 1894. viii, 80 pp.

A limited ed. of 600 copies printed for England.   *MPL*

ALLEN, William. Methodist minister.

The village reciter: [poems]; by William Allen. London: Robert Culley. [1896?]. [iv], 65 pp.

Published for the author.   *OXB*

ALLEYNE, Sarah Frances (1836–84). b. Clifton, Gloucestershire. Member of the council of Clifton High School for Girls, and secretary of the Oxford local examinations; she organized courses of lectures for women. Writer on Greek philosophy, and translator from the German. She is buried at Redland Green.

Verses; by Sarah Frances Alleyne. Printed London: Chiswick Press. 1885. vi, 76 pp.

Privately printed.   *OXB*

ALLEYNE-HARRIS, Robert

Twofold life: or, spirit songs; by R. Alleyne-Harris. London: Elliot Stock. 1893. x, 88 pp.   *OXB*

Whispers of 'the eternal': [poems]; by Robert Alleyne Harris. London: George Stoneman. [1890]. viii, 100 pp.   *OXB*

ALLINGHAM, Edward. Son of William Allingham, manager of the local bank at Ballyshannon, County Donegal. Brother of the poet William Allingham. Educated at Trinity College, Dublin; BA 1862, MA 1874. Practised law in Belfast.

New and original poems; by Edward Allingham. London: Reeves & Turner. 1890. vi, 159 pp.   *OXB*

ALLINGHAM, William (1824–89). Son of William Allingham, manager of the local bank at Ballyshannon, County Donegal. Educated there, entering his father's bank c. 1837. A customs officer in the civil service, 1846-70, first in Ireland then in London, where he became acquainted with Leigh Hunt. Sub-editor, then editor of *Fraser's Magazine*, 1874-79. In 1874 he married the artist Helen Paterson. He is buried at Ballyshannon.

Blackberries picked off many bushes: [poems]; by D. Pollex and others. Put in a basket by W. Allingham. London: G. Philip & Son. 1884. [iv], 172 pp.   *MPL*

Day and night songs; by William Allingham. New ed. London: G. Philip & Son. 1884. x, 157 pp.   *BL*

Evil May-Day, [and other poems]; by William Allingham. London: David Stott. [1882]. viii, 100 pp.   *MPL*

Flower pieces, and other poems; by William Allingham. With two designs by Dante Gabriel Rossetti. London: Reeves & Turner. 1888. x, 194 pp. il.   *EPL*

Flower pieces, and other poems; by William Allingham. With two designs by Dante Gabriel Rossetti. London: Longmans, Green. 1893. x, 194 pp. il.

    Another issue with cancels.   *★NUC*

Irish Songs and poems; by William Allingham. With nine airs harmonized for voice and pianoforte. London: Reeves & Turner. 1887. vi, 164 pp.   *OXB*

Life and phantasy: [poems]; by William Allingham. With frontispiece by Sir John Millais, a design by Arthur H. Hughes and a song for voice and pianoforte. London: Reeves & Turner. 1889. viii, 161 pp. il.   *OXB*

Thought and word: [poems]; and, Ashby Manor: a play in two acts; by William Allingham. With portrait, four designs for stage scenes by Mrs. Allingham, and a song with music. London: Reeves & Turner. 1890. viii, 185 pp.il., por.   *BL*

ALMA-TADEMA, Laurence (1865-1940). Daughter of the artist Sir Lawrence Alma-Tadema. Most of her life was spent in Kent. A novelist and short story writer, she contributed prose and verse to several magazines, including the *Yellow Book*.

Realms of unknown kings: [poems]; by Laurence Alma-Tadema. London: Grant Richards. 1897. xii, 78 pp.   *OXB*

ALMY, Percival Henry William. Of Torquay, Devon. Writer on the town.
 Scintillae carmenis: [poems]; by Percival H.W. Almy. London: Elliott Stock.
 1895. vi, 101 pp.   *OXB*

ALPHA CRUCIS, pseud. *see* **ADAMS, R.D.**, (Alpha Crucis, pseud.)

ALSOP, James Richard (1818–80). b. Bonehill, Tamworth, Staffordshire,
son of Richard Alsop, calico printer. Educated at Manchester Grammar
School, and Brasenose College, Oxford. Curate, West Houghton, Lanca-
shire, 1840–42, perpetual curate, 1842–67; vicar, Acton Trussell with Bednall,
Staffordshire, 1867 to his death. Essayist and reviewer in magazines.
 The prayer of Ajax, and other poems; by James R, Alsop. Printed Stafford: R. &
W. Wright. 1880. xii, 73 pp. por.
     Printed for private circulation.   *OXB*

**AMANDA'S FATE: OR, THE LEGEND OF RYE MONASTERY
(ILLUSTRATED)**. Rye: James Cole. [1887]. 16 pp. il.   *OXB*

AMATEUR, pseud.
 A few lyrics; by an amateur. London: C. Kegan Paul & Co. 1880. [vi], 56
pp. *OXB*

AMBLER, Benjamin George (1858–). Writer on Tennyson. Of The
Charterhouse, Charterhouse Square, London EC.
 The crucifixion, and other poems; by Benjamin George Ambler. London: W.
Poole. 1880. viii, 140 pp.   *OXB*
 A demon watch, and other poems; by Benjamin George Ambler. London:
William Poole. 1881. viii, 55 pp.   *OXB*
 Eddies and ebbs: [poems]; by Benjamin George Ambler. London: Elliot Stock.
1882. 26 pp.   *OXB*
 A leaf from Marc Anthony, and other poems; by Benjamin George Ambler.
London: Elliot Stock. 1887. 29 pp.   *OXB*
 On the summit, and other poems; by Benjamin George Ambler. London: Elliot
Stock. 1895. 38 pp.   *OXB*
 Voices from the void, and other poems; by Benjamin George Ambler. London:
Elliot Stock. 1881. ★

AMBOFILIUS, pseud.
 The marriage of time: a rhymed story; by Ambofilius. London: Tinsley Bros.
1881. [iv], 223 pp.   *OXB*

**"AMONG THE IMMORTALS": A POLITICAL SATIRE AND VIN-
DICATION, IN FOUR CANTOS**. London: Edward Stanford. 1880. 40
pp. *OXB*

AMOTT, Lennox *see* **AMOTT, Lennox R.P.C.**

AMOTT, Lennox R.P.C. Lived at The Grange, Kingsbury, near Tamworth, Staffordshire. Organist and choirmaster at Kingsbury Parish Church.

Chimes: [poems]; by Lennox Amott. Lewes: Farncombe & Co. 1887. 112 pp. *OXB*

Midsummer idylls, and other poems; by Lennox R.P.C. Amott. Lewes: J. Richards. 1882. [viii], 76 pp. *OXB*

The minstrel: a collection of poems; by Lennox Amott. Lewes: Farncombe & Co. 1883. [viii], 112 pp. *OXB*

Stray thoughts: a collection of verses; by Lennox R.P.C. Amott. Lewes: J. Richards. 1881. viii, 64 pp. *OXB*

AMYOT, Thomas Edward (1817–). b. Downing Street, London. Educated at Westminster School. Studied medicine at St Thomas's Hospital, London, and afterwards in Berlin and Paris; MRCS 1839, FRCS 1866. Practised in Diss, Norfolk, and neighbourhood for fifty years. President, East Anglian branch of the British Medical Association, he contributed papers to medical journals.

Verses and ballads; by Thomas Edward Amyot. Norwich: Agas H. Goose. 1897. [2], xiv, 184 pp. il. por. *OXB*

ANARCHIST, pseud. *see* **BARLAS, John Evelyn**, (Evelyn Douglas, pseud.), (Anarchist, pseud.)

ANDERDON, William Henry (1816–90). b. London, son of John L. Anderdon, West India [sic] merchant. Educated at King's College, London, Balliol College, Oxford, and University College, Oxford (scholar); BA 1839, MA 1842. Curate, Withyan, Kent, 1845, Reigate, Surrey, 1845–46; vicar, St Margaret's with Knighton, Leicester, 1846–50. Received into the Roman Catholic Church in Paris, 1850; ordained priest at Oscott, 1853; lecturer at Ushaw; dean of the Catholic University, Dublin, 1858-63; secretary to his uncle H.E. Manning, Archbishop of Westminster, 1865–68. He joined the Society of Jesus in 1874, giving missions and retreats in various parts of the country over many years.

Some verses of various dates; by W.H. Anderdon. London: Burns & Oates. 1888. 32 pp. *OXB*

ANDERSON, Alick Burnes, (Alick Burnes, pseud.) Of Oxford.

Wallasey: a tale of the Hundred of Wirral, and other poems; by Alick Burnes. Oxford: [Author?]. [1892]. xvi, 194 pp. il. *OXB*

ANDERSON, Basil Ramsay (1861-88). b. Unst, most northerly Shetland Island, son of a fisherman and one of six children. His father drowned at sea when he was five. A pupil-teacher in the parish school until the family moved to Edinburgh, where he entered a lawyer's office. Grand-uncle of Willa Muir.

Broken lights: poems and reminiscences of the late Basil Ramsay Anderson. Edited by Jessie M.E. Saxby. With glossary of Shetland terms by Gilbert Goudie. Edinburgh: R. & R. Clark; Lerwick: C. & A. Sandison. 1888. xxxvi, 128 pp. *OXB*

ANDERSON, G.F. Reynolds
The white book of the muses: [poems]; G.F. Reynolds Anderson. Edinburgh:
George P. Johnston. 1895. xiv, 223 pp.
A limited ed. of 666 copies. *OXB*

ANDERSON, George
The agnostic, and other poems; by George Anderson. Paisley: Alexander
Gardner. 1894. xii, 235 pp. por. *OXB*

ANDERSON, George W. (1856–). b. Strathbogie, Aberdeenshire. His
father died when he was fourteen and his mother two years later. He was
placed in the care of an instrument maker but ran away to join the Seaforth
Highlanders in 1874. Sent to India with the regiment in 1876, promoted
sergeant after the battle at Charasiab; took part in the Afghan War, 1878;
attached as mounted signaller to General Robert's staff during the second
campaign; became seriously ill on the march to Kandahar but soon recovered;
served in the Egyptian War, 1882. He returned to Scotland with the rank of
quartermaster-sergeant; his final posting was in Dublin. He was awarded four
war decorations and five clasps.
Lays of Strathbogie; and, The story of the Strath; by G.W. Anderson. With
several illustrations from drawings and photographs by the author. Dublin: R.
Chapman. 1891. 258 pp. il *TCD*
Seaforth songs, ballads, and sketches; by G.W. Anderson. With several
illustrations by the author. Printed Dublin: R. Chapman. 1890. 240 pp. il.,
por. *NLS*

ANDERSON, John (1822–97). b. Newburgh, Fife. His father was minister in
the parish of Dunbarney. Educated at St Andrews University; DD; completed
his training for the ministry at Edinburgh University. Appointed to St John's,
Dundee, then to St John's, Perth; from 1844 pastor at Kinnoull, near Perth. He
wrote for most of the leading magazines.
Sprigs of heather: or, the rambles of "may-fly" with old friends; by John Anderson.
Edinburgh: John Menzies & Co.; Perth: John Christie. 1884. viii, 163 pp.
Poetry and prose. *OXB*

ANDERSON, Matthew (1864–). b. Waterside, Dalmellington, Ayrshire.
Aged nine he was taken away from school to work on a farm; from twelve to
eighteen he worked underground in a coal mine, then went to South Wales.
He enlisted in the Royal Marine Artillery, serving as a runner for more than
three years. Joined Ayrshire Constabulary as a police constable at Colyton.
Poems of a policeman; by Matthew Anderson. Paisley: J. & R. Parlane;
Edinburgh: John Menzies & Co.; London: Houlston & Sons. 1898. 165 pp.
por. *NLS*

ANDERSON, Richard John (1848–1914). b. Ballybot, Newry, County
Down, son of Robert Anderson. Educated at Newry School, Queen's

College, and Belfast hospitals; MA, MD. After graduating he worked in Leipzig, London, Paris, Heidelberg and Naples; held senior scientific appointments in Ireland, including the chair of natural history, Queen's College, Galway. MRCS, FLS, JP.

The elephants: die Russel-Tiere – Proboscidea – Sslonn(U): a zoological mnemonic; by Richard John Anderson. Belfast: W. Erskine Mayre. 1895. 41 pp. *BL*

ANDERSON, Robert. Lived at 11 Station Road, Sandown, Isle of Wight.

Occasional pieces of verse and prose; by Robert Anderson. [Sandown, Isle of Wight]: [Author]. 1881. 32 pp. *BL*

ANDERSON, Thomas Scott (1853–1919). Son of Thomas Anderson, a Selkirk doctor. Educated at Merchiston Castle School, Edinburgh University, and Ecole de Médecine, Paris. He practised medicine professionally for a short time in Australia, where he formed a remarkable collection of Australian birds. On returning home he took to sheep farming. His recreations were foxhunting, shooting and natural history. Lived latterly at Ettrick Shaws, Selkirk. Master of Jed Forest Foxhounds.

Holloas from the hills: [poems]; by T. Scott Anderson. With illustrations by G. Denholm Armour. Jedburgh: T.S. Small. 1899. xii, 59 pp. il. *OXB*

ANDREWS, John, (J.A.) (1837–1906?). Son of Thomas R. Andrews of Wolverhampton, Staffordshire. Educated at Wadham College, Oxford; BA 1859. Student of Middle Temple, 1857.

The coming of spring, and other poems; by J.A. Printed Oxford: Geo. Bryan & Co. 1897. 40 pp. *OXB*

ANGLO-CATHOLIC, pseud.

Devotional verses; by an Anglo-Catholic. London: Masters & Co. 1888. 55 pp. *OXB*

ANGUS, William C. (1870–   ). b. Arbroath, Angus. He was apprenticed to a tinsmith but left to join the Black Watch at age of fifteen. His first experience of soldiering was in the Belfast riots of 1886; subsequently he was drafted to Malta, then to Gibraltar.

Under the shadow: songs of love and labour; by W.C. Angus. Arbroath: Brodie & Salmond. 1896. viii, 100 pp. *OXB*

ANLEY, Charlotte (1795?–1893). Novelist, essayist, and prison reformer. On behalf of Elizabeth Fry she investigated the conditions of female prisoners in New South Wales c. 1839. Lived latterly at 40 Grosvenor Place, Bath, where she died.

Sonnets, stanzas, and a crescendo composition; [by Charlotte Anley]. London: Remington & Co. 1884. viii, 98 pp. *OXB*

ANADOS, pseud. *see* **COLERIDGE, Mary**, (Anados, pseud.)

ANSLOW, Robert. Of Shrewsbury, Shropshire.
The defeat of the Spanish Armada (A.D. 1588): a tercentenary ballad (A.D. 1888);
by Robert Anslow. London: Elliott Stock. 1888. 40 pp.   *OXB*

ANSTEY, F., pseud. *see* **GUTHRIE, Thomas Anstey**, (F. Anstey, pseud.)

ANTAEUS, pseud. *see* **IBBETT, William Joseph**, (Antaeus, pseud.)

ANTI-JACOBIN, pseud.
A dream: or, the Irish landlord's lament, dedicated without permission to Messrs.
Gladstone, Bright, Parnell & Co., with an address to the landlords of Ireland, to defend
their just rights, &c.; by Anti-Jacobin. London: J.C. Hall. 1881. 16 pp.
    Title from cover.   *OXB*

ANTI-PUGNO, pseud.
The modern "P.R.,": or, the famous "running" (fighting) match in France, (March,
1988); by "Anti-Pugno". London: Roper & Drowley. [1888?]. 34 pp.   *BL*

APOLOGIST, pseud.
The epic of humanity: or, the quest of the ideal: [poems]; edited [i.e. written] by
an apologist. London: Kegan Paul, Trench, Trübner & Co., Ltd. 1898. [vi],
602 pp.   *OXB*

APPLEYARD, S., (S. A-Y-D)
Poems and rhymes; by S. A-Y-D. London: James Spiers. 1884. 50 pp.   *OXB*

AQUILA, pseud.
The passing of the poet, and other poems; by Aquila, London: Kegan Paul,
Trench, Trübner, & Co. Ltd. 1893. viii, 67 pp.   *OXB*

ARCHER, David Wallace. Of Kirriemuir, Angus.
Leaves from Logiedale; by David Wallace Archer. With introduction by J.M.
Barrie. Arbroath: Brodie & Salmond. 1889. 136 pp.
    Poetry and prose.   *OXB*

ARCHER, Mark. Biographer of William Hedley, inventor of railway
locomotion on the present principle, and writer on the coal trade of
Northumberland and Durham.
The ballad of Ben and Bill; by Mark Archer. With pictures from the pages of
"Judy". London: Ranken & Co. [1884]. 16 pp.   *OXB*
Political pieces, contributed to various papers; [by Mark Archer]. With illus-
trations by Arthur W. Allen. London: Ranken & Co. [1886]. [vi], 133 pp. il.
    Poetry and prose.   *OXB*

ARCHILOCHUS, pseud.
Sappho's soliloquy: a lament of unrequited love; by Archilochus. London:
Bevington & Co. 1886. [29] pp.
    Printed on one side of leaf only.   *BL*

ARGALL, Annie E. Of Truro, Cornwall. Writer on the county.
The inspiration of song, and other poems; by Annie E. Argall. Truro: Netherton & Worth. 1894. [iv], 156 pp. *BL*

ARGENT, Alice E. Of Chelmsford, Essex.
Poems; by Alice E. Argent. Chelmsford: Edmund Durrant & Co. 1890. viii, 126 pp. *BL*

ARGYLL, 8th Duke of *see* **CAMPBELL, George Douglas, Duke of Argyll**

ARGYLL, 9th Duke of *see* **CAMPBELL, John Douglas Sutherland, Duke of Argyll**

ARKWRIGHT, Sir John Stanhope (1872–1954). Son of John H. Arkwright of Hampton Court, Herefordshire. Educated at Eton College, and Christ Church, Oxford. Barrister and JP. Conservative MP for Hereford, 1900–12. Lived latterly at Kinsham Court, Presteigne, Radnorshire.
Montezuma: the Newdigate poem, 1895; by J.S. Arkwright. Oxford: B.H. Blackwell; London: Simpkin, Marshall, Hamilton, Kent & Co. 1895. 15 pp. *OXB*

ARMOUR, Margaret (18 –1943). b. Philpstoun House. West Lothian, daughter of Alexander H.H. Armour. Educated at George Watson's Ladies' College, Edinburgh, Edinburgh University, in Munich and in Paris. Translator of Wagner's operas. In 1895 she married W.B. Macdougall. Lived latterly at 28 Chalmers Street, Edinburgh.
The shadow of love, and other poems; by Margaret Armour. With drawings by W.B. Macdougall. London: Duckworth & Co. 1898. xiv, 124 pp. il.
A limited ed. of 500 copies. *OXB*
Songs of love and death; by Margaret Armour. Illustrated and decorated by W.B. Macdougall. London: J.M. Dent & Co. 1896. 136 pp. il. *OXB*
Thames sonnets and semblances; by Margaret Armour and W.B. Macdougall. London: Elkin Mathews. 1897. 64 pp. il.
Not joint authorship. Printed on one side of leaf only. *OXB*

ARMSTRONG, Andrew James (1848–). b. Scotland. His father died when he was an infant, leaving a family of five without support. After two years of schooling he became an errand boy in a draper's shop and afterwards in a bookseller's. Apprenticed to the cabinet-making trade, he attended evening school and completed his education. After following his profession for several years in England he settled in Kirkcudbright. Author of some prose tales and sketches.
Ingleside musings and tales told in rhyme; by Andrew J. Armstrong. With portrait of the author, and illustrations from original paintings by John Faed and Thomas Faed. Dalbeattie: Thomas Fraser. 1890. iv, 226 pp. il., por. *OXB*

ARMSTRONG, Arthur Coles. Lived at 25 Edward Street, Hampstead Road, London NW.

A tale from Boccaccio: poems; by Arthur Coles Armstrong. Westminster: Archibald Constable. 1897. viii, 89 pp.   *OXB*

ARMSTRONG, George Francis *see* **SAVAGE-ARMSTRONG, George Francis**

ARMSTRONG, George Francis Savage- *see* **SAVAGE-ARMSTRONG, George Francis**

ARNICA, pseud. *see* **KAY, William C.**, (Arnica, pseud.)

ARNOLD, Sir Edwin (1832–1904). b. Gravesend, Kent, son of a Sussex magistrate. Educated at King's School, Rochester, King's College, London, and University College, Oxford. Newdigate prizewinner, 1852. Assistant master, King Edward's School, Birmingham. In 1856 he was appointed principal of the Deccan College, Poona, India. Returned to England in 1861; joined the staff of the *Daily Telegraph*, eventually becoming editor. He attempted to interpret the life and philosophy of the East in English verse.

Golden pages (Kimpaku): being a birthday book; edited and arranged by Lady Tama Arnold. With twelve poems upon the months; by Sir Edwin Arnold. London: T.H. Burleigh. 1899. [184] pp.

 Blank diary pages, each month prefaced by a 2 pp. poem.   *BL*

In my lady's praise: being poems, old and new, written to the honour of Fanny, Lady Arnold, and now collected for her memory; by Sir Edwin Arnold. London: Trübner & Co. 1889. [ii], 144 pp.   *OXB*

 Also 2nd ed. 1889.

The light of the world: or, the great consummation; by Sir Edwin Arnold. London: Longmans, Green, & Co. 1891. [x], 295 pp.   *MPL*

 Also 2nd ed. 1891; 3rd ed. 1891.

The light of the world: or, the great consummation; by Sir Edwin Arnold. Illustrated after designs by W. Holman Hunt. New ed. London: Longmans, Green, & Co. 1896. [xii], 295 pp. il.   *OXB*

Lotus and jewel: containing "In an Indian temple", "A casket of gems", "A queen's revenge", with other poems; by Edwin Arnold. London: Trübner & Co. 1887. vi, 263 pp.   *MPL*

 Also 2nd ed. 1888.

Poems: national and non-oriental, (with some new pieces); selected from the works of Sir Edwin Arnold. London: Trübner & Co. 1888. viii, 375 pp.

 Cover-title is *Selected poems, national and non-oriental.*   *OXB*

 Also 2nd ed. 1888.

Potiphar's wife, and other poems; by Sir Edwin Arnold. London: Longmans, Green, & Co. 1892. vi, 136 pp.   *MPL*

The secret of death (from the Sanskrit), with some collected poems; by Edwin Arnold. London: Trübner & Co. viii, 406 pp.   *MPL*

The tenth muse, and other poems; by Sir Edwin Arnold. London: Longmans, Green, & Co. 1895. viii, 159 pp.   *LL*

ARNOLD, Frederick Sweet (1852–19). Son of Frederick A. Arnold, ironmonger of Devonport. Educated at Devonport & Stoke Grammar School, and King's College, Cambridge; MA 1883. Assistant master, Bedford Grammar School. Professor of English, Royal Oriental Institute, Naples.
Jordan: the Seatonian prize poem for 1883; by F.S. Arnold. Cambridge: Macmillan & Bowes. 1884. 32 pp. *BL*

ARNOLD, Matthew (1822–88). b. Laleham on the Thames, son of Thomas Arnold, the great headmaster of Rugby School. Educated at Rugby School, and Balliol College, Oxford. Newdigate prizewinner, 1843. Fellow of Oriel College, 1845. Taught at Rugby for a short time, then in 1847 became private secretary to Lord Lansdowne, President of the Council. In 1851 he began a career as inspector of schools.
BIBLIOGRAPHY: **SMART, Thomas Burnett**. *The Bibliography of Matthew Arnold*. London: J. Davy & Sons. 1892.

ARTHUR, J.K. Writer on Australia and New Zealand.
A bouquet of brevities: being practical maxims and refined sentiments, original and select: [poems]; by J.K. Arthur. With engravings. London: Leadenhall Press, Ltd; Simpkin, Marshall, Hamilton, Kent & Co., Ltd; New York: Charles Scribner's Sons. 1895. 146 pp. il. *BL*

ARUNDEL, Gerald
Light in darkness; by Gerald Arundel. Printed Trinidad: E.C. Fraser. 1898. 41 pp. *BL*
Pleasures of poesy: [poems]; by Gerald Arundel. [1894]. 52 pp. **BL*

ARUNDELL, Vere Monckton-, Lady Galway *see* **MONCKTON-ARUNDELL, Vere, Lady Galway**

ASH WOOD, pseud. *see* **ETCHES, James M.**, (Ash Wood, pseud.)

ASHBY, Anna E. Mrs Edmund Ashby of Glenburnie, Southampton.
Elidure, etc.: [poems]; by Mrs. Edmund Ashby. Printed Southampton: Foster & Roud. [1880?]. 56 pp.
Printed for private circulation. *BL*

ASHBY, Mrs Edmund *see* **ASHBY, Anna E.**

ASHBY-STERRY, Joseph (1838–1917). b. London. Educated privately, he studied painting, contributing drawings to *Punch* and other periodicals. Eventually giving up art for literature, he began writing novels and comic pieces.
The lazy minstrel: [poems]; by J. Ashby-Sterry. London: T. Fisher Unwin. 1886. xvi, 236 pp. *BL*
Also a limited special large paper ed. of 50 numbered copies signed by the author, 1886.
Also 2nd ed. 1886; 3rd ed. 1887; 4th ed. 1888.

ASHE, Emily, (R.M.E.A.). Wife of Robert Martyn Ashe of Langley House, Chippenham, Wiltshire.
  Twilight shadows, and other poems; by R.M.E.A. London: Griffith, Farran, Okeden & Welsh. [1886]. 141 pp.   *OXB*

ASHE, Robert. Educated at Trinity College, Dublin.
  On the tercentenary of Trinity College, Dublin: (being the Vice-Chancellor's prize poem for 1892); by Robert Ashe. Dublin: Hodges, Figgis, & Co., Ltd. 1892. [18] pp.   *TCD*

ASHE, Robert Martyn, (R.M.E.A.) (1807–85). Son of Robert Ashe of Broad Hinton, Wiltshire. Educated at Trinity College, Oxford; BA 1828, MA 1832. Of Langley House, Chippenham, Wiltshire, lord of the manor and patron of Langley Burrell.
  Twilight shadows, and other poems; by R.M.E.A. London: Griffith, Farran, Okeden & Welsh. [1886]. 141 pp.   *OXB*

ASHE, Thomas (1836-89). b. Stockport, Cheshire, son of a clergyman. Educated at St John's College, Cambridge. Curate, Silverstone, Northamptonshire, 1860. Taught mathematics at Leamington College, and subsequently at Queen Elizabeth's School, Ipswich. Later he became a man of letters in London and Paris. Edited an edition of S.T. Coleridge's works.
  Poems; by Thomas Ashe. Complete ed. London: George Bell & Sons. 1886. [2], vi. 334 pp.
    Half-title is *Poems and translations.*   *MPL*
  Songs of a year; by Thomas Ashe. London: Chiswick Press. 1888. viii, 84 pp.
    Privately printed.   *OXB*

ASHLEY, John Marks (1828–1909). b. Langham Place, London, son of Henry Ashley, solicitor of Greenhithe, Kent. Educated at King's College, London, Caius College, Cambridge, and the Royal College of Chemistry. Lecturer in chemistry at Hunterian School of Medicine, 1848–1855. Ordained, 1858; curate, Swanscombe, Kent, and lecturer at Greenhithe, 1859–67. LL.B 1860. Curate, St Peter's, Brighton, 1868-69; perpetual curate, St Peter's, Vere Street, London, 1869–73; vicar, Fewston, Otley, Yorkshire, 1873–1900.
  The Battle of Senlac, and other poems; by John M. Ashley. London: Samuel Tinsley & Co. 1880. vi, 178 pp.   *OXB*

ASHTON, J., (J.A.). Lived at 167 Norwood Road, Herne Hill, London SW.
  The last dream of General Gordon, before the fall of Khartoum: a poem; by J.A. Herne Hill: Anderson & Ashton. 1885. 32 pp. il.   *OXB*

ASHTON, Teddy, pseud. *see* **CLARKE, Charles Allen**, (Teddy Ashton, pseud.)

ASHWORTH, James George. Of Princetown, Dartmoor, Devon.
Gathered ears [poems]; by J.G. Ashworth. Truro: Heard & Sons. 1893. viii, 136 pp. *BL*

ASKHAM, John (1825–94). Shoemaker at Wellingborough, Northampton-shire. Librarian of the Literary Institute, Wellingborough, and a member of the first school board there, 1871; school attendance officer and sanitary inspector, 1874.
Sketches in prose and verse; by John Askham. With portrait and biographical sketch of the author. Northampton: S.S. Campion; Wellingborough: Thos. Collings. 1893. 247 pp. *★UCD*

ASSOCIATE OF THE VICTORIA INSTITUTE, LONDON, pseud.
The temptation of Jesus: a poem; by an associate of the Victoria Institute. London. Grantham: William Clarke; London: Simpkin, Marshall, & Co. 1882. [61] pp. *OXB*

ASTON, Marie. Of Stafford.
Linked lyrics; by Marie Aston. Congleton: Robert Head; London: Simpkin, Marshall & Co. 1887. [ii], 54 pp. *BL*

ATKINSON, Millicent L. Of Oldham, Lancashire.
Victoria our queen: a poem; by Millicent L. Atkinson. Printed Oldham: W.E. Clegg. 1897. 15 pp. *OXB*

ATKINSON, William Blake (1850?–19). Curate, St Martin's, Manchester, 1873–75, Cookley, Worcestershire, 1876– 77, Wishaw, Warwickshire, 1877–78; rector, Kington with Dormston, Worcestershire, 1879–86, Bradley, 1886–98. Lived latterly at Bishopswood, Hill Road, Weston-super-Mare, Somerset.
Pilgrim songs: poems, chiefly sacred; by W. Blake Atkinson. London: "Home Words" Publishing Office. [1884]. 91 pp. il. *OXB*
Songs in the night: poems on various subjects; by W. Blake Atkinson. London: Jarrold & Sons. 1893. 94 pp. *OXB*
Songs of faith, hope, and love: the collected poems of W. Blake Atkinson. London: Elliot Stock. 1899. xii, 200 pp. *OXB*

ATTENBOROUGH, Florence Gertrude, (Chrystabel, pseud.) A play-wright, she lived at Marlborough Road, Ealing, Middlesex.
"Cameos", and other poems: a volume of verse; by Florence G. Attenborough ("Chrystabel"). London: W. Reeves. 1898. viii, 168 pp. *BL*

AULD, Agnes Wellwood, (A.W.A.). Lived at Holmwood, Kilwinning, Ayrshire.
Souvenir of song: [poems]; by A.W.A. Ardrossan: Arthur Guthrie & Sons. [1896]. 103 pp. *NLS*

AUSTIN, Alfred (1835–1913). b. Headingley, Leeds, of Catholic parents. His father was a timber merchant. Educated at Stonyhurst College, Oscott College, and London University. Called to the Bar in 1857 but after practising for three years adopted literature as a profession; leader writer for the *Evening Standard*. 1866–96; editor of the *National Review* from 1883. Poet, dramatist, novelist and essayist, he was appointed poet laureate in 1896, succeeding Tennyson. The appointment caused an unfair standard to be applied to his work.
BIBLIOGRAPHY: **CROWELL, Norton B.** *Alfred Austin: Victorian.* Albuquerque, New Mexico: University of New Mexico Press. [1953].

AUTREMONDE, pseud. *see* **MILDMAY, Sir Aubrey Neville St. John** (Autremonde, pseud.)

AVELING, Henry. Writer on the Church psalter.
Poems and paragraphs; by Henry Aveling. London: Digby, Long & Co. 1899. viii, 186 pp.   *OXB*

AVELING, James Hobson (1828–92). Brother of Thomas Aveling, engine builder. Educated at Aberdeen University; medallist for anatomy, 1848; MB 1856, MD 1857, MRCS 1861. Lecturer on midwifery and diseases of women and children, Sheffield, where he founded Jessop Hospital, 1864. Practised at 1 Upper Wimpole Street, London, from 1871; consultant at several London hospitals. Author of works on gynaecology and obstetrics. Edited *The Obstetrical Journal*, 1873–76.
Fables: [poems]; by James H. Aveling. London: Longmans, Green, & Co. 1886. 185 pp.   *OXB*

AVENELL, Everard
The Lady Agatha's secret, and other poems; by Everard Avenell. London: J.S. Virtue & Co., Ltd. [1887]. 53 pp.   *OXB*

AXON, William Edward Armytage (1846–1913). b. Manchester. Chief librarian of Manchester Free Libraries until he joined the literary staff of the *Manchester Guardian* in 1874, retiring in 1905. A contributor to the *Dictionary of National Biography* and to *Encyclopaedia Britannica*. President of Lancashire & Cheshire Antiquarian Society. A frequent contributor to archaeological transactions and periodicals.
The Ancoats skylark, and other verses, original and translated; by William E.A. Axon. Manchester: John Heywood. 1894. 106 pp. il.   *MPL*

AZUCENA, pseud.
Confessions of a coquette, while staying at Scarboro', Whitby, & Bridlington; by Azucena. Printed Scarborough: E.T.W. Dennis. [1888]. 42 pp.   *OXB*

B

B. *see* **BISHOP, John B., (B.)**, (Aged Pilgrim, pseud.)

B., A.C. *see* **BARKER, A.C.**, (A.C.B.)

B., A.H. *see* **BOWIE, A.H.**, (A.H.B.)

B., C.S.
The Sunday "ABC": [poems]; by C.S.B. Illustrated by Oswald Fleuss. London: Roper & Drowley; F. Edwards & Co. [1890]. [54] pp. il. *BL*

B., D.M.
London sketches, and other poems; by D.M.B. Printed Maidstone: Young & Cooper. 1893. [iv], 77 pp. *BL*

B., E. *see* **PARKER, George Williams**, (E.B.)

B., E.H. *see* **BLAKENEY, Edward Henry**, (E.H.B.)

B., E.L.
A contrast, with some other verses; by E.L.B. Newport, Mon.: Stow Hill Bible & Tract Depot. [1899]. 61 pp. *★UCD*

B., E.L. *see* **BEVIR, Edward Lawrence**, (E.L.B.)

B., H. *see* **BELLOC, Hilaire**, (H.B.)

B., J.R. *see* **BLACKFORD, John Richard**, (J.R.B.)

B., J.T. *see* **BULLOCK, James Trower**, (J.T.B.)

B., M.
A miscellany in sonnets; by M.B. Printed London: Harrison & Sons. 1891. 22 pp. *BL*

B., M. *see* **BEALE, Mary**, (M.B.)

B., M.E. *see* **BECK, Mary Elizabeth**, (M.E.B.)

B., P.T.
Occasional verses; by P.T.B. [1886]. 66 pp. *★UCD*

B., S.
Janus: or, the perfidy of the Free Church of Scotland: a ditty; by S.B. Edinburgh: James Thomson & Son. 1896. 16 pp. *★UCD*

B., S. *see* **BLIGH, Samuel**, (S.B.)

B., V. *see* **THOMSON, James**, (B.V.)

B., W.R. Of Northampton.
Versiculi versicolores; [by] W.R.B. London: Williams & Norgate; Northampton: R. Harris & Son. 1898. 36 pp.   *OXB*

B., W.S. *see* **BRASSINGTON, William Salt**, (W.S.B.)

B.-S., A.
Poems; by A. B.-S. London: T. Woolmer. 1887. viii, 132 pp.   *OXB*

BABYLON: A POEM. London: Thomas Bosworth. [1884]. [viii], 120 pp.   *OXB*

BACKWARD LOOKING: VERSES, OCCASIONAL AND MISCEL-LANEOUS. Exeter: William Pollard & Co.; London: Simpkins [sic], Marshall, Hamilton, Kent & Co., Ltd. 1897. viii, 168 pp.   *OXB*

BADDELEY, St Clair *see* **BADDELEY, Welbore St. Clair**

BADDELEY, Welbore St. Clair (1856–   ). b. St Leonards-on-Sea, Sussex. Educated at Wellington College, Wokingham. Dramatist, novelist, and travel writer. Member of Royal Asiatic Society.
Bedoueen legends, and other poems; by W. St. Clair Baddeley. London: Robson & Kerslake. 1883. xvi, 144 pp.   *OXB*
Legend of the death of Antar: an eastern romance; also, Lyrical poems, songs, and sonnets; by Welbore St. Clair Baddeley. London: David Bogue. 1881. [xii], 212 pp.
     Spine-title is *The death of Antar.   OXB*
Lotus leaves: [poems]; by St Clair Baddeley. London: Trübner & Co. 1887. xii, 116 pp.   *OXB*
Love's vintage: [poems]; by W. St. Clair Baddeley. London: Sampson, Low, Marston, Searle, & Rivington, Ltd. 1891. xvi, 195 pp.   *OXB*
Tennyson's grave; by St. Clair Baddeley. London: William Heinemann. 1893. 16 pp.   *CU*

BAILDON, Henry Bellyse (1849–1907). b. Granton, near Edinburgh. At school he was a contemporary of Robert Louis Stevenson. He proceeded to Edinburgh, Cambridge and Freiburg Universities. Lecturer in English in Vienna, Glasgow, and Dundee. Hon. secretary of Edinburgh Philosophical Institute and of the university extension scheme in Edinburgh. Lived latterly at Murrayfield.
The rescue, and other poems; by Henry Bellyse Baildon. London: T. Fisher Unwin. 1893. 186 pp.   *OXB*

BAILEY, Albert Charles. Of Preston, Dorset.
Songs and sonnets; by a son of the soil, Albert Charles Bailey. Printed Dorchester: Henry Ling. 1897. 32 pp.   *OXB*

BAILEY, H.J.S.
Stray verses; by H.J.S. Bailey. London: Elliot Stock. 1898. [xii], 56, [27] pp.   *OXB*

BAILEY, James Lesingham (1860?–)
Tim, Tom, Tame: [poems]; [by James Lesingham Bailey]. [London]: J. Cartridge. 1886. xii, 157 pp.   *OXB*

BAILEY, John Robert (1851–94). b. Oxford. Educated at St John's College School, afterwards a chorister at Queen's College. He was articled to a solicitor and eventually qualified, holding positions successively at Worcester, Oldham and Bromyard until poor health forced him to resign. He moved to Leatherhead, Surrey, where he is buried.
Poems; by John Robert Bailey. Printed Edinburgh: R. & R. Clark. 1895. x, 68 pp. por.
    Privately printed.   *OXB*

BAIN, James Leith MacBeth, (James Macbeth, pseud.)
The opening of the gates: a mosaic of song; by James MacBeth. London: Kegan Paul, Trench, Trübner & Co., Ltd. 1897. viii, 320 pp.   *OXB*

BAIN, Robert (1865–19   ). b. Glasgow, son of Robert Bain. Educated at Hutchesons' Academy, Greenock. Taught at Kilblain Academy, Greenock. Lived at 148 Kenmure Street, Glasgow.
In Glasgow streets, and other poems; by Robert Bain. Glasgow: Henry Nicol. [1898]. [ii], 112 pp.   *OXB*

BAINES, Wilhelmina
Lays from legends, and other poems; by Wilhelmina Baines. London: W.H. Allen & Co. 1885. xvi, 144 pp.   *OXB*

BAKER, Arthur (1856?–19   ). Son of Robert Baker, factory inspector of Leamington, Warwickshire. Educated at Trinity Hall, Cambridge; BA 1878, MA 1883. Curate, St Matthew's, Cambridge, 1878–79; missionary, Norfolk Island, Melanesia, 1879-80; curate, Maker, Cornwall, 1882-84; chaplain in the Royal Navy, serving on many ships and at many naval bases, 1884–1901; perpetual curate, East Kennett, Wiltshire, 1901–07, Stonebridge Park, Willesden, 1908-19; preacher in London and St Albans, 1921–31. Lived latterly at Tolworth Park, Surrey.
Poems; by A. Baker. London: Bemrose & Sons. 1887. 44 pp.
    'Proceeds for a charity'.   *OXB*

BAKER, Charles, (Ex-Materialist, pseud). A Unitarian of Birmingham.
The new world of thought: [poems]; by an ex-materialist. Printed Luton: Albert H. Fensome. 1886. 127 pp.
 Title from cover. *BIP*

BAKER, Gulielma Alexander Wheeler (1831–86). b. Edgbaston, Birmingham, née Wheeler. A Quaker, she was educated at Ackworth, then at F. Dymond's School, Berkhamsted. In 1859 she married Morris Baker of Birmingham. Lived latterly at Woodhouse Lands, Harborne.
The consecration of the Temple, and other poems; by Gulielma A. Wheeler Baker. Harborne, Birmingham: Morris Baker. 1888. xiv, 221 pp. il., por. *BL*

BALCOMBE, Amy
A collection of verses, lyrics, and translations; by Amy Balcombe. London: Blades, East & Blades. 1897. xvi, 157 pp. *BL*

BALFERN, William Poole (1818–87). b. Hammersmith, London. Entered the Baptist ministry in 1848; he worked mainly in the London suburbs and at Brighton, Sussex. His hymns were published in the *Baptist Hymnal* and in a few Church of England collections. A frequent contributor to religious periodicals.
Pilgrim chimes, for the weeks of the year: [poems]; by W. Poole Balfern. London: "Home Words" Publishing Office. [1882]. 88 pp. il. *OXB*

BALL, Peter, (Philip Wentworth, pseud.) (1830–93). b. Southport, Lancashire, moving to Manchester early in life. His parents commenced business in Shudehill Market as wholesale fruiterers. He was apprenticed to the wire-working industry, rising to a position of trust. An ardent Conservative in north Manchester, and a member of the Primrose League, he was one of the founders of St George's School, Oldham Road.
April primrose poems, written in memoriam Earl of Beaconsfield, K.G., etc.; by Philip Wentworth. Radcliffe: T.H. Hayhurst. 1890. 19 pp.
 Cover-title is *Primrose poems*. *MPL*

BALLANTYNE, Jane Barclay. Daughter of James Ballantyne of Edinburgh, printer of Sir Walter Scott's works.
A summer trip to the Highlands, [and other poems]; by Jane B. Ballantyne. Printed Edinburgh: Ballantyne Press. 1880. 31 pp. *EPL*

BAMPFIELD, George (1827–1900). Son of Robert W. Bampfield, London surgeon. Educated at Tonbridge School, and Trinity and Lincoln Colleges, Oxford (scholar); BA 1849. Ordained deacon, 1850. Assistant master, St Nicholas Grammar School, Shoreham, Sussex, 1848–54; Fellow of St Nicholas College, 1854– 58. He entered the Roman Catholic Church in 1865, and was ordained priest. Founder of St Andrew's Institute, Barnet, its superior until his death.
Midsummer verses, and other poems; by G. Bampfield. Barnet: St Andrew's Press. 1894. 116 pp. *UCD*

BANCROFT, William (1864–19   ). b. Weaverham, Cheshire, son of John Bancroft, JP. Educated at Audlem Grammar School. Articled in the offices of Messrs A. & J.E. Fletcher, he was admitted solicitor in 1886, setting up practice at Northwich. A member of the Unionist Council of Cheshire. A pioneer of long-distance pigeon flying. Lived latterly at Mere Bank, Weaverham.

Lays of a salt town; by William Bancroft. London: Simpkin, Marshall, Hamilton, Kent & Co., Ltd. 1894. [viii], 160 pp.   *MPL*

BANKS, Edward (18   –84). Of Tettenhall, Wolverhampton, Staffordshire.
Waifs of rhyme: [poems]; by Edward Banks. Birmingham: Cornish Bros. 1884. xii, 134 pp.   *OXB*

BANNERMAN, Frances (1855–19   ). b. Halifax, Nova Scotia, of Welsh and Scottish ancestry, daughter of the Hon. A.G. Jones, Lieutenant Governor of Nova Scotia. In 1886 she married Hamlet Bannerman of Lytham, Lancashire. A talented artist, she exhibited at the Royal Academy, London, and the Salon, Paris. Live latterly in Italy.
Milestones: a collection of verses; by Frances Bannerman. London: Grant Richards. 1899. xii, 197 pp.   *OXB*

BARBER, Samuel. Educated at London University, and St Aidan's College. Curate, Bunbury, Cheshire, 1874–76, Tilmanstone, Kent, 1876–79; in Cumberland, at Maryport, 1881, Christ Church, Whitehaven, 1882, Grange-over-Sands, 1883, Staveley-in-Cartmel, 1886–87, Prestbury, Cheshire, 1888, Wythburn, Cumberland, 1890, West Newton, Cumberland, 1894–95, Sea-salter, Kent, 1895–96, St Petrock Minor, Cornwall, 1897–98, Broughton, Huntingdonshire, 1898–99.
Nature's orchestra, and other poems; by Samuel Barber. London: Swan Sonnenschein & Co., Ltd. 1896. vi, 106 pp.   *OXB*

BARBOUR, Robert William (1854–91). Educated at Edinburgh Collegiate School, and Edinburgh University. He became the Presbyterian minister at Cults, Aberdeenshire, but eventually resigned the ministry. Lived in the family home at Bonskeld, near Blair-Atholl, Perthshire.
Robert W. Barbour: letters, poems, and pensées. Printed Glasgow: Robert Maclehose. 1893. xxxii, 460 pp. por.   *OXB*

BARD OF DUNCLUG *see* **HERBISON, David**

BARD OF LONGDENDALE *see* **BARLOW, Thomas**

BARD OF LOUGH ERNE *see* **MAGENNIS, Peter**

BARD OF THOMOND *see* **HOGAN, Michael**

BARD OF THULE *see* **NICOLSON, Laurance James**

BARING, Maurice (1874–1945). b. London, son of Lord Revelstoke. Educated at Eton College, and Trinity College, Cambridge. He entered the diplomatic service, holding appointments successively in Paris, Copenhagen and Rome. In 1904 he turned to journalism, working as special correspondent in Manchuria, Russia, and the Balkans. During the First World War he served with Lord Trenchard in the Royal Air Force, attaining the rank of wing commander. Author of novels, plays, short stories, essays and sketches. *FRSL*
BIBLIOGRAPHY: **CHAUNDY, L.** *A bibliography of the first editions of the works of Maurice Baring.* London: Dulau & Co., Ltd. 1925.

BARING-GOULD, Sabine (1834–1924). b. Exeter, of an old Devon family. In early life he lived much in Germany and France. Educated at Clare College, Cambridge. Incumbent of Dalton, near Thirsk, Yorkshire, 1866; rector, East Mersea, Colchester, Essex, 1871, Lew Trenchard, Devon, 1881, having succeeded to the estate there on his father's death in 1872. A prolific writer, he produced sermons, theological works, histories, books of travel, and a whole series of popular antiquarian publications. Author of the hymn 'Onward, Christian Soldiers'.
  The building of Saint Sophia; by S. Baring-Gould. With introduction and notes by John Wharton. Manchester: John Green & Son; London: John Marshall & Co.; John Heywood. [189-]. 16 pp. (Green's scholastic series of poetry, 29). *MPL*

BARKER, A.C., (A.C.B.) (1818–92). b. Woodside, Aberdeen. He spent several years in America, where his verse appeared in periodicals.
  Fifty years' rhymes and reminiscences; [by] A.C.B. Aberdeen. 1880. 212 pp. il., por. *OXB*

BARKER, Henry James (1852–1934). Son of William Barker of Eccleshall, near Sheffield, Yorkshire. Educated at Westfield School, Sheffield, St John's College, London, and Trinity College, Dublin. Barrister of Middle Temple. He contributed to many magazines and the London daily press; gave occasional readings of his humorous works; studied the manners and customs of English gypsies; lectured on English literature to pupil teachers under London School Board. Lived at 2 Burstock Road, Putney, London SW.
  Lays and ballads of heroism; by Henry J. Barker. London: James Nisbet & Co. [1884]. 136 pp. *OXB*
  'Lisha Ridley the pitman, and other poems, including "Our curate", 'Farmer Gould's Story", "Ballads of heroism", "The picket", &c.; by Henry J. Barker. London: Jarrold & Sons. [1891]. 242 pp. il. *OXB*

BARKER, Horace Ross. Of Bury St Edmunds, Suffolk. Author of a history of the town.

Looking back, [and other poems]; by Horace Ross Barker. Printed Bury St. Edmunds: Catling. 1891. 48 pp. *OXB*

Shadows and sunshine: [poems]; by Horace Ross Barker. Printed Bury St. Edmunds: Barker. 1885. 48 pp. *OXB*

BARKER, John Thomas (1844–   ). b. Bramley, near Leeds, son of Benjamin Barker, a businessman. Engaged in commerce from the age of fifteen, he nevertheless wrote both prose and verse, sometimes in West Riding dialect, for the *Yorkshire Post* and other newspapers and periodicals.

The pilgrimage of memory: a romance of the Yorkshire moors, and other poems; by John Thomas Barker. London: Simpkin, Marshall, & Co.; Leeds: Walker & Laycock. [1886]. viii, 203 pp. *OXB*

BARLAS, John Evelyn, (Evelyn Douglas, pseud.), (Anarchist, pseud.) (1860–1914). Son of John Barlas of Rangoon, East Indies, gentleman. Educated at New College, Oxford. Barrister of Middle Temple.

Bird-notes: [poems]; by Evelyn Douglas. Printed Chelmsford, Essex: J.H. Clarke. 1887. 70 pp. *BL*

Holy of holies: confessions of an anarchist: [poems]. Printed Chelmsford: J.H. Clarke. 1887. 47 pp. *BL*

Love-sonnets; by Evelyn Douglas. Printed Chelmsford: J.H. Clarke. 1889. 72 pp. *JRL*

Phantasmagoria: "dream-fugues": [poems]; by Evelyn Douglas. Printed Chelmsford: J.H. Clarke. 1887. [ii], 65 pp. *BL*

Phantasmagoria: "dream-fugues": [poems]; by Evelyn Douglas. Chelmsford: A. Driver. 1887. [ii], 65 pp. *OXB*

Poems, lyrical and dramatic; by Evelyn Douglas. London: Trübner & Co. 1884. xiv, 238 pp. *OXB*

The queen of the hid isle: an allegory of life and art; Love's perversity: or, Eros and Anteros: a drama; by Evelyn Douglas. London: Trübner & Co. 1885. [vi], 257 pp.

Plays and 'The bloody heart', a long poem. *NLS*

Selections from Songs of a bayadere; and, Songs of a troubadour; by Evelyn Douglas. Printed Dundee: James P. Mathew & Co. 1893. 57 pp.

Cover-title is *Songs of a bayadere, and Songs of a troubadour*. *OXB*

BARLOW, George, (James Hinton, pseud.) (1847–1913). b. Westminster, London, son of George B. Barlow, master of the Crown Office. Educated at Harrow School, and Exeter College, Oxford. Some of his lyrics were set to music; he wrote the English version of the libretto of Gounod's *Ave Maria* at Gounod's request.

An actor's reminiscences, and other poems; by George Barlow. London: Remington & Co. 1883. xvi, 332 pp. *OXB*

The crucifixion of man: a narrative poem; by George Barlow. London: Swan Sonnenschein & Co. 1893. xx, 231 pp. por. *OXB*

The crucifixion of man: a narrative poem; by George Barlow. 2nd ed. London: Roxburghe Press. 1895. xx, 231 pp. por.   *OXB*

An English Madonna: [poems]; by James Hinton. London: Remington & Co. 1884. [2], x, 151 pp.   *OXB*

From dawn to sunset: Book I The song of youth; Book II The song of manhood; Book III The song of riper manhood; by George Barlow. London: Swan Sonnenschein & Co. 1890. xii, 498 pp.   *OXB*

From dawn to sunset: Book I The song of youth; Book II The song of manhood; Book III The song of riper manhood; by George Barlow. 2nd ed. London: Roxburghe Press. 1895. xii, 498 pp.   *OXB*

A life's love: [poems]; by George Barlow. New ed. London: Remington & Co. 1882. xvi, 342 pp.   *OXB*

A lost mother; by George Barlow. London: Swan Sonnenschein & Co. 1892. [iv], 153 pp.   *MPL*

Love-songs; by George Barlow. London: Remington & Co. 1880. [iv], 179 pp.   *OXB*

Loved beyond words: [poems]; by George Barlow. London: Remington & Co. 1885. xii, 227 pp.   *OXB*

Love's offering: [poems]; by James Hinton. London: Remington & Co. 1883. x, 144 pp.   *OXB*

The pageant of life: an epic poem, in five books; by George Barlow. London: Swan Sonnenschein & Co. 1888. xxxii, 443 pp.   *OXB*
      Also 2nd ed. 1889.

The pageant of life: an epic of man, in five books; by George Barlow. 3rd ed. London: Roxburghe Press. 1895. xxxii, 444 pp.   *OXB*

Poems real and ideal; by George Barlow. London: Remington & Co. 1884. x, 403 pp.   *OXB*

Song-bloom: [poems]; by George Barlow. London: Remington & Co. 1881. xii, 290 pp.   *OXB*

Song-spray: [poems]; by George Barlow. London: Remington & Co. 1882. xvi, 335 pp.   *OXB*

Time's whisperings: sonnets and songs; by George Barlow. London: Remington & Co. 1880. 105 pp.   *OXB*

BARLOW, Jane (1857–1917). b. Dublin, daughter of Rev. Dr Barlow who became Vice-Provost of Trinity College. She was educated at home and never married. A novelist and short story writer, she often wrote in Irish dialect. Lived at Raheny, County Dublin.

The end of Elfintown; by Jane Barlow. Illustrated by Laurence Housman. London: Macmillan & Co. 1894. [iv], 78 pp. il.   *MPL*
      Also a limited large paper ed. of 50 copies.

BARLOW, Thomas (1826–1904). b. Radcliffe, Lancashire, but at an early age moved to Hyde, Cheshire, where he became a calico printer. Later he moved to Dinting, spending the remainder of his life in the neighbourhood of Glossop. One of the first working-man magistrates of Glossop. Known as 'The Bard of Longdendale'. He is buried at Mottram.

Poems; by Thomas Barlow. London: Horace Cox. 1894. viii, 56 pp.   *OXB*

BARRASS, Alexander. A Durham miner. Friend of the poet Joshua Lax.

The Derwent Valley, and other poems; by Alexander Barrass. Printed Newcastle upon Tyne: J.M. Carr. 1887. vi, 218 pp.   *NPL*

The pitman's social neet: [poems]; by Alexander Barrass. Printed Consett: J. Dent. 1897. [iv], 96 pp. por.   *BL*

BARRAUD, Clement William (1843–19). Son of the artist William Barraud, and grandson of Paul P. Barraud, chronometer maker. Educated at Lancing College, and Stonyhurst College. Entered the Society of Jesus in 1862; priest in charge of the mission at Barbados, West Indies, then parish priest of New Amsterdam, British Guiana; spiritual father at St Bueno's College, St Asaph, North Wales. He published several plays.

Lays of the nights, [and other poems]; by Clement William Barraud. London: Longmans, Green, and Co. 1898. viii, 164 pp.   *OXB*

BARROW, Sir John Croker (1833–1900). b. Kensington Palace, London, son of Sir George Barrow. Educated at Harrow School, and University College, Oxford; BA 1855, MA 1858. Curate, St Philip's, Earls Court, London, 1858–59. Entered the Roman Catholic Church, 1859. Barrister, Lincoln's Inn, 1869. He succeeded his father as 3rd Bart in 1876. Lived at Eagle Lodge, Ramsgate, Kent.

"Mary of Nazareth": *a legendary poem, in three parts*; by Sir John Croker Barrow. London: Burns & Oates; New York: Catholic Publication Society Co. [1889]. 3 vols.   *OXB*

The seven cities of the dead, and other poems, lyrics, and sonnets; by Sir John Croker Barrow. London: Longmans, Green & Co. 1893. viii, 136 pp.   *OXB*

'Towards the truth': thoughts in verse; by Sir John Croker Barrow. London: Longmans, Green, & Co. 1885. [iv], 70 pp.   *OXB*

BARROWS, Harold Murdock (1861–1913). Son of Thomas W. Barrows of Wardington, Oxfordshire. Educated at Charterhouse. A solicitor with a practice in Walsall, Staffordshire. Died at Tettenhall.

Poems; by Harold Murdock Barrows. London: Simpkin, Marshall, & Co. 1887. 53 pp.   *OXB*

BARRY, Alice Frances

"A singer in the outer court": *a collection of songs and verses*; by Alice F. Barry. London: Biggs & Debenham. 1890. viii, 142 pp.   *OXB*

BARRY, Michael Joseph (1817–89). b. Cork, eldest son of M.J. Barry. A barrister, he was appointed a police magistrate in Dublin. Edited the *Cork Southern Reporter* from 1848; published verse in the *Nation*.

Heinrich and Leonore: an alpine story; Corregio, and some miscellaneous verses, original and translated; by Michael Joseph Barry. Dublin: Hodges, Figgis & Co.; London: Simpkin, Marshall, & Co. 1886. viii, 95 pp,   *OXB*

BARSAC, Louis, pseud. *see* **DAWSON, Joseph**, (Louis Barsac, pseud.)

BARTER, Charles (1820–   ). Son of Rev. Charles Barter, rector of Sarsdon, Oxfordshire. Educated at Winchester College, and New College, Oxford; BCL. Student of Inner Temple, 1844. Fellow of New College, 1849–53. he became a resident magistrate at Pietermaritzburg, South Africa.
Stray memories of Natal and Zululand: a poem; by Charles Barter. Printed Pietermaritzburg: Munro Bros. 1897. [vi], 136 pp.   *OXB*

BARTER, Laura Anna. Mrs Snow.
Led on; by Laura A. Barter. London: J. E. Hawkins & Co.[1882]. [16] pp. il., col. il.
  Printed on card.   *CU*

BARTLETT, Frederick R. A working man of the Black Country, living at Bilston, Staffordshire.
Flashes from forge & foundry: a volume of poems; by Fred. R. Bartlett. Bilston, Staffs,: Shakspeare [sic] Printing Co. 1886. [8], viii, 119 pp.
  Spine-title is *Poems*.   *BL*

BARTON, Joseph Edwin (1875–19   ). Educated at Crypt Grammar School, Gloucester, and Pembroke College, Oxford (scholar). Senior classics master at Bradford Grammar School, then headmaster successively at Crypt, Wakefield and Bristol Grammar Schools. President of several WEA branches. A writer for the *Saturday Review*, and a BBC radio broadcaster. President of the Incorporated Association of Headmasters, 1932.
Gibraltar: the Newdigate poem, 1897; by J. Edwin Barton. Oxford: B.H. Blackwell; London: Simpkin, Marshall, Hamilton, Kent & Co. 1897. 23 pp.   *OXB*

BARTON, William Robert. Civil servant, appointed to the Board of Trade, 1877; transferred to the Local Government Board in Ireland, 1881, then to the War Office, 1882. Retired 1908.
Poems; by William R. Barton. Printed [London]: W. Straker. 1889. 48 pp.   *★UCD*

BASS, Matilda (1832–80). b. Shelton Hall, Staffordshire. The family moved to Coventry, Warwickshire, after the death of her father. In 1856 she married James Bass of Olney, Buckinghamshire. She became well known as a preacher of evangelistic services at village halls throughout the county, and eventually further afield in England and Wales.
Silent ministry: poems; by Matilda Bass. London: Hamilton, Adams, & Co.; Leicester: Richard Lawrence. 1880. 94 pp.   *OXB*
Silent ministry: poems; by Matilda Bass. London: William Mack. 1881. viii, 63 pp.   *OXB*

BASSANIO, pseud. *see* **COUPLAND, John Arthur**, (Bassanio, pseud.)

BATE, John (18 –96). Ordained a Wesleyan Methodist minister, 1849; in the United States, 1851–60; on his return to England he ministered successively in twenty-three towns including Ely, Ashby-de-la-Zouche, Bedford and Walsall. Writer on Christian doctrine and the spiritual life. Died at Evesham, Worcestershire.

Christian Pharisees: (a poem in ten parts), and other poems; by John Bate. London: John Kensit. [c. 1890]. 232 pp. **UCD*

BATEMAN, Charles T. Tallent, (Webster Strelley, pseud.). Solicitor and antiquary.

The river of life: an allegory; by Webster Strelley. Manchester: Tubbs, Brook, & Chrystal. [1883]. 20 pp. *MPL*

BATEMAN, May. Educated at the Anglo-French College, Kensington. In the Boer War she acted as a special correspondent. Press organizer, National Baby Week campaign. Member of the Catholic Women's Housing Conference, and of the Invalid Children's Aid Association. A novelist and a contributor to many magazines including *Nineteenth Century* and *Fortnightly Review*. Lived in Beaufort Street, London SW.

Sonnets & songs; by May Bateman. London: Elkin Mathews. 1895. [viii], 56 pp. *BL*

BATH IDLER, pseud. *see* **WOOD, Martin Harvey Goulter**, (Bath Idler, pseud.)

BATTERSBY, C. Maud. Novelist.

Twilight and dawn: hymns, fragments and poems; by C. Maud Battersby. London: S.W. Partridge; Putney: Pearce & Co.; Dublin: Combridge & Co. [1899]. 96 pp. il., por. *OXB*

BATTERSBY, Caryl (1859?–1927). Son of James Battersby of Sheffield, Yorkshire. Educated at Sheffield Collegiate School, and Emmanuel College, Cambridge; BA 1881, MA 1884. Assistant master at Bradford Grammar School. Lived latterly at 35 West Street, Scarborough.

The song of the golden bough, and other poems; by Caryl Battersby. Westminster: Archibald Constable & Co. 1898. viii, 108 pp. *OXB*

BATTERSBY, Henry Francis Prevost, (Francis Prevost, pseud.) (1862–1949). Son of Major-General J.P. Battersby, his mother being a daughter of Sir John Dillon. Educated at Westminster School, and the Royal Military academies at Woolwich and Sandhurst; commissioned in the Royal Irish Rifles but resigned to become a journalist. Correspondent for the *Morning Post* in South Africa, 1899–1900; in Somaliland, 1902; special correspondent with the Prince of Wales in India, 1905–06. He rejoined the army to fight in France and Flanders in the First World War, in which he was gassed and wounded. Lived latterly at Creek End, Bosham, Sussex.

Fires of green wood: [poems]; by Francis Prevost. London: Kegan Paul, Trench & Co. 1887. [viii], 120 pp.   *OXB*

Melilot: [poems]; by Francis Prevost. London: Kegan Paul, Trench & Co. 1886. x, 158 pp.   *OXB*

BATTYE, Emma (18 –84). Of Huddersfield, Yorkshire. Died a young woman.

Poems; by Emma Battye. Huddersfield: Joseph Woodhead. 1884. 94 pp. por.   *BL*

BAUGHAN, Blanche Edith (1870–1958). b. Putney, London. Educated at Brighton High School, and Royal Holloway College, London University. A social worker, she was prominent in penal reform and other causes, becoming president of the Howard League for Penal Reform. She emigrated to New Zealand in 1900.

Verses; by B.E. Baughan. Westminster: Archibald Constable & Co. 1898. 144 pp.   *OXB*

BAXENDALE, Walter (1844?–1931). Irish. A Congregational minister.

A woodland mountain path, and other short poems; by Walter Baxendale. London: James Clarke & Co. 1894. 72 pp.   *OXB*

BAYLDON, Arthur Albert Dawson (1865–1958). b. Leeds, Yorkshire. Educated at Leeds Grammar School. He travelled widely in India, America, and other parts of the world. Lived in Hull for many years before emigrating to Australia; arriving in Brisbane in 1889, he contributed to the bush balladry of the 1890s.

Lays and lyrics; by Arthur A.D. Bayldon. London: George Bell & Sons; Hull: J.R. Tutin. 1887. xvi, 160 pp.   *OXB*

Poems; by Arthur A.D. Bayldon. Brisbane, Queensland: W.H. Wendt & Co. 1897. 140 pp.   *BL*

Poems; by Arthur A.D. Bayldon. Brisbane, Queensland: W.H. Wendt & Co. [1898]. 159 pp.

For private circulation only.   *BL*

The sphynx, and other poems; by Arthur A.D. Bayldon. Hull: J.R. Tutin. 1889. xiii, 73 pp.   *NUC★*

BAYLEY, George (1815–   ). Son of John S. Bayley of Portsmouth. Educated at Exeter College, Oxford, and New Inn Hall; BA 1843, MA 1844.

Ver-vert: (after the French of De Gresset); by George Bayley. London: Remington & Co. 1882. 34 pp.   *OXB*

BAYLEY, William. Well-known perfumer of 17 Cockspur Street, London. Translator from Greek and Latin poets.

Bouquet: [poems]; by William Bayley. London: Bayley's. 1883. xxii, 72 pp.   *MPL*

BAYNES, Robert Hall (1831–95). Son of Joseph Baynes, Baptist pastor at Wellington, Somerset. Educated at Bath, and St Edmund Hall, Oxford; BA 1856, MA 1859. Curate, Christ Church, Surrey, 1856–57, St John the Baptist, Hoxton, 1857–58; vicar, St Paul's Whitechapel, London, 1858-62, Holy Trinity, Maidstone, Kent, 1862–66, St Michael & All Angels, Coventry, 1866–79; rector, Toppesfield, Essex, 1879–80; vicar, Holy Trinity, Folkestone, Kent, 1880–85; hon, canon, Worcester Cathedral. He was sentenced to four months' imprisonment for obtaining food and lodging by false pretences in Oxford, and given other prison sentences in Bristol for theft and assault. Died after falling into the fire at his Oxford lodgings.

Hymns and other verses; by Canon Baynes. London: Sampson Low, Marston, Searle, & Rivington. [1887]. viii, 72 pp. *OXB*

BAYNTON, Roderic

Alkestis, and other poems; by Roderic Baynton. London: J. & E. Bumpus, Ltd. 1895. 80 pp. *OXB*

BEALE, Mary (M.B.)

Carmel, and other poems; by M.B. Printed Reading: J. J. Beecroft. 1889. viii, 82 pp.
    Printed for the author. *BL*
St John: a poem; by Mary Beale. London: Digby, Long & Co. [1892]. [iv], 35 pp. *CU*

BEALEY, Richard Rome (1828–87). b. Rochdale, Lancashire. Master-bleacher at Stand, Whitefield. A founder member of Manchester Literary Club and of Nottingham Literary Club. Awarded first prize by Liverpool Young Men's Temperance Association for the best original temperance song, 1886. Died at Nottingham.

Later-life jottings in verse and prose; by R.R. Bealey. Manchester: Tubbs, Brook, & Chrystal; London: Simpkin, Marshall & Co. 1884. 111 pp. *MPL*

BEASLEY, John Arthur Llewellyn. Of Kirby Muxloe, Leicestershire.

Poems; by J.A.L. Beasley. Leicester: Batty & Co. 1894–95. 2 vols. *OXB*

BEATTY, Pakenham (1855–1930). b. Maranha, Brazil, son of Pakenham W. Beatty, merchant of Dundalk, County Louth. Educated at Harrow School, and in Bonn and Paris. Studied for the Bar at Middle Temple but was never called. Lived latterly at 16A Gwendwr Road, West Kensington, London W.

Spretae carmina musae: First series: Songs of love and death; by Pakenham Beatty. London: George Bell & Sons. 1893. x, 141 pp. *OXB*
Three women of the people, and other poems; by Pakenham Beatty. London: Newman & Co. 1881. x, 180 pp. *BL*

BEATTY-KINGSTON, William (1837–1900). b. London. A clerk in the Public Record Office, 1852-56; vice-chancellor at the Austrian consulate in London, 1856, and in Cardiff, 1857–58. Special correspondent of the *Daily Telegraph* in Berlin, Vienna, and other cities; present in the campaigns of the Austro-Russian, Franco-German, and Russo-Turkish wars; member of the editorial staff of the *Daily Telegraph* from 1879. He contributed much verse to *Punch*, 1883-87; wrote for *The Lute* and other musical journals, and composed some pieces for piano.

Mr "hansom" lays: original verses, imitations, and paraphrases; by W. Beatty-Kingston. London: Chapman & Hall, Ltd. 1889. viii, 176 pp.   *OXB*

BEAUCLERK, Sidney De Vere (1866–1903). Son of Aubrey De Vere Beauclerk of Hill Street, Berkeley Square, London. Educated at Eton College, and Trinity College, Cambridge; BA 1887. He was admitted to Inner Temple, 1887, as son of Aubrey De Vere of Ardglass, County Down, name withdrawn 1902.

Poems; by Sidney De Vere Beauclerk. London. 1897. viii, 52 pp.
   Privately printed.   *OXB*

BEAUMONT, Frank. Schoolteacher.
   A Viking's raid, and other verses; by Frank Beaumont. Sheffield: J. Arthur Bain. 1891. 58 pp.   *BL*

BECK, Mary Elizabeth, (M.E.B.) (1823–1903). b. Dover, Kent, of Quaker parents. When she was nine the family moved to William Allen's Quaker 'Colony at Home', Lindfield, Sussex. She learned Greek, Latin, German, and science from Allen's protégés. Aged fourteen she went for a year to Sarah Sweetapple's school at Stoke Newington. She became a teacher and had a school at Leominster, Herefordshire. Travelled to Quaker missions in the Middle East and America; she was recorded a minister by Hereford & Radnor monthly meeting, 1874.

Birthday and other poems; by M.E.B. Printed Ashford: Headley Bros. 1890. 128 pp.   *OXB*

BECKENHAM, William
   In fear and dole: poems; by William Beckenham. London: Jas. Wade. 1882. 96 pp.   *OXB*

BECKER, John H. Writer in German, and translator.
   The seamless holy coat of Jesus Christ and Orendel of Trier; by John H. Becker. Printed London: Alexander & Shepheard. [1891?]. 16 pp. maps.   *BL*

BECKETT, Reginald A. Writer on the county of Essex.
   Post-mortem, and other poems; by Reginald A. Beckett. London: Rixon & Arnold. 1896. [vi], 61 pp.   *BL*

BEDFORD, Joseph Goodworth. Of Wrawby, Lincolnshire. Known as 'The Blind Poet of Wrawby'.
   A garland of poesy; by Joseph Goodworth Bedford. Hull: Charles Henry Barnwell. 1881. iv, 100 pp.   *BL*

BEDFORD, William
Love triumphant: a song of hope: [poems]; by William Bedford. London: Elliot Stock. 1898. [viii], 67 pp. *OXB*

BEDNALL, Jeannie
Sea spray, and other poems; by Jeannie Bednall. Illustrated by H.G. Baguley. London: Elliot Stock. 1894. 82 pp. *BL*

BEECHING, Henry Charles (1859–1919). Educated at Balliol College, Oxford. Rector, Yattendon, Berkshire. 1885-1900. Professor of pastoral theology, King's College, London, 1900; canon of Westminster, 1902; dean of Norwich, 1911; select preacher at Oxford, Cambridge and Dublin. He published sermons, and edited the works of Milton, Herbert, Vaughan and Drayton.
In a garden, and other poems; by H.C. Beeching. London: John Lane, The Bodley Head; New York: Macmillan & Co. 1895. x, 108 pp. *MPL*
Love's looking glass: a volume of poems; [by Henry Charles Beeching]. London: Percival & Co. 1891. [2], viii, 170 pp. *OXB*
St. Augustine at Ostia: the Oxford sacred poem; by H.C. Beeching. London: John Lane, The Bodley Head. 1896. 28 pp. *OXB*

BEEMAN, Thomas Oyler. (B.M.N.). Author of works on church ritual. Lived at 182 Earls Court Road, London, SW.
Protestant songs for troublous times; by B.M.N. London. 1891. 34 pp. *
    Also 2nd ed. 1891.
Protestant songs for troublous times; by B.M.N. 3rd ed., with additions. London: Alexander & Shepheard, Ltd. 1899. 108 pp. *BLD*

BEGBIE, Edward Harold (1871–1929). b. Fornham St Martin's, Suffolk, son of Rev. Mars H. Begbie. Journalist, editor, biographer, and popular writer on religious and social topics; biographer of General Booth of the Salvation Army; poet of the First World War. Lived latterly at Garden Court, Swanage, Dorset.
The god of fools, and other poems; by E. Harold Begbie. London: Digby, Long & Co. 1892. [viii], 76 pp. *OXB*

BEGG, Mary Millar. Of Giffnock, Renfrewshire.
My mother's marriage ring, and other poems; by Mary Millar Begg. Glasgow: David Bryce & Son. 1893. x, 172 pp. por. *OXB*

BEHENNA, Kathleen. Novelist.
The history of a soul; by Kathleen Behenna. London: Digby, Long & Co. [1896]. [viii], 104 pp. *OXB*

BELGIAN HARE, pseud. *see* **DOUGLAS, Lord Alfred**, (Belgian Hare, pseud.)

BELL, Anna (1850–94). b. The Grove, Basingstoke, Hampshire, daughter of Sheppard and Eliza Bell. A disease at the age of five resulted in lifelong lameness and she could only walk on crutches. She joined the Society of Friends in her twenties, organizing meetings for children at Alton. Lived at Reigate, Surrey, for some years then in 1883 settled in Ashford, Kent, with her sister.

Bible rhymes and Bible lessons, for Sunday schools and families; by Anna Bell and H.L.H. London: Samuel Bagster & Sons, Ltd; Boston, Mass.: H.L. Hastings. [1885]. 80 pp. *OXB*

BELL, Charles Dent (1818–98). b. Ballymaguigan, County Derry, son of Henry H. Bell, landowner. Educated at Edinburgh Academy, the Royal School, Dungannon, and Trinity College, Dublin; BA, MA, BD, DD. Curate, St Mary's, Reading, Berkshire, 1845–47, St Mary-in-the-Castle, Hastings, Sussex, 1847-54, St John's Chapel, Hampstead, 1854-61; vicar, Ambleside, Westmorland, 1861–72, Rydal, 1872; rector, Cheltenham, Gloucestershire, 1872–95; hon. canon of Carlisle from 1869.

Diana's looking glass, and other poems; by Charles D. Bell. London: Edward Arnold. 1894. viii, 152 pp. *OXB*

Poems old and new; by Charles D. Bell. London: Edward Arnold. 1893. viii, 326 pp. *OXB*

Songs in many keys; by Charles D. Bell. London: James Nisbet & Co. 1884. viii, 224 pp. *OXB*

Songs in the twilight; by Charles D. Bell. London: James Nisbet & Co. 1881. viii, 173 pp. *OXB*

BELL, Henry Thomas Mackenzie (1856–1930). b. Liverpool, son of Thomas Bell, merchant. Educated privately at home because of poor health. He lived and studied in Portugal, Spain, Italy, France and Madeira. In 1884 he settled in Ealing, London, becoming a professional writer; literary critic on staff of the *London Academy*; biographer of Christina Rossetti and a close personal friend. He stood as Liberal candidate for London County Council several times. Lived latterly at 8 Orme Square, London W.

Old year leaves: being verses revived; by H.T. Mackenzie Bell. London: Elliot Stock. 1883. xxiv, 308 pp. *OXB*

Old year leaves: being old verses revived; by H.T. Mackenzie Bell. New ed. London: T. Fisher Unwin. [1886]. xxiv, 308 pp. *BL*

Pictures of travel, and other poems; by Mackenzie Bell. With six illustrations. London: Hurst & Blackett, Ltd. 1898. 111 pp. il., por. *OXB*

Spring's immortality, and other poems; by Mackenzie Bell. London: Ward, Lock, & Bowden, Ltd. 1893. xii, 138 pp. *OXB*

Spring's immortality, and other poems; by Mackenzie Bell. With new prefatory note. 2nd ed. London: Ward, Lock, & Bowden, Ltd. 1895. xiv, 136 pp. *OXB*

Also 3rd ed. 1896.

Verses of varied life; by H.T. Mackenzie Bell. London: Elliot Stock. 1882. viii, 147 pp. *OXB*

BELL, Herbert. Writer on Albury, Surrey.
Uncut stones: poems; by Herbert Bell. London: George Redway. 1898. 68 pp. *OXB*

BELL, John Joy (1871–1934). b. Glasgow, son of James T. Bell, tobacco manufacturer. Educated at Kelvinside Academy, Glasgow, Morrison's Academy, Crieff, and Glasgow University, where he edited the university magazine. In 1898 he joined the staff of *The Scots Pictorial*, also contributing stories, sketches and verse to a number of London magazines, and writing regularly for Scottish newspapers.
The new Noah's ark: [poems]; [by] J.J. Bell. London: John Lane, The Bodley Head. 1899. 64 pp. col. il. *OXB*

BELL, Mackenzie *see* **BELL, Henry Thomas Mackenzie**.

BELL, Margaret Thomson (1833–90). Née Beveridge of Newmills, Tarryburn, Fife. Attended Circus Place School, Edinburgh, then Miss Bissett's. In 1862 she married Rev. Stephen Bell, Church of Scotland minister at Eyemouth, Berwickshire. She was killed in a carriage accident when the horses bolted.
Poems, and other pieces; by Margaret T. Bell. Edited, with a memoir, by her brother [D. Beveridge]. London: Leadenhall Press, Ltd; Simpkin, Marshall, Hamilton, Kent & Co., Ltd. [1894]. 191 pp. *BL*

BELL, Maria (18 –99). Novelist.
Songs of two homes; by Maria Bell. Edinburgh: Oliphant Anderson & Ferrier. 1899. xii, 140 pp. *BL*

BELL, Raimonde, pseud. *see* **JONES, James Pickering**, (Raimonde Bell, pseud.)

BELL, Robert (1845–1926). b. Alnwick, Northumberland, son of William A. Bell. Educated at Alnwick Grammar School, and Glasgow University; MB, MD, LRCS. From 1868 he was engaged in one of the largest medical practices in Glasgow; in 1876 he founded the Glasgow Hospital for Women, becoming senior physician; gave up general practice in 1896 for cancer research, moving to London to become a consultant in 1904. Lived latterly at 15 Half Moon Street, and at Colmonell, Ayrshire.
A physician's poems: patriotic, pastoral, pungent; by Robert Bell. Glasgow: David Bryce & Son. 1893. xii, 154 pp. *OXB*

BELLOC, Hilaire, (H.B.) (1870–1953). b. Paris, son of a French barrister and his English wife. Educated at The Oratory School, Birmingham, and Balliol College, Oxford, where he became president of the Oxford Union. A novelist, historian, essayist, and travel writer, he also published nonsense verse for children. Liberal MP for South Salford, 1906–13. A close friend of G.K. Chesterton.

The modern traveller: [poems]; by H.B. and B.T.B. London: Edward Arnold.
1898. 80 pp. il. (by B.T.B.).   *OXB*
Verses and sonnets; by Hilaire Belloc. London: Ward & Downey Ltd. 1896. 64
pp.
    Printed on card.   *BL*

BELSHAW, Mrs W.H. Of Ramsbottom, near Bury, Lancashire.
    Poems; by Mrs. W.H. Belshaw. Ramsbottom: Author. [1882]. 56 pp.
    For private curculation.   *BUP*

BENCKE, Albert Henry (1846–). Son of John A. Bencke of Liverpool.
Educated at Brasenose College, Oxford. Student of Middle Temple, called to
the Bar, 1873. Lived at Bentham, West Kirby, Liverpool. Served as lieutenant
in the Royal Lancashire Militia.
    Dantzick: or, the story of a picture, with other tales: [poems]; [by Albert Henry
Bencke]. London: Simpkin, Marshall & Co. 1880. x, 288 pp.   *OXB*

BENDALL, Gerard. Novelist.
    Ivy and passion-flower: [poems]; by Gerard Bendall. London: William
Heinemann. 1890. viii, 103 pp.   *OXB*
    Legends of the heart: [poems]; by Gerard Bendall. London: William Holmes.
1881. [viii], 142 pp.   *OXB*
    Musa silvestris: [poems]; by Gerard Bendall. London: Kegan Paul, Trench &
Co. 1884. viii, 63 pp.   *OXB*

BENDYSHE, Thomas, (Successor of Man, pseud.) (1828–). Son of John
Bendyshe of Barrington Hall, Cambridge. Student of Inner Temple, called to
the Bar, 1857. Translated the anthropological works of J.H. Blumenbach from
the German.
    The last Christian: an epic poem; by a successor of man. Dover: W.A. Smeeth.
[1884]. 3 vols.
    Printed and published for the author.   *BL*

BENECKE, Edward Felix Mendelssohn (1870–95). Educated at Haileybury, and Balliol College, Oxford. A Latin and Greek scholar, he published
several vols, one while still an undergraduate. He lost his life in the Alps, 16
July 1895, in his twenty-sixth year.
    The cross beneath the ring, and other poems; by the late E.F.M. Benecke. London:
Swan Sonnenschein & Co., Lim. 1897. viii, 94 pp.
    Spine-title is *Poems*.   *OXB*

BENHAM, Charles Edwin (1860-19). b. Colchester, Essex, son of
Edward Benham. Educated at Colchester Grammar School. Co-proprietor
and editor of *Essex County Standard*. Writer on Essex, and contributor to
scientific and other journals.
    Essex ballads, and other poems; by Charles E. Benham. With a prefatory note
by the Right Honourable the Countess of Warwick. Colchester: Benham &
Co. 1897. 91 pp.   *★UCD*

BENHAM, Sir William Gurney (1859–1944). b. Colchester, Essex, son of Edward Benham. Educated at Merchant Taylor's School. He entered business in 1875, becoming co-proprietor of *Essex County Standard*. A director of Benham & Co. and other companies. An alderman of Colchester, thrice mayor. Author of *Book of Quotations, Proverbs, and Household Words*, 1907. JP, FSA, FRHist.S. Lived at 9 Lexden Road, Colchester.

A story of Stourton, and other Wiltshire tales, told in verse; by W. Gurney Benham. London: Simpkin, Marshall & Co. 1883. [iv], 113 pp.   *OXB*

BENJAMIN, Joseph. Author of a series of penny recitations and dialogues.

The fate of the poets: an original poem; by Joseph Benjamin. Printed Liverpool: Dobb & Co. [1892]. 43 pp.   *OXB*

Love's triumph over beauty: a poetical romance; by Joseph Benjamin. Printed Liverpool: T. Dobb & Co. [1892]. 35 pp.   *OXB*

BENNETT, Arthur (1862–1931). b. Padgate, Lancashire, son of William Bennett. Educated at the People's College, Warrington, and Strathmore House School, Southport. A chartered accountant, he became secretary of Warrington Chamber of Commerce. A member of Warrington Town Council, and an overseer of the poor, he was particularly interested in town planning and smoke abatement. Lived at Paddington House, near Warrington.

The music of my heart: [poems]; by Arthur Bennett. Manchester: Palmer & Howe; London: Simpkin, Marshall & Co. 1889. 176 pp.   *OXB*

BENNETT, Edith M. Writer on mother and infant welfare.

The path of life: a poem; by Edith M. Bennett. London: Digby, Long, & Co. [1892]. [iv], 84 pp.   *OXB*

BENNETT, Lucy Ann (1850–1927). b. Green Farm, Falford, Gloucestershire, daughter of Charles Bennett. Educated at Penarth House, Clevedon, Somerset. A staunch Methodist, she made several visits to the Keswick Convention. In 1899 she moved with her parents to Stone, Gloucestershire. A frequent contributor to *The Christian*.

Alleluia songs; by Lucy A. Bennett (Y.E.T.). London: S.W. Partridge & Co. [1883]. 94 pp.   *OXB*

On the wing: scripture texts for each day in the month; with verses by Lucy A. Bennett, designs by Alice Price and F. Corbyn Price. London: Castell Bros. [1887]. [35] pp. il., col. il.

Printed on card.   *BL*

Open secrets, [and other poems]; by Lucy A. Bennett. London: Castell Bros. [1887]. [18] pp.   *BL*

Songs for Christmastide; by Lucy A. Bennett. London: Castell Bros. 1887. [24] pp.   *OXB*

Verses for Christmas and the new year; by Lucy A. Bennett. Book I. London: Castell Bros. 1885. [ii], 16 pp.   *OXB*

White hyacinths, and other poems; by Lucy A. Bennett. London: Marshall Bros. [1898]. xii, 164 pp.   *OXB*

BENNETT, Mary Anne. Née Grahame. Lived at Sparkford Rectory, Somerset.

Poems; by Mary Anne Bennett. London: Griffith, Farran & Co. 1894. 96 pp. *OXB*

BENNETT, Robert (1855-). b. Linlithgow, West Lothian, son of a pattern designer. The family moved to Rutherglen soon after his birth. He received an elementary education, and at the age of twelve went into the wholesale drapery trade, starting in business on his own account after eight years. Contributed prose and verse to the *Glasgow Weekly Herald*, the *Sunday School Magazine*, etc.

Poems and prose; by Robert Bennett. Illustrated. Printed Glasgow: William Sinclair. 1888. 163 pp. il. *★UCD*

BENNETT, Samuel Rowe, (Homer Michael Faustinetti, pseud.) Lived at 13 Arundel Gardens, Kensington Park Road, London W.

"Jenny": a poem; by Homer Michael Faustinetti. London: T. Fisher Unwin. [1883?]. [20] pp. il.

Cover-title is *Noctes Fumosae "Jenny"*. Printed on one side leaf only. *OXB*

BENNETT, William. Brother of Thomas Bennett. Educated at Glasgow University. A radical Unitarian minister, he held appointments successively in Canterbury, Aberdeen, Paisley, Guildford, Heywood and elsewhere.

A memorial volume of poetry and prose; by the late William & Thomas Bennett. With the funeral discourse preached in the Heywood Unitarian Church on the 22nd of January, 1882; by William Mitchell. Printed Manchester: Johnson & Rawson. 1882. viii, 152 pp.

Thomas Bennett's contribution is prose. *MPL*

BENNETT, William Cox (1820-95). b. Greenwich, London, son of a watchmaker. He carried on his father's business but also wrote for newspapers and became famous as a songwriter. On staff of the *Weekly Dispatch*, 1869–70. Member of the London council of the Education League. Lived at Hyde Cottage, Greenwich. Died at Blackheath.

"Locksley Hall": an appeal from "Locksley Hall sixty years after" to "Locksley Hall"; by W.C. Bennett. London: Hart & Co. 1887. 16 pp. *BL*

BENSON, Arthur Christopher (1862–1925). b. Wellington College, where his father Edward W. Benson, who later became Archbishop of Canterbury, was headmaster. Brother of the writer Robert Hugh Benson. Educated at Eton College (scholar), and King's College, Cambridge. Assistant master at Eton, 1885, housemaster, 1892–1903. Fellow of Magdalene College, Cambridge, 1904, Master, 1915–25. Writer of literary criticism, essays, novels, and biographer of D.G. Rossetti, Walter Pater, and Edward Fitzgerald. Wrote the words of the song 'Land of Hope and Glory'.

Le cahier jaune: poems; by Arthur Christopher Benson. Printed Eton: Geo. New. 1892. 99 pp.

Privately printed. *OXB*

Lord Vyet, and other poems; Arthur Christophe Benson. London: John Lane, The Bodley Head. 1897. viii, 74 pp. *MPL*

Lyrics; by Arthur Christopher Benson. London: John Lane; New York: Macmillan & Co. 1895. xii, 189 pp.

A limited ed. of 550 copies printed for England. *MPL*

Poems; by Arthur Christopher Benson. London: Elkin Mathews & John Lane. 1893. xvi, 192 pp.

A limited ed. of 550 copies. *MPL*

The professor: [poems]; by Arthur Christopher Benson. Eton: George New. 1895. 51 pp.

A limited ed. of 100 numbered copies privately printed. *OXB*

Thomas Gray; by Arthur Christopher Benson. Eton: R. Ingalton Drake. 1895. [vi], 10 pp.

Privately printed *OXB*

BENT, Morris, (Maurice Penderrick, pseud.) (1852–19). b. Plymouth, Devon, son of Surgeon-General John Bent. Educated at Manchester Grammar School, and Trinity College, Dublin. An army major, he served in Egypt, 1882, and the Sudan, 1884–86. During the First World War he was re-employed in recruiting and intelligence. Lived at Deerswell, Bovey Tracey, Devon.

Sonnets and miscellaneous poems; by Maurice Penderrick. London: Simpkin, Marshall & Co. 1880. viii, 146 pp. *OXB*

BENTHALL, John (1806?–87). b. Totnes, Devon, son of William S. Benthall. Educated at Westminster School, and Trinity College, Cambridge; BA 1828, MA 1831. Assistant master, Westminster School, 1828–46. Ordained, 1830; chaplain to the Marquess Of Ailsa, 1846–73; vicar, Willen, Buckinghamshire, 1852-87.

Gleanings in the harvest field: or, thoughts in verse on portions of the church services; by John Benthall. Printed Newport Pagnell: J. Line. 1882. [vi], 184 pp.

Printed for private circulation. *OXB*

BENTLEY, Henry Cumberland (1860–). b. Woodlesford, Yorkshire, son of Henry Bentley of Scrivelsby Court, Lincolnshire. Educated at Eton College, Trinity Hall and Jesus College, Cambridge.

Poems; by H. Cumberland Bentley. London: Hatchards. 1894. 50 pp. il. *UCD★*

Songs and verses; by H. Cumberland Bentley. London: Chapman & Hall, Ltd. 1892. [iv], 143 pp. il. *OXB*

BERESFORD, Edward Marcus (1836–96). Son of Major William Beresford, MP for North Essex. Educated at Eton College. Ensign, 51st Foot, Scots Fusilier Guards, 1854; served in the Crimea, 1855–56; captain, 1864; retired with hon. rank of major-general, 1885. Died at the Earl of Arran's house, Queen Anne's Mead, Windsor.

Songs and shadows: [poems]; by E.M. Beresford. London: Digby, Long & Co. [1897]. viii, 99 pp. *OXB*

BERESFORD, Gilbert (1812–99). b. Trowbridge, Wiltshire. Brother of Francis M. Beresford, MP for Southwark. Educated at St John's College, Cambridge; BA 1835, MA 1838. Fellow of St John's 1835–49. Ordained, 1840; rector, Hoby-cum-Rotherby, Leicestershire, from 1843; rural dean, Goscote, and hon. canon of Peterborough.

Poems; by Gilbert Beresford. London: James Nisbet. 1891. viii, 104 pp. *OXB*

The stream of talent, and other poems; by Gilbert Beresford. London: James Nisbet & Co. 1882. iv. 122 pp. *OXB*

BERETON, Ford pseud. *see* **CROCKETT, Samuel Rutherford**, (Ford Bereton, pseud.)

BERRY, Lizzie (1847–   ). b. Great Bowden, Leicestershire, of poor parents. She lived at Otley.

Day dreams: a collection of miscellaneous poems; by Lizzie Berry. Otley: William Walker & Sons. 1893. 319 pp. *UCD*

Heart sketches: original miscellaneous & devotional poems; by Lizzie Berry. With portrait of authoress. Otley: William Walker & Sons. 1886. 320 pp. por. *OXB*

BERTRAM, pseud.

By your leaves, gentle men!: a poem in reply to Mr. W. Watson's "Apologia", and some other poems and fragments; by "Bertram". London: Simpkin, Marshall, Hamilton, Kent & Co. 1896. 80 pp. *OXB*

BESEMERES, Jane. Writer of elementary school books.

Vanished faces, and other poems; by Jane Besemeres. London: James Nisbet & Co. 1884. 110 pp. *BL*

BEST, Kenelm Digby (1835?–   ). Son of John R.D. Best of Botley Grange, Hampshire, a well-known writer. Educated at Ampleforth College, St Edmund's College, Ware, and Oxford University. Ordained Roman Catholic priest, 1858. He was connected with The Oratory, Brompton Road, Kensington, London SW.

The seven dolours: [poems]; by Kenelm Digby Best. 3rd ed. London: Burns & Oates; New York: Catholic Publication Society. [1889]. [iv], 55 pp. *OXB*

BETHAM, Burton

Twenty-odd: [poems]; by Burton Betham. London: Reeves & Turner. 1894. 58 pp. *OXB*

BETHAM-EDWARDS, Matilda (1836–1919). b. Westerfield Hall, Suffolk, daughter of a farmer. Cousin of Amelia Blandford Edwards, novelist and Egyptologist. Largely self-educated to a very high standard, she travelled widely in France. In 1864 she settled in London, becoming a friend of George Eliot, and moving in prominent literary circles. A prolific novelist, she also wrote on French life and topography.

The golden bee, and other recitations; by M. Betham-Edwards. London: Dean & Son Ltd. [189–). 83 pp. (Dean's books for elocutionists).   *OXB*

Poems; by Miss Betham-Edwards. London: Kegan Paul, Trench & Co. 1884. x, 155 pp.   *OXB*

BETTS, E. St. G.
Sun and mist: poems; by E. St. G. Betts. London: T. Fisher Unwin. 1897. 76 pp.   *OXB*

BEVAN, Frances (1827–1900). b. Oxford, daughter of Rev. Philip N. Shuttleworth, Warden of New College, afterwards Bishop of Chichester. In 1856 she married R.C.L. Bevan of the Lombard Street banking firm. Hymn writer.
Service of song in the house of the Lord: [poems]; by Frances Bevan. London: Hatchards. 1884. [iv], 118 pp.   *OXB*

BEVINGTON, Louisa Sarah (1845–). Freethinker, and essayist on evolutionary science, she contributed articles to various periodicals including *Nineteenth Century*, *Progress* and *Liberty*, the last-named a journal of anarchistic communism. She married a Munich artist named Guggenberger, and moved to Germany in 1883.
Liberty lyrics: [poems]; by L.S. Bevington. London: James Tochatti, "Liberty" Press. 1895. 16 pp.   *OXB*

Poems, lyrics, and sonnets; by L.S. Bevington. London: Elliot Stock. 1882. 159 pp.   *BL*

BEVIR, Edward Lawrence, (E.L.B.). Writer on the Bible. Of London.
The storm, and some other verses; by E.L.B. London: G. Morrish. [1892]. 32 pp.   *OXB*

BEWLEY, Edward White (1830–19). b. Moulsham, Essex, son of Thomas Bewley, iron founder of Chelmsford. Educated privately. Articled to John H. Thursfield of Wednesbury, Staffordshire, and admitted a solicitor, 1861. In practice at Gravesend, Kent, from 1866; clerk to Gravesend Borough Justices from 1874. He contributed papers to *Law Magazine*.
Dudley Castle in the Black Country; Little Mabel's note-book; and, Lucy's album; by Edward White Bewley. London: Wyman & Sons. 1884. [iv], 107 pp.   *OXB*

Idonea: a tale of the twelfth century; by Edward White Bewley. London: Digby & Long. [1890]. viii, 100 pp.   *OXB*

Perla: a legend of Tequendama; by Edward White Bewley. London: Wyman & Sons. 1888. [iv], 51 pp.   *OXB*

BEWLEY, John. Apprenticed to a shoemaker at Crookdale, near Wigtown, Cumberland. Lived at Blennerhasset.
Bewley's day dreams: a series of poetical pieces; by John Bewley. Mealsgate: W. Tate. 1891. 31 pp.
      Title from cover.   *BL*

BIBLE STUDENT, pseud. *see* **W., T.A.**, (Bible Student, pseud.)

BICKERSTAFF, Joseph Benjamin
Philomath triumphant, and other poems; by Joseph Benjamin Bickerstaff. London: William Andrews & Co. 1897. [vi], 56 pp.   *OXB*

BICKERSTETH, Edward Henry (1825–1906). Son of Edward Bickersteth. Educated at Trinity College, Cambridge; BA 1847, MA 1850. Seatonian prizewinner, 1854. Ordained, 1848; curate, Banningham, Norfolk, then Christ Church, Tunbridge Wells; rector, Hinton-Martell, Dorset, then Christ Church, Hampstead; Dean of Gloucester, 1885; Bishop of Exeter, 1885-1900. He published many devotional works, and edited several hymnals.
From year to year: poems and hymns for all the Sundays and holy days of the Church; by E.H. Bickersteth. London: Sampson Low, Marston, Searle, & Rivington. 1884. xvi, 232 pp.   *OXB*
    Also 2nd ed. 1884; 3rd ed. [1896].

BIDDER, George (1863–1953). b. Kensington, London, son of George P. Bidder, QC, of Mitcham, Surrey. Educated at Harrow School, and Trinity College, Cambridge. Marine biologist engaged in research on sponges at Naples, Plymouth and Cambridge; lecturer at Cambridge University, 1894 and 1920–27. Owner of the steam-trawler *Huxley*, the British research vessel on the international exploration of the North Sea. Proprietor of Parker's Hotel, Naples, 1889–1922; managing director, Carnock Chase Colliery Co., 1897–1908; also held other directorships. Lived at Cavendish Corner, Cambridge.
By southern shore: [poems]; [by] George Bidder. Westminster: Archibald Constable & Co. 1899. 128 pp.   *OXB*
Merlin's youth, [and other poems]; by George Bidder. Westminster: Archibald Constable & Co. 1899. 70 pp.   *OXB*

BIGGER, Samuel Lenox L. (1809?–91). b. Belfast, with which he had family connections. Educated at Trinity College, Dublin; BA 1830, MA 1832, MB 1834. Engaged on a medical career; Fellow of the Academy of Medicine. He is buried at Mount Jerome Cemetery, Dublin.
The collegians: a poem in fourteen cantos; by S. Lenox L. Bigger. Dublin: Hodges, Figgis, & Co.; London: Simpkin, Marshall, & Co. 1882. [iv], 465 pp.   *OXB*
Elijah, the prophet of fire; by S. Lenox L. Bigger. Dublin: Hodges, Figgis, & Co.; Edinburgh: Andrew Elliot. 1885. 140 pp. il.
    Cover-title is *The prophet of fire*.   *OXB*
A triplet of poems, Christmas, 1886; by S. Lenox L. Bigger. Dublin: Hodges, Figgis, & Co.; London: Simpkin, Marshall, & Co. 1886. 79 pp. il.   *TCD*

BIGNOLD, Thomas Frank (1837?–87). b. Norwich, son of Thomas Bignold. Educated at Caius College, Cambridge (scholar); BA 1859. Entered the Bengal Civil Service, 1859; assistant magistrate, 1860; magistrate at Balasore, 1874; district and sessions judge, 1879; retired in 1886, settling in Tasmania. Died in Melbourne.

Leviora: being the rhymes of a successful competitor; by Thomas Frank Bignold. Calcutta: Thacker, Spink & Co.; London: W. Thacker & Co. 1888. x, 207 pp. *OXB*

BILL O' TH' HOYLUS END, pseud. *see* **WRIGHT, William**, (Bill o' th' Hoylus End, pseud.)

BILLINGTON, William (1827?–84). b. Samlesbury, Lancashire, son of a road contractor who also worked as a handloom weaver and basket-maker. He received very little schooling, entering a mill at an early age to learn throstle spinning. The family moved to Blackburn, where he worked in the mills and made considerable progress in self-education. By saving he went into business as a publican at The Nag's Head, Northgate. He was known as 'The Blackburn Poet'; much of his verse is in dialect.
Lancashire songs, with other poems and sketches; by William Billington. Blackburn: J.G. & J. Toulmin. 1883. [xii], 148 pp. *OPL*

BINGHAM, Mrs Ashton
The autumn leaf poems; by Mrs Ashton Bingham. Printed Edinburgh: Colston & Co. 1891. viii, 104 pp. *BL*

BINGLEY, Robert Mildred (1829–97). Son of Henry Bingley of Woodford, Essex. Educated at Charterhouse, and Trinity College, Cambridge. Ordained 1853; curate, Eastry, Kent, 1853; rector, Braiseworth, Suffolk, where he built the church, from 1853 until his death. Seven stained glass memorial windows were erected by his widow and children, and dedicated in 1900.
Border-lands: [poems]; by Robert Mildred Bingley. London: Henry Frowde. 1893. viii, 92 pp. *OXB*
Also 2nd ed. 1894

BINYON, Laurence (1869–1943). b. Lancaster, son of a clergyman. A cousin of Stephen Phillips. Educated at St Paul's School (scholar), and Trinity College, Oxford (scholar). Entered the Department of Printed Books, British Museum, 1893; transferred to Department of Prints and Drawings, 1895; assistant keeper, 1909; deputy keeper, Oriental Prints & Drawings, 1913-32. An authority on oriental painting and other branches of art, he lectured in the United States and Japan. President, English Association, 1933-34.
First book of London visions: [poems]; by Laurence Binyon. London: Elkin Mathews. 1896. [ii], 32 pp. (Shilling garland, 1). *OXB*
First book of London visions: [poems]; by Laurence Binyon. [2nd ed., revised]. London: Elkin Matthews. 1896. 32 pp. (Garland of new poetry, I). *MPL*
Lyric poems; by Laurence Binyon. London: Elkin Mathews & Io [sic] Lane. 1894. xii, 92 pp.
A limited ed. of 300 copies. Spine-title is *Poems*. *MPL*
Persephone: the Newdigate poem, 1890; by Laurence Binyon. Oxford: B.H. Blackwell; London: Simpkin, Marshall & Co. 1890. 15 pp. *OXB*
Poems; by Laurence Binyon. Oxford: Daniel. 1895. [viii], 56 pp.
A limited ed. of 200 numbered copies. *TCD*

Porphyrion, and other poems; by Laurence Binyon. London: Grant Richards. 1898. [viii], 150 pp. *OXB*

The praise of life: [poems]; by Laurence Binyon. London: Elkin Mathews. 1896. [ii], 32 pp. (Garland of new poetry). *MPL*

The praise of life: [poems]; by Laurence Binyon. London: Elkin Mathews. 1896. [ii], 32 pp. (Shilling garland, VI). *OXB*

Second book of London visions: [poems]; by Laurence Binyon. London: Elkin Mathews. 1899. 36 pp. (Garland of new poetry). *MPL*

BIRD, Robert (1854–   ). b. Govan, Lanarkshire, son of David Bird, lawyer. Educated at Glasgow College, taking honours in Scottish law before joining his father's practice in Glasgow. A Quaker, he was organizer of the Liberal Unionist Association; vice-president, Glasgow Peace Society; vice-chairman of council, Scottish Society of Literature & Art; member of the Ruskin Society, and the Glasgow Ballad Club.

The falls of Clyde, and other poems; by [Robert Bird]. Paisley: Alexander Gardner. 1888. 119 pp. il. *OXB*

Law lyrics; by [Robert Bird]. Glasgow: Wilson & McCormick. 1885. 88 pp. *OXB*

   Also 2nd ed. 1887; New ed. (abridged) 1888.

More law lyrics; by Robert Bird. Edinburgh: William Blackwood & Sons. 1898. xiv, 136 pp. *MPL*

BIRD, Robert J. Golding- *see* **GOLDING-BIRD, Robert J.**

BIRKS, Herbert Alfred (1856–1923). b. Kelsall, Hertfordshire, son of Thomas R. Birks. Educated at Repton School, and Trinity College, Cambridge; BA 1878, MA 1882. Seatonian prizewinner, 1890. Curate, St Andrew's, Nottingham, 1880–81; assistant tutor, London College of Divinity, 1881–85; curate, Hornsey Rise, Middlesex, 1884–85, Chigwell, Essex, 1885–95; vicar, Churchstow with Kingsbridge, Devon, 1895–1921; chaplain to the forces, 1915–21. Lived latterly at Dawlish, Devon.

Sonnets for saints' days and holy days; by H.A. Birks. London: Society for Promoting Christian Knowledge; New York: E. & J.B. Young & Co. [1890]. 48 pp. *OXB*

BIRMINGHAM, Andrew B. A Galway man. Died pre– 1912.

Poems; by Andrew B. Birmingham. Dublin. 1881. ★

BIRTLES, William. Of Great Salkeld, Cumberland.

Musings o'er flood and fell: [poems]; by William Birtles. Manchester: John Heywood. 1882. viii, 108 pp.

   Spine-title is *Poems*. *OXB*

BISHOP, John B., (B.), (Aged Pilgrim, pseud.). A Scottish businessman, he lived at Bruntsfield Place, Edinburgh.
Heart melodies of an aged pilgrim; by [B.]. Edinburgh: Andrew Stevenson. 1891. viii, 164 pp. *BL*

BISHOP, Kate (1869–19). b. St Mary's, Orkney Islands. Daughter of an estate agent who practised in North Wales and Sussex.
A life's requiem, and other poems; by Kate Bishop. London: E. Marlborough; Northampton: S.S. Campion. 1890. [viii], 199 pp. *BL*

BLACK, Ebenezer
Early songs and lyrics; by Ebenezer Black. Edinburgh: William Brown. 1886. 158 pp. *OXB*

BLACKBURN, Osburn (1870–96). b. Edinburgh, son of an outfitter. Educated at Newington Academy, and St James's Episcopal School. His juvenile verses were written for London birthday and Christmas card manufacturers. A frequent contributor to the *Weekly Scotsman, Reformer*, etc. Several of his poems were set to music.
Twilight thoughts: [poems]; by Osburn Blackburn. Paisley: Alexander Gardner. 1896. 199 pp. por. *OXB*

BLACKBURN POET *see* **BILLINGTON, William**

BLACKFORD, John Richard, (J.R.B.).
The three bills: the great will, the lesser will, and the little bill: a political satire; by J.R.B. London: William Poole. 1881. 15 pp. *OXB*

BLACKIE, John Stuart (1809–95). b. Glasgow of Kelso ancestry. Educated at Aberdeen and Edinburgh Universities, and at Gottingen, Berlin and Rome. Passed advocate at the Edinburgh Bar. Professor of humanity, Marischal College, Aberdeen, 1841–52, then professor of Greek at Edinburgh until 1882. He took an active part in educational reform; raised funds for the foundation of a Celtic chair at Edinburgh. Wrote on moral and religious philosophy.
Lays of the highlands and islands; by John Stuart Blackie. London: Walter Scott. 1883. 302 pp. *LL*
Messis vitae: gleanings of song from a happy life; by John Stuart Blackie. London: Macmillan & Co. 1886. x, 204 pp. *MPL*
The selected poems of John Stuart Blackie. Edited with an appreciation by Archibald Stodart Walker. With a portrait after the painting by J.H. Lorimer. London: John Macqueen. 1896. xii, 301 pp. por. *MPL*
A song of heroes: [poems]; by John Stuart Blackie. Edinburgh: William Blackwood & Sons. xiv, 256 pp. *MPL*

BLACKMORE, Richard Doddridge (1825–1900). b. Longworth, Berkshire. Educated at Blundell's School, and Exeter College, Oxford. Called to the bar, Middle Temple, 1852; practised for c. twelve years as a conveyancer, then left the law for literature, combining writing with management of a market garden at Teddington-on-Thames, Middlesex. A successful novelist, he contributed articles on gardening and fruit-growing to *Chambers's Encyclopaedia*. Lived at Gomer House, Teddington, from 1858 until his death.
   Fringilla: some tales in verse; by Richard Doddridge Blackmore. Pictured by Louis Fairfax-Muckley. With III drawings by James Linton. London: Elkin Mathews. 1895. [viii], 128 pp. il. *MPL*
     Also a limited ed. of 25 copies, 1895.

BLACKWOOD, James Stevenson (1805–82). Son of Pinkstan Blackwood of Killyleagh, County Down. Educated at Trinity College, Dublin; BA, LL.B, LL.D. Admitted to Gray's Inn, London, but did not follow law. Vicar, Middleton Tyas, Yorkshire.
   The paradox of life: or, Christian Koheleth: a poem, with a sheaf of sacred sonnets and other poems; by James S. Blackwood. London: James Nisbet & Co. 1881. [iv], 119 pp. *OXB*

BLAIKIE, John Arthur (1850–   ). Author and journalist.
   Love's victory: lyrical poems; by John Arthur Blaikie. London: Percival & Co. 1890. xii, 128 pp. *OXB*

BLAKE, Emilia Aylmer *see* **GOWING, Emilia Aylmer**

BLAKE, C.J. Novelist.
   Bernard and Constantia, and other poems; by C.J. Blake. London: Digby, Long & Co. [1892]. viii, 55 pp. *OXB*

BLAKENEY, Edward Henry, (E.H.B.) (1861–1955). b. Mitcham, Surrey, son of William Blakeney, paymaster-in-chief, Royal Navy. Educated at Westminster School, and Trinity College, Cambridge; BA 1891, MA 1895. Headmaster, Sandwich Grammar School, Kent, 1895-1901, Sir William Borlase's School, Marlow, Buckinghamshire, 1901–04, King's School, Ely, 1904-18; assistant master, Winchester College, 1918-30. Lecturer in English literature, Southampton University, 1929-31. Lived latterly at 17 Edgar Road, Winchester.
   Driftwood: or wayside musings in verse; by Edward Henry Blakeney. Printed Ramsgate: Sutton & Goodchild. 1893. 20 pp. *OXB*
   The exile's return, and other poems; by E.H.B. Cambridge: J. Palmer; London: G.J. Palmer. 1890. viii, 58 pp. *BL*
   Poems by two friends: Edward Henry Blakeney and D. Morrieson Panton. Cambridge: J. Palmer; London: G.J. Palmer. 1892. viii, 44 pp.
     Not joint authorship. *OXB*

Voices after sunset, and other poems; by Edward Henry Blakeney. With illustrations by H. Maurice Page. Printed London: Gresham Press, Unwin Bros. [1897]. 88 pp. il.
    A limited ed. of 251 numbered copies. *OXB*

BLASE MAN, pseud. *see* **HERON-ALLAN, Edward**, (Blasé Man, pseud.)

BLATCHFORD, Ambrose Nichols (1842–1924). b. Plymouth, Devon, son of James Blatchford. Educated at Old Tavistock Grammar School, and London University. He studied for the ministry; appointed minister to the Ancient Society of Protestant Dissenters assembling in Lewin's Mead; manager and secretary of Lewin's Mead British Schools. President of Bristol Cambrian Society, 1893; second president, Society of Devonians in Bristol.
    Idylls of Old Greece; by Ambrose N. Blatchford. Bristol: J.W. Arrowsmith; London: Simpkin, Marshall, Hamilton, Kent & Co. Ltd. [1899]. 186 pp. *OXB*

BLAYDS, Charles Stuart *see* **CALVERLEY, Charles Stuart**

BLECKLY, Henry (1812–90). b. Ipswich, Suffolk. Educated at Ackworth School. Partner and manager of a small iron business at Warrington, Lancashire, which amalgamated with the Wigan collieries of Messrs Pearson & Knowles; he became chairman of the new company. One of the earliest members of the Iron & Steel Institute; founder of Warrington Chamber of Commerce. Vice-chairman of Liverpool quarter sessions for many years. Lived at West Wood, Altrincham, Cheshire.
    Verses in controversy; by Henry Bleckly. Manchester: J.E. Cornish. 1884. 24 pp. *MPL*

"The BLESSED HOPE". London: William & Norgate. [1881]. [8], viii, 236 pp. *OXB*

BLEVINS, Louisa. Of Romsey, Hampshire.
    Tears and smiles: [poems]; by Louisa Blevins. Romsey: C.L. Lordan. 1880. [viii], 64 pp. *OXB*

BLEW, William John, (Storicus, pseud.) (1804–94). b. Westminster, London, son of William Blew. Educated at St Nicholas's School, Ealing, and Wadham College, Oxford; BA 1830, MA 1832. Curate, Nuthurst, Sussex, 1832–40, St Anne's, Soho, London, 1840–42; minister, St John's Chapel, Milton next Gravesend, 1842–50. Hymn writer, and translator from the Greek. Lived at 6 Warwick Street, Pall Mall, London, from 1850 to his death.
    English babes and Irish bullies: lays of old Rome for old England; by Storicus. London: Kennett, Towerzey, & Co. 1890. [6], viii, 58 pp. *OXB*

BLIGH, Samuel, (S.B.) (1806-85). Of Tooting-Graveney, Surrey.
    Poems, 1806 to 1885; by S.B. Printed Guildford: Billing & Sons. 1886. [vi], 56 pp.il.
    Privately printed. BL copy is interleaved with author's MS. notes. *BL*

BLIND, Mathilde (1841–96). b. Mannheim, Germany, daughter of a banker named Cohen. She subsequently adopted the name of her stepfather, Karl Blind, exiled for involvement with the 1849 Baden insurrection. The family settled in London, where she received an English education. A champion of women's rights, she wrote biographies of George Eliot and Madame Roland, and translated the journal of Marie Bashkirtseff. She died in London, bequeathing the greater part of her estate to Newnham College, Cambridge.

The ascent of man, [and other poems]; by Mathilde Blind. London: Chatto & Windus. 1889. viii, 200 pp.   *MPL*

The ascent of man, [and other poems]; by Mathilde Blind. With an introduction by Alfred R. Wallace. London: T. Fisher Unwin. 1899. xvi, 192 pp. por.   *OXB*

Birds of passage: songs of the orient and occident; by Mathilde Blind. London: Chatto & Windus. 1895. viii, 147 pp.

   A limited ed. of 250 copies.   *OXB*

   Also 2nd ed. 1896.

Dramas in miniature: [poems]; by Mathilde Blind. With a frontispiece by Ford Madox Brown. London: Chatto & Windus. 1891. vi, 114 pp. il.   *MPL*

The heather on fire: a tale of the Highland Clearances; by Mathilde Blind. London: Walter Scott. 1886. [viii], 118 pp.   *MPL*

The prophecy of Saint Oran, and other poems; by Mathilde Blind. London: Newman & Co. 1881. viii, 135 pp.   *MPL*

A selection from the poems of Mathilde Blind. Edited by Arthur Symons. London: T. Fisher Unwin. 1897. xii, 147 pp. por.

   Spine-title is *Poems*.   *OXB*

Songs and sonnets; by Mathilde Blind. London: Chatto & Windus. 1893. viii, 120 pp.   *MPL*

BLIND POET OF WRAWBY *see* **BEDFORD, Joseph Goodworth**

BLIND PREACHER *see* **MATHESON, George**

BLOOMER, Frederick

Annie Wray: a poem: by Frederick Bloomer. London: A. White & Co. 1884. 108 pp.

   A limited ed. of 500 copies.   *OXB*

BLUNT, Wilfrid *see* **BLUNT, Wilfrid Scawen**

BLUNT, Wilfrid Scawen, (Proteus, pseud.) (1840–1922). b. Petworth, Sussex, son of a landowner. Educated at Pyrford, Hampshire, Stonyhurst College, and Oscott College. He entered the diplomatic service in 1858, serving successively in Athens, Frankfurt, Madrid, Paris, Lisbon, Buenos Aires, and Berne. In 1869 he married Lady Anne Noel, grand-daughter of Lord Byron. Travelled in Arabia and the Moslem East, 1877–81. With his wife he founded the Crabbet Arabian Stud, Sussex, 1878. An enthusiastic supporter of the nationalist movements in Egypt and in Ireland, he was imprisoned for activity in the Irish Land League, 1888.

Esther; Love lyrics; and, Natalia's resurrection; by Wilfrid Scawen Blunt. London: Kegan Paul, Trench, Trübner & Co., Ltd. 1892. vi, 248 pp. *MPL*

Griselda: a society novel in rhymed verse; [by Wilfrid Scawen Blunt]. London: Kegan Paul, Trench, Trübner, & Co. Ltd. 1893. 127 pp. *OXB*

In vinculis: [poems]; by Wilfrid Scawen Blunt. London: Kegan Paul, Trench & Co. 1889. x, 64 pp. por. *OXB*

The love-lyrics & songs of Proteus; by Wilfrid Scawen Blunt; with The love-sonnets of Proteus; by the same author now reprinted in their full text with many sonnets omitted from the earlier editions. Printed [Hammersmith]: [William Morris at the Kelmscott Press]. 1892. [x], 251 pp. *JRL*

The love sonnets of Proteus. With frontispiece by the author. London: C. Kegan Paul & Co. 1881. xii, 120 pp. il. *OXB*

Also 2nd ed. 188–; 3rd ed. 1882, 4th ed. 1885.

A new pilgrimage, and other poems; by Wilfrid Scawen Blunt. London: Kegan Paul, Trench & Co. 1889. xvi, 183 pp. *OXB*

The poetry of Wilfrid Blunt. Selected and arranged by W. E. Henley and George Wyndham. London: William Heinemann. 1898. xiv, 283 pp. *OXB*

The wind and the whirlwind; by Wilfrid Scawen Blunt. London: Kegan Paul, Trench, & Co. 1883. 42 pp. *OXB*

The wind and the whirlwind; by Wilfrid Scawen Blunt. Boston, [Mass.]: Benj. R. Tucker. 1884. 30 pp. *OXB*

BODLEY, George Frederick (1827–1907). Descendent of Thomas Bodley, scholar and diplomat. He trained as an architect, a pupil of Sir Gilbert Scott from 1845 to 1850; designed many churches and private houses world-wide; an exponent of fourteenth-century English Gothic style. Friend of Burne-Jones, William Morris, and others in the Pre-Raphelite Brotherhood.

Poems; by G.F. Bodley. London: George Bell & Sons. 1899. viii, 169 pp. *OXB*

BODMER, Friederica, (Granny, pseud.)

Six ballads about King Arthur; [by a granny]. London: Kegan Paul, Trench. & Co. 1881. [viii], 80 pp. il. *OXB*

BOLITHO, William (18 –94). Member of a family of bankers in Penzance, Cornwall. Lived at Ponsandane, Penzance.

Nugae: a rhyming melody; by William Bolitho. Printed Plymouth: W. Brendon & Son. 1891. viii, 53 pp.

Printed for private circulation. *OXB*

BONAR, Horatius (1808–89). b. Edinburgh, son of James Bonar, solicitor. Educated at Edinburgh High School, and Edinburgh University. Entered the Church of Scotland ministry; appointed minister at Kelso, 1837; joined the Free Church at the disruption in 1843: minister of Chalmers Memorial Church, Edinburgh, 1866. Moderator of the General Assembly of the Free Church, 1883. Published hymns and religious tracts, and edited several religious journals.

My old letters: [poems]; by Horatius Bonar. London: James Nisbet & Co. 1880. 2 vols. *MPL*

Songs of love and joy: poems; by Horatius Bonar. London: H.J. Drane; New York: E.P. Dutton & Co. [1888]. [32] pp. col. il.

Printed on card. *TCD*

"Until the day break", and other hymns and poems left behind; by Horatius Bonar. London: Hodder & Stoughton. 1890. xvi, 284 pp. *OXB*

BOND, Richard Warwick (1857–1943). Son of Rev. Richard S. Bond of Hindley, Lancashire. Educated at Bromsgrove School, and Queen's College, Oxford; BA 1880, MA 1887. Lecturer to the Oxford extension delegacy from 1886. Sometime editor of *Saint George*, the Ruskin quarterly. Lived latterly at Lynwood, Tattenhall Drive, The Park, Nottingham.

Another sheaf: [poems]; by R. Warwick Bond. London: Elkin Mathews. 1898. 95 pp. il. *OXB*

At Stratford Festival: a poem; by R. Warwick Bond. London: Lawrence & Bullen. 1896. 30 pp. il. *OXB*

The immortals, and other poems; by R. Warwick Bond. London: T. Fisher Unwin. 1890. 64 pp. *OXB*

An ode to the sun, and other poems; by R. Warwick Bond. London: Kegan Paul, Trench, Trübner & Co., Ltd. 1892. [viii], 122 pp. *OXB*

BONE ET FIDELIS: A POEM. London: Elliot Stock. 1882. x, 70 pp. *OXB*

BOOK OF CHAINS: [poems]. London: Swan Sonnerschein & Co., Ltd. 1897. xii, 107 pp. *OXB*

BOOTH, Eva Gore- *see* **GORE-BOOTH, Eva**

BORASTON, John Maclair, (Aston Claire, pseud.). Of Stretford, Lancashire. A member of the north-west branch of the British Astronomical Association, to which he contributed papers. Writer on British birds.

Claudio and Fida, and other poems; by Aston Clair. London: London Literary Society. [1886]. [viii], 128 pp. *MPL*

Philaster, and other poems; by Aston Clair. London: T. Fisher Unwin. 1888. viii, 206 pp. *MPL*

BOTT, Thomas Herrivel. Of Stechford, Worcestershire.

Robinson Crusoe in verse; by Thomas H. Bott. London: Simpkin, Marshall & Co.; Birmingham: Midland Educational Co. [1882]. 173 pp. il. *OXB*

BOTTOMLEY, Gordon (1874–1948). b. Keighley, Yorkshire. Educated at Keighley Grammar School. He settled in the Lake District. Ill-health obliged him to restrict his activities. A student of the Elizabethans, he led a revival of verse-drama.

The mickle drede, and other verses; written by Gordon Bottomley. Printed Kendal: T.Wilson. 1896. [viii], 102 pp. *OXB*

Poems at White-Nights: a book of verse; written by Gordon Bottomley. London: Sign of the Unicorn. 1899. 96 pp. (Unicorn books of verse, 5).   *OXB*

BOULDING, James Wimsett. A clergyman.
Fables and fancies: grave, humorous and pathetic: a book for children and children of a larger growth: [poems]; by J. Wimsett Boulding. London: Jarrold & Sons. [1897]. 181 pp.   *OXB*

BOULTON, Sir Harold (1859–1935). Elder son of Sir S.B. Boulton. Educated at Harrow School, and Balliol College, Oxford. Captain, Queen's Own Cameron Highlanders Militia; captain, City of London Yeomanry, Rough Riders, 1914–17. He held many public appointments. Lived at Copped Hall, Camberley, Surrey, and Inch Kenneth, Argyll.
Songs, sung and unsung; by Harold Boulton. London: Simpkin, Marshall, Hamilton, Kent & Co., Ltd; New York: Charles Scribner's Sons. [1894]. 2 vols.   *OXB*

BOUNDY, T. Lived at 59 Walton Street, Gateshead, County Durham.
An essay on ambition: a poem; by T. Boundy. Gateshead: Author. [1883]. 16 pp.   *BL*

BOURDILLON, Francis William (1852–1921). Son of Rev. F. Bourdillon. Educated at Haileybury, and Worcester College, Oxford (scholar). Appointed resident tutor to Prince and Princess Christian at Cumberland Lodge. Later, at Eastbourne, he prepared private pupils for university entrance. Lived latterly at Buddington, near Midhurst, Sussex.
Ailes d'alouette: [poems]; [by] F.W. Bourdillon. Oxford: H. Daniel. 1890. [vii], 64 pp.
   A limited ed. of 100 numbered copies.   *OXB*
Among the flowers, and other poems; by Francis W. Bourdillon. Cheaper issue. London: Marcus Ward & Co. 1883. [ii], 176 pp.   *NLW*
Chryseis, [and other poems]; [by Francis William Bourdillon]. Oxford: B.H. Blackwell. 1894. [vi], 47 pp.   *BL*
A lost god; by Francis W. Bourdillon. With illustrations by H.J. Ford. London: Elkin Mathews at the sign of The Bodley Head. 1891. 60 pp. il.
   A limited small paper ed. of 500 copies.   *OXB*
   Also a limited large paper ed. of 50 copies.
Love in a mist: [poems]; by [Francis William Bourdillon]. Oxford: B.H. Blackwell. 1892. [iv], 100 pp.   *BL*
Love lies bleeding: [poems]; [by Francis William Bourdillon]. Oxford: B.H. Blackwell. 1891. [iv], 83 pp.   *BL*
Miniscula: lyrics of nature, art and love; by Francis William Bourdillon. London: Lawrence & Bullen, Ltd. 1897. xii, 112 pp.   *OXB*
Sursum corda, [and other poems]; by F.W. Bourdillon. London: T. Fisher Unwin. 1893. 144 pp.   *OXB*

BOUSTEAD, Christopher Murray. A road-man of Keswick, Cumberland.
Rustic verse and dialect rhymes; by Christopher Murray Boustead. Printed
Keswick: T. Bakewell. 1892. viii, 88 pp.   *MPL*

BOWEN, Charles, Lord Bowen (1835–94). b. Chepstow, Monmouthshire.
Educated at Rugby School, and Balliol College, Oxford; Fellow of Balliol,
1857. Called to the Bar, Lincoln's Inn, 1861; bencher, 1879; joined the Western
circuit; junior counsel against claimant in the Tichbourne case, 1871–74;
appointed judge of Queen's Bench, and knighted, 1879; Lord of Appeal,
receiving a life peerage, 1893. He published translations of Virgil, and other
writings.
Lord Bowen: a biographical sketch, with a selection from his verses; by Sir Henry
Stewart Cunningham. London: John Murray. 1897. viii, 252 pp. por.   *BL*

BOWEN, Edward Ernest (1836–1901). b. Chepstow, Monmouthshire.
Brother of Charles, Lord Bowen. Educated at King's College, London, and
Trinity College, Cambridge (scholar); Fellow of Trinity, 1859. A master at
Harrow School, 1859–1901; in 1872 he wrote the Harrow School song 'Forty
Years On'. An all-round sportsman, he was a Liberal in politics, and a writer
on military and theological topics.
Harrow songs, and other verses; by Edward E. Bowen. London: Longmans,
Green, & Co. 1886. viii, 80 pp.   *OXB*

BOWEN, Herbert Courthope (1848–1909). b. Trinidad, West Indies.
Educated at Corpus Christi College, Cambridge; BA 1870, MA 1874.
Assistant master, Dulwich College, 1870, Highstead School, Torquay, 1871–
73, city of London School, 1873–76; headmaster, Hackney Downs School,
1876–81; principal, Finsbury Training College for Teachers, 1882–86; lec-
tured on education at Cambridge, 1884–98. A founder of the Teachers' Guild.
Writer on comparative religion. Lived at 14 Castletown Road, West
Kensington, London W.
Blossom from an orchard: poems, songs, and sonnets; by H. Courthope Bowen.
London: David Stott. 1885. 141 pp.   *OXB*

BOWER, Selina A. Miscellaneous writer.
*From Advent to Advent: or, pieces in prose and poetry, on subjects selected from
Sunday services*; by Selina A. Bower. London: Jarrold & Sons. [c. 1884]. 219
pp.   **UCD*

BOWES, Fanny
The house beautiful, and other poems; [by Fanny Bowes]. Glasgow: Robert
Maclehose & Co. 1896. 39 pp. por.
   For private circulation.   *CU*

BOWES, William
Our little Nell; by William Bowes. [1895]. 16 pp.   *OXB*

BOWIE, A.H., (A.H.B.). Kinsman of John Spreull, 1646–1722.

The martyr's crest: memorial of (Bass) John Spreull; by A.H.B. Printed Glasgow: Robert Maclehose. 1886. [iv], 20 pp. por.

Printed for private circulation. *BL*

BOWLES, Frederick G. (18 –19). Song writer. The English representative for Talia (Teatro Libero), Milan. Lived at Dunedin, Stockton-on-Tees, County Durham.

In the wake of the sun: a book of verse; written by Fred G. Bowles. London: Sign of the Unicorn. 1899. 89 pp. (Unicorn books of verse, 4). *OXB*

BOWLES, George Stewart (1877–1955). Son of T. Gibson Bowles. Educated at Trinity College, Cambridge. Entered the Royal Navy, 1891, serving as sub-lieutenant on HMS *Tourmaline;* he resigned his commission on attending Trinity College, 1898. barrister of Inner Temple, 1901. Conservative MP for the Norwood Division of Lambeth, London, 1906–10. Lived latterly at Clives, Boxted, Colchester, Essex.

A gun-room ditty box; by G. Stewart Bowles. With a preface by Rear-Admiral Lord Charles Beresford. London: Cassell & Co. Ltd. 1898. 116 pp.

Poetry and prose. *OXB*

BOWLING, Edward Woodley (1837–1907). Son of Thomas R. Bowling, a physician practising in Nice. Educated at King Edward's School, Birmingham, and St John's College, Cambridge; BA 1860, MA 1863. Fellow of St John's, 1862–73. Assistant master, Bromsgrove School, 1860–62. Ordained, 1868; curate, Newton, Cambridgeshire, 1867–73; rector, Houghton Conquest, Bedfordshire, 1873–97. Contributor to *Punch* and other periodicals. Lived latterly at 21 Amherst Avenue, Ealing, London W.

"The message to the angel of the church in Sardis" – Rev. III, 1–6: the Seatonian prize poem for 1886; by Edward Woodley Bowling. Cambridge: Macmillan & Bowes. 1887. 16 pp. *OXB*

"On earth peace": the Seatonian prize poem for 1887; by Edward Woodley Bowling. Cambridge: Deighton, Bell & Sons; London: George Bell & Sons. 1888. 16 pp. *OXB*

Sagittulae: random verses; by E.W. Bowling. London: Longmans, Green, & Co.; Cambridge: W. Metcalfe & Son. 1885. viii, 196 pp. *OXB*

St Paul and Felix: the Seatonian prize poem for 1880; by Edward Woodley Bowling. Cambridge: Deighton, Bell & Co; London: George Bell & Sons. 1880. 16 pp. *OXB*

BOWNES, James (1845–1907). Son of James Bownes of Cirencester, Gloucestershire. Educated at Cheltenham College, and Trinity College, Cambridge; BA 1869, MA 1872. Curate, St Paul's, Congleton, Cheshire, 1869–72, Charlton King's, Gloucestershire, 1872; vicar, Creech St Michael, Somerset, 1872–1901.

Randolph, Lord De Vere, and other poems; by James Bownes. London: Swan Sonnenschein & Co. 1895. viii, 128 pp. *OXB*

A vision of martyrs, and other poems; by James Bownes. London: J. Masters & Co. 1887. 165 pp.   *OXB*
   Also revised ed. 1892.

BOWSTEAD, Joseph (1831?–1907). Educated at Queen's College, Oxford; BA 1853, MA 1856. Curate, Alston, Cumberland, 1854–57, Whickham, County Durham, 1857–60, Etherley, 1861–66, St John's Lee, Northumberland, 1866–73; vicar, Soulby, Kirby Stephen, Westmorland, from 1873.
   Poems; by J. Bowstead. Printed Appleby: J. Whitehead. 1881. xii, 88 pp.   *OXB*

BOX, John. Taught at Dorking Grammar School, Surrey.
   The deluge: a poem, Books I to IV; by John Box. London: John Marshall & Co. 1882. x, 150 pp.   *BL*
   A metrical history of England; by John Box. London: John Marshall & Co. 1882. 46 pp.
      Cover-title is *Metrical England*.   *OXB*
   Noe and Noemah; by John Box. London: John Marshall & Co. [1885?]. [171] pp.   *OXB*

BOYCE, John Cox (1826?–89). Son of John Boyce of Birmingham. Educated at Magdalen Hall, Oxford; BA 1854, MA 1859. Curate, Topcliffe, Yorkshire, 1856–64; perpetual curate, Marton-le-moor, near Ripon, 1859–64; domestic chaplain to Lord Borthwick, 1881–85; rector, Cornwell, Oxfordshire, from 1885.
   The Sea of Galilee: a mirror of the Church's future: a poem in five books; by J.C. Boyce. Oxford: Parker & Co. 1886. [viii], 110 pp.   *OXB*

BOYD-MUSHET, William (18 –87?). A relative of Dr William Mushet, eminent Irish physician. Educated at London University; MB, MRCP. Resident physician at St Marylebone Infirmary, at North London Hospital for Consumption, and at the Jews' Hospital; practised in Cheshire. Author of medical works.
   The age of clay (Aetas argillacea): I Morals, II A rhythmic satire; by William Boyd-Mushet. London: Wyman & Sons. 1883. [viii], 176 pp.   *OXB*

BOYLE, Emily Charlotte, Countess of Cork & Orrery (1828–1912). Daughter of the 1st Marquis of Clarincade. In 1854 she married Richard Edmund St Lawrance Boyle, 9th Earl of Cork & Orrery. Lived at 40 Charles Street, Mayfair, London, and at Marston Biggott, Frome, Somerset.
   Memories and thoughts: [poems]; by the Countess of Cork. Followed by a hitherto unpublished poem by George Canning. London: George Bell & Sons. 1886. xii, 142 pp.   *OXB*

BRABOURNE, Percy
   Recitations, and other poems; by Percy Brabourne. London: Elliot Stock. 1889. [iv], 108 pp.   *OXB*

BRACKENBURY, Catherine Ada. Of Harringay, London. Died aged twenty-one.

A legacy of verse; by Catherine Ada Brackenbury. London: George Routledge & Sons, Ltd. 1893. 192 pp. *BL*

BRADFIELD, Mary Bertha. Miss Bradfield.

Songs of faith and hope and love; by Mary Bertha Bradfield. London: Charles H. Kelly. 1898. 112 pp. *BL*

BRADFORD, John. Of Hereford?

Poems: original and translated; by John Bradford. Hereford: F.S. Prosser; Bristol: Austin & Oates. 1885. [xiv], 107 pp. *BL*

BRADLEY, Katherine Harris, (Michael Field, pseud. with Edith Emma Cooper), (Arran Leigh, pseud.) (1848-1914). Daughter of a Birmingham tobacco manufacturer. Educated privately, at Newnham College, Cambridge, and the Collège de France, Paris. The devoted companion of her niece, Edith Emma Cooper, they lived together successively in Bristol, Reigate and Richmond, Surrey. In collaboration they wrote twenty-seven tragedies and eight volumes of verse, operating in such close affinity that their work appeared to be that of a single author. They became Roman Catholics in 1907, and died of cancer within a year of each other.

Bellerophôn: [a play]; [and], [Poems]; by Arran and Isla Leigh. London: C. Kegan Paul & Co. 1881. [vi], 182 pp. *OXB*

Long ago: [poems]; by Michael Field. London: George Bell & Sons. 1889. [viii], 133 pp. il.

A limited ed. of 100 numbered copies. *OXB*

Sight and song: [poems]; written by Michael Field. London: Elkin Mathews and John Lane at the sign of The Bodley Head. 1892. x, 127 pp.

A limited ed. of 400 copies. *BL*

Underneath the bough: a book of verses; by Michael Field. London: George Bell & Sons. 1893. [viii], 138 pp.

A limited ed. of 150 copies. *BL*

Also [Revised and decreased ed.] 1893.

Underneath the bough: a book of verses; by Michael Field. Portland, Maine: Thomas B. Mosher. 1898. [vi], 94 pp. (Old world series). *BL*

BRADLEY, Reuben. Of Shrewsbury, Shropshire?

The flute of Athena, and other poems; by Reuben Bradley. London: Elliot Stock; Shrewsbury: Adnitt & Naunton. 1894. viii, 202 pp. *OXB*

BRADSHAW, George Butler (1822?-1901). An Irishman, an eccentric character, a professor and examiner at the Science & Art Department, South Kensington, allegedly dismissed on account of his nationality. He became a clergyman at New Maldon, Surrey. Died as a result of burns received in a fire at his lodgings.

The gossiping tongue, and other salutary satires: [poems]; by George Butler Bradshaw. 2nd ed. Clapham: A. Bachhoffner; London: Hamilton, Adams & Co. 1880. 69 pp. *OXB*

"Mamma, is Jesus dead?": *a true and thrilling story of a holy Christian mother and her innocent infant son; with six other poems, suitable to the subject*; by George Butler Bradshaw. London: C.A. Mason. 1895. 24 pp. (Heart's-ease series of un-sectarian . . . poems for the people, I). *OXB*

Poetical portraits of the good, the gifted, the brave, and the beautiful, with other poems; by George Butler Bradshaw. Subscribers' ed. New Maldon, Surrey: Author. 1882. xxviii, 322 pp.

Private ed. obtainable from author only. *BL*

Stirring ballads for the people: 1. Don't give up; 2. Nothing to eat; 3. The tippler; 4. Jimmy Joyce; by George Butler Bradshaw. London: George Stoneman. 1892. 4 vols in 1.

Title from cover. *OXB*

BRADY, Barney, pseud. *see* **PARKES, William Theodore**, (Barney Brady, pseud.)

BRAGG, John (1821–98). b. Birmingham, son of Thomas P. Bragg, manufacturing jeweller. He began work as a cooper then joined the family business with his brother. They were the first to employ professional designers, modellers and draughtsmen. A talented landscape painter and water colourist, his works were exhibited in London, Leeds and Birmingham. A Sunday school teacher, and a member of Birmingham Temperance Society, he lived at Hamstead Mount, Handsworth.

Sonnets and short poems (Second series); by John Bragg. Printed Leeds: Alfred W. Inman. 1890. x, 128 pp. por.

For presentation only. *BL*

BRAITHWAITE, Adeline. Miss Braithwaite. Writer on foreign missions.

Scripture spoil in sacred song: [poems]; by Adeline Braithwaite. London: James Nisbet & Co. 1886. viii, 119 pp. *OXB*

BRAITHWAITE, Joseph Bevan (1818–1905). Son of Isaac Braithwaite of Kendal, Westmorland. Student of Middle Temple, called to the Bar, 1843. He married the daughter of a Banbury solicitor. Lived in London.

Paul the apostle: a poem; by Joseph Bevan Braithwaite. London: Seeley & Co. 1885. 178 pp. *OXB*

BRAITHWAITE, William Charles (1862–1922). Son of Joseph Bevan Braithwaite of London. Educated at Oliver's Mount School, Scarborough, and University College, London. Practised as a barrister until 1896 then became a partner in Gillett & Co., bankers of Banbury and Oxford. Writer on Quakerism and other religious topics. Lived latterly at Castle House, Banbury.

Monodies; by [William Charles Braithwaite and Silvanus Phillips Thompson]. Printed Chiswick: Chiswick Press. 1892. 24 pp.

A limited ed. of 100 numbered copies, privately printed for the Westminster Portfolio Society. Not joint authorship. *OXB*

BRAMHALL, Mae St John

Japanese jingles: being a few little verses, which have appeared before in the "Japanese Gazette"; by Mae St John Bramhall. Tokyo, Japan: T. Hasegawa. 1891. [66] pp. col. il.

Printed on crepe paper. Cover-title is *Niponese rhymes and Japanese jingles*. *BL*

Also 2nd ed. 1893 [i.e. 1892].

BRAMSTON, Francis Thomas (1843–1916). Son of William Bramston of Paddington, London. Educated at St Paul's School, and Trinity College, Cambridge; BA 1863. MA 1872. Curate, Layham, Suffolk, 1865–85; Polstead, 1885–87; vicar, Wootton-Wawen, Warwickshire, 1887–1916.

Victoria, queen and empress, 1837–1897; by F.T. Bramston. Printed London: Eyre & Spottiswoode. [1897]. 15 pp.

Printed for the author. *OXB*

BRANCO, C.

The lifting of the veil, and other pieces: [poems]; by C. Branco. London: Swan Sonnenschein & Co. 1892. iv, 235 pp. *OXB*

BRANT, Alfred Charles

The demagogues: a poetic drama, and other poems; by Alfred Charles Brant. London: W. Stewart & Co. [1894]. 64 pp. *OXB*

BRASSINGTON, William Salt, (W.S.B.) (1859–1939). Son of William R. Brassington of Lichfield, Staffordshire. Educated at Edgbaston Proprietary School, and Oxford University. A director of Barker & Allen, Ltd, metal manufacturers of Birmingham. Librarian and curator, Shakespeare Memorial Theatre, and hon. chief librarian, Stratford-upon-Avon Public Library. Writer on historic bookbinding. Lived latterly at Sandcroft, Uphill, Weston-super-Mare, Somerset.

The legend of Uphill Church: a lay of Saint Nicholas; compiled from local tradition, with original illustrations engraved from pen and ink drawings; by W.S.B. King's Heath: Pritchard Bros. 1887. [16] pp. il.

Cover-title is *A Somersetshire legend*. *OXB*

BRAYE, Lord *see* VERNEY-CAVE, Alfred, Lord Braye

BREEZE, Ryder E.N.

Lays of the Scottish Highlands; Home rule in 1897, and other poems; by Ryder E.N. Breeze. London: Ward & Downey. 1893. viii, 200 pp. *OXB*

BREMNER, James, (MacBremen, pseud.)
Breezes from John o' Groats: [poems]; by MacBremen. Paisley: Alexander
Gardner. 1896. 224 pp.   *OXB*

BREMONT, Anna De, Comtesse. Née Dunphy. English wife of Comte
Leon De Brémont, Chevalier de Légion d'Honneur.
Love poems; by Anna, Comtesse De Brémont. Cape Town: Argus Printing &
Publishing Co., Ltd. 1889. 80 pp.   *BL*
Sonnets and love poems; by Anna, Comtesse De Brémont. Printed New York:
J.J. Little & Co. 1892. viii, 121 pp.
A limited ed. of numbered copies.   *BL*

BRENON, Edward St. John- *see* **ST. JOHN-BRENON, Edward**

BRENT, John (1808–82). b. Rotherhithe, Kent, son of a shipbuilder. He held
appointments in Canterbury Corporation. FSA, 1853. An antiquary, novelist,
and contributor to various archaeological publications. Member of the British
Archaeological Association and other learned societies.
The poetical works of the late John Brent. Revised ed. London: W. Kent & Co.
1884. 2 vols.
Cover-title is *Poems*.   *OXB*

BRERETON, John Le Gay (1827–86). b. Bawtrey, Yorkshire. A Quaker, he
was educated at Ackworth School. Studied medicine at Edinburgh and St
Andrews, practising at Bradford for many years. In 1857 he married Mary
Tongue. They settled in Sydney, Australia, where he built up a large practice.
He brought about radical reforms in the country's lunatic asylums. Eventually
he became a Swedenborgian.
Beyond, and other poems; by John Le Gay Brereton. Sydney: Turner &
Henderson. 1886. 100 pp.   *BL*
The goal of time: a poem; by John Le Gay Brereton. Melbourne: George
Robertson. 1883. 56 pp.   *BL*
The triumph of love: [poems]; by John Le Gay Brereton. Sydney: Turner &
Henderson; London: James Speirs. 1887. 156 pp.   *OXB*

BRERETON, Joseph Lloyd (1822–1901). Educated at Rugby School, and
University College, Oxford, Oxford; BA 1846, MA 1857; Newdigate
prizewinner, 1844. Rector, West Buckland, Devon, 1852–67, Little Mass-
ingham, King's Lynn, Norfolk, 1867–1901. He advocated national education
on a county basis, establishing county schools in Devon, 1858, and in
Norfolk, 1871. He was permanently injured in a railway accident in 1882.
Musings in faith, and other poems; by Joseph Lloyd Brereton. Cambridge:
Macmillan & Bowes. 1885. viii. 148 pp.   *OXB*
A triplet for Christmas: 1. A paean; 2. An allegory; 3. Chit-chat; [by] Joseph
Lloyd Brereton. Printed London: Jarrold & Sons. [1887]. 3 vols in 1.   *OXB*

BRETT, Reginald Baliol, Lord Esher (1852–1930). Educated at Eton College, and Trinity College, Cambridge. Private secretary to the Marquess of Hartington, 1875-85. Liberal MP for Penrhyn & Falmouth, 1880–85. Moved to Orchard Lea, near Windsor, and was admitted to Queen Victoria's private circle. He succeeded his father, the 1st Viscount, in 1899. Superintended the funeral of Queen Victoria, and the coronation of Edward VII. His London home was 2 Tilney Street, W.

Foam: [poems]; [by Reginald Baliol Brett]. London: Macmillan & Co. 1893. viii, 102 pp. *OXB*

BREVIOR, Thomas, pseud. *see* **SHORTER, Thomas**, (Thomas Brevior, pseud.)

BREWSTER, Emily. Daughter of Guybon Damant, surgeon of Lammas, Norfolk. In 1870 she married Rev. Waldegrave Brewster, rector of Middleton, Lancashire, 1870–88.

Collect, epistle and gospel teachings, for the Sundays of the Christian year: [poems]; by Emily Brewster. London: Skeffington & Son. 1890. [iv], 89 pp. *OXB*

BRIDGE, Arthur (1854–19). b. Upton Park, Slough, Buckinghamshire, son of Colonel George Bridge. Educated privately. Chaplain in India: Hissar, 1879–82, Peshawar, 1882–84, Multan, 1885–90, Jollundur, 1892–95; rector, Worth, Sussex, from 1896. He owned fifteen acres in Sussex. Vice-president, National Dahlia Society. FRHS.

Poems; by Arthur Bridge. London: Richard Bentley & Son. 1882. x, 309 pp. *OXB*

BRIDGES, Guy J. Novelist. Of Exeter, Devon?

Imaginations in verse; by G.J. Bridges. London: "Commercial Exchange"; Exeter: William Pollard & Co. 1898. [ii], 50 pp. *OXB*

The second mate, and other poems; by G.J. Bridges. London: L. Lloyd. 1899. 44 pp. *OXB*

BRIDGES, John Affleck (1833?–). b. Walmer, Kent, son of John T. Bridges. Educated at Christ Church, Oxford.

In a village: [poems]; by John A. Bridges. London: Elkin Mathews. 1898. viii, 72 pp. *OXB*

BRIDGES, Robert (1844–1930). b. Walmer, Kent, son of John Bridges. Educated at Eton College, and Corpus Christi College, Oxford; BA 1867. Qualified in medicine at St Bartholomew's Hospital, London; MB, MRCP. Held appointments at St Bartholomew's, at Great Ormond Street Children's Hospital, and in general practice until his retirement in 1881. He settled at Yattendon, Berkshire, before moving to Boar's Hill, Oxford, in 1907. Critic of Milton and Keats. Co-founder of the Society for Pure English. Poet laureate from 1913.

BIBLIOGRAPHY: **McKAY, George L:** *A bibliography of Robert Bridges.* New York: Columbia University Press; London: Oxford University Press. 1932.

BRIDGES, William. Educated at St Bees School. Ordained 1846; perpetual curate, Lysse, Hampshire, 1847–58; curate, St Peter's, Preston, Lancashire; chaplain, Manchester Union, 1860–71; curate, Holme St Cuthbert, Cumberland, 1871–72; vicar, Holme-Cultram, Maryport, from 1872.
The reign of grace: whereby saving faith may be discerned from a natural and formal profession of religion: [poems]; by W. Bridges. [London]: Marshall Bros. [1885]. 80 pp.　*OXB*

BRIDGETT, Thomas Edward (1829–99). Educated at St John's College, Cambridge. He entered the Roman Catholic Church in 1850; joined the Redemptorist order, becoming a priest in 1856; founded the Confraternity of the Holy Family, Limerick, 1868. Writer on the history of the Reformation.
Sonnets and epigrams on sacred subjects; by T.E. Bridgett. London: Burns & Oates, Ltd; New York: Benziger Bros. 1898. xii, 79 pp.　*OXB*

BRIEFLESS BARRISTER, pseud. *see* **WILLIAMS, James**, (Briefless Barrister, pseud.)

BRIERLEY, Ben (1825–96). b. Failsworth, Lancashire, son of a handloom weaver. He attended the village school until his sixth year, when his parents moved to Hollinwood. Educated at night school, and at the Primitive Methodist Sunday school. Worked as a handloom weaver, and later as a silk-warper. In 1863 he became sub-editor of the *Oldham Times*. A founder of Manchester Literary Club, he edited the popular *Ben Brierley's Journal*, 1869–91. His works were written largely in the dialect of South Lancashire, and he was in demand as a dialect reciter.
Spring blossoms and autumn leaves: [poems]; by Ben Brierley. Printed Manchester: J. Andrew & Co. 1893, xvi, 154 pp. il.　*MPL*

BRIERLEY, Thomas (1820–1909). Of Alkrington, near Middleton, Lancashire. Educated at Joseph Fielding's School. One of the last of the Middleton home silk weavers. An educated man, he always spoke in the broad local dialect.
The countrified pieces of Thomas Brierley. Printed Oldham: W.E. Clegg. 1894. viii, 208 pp.
　　Poetry and prose.　*BL*
Short poems, with pepper and salt in; by Thomas Brierley. Manchester: John Heywood; London: Simpkin, Marshall, & Co. [1892?]. 32 pp.　*OPL*

BRIGGS, Edith M., (Eta, pseud.) (1867–). b. Westfield House, Wyke, near Bradford, Yorkshire, daughter of Jonas Briggs, woollen manufacturer. Educated at St Andrews University. Lived latterly at Clare Villas, Wyke.
Poems; by Eta. Printed London: Cassell & Co., Ltd. [c.1890]. 80 pp.　*UCD*

BRIGGS, Jonas (1821?–91). Native of Wyke, near Bradford, Yorkshire, where his father was a corn miller. He entered the worsted trade, becoming a partner at Bowling Mills, employing nearly a thousand workpeople. A member of the Liberal Party until 1885 when he became a Unionist.

The miscellaneous poems of the late Jonas Briggs. Printed Bradford: Knight & Forster. [1892?]. 60 pp.

Spine-title is *Poems.* BL

BRIGHT, William (1824–1901). Educated at Rugby School, and University College, Oxford: BA 1846, MA 1849, DD 1869; Fellow of University College, 1847–68. Theological tutor, and Bell lecturer in ecclesiastical history, 1851–58; regius professor in ecclesiastical history, and canon of Christ Church, 1868–1901. Hymn writer and popular lecturer.

Iona, and other verses; by William Bright. London: Rivingtons. 1886. xii, 154 pp. *OXB*

BRINE, Emily. Wife of Rear-Admiral Lindesay Brine, who served in the Royal Navy, 1847–94. Lived latterly at Oystermouth, near Faversham, Kent.

Allington, and other poems; by E. Brine. London: Simpkin, Marshall, & Co.; Swansea: Charles F. Edwards. 1884. xvi, 255 pp. por. *OXB*

BRITISH MATRON, pseud. *see* **WATTS-JONES, Hannah**, (British Matron, pseud.)

BRITTAIN, Frank Smith. Lived at 33 Bristol Street, Birmingham.

Oscar and Esther, and other poems; Frank Smith Brittain. London: Wyman & Sons. 1883. viii, 110 pp.

Spine-title is *Poems.* *OXB*

BRITTON, John James. Editor of *The Midland Magazine and Monthly Review*.

The lay of the Lady Ida, and other poems; by J.J. Britton. London: Remington & Co. 1883. viii, 280 pp. *OXB*

A sheaf of ballads (mainly from old world sources); to which are added, Carrella: a love story, and other poems; by J.J. Britton. London: Elliot Stock. 1884. vi, 160 pp. *BL*

BROCKBANK, William Edward

Ashtorel, and other poems; by William Edward Brockbank. London: Kegan Paul, Trench, Trübner, & Co. Ltd. 1893. viii, 135 pp. *OXB*

Poems and songs; by W.E. Brockbank. London: T. Fisher Unwin. 1897. x, 180 pp. *OXB*

BROCKMAN, Lewis

Poems; by Lewis Brockman. London: Horace Cox. 1894. viii, 216 pp. *OXB*

BROCKMAN, Louisa

Bright thoughts: text book for every day of the Church's year. Poetry by Louisa Brockman. Introduction by C.A. Keightley. London: Digby, Long & Co. [1897]. xii, 116 pp. *OXB*

BRODIE, Elizabeth Rowton. Mrs Brodie. Of Hereford?
Miscellaneous poems; by Elizabeth Rowton Brodie. Printed [Hereford]: Offices of the "Hereford Times". [1880?]. 47 pp.   *BL*

BRODIE, Erasmus Henry (1832?–   ). Son of William B. Brodie of Salisbury, Wiltshire, gentleman. Educated at Trinity College, Oxford (scholar); BA 1855, MA 1860. HM inspector of schools, Manchester.
Lyrics of the sea; Varieties in verse; Translations; Sonnets; by E.H. Brodie. London: George Bell & Sons. 1887. vi, 204 pp.   *OXB*
Sonnets; by E.H. Brodie. London: George Bell & Sons. 1885. xvi, 155 pp.   *MPO*

BRODIE, Staunton. Playwright.
Poetical stories; by Staunton Brodie. London: Digby, Long & Co. [1898]. vi, 194 pp.   *OXB*
Songs of the country; by Staunton Brodie. With vignettes by the author. London: Remington & Co. 1885. viii, 90 pp. il.   *OXB*

BRODRICK, Albert. Lived some time in South Africa.
A wanderer's rhymes; [by] A. Brodrick. London: Wilkinson Bros., Ltd. [1898]. 280 pp. por.   *BL*

The BROKEN MAST: OR, SKETCHES FROM THE LIFE OF ONE ADMITTED TO DR BARNADO'S VILLAGE HOME. With preface by W. Meynell Whittemore. London: George Stoneman. 1886. 32 pp. il.
'Profits will be given to the fund for building a new cottage in the Girls' "Village Home" at Ilford, Essex'.   *OXB*

BROOKE, Emma Fairfax, (E. Fairfax Byrrne, pseud.) (1859?–1926). b. Cheshire, daughter of an industrialist. Educated at Newnham College, Cambridge. She moved to London in 1879, living in Hampstead for the rest of her life. Associated with the London School of Economics, she published surveys of the working conditions of women. Member of the Fabian Society.
Millicent: a poem; by E. Fairfax Byrrne. London: C. Kegan Paul & Co. 1881. [vi], 262 pp.   *MPL*

BROOKE, Mrs George. Of Batley, Yorkshire?
Poems: by Mrs. George Brooke. Printed Batley: J.S. Newsome. 1882. 166 pp.   *★UCD*

BROOKE, Stopford Augustus (1832–1916). b. Letterkenny, County Donegal. Educated at Trinity College, Dublin. Curate in London, at St James's Chapel, 1866–76, then at Bedford Chapel, Bloomsbury, 1876–95. Appointed chaplain to Queen Victoria in 1867, he became one of the foremost London preachers before resigning from the Church of England in 1880 and adopting Unitarian views. Writer on English literature, including studies of Milton, Tennyson and Browning. Died at Ewhurst, Surrey.
Poems; by Stopford A. Brooke. London: Macmillan & Co. 1888. viii, 284 pp.   *MPL*

BROOKS, Clifford
The wanderer in the land of Cybi, and other poems (1886–1893); by Clifford
Brooks. London: Horace Cox. 1894. viii, 150 pp.   *OXB*

BROTHER GAUGER, pseud.
At Robin's grave, a hundred years after: a rough rhyme; by a brother gauger.
Printed Banbury: Cheney & Sons. 1896. 22 pp.   *OXB*

BROTHERTON, Mary. Née Irwin. Novelist.
Rosemary for remembrance: [poems]; by Mary Brotherton. London: John Lane,
Bodley Head. 1895. [ii], 75, [22] pp.   *OXB*

BROUGH, Robert (1872–1905). b. Invergordon, Ross-shire. Educated in
Aberdeen and Glasgow, he studied art at Aberdeen Art School, and the Royal
Scottish Academy, Edinburgh. A portrait painter and compositor, he was a
member of the International Society of Sculptors, Painters, & Graveurs, and
of the Society of Portrait Painters. Lived latterly at 33 Tite Street, Chelsea,
London SW.
Tips for typos: or, rhymes to rub off rust; by Robert Brough. Printed Glasgow:
William Hodge & Co. 1890. viii, 128 pp. por.   *NLS*

BROWN, Annie Johnson- *see* **JOHNSON-BROWN, Annie**

BROWN, Campbell Rae- *see* **RAE-BROWN, Campbell**

BROWN, Colin Rae- *see* **RAE-BROWN, Colin**

BROWN, Frederick Rivers. Of Colchester, Essex?
Ave, Victoria!; by Frederick Rivers Brown. Colchester: Wright & Sons. 1897.
36 pp.   *OXB*

BROWN, Henry Rowland, (Oliver Grey, pseud.) (1865– 1905). b. Pinner,
Middlesex, son of Henry Brown. Educated at Rugby School, and University
College, Oxford; BA 1887. Student of Lincoln's Inn, called to the Bar, 1889.
The rhymes and rhapsodies of Oliver Grey. London: George Routledge & Sons,
Ltd. 1898. xiv, 208 pp.   *OXB*
    Also [2nd ed.] 1898.

BROWN, J.E.A.
From Advent to All Saints: verses suggested by the epistles and gospels; by J.E.A.
Brown. London: Griffith, Farran, Okeden & Welsh. [1889]. xiv, 154
pp.   *OXB*

BROWN, James, (J.B. Selkirk, pseud.) (1832–1904). b. Galashiels, Selkirk-shire, spending his childhood in the neighbouring town of Selkirk. Educated at Selkirk Grammar School, and Edinburgh Institute. His family were woollen manufacturers in Selkirk for several generations, and he joined the firm until it failed in 1870. A frequent contributor to *Blackwood's Magazine* and *Chambers's Journal*, he took an active part in local civic affairs.
  Poems; by J.B. Selkirk. London: Kegan Paul, Trench & Co. 1883. viii, 263 pp.   *OXB*
  Poems; by J.B. Selkirk. Edinburgh: William Blackwood & Sons. 1896. x, 292 pp.   *OXB*

BROWN, James Walter. Of Cumberland. Writer on the town of Carlisle.
  Lyrics and songs; by James Walter Brown. Carlisle: Chas. Thurnam & Sons. 1893. 96 pp.   *OXB*

BROWN, John (1812–90). b. Horncastle Workhouse, Lincolnshire. Received a very limited education before being apprenticed to a cabinet maker. He ran away to sea as a cabin boy and travelled to Russia. On his return to Horncastle he was sent to London to learn the trade of a house painter and glazier. Known as 'The Horncastle Laureate'.
  Literae laureate: or, a selection from the poetical writings in Lincolnshire language; by John Brown. With introduction, life, and explanatory notes by J. Conway Walter. Horncastle: W.K. Morton. 1890. xliv, 156 pp.   *OXB*

BROWN, John. b. Alexandria, Dumbartonshire. His parents soon moved to Glasgow, then to Dumbuck on the Strath of Clyde. After six years the family returned to Glasgow, where he was apprenticed to a pattern-maker, following that occupation all his life. When qualified he remained in Glasgow, apart from seven years spent in Manchester.
  Poems and songs; by John Brown. Glasgow: Thomas D. Morison; London: Hamilton, Adams, & Co. 1883. 103 pp.   *OXB*
  Wayside songs, with other verse; [by John Brown]. Glasgow: Wilson & McCormick. 1883. xii, 144 pp.   *NLS*
  Wayside songs, with later lyrics; by John Brown. New ed. Glasgow: Frederick W. Wilson & Brother. 1887. xii, 168 pp.   *BPL*

BROWN, John Henry (1859–   ). Of Nottingham. Playwright, and writer on Nottingham Castle.
  The rambler's calendar: [poems]; by J. Henry Brown. London: B. Quaritch; Nottingham: T. Forman & Sons. 1882. 111 pp.   *MPL*

BROWN, John Joseph. Son of George W. Brown, banker of Whitehaven, Cumberland. Student of Middle Temple, 1877, called to the Bar, 1880. Equity draughtsman and conveyancer.
  The vision of Barabbas, and other poems; [by John Joseph Brown]. London: Henry Frowde. 1891. [viii], 103 pp.   *TCD*

BROWN, Jones, pseud. *see* **MUNBY, Arthur Joseph**, (Jones Brown, pseud.)

BROWN, Middlemass. Scottish.
Aspects of life: poems; by Middlemass Brown. Glasgow: Morison Bros. 1894.
77 pp.   *OXB*
The vale of life; and, Pilgrim songs; by Middlemass Brown. Glasgow: Morison
Bros. 1895. 95 pp.   *OXB*

BROWN, Reuben William. Of Leicester.
The vicar's dream, and other poems; by Reuben William Brown. London: James
Blackwood & Co. [1895]. 120 pp.   *OXB*

BROWN, Robert (1844–1912). b. Barton-upon-Humber, Lincolnshire. Educated at Cheltenham College. A solicitor and registrar of the county in his
native town. Writer of numerous works on mythology and religions. A
frequent contributor to the *Academy, Archaeologia*, etc. Member of the Society
of Biblical Archaeology.
Tellis and Kleobeia, [and other poems]; by Robert Brown. London: David
Nutt. 1895. [vi], 126 pp.   *OXB*
A trilogy of the life-to-come, and other poems; by Robert Brown. London: David
Nutt. 1887. viii, 148 pp.   *OXB*

BROWN, Thomas Edward (1830–97). b, Douglas, Isle of Man, son of a
clergyman. Educated at King William's College, and Christ Church, Oxford.
Fellow of Oriel College, 1854–58. Vice–principal, King William's College,
1858–61; headmaster of Crypt School, Gloucester, 1861–64; one of the
original staff masters at Clifton College, where he remained for nearly thirty
years. Curate, St Barnabas's, Bristol, 1884-93.
The doctor, and other poems; by T.E. Brown. London: Swan Sonnenschein,
Lowrey & Co. 1887. [vi], 385 pp.   *MPL*
Fo'c's'le yarns; including, Betsy Lee, and other poems; [by Thomas Edward
Brown]. London: Macmillan & Co. 1881. [viii], 291 pp.   *OXB*
  Also New ed. 1889.
The Manx witch, and other poems; by T.E. Brown. London: Macmillan & Co.
1889. [viii], 261 pp.   *OXB*
Old John, and other poems; by T.E. Brown. London: Macmillan & Co. 1893.
xii, 250 pp.   *MPL*
Tommy Big-eyes; by [Thomas Edward Brown]. Douglas, [Isle of Man]: James
Brown & Son. [1880]. 78 pp.   *BL*

BROWN, W. Wallace. Rev. Brown of Brookhill.
Christ, the life of lives, with other poems; by W. Wallace Brown. London:
Marcus Ward & Co., Ltd. 1887. 72 pp.   *OXB*

BROWNE, Alfred Hall, (Two Idle Bees, pseud. with Amelia Browne).
Alphabetical fancies, rhymed riddles, & local lays; by two idle bees. [1891]. 45 pp.
    Title from cover. *BL*

BROWNE, Amelia, (Two Idle Bees, pseud. with Alfred Hall Browne).
Alphabetical fancies, rhymed riddles, & local lays; by two idle bees. [1891]. 45 pp.
    Title from cover. *BL*

BROWNE, John Hutton Balfour. Son of William A.F. Browne, commissioner in lunacy for Scotland. Student of Middle Temple, called to the Bar, 1870. Registrar and secretary to the Railway Commissions, 1874–82. Member of the Midland circuit. Lived at 88 Claverton Street, London SW.
    Moods; [by John Hutton Balfour Browne]. Glasgow: James Maclehose. 1881. vi, 224 pp. *OXB*
    Poems, sonnets, songs, and verses; by [John Hutton Balfour Browne]. London: George Bell & Sons. 1894. viii, 151 pp. *TCD*
    The professor, and other poems; by [John Hutton Balfour Browne]. London: Kegan Paul, Trench, Trübner & Co. Ltd. 1892. viii, 155 pp. *TCD*

BROWNE, Marie Hedderwick (1857–   ). b. Ireland, daughter of John Hedderwick of Glasgow, where her girlhood was spent. On her marriage in 1879 she moved to London. A frequent contributor to *London Society*, *Chambers's Journal*, *The Girls' Own Paper*, etc. A number of her songs were published, with musical settings by various composers.
    A spray of lilac, and other poems and songs; by Marie Hedderwick Browne. London: Isbister & Co. Ltd. 1892. viii, 104 pp. *BL*

BROWNE, Matthew, pseud. *see* **RANDS, William Brighty**, (Matthew Browne, pseud.)

BROWNE, S., (Dunelmiae Filius, pseud.)
    Leaves from the mind's diary: being poems of thought and reflection; by Dunelmiae Filius. Oxford: John Oliver. [1880]. 16 pp. *OXB*
    Leaves from the mind's diary: being poems of thought and reflection; by Dunelmiae Filius. Printed Oxford: John Oliver. [1891]. 60 pp. *OXB*

BROWNE, Wilfrid
    The fisher of Le Brunn: a story in verse; by Wilfrid Browne. London: H.R. Allenson. [1896]. 19 pp. *BL*

BROWNING, Robert (1812–89) b. Camberwell, London, son of a Bank of England official. Educated at home, and at the Rev, Thomas Ready's school at Peckham; attended London University, 1829–30. Having embarked on a career as a poet, he also worked at writing for the theatre. He visited Russia, 1833, and Italy, 1834. After his marriage to Elizabeth Barrett in 1846, they lived in Pisa, 1846, and in Florence, 1847–61. He settled in London after his wife's death in 1861.

BIBLIOGRAPHY: **WISE, Thomas J.** *A complete bibliography of the writings in prose and verse of Robert Browning.* Folkestone: Dawsons of Pall Mall. 1971.
Reprint of the original 1897 limited ed. of 50 copies.

BROWNLIE, John (1857–) b. Glasgow. Educated at Glasgow University where he studied theology. Ordained in the Free Church of Scotland, he was assistant to the Rev. Andrew Urquhart at Portpatrick, Wigtownshire. Appointed chaplain to the Ayr & Galloway Volunteers, 1885.
Hymns of our pilgrimage; by John Brownlie. London: James Nisbet & Co. 1889. 136 pp. *BL*
Pilgrim songs (Third Series); by John Brownlie. London: James Nisbet & Co. 1892. 76 pp. *BL*
The rest of God; by John Brownlie. London: James Nisbet & Co. 1894. 45 pp. *OXB*
The rest of God; by John Brownlie. Stirling: Drummond's Tract Depot; London: S.W. Partridge & Co. [1899]. 32 pp.
Title from cover. *OXB*

BRUCE, George (1825–). b. St Andrews, Fife. Left an orphan aged fourteen. Apprenticed to a joiner, he went to London for a short time as a journeyman but returned to St Andrews to start his own business as a contractor for large engineering projects in the area. A town councillor for St Andrews and a member of the school board, he was also local correspondent for the *Dundee Advertiser*.
Poems and songs; by George Bruce. Printed Dundee: John Leng & Co. 1886. 338 pp. *BL*

BRYAN, Daniel. Of Sheffield, Yorkshire.
Among the tombs: an original poem, in five cantos; by Daniel Bryan. Sheffield: Pawson & Brailsford. [1885]. 17 pp. *OXB*
Poetic biographical sketches of Earl Beaconsfield; by Daniel Bryan. 2nd ed. Sheffield: Pawson & Brailsford; London: Simpkin, Marshall & Co. [1882]. [iv], 112 pp. *OXB*
Poetic essay on the life and times of her most gracious majesty, Queen Victoria: or, the truth about England: an historical poem in three cantos; by Daniel Bryan. Sheffield: Author. [1893]. 48 pp.
Cover-title is *The life and times of Queen Victoria*. *OXB*

BRYAN, John. Lived at 3 Scylla Road, Peckham Rye, London SE.
Harcourt's dream; Don Quixote & Sancho Panza; Tommy Pop; Life: a selection of poetical sketches; by John Bryan. Printed [London]: Simpkins. [1894]. 15 pp.
Title from cover. *OXB*

BUCHAN, Alexander Winton (1814–87?). b. Kilmarnock, Ayrshire, son of working people. He received a good education, becoming a teacher at Underhills, Craigie, at the early age of seventeen. Head teacher of the school at Irvine, 1838–43, then at St James's Parish School, Glasgow; later moved to West Regent Street school, then to Bath Street Academy. He attended Glasgow University part-time. Member of Glasgow St Andrew Society.

Poems of feeling; by Alexander Winton Buchan. Glasgow: Thomas Murray & Son. 1884. 200 pp. *BL*

The vision stream: or, the song of man: an allegory, in six books; by Alexander Winton Buchan. London: Houston & Sons. 1887. 164 pp. *OXB*

BUCHAN, John (1847–1911). b. Peebles, son of John Buchan, writer to the signet. Educated at Peebles, and at Edinburgh University. Ordained a Free Church of Scotland minister, 1873, serving successively in Broughton, Perth, Pathhead near Kirkcaldy, and Glasgow. Father of John Buchan, 1st Lord Tweedsmuir, and of the novelist Anna Buchan, (O. Douglas, pseud.).

Tweedside echoes and moorland musings: [poems]; by John Buchan. Edinburgh: John Maclaren & Son. 96 pp. *BL*

BUCHANAN, David (1811–93). b. Hillhead, Dunbartonshire, the youngest of six sons. He became a handloom weaver, eventually joining a brother in a manufacturing business.

Man and the years, and other poems; by David Buchanan. Selected and edited, with a biographical sketch, by William Freeland. Glasgow: James Maclehose & Sons. 1895. xxiv, 280 pp.

Spine-title is *Poems*. *OXB*

BUCHANAN, David Wills (1844–   ). b. Dundee, Angus. Orphaned at four, he was brought up at Blackwater, Glenshee, attending school until he was nearly fourteen. He worked with farmers in Glenshee, then became a van driver in Blairgowrie, Perthshire, then a storekeeper in a large shipbuilding yard in Dundee. Precentor in Cray Free Church, and a collector of the Dundee Burial Society.

Leisure lays, by David Wills Buchanan. With biographical introduction by John Paul. Printed Dundee: R.S. Barrie. 1899. 136 pp. por. *BL*

BUCHANAN, Francis (1825–   ). b. Perth. Educated at Kinnoul School. Wanting to become a sailor, he ran away from home at fifteen but was brought back and apprenticed to a draper. After marriage he settled in Sheffield, Yorkshire. Incapacitated from work by an accident, he contributed to local and Scottish newspapers. Lived at 187 Fowler Street, Sheffield.

Sparks from Sheffield smoke: a series of local and other poems; by Francis Buchanan. Sheffield: Leader & Sons. [1882]. viii, 92 pp. *OXB*

BUCHANAN, Robert *see* **BUCHANAN, Robert Williams**

BUCHANAN, Robert Williams (1841–1901). b. Caverswell, Staffordshire, of Scottish parents. The family moved to Glasgow, and he was educated at Glasgow High School, and Glasgow University, where his closest friend was David Gray (1836–61). His father, a tailor, was a noted socialist and follower of Robert Owen. He went to London in 1860, writing for the *Athenaeum* and other journals. A novelist, playwright and critic, he was financially ruined by an unwise speculation. Died of a stroke at Streatham.

The ballad of Mary the mother: a Christmas carol, [and other poems]; by Robert Buchanan. London: Author. 1897. [viii], 154 pp.   *OXB*

Ballads of life, love, and humour; by Robert Buchanan. With a frontispiece by Arthur Hughes. London: Chatto & Windus. 1882. xii, 255 pp. il.   *MPL*

The Buchanan ballads, old and new; by Robert Buchanan. London: John Haddon & Co. 1892. 112 pp. il. (Buchanan's poems for the people, 1).   *OXB*

The city of dream: an epic poem; by Robert Buchanan. London: Chatto & Windus. 1888. xvi, 364 pp. il.   *MPL*

The devil's case: a bank holiday interlude; by Robert Buchanan. London: Author. [1895]. x, 169 pp. il.   *OXB*

The earthquake: or, six days and a sabbath: the first three days; by Robert Buchanan. London: Chatto & Windus. 1885. [viii], 236 pp.   *OXB*

The new Rome: poems and ballads of our Empire; by Robert Buchanan. London: Walter Scott, Ltd. [1899]. 390 pp.   *MPL*

The outcast: a rhyme for the time; by Robert Buchanan. With illustrations by Rudolf Blind, Peter Macnab, Hume Nisbet, etc. London: Chatto & Windus. 1891. [viii], 200 pp. il.   *OXB*

Also 1st cheap ed. published by author [1896].

Poems and love lyrics; by Robt. W. Buchanan. Glasgow: Thomas Murray & Son; Edinburgh: Sutherland & Knox; London: Hall Virtue, & Co. [188–]. [2], viii, 146 pp.   *MPL*

The poetical works of Robert Buchanan. With a portrait of the author. London: Chatto & Windus. 1884. viii, 534 pp. por.   *OXB*

Selected poems of Robert Buchanan. With a frontispiece by Thomas Dalziel. London: Chatto & Windus. 1882. viii, 298 pp. il.   *MPL*

The wandering Jew: a Christmas carol; by Robert Buchanan. London: Chatto & Windus. 1893. viii, 151 pp.   *MPL*

BUCHANAN, Sidney James, (Salisbury Curate, pseud.) (1864-19). b. Great Wishford, Wiltshire, son of Archdeacon Thomas B. Buchanan. Educated at Winchester College, and New College, Oxford (scholar); BA 1887, MA 1894. Curate, St Edmund's, Salisbury, 1890–98, Southbroom, 1898–1900, Poulshot & Rowde, 1900–05; vicar, Berwick Bassett & Winterbourne Monkton, from 1905.

Salisbury Cathedral: a sacred poem; by a Salisbury curate. Salisbury: Brown & Co.; London: Simpkin, Marshall, Hamilton, Kent & Co., Ltd. 1895. 16 pp.   *OXB*

BUCKLE, Anthony (1838–). b. Barden, Yorkshire. Educated in Richmond, then trained as a schoolmaster at the Training College, York, where he became a teacher. Appointed assistant to HM Inspector of Schools, 1863. Took BA degree at London, 1865. Elected superintendent of Yorkshire School for the Blind, 1869. He took up the art of etching, becoming extremely skilful.

Lyrics and sonnets of northern lands; by A. Buckle. Illustrated with etchings and mezzotints by the author. Leeds: Richard Jackson. 1889. 115 pp. il.

A limited ed. of 300 numbered copies. *OXB*

Yorkshire etchings, with sonnets and descriptions; by A. Buckle. Leeds: Richard Jackson. 1885. [85] pp. il.

A limited ed. of 500 numbered copies. Printed on one side of leaf only. *OXB*

BUCKLER, Alexander. Of Beckenham, Kent. Member of the Wanderers Club, Pall Mall, London.

Tales and legends in verse; by Alexander Buckler. 2nd ed., with additions. London: Griffith & Farran; New York: E.P. Dutton & Co. 1880. [iv], 83 pp. *OXB*

Word sketches in Windsor: [poems]; by Alexander Buckler. London: Digby, Long & Co. 1897. 127 pp. *OXB*

BUDDEN, M.G.

Poems; by M.G. Budden. London: Digby & Long. [1890]. 63 pp. *BL*

BUFFO BARD, pseud.

Bad ballads; by a buffo bard. London: Peter Lane & Co. [188–]. 136 pp. **UCD*

BULKELEY, Henry John (1841?–19). Son of George T. Bulkeley of Horton, Buckinghamshire. Educated at Lincoln College, Oxford; BA 1864, MA 1866. Curate, Sulham, Berkshire, 1866–68, Shiplake, 1868–70, Giggleswick, Yorkshire, 1871–72, St Mary's, Bryanston Square, London, 1874–79; vicar, Lanercost with Kirkcambeck, Cumberland, 1879–90; rector, Morpeth, Northumberland, 1890–1906; Hon. canon, Newcastle upon Tyne Cathedral, 1901–06; rector of Codrington from 1906.

Alypius, and other poems, abroad and at home; by H.J. Bulkeley. London: Kegan Paul, Trench, Trübner & Co., Ltd. 1890. 170 pp. *OXB*

BULLEN, Peter, (Boleyne Reeves, pseud.) (1820–1905). b. Cork, Ireland. Harpist and composer.

Cassiope, and other poems; by Boleyne Reeves. London: Kegan Paul, Trench, Trübner & Co., Ltd. 1890. viii, 212 pp. *MPL*

BULLOCH, John Malcolm (1867–19). b. Aberdeen, son of John Bulloch. Educated at Aberdeen Grammar School, and Aberdeen University; MA 1888, LL.D 1921. Editor, *The Sketch*, 1893–99; dramatic critic, *Daily Courier*, 1896; assistant editor, *The Sphere*, 1899; dramatic critic, *The Tatler*, 1901-06, *The*

Sphere, 1906-09; editor, *The Graphic*, 1909-24. Prolific writer, editor and compiler, interested in Gordon genealogy.

Certain college carols: [poems]; by John Malcolm Bulloch. Aberdeen. 1894. 32 pp.
> A limited ed. of 50 numbered copies, printed for private circulation. *OXB*

College carols; by John Malcolm Bulloch. Aberdeen: D. Wyllie & Son. 1894. 80 pp il. *BL*

Miniatures painted for divers good patrons, and herewith reframed, Christmas, A.D. MDCCCXCV: [poems]; by John Malcolm Bulloch. Aberdeen: Albany Press. 1895. [16] pp.
> Title from cover. *BL*

BULLOCK, James Trower, (J.T.B.). Educated at Eton College. Practised as a solicitor at Debenham, Suffolk.

Stray leaves from the road side: illustrating country life, strange events, queer folk, eccentric tales, etc., etc.: [poems]; by J.T.B. London: Provost & Co. 1880. iv, 116 pp. *CU*

BULWER-LYTTON, Edward Robert, Lord Lytton, (Owen Meredith, pseud.) (1831–91). Only son of the novelist Edward G.E. Bulwer-Lytton, 1st Baron Lytton. Educated at Harrow School, and at Bonn. In 1849 he went to Washington as attaché and private secretary to his uncle Sir Henry Bulwer. He was subsequently attaché, consul or chargé d'affaires at Florence, Paris, the Hague, St Petersburg, Constantinople, Vienna, Belgrade, Athens, Lisbon and Madrid. In 1873 he succeeded his father as 2nd Baron Lytton. Appointed Viceroy of India, 1876; made Earl of Lytton on his resignation, 1880. Sent as ambassador to Paris, where he died.

After paradise: or, legends of exile, with other poems; by Robert, Earl of Lytton (Owen Meredith). London: David Stott. 1887. [iv], 232 pp. *UCD*

Glenaveril: or, the metamorphoses; by the Earl of Lytton. In two volumes. London: John Murray. 1885. 2 vols. *UCD*

Glenaveril: or, the metamorphoses: a poem in six books; by the Earl of Lytton. London: John Murray. 1885. 6 vols. *OXB*

Marah: [poems]; by Owen Meredith. London: Longmans, Green, & Co. 1892. x, 203 pp. *JRL*
> Also 2nd ed. 1892.

Poems of Owen Meredith (the Earl of Lytton). Selected, with an introduction, by M. Betham-Edwards. Authorised ed. London: Walter Scott. [189–]. xxiv, 250 pp. (Canterbury poets). *OXB*

Selected poems; [by] the Earl of Lytton (Owen Meredith). New ed. London: Longmans, Green, & Co. 1894. xxx, 426 pp. *UCD*

BUMSTEAD, Mary E. With her aunt she ran a boarding and day school for girls at Leicester Street, Southport, Lancashire.

Heart breathings: [poems]; by Mary E. Bumstead. 3rd ed. Printed Southport: Thomas Greener. 1888. 64 pp. *BL*

Heart breathings: [poems]; by Mary E. Bumstead. 4th ed. Printed Southport: Fortune & Chant. 1894. 94 pp.   *UCD*

BURBRIDGE, John. Curate, Chesterfield, Derbyshire, 1856– 57; perpetual curate, St Stephen's, Sheffield, 1858–75; vicar, Emmanuel Church, Liverpool, 1875–87; rural dean, Toxteth, 1886– 95; perpetual curate, St Michael's, Toxteth Park, 1886–96; hon. canon, Liverpool. Lived latterly at 44 Duke Street, Southport.
Poems, including, My study chair, Trifles, Thoughts by the way; by John Burbidge. London: J. Nisbet & Co.; Liverpool: J.A. Thompson & Co. 1891. 144 pp.   *★UCD*
Trifles, and miscellaneous poems; by John Burbidge. London: Marshall Bros; J. Nisbet & Co.; Liverpool: J.A. Thompson. 1885. 112 pp.   *OXB*
'We would see Jesus': sacred poems; by John Burbidge. London: George Philip & Son; Liverpool: Philip, Son & Nephew. 1882. 81 pp.   *OXB*

BURDEN, George. Novelist. Lived at 23 Sparkenhoe Street, Leicester.
The months, and other poems; by George Burden. London: E. Marlborough; Leicester: F. Hewitt; Author. [1883]. 100 pp.   *OXB*

BURGESS, Alexander, (Poute, pseud.) (1807–85). b, Lalathan, Fife. Educated at the parish school of Kennoway. Choirmaster, an accomplished musician and a successful teacher of dancing. Known as 'The Fife Paganini', his fame as a violinist was only local. He drowned at Whin Quarry, Starr, Fife.
"Poute!": being poutry, poetry and prose; by the late Alexander Burgess. Cupar-Fife: A. Westwood & Son; Edinburgh: John Menzies & Co. [1890]. x, 125 pp.   *BL*

BURGESS, James John Haldane (1862–1927). b. Lerwick, Shetland. Educated at Anderson Institute, Lerwick. Blind from 1887, he entered Edinburgh University, graduating in 1889. Author and private teacher, he contributed short stories, articles and verse to various periodicals. Editor of *The Shetlander*.
Shetland sketches and poems . . . ; by J. J. Haldane Burgess. Lerwick: H. Morrison. [1886]. [vi], 128 pp.   *OXB*

BURGH, Hugh Nicholas
Unpainted pictures, and other fragments in verse; by Hugh Nicholas Burgh. London: Elliot Stock. 1899. viii, [24] pp.   *OXB*

BURGHCLERE, Lord *see* **GARDNER, Herbert**, Lord Burghclere.

BURGON, John William (1813-88). b. Smyrna, son of a merchant who moved to London in 1814. Educated at Blackheath, London University, and Worcester College, Oxford; Newdigate prizewinner, 1845; Fellow of Oriel College, 1846. Curate successively at West Ilsley, Berkshire, Worton, and Finmere, Oxfordshire; appointed vicar, St Mary's, Oxford, 1863; Gresham professor of divinity, 1867; dean of Chichester, 1876. Reactionary in university politics, he published sermons and works of religious controversy. *Poems (1840 to 1878)*; by John William Burgon. London: Macmillan & Co. 1885. 148 pp. *OXB*

BURKE, Christian (1859–1944). Novelist, and author of religious works.
The flowering of the almond-tree, and other poems; by Christian Burke. Edinburgh: William Blackwood & Sons. 1896. x, 146 pp. *OXB*

BURLAND, John Burland Harris- *see* **HARRIS-BURLAND, John Burland**

BURN, Peter. Of Brampton, Cumberland.
Poems; by Peter Burn. London: Bemrose & Sons; Carlisle: G. & T. Coward. 1885. xvi, 389 pp. *UCD*

BURNETT, Alice Christina. Of Exeter, Devon?
Thoughts from the drama of life: a collection of short poems; by Alice Christina Burnett. London: Commercial Exchange; Exeter: William Pollard & Co. 1897. 47 pp *UCD*

BURNS, Dawson (1828–1909). Son of Rev. Jabez Burns of Oldham, Lancashire. A temperance reformer, he became secretary of the National Temperance Society, 1846. Baptist pastor at Salford, Lancashire, 1851, he helped to found the United Kingdom Alliance, 1853. Wrote for *Alliance News*, and actively promoted temperance legislation. A director of the Liberator Building Society which failed in 1892.
Oliver Cromwell, and other poems; by Dawson Burns. London: S.W. Partridge & Co. [1887]. 104 pp. *OXB*
Rays of sacred song for the church and the home; by Dawson Burns. London: S.W. Partridge & Co. [1884]. 176 pp. *OXB*

BURNS, Thomas (1848–   ). b. Eckford, Roxburghshire. Received very little schooling, starting work on a farm at age of nine; moved south to work on a farm at Ford, Northumberland. He began to educate himself, and in 1876 joined the police force at Newcastle-upon-Tyne. After three years he was appointed school board officer. His verse was published in local newspapers.
Chimes from nature: [poems]; by Thomas Burns. With introduction by James Graham Potter. Newcastle-upon-Tyne: J.M. Carr. 1887. xvi, 174 pp. por. *UCD*
Flowers from philosophy: [poems]; by Thomas Burns. Newcastle-upon-Tyne: J.M. Carr. 1890. [vi], 200 pp. *UCD*
Poems; by Thomas Burns. With introduction by James Graham Potter. Newcastle-upon-Tyne: J.M. Carr. 1885. x, 111 pp. *UCD*

BURNS OF BRADFORD *see* **PRESTON, Benjamin**

BURNSIDE, Helen Marion (1844–1923). b. Bromley Hall, daughter of John F. Burnside. Educated at home. A talented artist, she exhibited at the Royal Academy, 1863, and at the Society of Lady Artists, 1897; designer to the Royal School of Needlework, 1880–89. Editor to Messrs Raphael Tuck & Co., 1889–95. Prolific writer of songs, poems, tales, and card verses. Lived latterly at Up Down House, Windlesham, Surrey.
  Christmas lights: poem; by Helen Marion Burnside. Designed by J. Pauline Sunter. London: Raphael Tuck & Sons. [1890]. 24 pp. il., col. il.
    Printed on card.   *OXB*
  Drift weed: verses & lyrics; by Helen Marion Burnside. [London]: Hutchinson & Co. [1897]. xvi, 274 pp.   *OXB*
  The three angels: or, faith, hope, and love; by Helen Marion Burnside. Illustrated by Alice Price and F. Corbyn Price. London: Raphael Tuck & Sons. [1890]. [16] pp. il.
    Printed on card.   *BL*

BURRARD, William Dutton (1861–1938). Son of Lieutenant-Colonel Sidney Burrard, Grenadier Guards. Educated at Wellington. Entered the Royal Artillery, 1882; adjutant, north-western district, 1896–99; promoted major, 1899; formed 96th Royal Field Artillery, 1899; retired 1903. Colonel commanding the Lancashire Royal Garrison Artillery, 1904–09; commandant, No. 6 Artillery Training School, 1916; served at GHQ, 3rd Echelon, France, 1916–19.
  Out of the depths: poems; by W. Dutton Burrard. London: Kegan Paul, Trench, Trübner, & Co. Ltd. 1892. [viii], 95 pp.   *OXB*

BURROWS, Harold. LL.B.
  The prelude: [poems]; by Harold Burrows. London: T. Fisher Unwin. 1890. vi, 81 pp.   *OXB*

BURROWS, Henry William (1816–92). Son of Montagu Burrows of Malta. Educated at St John's College, Oxford; BA 1837, MA 1841, BD 1846. Vicar, Edmonton, Middlesex, 1878–82; canon of Rochester, 1881.
  The Knights of St. John: (second for the Newdigate in 1836); by H.W. Burrows. [Oxford]. [1892]. 16 pp.
    For private circulation.   *OXB*

BURTON, Henry (1840–19). b. Swannington, Leicestershire, son of Henry Burton. Educated at Griffydam Wesleyan day school, and Beloit College, United States; spent two years as a local preacher in the Methodist Episcopal Church. Lived latterly at Charnwood, West Kirby, Cheshire.
  Wayside songs of the inner and the outer life; by Henry Burton. London: T. Woolmer. [1886]. xiv, 190 pp.   *BL*

BUSHBY, Dudley Charles (1864–   ). b. London, son of Henry J. Bushby, metropolitan magistrate. Educated at Eton College, and Trinity College, Oxford. Lived at Antwerp, Belgium, c. 1888.

The royal shepherdess, and other poems; by Dudley Charles Bushby. London: Digby, Long & Co. 1897. [viii], 44 pp.   *OXB*

BUTLER, Arthur Gray (1831–1909). Son of Dr George Butler. Educated at Rugby School, and University College, Oxford; president of the Oxford Union, 1853; Fellow of Oriel College, 1856. A master at Rugby School, 1858–62; headmaster, Haileybury, 1862–67. Dean and tutor, Oriel College, 1875–97; hon. Fellow, 1907.

Harold: a drama in four acts, and other poems; by Arthur Gray Butler. London: Henry Frowde. 1892. viii, 226 pp.   *MPL*

BUTLER, George William (1839?–   ). Son of Thomas Butler of Chelsea, gentleman. Educated at University College, Oxford; BA 1861, MA 1864. curate, Tincleton, Dorset, 1862–64, Bollington, Cheshire, 1865–68; chaplain, training ship *Akbar*, 1868–71; curate, Stanhope, Durham, 1871–72, Christ Church, Sparkbrook, Birmingham, 1879; rector, West Knighton with Broad Mayne, Dorset, from 1880.

Rebekah: a narrative from holy scripture; told in hexameter verse; by George William Butler. London: S.W. Partridge & Co. 1899. 32 pp.   *OXB*

BYLES, Charles Edward (1873–19   ). b. London, son of Dr James C. Byles, physician of Hackney, London. Educated at Uppingham School, and St John's College, Cambridge; BA 1895. Sub-editor of the *Illustrated London News*. Lived at 90 Ridgmount Gardens, London WC.

Random rhymes; Sins and cynicisms; Cam carols; by C.E. Byles. London: Bouverie Press, Ltd. [1896]. 58 pp.

Cover-title is *From grave to gay*.   *UCD*

BYNG, Lancelot Cranmer- *see* **CRANMER-BYNG, Lancelot**, (Paganus, pseud.)

BYRNE, Edmund John, (Singer from the South, pseud.)

Without a god; by a singer from the south. London: Kegan Paul, Trench, Trübner & Co., Ltd. 1899. [iv], 584 pp.   *OXB*

BYRON, May *see* **GILLINGTON, Mary Clarissa**.

BYRRNE, E. Fairfax, pseud. *see* **BROOKE, Emma Frances**, (E. Fairfax Byrrne, pseud.)

C

C., A. Of Liverpool.
Imaginary stories of the Isle of Man: [poems]; by A.C. Liverpool. [1894]. [iv], 17 pp. il., map. *OXB*

C., B.E.J.
A fool's "passion", and other poems, by B.E.J.C. London: Eglington & Co. 1892. [iv], 76 pp. *BL*

B., Beatrix S.
'Benediction': a meditation in verse; [by Beatrix S.C.]. London: Elliot Stock. 1892. 16 pp. *OXB*

C., D. *see* **CRONIN, Daniel**, (D.C.)

C.,E. Of Glasgow.
An exhibition ode and city poem; by E.C. Glasgow: James Hedderwick & Sons; Edinburgh: John Menzies & Co. 1888. [iv], 68 pp. *OXB*

C., E.C.L. *see* **CAMPBELL, Lady Evelyn Caroline Louisa**, (E.C.L.C.)

C., H. Of London?
Early poems; by H.C. Printed Clapham: A. Bachhoffner. 1894. 55 pp. *UCD*

C., H.D. *see* **CATLING, Harry Debron**, (H.D.C.)

C., J. Of Falkirk, Stirlingshire?
A modern rhyming chronicle "A spark from the fire", as an appeal to all sections and connections of the British race (to the great American brotherhood), and to every nationality, province and dependency in connection with or under the protection of "The Greater Britain", recognised as the British Empire . . . ; by J.C. Printed Falkirk: "Mail" Printing Works. [c. 1896]. 16 pp.
Title from cover. UCD

C., J.A. *see* **COLBECK, James Alfred**, (J.A.C.)

C., K.
Songs of many days; by K.C. London: Marcus Ward & Co. 1882. 99 pp. *OXB*

C., L.E.
The collects in verse; by L.E.C. Printed London: J. Masters & Co. [1888]. 64 pp. *OXB*

C., Mrs L.T.

Songs under His shadow: original, and translated from the German; by Mrs. L.T.C. London: S.W. Partridge & Co. [1880]. [viii], 112 pp.   *OXB*

C., M.E.

The legend of St. Christopher; [by M.E.C.]. London: Catholic Truth Society. [1896]. 20 pp. (Devotional series).   *BL*

C., O.S *see* **WALKER, W.A.**, (O.S.C.)

C., S. *see* **CROFT, S.**, (S.C.)

C., S.M.

Random rhymes; by S.M.C. Manchester: John Heywood. [1893]. viii, 134 pp.   *OXB*

C.3.3., pseud. *see* **WILDE, Oscar**, (C.3.3., pseud.)

C., W.E.

Elvinor: a poem; by W.E.C. London: William Poole. [1880]. viii, 240 pp.   *UCD*

CAILLARD, Emma Marie (1852–   ). A miscellaneous writer, she contributed to *Contemporary Review*, *Hibbert Journal*, etc. Lived at 6 Albany Mansions, Albert Bridge Road, London SW.

Charlotte Corday, and other poems; by Emma Marie Caillard. London: Kegan Paul, Trench & Co. 1884. xii, 99 pp.   *BL*

The lost life, and other poems; by E.M. Caillard. London: Eyre & Spottiswoode. 1889. viii, 191 pp.   *BL*

A poem of life, [and other poems]; by Emma Marie Caillard. London: London Literary Society. [1884]. viii, 120 pp.   *OXB*

CALAMO CURRENTE, pseud. *see* **McHARDY, James**, (Calamo Currente, pseud.)

CALDER, John Fraser (1825–91). b. Campbeltown, Argyllshire. Educated at Edinburgh University. A solicitor with his own practice in Dundee.

Fragments: [poems]; by John Fraser Calder. With introductory biographical sketch. Coupar Angus: Comerton Private Printing Press. 1897. xvi, 65 pp. il.   *UCD*

CALDER, Robert McLean (1841–95). b. Duns, Berwickshire. In 1846 the family moved to Polwarth. Apprenticed to his uncle, a draper in Duns, he later went to London to take up a post at Marshall & Snelgrove, Oxford Street. He sailed for New York in 1866, settling in Chatham, Ontario; returned to London in 1882 to work in the shoe-trimming and embroidery trade.

A Berwickshire bard: the songs and poems of Robert McLean Calder. Edited, with introductory memoir, by W.S. Crockett. Paisley: J. & R. Parlane; Edinburgh: John Menzies & Co.; London: Houlston & Sons. 1897. 306 pp. il., por.   *OXB*

CALLANAN, Helena. Of the Asylum for the Blind, Infirmary Road, Cork, Ireland.
Verses old and new; by Helena Callanan. Printed Cork: Eagle Works. 1899. 108 pp.   *CU*

CALOW, Robert
Agnes; The bower of souls, and other poems; by Robert Calow. London: Remington & Co., Ltd. 1893. [vi], 303 pp.   *OXB*

CALVADOS, J.S. De *see* **DE CALVADOS, J.S.**

CALVERLEY, Charles Stuart (1831–84). b. Martley, Worcestershire, son of Rev. Henry Blayds, who assumed the name Calverley in 1852. Educated at Harrow School, Balliol College, Oxford, and Christ's College, Cambridge; Fellow of Christ's College, 1858. Called to the Bar, Inner Temple, 1865, and settled in London. A fall on ice in the winter of 1866-67 ended what might have been an exceptional career. Translator of Theocritus.
The literary remains of Charles Stuart Calverley. With a memoir by Walter J. Sendall. With portrait and illustrations. London: George Bell & Sons; Cambridge: Deighton, Bell & Co. 1885. x, 282 pp. il., por.   *MPL*
     Also 2nd ed. 1885; 3rd ed. 1892; Works, vol. I 1896.

CAMBRIDGE, Ada (1844–1926). b. Wiggenhall, St Germains, Norfolk, second of the ten children of Henry and Thomasine Cambridge. In 1870 she married George Frederick Cross, a young curate. They emigrated to Victoria, Australia, where Cross served as an Anglican minister in a succession of parishes, moving to Williamstown in 1893. She wrote romantic novels and contributed stories to newspapers and magazines, and is regarded as the first writer of prose and verse in Australia to be concerned with the socially disadvantaged.
Unspoken thoughts: [poems]; [by Ada Cambridge]. London: Kegan Paul, Trench & Co. 1887. vi, 143 pp.   *OXB*

CAMBRIDGE UNDERGRADUATE, pseud.
Khartoum, and thither: a poem; by a Cambridge undergraduate. Manchester: Heywood & Son; London: H. Vickers. 1885. 64 pp.   *OXB*

CAMERON, W.N. Of Aberdeen.
Poems: democratic and local; by W.N. Cameron and W.S. Rennie. Aberdeen. 1894. 24 pp.
     Not joint authorship. Title from cover.   *WCM*

CAMPBELL, Arthur
Songs of the pinewoods; by Arthur Campbell. London: Horace Cox. 1894. iv, 90 pp.   *OXB*

CAMPBELL, Mrs Colin G. *see* **CAMPBELL, Gertrude Elizabeth**, Lady Colin Campbell

CAMPBELL, Lady Evelyn Caroline Louisa (E.C.L.C.) (1851–). Daughter of the 2nd Earl Cawdor. Her mother had been a maid-of-honour to Queen Victoria. The family had homes at 74 South Audley Street, London, Stackpole Court, Pembrokeshire, Golden Grove, Llandilo, Carmarthenshire, and Cawdor Castle, Nairnshire.
Songs by the way; by E.C.L.C. London: Kegan Paul, Trench, Trübner, & Co. Ltd. 1894. viii, 75 pp. *UCD*

CAMPBELL, George Douglas, Duke of Argyll (1823– 1900). b. Ardencaple Castle, Dumbartonshire. He succeeded his father as 8th Duke in 1847. Served in several Liberal governments as Lord Privy Seal (twice), Postmaster-General, and Secretary of State for India. An independent and fearless statesman, he resigned his last public office through his disapproval of Gladstone's Irish land bill. Published works on politics, science, and religion.
The burdens of belief, and other poems; by the Duke of Argyll. London: John Murray. 1894. 131 pp. *MPL*
Crux muni: or, burdens of belief; by the Duke of Argyll. Printed London: Spottiswoode & Co. 1893. 32 pp.
　Privately printed. *BL*
Poems; by the Duke of Argyll. Printed Edinburgh: David Douglas. 1898. 48 pp.
　Privately printed. *OXB*

CAMPBELL, Gertrude Elizabeth, Lady Colin Campbell (1861–1911). Daughter of Edward M. Blood of Brickhill, County Clare. Educated in England and France. She married Lord Colin Campbell, son of the 8th Duke of Argyll, in 1881; obtained a separation from him on grounds of cruelty, and became a widow in 1895. Art critic of *The World*. Lived latterly at 67 Carlisle Mansions, Victoria, London SW.
Father Damien, and other poems; by Mrs. Colin G. Campbell. Oxford: A.R. Mowbray & Co. [1899]. viii, 95 pp. facsim. *OXB*

CAMPBELL, John. b. Oban, Argyllshire. The family moved to Ledaig when he was an infant. Aged seventeen he went to work in a Glasgow warehouse, remaining six years. He returned home because of poor health, becoming post-master at Ledaig. Often wrote in the Gaelic.
Yggdrassil, and other poems; by John Campbell. London: John Macqueen. 1898. viii, 185 pp. *OXB*

CAMPBELL, John Douglas Sutherland, Duke of Argyll (1845–1914). b. London, eldest son of the 8th Duke of Argyl. Known by the courtesy title of Marquis of Lorne. Elected MP for Argyllshire in 1868, becoming private secretary to his father at the India Office. In 1871 he married Princess Louise, fourth daughter of Queen Victoria. Governor-General of Canada, 1878–83. Elected Unionist MP for South Manchester, 1895. He succeeded his father as 9th Duke in 1900. Miscellaneous writer.

Memories of Canada and Scotland: speeches and verses; by the Marquis of Lorne. London: Sampson Low, Marston, Searle, & Rivington. 1884. xii, 360 pp.   OXB

   Also same ed. published in Montreal by Dawson Bros 1884.

Rome under Pius, and Italy under Rome, 1867–1887; by the Marquis of Lorne. London: Thomas Ogilvie Smith. 1888. [iv], 45 pp.   OXB

CAMPBELL, Robert (1837–   ). b. Barr, Ayrshire. His father died when he was four and he was brought up by his grandfather, a farmer of New Cumnock, who later moved to Kintyre, Argyllshire. Educated at New Cumnock, for a short time a pupil-teacher. He entered the Divinity Hall of the United Presbyterian Church in Edinburgh; ordained minister of Canon Street Church in 1863, then moved to Aldershot, Hampshire, and afterwards to the Albion Presbyterian Church, London Wall; eventually he was transferred to Calton Church, Glasgow.

Ivie, and other poems; by Robert Campbell. Glasgow: R. Robertson. 1896. 159 pp.   *UCD

CAMPBELL, Mrs Robert Burleigh

Palm leaves from Ceylon, and other poems; by Mrs. R. Burleigh Campbell. Epsom: John Snashall. 1885. [2], x, 117 pp.   OXB

CAMPBELL, Thomas. b. Lisnagarvey, Lisburn, County Down. A mill-worker, he lived at Low Road, Lisburn.

Lays from Lisnagarvey; by Thomas Campbell. Belfast: John Reid & Co. 1884. 136 pp.   NLI

CAMPBELL, Thomas A. Roman Catholic priest in northern Ireland, probably at Newry, County Down.

Saint Mary Magdalen: a poem; by Thomas A. Campbell. Newry: "Newry Reporter" Steam Printing Works. [1889]. 118 pp.   NLI

CAMPION, Hubert Craigie, (Two Undergrads, pseud. with Sydney Haldane Olivier). (1861?–82). Son of Hubert Campion of Ramsgate, Kent. Educated at Keble College, Oxford (scholar). Died February 1882.

Poems and parodies; by two undergrads. Oxford: B.H. Blackwell. 1880. 24 pp.   OXB

CANTON, William (1845–1926). b. Island of Chusan in the China Sea but the greater part of his childhood was spent in Jamaica. Engaged in miscellaneous literary and educational work, he was a journalist in London and Glasgow, for a time on staff of the *Glasgow Herald*. Hymn writer, and author of a history of the British & Foreign Bible Society, 5 vols, 1904–10.

The invisible playmate: a story of the unseen, with appendices; by William Canton. London: Isbister & Co. Ltd. 1894. 95 pp.

   Poetry and prose. Includes *Rhymes about a little woman*.   BL

The invisible playmate; and, W.V. her book; by William Canton. With two illustrations by C.E. Brock. London: Isbister & Co. Ltd. 1897. xii, 235 pp. il.

   Poetry and prose.   TCD

A lost epic, and other poems; by William Canton. Edinburgh: William Blackwood & Sons. 1887. x, 216 pp. *UCD*

W.V. her book, and various verses; by William Canton. With two illustrations by C.E. Brock. London: Isbister & Co. Ltd. 1896. 175 pp. il.
Poetry and prose. *BL*

CAP AND BELLS, pseud. *see* **WALTERS, John Cuming**, (Cap and Bells, pseud.)

CAPERN, Edward (1819–94). b. Tiverton, Devon, son of a baker. He worked in a lace factory at Barnstaple, 1827–47; rural letter-carrier in the Bideford area, 1847–68. Lived at Harborne, near Birmingham, 1868–84, lecturing in the midland counties for many years. W.S. Landor pronounced him 'a noble poet'. Known as 'The Rural Postman of Bideford'.
Sungleams and shadows: [poems]; by Edward Capern. London: Kent & Co.; Birmingham: Cornish Bros; Houghton & Hammond. 1881. xvi, 324 pp. *OXB*

CAPPER, Elizabeth Naish (1818–1907). b. Potterne Farm, Devizes, Wiltshire, daughter of Samuel and Elizabeth Capper, Quakers. She lived most of her life in Bristol, working for the Salvation Army, and the Friends' Home Mission.
Voices of the twilight, and other poems: by E.M. Capper. With a few translations. London: Saml. Harris & Co.; Leominster: Orphans' Printing Press. [1882]. [iv], 108 pp. il. *OXB*

CARGILL, Alexander (1853–). b. Leith, Midlothian, son of the master of Leith Academy, a descendant of the famous covenanter Donald Cargill. He studied for the ministry but instead took up a commercial career in banking. Contributed verse to the *Scotsman* and to English magazines.
Scraps from a pedlar's wallet: being original sonnets, songs, etc.; by Alexander Cargill. Edinburgh: Oliphant, Anderson, & Ferrier. 1883. 64 pp. *OXB*

CARMICHAEL, Daniel (1826–). b. Alloa, Clackmannanshire, son of a stonemason. Apprenticed to the engineering trade in Edinburgh; on completing his apprenticeship he went to Glasgow, working in various engineering shops on the Clyde for several years. In 1862 he moved to Liverpool, employed in a large engineering works on the Mersey. Contributed sketches and prose to the *Scottish Reader, Ladies' Journal*, etc.
Cosietattle, and other poems; by Daniel Carmichael. Liverpool: Author. 1888. viii, 296 pp. *UCD*
Rhyming lilts and Doric lays; by Daniel Carmichael. Printed by the author. 1880. ★

CARMICHAEL, Peter (1897–). Educated at a small village school. He began to earn his living at the age of ten, attending evening classes for many years to continue his education. Became the station-master at Douglas, Lanarkshire.

Clydesdale poems; by Peter Carmichael. Hamilton: W. Naismith; Glasgow: J. Menzies & Co. 1884. 303 pp.   *OXB*

   Also 2nd ed. 1885.

CARMICHAEL, Walter Scott. Studied medicine at Edinburgh University; MD, LM, 1835; Fellow of the Obstetrical Society of Edinburgh. Member of the general council of Edinburgh University. A parochial medical officer in practice in Pilrig Street. A Freemason.

   Miscellanea poetica; by Walter Scott Carmichael. Printed Edinburgh: Colston & Son. 1883. viii, 90 pp.

      Printed for private circulation.   *OXB*

CARNEGIE, James, Lord Southesk (1827–1905). b. Edinburgh, son of Sir James Carnegie, 5th Bart. Educated at Edinburgh Academy, and the Royal Military College, Sandhurst. Served as an ensign in the 92nd Highlanders, then commissioned in the Grenadier Guards. He succeeded his father as 6th Bart in 1849; obtained the title, forfeited in 1715, of Earl of Southesk. An antiquary, he collected gems, pictures, and Asiatic cylinders. Hon. LL.D, St Andrews, 1872, and Aberdeen, 1875.

   The burial of Isis, and other poems; by the Earl of Southesk. Edinburgh: David Douglas. 1884. xvi, 478 pp.   *OXB*

CARNIE, William. b. Aberdeen. Trained as an engraver. While still young he became an Inspector of the Poor. Having studied music he was appointed precentor in the parish church of Banchory Devenick. In 1853 he was made sub-editor of the *Aberdeen Herald*, acting as a professional shorthand writer. He was known all over Scotland as a music critic of the highest order.

   Waifs of rhyme, [and other poems]; [by William Carnie]. Aberdeen: J. & J.P. Edmond & Spark. 1887. viii, 63 pp.

      A limited ed. of 200 numbered copies.   *OXB*

   Waifs of rhyme, [and other poems]; [by William Carnie]. Aberdeen: Lewis Smith & Son. 1890. viii, 82 pp.   *OXB*

CARPENTER, Albert L.

   Edmund: a metrical tale; by Albert L. Carpenter. London: Elliot Stock. 1898. [iv], 79 pp.   *OXB*

CARPENTER, Edward (1844–1929). b. Brighton, Sussex. Educated at Trinity Hall, Cambridge; Fellow of Trinity, 1868. He took holy orders, and served in the Anglican ministry, 1869–74. Joined the university extension movement. In 1877 he visited the United States, meeting Emerson, Holmes, Lowell and Whitman. He became a socialist in 1883, influenced by William Morris. Settling at Millthorpe, a Derbyshire hamlet near Chesterfield, he engaged in literary work, market gardening, and sandal making. A prominent lecturer on socialism, he rejected his own social class. In 1922 he moved to Guildford, Surrey.

Towards democracy; [by Edward Carpenter]. Manchester: John Heywood. 1883. [iv], 119 pp.
> Poetry and prose. *MPL*
> Also 2nd ed. 1885.

Towards democracy; [by] Edward Carpenter. 3rd ed. London: T. Fisher-Unwin. 1892. viii, 368 pp. *MPL*
> Also re-issue of 3rd ed. published by Labour Press, Manchester, 1896.

CARPENTER, Joseph Edwards (1813–85). b. London. Wrote for magazines at an early age. Producer of musical entertainments, and author of more than 2,500 songs and duets. He edited *Penny Readings in Prose and Verse*, 1865–67. Writer on elocution and public speaking. Lived at 20 Norland Square, Notting Hill, London W.
My jubilee volume: [poems]; by Joseph Edwards Carpenter. Printed London: Clayton & Co. 1883. xvi, 335 pp.
> Printed for the author. *CU*

CARR, Francis, (Aelian Prince, pseud.) (1834–94). b. Newcastle upon Tyne. Secretary and manager, for many years, of the co. running steamers between Newcastle and Tynemouth; secretary of Lloyd's Tyne Public Chain & Anchor Testing Co.; timber merchant at Newcastle. Lived at The Willows, Walker.
Love's moods: [poems]; by Aelian Prince. London: E.W. Allen. [1885]. [iv], 104 pp. *MPL*
Of Joyous Gard; by Aelian Prince. London: E.W. Allen. 1890. [iv], 139 pp. *OXB*
Of Palomide, famous knight of King Arthur's round table; by Aelian Prince. London: E.W. Allen. 1890. 102 pp. *OXB*

CARR, George. Of Crook, Northumberland.
Bonnie Blanchland: a descriptive poem; by Geo. Carr. Printed Crook: W.J. Best. [189-]. 24 pp. *NPL*

CARRINGTON, Henry (1814–1906). Son of Sir Edmund Carrington, first Chief Justice of Ceylon. Educated at Charterhouse and Caius College, Cambridge. Rector, Monks Eleigh, Suffolk; dean and rector of Bocking, Essex.
The siren: [poems]; by Henry Carrington. London: Elliot Stock. 1898. viii, 148 pp. *OXB*

CARROLL, Lewis, pseud. *see* **DODGSON, Charles Lutwidge**, (Lewis Carroll, pseud.)

CARUS-WILSON, Mary Louisa Georgina (18 –19). Daughter of Colonel Martin Petrie. Educated at University College, London. In 1893 she married Professor Charles Ashley Carus-Wilson. Her prose works went through several eds in Britain and the United States. Lived latterly at Hanover Lodge, Kensington Park, London W.
Tokiwa, and other poems; by Mrs. Ashley Carus-Wilson (Mary L.G. Petrie). London: Hodder & Stoughton. 1895. viii, 357 pp. *BL*

CASEY, James (1824–1909). b. Riverston, County Sligo. Trained for the Roman Catholic priesthood at Maynooth, ordained c. 1857; served first at Ballygar, County Galway, then at Sligo; principal, St John's Seminary, 1860–73; parish priest, Athleague, Roscommon, from 1873; canon. Prolific writer in prose and verse, devoted to the Irish language, and a popular temperance poet.

The spouse of Christ: or, the church of the crucified: a dogmatic and historic poem, in four parts; by James Casey. Parts I and II. Dublin: James Duffy & Co., Ltd. 1897. [iv], 87 pp.
    Cover-title is *The Church of Christ.*   OXB
Verses on doctrinal and devotional subjects; by James Casey. Dublin: James Duffy & Sons. 1882. viii, 152 pp.   OXB

CASSELS, C.J.H.
New songs of the north (without music); by C.J.H. Cassels. Illustrated. Edinburgh: J. & J. Gray & Co. 1893. viii, 151 pp. il.   BL
Rhymes of the times; by C.J.H. Cassels. Edinburgh: R. Grant & Son; London: Simpkin, Marshall, & Co. 1891. x, 86 pp.   OXB

CASTLE, Joseph (1859–19). b. Oxford, son of Frederick Castle, gentleman. Educated at Hertford College, Oxford; BA 1885, MA 1894. Curate, Lydd, Kent, 1885–89, Lynstead, 1890–91, Faversham, 1891–98; vicar, Leysdown with Harty, Sheerness, and coastguard chaplain from 1898.
Dungeness ballads; by Joseph Castle. Printed Ashford: H.D. & B. Headley. 1887. 39 pp.   OXB

CATLING, Harry Debron, (H.D.C.), (Two Bachelors, pseud. with A.W. Burke Peel) (1869–1939?). Son of James Catling, auctioneer and estate agent of Cambridge. Educated at Perse School, and St John's College, Cambridge; BA 1892, MA 1904. Lived latterly at 53 Burleigh Street, Cambridge.
Versatile verses on the 'varsity, etc.; by two bachelors. Cambridge: J. Hall & Son. 1896. [iv], 31 pp.   OXB
Women's degrees: [poems]; by H.D.C. Cambridge: J. Hall & Son. 1897. [iv], 20 pp.   OXB

CATO, pseud.
Cato redivivus: a satirical review; [by Cato]. London: Hamilton & Adams. 1881. 32 pp.   OXB

CAUX, John William *see* **DE CAUX, John William**

CAVE, Alfred Verney- *see* **VERNEY-CAVE, Alfred, Lord Braye**

CAYLEY, Charles Bagot (1823–83). b. St Petersburg, son of Henry Cayley, merchant. Educated at King's College School, London, and Trinity College, Cambridge; BA 1845. Translator of Dante, Aeschylus, Homer and Petrarch. At one time he was engaged to marry Christina Rossetti.
Poems and translations; by Charles Bagot Cayley. London: Brain & Co. 1880. 80 pp. il.   *NUC

CAYZER, Sir Charles William (1869–1917). b. Bombay, son of Sir Charles Cayzer. Educated at Rugby School, and Christ Church, Oxford. Shipowner, partner in Cayzer, Irvine & Co.; director, Clan Line Steamers, Ltd, 1890–1911. He succeeded his father as 2nd Bart, 1916. Lived at 22 Lewes Crescent, Brighton, and at Dunsdale, Frodsham, Cheshire.

Amy Robsart, and other poems; by Charles W. Cayzer (the younger). Oxford: James Parker. [1893]. xii, 60 pp.   OXB

Poems of love and nature; by Charles W. Cayzer. London: Elliot Stock. 1896. x, 118 pp.   OXB

CECIL, Lady Frances H., pseud. *see* **SAYERS, Frances H.**, (Lady Frances H. Cecil, pseud.)

CECIL, Henry

Aleck; [by Henry Cecil]. Printed Cambridge: J. Palmer. [1885]. 23 pp.   OXB

CHADWICK, George Alexander (1840–1923). Educated at Trinity College, Dublin; BA 1862, MA 1867, BD 1876, DD 1877. Curate, St Anne's, Belfast, 1868–70; vicar, St James's, Belfast, 1870–72; prebendary, Tynan, Armagh Cathedral, 1873–85; dean of Armagh, 1886–96; chaplain to Lord Lieutenant, 1885–87; Bishop of Derry & Raphoe, 1896–1916.

"As one that serveth"; sacred poems; by George Alex. Chadwick. London: Elliot Stock. 1880. xii, 155 pp.   OXB

CHADWICK, Sheldon. Son of Jeremiah Chadwick, city missionary of Manchester. He lived in London.

Working and singing: poems, lyrics, and songs on the life-march; by Sheldon Chadwick. London: Edwin Benson. 1895. viii, 189 pp.

Cover-title is *Poems, lyrics & songs on the life march*.   BL

CHALLINOR, William (1821–96). b. Leek, Staffordshire, son of William Challinor. Educated at King William's College, Isle of Man, and Trinity College, Dublin; BA 1847, MA 1879. A solicitor at Leek from 1842. Writer on the Court of Chancery, worker for Chancery reform, and Leek local historian.

Lectures, verses, speeches, reminiscences, &c.; by William Challinor. Leek: M.H. Miller; London: Bemrose & Sons. 1891. xii, 3–368 pp. por.   OXB

CHALMERS, Andrew. Clergyman of St John's, Wakefield, Yorkshire.

A Red Cross romance; by Andrew Chalmers. London: Simpkin, Marshall & Co.; Aberdeen: D. Wyllie & Son. 1893. 102 pp.   OXB

CHAMBERLAYNE, William John (1821–1910). Entered the army in 1842; his appointments included fort adjutant, Bahamas, 1850–53, staff colonel, Mauritius, 1872–77; retired with rank of lieutenant-general, 1882. Lived latterly at Las Flores, Springfield Road, Torquay, Devon.

Poems: Part I: The tropic bird; Part II: The enchanted land; by General W.J. Chamberlayne. London: Smith, Elder, & Co. [1892]. 2 vols in 1.   *NUC

CHAMELEON, pseud.
Children of to-day; by Chameleon. Printed Glasgow: Robert Maclehose & Co.
1896. 51 pp. *★UCD*

CHANCELLOR, Frederic J. Dramatist.
Poems of the fancy & imagination; by Frederic J. Chancellor. Printed London:
Burdett & Co. [1885]. [ii], 66 pp. *OXB*

CHANTREY, P.
Life's inner life: (poetic pensée); by P. Chantrey. London: Remington & Co.
1888. xii, 242 pp. *OXB*

CHAPLIN, Mrs M.A. Of Galleywood, Essex.
Chimes for the times: [poems]; by Mrs M.A. Chaplin. With a preface by the
Rev. W. Lancelot Holland. London: William Wileman; E. Wilmshurst. 1891.
xiv, 126 pp. *BL*
Sunlit spray from the billows of life: [poems]; by Mrs. M.A. Chaplin. London:
G. Stoneman; R. Banks & Son. 1898. 110 pp. por. *BL*

CHAPMAN, Edward John (1821–1904). English–Canadian mineralogist.
Professor of mineralogy, University College, London, 1849–53, and Toronto
University, 1853–95. Published research on the fossils and minerals of
Canada.
A drama of two lives; The snake-witch; A Canadian summer-night, and other poems;
by E.J. Chapman. London: Kegan Paul, Trench, Trübner & Co. 1899. [vi], 98
pp. *MPL*

CHAPMAN, Elizabeth Rachel (1827–96). b. Woodford, Essex, into a
family originally from Whitby, Yorkshire; connected with the Gurneys of
Norwich, and lineally descended from Elizabeth Fry. She published novels
and essays, and was interested in the social and philanthropic movements of
the day.
A little child's wreath;by Elizabeth Rachel Chapman. London: Elkin Mathews
and John Lane; New York: Dodd Mead & Co. 1894. [vi], 43 pp.
  Of this ed. 350 copies were printed for England and 200 copies for
America. *OXB*
The new purgatory, and other poems; by Elizabeth Rachel Chapman. London:
T.Fisher Unwin. 1887. 158 pp. *OXB*

CHAPMAN, James (1835–88). b. Upper Banchory, Kincardineshire, son of a
country blacksmith who also leased a farm. After an elementary education he
worked on the farm until the age of twenty-four when he went to Glasgow,
working as an attendant at Gartnavel Asylum. Move to Partick, where he was
employed as a detective office, then as a sanitary officer for the burgh.
"Ecce homo", and other poems; by James Chapman. With frontispiece, &c,
drawn and engraved by the author. Partick: John Thomlinson. 1883. 152 pp.
il. *EPL*
The Scots o' langsyne, and other poems; by James Chapman. Memorial vol.
Printed Glasgow: James Macnab. 1888. viii. 104 pp. *NLS*

CHAPMAN, Joseph Thomas. Lived at Derby Villas, St John's Road, Bedminster, Bristol.

Meditative poems; and, An essay on happiness; by Joseph Thomas Chapman. Bristol: J.W. Arrowsmith; London: Simpkin, Marshall, Hamilton, Kent and Co. Ltd. [1892]. 150 pp. *UCD*

Poems; by Joseph Thomas Chapman. Bristol: J.W. Arrowsmith; London: Simpkin, Marshall & Co. 1889. [iv], 67 pp. *OXB*

CHAPMAN, Thomas, (Joseph, pseud.) (1844–88). b. Falla, Lanarkshire. He began his working life as a cowherd then became a ploughman. Largely self-educated, he joined the police force at Maryhill, near Glasgow; transferred to Hawick, Roxburghshire, becoming a sergeant in the county police.

Contentment, and other poems; by Thomas Chapman (Joseph). Kelso: J. & J.H. Rutherfurd. 1883. viii, 148 pp.
    Spine-title is *Poems*. *UCD*

CHARLES, Beatrice Ethel. Of Walsall, Staffordshire?

Songs in the night; by Beatrice Ethel Charles. London: Simpkin, Marshall, Hamilton, Kent & Co., Ltd; Walsall: W. Henry Robinson. 1894. [viii], 104 pp. *OXB*

CHARLES, Elizabeth Rundle (1828–96). b. Tavistock, Devon, daughter of the local MP. Educated at home by governesses and tutors. In 1851 she married Andrew P. Charles, owner of a soap and candle factory at Wapping, East End of London. When he died in 1868 she was left impoverished but was able to support herself by her writing, moving to Victoria Street, Westminster. She founded the home for the dying known as 'Friedenheim' in Hampstead in 1885. One of the first meetings of the Metropolitan Association for Befriending Young Servants was held at her house.

Songs of many seasons; by [Elizabeth Rundle Charles]. London: T. Nelson & Sons. 1882. 237 pp. *OXB*

Songs old and new; by Elizabeth Rundle Charles. Collected ed. London: T. Nelson & Sons. 1887. 340 pp. *BL*

Songs old and new; by Elizabeth Rundle Charles. Collected ed. London: Society for Promoting Christian Knowledge; New York: E. & J.B. Young & Co. 1894. viii, 340 pp. *TCD*
    Also Collected ed. 1896.

CHEEM, Aliph, pseud. *see* **YELDHAM, Walter**, (Aliph Cheem, pseud.)

CHESTER, Greville John (1839–92). b. Denton, Norfolk, son of Rev. William Chester, rector. Educated at Balliol College and St Mary Hall, Oxford; BA 1853. Ordained 1856; curate, Crayke, Yorkshire, 1855–57; perpetual curate, St Jude's, Moorfields, Sheffield, 1858–65; incumbent, St Luke's, Barbados, 1867–68. Founder of Sheffield Naturalists' Society. A well-known Egyptologist, he wintered in Egypt for many years.

Ella Cuthullin, and other poems, old and new; by Greville J. Chester. London: Marcus Ward & Co. 1883. [iv], 251 pp. *OXB*

CHESTER, Norley, pseud. *see* **UNDERDOWN, Emily**, (Norley Chester. pseud.)

CHIEL AMANG THE CLASSES AND THE MASSES TAKIN' NOTES, pseud.
A nineteenth century satire, with other rhymes for other times; by a chiel amang the classes and the masses takin' notes. London: Eden, Remington & Co. 1891. [viii], 338 pp.   *OXB*

CHILD, Gilbert William, (Oxoniensis, pseud.) (1832–96). b. Hackney, London, son of Samuel P. Child. Educated at Clapton Grammar School, and Exeter College, Oxford: BA 1854, MA 1856, MB 1857, MRCP 1858, MD 1859, FRCP 1871. Examiner in medicine, Oxford University, 1863, in natural science, 1867. He practised in Oxford, retiring c. 1882. Master of the Clothworkers' Co., London, 1891–92. Writer of three reports on the sanitary conditions in Oxford, physiological papers, etc.
Juvenal in Piccadilly; by Oxoniensis. London: Vizetelly & Co. 1888. 32 pp.   *OXB*

CHILD-LIFE AND ITS LESSONS: [poems]. London: Thomas Richardson & Son. 1881. 101 pp.   *OXB*

CHILD OF MARY, pseud. *see* **H., A.**, (Child of Mary, pseud.)

CHILDE-PEMBERTON, Harriet Louisa. Daughter of Charles O. Childe-Pemberton of Millichope Park, Church Stretton, high sheriff of Shropshire. Her London home was at 12 Portman Street, W.
Dead letters, and other narrative and dramatic pieces; by Harriet L. Childe-Pemberton. London: Ward, Lock & Co., Ltd. 1896. viii, 126 pp.
    Poetry and prose.   *BL*
In a Tuscan valley, and other poems; by Harriet L. Childe-Pemberton. London: Griffith, Farran, Okeden & Welsh. [1890]. 144 pp.   *BL*
"Prince", a story of the American War, and other narrative poems, adapted for reading and recitation; by Harriet Childe-Pemberton. London: Ward, Lock & Co. [1883]. 145 pp. (Original readings and recitations).   *BL*

CHIMES FROM A POET'S BELFRY. London: Elliot Stock. 1886. [viii], 152 pp.   *OXB*

CHLORIS, pseud. Of Dublin?
Dream-wreaths and scattered leaves: [poems]; by Chloris. London: James Nisbet & Co. Ltd. 1898. 136 pp.   *OXB*

CHOLMONDELEY-PENNELL, Henry (Harry) (1836–1915) b. London, son of Sir Charles H. Pennell. Educated by private tutor. He entered the civil service, 1853; inspector of sea fisheries, 1866–75; selected to initiate commercial and other reforms in Egypt, 1875; later appointed director-general of interior commerce. A keen sportsman, he wrote several books on fishing and fisheries; a contributor to *Punch*. Lived latterly at 46 Palace Mansions, Chelsea, London.

'From grave to gay': a volume of selections form the complete poems of H. Cholmondeley-Pennell. London: Longmans, Green, & Co. 1884. xii, 170 pp. por. *MPL*

CHRISTIAN, Owen, pseud. *see* **CURWEN, Henry**, (Owen Christian, pseud.)

CHRISTIE, Albany James (1817?–91). Son of Albany H. Christie of Chelsea, London. Educated at Oriel and Queen's Colleges, Oxford; Fellow of Oriel, 1840–45. Member of the Society of Jesus, ordained priest of the Westminster archdiocese; attached to the Jesuit churches in Farm Street and Mount Street, London, from 1868. Lecturer and playwright.

Chimes for holy-days, from "The end of man": [poems]; by Albany J. Christie. [Roehampton]: Manresa Press. 1890. viii, 98 pp. OXB

The end of man, in four books; by Albany James Christie. London: Kegan Paul, Trench & Co. 1886. xii, 437 pp. il. *OXB*
   Also 2nd ed. 1886.

The end of man, in four books; by Albany James Christie. 3rd ed. London: Burns & Oates, Ltd; New York: Catholic Publication Society Co. 1886. viii, 254 pp. *OXB*
   Also 4th ed. 1888.

Rosary verses; by Albany J. Christie. London: Catholic Truth Society. [1889]. 16 pp. *OXB*

CHRISTIE, Edward Richard, (Julian Home, pseud.) (1858?–89). Educated at Christ's College, Cambridge. Ordained, 1882; curate, St John the Evangelist, Clapham, London, 1882-83. Headmaster of West Kent Grammar School, Brockley, 1885, and of Magdalen College School, Oxford, 1886–88.

"Home they brought her warrior dead": an in memoriam to the late Prince Imperial of France; by Julian Home. London: Newman & Co. [1880]. [vi], 200 pp. *OXB*

CHRISTIE, Nimmo. Of Hexham, Northumberland.

Lays and verses; by Nimmo Christie. London: Longmans, Green, & Co. 1896. viii, 80 pp. *OXB*

CHRISTIE, William, (Stable Boy, pseud.). Of Hexham, Northumberland.

Three leal and lowly laddies: Mauricewood pit disaster, Midlothian, September, 1889: [poems] to the memory of three pony boys; by a stable boy. Manchester: John Heywood. [1889]. [23] pp. *MPL*

CHRYS, pseud. Educated at Oxford University; MA.

Sonnets and quatorzains; by Chrys. London: Cassell & Co., Ltd; Bournemouth: E.M. & A. Sydenham. [1887]. x, 145 pp. *OXB*

CHRYSTABEL, pseud. *see* **ATTENBOROUGH, Florence Gertrude**, (Chrystabel, pseud.)

CHURCH, Alfred John (1829–1912). b. London, son of a solicitor. Educated at King's College, London, and Lincoln College, Oxford. Ordained 1853; curate, Charlton, Wiltshire, 1853–56. Assistant master, Royal Institution School, Liverpool, and Merchant Taylors' School, London, 1857–70; head-master, Henley Grammar School, 1870–73, and Retford Grammar School, 1873–80; professor of Latin, University College, London, from 1880. He retired from teaching in 1892, taking up a living at Ashley St James, Wiltshire. Classical scholar, and author of historical tales for boys.

The legend of Saint Vitalis, and other poems; by Alfred J. Church. Oxford: B.H. Blackwell; London: Seeley & Co. 1887. viii, 61 pp.   *LL*

CHURCH, Sir Arthur Herbert (1834–1915). b. London, son of John T. Church. Educated at King's College, London, Royal College of Chemistry, and Lincoln College, Oxford. Professor of chemistry, Royal Agricultural College, Cirencester, 1863–79; lecturer, Cooper's Hill, 1888–90; professor of chemistry, Royal Academy of Arts, 1879–1911. President, Mineralogical Society, 1898–1901. Discoverer of turacin, an animal pigment, a native cerium phosphate, and other new minerals.

Flower and bird posies: [poems]; by A.H. Church and R.H. Soden-Smith. Shelsley, Kew Gardens: Authors. 1890. [1], viii, 33 pp.
    Not joint authorship.   OXB

CHURCHILL, Rosie
    Poems and song words; by Rosie Churchill. London: Simpkin, Marshall & Co.; Sandown, I.W.: W. Beavan Martin. [1889]. 48 pp.   *OXB*

CHURCHMAN, pseud.
    Silence versus the Athanasian chorus: an appeal; by a churchman. London: William Ridgway. 1881. 39 pp.   *OXB*

CITIE BARDE, pseud. Of Crouch End, London.
    Poems of ye citie, with manie another dittie; by a citie barde. London: Simpkin, Marshall, Hamilton, Kent & Co., Ltd. 1895. viii, 96 pp.
    Poetry and prose.   *BL*

CLAIR, Aston, pseud. *see* **BORASTON, John Maclair**, (Aston Clair, pseud.)

CLARE, Mavis. Of London W.
    Jottings in verse; by Mavis Clare. London: Simpkin, Marshall & Co. Ltd; Liverpool: Edward Howell. 1899. [vi], 37 pp.   *OXB*

CLARK, Henry W.
Behind the veil, and other poems; by Henry W. Clark. London: Hatchards. 1886. iv, 91 pp. *OXB*

CLARK, Hugh, (Heone, pseud.) (1832–) b. North Ayrshire.
Poems for the period; by Heone. Edited by Henry Reid. Irvine: Charles Murchland. 1881. xiv, 222 pp. **NUC*

CLARK, J.T.
Selections from poems; by J.T. Clark. Edinburgh: J. Gardner Hitt. 1898. 32 pp.
  Cover-title is *Poems* *OXB*

CLARK, John Aubrey (1826?–89). Of Street, Somerset. Contributed verse and prose to the *Village Album*, started in Street, 1856.
In remembrance: selected verses and essays, written from 1839 to 1889; by John Aubrey Clark. Printed London: Headley Bros. 1897. xvi, 351 pp. por.
  Printed for private circulation. *TAU*

CLARK, John William
Henry the Eighth (a burlesque); and, Miscellaneous poems; by John William Clark. London: Milton Smith & Co. 1886. 136 pp.
  Cover-title is *Miscellaneous poems*. *BL*

CLARK, Kate McCosh. Mrs McCosh of London. She travelled to New Zealand to collect Maori tales and legends.
Persephone, and other poems; by K. McCosh Clark. London: Sampson Low, Marston & Co. 1894. x, 192 pp. *OXB*

CLARK, Charles Allen, (Teddy Ashton, pseud.) (1863–1935). b. Bolton, Lancashire, of working class parents. On leaving school he worked in a cotton mill, eventually becoming a journalist; started the popular local journal *Teddy Ashton's Weekly*. Writer of fiction with a communistic slant, he was the founder of the Lancashire Authors' Association. Lived latterly in Blackpool.
"Voices", and other verses; by C. Allen Clarke. London: 'Clarion' Office; Manchester: Labour Press Society Ltd. 1895. 120 pp. *WCM*

CLARKE, Frank Harold. Of Wisbech, Cambridgeshire?
On fenland reeds: [poems]; by Frank Harold Clarke. Printed Wisbech: W. Poyser. 1899. [iv], 24 pp. *OXB*

CLARKE, Henry (1804–80). Educated at Trinity College, Dublin; BA 1825, MA 1858. Ordained 1829; rector of Northfield with Cofton Hackett and Bartley Green. Birmingham, from 1834.
Memorials of Henry Clarke: [poems]. Printed London: National Press Agency, Ltd. [c. 1881]. viii, 109 pp.
  For private circulation. *BIP*

CLARKE, Henry Savile (1841–93). Playwright, author of comic opera and musical plays, he edited *The Court Journal* for some years; contributed many verses to *Punch* from 1867. Member of the Garrick Club. He is buried at Kensal Green Cemetery.

"A little flutter": stage, story, and stanza; by H. Savile Clarke. London: Henry & Co. [1892]. viii, 205 pp. por. (Whitefriars library of wit and humour, second series). *TCD*

The modern Macbeth, and other political verses; by H. Savile Clarke. London: "Court Circular" Office. [1885]. 44 pp. *OXB*

CLARKE, Herbert Edwin (1852–1912). b. Chatteris, Isle of Ely, Cambridgeshire. His parents were Quakers, and he was educated at the Quaker schools at Hertford and Sidcot. In 1873 he went to London, taking a post in the office of Elder & Co., becoming company secretary and remaining with the firm until his death. After his marriage in 1883 he settled at Forest Hill, then moved to Beckenham. A member of Croydon Literary Circle. Friend of Philip Bourke Marston.

Poems and sonnets; by Herbert E. Clarke. London: Simpkin, Marshall, Hamilton, Kent & Co. Ltd. 1895. xii, 140 pp. *OXB*

Storm-drift: poems and sonnets; by H.E. Clarke. London: David Bogue. 1882. [vi], 249 pp. *OXB*

Tannhäuser, and other poems; by Herbert E. Clarke. London: Bertram Dobell. 1896. vi, 166 pp. *MPL*

CLARKE, Mary Cowden- *see* **COWDEN-CLARKE, Mary**

CLARKE, Samuel Childs (1821–1903). Son of James Clarke of Devonport. Educated at Queen's College and St Mary Hall, Oxford; BA 1844, MA 1846. Curate, Thorverton, Devon, 1844–46, Dawlish, 1846–48; vicar, St Thomas-by-Launceston, 1848–75, Thorverton Cullompton from 1875. Hymn writer.

Festival and other hymns for church tides, and occasional services, together with litanies and carols for various seasons, and songs sacred and secular; by S. Childs Clarke. London: Skeffington & Son. 1896. xvi, 323 pp. *BL*

Memorial tributes, inscribed from time to time to members of the royal family of England, on events connected with the reign of her most gracious majesty, Queen Victoria; by S. Childs Clarke. London: Skeffington & Son. 1894. 39 pp. *OXB*

CLAYTON ADAMS, Mary Frances (1838–1920). Second daughter of Martin Farquhar Tupper. Lived at Albury House, Tillingbourne, Surrey. In 1871 she married John Clayton Adams, landscape artist, setting up home at Ewhurst, near Albury. They had a son and a daughter.

Out in the sunshine, [and other poems]; by Mrs Clayton Adams. Illustrated by J. Clayton Adams and other artists. London: George Stoneham. [1893]. 40 pp. il. *OXB*

CLEARY, Thomas Stanislaus (1851–98). b. Dublin. Worked as a journalist in Dublin, a constant contributor to various Irish and American periodicals. He wrote largely for the *Weekly Irish Times* but edited the *Clare Independent* for a time. Died suddenly at Killaloe and is buried at Glasnevin.

Songs of the Irish land war; by Thomas S. Cleary. Dublin: W.P. Swan. 1888. 54 pp. *BL*

Twitterings at twilight: [poems]; by T.S. Cleary. Dublin: M.H. Gill & Son. 1883. 92 pp. *OXB*

CLELAND, John (1835–1924). b. Perth, son of John Cleland, surgeon. Educated at Edinburgh High School, and Edinburgh University; MD, DSc, LL.D, FRS. In 1863 he was appointed professor of anatomy and physiology, Queen's College, Galway, and in 1877 regius professor of anatomy, Glasgow University. He published numerous scientific works in his field. Lived latterly at Drumclog, Crewkerne, Somerset.

Scala naturae, and other poems; by John Cleland. Edinburgh: David Douglas. 1887. viii, 151 pp. il. *UCD*

CLELAND, William, (Gama, pseud.). He and his wife Mary were the parents of twin boys born 23 January 1867, who died a few weeks after birth.

Loved, lost, and found: memorial verses; by Gama. Liverpool: Edward Howell; London: Simpkin, Marshall & Co. Ltd. 1895. [vi], 36 pp. *UCD*

Also 2nd ed. 1895.

CLERKE, Ellen Mary (1840-1906). b. Skibereen, County Cork, sister of Agnes Mary Clerke, historian of astronomy. A novelist, she also wrote in German and Italian for various European newspapers. She and her sister lived together all their lives, dying in London within a year of one another.

The flying Dutchman, and other poems; by E.M. Clerke. London: W. Satchell & Co. 1881. iv, 107 pp. *BL*

CLIFF, Maria

Poems on true incidents, and other poems, 1885–1892; by Maria Cliff. London: Kegan Paul, Trench, Trübner & Co., Ltd. 1893. viii, 278 pp. *BL*

CLIFFE, Francis Henry. Novelist and dramatist.

The Persian vizier, and other poems; by Francis Henry Cliffe. London: Remington & Co., Ltd. 1894. [iv], 103 pp. *OXB*

CLIFFORD, Sir Charles (1813–93). b. Mount Vernon, Liverpool, son of George L. Clifford. Educated at Stonyhurst College. One of the early settlers in Wellington, New Zealand, arriving 1843. He was elected to the first parliament, 1854, serving as speaker, 1854-60. Knighted, 1858, created bart, 1887. Died in London, and is buried at Clifford, near Tadcaster, Yorkshire.

Verses; by Sir Charles Clifford. [c. 1886]. [ii], 19 pp. *UCD*

CLIFTON POET *see* **GABBITASS, Peter**

CLONTARF, pseud. *see* **O'BRIEN, Thomas**, (Clontarf, pseud.)

CLOSE, Jarvis William. Educated at Queen's College, Oxford (exhibitioner).
Poems; by Jarvis William Close. Printed London: J. Liges & Co. 1882. [x], 99 pp.
Printed for private circulation. *OXB*

CLOSE, Richard Inge
The world's need: a poem; by Richard Inge Close. London: Digby, Long & Co. [1893]. 30 pp. *OXB*

CLOUGH, John. Of Westhoughton, near Bolton, Lancashire.
A tragedy: the burning of Westhoughton Cotton Mill in 1812: a poem; by John Clough. Bolton: 'Journal' Office. 1882. 20 pp.
Cover-title is *The burning of Westhoughton Mill*. *WCM*

CLOUGH, R.L.
During twelve years of Gladstone's leadership (1868–81); by R.L. Clough. London: Chapman & Hall, Ltd. 1885. [viii], 160 pp. *OXB*
Election lyrics; by R.L. Clough. London: Chapman & Hall, Ltd. 1885. viii, 113 pp. *OXB*

CLOWES, Sir William Laird- *see* **LAIRD-CLOWES, Sir William**.

CLYNE, Norval (1817–88). b. Ballycastle, Country Antrim, son of Captain John Clyne, Royal Scots Regiment. Educated at Aberdeen Grammar School, and Marischal College, Aberdeen. Member of the Society of Advocates, Aberdeen, its secretary and factor for many years. Writer on Scottish ballads and Jacobite poetry. Lived at 6 Golden Square, Aberdeen.
The lost eagle, and other verses; by Norval Clyne. Printed Aberdeen: G. Cornwall & Sons. 1880. [viii], 47 pp.
For private circulation. *OXB*

COBBE, Frances Power (1822–1904). b. Newbridge, near Dublin, daughter of a country gentleman and magistrate. Educated in Brighton, Sussex. After her father's death she travelled abroad in Italy and the East. She engaged in philanthropic and reformatory work with Mary Carpenter in Bristol, and became a busy journalist; leader writer for the *Echo*, 1868–75. Feminist, social reformer, philosopher, and a prominent anti-vivisectionist.
Rest in the Lord, and other small pieces: [poems]; by Frances Power Cobbe. Printed London: Pewtress & Co. 1887. viii, 47 pp.
'For private gift only'. *BL*

COBBETT, John Meredith.
Ephemera: a collection of occasional verse; by J.M. Cobbett. Oxford: Alden & Co. Ltd; London: Simpkin, Marshall, Hamilton, Kent & Co. Ltd. 1898. [vi], 70 pp. *OXB*

COBBETT, Maria. Mrs Cobbett. An octogenarian in 1880.
Poems; by Maria Cobbett. 1880. viii, 88 pp.
Printed for private circulation. *BL*

COBBY, Eleanor F. Of Bognor, Sussex?

The auto-biography of war: being a brief account of its private pedigree and public transactions; by Eleanor F. Cobby. Bognor: Henry Lovett. [1884?]. 16 pp.   *BL*

COCHRANE, Alfred (1865–1948). b. Mauritius, son of Rev. C. Cochrane. Educated at Repton School, and Hertford College, Oxford; BA 1888, MA 1891; in the University cricket eleven, 1885, 1886, 1888. Secretary to Sir W.G. Armstrong at Whitworth & Co., Elswick Works, Newcastle upon Tyne. He contested the Tyneside division of Northumberland, 1910; member of the River Tyne Commission, 1912-27. Lived latterly at Elm Hurst, Batheaston, Somerset.

The kestrel's nest, and other verses; by Alfred Cochrane. London: Longmans, Green & Co. 1894. vii, 76 pp.   *OXB*

Leviore plectro: (occasional verses); by Alfred Cochrane. London: Longmans, Green & Co. 1896. viii, 82 pp.   *OXB*

COCKLE, Mrs Moss *see* **MOSSCOCKLE, Rita Frances**, (Mrs Moss Cockle).

CODD, John. Architect; ARIBA.

A legend of the Middle Ages, and other songs of the past and present; by John Codd. London: Kegan Paul, Trench, Trübner & Co., Ltd. 1890. [viii], 148 pp.   *OXB*

Voices of the Thames, and other poems; by John Codd. Printed Frome: Butler & Tanner. 1897. [viii], 183 pp.

Printed for private circulation only.   *OXB*

COGHILL, Annie Louisa (1836-1907). Née Walker. In her teens she spent some time in the Canadian backwoods. On her return to England she married Harry Coghill of Coghurst.

Oak and maple: English and Canadian verses; by Mrs E. Coghill (Annie L. Walker). London: Kegan Paul, Trench, Trübner & Co. Ltd. 1890. x, 114 pp.   *OXB*

COGHILL, James (1854–   ). b. Edinburgh, son of a master mason. While he was still an infant the family moved to Glasgow, where he attended various schools until 1865. The family moved again to Ardoch, then to Dumbarton. In 1868 he started work as an apprentice mason, eventually joining the family firm. He entered Glasgow University in 1873 but was not a successful student. Lived at 16 Preston Street, Govan Hill, Glasgow.

Poems, songs, and sonnets; by James Coghill. Subscribers' ed. Glasgow: Robert L. Holmes. 1890. 191 pp.   *OXB*

COLBECK, James Alfred, (J.A.C.) (18 –80).

Poems; by J.A.C. In memoriam, July 14, 1880. Printed London: R. Clay, Sons, & Taylor. 1881. 64 pp. il.

Cover-title is *In memoriam, J.A.C.*   *UCD*

COLBURN, George (1852–   ). b. Laurencekirk, Kincardineshire, of work-ing-class parents with a large family. They moved to Stonehaven when he was nine. He attended school for a short time, working on the land in the summer. Aged fourteen he was sent to Montrose to learn the grocery trade. He went to America for three years but ill-health compelled him to return to Scotland. Contributed prose and verse to local newspapers and magazines.

Poems: historical and descriptive; by George Colburn. With introduction by D.H. Edwards. [Brechin]: Brechin Advertiser Office. [1884]. 124 pp.   *NLS*

Poems on mankind and nature; by George Colburn. Glasgow: Maclaren & Sons. 1891. 442 pp. por.   *MPL*

COLBY, Frederic Thomas (1827–99). b. St Andrews, Plymouth, Devon, son of Thomas Colby, Captain, RN. Educated at Shrewsbury School, and Exeter College, Oxford; Fellow of Exeter, 1849–75, bursar, 1856–69. Ordained, 1850; vicar, South Newington, Oxfordshire, 1869–70; rector, Little Cheney, Dorset, 1875; resigned 1893. Writer on Devon genealogy; FSA.

Verses & translations; by Frederic Thomas Colby. Printed Exeter: William Pollard & Co. 1898. 19 pp.

Printed for private circulation. Title from cover.   *BL*

COLE, John Cowden- *see* **COWDEN-COLE, John**

COLE, Owen Blayney (1808–86). Son of Henry Cole of Twickenham, Middlesex. Educated at Christ Church, Oxford; BA 1830. Of Brandrum, County Monaghan, he lived latterly at Portishead, Somerset.

Christmas and new-year carols, &c.; by Owen Blayney Cole. Portishead: Author. 1880. 16 pp.

Cover-title is *Christmas carols*.   *BL*

Eyolf and Astrida: an Icelandic saga; with, Christmas & new-year carols. &c.: by Owen Blayney Cole. Portishead: Author. 1881. 24 pp. por.   *BL*

Floralia: or, posies from our nursery-garden, &c.: poems; by Owen Blayney Cole. Portishead: [Author]. 1880. 36 pp. por.   *TAU*

The heron, and other familiar ballads; with, Christmas and new-year carols; by Owen Blayney Cole. Portishead: [Author]. 1883. 24 pp. col. il.   *BL*

The lily of Llandaff, and other rimes; by Owen Blayney Cole. Portishead: [Author]. 1884. 40 pp. por.   *BL*

The midnight ride: an Irish legend dramatised; with, Christmas & new-year carols, &c.; by Owen Blayney Cole. Portishead: [Author]. 1886. 40 pp. il.   *BL*

The minuet: a chorographic poem; by Owen Blayney Cole. Portishead: [Author]. 1885. 20 pp. il.   *BL*

Neoterocomia: being addenda to "Our village": [poems]; by Owen Blayney Cole. Portishead: [Author]. 1883. 32 pp. col. il.   *BL*

The will in the walls, and other ballads; by Owen Blayney Cole. Portishead: [Author]. 1880. 24 pp. por.   *BL*

COLE, Thomas E., (Podd, pseud.)
The love songs of "Podd", including sonnets on Worcester. Birmingham: Cornish Bros; Wolverhampton: Barford & Newitt. 1884. [vii], 164 pp. il. *OXB*

COLERIDGE, Ernest Hartley (1846–1920). Son of Samuel Taylor Coleridge's son Derwent. Educated at Oxford University. Secretary to the Lord Chief Justice of England, 1894. He edited his grandfather's letters and selections from his notebooks, also Byron's poetical works, 7 vols, 1898–1903.
Poems; by Ernest Hartley Coleridge. Printed Chertsey: Frank E. Taylor. 1881. viii, 72 pp.
   Title page states 'Not published'. *OXB*
Poems; by Ernest Hartley Coleridge. London: John Lane The Bodley Head. 1898. 108 pp. *OXB*

COLERIDGE, Mary, (Anodos, pseud.) (1861–1907). b. London, daughter of Arthur Coleridge, clerk of assize and a nephew of Samuel Taylor Coleridge. Educated privately, partly by the poet William Cory Johnson. She devoted much time to teaching working women in her own home, and gave lessons in English literature at the Working Women's College. Essayist and novelist, her poems were praised by Binyon, Bridges, and Edward Thomas. She was a close friend of Henry and Margaret Newbolt. Died at Harrogate, Yorkshire.
Fancy's following: [poems]; by Anodos. Oxford: Daniel. 1896. [vii], 60 pp.
   A limited ed. of 125 numbered copies. *OXB*
Fancy's guerdon, [and other poems]; by Anodos. London: Elkin Mathews. 1897. 30 pp. (Shilling garland, VII). *OXB*

COLERIDGE, Stephen (1854–1936). Son of 1st Baron Coleridge. Educated at Trinity College, Cambridge. Barrister, Middle Temple, 1866; clerk of assize, South Wales circuit, 1890–1936. He lectured and wrote on English literature. An anti-vivisectionist and founder of the National Society for the Prevention of Cruelty to Animals.
Fibulae: [poems]; by the Hon. Stephen Coleridge. London: Kegan Paul, Trench & Co. 1889. 44 pp. *OXB*

COLLER, Edwin. Journalist of Chelmsford, Essex, for many years on staff of *The Essex Weekly News*.
Homespun yarns: [poems]; by Edwin Coller. London: John & Robert Maxwell. [1884]. viii, 246 pp. *BL*

COLLETT, John (1832–   ). b. Westerham, Kent, son of Rev. Robert H. Collett. Educated at Wadham College, Oxford.
The story of St. Stephen, and other poems; by John Collett. London: Longmans, Green, & Co. 1883. viii, 202 pp. *OXB*

COLLIN, Stephen. Lived at 11 Ripon Villas, Brunswick Avenue, Hull, Yorkshire.
Summer and wayside poems; by Stephen Collin. Hull: Author. 1887. xii, 142 pp.   *OXB*

COLLINGS, Linda Bonamy M. Of Guernsey, Channel Islands?
A rhyming record of English history, and other poems; by Linda B.M. Collings. London: Digby, Long & Co. [1892]. viii, 51 pp.   *BL*

COLLINGWOOD, William Gershom (1854–1932). b. Liverpool. Educated at Liverpool College, University College, Oxford, and the Slade School, London. Painter, writer, antiquarian, lecturer on art, and an authority on geology. A friend of John Ruskin, he lived at Gillhead, Windermere, Westmorland.
A book of verses; by W. Gershom Collingwood. Orpington, Kent: George Allen. 1885. x, 94 pp.   *OXB*

COLLINS, William John Townsend, (Member for the West Ward, pseud.) (1868-19). b. Stratford-upon-Avon, Warwickshire, and educated locally. Trained as a journalist on the *Herald*. He played Rugby football for Stratford and in London, where he reported matches for the *Evening News*; moved to Newport in 1892 as a reporter for the *South Wales Argus*; appointed editor, 1917.
West Ward rhymes, and other verses; by the member for the West Ward. Newport: A.W. Dawson, Ltd. 1898. 80 pp.   **UCD*

COLMORE, G., pseud. *see* **RENTON, Gertrude,** (G. Colmore, pseud.)

COLOMB, George Hatton. Colonel, Royal Artillery. Irish novelist and playwright; FSA.
The Cardinal Archbishop: a Spanish Legend in twenty-nine cancions; by Colonel Colomb. London: C. Kegan Paul & Co. 1880. viii, 179 pp.   *BL*
The Cardinal Archbishop and the invincible armada (1588): a Spanish legend, in twenty-nine cancions, with rhymed introduction; by Colonel Colomb. New ed. London: W.H. Allen & Co. 1889. xiv, 179 pp.   *BL*
      Also re-issue 1892.

COLQUHOUN, John (1805–85). b. Edinburgh, second son of Sir James Colquhoun of Luss. Educated in Edinburgh, at a private school in Lincolnshire, and Edinburgh University. Ensign in 33rd Foot Regiment, 1828; lieutenant, 4th Dragoon Guards from 1829 to 1834, when he sold out. An expert in country sports and natural history. Lived at Crosshill, Ayrshire, and Royal Terrace, Edinburgh.
Poems and prose pieces; by John Colquhoun. Glasgow: W. & R. Holmes. 1894. viii, 138 pp.   *NLS*

COMFORT, Robert. Member of the Brotherhood of the Royal Society of Labour, an anti-capitalist organization. Lived at Henry Street, Bury, Lancashire.
Might against right; The critic, and other poems; by Robert Comfort. Bury: Author. [189–]. 66 pp. *UCD*

COMLEY, James. Of Hereford?
Poems, chiefly sacred; by James Comley. Hereford: Wilson & Philips. [1892]. 68 pp. *BL*

CONAN; LADY BRIDE, AND OTHER POEMS. London: Pickering & Co. 1885. [iv], 159 pp. *UCD*

The CONQUEST OF CONSTANTINOPLE BY THE CRUSADERS: A SONG OF ISRAEL, AND OTHER POEMS. London: Kegan Paul, Trench, Trübner & Co. Ltd. 1898. [vi], 122 pp. *OXB*

CONSERVATIVE OF "THE FOURTH PARTY", pseud.
To Sir Stafford; by a Conservative of "The fourth party". London: E.W. Allen. 1883. 16 pp. *OXB*

CONWAY, Hugh, pseud. *see* **FARGUS, Frederick John**, (Hugh Conway, pseud.)

COOK, Eliza (1818–89). b. Southwark, London, youngest of the eleven children of a brazier. When she was nine the family went to live on a small farm at Horsham, Sussex. Almost entirely self-educated, she contributed to many magazines, and in 1849 brought out a magazine for family reading called *Eliza Cook's Journal*, which was highly successful. In 1863 she received a civil list pension of £100 a year. She became something of a confirmed invalid, and died at Thornton Hill, Wimbledon.
The poetical works of Eliza Cook. Complete ed., with explanatory notes, etc. London: Frederick Warne & Co. [1882]. xvi, 624 pp. il., por. (The "Lansdowne poets"). *MPL*
The poetical works of Eliza Cook. Complete ed. With explanatory notes, &c. New York: T.Y. Crowell & Co. [1882]. xvi, 558 pp. *BL*

COOK, Ellen (18 –19). Wife of Canon Cook of Rochdale, Lancashire. Lived at Elwick Hall, Castle Eden.
Humphrey Gray, with sundry poems; by Ellen Cook. Printed Rochdale: J. Dawson. 1888. [vi], 23 pp. *RPL*
On the threshold, [and other poems]; by Ellen Cook. West Hartlepool: J. Taylor. 1899. 31 pp. *RPL*

COOK, Flavel Smith (1827?–1900). b. Rame, near Devonport, son of James Cook, MD. Educated at Trinity College, Dublin; BA 1853, MA, BD, DD 1880. Ordained, 1854; curate, Millbrook, near Devonport, 1853–55; vicar, Liskeard, Cornwall, 1863–71, Christ Church, Clifton, Bristol, 1871–76; chaplain, Lock Hospital, London, 1876–91. Lived at Priory Lawn, High Street, Cheltenham, Gloucestershire.

Avena: musings in rhyme; by Flavel S. Cook. London: James Nisbet & Co. 1886. viii, 207 pp. *UCD*

COOK, Keningale (1846–86). Son of Rev. Robert K. Cook, vicar of Smallbridge, near Rochdale, Lancashire. Educated at Rugby School, and Trinity College, Dublin; BA 1866, MA, LL.B, LL.D 1875. Clerk in the General Post Office, London, 1868–74; partner in a firm of stockbrokers in Throgmorton Street from 1874. He married Minna M. Collins, only child of novelist Mortimer Collins. Published translations from works of French, Greek and Latin writers.

The guitar player, with sundry poems; by Keningale Cook. London: Pickering & Co. 1881. vi, 138 pp. *OXB*

COOKE, Robert Humphrey. Qualified in medicine and surgery at Guy's Hospital, London; FRCS 1860; surgeon to the Warehouseman & Travellers' Provident Association, and to the Asylum for Fatherless Children. Contributed a paper on epidemic diseases of children to the *Psychological Journal*, 1853.

The word; and, The Life; [by Robert Humphrey Cooke]. Printed London: G. Mitton. 1883. [viii], 112 pp. *OXB*

COOKSON, Elizabeth, (Old Lady, pseud.). Mrs Cookson. Of the Isle of Man?

A tour in Switzerland, [and other poems]; by an old lady. London: Wyman & Sons. 1888. [viii], 51 pp. *OXB*

COOKSON, Fife *see* **FIFE-COOKSON, John Cookson**

COOKSON, George (1871?–). b. Frome, Somerset, son of Edgar W. Cookson, captain, RN. Educated at Clifton College, and Lincoln College, Oxford.

Poems; by George Cookson. London: A.D. Innes & Co. 1897. viii, 104 pp. *OXB*

COOKSON, John Cookson Fife- *see* **FIFE-COOKSON, John Cookson**

COOKSON, Mrs, (Old Lady, pseud.) *see* **COOKSON, Elizabeth**, (Old Lady, pseud.)

COOPER, Edith Emma, (Michael Field, pseud. with Katherine Harris Bradley), (Isla Leigh, pseud.) (1846–1913). b. Kenilworth, Warwickshire, daughter of a merchant. The devoted companion of her aunt, Katherine Harris Bradley, they lived together successively in Bristol, Reigate and Richmond, Surrey. In collaboration they wrote twenty-seven tragedies and eight volumes of verse, operating in such close affinity that their work appeared to be that of a single author. They became Roman Catholics in 1907, and died of cancer within a year of each other.

Bellerophôn: [a play]; [and], [Poems]; by Arran and Isla Leigh. London: C. Kegan Paul & Co. 1881. [vi], 182 pp. *OXB*

Long ago: [poems]; by Michael Field. London: George Bell & Sons. 1889. [viii], 133 pp. il.

A limited ed. of 100 numbered copies. *OXB*

Sight and song: [poems]; written by Michael Field. London: Elkin Mathews and John Lane at the sign of The Bodley Head. 1892. x, 127 pp.

A limited ed. of 400 copies. *BL*

Underneath the bough: a book of verses; by Michael Field. London: George Bell & Sons. 1893. [viii], 138 pp.

A limited ed. of 150 copies. *BL*

Also [Revised and decreased ed.] 1893.

Underneath the bough: a book of verses; by Michael Field. Portland, Maine: Thomas B. Mosher. 1898. [vi], 94 pp. (Old world series). *BL*

COOPER, Elise. Writer on needlework for children.

The queen's innocent, with other poems; by Elise Cooper. London: David Stott. 1886. [iv], 228 pp. *OXB*

COOPER, John Dunning. Of Wolverhampton, Staffordshire.

Prometheus bound, (from the Greek of Aeschylus); and, Original poems; by John Dunning Cooper. London: Simpkin, Marshall, Hamilton, Kent & Co., Ltd; Wolverhampton: John Steen & Co. [1890]. [viii], 124 pp. *OXB*

COOPER, Joseph (1810–90). b. Thornsett, near New Mills, Derbyshire, son of John and Mary Cooper. His father died when he was a child so he was compelled to work from the age of seven, attending Sabbath school. He went into business in Manchester, and joined Manchester Literary Club. A member of Manchester & Salford Temperance Union, his temperance verses had a large circulation – a consignment was sent to the Crimea for use of English soldiers before Sebastopol. He retired to Eaves Knoll, New Mills, serving on the local board of guardians.

Helping God to make the flowers grow, with other original poems, hymns, songs, dialogues, recitations, etc.; by Joseph Cooper. Manchester: Brook & Chrystal. 1889. xiv, 11-268 pp. il. por. *MPL*

COOPER, Oliver. Of Manchester?

Tales and ballads; by Oliver Cooper. First series. Manchester: John Heywood. 1889. 32 pp. (Booklet series). *OXB*

COOPER, Robert Thomas. Educated at Trinity College, Dublin; MB, M.Ch 1865, MD 1870, MA 1883. Resident physician, General Lying-In Hospital, Lambeth, London, 1874. Lived at 30A George Street, Hanover Square, and at 17 Stanley Gardens, Kensington Park. Writer on diseases of the ear; contributed papers to Dublin and London medical journals.

A forest poem; by Robert Thomas Cooper. London: David Stott. 1893. 16 pp. *OXB*

Phil Carcas' boat, and other poems; by Robert T. Cooper. London: David Stott. 1893. [viii], 72 pp. *OXB*

CORBETT, Frederick St. John (1862–1919). b. Dublin, son of Dr John Corbett. Educated at Trinity College, Dublin; BA 1884, MA 1887. Ordained 1887; curate, Hunslet, Leeds, 1885–91; chaplain, Leeds Rifles, 1886–93; curate, St Michael's, Chester Square, London, 1891–96; rector, Long Marton, Westmorland, 1896–1903; chaplain to high sheriff of Westmorland, 1901; dean, Sion College, and lord of the manor of Bradwell, Essex, 1917. A pioneer of church finance reform, he held many church administrative posts.

Echoes of the sanctuary: [poems]; by F. St. John Corbett. London: Skeffington & Son. 1892. viii, 52 pp. *OXB*

CORBETT, W. (18 –91). Native of Cumberland or Westmorland. The agent in Manchester for the publishers Blackie & Co.

England's decline, and other poems; by W. Corbett. Manchester: John Heywood. 1888. 142 pp. *OXB*

CORBOULD, Maria

Miscellaneous poems, etc., etc.; by Maria Corbould. Printed London: J. Wakeham & Son. 1886. 240 pp.

Spine-title is *Poems*. *UCD*

CORDER, Annie

Songs in many moods; by Nina Frances Layard; [and], *The wandering albatross, etc.*: [poems]; by Annie Corder. London: Longmans, Green, & Co. 1897. viii, 126 pp. *BL*

CORK, Countess of *see* **BOYLE, Emily Charlotte**, Countess of Cork & Orrery

CORNISH, Fraser

Week by week: [poems]; by Fraser Cornish. London: Macmillan & Co. 1894. [vi], 112 pp. *OXB*

CORRIE, C.J.

Billy, and other ballads; by C.J. Corrie. Bristol: J.W. Arrowsmith; London: Simpkin, Marshall & Co. 1886. 79 pp. *OXB*

CORRIE, Theodora. Novelist.

Siberian echoes; by Theodora Corrie. Printed Edinburgh: T. & A. Constable. 1896. 104 pp.

Poetry and prose. Privately printed. *⋆NUC*

CORRY, Helen M. Wife of Thomas Hughes Corry, Irish botanist and writer. Lived at Mentone, south of France.

Dual songs; by Thomas H. Corry, and by his wife [Helen M. Corry]. Together with a short memoir of her husband's literary life. Belfast: William Mullan & Son. 1887. xvi, 248 pp. col. il., por.   *UCD*

Songs of two: [Thomas Hughes Corry and Helen M. Corry]. Printed Belfast: Alexander Mayne. 1881. 64 pp.   *BL*

CORRY, Thomas Hughes (1859–83). b. Belfast, son of Robert W. Corry, shipowner. Educated at Queen's College, Belfast, and Caius College, Cambridge; BA 1883, FLS, FZS. Assistant curator of the herbarium, and University demonstrator in botany. He published papers in the *Transactions* of the Linnean Society. Accidentally drowned in Loch Gill, County Sligo, when on a botanical expedition.

Dual songs; by Thomas H. Corry, and by his wife [Helen M. Corry]. Together with a short memoir of her husband's literary life. Belfast: William Mullan & Son. 1887. xvi, 248 pp. col. il., por.   *UCD*

Songs in the sunlight: the last poems of Thomas H. Corry. Belfast: William Mullan & Son. 1883. [xii], 96 pp.   *BL*

Songs of two: [Thomas Hughes Corry and Helen M. Corry]. Printed Belfast: Alexander Mayne. 1881. 64 pp.   *BL*

A wreath of wind-flowers, [and other poems]; by Thomas H. Corry. Printed Belfast: Alexander Mayne. 1882. [2], viii, 95 pp.
Printed for private circulation.   *BL*

CORVUS-REX, pseud. *see* **CROKER-KING, Charles**, (Corvus Rex, pseud.)

CORY, Constance E. Of Bath?

The harvest of fruit; by Constance E. Cory. London: A.D. Innes & Co. Ltd.; Bath: S.W. Simms. 1898. viii, 119 pp.
Poetry and prose.   *OXB*

Seeds & blossoms; by Constance E. Cory. Bath: S.W. Simms. 1897. viii, 86 pp.
Poetry and prose.   *BL*

COSTER, George Thomas (1835–1912). b. Chatham, Kent. Studied at New College, London, entering the Congregational ministry in 1859; his appointments included minister at Fish Street, Hull, Yorkshire, and Whitby Congregational Church. An active worker in movements for the social advancement of the people. He contributed to the *Book of Congregational Hymns*.

Gloria Christi: verses; by G.T. Coster. London: H.R. Allenson. [1896]. [vi], 97 pp.   *OXB*

Poems; by George Thomas Coster. New ed., revised, with additions. London: Elliot Stock. 1890. xii, 180 pp.   *UCD*

Poems and hymns; by George T. Coster. London: T. Fisher Unwin. [1882]. viii, 214 pp.   *OXB*

Red roofs, and other poems; by George T. Coster. London: Elliot Stock. 1886. 64 pp. *UCD*

COSTLEY, Thomas (1837–1900). b. Megaberry, near Belfast, of poor parents. Apprenticed at an early age to hand-loom handkerchief weaving, following his trade in Belfast, Glasgow, and Pendleton, Salford. In 1875 he commenced business as an estate agent, succeeding in building up the firm Messrs Thomas Costley & Sons. A poor law guardian of Salford, and an active member of literary societies and coteries in Manchester and district. Lived latterly in Southport.

Sketches of Southport, and other poems; by Thomas Costley. Manchester: Barber & Farnworth. [1899]. xx, 140 pp. il. *OXB*

COTSWOLD ISYS, pseud. *see* **GLOVER, Richard H.**, (Cotswold Isys, pseud.)

COTTRELL, George (1839–). b. Walsall, Staffordshire. For many years he practised as a solicitor in London but moved to York in 1887 as editor of the *York Daily Herald*; became an active contributor to literary journals and the daily press.

The banquet: a political satire; by [George Cotterell]. Edinburgh: William Blackwood & Sons. 1885. [viii], 101 pp. *UCD*

Also New ed. 1885.

Poems: old and new; by George Cotterell. London: David Nutt. 1894. xii, 228 pp.

A limited ed. of 400 copies. *TCD*

COTTON, Mrs F. Percy, (Ellis Walton, pseud.)

Lyrics; by Ellis Walton (Mrs. F. Percy Cotton). London: Elliot Stock. 1895. xii, 60 pp. *OXB*

Seven love-songs, and other lyrics; by Ellis Walton (Mrs. F. Percy Cotton). London: Elliot Stock. 1894. xii, 60 pp. *BL*

COTTON, John, (Odd Fellow, pseud.). b. Bromsgrove, Worcestershire, son of William Cotton, estate agent and surveyor. Educated near Wolverhampton. He practised as an architect in Birmingham until 1890, when he became a landscape painter in oil and watercolour in Oxford, Leamington, and Birmingham. FRIBA. Lived at 53 Gladstone Road, Sparkbrook.

Election squibs, ballads & broadsides, with other impromptu verses; by John Cotton. Printed Birmingham: J.L. Allday. [1887]. 23 pp.

Private reprint. Title from cover.

Sceptical musings, and other verses: or, thoughts on odd themes at odd times; by an old fellow. Birmingham: [Author?]. 1890. 51 pp. *BL*

Song and sentiment: lyrical and other verses; by John Cotton. London: Simpkin, Marshall, Hamilton, Kent & Co., Ltd. 1891. [xii], 156 pp. il. (by the author). *OXB*

Thoughts and fancies: poems and occasional verses; by John Cotton. London: Simpkin, Marshall, Hamilton, Kent & Co. Ltd. 1897. [viii], 148 pp. *OXB*

COUCH, Sir Arthur Quiller-, ('Q') *see* **QUILLER-COUCH, Sir Arthur**, ('Q').

COULSON, Frederick Raymond (1864–1922). b. London. Journalist on the literary staff of the *Sunday Chronicle*, writing as Vexatus and Democritus; contributed articles, verse, and short stories to various periodicals; he also wrote songs and monologues. Lived latterly at 68 Corringham Road, Golders Green, London NW. His son, the poet Leslie Coulson, was killed in action in the First World War.

A jester's jingles; by F. Raymond Coulson. Illustrated by H. Penfold Jenner and J. Dodworth. London: Skeffington & Son. 1899. xii, 119 pp. il. *MPL*

COULTER, Frederic W.

England's glory: a poem dedicated to the English nation, and commemorating the royal and joyful sixtieth year of the magnificent reign of Victoria . . .; by Frederic W. Coulter. London: Digby, Long & Co. [1897]. 56 pp. *OXB*

COUNT ERNEST, pseud. *see* **THURSTAN, Frederick William**, (Count Ernest, pseud.)

COUNTRY COUSIN, pseud.

Hill-a-hoy-o, [and other poems]; by a country cousin. Paisley: Alexander Gardner. 1892. 129 pp. *OXB*

COUNTRY CURATE *see* **MacHALE, M.J.**

COUPER, Robert Mackenzie. Lived at 9 Gloucester Road, Trowbridge, Wiltshire.

Robin's lays: poems incidental and miscellaneous; by Robert Mackenzie Couper. Trowbridge, Wilts.: John Diplock. 1881. xii, 100 pp. *UCD*

COUPLAND, John Arthur, (Bassanio, pseud.), (Ganymede, pseud.). Dramatist.

Actaeon, and other poems; by Bassanio. London: Elliot Stock. 1885. iv, 63 pp. *OXB*

Paris and Helen; and, Endymion; by J.A. Coupland. London: E.W. Allen. [1883]. 86 pp. *OXB*

Penelope, and other poems; [by John Arthur Coupland]. London: Trübner & Co. 1888. vi, 62 pp. *OXB*

Pipings: [poems]; by John Arthur Coupland. London: Sold by John Ferries. 1894. 64 pp. *BL*

The temple of fame, and other poems; by Ganymede. London: Griffith, Farran, Okeden & Welsh. 1891. [vi], 87 pp. *OXB*

The valley of idleness, and other poems; by J.A. Coupland. London: E.W. Allen. [1884]. 200 pp.

Spine-title is *Poems*. *OXB*

COURTENAY, L.B., (Patch, pseud.)

Translations and imitations: [poems]; by Patch (L.B. Courtenay). [1892]. [ii], 26 pp. *BL*

COURTHOPE, William John (1842–1917). Son of Rev. William Court-hope, Sussex clergyman. Educated at Harrow School, and New College, Oxford; BA 1866, MA 1877; Newdigate prizewinner, 1863, Chancellor's English essay prize, 1869. Entered the Education Office, 1869; civil service commissioner, 1887–1907. Professor of poetry, Oxford, 1895–1900. Editor of Alexander Pope's works, biographer of Pope and Joseph Addison, and author of *History of English Poetry*, 6 vols, 1895–1910.

  The longest reign: an ode on the completion of the sixtieth year of the reign of her majesty Queen Victoria; by William John Courthope. Oxford: Clarendon Press. 1897. 16 pp.

    Cover-title is *Ode on the completion . . .*   *OXB*

COUSINS, James Henry (1873-1956). b. Belfast. Educated at a national school, he became a clerk, then private secretary to the Lord Mayor of Belfast. He moved to Dublin in 1897, working as a clerk in a shipping office. Wrote a number of plays, acting in small parts for the newly formed National Theatre Society, where he met Yeats and other writers of the literary revival. In 1913 he left for India where he spent the rest of his life.

  Ben Madighan, and other poems; by James H. Cousins. With introduction by John Vinycomb. Illustrated. Belfast: Marcus Ward & Co., Ltd. [1895]. 108 pp. il., por. *OXB*

COUTTS, Francis Burdett Money- *see* **MONEY-COUTTS, Francis Burdett**

COVENTRY, Mary, (Moi-même, pseud.). Said to be Sister Mary, an Irish nun. She contributed to the *Cork Examiner* under her pseud.

  Poems of the past; by Moi-Même. Dublin: M.H. Gill & Son. 1890. 332 pp. *BL*

COWAN, Isa, (Isa, pseud.). Of Newton Stewart, Galloway. Educated in local schools.

  The banks o'Cree, and other poems; by Isa. 2nd ed., enlarged. Newton-Stewart: W.S. M'Credie; Wm Anderson. 1886. [iv], 210 pp. *NLS*

COWAN, Samuel Kennedy (1850–). b. Lisburn, County Antrim. Edu-cated at Trinity College, Dublin; BA 1871, MA 1874. Many of his poems were set to music as songs. Lived at Bangor, County Down.

  A broken silence: some stray songs; by Samuel K. Cowan. London: Marcus Ward & Co. 1883. 147 pp. *BL*

  Idylls of Ireland: some Celtic legends done into metre; by Samuel K. Cowan. London: Marcus Ward & Co., Ltd. 1896. 72 pp. *OXB*

  Jemima Jinkings, and other jingles; by Samuel K. Cowan. Printed Newry: 'Newry Telegraph' Office. 1892. 72 pp. *BL*

  Laurel leaves; or, lays of a laureate; by Samuel K. Cowan. Belfast: M'Caw, Stevenson & Orr. 1885. 69 pp. *TCD*

COWDEN-CLARKE, Mary (1809–98). b. London, daughter of Vincent Novello, organist and composer. She spent some years in Boulogne as a governess. In 1828 she married Charles Cowden-Clarke, schoolmaster and friend of John Keats. Her *Complete Concordance to Shakespeare was* published in 1845; from 1853 to 1856 she edited the *Musical Times*. In 1856 they went to live in Italy.

Honey from the weed: verses; by Mary Cowden-Clarke. London: C. Kegan Paul & Co. 1881. xii, 350 pp. *MPL*

Memorial sonnets, etc.; by Mary Cowden Clarke. Printed London: Novello, Ewer. 1888. 112 pp. *★NUC*

A score of sonnets to one object; by Mary Cowden Clarke. London: Kegan Paul, Trench. 1884. 28 pp. *★NUC*

Verse-waifs: [poems] forming an appendix to, Honey from the weed; by Mary Cowden Clarke. London: Kegan Paul, Trench. 1883. viii, 79 pp. *★NUC*

COWDEN-COLE, John. Educated at St David's College, Lampeter; graduated 1st class theological honours, 1871. Curate, St Mark's, Bolton-le-Moors, Lancashire, 1871–72, Kirkham, and chaplain to Fylde Union, 1873–75; Landrake, Cornwall, 1875–79; vicar, Upton, Somerset, 1879-99. Of Thorley Vicarage, Yarmouth, Isle of Wight, 1905.

The bride and the bridegroom: being sonnets and other verse for the Church's year; by J. Cowden-Cole. London: Houlston & Sons. 1882. 120 pp. *OXB*

The loves of Tibullus: his rustic elegies, etc.: [poems]; by J. Cowden-Cole. London: Houlston & Sons. 1890. xii, 249 pp. *OXB*

New year reflections, etc.: [poems]; by J. Cowden-Cole. London: Houlston & Sons. 1887. 128 pp. *OXB*

COWELL, Elizabeth. Of Cambridge.

Leaves of memory: [poems]; by Elizabeth Cowell. London: Seeley & Co., Ltd. 1892. [viii], 89 pp. *BL*

COWLEY, Percy Tunnicliff. Writer on the Scottish Highlands.

Poems; by Percy Tunnicliff Cowley. London: Trübner & Co. 1881. 89 pp. *OXB*

COX, Harding (1854-1944). Son of Edward W.H. Cox of, Mill Hill, Middlesex. Educated at Harrow School, and Trinity College, Cambridge; BA 1877. Admitted Inner Temple, 1876. Vice-chairman and trustee of *The Field*, 1879–1906, and connected with other periodical publications. Captain, Duke of Cambridge's Hussars; in 29th and later 35th Co., Royal Defence Corps, in the First World War. Author, journalist, artist, musical composer, and dramatic critic. Master of Old Berkeley Foxhounds.

Six pieces for recitation; by Harding Cox. London: Griffith & Farran. [1884]. viii, 40 pp. *OXB*

COX, Mary M. Teacher of piano and singing. Lived at 18 Carlton Crescent, Southampton.
Poems; by Mary M. Cox. London: George Bell & Sons. 1889. viii, 72 pp.   *OXB*

COX, Ponsonby
The opening of the line: a strange story of dogs and their doings; by Ponsonby Cox. Illustrated by J.H. Oswald Brown. Edinburgh: William Blackwood & Sons. 1886. 58 pp. il.   *OXB*

COXON, Annie Hetherington
From heatherland: [poems]; by Annie Hetherington Coxon. London: Digby, Long & Co. [1896]. 132 pp.   *OXB*

COZENS, Emily. Of little Wittenham, Berkshire.
Bertha: a tale of the New Forest; The miser's dream, and the remainder of the historical and other poems hitherto unpublished; composed by Emily Cozens. Printed London: W.H. & L. Collingridge. 1880. viii, 156 pp.
    Printed for the author.   *OXB*
A metrical history of England, from the landing of Julius Caesar to the close of the reign of King Edward II; composed by Emily Cozens. Wallingford: W. Payne & Son. 1896. xii, 130 pp. il., por.   *OXB*

CRADDOCK, Thomas. Critic, religious writer, biographer of Charles Lamb. Of Wisbech, Cambridgeshire.
Man and nature: poems written long ago; [by Thomas Craddock]. Liverpool. [1885]. [vi], 108 pp.
    Privately printed.   *NUC*

CRAFTON-SMITH, Adele, (Nomad, pseud.)
Lyrics; by "Nomad". London: Jarrold & Sons. 1899. 72 pp.   *OXB*

CRAIG, Finley
Sunshine and shade: tales from many lands, in verse; by Finley Craig. London: Simpkin, Hamilton & Co.; Edinburgh: Andrew Elliot. 1894. [viii], 157 pp.   *OXB*

CRAIG, John Duncan (1831?–1909). Educated at Trinity College, Dublin; BA 1851, MA 1857, BD & DD 1869. Chaplain, Irish Convict Service; perpetual curate, Temple-Breda; curate, Youghal, County Cork; vicar, Kinsale; chaplain, Molyneux Asylum, 1873-84; incumbent, Holy Trinity City & Diocese from 1884.
Bruno!, with other ballads of the Irish reign of terror; by J. Duncan Craig. Dublin: Sealy, Bryers, & Walker. 1888. 52 pp.   *OXB*

CRAIG, Robert Smith
In Borderland: Border and other verses; by R.S. Craig. With illustrations by John Wallace. Hawick: W. & J. Kennedy. 1899. [viii], 64 pp. il. *OXB*

CRAIG, William Alexander. Manager of the Hibernian Bank, Dublin. He contributed verse to the *Irish Times*. Member of the Royal Irish Academy.
Poems and ballads; by W. Alexander Craig. Dublin: Hodges, Figgis, & Co.,Ltd; London: Simpkin, Marshall, Hamilton, Kent, & Co., Ltd. 1899. viii, 206 pp. *CU*

CRAIGMYLE, Bessie *see* **CRAIGMYLE, Elizabeth (Bessie)**.

CRAIGMYLE, Elizabeth (Bessie). b. Strawberry Bank, Aberdeen, daughter of a scholar and bookman. Educated at Aberdeen High School, and at St Andrews, Aberdeen, and London Universities. She became a lecturer at Bishop Otter College, Chichester. Translator from the Greek, French and German, she published an edition of Goethe's *Faust*.
Poems and translations; by Bessie Craigmyle. Aberdeen: J. & J.P. Edmond & Spark. 1886. viii, 134 pp. *OXB*

CRAIK, Dinah Maria (1826–87). b. Stoke-on-Trent, Staffordshire, daughter of Thomas Mulock, a nonconformist clergyman. She settled in London c. 1846, at first writing children's books but later producing a series of successful novels, the best known of which is *John Halifax, Gentleman*. In 1864 she married George L. Craik, a partner in Macmillan & Co., publishers. Her home was Shortlands, near Bromley, Kent, where she died from a heart attack in 1887.
Poems; by [Dinah Maria Craik]. London: Macmillan & Co. 1888. xvi, 398 pp. *OXB*
Thirty years: being poems new and old; by [Dinah Maria Craik]. London: Macmillan & Co. 1880. xiv, 412 pp. *MPL*
Thirty years: being poems new and old; by [Dinah Maria Craik]. London: Macmillan & Co. 1881. xiv, 359 pp. *BL*

CRANE, Walter (1845-1915). b. Liverpool, son of a portrait painter. Apprenticed to W.J. Linton, wood engraver. He illustrated several series of picture books, chiefly for children, 1863-96. Master of the Art-Workers Guild, 1888-89; twice president, Arts & Crafts Exhibition Society. Principal, Royal College of Art, South Kensington, 1898. Associated with William Morris in the Socialist League.
Renascence: a book of verse; by Walter Crane. London: Elkin Mathews at the sign of The Bodley Head. 1891. [1], xiv, 165 pp. il. (by the author).
A limited small paper ed, of 500 numbered copies, 350 copies for England and 150 copies for America. *TCD*
The sirens three: a poem; written and illustrated by Walter Crane. London: Macmillan & Co. 1886. [vi], 26, [44], pp. il. *MPL*

CRANMER-BYNG, Lancelot, (Paganus, pseud.) (1872–1945). Son of Lieutenant-Colonel Alfred M. Byng of Quendon Hall, Newport, Essex. Educated at Wellington School, and Trinity College, Cambridge. He popularized the study of oriental languages, and was interested in the literary movements of the early 1890s. JP and alderman of Essex. Lived at Foley Mill, Thaxted.

Daisies of the dawn, [and other poems]; by L. Cranmer-Byng. Guernsey: T.B. Banks & Co. [1896]. 112 pp.   GPR

Poems of paganism: or, songs of life and love; by "Paganus" (L. Cranmer-Byng). London: Roxburghe Press. 1895. 112 pp.   UCD

Voices in the twilight: [poems]; by L. Cranmer-Byng. London: Watts & Co. 1897. 88 pp.   UCD

CRAVEN, Carey Williams (1855–   ). b. Keighley, Yorkshire, son of leading bookseller. Edited the Keighley and Airedale Tattler [sic] for two years. In 1886 he commenced business on his own account as a printer and stationer. Wrote the introduction to Craven's Directory of Keighley, Bingley and Skipton. Interested in local affairs, he became a Keighley town councillor and a member of the local school board.

The Eiffel Tower, and other poems; by C.W. Craven. Keighley: 1889.★

Poems; by C.W. Craven. Keighley: E. Craven. 1889. viii, 128 pp.   BL

With Mr. Butterfield on the continent: letters descriptive of a tour through France, Italy, and Switzerland; together with, New poems; by C.W. Craven. Printed Keighley: E. Craven. 1885. 70 pp.   OXB

A wreath of flowers: short poems; by C.W. Craven. 1884. 32 pp.   BL

CRAWFORD, Howard

An atonement of east London, and other poems; by Howard Crawford. Edinburgh: William Blackwood & Sons. 1890. viii, 140 pp.   OXB

CRAWFORD, John Howard (1854–   ). b. Edinburgh. He studied theology at Edinburgh University; MA; awarded Professor Blackie's prize for English verse. Parish minister, Abercorn, South Queensferry, 1881. University lecturer, St George's Training College, and chaplain to the Lord High Commissioner. Composed songs and hymn tunes.

A circle of the soul: poems of the spiritual life; by John Howard Crawford. Edinburgh: James Gemmell. 1889. xii, 194 pp.   OXB

CRAWFORD, S. Henry. Of Harrow, Middlesex.

Agatha's curse: (a tragedy), and other poems; by S. Henry Crawford. Harrow: William J. Overhead. 1889. 104 pp.   OXB

The banished son: (a tragedy), and other poems; by S. Henry Crawford. London: J.F. Willis. 1884. 112 pp.   BL

Day-dreams of youth, and other poems; by S. Henry Crawford. Harrow: William J. Overhead. 1886. 120 pp.   BL

CRAWFORD, William P. Lived at 72 M'Kinlay Street, Glasgow.
Leisure lays; by William P. Crawford. Printed Glasgow: W.N. Leitch. 1881.
80 pp. *NLS*

CRAWHALL, Joseph (18 –1913). b. Morpeth, Northumberland. Educated
at King's College. He studied art under Aime Morot in Paris; gold medallist,
Munich; silver medallist, Paris. Lived latterly at Brandsby, Easingwold,
Yorkshire.
Border notes & mixty-maxty; by Joseph Crawhall. [Newcastle upon Tyne]:
[Andrew Reid]. 1880. [ii], 142 pp. il., col. il.
    Poetry and prose. A limited facsim. ed. of 50 copies, 'impressions from
wooden blocks cut by the author out of his own head'.
A jubilee thought, imagined & adorn'd; by Joseph Crawhall. Newcastle-upon-
Tyne: Mawson, Swan, & Morgan. 1887. [iii], 77 pp. col. il. (by the author).
    A limited ed. of 50 copies on large paper, hand coloured. *BL*
Olde tayles newlye relayted, enryched with all ye ancyente embellyshmentes; [by
Joseph Crawhall]. [London]: Leadenhall Press. 1883. 15 vols in 1. il. (by the
author).
    Poetry and prose. *BL*
Several sovereigns for a shilling: [poems]; adorned by Joseph Crawhall. London:
Hamilton, Adams, & Co.; Newcastle on Tyne: Mawson, Swan, & Morgan.
1886. 24 pp, il. (by the author). *BL*

CRAWLEY, Richard (1840–93). Educated at Marlborough College, and
University College, Oxford; Fellow of Worcester College, 1866–80. Barris-
ter, Lincoln's Inn, 1869. Translator of Thucydides.
Election rhymes; by Richard Crawley. Edinburgh: William Blackwood &
Sons. 1880. 24 pp. *OXB*

CREALOCK, W.M.
Scraps by a sailor: or, rhymes of the land and sea; by W.M. Crealock. London:
Wyman & Sons. 1888. [ii], 64 pp. *OXB*

CREDO, pseud.
Professor Tyndall's denial of the soul and assumption of fatalism: a poem; by Credo.
London: Simpkin, Marshall & Co.; Manchester: Tubbs, Brook, & Chrystal.
[1883]. 59 pp. *MPL*

CREMER, Gabriel Henry (1850–). Son of Henry Cremer of Barnes,
Surrey, gentleman. Educated at Winchester College, and New College,
Oxford (scholar); BA 1870.
A vision of empires; by G.H. Cremer. Oxford: Parker & Co. 1890. xii, 491 pp.
il. *OXB*

CRERAR, Duncan MacGregor (1838–). b. Amulree, Perthshire, son of
Alexander Crerar. He was intended for the ministry but the early death of his
father prevented this. In 1857 he went to Canada, spending nine years there,
mainly in business. For a time he was in the Active Militia, serving on the

frontier during the 1865 Fenian troubles; gazetted hon. lieutenant. After his discharge he move to New York.
   Robert Burns: an anniversary poem; by Duncan MacGregor Crerar. London: Marcus Ward & Co. Ltd. 1885. [31] pp. il.
      Printed on one side of leaf only.   *OXB*

CRIGHTON, James. Of Tarrybank.
   Rural notes: [poems]; by James Crighton. Arbroath: T. Buncle. 1886. viii, 214 pp.   *OXB*

CRIPPS, Henry
   Sacred poems; by Henry Cripps. Sutton: William Pile. [1892]. [iv], 36 pp.
      For private circulation only.   *OXB*

CRISFORD, K. Of Eastbourne, Sussex.
   Rugged rural rhymes; by K. Crisford. Eastbourne: W.H. Christian. 1898. x, 154 pp. por.   *UCD*

CRITO, pseud.
   Erin at peace: or, the union unique: a response to Lady Florence Dixie's fine effusion, entitled "Out of the land of bondage"; by Crito. Printed Lancaster: R. Lamb. 1887. 16 pp.   *OXB*

CROASDAILE, Edward
   Heart harmonies: poems, songs, and sonnets; by Edward Croasdaile. London: Elliot Stock. 1883. [2], viii, 142 pp.   *BL*
   The lady of the tower: lyrical romance, in six cantos; by Edward Croasdaile. London: Elliot Stock. 1885. [ii], 77 pp.   *OXB*

CROCKETT, Samuel Rutherford. (Ford Berêton, pseud.) (1860–1914). b. near Laurieston, Kirkcudbrightshire. Educated at Edinburgh University, where he supported himself by writing for the press. Entered New College as a student of divinity; ordained in the Church of Scotland, 1886; minister at Penicuik, Midlothian, until 1895 when he resigned to write full time as a novelist.
   Dulce cor: being the poems of Ford Berêton. London: Kegan Paul, Trench & Co.. 1886. xii, 201 pp. por.   *OXB*

CROFT, S., (S.C.). Writer on French and German grammar. Of Ely, Cambridgeshire?
   Christmas with the Holy Child: a poem; by S.C. London: Skeffington & Son. [1891]. 37 pp.   *OXB*

CROFTS, Thomas. Lived at The Orchard, Belper, Derbyshire.
   A castle in the air, and other poems; by Thomas Crofts. Printed Derby: Bemrose & Sons, Ltd. [1892]. viii, 247 pp. por.   *OXB*

CROKER-KING, Charles, (Corvus-Rex, pseud.). Son of Dr Charles Croker-King. Educated at Cheltenham College.
Tennyson: the prize poem, 1893, Cheltenham College; by Charles Croker-King ("Corvus Rex"). Printed Cheltenham: Cheltenham Chronicle & Gloucestershire Echo. 1893. 19 pp. *OXB*

CRONIN, Daniel?, (D.C.)
Poems; by D.C. London: Henry S. Warr. [1880]. 157 pp. **UCD*

CROSBIE, Robert (1820–90). b. Darnick, near Melrose, Roxburghshire. Lived at Innerleithen, Peeblesshire.
Poems and songs; by Robert Crosbie. [2nd ed.]. Galashiels: W. Smith Elliot. 1888. 184 pp.
Printed and published for the author. *OXB*

CROSLAND, Thomas William Hodgson (1868–1924). Son of William Crosland of Leeds. Educated privately. A contributor to many periodicals, he was assistant editor of *Outlook*, 1899–1902; editor of *English Review*, 1905; assistant editor of *Academy*, 1908–11. Lived latterly at Mitcham House, Mitcham Street, Marylebone, London NW.
The absent-minded mule, and other occasional verses; by T.W.H. Crosland. London: At the Sign of the Unicorn. 1899. 32 pp. *OXB*
Other people's wings: parodies and occasional verses; by T.W.H. Crosland. London: At the Sign of the Unicorn. 1899. 32 pp. *OXB*
The pink book: being verses good, bad and indifferent; by T.W.H. Crosland. Brighton: Guy & Co. 1894. 64 pp. *OXB*

CROSS, Albert Francis (1863–19). b. Loughborough, Leicestershire. A journalist, his first job was writing sporting articles for the *Leicester Advertiser*. The first managing director of Nuneaton Observer Co. Ltd, he was editor/proprietor of *Nuneaton Chronicle*. He founded the George Eliot Fellowship. Lived at The Lawns, Nuneaton, Warwickshire.
Songs and sonnets; by Albert Francis Cross. Leeds: J.S. Fletcher & Co. 1884. viii, 63 pp. *OXB*
Virginia, and other poems; by Albert Francis Cross. Bradford: Percy Lund & Co.; London: Swan Sonnenschein & Co. [1887]. 96 pp. *OXB*

CROSS, E.J. Mrs J. Taylor Cross.
Waifs and strays, with other lays; by Mrs. J. Taylor Cross. London: Swan Sonnenschein, Le Bas & Lowrey. 1886. viii, 71 pp. *BL*
Also 2nd ed. 1887.

CROSS, Mrs J. Taylor *see* **CROSS, E.J.**

CROSS, Mary (1860–). b. Liverpool. A novelist, she was a frequent contributor of verse and prose to *Household Words* and numerous other periodicals. She lived in Glasgow.

Poems; by Mary Cross. Edinburgh: Oliphant, Anderson & Ferrier. 1892. 64 pp. *OXB*

CROSS, William (1804–86). b. Paisley, Renfrewshire, son of handloom weaver. He received little or no schooling, and was first employed as a draw-boy in the textile trade; became a pattern-drawer, going into partnership with a shawl manufacturer, and eventually starting his own business in 1832. By 1839 the textile trade was depressed and he could no longer continue. He was appointed editor of a provincial newspaper but became penniless after an attempt to purchase an old-established newspaper. Eventually he resumed business as a tartan manufacturer.

Songs and miscellaneous poems, written in rare intervals of leisure in the course of a busy life; by William Cross. Glasgow: Kerr & Richardson. 1882. viii, 116 pp.
   Spine-title is *Songs and poems*. *NLS*

CROSSLEY, William. Of Wakefield, Yorkshire.
   Christus victor: the great temptation; by William Crossley. London: Elliot Stock. 1899. xvi, 283 pp. *OXB*

CROWLEY, Aleister *see* **CROWLEY, Edward Alexander** (Aleister)

CROWLEY, Edward Alexander (Aleister), (Gentleman of the University of Cambridge, pseud.) (1875–1947). Son of Edward Crowley of Streatham, London, a wealthy brewer. Educated at schools in Leamington and Warwick, Tonbridge School, Malvern College, and Trinity College, Cambridge. Interested in magic, he joined the Order of the Golden Dawn, a group of theosophists involved in cabbalistic magic. He lived at Cefalu, Sicily, where he claimed to practise 'white magic'. Failed in a libel action against publishers Constable & Co. Ltd and others.

Aceldama: a place to bury strangers in: a philosophical poem; by a gentleman of the University of Cambridge. London. 1898. 29 pp.
   A privately printed limited ed. of 100 numbered copies: 2 copies on vellum, numbered 1, 2; 10 copies on Japanese vellum, numbered 3–12; 88 copies on hand–made paper, numbered 13–100. *OXB*

Jephthah, and other mysteries, lyrical and dramatic; by Aleister Crowley. London: Kegan Paul, Trench, Trübner & Co., Ltd. 1899. xxii, 224 pp. *OXB*

Songs of the spirit; by Aleister Crowley. London: Kegan Paul, Trench, Trübner & Co. 1898. x, 110 pp. *OXB*

The tale of Archais: a romance in verse; by a gentleman of the University of Cambridge. London: Kegan Paul, Trench, Trübner & Co. 1898. viii, 89 pp. *OXB*

White stains: the literary remains of George Archibald Bishop, a neuropath of the Second Empire: [poems]; [by Edward Alexander Crowley]. Nouveau Phèdre à Lui Moins Dure. 1898. [iv], 131 pp.
   A limited ed. of 100 numbered copies. *BL*

CROWLEY, Elfrida Mary (1863–92). b. Croydon, Surrey, daughter of Alfred and Catherine Crowley, Quakers. She suffered from asthma all her life, spending winters in Egypt and the French Riviera. Lived at Bramley Oaks, Croydon.

Poems; by Elfrida Mary Crowley. Selected and arranged by her. Croydon: Roffey & Clark. 1892. [viii], 74 pp.

Includes an appendix of prose. *BL*

CRUSE, Jesse. London postman, a lay preacher in the Primitive Methodist Connexion, and a total abstainer. Lived at 19 Kynaston Road, and later at 66 Nevill Road, Stoke Newington, London N.

God's faithfulness: containing eleven original poems on important themes; by Jesse Cruse. London: Author. 1899. [ii], 30 pp.

Title from cover. *OXB*

Labour of love: containing twelve original poems on moral & religious subjects; by Jesse Cruse. London: [Author]. 1898. [ii], 30 pp.

Title from cover. *OXB*

Link to link: or, stirring contemplations: [poems]; by [Jesse Cruse]. With introduction by James Wood. London: Houlston & Sons. 1885. 116 pp. *OXB*

A little casket: containing twenty original poems on several topics; by Jesse Cruse. London: Author. 1895. [ii], 30 pp.

Title from cover. *OXB*

A living coal, fresh from the altar, and other original poems; by Jesse Cruse. London: Author. [1894]. [ii], 30 pp.

Title from cover. *OXB*

Nature and revelation: containing twelve original poems on various themes; by Jesse Cruse. London: Author. 1894. [ii], 30 pp.

Title from cover. *OXB*

Patience of hope: containing twelve original poems on various subjects; by Jesse Cruse. London: Author. 1899. 29 pp.

Title from cover. *BL*

A poor man's logic: containing twelve original poems on moral & sacred themes; by Jesse Cruse. London: [Author]. 1896. [ii], 30 pp.

Title from cover. *OXB*

The prophet Jonah, and nine other original poems on moral and sacred subjects; by Jesse Cruse. London: Author. 1895. [ii], 30 pp. *OXB*

A small cargo, of fourteen original poems on various subjects; by Jesse Cruse. London: [Author]. 1897. [ii], 30 pp.

Title from cover. *OXB*

Step by step: containing fourteen original poems on various subjects; by Jesse Cruse. London: Author. 1894. [ii], 30 pp.

Title from cover. *OXB*

Suffering and glory: containing thirteen original poems on moral & sacred themes; by Jesse Cruse. London: [Author]. 1893. [ii], 30 pp.

Title from cover. *OXB*

A sun and shield: containing thirteen original poems on sacred & moral subjects; by Jesse Cruse. London: Author. 1896. [ii], 30 pp.

    Title from cover. *OXB*

Thoughts in rhyme: or, a blind man's poems; by Jesse Cruse. With introduction by W.H. Pearson. London: Houlston & Sons. 1883. [iv], 108 pp.

    Cover-title is *A blind man's poems*. *OXB*

Time & purpose: containing eleven original poems on important themes; by Jesse Cruse. London: [Author]. 1897. [ii], 30 pp.

    Title from cover. *OXB*

Work of faith: containing fifteen original poems on important themes; by Jesse Cruse. London: [Author]. 1898. [ii], 30 pp.

    Title from cover. *OXB*

CULLEN, John (1837–1914). Son of John Cullen. Educated at a grammar school, Trinity College, Dublin, and St Aidan's, Cheshire; DD. Curate, St George's, Wigan, Lancashire, Knipton, and Bottesford, Leicestershire; vicar, Radcliffe-on-Trent, from 1874. He rebuilt Radcliffe Church, and raised large sums of money for charitable purposes. A missioner of the Church Parochial Mission Society. Well known as a preacher.

Poems and idylls; by John Cullen. London: Hatchards. 1882. xii, 216 pp. *OXB*

Poems and idylls; by John Cullen. London: S.W. Partridge & Co. 1893. 280 pp. *OXB*

Songs of consolation; by John Cullen. London: S.W. Partridge & Co. 1893. 47 pp. *OXB*

CULLINGWORTH, William

Life's golden age: or, juvenile congress: [poems]; by William Cullingworth. London: Digby, Long & Co. [1895]. viii, 132 pp. *OXB*

CUMBRIAN, pseud.

The Cumbrian brothers: or, how we raise the revenue; by a Cumbrian. London: Wyman & Sons. 1885. 66 pp. *OXB*

CUMING, Ann Bagwill

Night thoughts and day dreams: [poems]; by Ann Bagwill Cuming. Printed London: T.J. Molyneaux. 1880. 163 pp.

    Printed for private circulation only. *★UCD*

CUMPSTON, William Henry. Lived at Maple Grove, Newington, Hull, Yorkshire.

Glimmerings of truth: being a collection of poems; by William Henry Cumpston. Hull: A. Brown & Sons; London: Simpkin, Marshall, & Co. 1887. xii, 108 pp. *OXB*

CURRIE, James (1829–90). b. Selkirk. Aged nine he was working eleven hours a day in a woollen factory. He joined the 79th Cameron Highlanders and was sent to the Crimea, losing his right arm in the fighting. After discharge on a pension he became a post-runner in Selkirk, then worked for the millowners Messrs Cochrane of Galashiels.

Poems and songs; by James Currie. With biographical sketch by Charles Rogers. Printed Glasgow: George Bogie. 1883. viii, 200 pp.

Printed for the author. *BL*

CURRIE, Mary Montgomerie, Lady, (Violet Fane, pseud.) (1843–1905). b. Littlehampton, Sussex, daughter of C.J.S. Montgomerie Lamb, and grand-daughter of the 11th Earl of Eglinton. Educated privately. In 1864 she married Henry S. Singleton, Irish landowner who died in 1893. She then married Sir Philip H. Currie of the diplomatic corps, afterwards Lord Currie, accompanying him to Constantinople, 1894, and to Rome, 1898–1903. Lived latterly at Hawley, Hampshire. Essayist, novelist and dramatist.

Autumn songs; by Violet Fane. London: Chapman & Hall Ltd. 1889. viii, 85 pp. *OXB*

Betwixt two seas: poems and ballads (written at Constantinople and Therapia); by Violet Fane. London: John C. Nimmo. 1900 [i.e. 1899]. viii, 106 pp.

A limited ed. of 260 numbered copies for England and America on Arnold's hand-made paper. *BL*

Collected verses; by Violet Fane. London: Smith, Elder, & Co. 1880. vi, 101 pp. *UCD*

Poems; by Violet Fane. With portrait engraved by E. Stodart. London: John C. Nimmo. 1892. 2 vols. por.

A limited ed. of 365 numbered copies printed for England and America on Arnold's hand-made paper. *JRL*

Under cross and crescent: poems; by Violet Fane. London: John C. Nimmo. 1896. viii, 129 pp.

A limited ed. of 260 numbered copies printed for England and America on Arnold's hand-made paper. *OXB*

CURTIUS, pseud.

Pentagon parodies; and, Phallic hymn; by Curtius. [Oxford]: [James Thornton]. 1881. 27 pp.

For private circulation. *OXB*

CURWEN, Annie Isabel

Poems; by Annie Isabel Curwen. Printed Barrow-in-Furness: Barrow Printing Co. [1899]. 284 pp. por. *UCD*

CURWEN, Henry, (Owen Christian, pseud.) (1845–92). b. Workington, Cumberland, son of a clergyman. Educated at Rossall School. He worked in London for the publisher John Camden Hotten. In 1876 he went to India as assistant editor of *The Times of India*, eventually becoming editor, then joint proprietor. In failing health he died during the return voyage. Published novels, essays, short stories, and translations.

Poems; by Owen Christian. London: Kegan Paul, Trench & Co. 1885. vi, 117 pp. *OXB*

CUSACK, Mary Frances. Sister Mary Francis Clare, known as 'The Nun of Kenmare'.
Cloister songs ; by Sister Mary Frances Clare. London. 1881. *

CUST, Sir Reginald John (1828–1912). b. Shavington Hall, Shropshire, third son of Hon. Rev. Henry Cockayne Cust, Canon of Windsor. Educated at Eton College, and Trinity College, Cambridge. He travelled in Palestine, Russia, Algeria, 1852–55. Barrister, Lincoln's Inn, 1856; assistant commissioner, West Indian Incumbered Estates Court, 1865–87; chief commissioner, 1887–92.
Early poems; by Sir Reginald John Cust. London: Kegan Paul, Trench, Trübner & Co., Ltd. 1892. xiv, 87 pp.   *OXB*

CUST, Robert Needham, (Lifelong Thinker and Wanderer, pseud.), (Sufferer, pseud.) (1821–1909). b. Cockayne Hatley, Bedfordshire, second son of Hon. Rev. Henry Cockayne Cust, Canon of Windsor. Educated at Eton College, East India College, Haileybury, College of Calcutta, and Edinburgh University; LL.D 1885. Barrister, Lincoln's Inn, 1857. In the Indian Civil Service, 1843–68. Secretary of Royal Asiatic Society, 1878–99. Writer on oriental philology and religion.
Poems of many years and many places, 1839–1887; by a lifelong thinker and wanderer. London: Longmans, Green, & Co. 1887. xii, 252 pp.   *MPL*
Poems of many years and many places, 1836–1897; by a lifelong thinker and wanderer. Second series. Hertford: Stephen Austin & Sons. 1897. [xviii], 279 pp. il., por.
    For private circulation.   *MPL*
Songs of Anglo-Indian life; by a sufferer. With eight wood engravings. London: Elliot Stock. 1889. 86 pp. il.   *MPL*

CUSTANCE, Olive (1874–1944). Daughter of Colonel Frederic H. Custance, Grenadier Guards, of Weston Old Hall, Norfolk. When she was sixteen she fell in love with the young poet John Gray, but he was destined to remain unmarried and become a Roman Catholic priest. She was one of several notable women writers associated with the publishing house of John Lane, contributing to the *Yellow Book* and other magazines. In 1902 she became engaged to the Hon. George Montagu but married Lord Alfred Douglas, son of the Marquess of Queensbury, by special licence on 4 March of that year.
Opals: [poems]; by Olive Custance. London: John Lane, The Bodley Head. 1897. vi, 75 pp.   *BL*

CUTHBERT, James Aitken. Of Bishopbriggs, Lanarkshire.
Napoleon, and other poems and lyrics: being a selection of pieces, Scotch and English, with music; by James A. Cuthbert. Glasgow: Thomas Murray & Son. 1891. 59 pp.   *NLS*
Samiasa: or, heaven regained; by James A. Cuthbert. Glasgow: Thomas Murray & Son, Ltd. 1893. 116 pp.   *OXB*

CUTHBERTSON, William. Novelist and short story writer.
By shore and wood: [poems]; by W. Cuthbertson. Edinburgh: James Thin. 1899. 159 pp. *OXB*

CYGNET, pseud.
Brentley Hall, and other poems; by Cygnet. London: London Literary Society. [1886]. [vi], 75pp. *OXB*

CYNIC, pseud.
A sonnet; by Cynic. Printed [London]: Bickers & Son. 1885. [42] pp.
A limited ed. of 100 copies, printed for private circulation. *OXB*

D. *see* **DAVIES, John Henry**, (D.), (J.H.D.)

D., A.
Little wings: [poems]; by A.D. London: J. Masters & Co. 1891. 48 pp. *OXB*
Thoughts for holy seasons: [poems]; by A.D. London: John Masters & Co. 1892. 47 pp. *OXB*

D., A.E.
Poems; by A.E.D. London: Griffith, Farran, Okeden & Welsh. 1885. 96 pp. *OXB*

D., A.J.G. *see* **DUFF, Anna Julia Grant**, (A.J.G.D.)

D., B.
Ballerina: a poem; Eidelweiss: a romance; by B.D. London: Gilbert & Field. 1890. [ii], 109 pp. *OXB*
Poems; by B.D. [c. 1880]. [vi], 75 pp.
Unpublished. *OXB*
Swan songs; by B.D. London: Gilbert & Field. [1892]. [iv], 200 pp. *OXB*

D., F.T. *see* **DOWDING, Frederick Townley**, (F.T.D.)

D., G.
The prince: a poem; by G.D. London: Elliot Stock. 1880. [viii], 80 pp. *OXB*

D., H.
Songs of the new age; by H.D. London: James Speirs. 1899. viii, 200 pp. *OXB*

D., J.H. *see* **DAVIES, John Henry**, (D.), (J.H.D.)

DACCORD, Michael
"Pebbles", [and other poems]; by Michael Daccord. London: Remington & Co. 1884. xvi, 147 pp.   *OXB*

DAGONET, pseud. *see* **SIMS, George Robert**, (Dagonet, pseud.)

DALE, Philip
Voices from Australia: [poems]; by Philip Dale and Cyril Haviland. London: Swan Sonnenschein & Co. 1892. iv, 288 pp.
    Not joint authorship.   *TCD*

DALE, Sarah, (Essdee, pseud.). b. Ashton-under-Lyne, Lancashire. Née Schofield. She did not attend school but was taught to read and write by her mother. Employed in a cotton mill.
Adelia, and other poems; by [Sarah Dale]. Printed Ashton-under-Lyne: J. Andrew & Co. 1883. 88 pp.   *OXB*
Merriky letters, with other rhymes of old and New England; by Essdee. Huddersfield: John Coldwell. [189–?]. xii, 232 pp.   *TPL*

DALMAS, H.P. Emeric De St. *see* **DE ST. DALMAS, H.P. Emeric**

DALMON, Charles William (1872–). Contributed to the *Yellow Book*, *Nineteenth Century*, and other periodicals. Lived at The White House, Trottiscliffe, West Malling, Kent.
Minutiae: [poems]; by Charles William Dalmon. London: Digby, Long & Co. [1892]. viii, 77 pp.   *OXB*
Song favours, [and other poems]; [by] C.W. Dalmon. London: John Lane The Bodley Head; Chicago: Way & Williams. 1895. [x], 77 pp.   *OXB*

DALRYMPLE, C. Elphinstone- *see* **ELPHINSTONE-DALRYMPLE, C.**

DALSTON, Frank Hardinge
Twelve poems; by Frank Hardinge Dalston. Printed [London]: [Private Press of Frederick Arthur Crisp]. 1898. [viii], [23] pp.
    Printed on one side of leaf only.   *OXB*

DALY, Brian. Writer of music hall songs; biographer of Albert Chevalier and others.
"Fancy free": a book of verse; by Brian Daly. London: Samuel French. [1893]. 64 pp.   *OXB*

DALY, Mary Anne. Of Dublin. One of four sisters.

A retrospect: being memorials of some who have long since departed this life; [by Mary Anne Daly]. Dublin: G. Herbert. 1882. 175 pp. por.   *NUC

DALY, Nicholas. Of Cork.

"Upbraid not Eve": an allegorical poem in 7 parts; by Nicholas Daly. Cork: Purcell & Co. 1893. 51 pp.   OXB

DALZIEL, George, (G.D.) (1815–1902). Eldest of the Dalziel brothers and joint founder of the London firm of illustrators and wood engravers started in 1859. A prolific company, they produced engraving blocks for the *Illustrated London News* and *Punch*, and for the leading artists of the day.

In memoriam; by George Dalziel. [London?]. [1888]. 93 pp.

   Printed for private circulation.   BL

Mattie Grey, and other poems; by G.D. Printed London: Dalziel Bros, Camden Press. [1884?]. x, 244 pp.

   Printed for private circulation.   OXB

Pictures in the fire, and other thoughts in rhyme and verse; by George Dalziel. Printed London: Dalziel Bros, Camden Press. [1887]. xii, 256 pp.

   Printed for private distribution.   MPL

Unconsidered trifles; [and other poems]; by George Dalziel. London: Elliot Stock. 1898. xii, 232 pp.   OXB

DANIEL, Harold C. (1866–   ). b. Loughton, Essex, son of a wealthy London merchant who became bankrupt. Educated at the City of London Freeman's Orphans School. He became a clerk, correspondent and manager. Lived latterly in Cambridge.

Love's minstrel, and other poems; by H.C. Daniel. London: W.W. Morgan & Son. 1892. 56 pp.   *UCD

DARBY, John Nelson (1800–82). b. London. Educated at Westminster School, and Trinity College, Dublin. Called to the Bar, 1835, then took holy orders. After holding a brief curacy he joined the Plymouth Brethren in 1827, establishing congregations in Switzerland. In 1847 he founded the Darbyites, an exclusive section of the sect. A theological writer, he made several visits to Canada and the United States.

Spiritual songs; [by] J.N. Darby. Dublin: 13 Westland Row. 1883. xiv, 96 pp.   OXB

Spiritual songs; [by] J.N. Darby. 2nd ed., revised. London: James Carter. 1893. xvi, 98 pp.   OXB

DARBYSHIRE, E. Of Sheffield, Yorkshire.

Ballads, poems, and recitations; by E. Darbyshire. Printed Sheffield: J. Wrigley. 1885. 144 pp.   OXB

DARLING, Elizabeth

Spare moments: a little book of poems; by Elizabeth Darling. Kingston: British Whig Steam Presses. [c. 1880]. 25 pp.   *NUC

DARLING, Isabella F. (1861–1903). b. Stane, Shotts, Lanarkshire, second of ten children. When she was eight the family moved to Glasgow, where she attended Glasgow Free Church Normal School. Contributed to the *Glasgow Herald*, the *People's Friend*, and other periodicals.

Poems and songs; by Isabella F. Darling. Glasgow: Hay Nisbet & Co.; Edinburgh: John Menzies & Co.; London: Simpkin, Marshall, & Co. 1889. 240 pp.   *BL*

Whispering hope: [poems]; by Isabella F. Darling. Edinburgh: John Menzies & Co.; London: Simpkin, Marshall & Co. 1893. 240 pp. por.   *BL*

DASH, Blancor, pseud. *see* **HILL, A.E.**, (Blancor Dash, pseud.)

DAVEN, pseud. *see* **DAVENPORT, David**, (Daven, pseud.)

DAVENPORT, David, (Daven, pseud.) (1861–19   ). b. Welford-on-Avon, Gloucestershire, son of Rev. James Davenport. Educated at St Columba's College, Ireland, and Oriel College, Oxford; BA 1882, MA 1889. Curate, St David's, Birmingham, 1889; rector, Stonton Wyville, Leicestershire, 1906.

Blurs and blottings: a miscellany of verse; by Daven. Birmingham: Cornish Bros; London: Simpkin, Marshall & Co., Ltd. 1892. [x], 81 pp.   *OXB*

Epictetus; Letters from the colonial mail, and other poems; by David Davenport. London: George Bell & Sons. 1894. vi, 110 pp.   *OXB*

Wroxall Abbey, and other poems; by David Davenport. London: Kegan Paul, Trench, Trübner & Co. Ltd. 1898. 99 pp.   *OXB*

DAVIDSON, John (1857–1909). b. Barrhead, Renfrewshire, son of an Evangelical Union minister. Educated at the Highlanders Academy, Greenock, and briefly at Edinburgh University. He worked in a chemical laboratory, then became an assistant to the public analyst, 1871-72. He taught at schools in Glasgow, Perth, Paisley, Crieff, and Greenock until 1890 when he took up journalism in London. Playwright, short story writer, translator and novelist, he was reader for the publishers Grant Richards, and a member of the Rhymers' Club. From 1907 he lived in Penzance, Cornwall, where he committed suicide by drowning.

Ballads & songs; by John Davidson. London: John Lane, The Bodley Head; Boston, [Mass.]: Copeland & Day. 1894. vi, 132 pp.   *OXB*

   Also 2nd & 3rd eds 1894; 4th ed. 1895; 5th ed. 1898.

In a music hall, and other poems; by John Davidson. London: Ward & Downey. 1891. viii, 120 pp.   *MPL*

The last ballad, and other poems; by John Davidson. London: John Lane. 1899. vi, 187 pp.   *MPL*

New ballads; by John Davidson. London: John Lane, The Bodley Head. 1897. 112 pp.   *MPL*

   Also 2nd ed. 1897.

DAVIES, Arthur M. Educated at Jesus College, Oxford (scholar); MA.

Grecian rhymes and ballads, with a few other minor poems; by Arthur M. Davies. Printed Morpeth: D.F. Wilson. 1886. 72 pp.   *NPL*

DAVIES, Edward. Of Cheltenham, Gloucestershire.
Conquest of England by the Normans: by Edward Davies. Cheltenham: John J. Banks; London: Simpkin, Marshall, Hamilton, Kent & Co. [1896]. 99 pp.
 Poetry and prose. *OXB*
Legend and lay: the poetical works of Edward Davies. With six illustrations by Ed. J. Burrow. London: Simpkin, Marshall, Hamilton, Kent & Co.; Cheltenham: J.J. Banks. [1894]. [iv], 70 pp. il. *UCD*

DAVIES, Edward William Lewis (1812–94). Son of William Davies of Eglwysilan, Glamorgan. Educated at Jesus College, Oxford; BA 1836, MA 1838; cox of the Oxford boat in the second boat race against Cambridge. Ordained 1837; vicar, Adlingfleet, Yorkshire, 1852–75; rural dean, 1885–75. He kept otter hounds and was known as 'Otter Davies'. Lived latterly at 29 Circus, Bath.
The collects, rendered into plain, easy verse for school and family use; by E.W.L. Davies. London: Samuel Bagster & Sons; Bath: William Lewis & Son. [1882]. 32 pp. *OXB*

DAVIES, John Henry, (D.), (J.H.D.) (1850–93). Son of Rev. Nathaniel Davies, rector of Mount Bures, Essex. Educated at Jesus College, Oxford (scholar). Curate, Brindle, Lancashire, 1876–77, Tendring, Essex, 1877–78, Mount Bures, 1879–87; rector, Mount Bures, 1887 to his death.
Albion's fall: a prophecy of doom; [by J.H.D.]. London: E.W. Allen. 1880. 23 pp. *OXB*
Chips: another "tribute of song"; by [J.H.D.]. London: E.W. Allen. 1884. 17 pp. *OXB*
Random rhymes (1865 to 1885); [by John Henry Davies]. London: Griffith, Farran, Okeden & Welsh. 1886. [ii], 264 pp. *BL*
Some Welsh legends, and other poems; by John H. Davies. Sudbury: Henry C. Pratt. 1893. [4], iv, 325 pp. *NLW*
 Also 2nd ed. 1893.
Somebody: a sketch; [by D.]. London: E.W. Allen. 1882. 16 pp. *BL*

DAVIES, Joseph. Dramatist. Lived at The Oldwarps, Warrington, Lancashire.
The cruise of the steam yacht "Ceylon" to the West Indies, in the spring of 1887; [by Joseph Davies]. London: Ben George. 1887. 43 pp. *BL*

DAVIES, Otter *see* **DAVIES, Edward William Lewis**

DAVIN, Nicholas Flood (1843–1901). b. Kilfinnane, County Limerick. Educated at Queen's College, Cork. Called to the Bar, Middle Temple, 1868. Parliamentary reporter in the House of Commons; special correspondent for the *Irish Times* and *London Standard* in the Franco-German War. In 1872 he went to Canada, becoming a prominent journalist and politician, noted as an orator. Elected three times to the Canadian parliament, he was secretary to several government commissions. He shot himself.

Album verses, and other poems; by Nicholas Flood Davin. Printed Ottawa: MacLean, Roger & Co. 1882. 32 pp.   *BL*

Eos: a prairie dream, and other poems; by Nicholas Flood Davin. Printed Ottawa: Citizen Printing & Publishing Co. 1884. 36 pp.   *OXB*

Eos: an epic of the dawn, and other poems; by Nicholas Flood Davin. Regina, N.W.T.: Leader Co. Ltd. 1889. viii, 5–141 pp. por.   *BL*

DAVIS, Emily *see* **PFEIFFER, Emily**

DAVIS, Thomas (1804–87). b. Worcester, son of Rev. Richard F. Davis, rector of Pendock. A solicitor at Worcester, 1825–28. Entered Queen's College, Oxford; BA 1832, MA 1835. Ordained, 1833; curate, All Saints, Worcester, 1833–40; perpetual curate, St John's, Roundhay, near Leeds, from 1840. In 1871 he was appointed chaplain of the reformatory ship *Akbar* anchored in the Mersey. Hymn writer.

Thoughts in prose and verse for every Sunday and the greater holy days in the year: selected from the writings of T. Davis. Edited by his widow. Printed Leeds: Thomas Watson. 1896. 127 pp.

Half-title is *Sabbath thoughts*.   *NLW*

DAVIS, Thomas. Lived at Bleak House, Hill Top, West Bromwich, Staffordshire.

The poet's wreath: [poems]; by Thomas Davis. West Bromwich: [Author]. 1892. x, 220 pp.   *OXB*

DAVIS, William Henry. Lived at Meonstoke, Hampshire.

The bride of Albion, and other poems; by William H. Davis. London: E.W. Allen. 1880. 59 pp.   *OXB*

DAVISON, Henry. Son of James W. Davison.

Dove sono: [poems]; [by Henry Davison]. London: Kegan Paul, Trench, Trübner, & Co. Ltd. 1894–95. 2 vols.

2nd vol. is described as Part two.   *TCD*

Other poems; [by Henry Davison]. London: David Stott. 1891. 38 pp.   *BL*

Poems; by Henry Davison. London: David Bogue. 1884. [viii], 40 pp.   *OXB*

DAWE, Frances. Lived at Smarden, Kent.

The silver cord: a book of poems; by Frances Dawe. London: Elliot Stock. 1888. xvi, 144 pp.   *OXB*

DAWE, William. Novelist.

Sketches in verse; by William Dawe. London: Kegan Paul, Trench & Co. 1889. vi, 128 pp.   *OXB*

Sydonia, and other poems; by William Dawe. London: Wyman & Sons. 1885. [iv], 112 pp.   *OXB*

DAWSON, Alfred. Educated at Christ's College, Cambridge.
Keta, and other poems; by Alfred Dawson. London. 1885. iv, 380 pp.
Printed for private circulation. *BL*

DAWSON, Benjamin Clapham. Of Bramley, Leeds.
Poems, ballads and love lyrics; by Benjamin Clapham Dawson. Leeds: T.
Tweedie. 1891. xvi, 161 pp. *OXB*

DAWSON, Catharine Amy *see* **DAWSON-SCOTT, Catharine Amy**

DAWSON, Christopher *see* **DAWSON, Christopher Murray**

DAWSON, Christopher Murray (1826–). b. Cupar, Fife. His parents
settled in Coldstream, Berwickshire, c. 1830. Educated in the parish school
there, serving as pupil-teacher for five years. He was appointed English master
at Madras Academy, Cupar; in 1846 he became parish schoolmaster of
Abercorn, Firth of Forth. A popular lecturer on historical, literary and
scientific subjects, and a speaker at public meetings.
Avonmore, and other poems; by Christopher Dawson. London: James Nisbet &
Co. 1891. viii, 309 pp. *OXB*
"The justice stone": or, the last sacrifice, and other poems; by Christopher Murray
Dawson. Edinburgh: R.W. Hunter. 1899. xii, 344 pp. il., por. *OXB*

DAWSON, Ethel. Writer of stories for girls.
The log book: [poems]; by H.G. Groser & E. Dawson. Illustrated by A. Wilde
Parsons. London: Ernest Nister. [1897]. [16] pp. col. il.
Not joint authorship. Printed on card. *BL*

DAWSON, Forbes (1860–19). b. Alfrick, Worcestershire, son of Rev. B.V.
Dawson, vicar of Alfrick who afterwards became a Roman Catholic priest.
Educated in Normandy, and at Ushaw College. He went to New Zealand
when in his teens, and was a steeplechase jockey for a time before joining a
travelling company of actors touring the colonies. In 1884 he toured the
United States with Madame Modjeska's Company. He appeared at most of
the London theatres.
Cross country ballads; by Forbes Dawson. London: Samuel French. [1891]. 64
pp. *OXB*

DAWSON, Joseph, (Louis Barsac, pseud.) (1842–19). b. Shincliffe. County
Durham, son of George Dawson. Educated at East Keswick Academy, near
Leeds. A Methodist minister, he was engaged in preaching, lecturing, and
literary work, contributing to the *Spectator*, *Pall Mall Gazette*, and other
journals. Lived latterly at Wychling Over, Westwell, Ashford, Kent.
Shadows and fire-flies: a book of verse; written by Louis Barsac. London:
Unicorn Press. 1898. 88 pp. (Unicorn books of verse, 1). *OXB*
Also 2nd ed. 1898.

DAWSON, William James (1854–1928). b. Towcester, Northamptonshire, son of Rev. W.J. Dawson, Wesleyan minister. Educated at Kingswood School, Bath, and trained for the Wesleyan ministry at Didsbury College, Manchester. From 1875 he held appointments in London, Glasgow and Southport. He was a popular lecturer on historic subjects. In 1892 he resigned from the ministry, becoming pastor of the Highbury Quadrant Congregational Church, London, until 1906.

Poems and lyrics; by W.J. Dawson. London: Macmillan & Co. 1893. viii, 140 pp.   *OXB*

A vision of souls, with other ballads and poems; by W.J. Dawson. London: Elliot Stock. 1884. vi, 212 pp.   *OXB*

DAWSON-SCOTT, Catharine Amy (18 –1934). b. Dulwich, daughter of Ebenezer and Catharine Dawson. Educated at the Anglo-German College, Camberwell. She started earning her living as a secretary aged eighteen. In the First World War she organized the Women's Defence League, which trained women to take the place of men conscripted into the services. Founded the Tomorrow Club, 1917, and P.E.N., 1921.

Idylls of womanhood; by C. Amy Dawson. London: William Heinemann. 1892. [vi], 120 pp.   *OXB*

Sappho; by C.A. Dawson. London: Kegan Paul, Trench & Co. 1889. [vi], 210 pp.   *OXB*

DEACON, Alfred W. Newport, pseud. *see* **O'SHAUGHNESSY, Arthur William Edgar**, (Alfred W. Newport Deacon, pseud.)

DEAN, George Alfred (1816?–98). b. Essex. His father owned a landed estate which he personally managed. Became an architect and surveyor with offices in Lancaster Place, London. He specialized in farm buildings and estates, and was agent for Sir Thomas Hesketh at Towcester, Northamptonshire. He laid out the royal model farm at Osborne, Isle of Wight, c. 1845. Active in Northamptonshire political life as a Conservative. Lived at The Grange, Pattishall, near Towcaster.

Poems on social, educational, national, patriotic and other subjects; by G.A. Dean. Towcester: E. Hunt. [c. 1896]. 94 pp.   *★UCD*

DEAN, Josiah. Lived at 68 Roman Road, Barnsbury, London N.

Ben Rool's wedding: a poetical work, introducing an amusing tale of the shy lovers, and the old custom of the marrowbones & cleavers; written and published by J. Dean. Barnsbury, N.: Author. [1889]. 16 pp.   *OXB*

DEANE, Anthony Charles (1870–1946). Son of H.C. Deane, barrister of Cheltenham, Gloucestershire. Educated at Wellington College, and Clare College, Cambridge; BA 1892, MA 1896. Student, Lincoln's Inn, 1891. Ordained, 1894; curate, Barcombe, Sussex, 1893–96, Christ Church, Walcot, Bath, 1896–98, Gnossal, Staffordshire, 1898–1901, Midhurst, Sussex, 1901–03; vicar, Holy Trinity, Malvern, and rural dean of Powyke, 1909–13,

Hampstead, 1913–16, All Saints, Knightsbridge, 1917–29; canon, St George's, Windsor, 1929–40; chaplain to HM the King from 1934.

Frivolous verses; by Anthony C. Deane. Cambridge: Redin & Co.; London: Simpkin, Marshall, Hamilton, Kent & Co. 1892. [viii], 56 pp. *OXB*

Holiday rhymes; by Anthony C. Deane. London: Henry & Co. 1894. viii, 128 pp. *OXB*

Leaves in the wind: [poems]; by Anthony C. Deane. London: Elliot Stock. 1896. viii, 91 pp. *OXB*

Poems; by Anthony C. Deane. Wellington College Station: George Bishop. 1889. 48 pp. *BL*

DEANS, George. Of Tweedside.

Harp strums: [poems]; by George Deans. Kelso: J. & J.H. Rutherfurd; Glasgow: A.F. Sharp & Co. 1890. xiv, 223 pp. *NLS*

DEAS, Christie. A Scot from the Border country.

Poems; by Christie Deas. Selkirk: George Lewis & Co. 1897. xii, 69 pp. *EPL*

DEAS, Elizabethan Ann (Lizzie), (Fauvette, pseud.). b. Edinburgh, daughter of Sir George Deas, Scottish judge. She contributed verse to various magazines and newspapers under the pseud. Fauvette. Lived latterly at Villa Sommer, Ems, Prussia.

Flower legends from many lands: [poems]; by Lizzie Deas. London: Digby, Long & Co. [1895]. 48 pp. *OXB*

Poem pictures with other lyrics; by Fauvette. London: T. Fisher Unwin. 1889. viii, 128 pp. *OXB*

DEAS, Lizzie *see* **DEAS, Elizabeth Ann (Lizzie)**, (Fauvette, pseud.)

DE BLAQUIERE, Anna Maria, Lady (18 –94). Only child of J. Wormald of Upper Harley Street, London. In 1862 she married William Barnard De Blaquiere, 5th Baron. Lived at Springfield, Crawley, Sussex, and Brockworth Manor, Gloucestershire.

Poems; by Anna Maria De Blaquiere. Crawley. 1882. 26 pp. ⋆

DEBORAH, pseud. *see* **KYD, Jean**, (Deborah, pseud.)

DE BREMONT, Anna, Comtesse *see* **BREMONT, Anna De**, Comtesse

DE CALVADOS, J.S.

Levana and our ladies of sorrow; by J.S. De Calvados. London: Kegan Paul, Trench & Co. 1888. 29 pp. il. (by M. Tuke). *OXB*

DE CAUX, John William. Writer on sea fishing and fisheries, and on the licensed victuallers' trade.
The cruise of the "Bunch of Roses": a tale of fisher-life at sea; by J.W. De Caux. Great Yarmouth: A. & W. Huke; London: Simpkin & Co. [1887]. 35 pp. il.   OXB

DE FONBLANQUE, Ethel Maud. Daughter of Albany De Fonblanque. Educated in Dresden, Florence and Brussels. She was married first to Arthur Chester-Master, formerly of the 5th Lancers and secondly to Arthur Harter. A novelist, she was a member of the British Italian League, and founder of the Anglo-Italian Literary Society. Lived at 45 Costa San Giorgio, Florence, and at 33 Montpelier Square, London SW.
A chaplet of love poems; by Ethel M. De Fonblanque (Mrs Arthur Harter). London: Leonard Smithers & Co. 1889. viii, 130 pp. il., por.   BL
Disillusion, and other poems; by Ethel M. De Fonblanque. London: T. Fisher Unwin. 1887. 64 pp.   BL
Poems; by Ethel Maud De Fonblanque. London: May be obtained at Bolton's Library, Knightsbridge. [1880], vi, 90 pp.   BL

DE FRAINE, John. Lived at White Hall, West Wickham, Cambridgeshire.
Happy thoughts for young and old; by John De Fraine. West Wickham, Cambridgeshire: Author. 1892. 58 pp.
Poetry and prose.   OXB

DE GRUCHY, Augusta. Novelist.
Under the hawthorn, and other verse; by Augusta De Gruchy. London: Elkin Mathews & John Lane at The Bodley Head. 1893. [iv], 85 pp.
A limited ed. of 30 numbered copies printed on Japanese vellum.   BL

DE KANTZOW, Theodosia
Poems, original and translated; by Theodosia De Kantzow. London: Chiswick Press. 1896. 24 pp.
Privately printed.   BL

DELL, John Henry (1832–88). Landscape painter and etcher. He exhibited many pictures at the Royal Academy and other galleries. Lived at Aden Cottage, Thorpe Green, Chertsey, Surrey, 1860–85, and at 5 Montera Road, New Maldon, from 1885.
The dawning grey: [poems]; by J.H. Dell. With illustrations by the author. London: Simpkin, Marshall, & Co. [1885]. viii, 216 pp. il.   OXB

The DELUGE: A POEM. Books I to IV. London: Elliot Stock. 1881. viii, 148 pp.   OXB

DELUSCAR, Horace *see* **DELUSKAR, Horace,**

DE LUSIGNAN, Marie, Princess.
  Scraps: [poems]; [by] Princess De Lusignan. London: Chapman & Hall Ltd. 1887. [iv], 66 pp. *OXB*

DELUSKAR, Horace. Of Hanwell, Middlesex?
  Battle of Flodden, [and other poems]; by Horace Deluskar. Hanwell: Anderson & Co. [1896]. [32] pp.
    Title from cover. *OXB*
  Deluscar's Merris, and other poems; by Horace Deluscar. London: Gay & Bird. 1899. xiv, 276 pp.
    Cover-title is *Songs to Merris.* *OXB*
  Lemel lyrics; by Horace Delusskarr. Hanwell: Anderson & Co. 1897. [46] pp. *OXB*
  Sonnets; [by Horace Deluskar]. Hanwell: Anderson & Co. [1896]. [34] pp. *OXB*

DELUSSKARR, Horace *see* **DELUSKAR, Horace**

DENMAN, George (1819–96). Son of Lord Denman, Lord Chief Justice. Educated at Repton School, and Trinity College, Cambridge; BA 1842, MA 1845; he rowed in the Cambridge boat against Oxford, 1841 and 1842; Fellow of Trinity, 1843. Barrister, Lincoln's Inn, 1846; joined the home circuit; counsel to Cambridge University, 1847–72; QC, 1861; judge, 1875. MP for Tiverton, Devon, 1859–65 and 1866–72. A distinguished high court judge, he retired in 1892. Lived at 8 Cranley Gardens, London.
  Intervalla: verses, Greek, Latin and English; by George Denman. Printed Cambridge: At the University Press. 1898. xiv, 96 pp.
    For private circulation. *MPL*
  The story of the kings of Rome, in verse; by the Hon. G. Denman. London: Trübner & Co. 1889. 62 pp. *OXB*

DENNING, John Renton. Served as private, 1st Battalion, Rifle Brigade, stationed at Poona, India, c. 1878.
  Poems and songs; by John Renton Denning. Bombay: Education Society's Press, Byculla. 1888. [xii], 275 pp. *OXB*
  "Soldierin'": *a few military ballads*; by J.A.N. (John Renton Denning). Bombay: Indian Textile Journal Co., Ld. 1899. [viii], 68 pp. *BL*

DENNIS, John. Of Brighton, Sussex.
  Verses; by John Dennis. London: Chiswick Press. 1898. [vi], 58 pp.
    Privately printed. *BL*

DENT, Amelia Jane. Née Campbell, she married William Dent. Lived in Ceylon for several years.
   Ceylon: a descriptive poem, with notes; by Mrs. William Dent. London: Kegan Paul, Trench & Co. 1886. 32 pp.   *OXB*

DENT, Mrs William *see* **DENT, Amelia Jane**

DE QUETTEVILLE, Philip Winter (1831?–1915). b. Jersey. Educated at Peterhouse, Cambridge; BA 1853, MA 1856. Ordained, 1858; curate, East Dean, Sussex, 1859–62. Assistant master, St Mary & St Michael School, Lancing. Curate, Bix, Oxfordshire, 1865, Stodmarsh, Canterbury, Kent, 1866–68, Littleworth, Berkshire, 1873–74; chaplain at Rotterdam, 1874–76. Lived latterly at Trinity, Jersey.
   The empty tomb, with other poems; by P.W. De Quetteville. London: Swan Sonnenschein & Co., Ltd. 1896. iv, 251 pp.   *GPR*

DERFEL, Robert Jones, (Munullog, pseud). (1824–1905). b. Llandderfel, Merionethshire, son of Robert Jones. At an early age he moved to Manchester, and for some time was a commercial traveller in drapery. He opened a bookshop in Manchester which proved a failure but succeeded in establishing a sound business as a printer. A voluminous writer on socialistic subjects, both in English and in Welsh. Adopted the name Derfel.
   Hymns and songs for the church of man; by Munullog. Printed Manchester: Author. [1890]. 128 pp.   *MPL*
   Musing for the masses: [poems]; [by Robert Jones Derfel]. [Manchester]: [Author]. [1895]. 32 pp.
      Title from cover.   *MPL*
   Social songs; by Munullog. Manchester: Author. [1890]. 166 pp.   *MPL*

DERRY, E.
   Love: a poem in five cantos; by E. Derry. Printed London: Arliss Andrews. 1898. 110 pp.   *OXB*
   Rhymes of road, rail, & river; by E. Derry. Bristol: J.W. Arrowsmith; London: Simpkin, Marshall, Hamilton, Kent & Co. Ltd. [1899]. 127 pp.   *OXB*
   Sophonisba: or, the prisoner of Alba, and other poems; by E. Derry. London: Digby, Long & Co. 1896. viii, 223 pp.   *BL*

DE ST. DALMAS, H.P. Emeric. Writer on the Great Pyramid. Lived at Aubrey Lodge, Merton Park, Surrey.
   The mystery unveiled: or, an exhibition of the divine purpose in man's creation, fall and redemption: [poems]; by H.P.E. De St. Dalmas. London: John F. Shaw & Co. 1896. viii, 176 pp.   *OXB*

DE TABLEY, Lord *see* **WARREN, John Leicester, Lord De Tabley**

DE TEISSIER, George Frederick (1821–90). Son of James De Teissier of Epsom, Surrey. Educated at Corpus Christi College, Oxford; BA 1842, MA 1845, BD 1853; Fellow and tutor of Corpus Christi, 1847–56. Curate, St Peter-Le-Bailey, Oxford, 1855–56; rector, Church and Chapel Brampton, Northamptonshire, 1856–76; rural dean, Haddon, 1864–76; rector, Childrey, Berkshire, 1876–82. Lived latterly at West Street, Chichester, Sussex.

The guardian angel, and other poems; by G.F. De Teissier. London: W. Skeffington & Son. 1884. 67 pp. *BL*

Miscellaneous poems; by G.F. De Teissier. London: Houlston & Sons. 1886. viii, 192 pp. *OXB*

Parochial sketches, and other verses; by G.F. De Teissier. London: W. Skeffington & Son. 1883. [iv], 59 pp. *OXB*

DE VERE, Aubrey (1814-1902). b. Adare, County Limerick, third son of Sir Aubrey De Vere, poet and dramatist. Educated at Trinity College, Dublin. He was greatly influenced by Wordsworth, whom he met in 1841; became a friend of Newman and Manning, and in 1851 was received into the Roman Catholic Church; appointed by Newman to the nominal post of professor of political and social affairs in the new Catholic University, Dublin, 1854. Keenly interested in Irish affairs, he published several prose works on public questions.

Aubrey De Vere's poems: a selection. Edited by John Dennis. London: Cassell & Co., Ltd. 1890. 283 pp. *TCD*

The foray of Queen Maeve, and other legends of Ireland's heroic age: [poems]; by Aubrey De Vere. London: Kegan Paul, Trench and Co. 1882. xxviiii, 233 pp. *UCD*

Legends and records of the Church and Empire: [poems]; by Aubrey De Vere. London: Kegan Paul, Trench & Co. 1887. xxviii, 311 pp. *OXB*
Also New ed. 1887.

Mediaeval records and sonnets; by Aubrey De Vere. London: Macmillan & Co. 1893. xx, 270 pp. *MPL*

The poetical works of Aubrey De Vere. London: Kegan Paul, Trench & Co. 1884–98. 6 vols. *OXB*

Saint Peter's chains: or, Rome and the Italian revolution: a series of sonnets; by Aubrey De Vere. London: Burns & Oates, Ld; New York: Catholic Publication Society Co. [1888]. xii, 55 pp. *OXB*

Selections from the poems of Aubrey De Vere. Edited with a preface by George Edward Woodberry. New York: Macmillan & Co. 1894. xx, 310 pp. por. *OXB*

DE VERE, Sir Stephen Edward (1812–1904). Son of Sir Aubrey De Vere and brother of Aubrey De Vere. Educated at Trinity College, Dublin. Called to the Irish Bar, 1836. He became a Roman Catholic in 1848. MP for Limerick, 1854–59, he also served as deputy lieutenant and JP for the county. Succeeded his brother as 4th Bart, 1880.

Grave and gay: verses of many years; [by Sir Stephen Edward De Vere]. Printed London: Charles Skipper & East. 1883. [iv], 71 pp.
　　For private circulation only. Cover-title is *Poems*.   *OXB*

Translations from Horace, &c.; by Sir Stephen E. De Vere. With Latin text. London: George Bell & Sons; Dublin: M.H. Gill & Son. 1885. xvi, 70 pp.   *OXB*

Translations from Horace, and a few original poems; by Sir Stephen De Vere, Bart. With Latin text. 2nd ed. enlarged. London: George Bell & Sons. 1886. xxviii, 223 pp.   *NLS*

DE W., H. *see* **DE WINDT, Henry, (H. De W.)**

DEWAR, Alexander (1822?–83). b. Crathie, Aberdeenshire. He entered Glasgow College intending to become a minister. Spent some time in missionary work in Dunfermline, then became involved in business in Liverpool. Settled in Ormskirk, Lancashire, as a Congregational minister.
　　The grave of love, and other poems; by Alexander Dewar. London: Elliot Stock. 1883. iv, 144 pp.   *OXB*

DEWES, Adrian (1865–80). Sent to Shrewsbury School in January 1880; he contracted typhoid fever from which he died on 30 March 1880.
　　Firstfruits: [poems]; by Adrian Dewes. Edited, with a short memoir, by Ursula Mary Dewes. Printed London: Gilbert & Rivington. [1881]. xii, 124 pp. por.   *OXB*

DE WINDT, Henry, (H. De W.). World-wide traveller.
　　Ennui de voyage: [poems]; [by H. De W.]. Printed London: Leadenhall Press. [1889]. 65 pp.
　　Title from cover.   *OXB*

DEY, Agnes Christall (1861–95). b. Aberdeen. At an early age she went to Edinburgh, where most of her life was spent as a teacher. In 1894 she married Rev. Alexander Westwater, minister of West Port Free Church, Hawick, Roxburghshire.
　　Songs and poems; by Agnes Christall Dey. With introduction by Rev. J.H. Wilson. Paisley: J. & R. Parlane; Edinburgh: John Menzies & Co.; MacNiven & Wallace. 1896. 123 pp. por.   *BL*

DICK, Cotsford (1846–1911). Son of Charles G. Dick, barrister. Educated at private schools, and Worcester College, Oxford. Composer of many songs and piano pieces. An invalid for many years, he lived at 115 St George's Road, London SW.
　　The model, and other poems; by Cotsford Dick. London: Elliot Stock. 1886. viii, 106 pp.   *OXB*

　　The ways of the world: vers de société; by Cotsford Dick. London: George Redway. 1896. 120 pp.   *OXB*

DICK, Robert (1849–89). b. Langlands Brae, Kilmarnock, Ayrshire, spending his life in the town. While still a child he worked in a factory for sixpence a week; apprenticed to a printer at thirteen, he attended evening classes to complete his education; worked for Messrs Smith Bros, printers, for over twenty years.

Tales and poems; by Robert Dick. Kilmarnock: Dunlop & Drennan. 1892. viii, 248 pp. *BL*

DICKINS, Clara Swain. Third daughter of the poet Charles Swain of Manchester. She married Thomas Dickins, MP.

Margaret and margarites: [poems]; by Clara Swain Dickins. London: Sampson Low, Marston & Co. Ltd. 1896. viii, 112 pp. *MPL*

Sonnets, sacred and secular; by Clara Swain Dickins. London: Simpkin, Marshall, & Co.; Manchester: J.E. Cornish. 1886. xvi, 202 pp. *MPL*

DICKINSON, Goldsworthy Lowes (1862–1932). Educated at Charterhouse, and King's College, Cambridge; Fellow of King's 1886–1920; lecturer in political science, 1896–1920. A pacifist, humanist and historian, he worked actively for the foundation of a 'League of Nations'. Lived latterly in Edwardes Square, Kensington, London W.

Jacob's ladder; by G. Lowes Dickinson. Printed [London]: Monotype Printing Co., Ltd. [1887]. 24 pp. *OXB*

Poems; [by Goldsworthy Lowes Dickinson]. [London]: Chiswick Press. 1896. vi, 68 pp.

Privately printed. *OXB*

DICKINSON, H.R.

Sentimental and absurd rhymes; by H.R. Dickinson. London: A. & F. Denny. [1898]. [80] pp. il. *BL*

DICKINSON, William (1798?–1882). b. Kidburngill, Cumberland. Educated in Workington. He became a farmer, land-surveyor and valuer, owning two farms and numerous agencies. High constable for Allerdale, 1829–68. FLS. Built a house named Newlands in Workington, and lived there until his death.

Uncollected literary remains of William Dickinson: being a series of pieces in prose and verse, arranged from the author's manuscripts by W. Hodgson. With portrait and brief memoir. Printed Carlisle: G. & T. Coward. 1888. xvi, 255 pp.

Spine-title is *Literary remains*. *OXB*

DIETZ, Ella (1856–). Mrs Clymer. She became an actress but left the stage in 1881.

The triumph of life: mystical poem; by Ella Dietz. London: E.W. Allen. 1885. [viii], 352 pp. *OXB*

The triumph of time: mystical poem, a sequel to, The triumph of love; by Ella Dietz. London: E.W. Allen. 1884. 228 pp. *OXB*

DILLON, Arthur. Dramatist.
Gods and men: [poems]; by Arthur Dillon. London: Kegan Paul, Trench, &
Co. 1887. [vi], 131 pp. *OXB*
Gods and men: [poems]; by Arthur Dillon. London: Eden, Remington & Co.
1892. [iv], 312 pp. *OXB*
River songs, and other poems; by Arthur Dillon. Illustrated by Margery May.
London: Kegan Paul, Trench, & Co. 1882. [viii], 128 pp. il. *OXB*
    Also New ed. 1893, published by Remington & Co., Ltd.

DISNEY, Thomas (1854?–   ). Son of James Disney of Armagh. Educated at
Merton College, Oxford; BA 1878. Composer of hymns and songs. Lived at 8
Westhill Road, London SW.
    Cricket lyrics; by T. Disney. London: Digby, Long & Co. [1897]. 49
pp. *OXB*

DIX, William Chatterton (1837–98). b. Bristol. Educated at Bristol Gram-
mar School. A hymn writer, many of whose hymns are in common use in
Britain and America. Died at Cheddar, Somerset.
    My lady poverty, and other verses; by William Chatterton Dix. Oxford:
Mowbray & Co. [1891]. iv, 107 pp. *OXB*

DIXIE, Lady Florence (1857–1905). b. London, née Douglas, daughter of
the 7th Marquess of Queensbury. In 1875 she married Sir Alexander Dixie.
She travelled extensively, hunting big game on several continents; explored
unknown Patagonia. Acted as war correspondent for the *Morning Post* in the
Zulu War. A keen champion of women's rights, she advocated complete sex
equality.
    Waifs and strays: or, the pilgrimage of a Bohemian abroad; by Lady Florence Dixie,
written when a child, between 1870 and 1873. London: Griffith, Farran,
Okeden & Welsh, [1884]. 60 pp. *BL*

DIXON, Constance E. Aged sixteen she was invited by Oscar Wilde to join
the staff of his paper *Woman's World*, an invitation to which she readily agreed.
    The chimneypiece of Bruges, and other poems; by Constance E. Dixon. London:
Elliot Stock. 1886. viii, 131 pp. *BL*

DIXON, George
    Recreations in verse; by George Dixon. Manchester: John Heywood. 1884. 243
pp. por. *★UCD*

DIXON, Richard Watson (1833–1900). b. Islington, London, son of Dr
James Dixon, Wesleyan minister. Educated at King Edward's School,
Birmingham, and Pembroke College, Oxford. Took Anglican orders; curate
in London, at St Mary-the-Less, Lambeth, 1858–61, and St Mary's, Newington Butts, 1861. Assistant master, Highgate School, 1861–62; second
master, Carlisle High School, 1862–68. Minor canon and hon. librarian,
Carlisle Cathedral, 1868–75, hon. canon, 1874; vicar, Hayton, Cumberland,
1875–83, Warkworth, Northumberland, 1883–1900. Author of a scholarly
history of the Church of England in the Reformation period.

Lyrical poems; by Richard Watson Dixon. Printed Oxford: H. Daniel, Fellow of Worcester College. 1887. [viii], 64 pp.

> A limited ed. of 105 numbered copies. *OXB*

Mano: a poetical history of the time of the close of the tenth century, concerning the adventures of a Norman knight, which fell in Normandy part in Italy, in four books; by Richard Watson Dixon. London: George Routledge & Sons. 1883. xvi, 192 pp. *OXB*

> Also 2nd ed. 1891.

Odes and eclogues; by Richard Watson Dixon. Printed Oxford: Henry Daniel. 1884. [vi]. 40 pp.

> A limited ed. of 100 numbered copies. *OXB*

Songs and odes; by R.W. Dixon. London: Elkin Mathews. 1896. 31 pp. (Garland of new poetry, I). *MPL*

> Also issued in Shilling garland series, V.

The story of Eudocia & her brothers; by Richard Watson Dixon. Printed Oxford: H. Daniel, Fellow of Worcester College. 1888. viii, 38 pp.

> A limited ed. of 50 numbered copies. *OXB*

DOAKE, Margaret, (Sheila, pseud.)

Sketches from nature: a book of verses; by Sheila. London: Kegan Paul, Trench, Trübner & Co., Ltd. 1891. [2], vi, 102 pp. *OXB*

DOBELL, Elizabeth Mary Fordham (1828–1908). b. Hertfordshire, sixth in a family of nine children. She married Horace Dobell, physician. Lived at 84 Harley Street, London, and Streate Place, Bournemouth, Hampshire.

Ethelstone, Eveline, and other poems: or, legends of the castle and tales of the village; by Elizabeth Mary Fordham Dobell. London: C. Kegan Paul & Co. 1881. x, 303 pp. *BL*

In the watches of the night: poems (in eighteen volumes); by Mrs. Horace Dobell. London: Remington & Co. 1884--88. 18 vols. *OXB*

DOBELL, Mrs Horace *see* **DOBELL, Elizabeth Mary Fordham**

DOBIE, George (1824–). Lived at 9 Priestfield Road, Edinburgh. FSA Scotland.

Poems; by George Dobie. Printed Edinburgh: Morrison & Gibb. 1883. 232 pp. *OXB*

Rambling rhymes; by George Dobie. [Edinburgh]: T. & A. Constable. 1895. viii, 157 pp.

> Privately printed. *OXB*

DOBSON, Austin (1840–1921). b. Plymouth, Devon, son of a civil engineer. When he was eight the family moved to Holyhead, Anglesey, Wales. Educated at Beaumaris Grammar School, a private school in Coventry, and the Gymnase of Strasburg. In 1856 he became a clerk in the Board of Trade where he served until 1901, retiring as departmental head. A prolific writer of literary studies. Council member of the Society of Authors, and the Royal Literary Fund.

BIBLIOGRAPHY: **MURRAY, Francis Edwin.** *A bibliography of Austin Dobson.*
Derby: Frank Murray. 1900.

DOCEO, pseud.
  Phil's octave: their eight nights' entertainment: [poems]; by Doceo. London:
Digby, Long & Co. [1896]. [iv], 76 pp.   *OXB*

DODD, Godfrey
  Blossom and weed, [and other poems]; by Godfrey Dodd. London: Gay &
Bird. 1898. 30 pp.   *OXB*

DODGSON, Charles Lutwidge, (Lewis Carroll, pseud.) (1832–98). Son of
the vicar of Daresbury, Cheshire. Educated at Rugby School, and Christ
Church, Oxford; BA 1854, MA 1857; lecturer in mathematics, Oxford
University, 1855–81. Ordained deacon, 1861. Author of *Alice's Adventures in
Wonderland*, and other books for children. Lived in Oxford.
  Rhyme? and reason?: [poems]; by Lewis Carroll. With sixty-five illustrations
by Arthur B. Frost and nine by Henry Holiday. London: Macmillan & Co.
1883. xii, 216 pp. il.   *MPL*
  Three sunsets, and other poems; by Lewis Carroll. With twelve fairy-fancies by
E. Gertrude Thomson. London: Macmillan & Co.; New York: Macmillan
Co. 1898. [xii], 68 pp. il.   *MPL*

DOHERTY, Austin. Composer. Lived at 1 Caxton Villas, Ashfield Road,
Urmston, Lancashire.
  Nathan Barlow: sketches in the retired life of a Lancashire butcher, in verse; by
Austin Doherty. Manchester: John Heywood. 1884. 101 pp.   *MPL*
    Also 2nd ed. [1885?].

DOLORES: A THEME WITH VARIATIONS, IN THREE PARTS.
London: C. Kegan Paul & Co. 1880. xii, 217 pp.   *OXB*

DOMAN, Henry. Of Lymington, Hampshire.
  Songs in the shade; by Henry Doman. London: Simpkin, Marshall, & Co.;
Lymington: Author. 1881. xvi, 224 pp. il. (by J.H. Dell).   *OXB*

DOMENICHETTI, Richard Hippisley (1863–). b. Stoke Damerel,
Devon, son of Dr Richard Domenichetti of Louth, Lincolnshire. Educated at
Haileybury, and Oriel College, Oxford; BA 1886. Ordained a Roman
Catholic priest; served at Brompton Oratory, London.
  The quest of Sir Bertrand, and other poems; by R.H. Domenichetti. With a
frontispiece by Mrs. Traquair. London: W.H. Allen & Co. 1890. viii, 212 pp.
il.   *OXB*
    Also New ed. 1893.
  The Thames: Newdigate prise poem, 1885; by Richard Hippisley Domenichetti.
Oxford: A. Thomas Shrimpton & Son; London: Simpkin, Marshall, & Co.
1885. 19 pp.   *OXB*

DONNE, Alicia. Lived at 29 Nicholas Street, Chester.

Peeps into bird life: [poems]; by Alicia Donne. With a prelude by the Lord Bishop of Wakefield. Chester: Phillipson & Golder; London: Simpkin, Marshall & Co. 1896. [viii], 112 pp. *OXB*

D'ORSEY, Alexander James Donald. b. Haunchwood House, Nuneaton, Warwickshire. Educated at Glasgow University. Ordained 1847. Incumbent, St John's, Anderston, Glasgow, and English master, Glasgow High School, until 1850. He lived in Madeira, 1850–59, founding an English school and a mission to seamen; raised £12,000 by subscription in London for the islanders of Madeira suffering from famine and cholera, 1856. Chaplain and lecturer in English history, Corpus Christi College, Cambridge, 1860–64. Lecturer, King's College, London, 1864–90, then professor of public reading.

Calderón: a poem in honour of the second century of the immortal poet; by Alexander J.D. D'Orsey. London: Simpkin, Marshall & Co.; Waters. 1881. 16 pp.
Title from cover. *OXB*

DOUDNEY, Sarah. b. Portsmouth, daughter of G.E. Doudney, owner of soap works in Portsmouth and Plymouth. Educated privately, and at Mrs Kendall's school at Southsea. She began contributing to magazines at an early age, and her many novels had a considerable vogue in their day. Lived mainly in London but died at Oxford.

Drifting leaves: [poems]; by Sarah Doudney. London: Marcus Ward & Co. Ltd. [1892]. 32 pp. col. il. *BL*

Violets for faithfulness: [poems]; by Sarah Doudney. London: Marcus Ward & Co., Ltd. [1893]. [24] pp. col. il. *BL*

Voices in the starlight; by Sarah Doudney. Illustrated by Edith Berkeley. London: Marcus Ward & Co. Ltd. [1892]. [16] pp. col. il. *BL*

DOUGHTY, George Bell (1865?–19). Educated at London University; BA 1886. Curate, St Michael & All Angels, Sydenham, Kent, 1887-89, Wanstead, Essex, 1889–1901; rector, St Peter-upon-Cornhill, City of London, 1901. Lived latterly at 27 Westbourne Gardens, London W.

Saint Peter: a fragment, and other verses; by Geo. Bell Doughty. London: Horace Marshall & Son. 1892. 48 pp. *OXB*

DOUGLAS, Lord Alfred, Belgian Hare, pseud.) (1870–1945). b. Ham Hill, near Worcester, son of the 8th Marquess of Queensberry. Educated at Winchester College, and Magdalen College, Oxford. His friendship with Oscar Wilde led to the latter's imprisonment for homosexual practices. Editor of the *Academy*, 1907–10. He was involved in many legal actions, and in 1923 was sentenced to six months for publishing a libel on Winston Churchill.

The city of the soul, [and other poems]; [by Lord Alfred Douglas]. London: Grant Richards. 1899. viii, 110 pp. *OXB*

The Duke of Berwick: a nonsense rhyme; by the Belgian hare. Illustrated by Tony Ludovici. London: Leonard Smithers & Co. [1899]. 43 pp. col. il.
Printed on one side of leaf only. *OXB*

Poems; [by] Lord Alfred Douglas. Paris: Mercure de France. 1896. [xii], 201 pp. por.

Parallel English and French texts. Cover-title is *Poèmes*.
Also identical 'fine paper' ed. 1896.
Tails with a twist: the verses; by "Belgian Hare". The pictures by E.T. Reed.
London: Edward Arnold. [1898]. 72 pp. col. il.   *OXB*

DOUGLAS, Evelyn, pseud. *see* **BARLAS, John Evelyn**, (Evelyn Douglas,
pseud.)

DOUGLAS, Frederick. Lived at The Elms, Ramsgate, Kent.
Patriots and place hunters: a satire; by Frederick Douglas. Ramsgate: Henry E.
Boulter. [1892]. 15 pp.   *OXB*

DOUGLAS, Sir George *see* **DOUGLAS, Sir George Brisbane.**

DOUGLAS, George A.H. (1850–   ). b. in 'The Vennel', Edinburgh.
Attended elementary schools in Edinburgh, and the Dollar Institution.
Apprenticed to Macniven & Cameron, wholesale stationers, staying for
thirteen years, the last five as the firm's representative from Shetland to
Berwick-on-Tweed. He started his own business in Glasgow, c. 1881. Wrote
articles on Egyptian architecture.
Sir William Wallace, and other poems; by G.A.H. Douglas. Glasgow: G.A.H.
Douglas & Co; John Menzies & Co. [188–). 261 pp.   *BL*

DOUGLAS, Sir George Brisbane (1856–1935). b. Kelso, Roxburghshire,
son of Sir George H. Douglas. Educated at Harrow School, and Trinity
College, Cambridge; BA 1878, MA 1881. Succeeded his father as 5th Bart,
1885. He discontinued the additional name Scott as used by his father and
grandfather. Lecturer in Scottish literature, Glasgow University, 1911. JP and
deputy lieutenant of Roxburghshire. A prolific writer on literary subjects, and
historian of the Border counties. Lived at Springwood Park, Kelso.
The fireside tragedy: a play; by Sir George Douglas. Edinburgh: David
Douglas. 1887. [iv], 144 pp.
   Includes *Poems*.   *OXB*
A love's gamut, and other poems; [by Sir George Brisbane Douglas]. London:
C. Kegan Paul & Co. 1880. vi, 122 pp.   *OXB*
Poems of a country gentleman; by Sir George Douglas. London: Longmans,
Green, & Co. 1897. viii, 75 pp.   *OXB*

DOUGLAS, Harry
Idylls of the home, in three books; by Harry Douglas. London: Spencer Blackett.
1889. [viii], 246 pp.   *OXB*

DOUGLAS, John Sholto, Lord Queensberry (1844–1900). Succeeded his
father as 8th Marquess in 1858; a representative peer for Scotland, 1872–80.
He married twice, the first marriage ending in divorce, the second in
annulment. Best known as a patron of boxing, the 'Queensberry rules' being
drawn up under his supervision, 1867. Lived at Kinmount Castle, Dumfriesshire, and Glen Stuart, Annan.
The spirit of the Matterhorn; by Lord Queensberry. London: Watts & Co.
[1880]. 30 pp.   *OXB*

The spirit of the Matterhorn; by Lord Queensberry. London: W. Mitchell. 1881. 31 pp.
Published for the author. *OXB*

DOUGLAS-SCOTT, Charles Henry Montagu- *see* MONTAGU-DOUGLAS-SCOTT, Charles Henry

DOVETON, Frederick Bazett (1841–1911). b. Exeter, Devon, son of Captain Doveton, Royal Madras Fusiliers. Educated privately in Bristol and Putney. Joined the Royal Canadian Rifles, 1861; entered the Army Control Depot, 1868; retired, 1879. Afterwards his time was spent as a man of letters. Lived at Karsfield, Torquay, Devon.
Sketches in prose and verse; by F.B. Doveton. London: Sampson, Low, Marston, Searle, & Rivington. 1886. xvi, 500 pp. *OXB*
Also New ed. 1888.
Snatches of song; by F.B. Doveton. London: Wyman & Sons. 1880. xii, 140 pp. *MPL*
Songs grave and gay; by F.B. Doveton. London: Horace Cox. 1893. xii, 267 pp. *OXB*

DOW, Margaret Russell. b. Edinburgh, daughter of John Dow. Educated in Edinburgh. She later lived with her brother Rev. John A. Dow, minister at Strathmiglo, Fife. Hymn writer.
Lays for leisure hours; by Margaret Russell Dow. Edinburgh: Andrew Elliot. [1882]. xvi, 230 pp. *OXB*
Lays for leisure hours; by Margaret Russell Dow. Revised and enlarged [ed.]. Edinburgh: Norman M'Leod. 1892. xx, 428 pp. por. *OXB*
Songs of nature, and other poems; by Margaret Russell Dow. Printed [Edinburgh]: Edinburgh Press. 1898. xii, 228 pp. *BL*

DOWDING, Frederick Townley, (F.T.D.) (1850–80). b. Devizes, Wiltshire. Educated at Eton College, and St John's College, Oxford. Rowed in the boat race against Cambridge, 1873. He was appointed professor of English literature in the native college at Chinsurah, India, then promoted to a position in the Indian Civil Service at a similar college at Rampora Baulcah; became the instructor and companion to the Nizam of Hyderabad, a minor. Died of typhoid fever at Hyderabad, aged twenty-nine.
Under the pipal: [poems]; by F.T.D. London: Roworth & Co. Ltd. 1883. xvi, 143 pp. *OXB*

DOWMAN, James
Shreds and patches: [poems]; by James Dowman. Aberdeen: W Jolly & Sons. 1896. 124 pp. *OXB*

DOWN, Eliza. Of Torrington.
Athelney, and other poems, including 'Kenwith' and 'Messeria'; by Eliza Down. London: George Bell & Sons. 1884. viii, 329 pp. *BL*

DOWNE, Mark. Of Colchester, Essex?
Essex ballads, and other poems; by Mark Downe. Colchester: Benham & Co.;
London: E. Marlborough & Co. 1895. 76 pp. il.   *OXB*

DOWNHAM, Frederick Linstead (1857–19   ). b. Beckenham, Kent, son of
Francis Downham. Educated at a private school in Beckenham, and King's
College, London. Curate, Emmanual Church, Everton, Liverpool; vicar, St
Simon & St Jude's, Anfield. Hon. secretary of Walton Rural Deanery from
1896; joint hon. secretary of Liverpool Diocesan Church of England
Temperance Society from 1906.
Sonnets addressed to Christ, and other poems; by Frederick Linstead Downham.
London: J. Nisbet & Co.; Liverpool: J. Albert Thompson. 1885. 165
pp.   *★UCD*

DOWSON, Ernest (1867–1900). b. Lee, Kent, son of an East End dry dock
owner. Educated in England and on the continent. Went up to Queen's
College, Oxford, but did not take a degree. He led a Bohemian life in London,
working intermittently at the dry dock, 1888–93. A friend of Yeats, he was a
founder-member of the Rhymers' Club. He moved to France, making a living
by translating, 1894–99.
Decorations: in verse and prose; by Ernest Dowson. London: Leonard Smithers
& Co. 1899. xii, 51 pp.   *OXB*
Verses; by Ernest Dowson. London: Leonard Smithers. 1896. xii, 58 pp.
    A limited ed. of 350 numbered copies, 300 small paper copies on handmade
paper, 30 large paper copies on Japanese vellum.   *OXB*

DOWSON, Thomas. Lived at 90 Conway Street, Birkenhead, Cheshire.
Sir John Stanley of Knowsley and his successors, in heroic verse; by Thomas
Dowson. Birkenhead: H. C. Robinson; Liverpool: D. Scott & Sons. [1888].
[vi] 120 pp.   *BL*

DOYLE, Sir Arthur Conan (1859–1930). b. Edinburgh, son of Irish Catholic
parents, his father a clerk in the Exchequer Office in Edinburgh. Educated at
Stonyhurst College, he studied medicine at Edinburgh University. After
working as a ship's doctor for two years he started a medical practice at
Southsea, Portsmouth, in 1882. Served as a physician with the troops in the
Boer War. He was knighted in 1902. A popular novelist, known for the
creation of the fictional detective Sherlock Holmes, his writing made him rich.
In his later years he became interested in spiritualism.
Songs of action; by A. Conan Doyle. London: Smith, Elder, & Co. 1898. viii,
136 pp.   *MPL*

DOYLE, Ezra. A Yorkshireman, he sometimes wrote in the local dialect.
Polly's gaon: or, merriment in dress and the folly of pride, [and other poems]; by
Ezra Doyle. Printed London: W. Nicholson & Sons. [1880?]. 50 pp.
    Printed for the author.   *BL*

DOYLE, Michael
Cause; by Michael Doyle. London: Kegan Paul, Trench & Co. 1889. [iv], 382 pp. *OXB*

DRAGON, pseud. Of Hertfordshire.
The Hertfordshire Hunt: a poem, dedicated to the members and supporters of the Hunt; by Dragon. London: A.H. Bailey & Co. 1880. 16 pp.
'Proceeds will be devoted to the Royal Agricultural Benevolent Institution'. *OXB*

DRAKE, John (1846–). b. Edinburgh. After receiving only a limited education he became a tailor's boy. Aged twelve he went to Glasgow, taking a succession of humble jobs; for some time he was a book-keeper in a wine merchant's establishment. Lived at 47 Renfrew Street, Glasgow.
The crofter, and other poems; by John Drake. Printed Glasgow: Gillespie Bros. 1888. 88 pp. *NLS*
Jock Sinclair, and other poems; by John Drake. Printed Glasgow: Thomas Gillespie. 1890. 256 pp. *NLS*
    Also [New ed.] 1890.
The Lion of Scotland: a tale of 1298; [by John Drake]. Printed Glasgow: John Horn. 1897. 240 pp. por. *UCD*

DRAMATIC DRIVELLERS: OR, ART PROFANED: A SATIRE.
Northampton: Author. [c. 1892]. [ii], 29 pp. *OXB*

A DREAM QUEST: A POEM IN THE STANZA OF SPENCER.
London: Truslove & Hanson. 1898. 62 pp. *OXB*

DRENNAN, John Swanwick (1809–93). b. Dublin. Educated at Trinity College; BA 1831, MB 1833, MD 1854. He practised medicine in Belfast. Some of his verse appeared in the *Nation* over his initials.
Poems and sonnets; by John Swanwick Drennan. London: Kegan Paul, Trench, Trübner & Co. Ltd. 1895. xii, 188 pp. *OXB*

DRESDEN, C.F.B.
Life thoughts: [poems]; [by C.F.B. Dresden]. London: Kegan Paul, Trench & Co. 1883. [viii], 73 pp. il. *OXB*

DRINKWATER, Albert Edwin (1852–19). b. Warwick, son of George Drinkwater, gentleman. Educated at Magdalen College School, and Merton College, Oxford (postmaster); BA 1876, MA 1878. Actor, dramatist and manager, he first appeared on stage in 1886. He played a number of Shakespearean roles in London and on tour. Secretary of the Incorporated Stage Society, 1906–12. Lived at 3 St Stephen's Square, London W.
Plays and poems; by Albert E. Drinkwater. London: Griffith, Farran, Okeden & Welsh. [1885]. [viii], 151 pp. *OXB*

DRUERY, Charles Thomas. Botanist, an expert on British ferns. Lived at Fernholme, Windsor Road, Forest Gate, Essex.

The rocking of the lilies, and other poems, grave and humorous; by Charles T. Druery. Printed London: Clayton & Co. [1882]. viii, 215 pp.

Printed for the author. *BL*

DRUMMOND, Hamilton (1857–1935). An Irishman, son of a Dublin JP. A successful novelist, he wrote historical romances.

Herod, and other poems; by Hamilton Drummond. London: Kegan Paul, Trench, Trübner, & Co. Ltd. 1893. [viii], 152 pp. *OXB*

Sir Hildebrand, and other poems; by Hamilton Drummond. Dublin: Hodges, Figgis, & Co. 1882. iv, 91 pp. *OXB*

DUDLEY, Robert. Artist and prolific illustrator.

Monthly maxims: rhymes and reasons to suit the seasons, and pictures new to suit them too; by Robert Dudley. London: Thos. De La Rue & Co. [1882]. [61] pp. il., col. il.

Printed on card. *OXB*

DUFF, Anna Julia Grant-, Lady *see* **GRANT-DUFF, Anna Julia**, Lady

DU MAURIER, George (1834–96). b. Paris of an English mother and French father. Educated in France but studied chemistry at University College, London. He returned to Paris in 1856 to study art then moved to Antwerp, becoming a pupil of De Keyser and Van Lerius, 1857–60. In 1859 he lost the sight of one eye but joined the staff of *Punch* in 1860 as an illustrator, making regular literary contributions in verse and prose. A novelist, he achieved great success with *Trilby*.

Legend of Camelot: pictures and poems, &c.; by George Du Maurier. London: Bradbury, Agnew, & Co. Ld. 1898. [203] pp. il.

Printed on one side of leaf only. *BL*

DUNCAN, John Garrow (1872–19). b. Botriphnie, son of John Duncan. Educated at Aberdeen University; MA 1892, BD 1897. In 1896 he adopted the name John Garrow Duff. Appointed minister of Macduff, Banffshire, 1901.

Tramps and troubadours: [poems]; by John Garrow Duncan. London: Digby, Long & Co. 1898. vi, 237 pp. *OXB*

DUNELMIAE FILIUS, pseud. *see* **BROWNE, S.**, (Dunelmiae Filius, pseud.)

DUNLOP, Margaret J. Of Kilmarnock, Ayrshire?

Poems; by Margaret J. Dunlop. Printed Kilmarnock: Dunlop & Drennan. 1897. [viii], 230 pp.

Includes *Tales*. *UCD*

DUNLOP, Thomas (1839–). b. Kilmarnock, Ayrshire. He studied theology at Edinburgh University. Minister of the United Presbyterian Church at Balfron, Stirlingshire, for several years, then at Bristol Church, Edinburgh, then at Emmanuel Congregational Church, Liverpool.

John Tamson's bairns, and other poems; by Thomas Dunlop. Edinburgh: Andrew Elliot. 1897. xii, 300 pp.   *UCD*

DUNTON, Theodore Watts- *see* **WATTS-DUNTON, Theodore**

DUVAL, Claude (1844?–84). Taught French at Manchester Grammar School. Lived at 48 Portsmouth Street, Chorlton, Manchester, then at Heaton Chapel, Cheshire.

Fanny: sonnets and poems; by Claude Duval. Manchester: Abel Heywood & Son; London: Simpkin, Marshall, & Co. [1880]. viii, 183 pp.   *OXB*

DYMOND-STUCKEY, Harry. Son of William Young Stuckey of Clevedon, Somerset.

Songs of the spirit: poems; by Harry Dymond-Stuckey. London: W.R. Price Little. [1893]. 32 pp.

 Title from cover.   *OXB*

E

E., A. *see* **RUSSELL, George William**, (A.E.)

E., A.B.

The conventiad, and other poems; by A.B.E. London: Samuel Tinsley & Co. 1880. [viii], 128 pp.   *OXB*

E., E.R. *see* **ECKERSLEY, Edmund Ryley**, (E.R.E.)

E., M. *see* **EDMONDS, Mary**, (M.E.)

E., M. *see* **EVANS, Margaret**, (M.E.)

E., S.

The legend of Dahut, and other poems; by S.E. London: Wells Gardner, Darton, & Co. [1891]. [viii], 55 pp.   *OXB*

E., Sister. Of the Community of Saint John the Baptist, Clewer, Berkshire.

On the wings of a dove: or, the life of a soul: [poems]; by Sister E. With nine illustrations. London: Griffith & Farran; New York: E.P. Dutton & Co. 1881. 48 pp. il.   *BL*

EAGLE, H. Served in the Royal Marines.
Songs of the camp and field; by H. Eagle. Printed Portsea: Times & Mail
Printing Works. [1888]. 23 pp.
    Title from cover. *OXB*

EAREE, William. Anglican clergyman, trained at St Bees College. Evening
lecturer, Cockermouth, Cumberland, and chaplain, Cockermouth Union,
1847–66; perpetual curate, Setmurthy, 1851–56. Headmaster, Cockermouth
Grammar School, 1859–66; lecturer, St Philip's, Birmingham, 1866–70.
Rector, Alphamstone, Essex, from 1870.
Lyrics of a life; by William Earée. Printed Edinburgh: Banks & Co. 1896. xvi,
330 pp. por. *UCD*

EARLE, George Chester (1870–   ). b. Swanwick, near Bath, son of Rev.
John Earle, professor of Anglo-Saxon. Educated at Keble College, Oxford;
BA 1892. Writer of school textbooks.
"Love's not time's fool": [poems]; by George Earle. Manchester: Labour Press
Ltd. [c. 1896]. 35 pp. *UCD*

EARLE, May
Cosmo Venucci, singer, and other poems; by May Earle. London: Kegan Paul,
Trench, Trübner & Co. Ltd. 1890. [vi], 150 pp. *UCD*
The quest of fire: [poems]; by May Earle. London: T. Fisher Unwin. 1894. 165
pp. *UCD*

EARLE, Walter (1839–1922). b. High Ongar, Essex, son of Henry J. Earle.
Educated at Marlborough College, and St John's College, Cambridge; BA
1861, MA 1865. Assistant master, Uppingham School, 1862–73; founder and
headmaster of Yarlet Hall School, 1873–87, of Bilton Grange School, 1887–
1902. Lived latterly at Reigate, Surrey.
Thought sketches: poems; by Walter Earle. London: George Allen. 1899. x, 259
pp. il., por. *UCD*

EAST AND WEST: OR, ALEXANDER'S DEATH, [and other poems].
London: George Bell & Sons. 1892. [viii], 163 pp. *OXB*

EASTWOOD, John R. Lived at 138 Bedford Road, Rock Ferry, Cheshire.
Fireside poems; by J.R. Eastwood. London: George Philip & Son. 1896. xiv,
189 pp. por. *OXB*
Poems for little people and those of larger growth; by J.R. Eastwood. London:
Simpkin, Marshall & Co. 1887. x, 182 pp. *OXB*
Poems for little people and those of larger growth; by J.R. Eastwood. London:
George Philip and Son. 1896. x, 182 pp. *UCD*

EATON, William Andrew. Of London.

Original readings and recitations, pathetic and humorous, in prose and verse; by W.A. Eaton. London: Islington Gazette Offices; Simpkin, Marshall, Hamilton, Kent, & Co. 1893. 70 pp. *★UCD*

Poems from the pavement; by W.A. Eaton. London: Islington Gazette Offices; Marshall Bros; H. Vickers. 1886. 64 pp. *★UCD*

EBBS, Ellen H.

The inner light, and other poems; by Ellen H. Ebbs. London: Digby, Long & Co. [1897]. viii, 44 pp. *OXB*

EBSWORTH, Joseph Woodfall (1824–1908). Brought up in Edinburgh, where his father kept a bookshop. After studying art, he was employed in Manchester by Faulkner Bros, lithographers. He contributed verse and prose to the Scottish press. Entered St John's College, Cambridge; BA 1864, MA 1867. Took Anglican orders, 1864; curate, Bradford, Yorkshire; vicar, Molash, Kent, 1871–94.

Cavalier lyrics: 'for church and crown'; by J.W. Ebsworth. London: Stephen Austin & Sons. 1887. xxxvi, 200 pp. il.

A limited ed. of 125 numbered copies printed for private circulation and signed by the author. *JRL*

ECHO, pseud.

Nouvelle noblesse: or, the cuckoo, chemical, coal, cotton and collops company, unlimited: [poems]; by Echo. [London]: John Bale & Sons. 1896. 65 pp. *OXB*

ECKERSLEY, Edmund Ryley, (E.R.E.),(One of Those Who Loves His Fellow Men, pseud.) (1857–). b. Bolton, Lancashire. Admitted a solicitor in 1879, practising in the town for many years. Served on Bolton town council, 1889–91; member of the board of guardians.

Human sympathy: a collection of rough blocks of verse; by "one of those who loves his fellow men" [E.R.E.]. Bolton: A. Green (Stead's). 1887. 67 pp.

'Published by express desire, and for private circulation only'. *BOP*

ECOSSAIS–ANGLAIS, pseud.

Lothian campaigns: a political exhibition: [poems]; by Ecossais–Anglais. Manchester: J.P. Muir & Co. 1885. xii, 109 pp. *NLS*

ECRITT, W.H. Taken from school and sent to work, aged nine. Lived at 18 Artillery Terrace, Guildford, Surrey.

Heart-throbs: [poems]; by W.H. Ecritt. London: Harrison & Sons. 1891. x, 114 pp. *OXB*

Poems: Lyrics for the crowd; and, Night musings; by W.H. Ecritt. London: Harrison & Sons. 1886. 117 pp. *OXB*

EDELSTEN, Jane (1818–   ). A married woman with children.
Sweet thoughts: [poems]; by Jane Edelstein. Printed London: Skeffington & Son. 1895. viii, 36 pp.
    Printed for private circulation.   *OXB*

EDMOND, Grand-Père, pseud. *see* **GRAND-PERE EDMOND**, pseud.

EDMONDS, Elizabeth Mayhew. Mrs Edmonds, née Waller.
Hesperas: rhythm and rhyme; by E.M. Edmonds. London: Kegan Paul, Trench & Co. 1883. vi, 166 pp.   *OXB*

EDMONDS, Mary, (M.E.). Of Stamford, Lincolnshire.
Poems; by M.E. [1896]. [viii], 159 pp. il., por.   *OXB*

EDWARDS, Basil (1847?-19   ). Educated at Gonville & Caius College, Cambridge; BA 1868, MA 1972. Ordained, 1869; curate, Trowbridge, Wiltshire, 1869–73, St Mary's, Gateshead, County Durham, 1873–74, St Ann's, Newton Heath, Manchester, 1874–75, Christ Church, Streatham, London, 1875–77; rector in Gloucestershire, at Blaisdon, 1877–89, and at Ashleworth from 1890.
Songs of a parish priest; by Basil Edwards. Orpington, Kent: George Allen. 1888. xvi, 141 pp.   *OXB*
    Also 2nd ed.   ★; 3rd ed. 1892.

EDWARDS, Griffith, (Gutyn Padarn) (1812–93). b. Llanberis, Caernarvonshire. Rev. MA, FRHS. Vicar of Llanyblodwel, Oswestry, Shropshire; appointed to Llandgadfen parish, Montgomeryshire, in 1863 but resigned in 1892 because of poor health. National Eisteddfod prizewinner. Died at Welshpool in retirement.
The works of the Rev. Griffith Edwards (Gutyn Padarn). Edited by Elias Owen. London: Elliot Stock. 1895. xx, 296 pp. il., por.   *NLW*

EDWARDS, James H., (Jim, pseud.). Of Byethorn.
Jingles; by "Jim". Printed Newcastle-upon-Tyne: Daily Journal Office. 1887. vi, 128 pp.   *NPL*

EDWARDS, Joseph, (Agriklar, pseud.). From the west of England. He emigrated to Willoughby, Ohio, United States.
Poems: humorous and philosophical; by Agriklar. New series. London: Griffith & Farran; Bristol: J.W. Arrowsmith. [1883]. [ii], 140 pp.   *OXB*
Poems: humorous and philosophical; by Agriklar. A new series with the latest additions. Bristol: John Wright & Co.; London: Houlston & Sons. [1887]. viii, 165 pp. por.   *BL*

EDWARDS, Matilda Betham- *see* **BETHAM-EDWARDS, Matilda**

EDWARDS, Robert John, (Edward Johns, pseud.) (1851?–19). Educated at Jesus College, Oxford; BA 1872. Ordained, 1874; curate, Caernarvon, 1873–76; vicar, Corris, Merionethshire, 1876–1907; rector, Llangefni with Tregaian, Anglesey, from 1907.
Welsh legends in humorous English verse; by Edward Johns. Aberystwyth: Evans Bros. 1899. 51 pp. *OXB*

EDWARDS, Thomas (1857–). b. Milnab, near Crieff, Perthshire, son of the miller. He left school in his fifteenth year, and was sent to learn the house-painting business. On finishing his apprenticeship he went to Edinburgh for a time then returned to Crieff. Contributed to the *Glasgow Herald, People's Friend*, etc.
Strathearn lyrics, and other poems; by Thomas Edwards. Paisley: Alexander Gardner; Crieff: David Philips. 1889. 178 pp.
 Spine-title is *Poems and lyrics. OXB*

EDWARDS, Thomas, Minister of Salem Chapel, Tunbridge Wells, Kent.
Nature-poems (and others); by Thomas Edwards. Printed Tunbridge Wells: Lewis Hepworth & Morriss, Ltd. 1893. [iv], 52 pp. *OXB*

EGERTON-WARBURTON, Rowland Eyes (1804–91). Educated at Eton College, and Corpus Christi College, Oxford. High sheriff of Cheshire, 1833. Lived at Arley Hall, Northwich
Twenty-two sonnets; by R.E. Egerton Warburton. With illustrations. London: Pickering & Co. 1883. [iv], 26 pp. il. *UCD*

ELAN, pseud.
Fleeting fancies: a collection of miscellaneous poems, to which are added, Charades and enigmas; by Elan. London: W.H. Beer & Co. 1886. 152 pp. *OXB*

ELDRYTH, Maud, pseud. *see* **NORWOOD, J.F.**, (Maud Eldryth, pseud.)

ELFED, pseud. *see* **LEWIS, Howell Elvet**, (Elfed)

ELIOT, George, pseud. *see* **EVANS, Mary Ann**, (George Eliot, pseud.)

ELIZABETH, pseud.
"Behold the man!": being the six-fold trial of Jesus Christ, Our Lord and saviour, with other shorter poems and hymns; [by Elizabeth]. London: James Nisbet & Co. [1888]. 110 pp. ("For Jesus' sake only" series, 1). *OXB*

ELLER, pseud. *see* **ELLERMAN, Anne Elizabeth**, (Eller, pseud.)

ELLER, Mrs Thorald
Verses; by Mrs Thorald Eller. London. 1897. 112 pp. *

ELLERMAN, Anne Elizabeth, (Eller, pseud.)
Ingatherings; by Eller. London: William Andrews & Co. 1897. viii, 184 pp.
Poetry and prose. BL

ELLIOT, Lady Charlotte (1839–80). Daughter of Sir James Carnegie, and sister of the 6th Earl of Southesk. She was married twice, in 1860 to T. Scrymsoure-Fothringham, and in 1868 to Frederick B. Elliot, son of Lord Minto.

Mary Magdalene, and other poems; by Lady Charlotte Elliot. Printed Edinburgh: For the Earl of Southesk. 1880. x, 80 pp.

Not published. A limited impression of 50 copies.   *BL*

ELLIOT, W. Scott- *see* **SCOTT-ELLIOT, W.**

ELLIOTT, Emily Steele (1836–97). b. Brighton, Sussex, daughter of Rev. Edward B. Elliott of St Mark's Church. She contributed hymns to several choir manuals, and edited the *Church Missionary Juvenile Instructor* for six years. Some of her hymns were published in *Under the Pillow*, a cheap, large-type hymn book for hospitals, infirmaries and the sick generally. Lived at 66 Mildmay Park, Ball's Pond Road, London N.

Glad voices: verses; by E.S. Elliott, from, Chimes of consecration. Arranged by E. St. B. Holland. London: James E. Hawkins; New York: Fleming H. Revell. [1890]. [18] pp. il., col, il.

Printed on card.   *CU*

You may pick the daisies; by E.S. Elliott. London: James E. Hawkins. [1890]. [20] pp. il.

Printed on card.   *CU*

ELLIOTT, Jane, pseud. *see* **RIGG, Caroline**, (Jane Elliott, pseud.)

ELLIOTT, Robinson

Treasures of the deep, and other poems; by Robinson Elliott. London: Elliot Stock. 1894. viii, 118 pp.   *OXB*

ELLIS, Edwin John. Artist, illustrator, and novelist.

Fate in Arcadia, and other poems; by Edwin J. Ellis. With illustrations by the author. London: Ward & Downey. 1892. x, 205 pp. il.   *OXB*

Seen in three days; written, drawn & tinted by Edwin J. Ellis. London: sold by Bernard Quaritch. 1893. [119] pp. il.

Printed on one side of leaf only.   *OXB*

When is your birthday?: a year of good wishes: a set of twelve designs; by Edwin J. Ellis. With sonnets by the artist. London Field & Tuer; Simpkin, Marshall & Co.; Hamilton, Adams & Co.; New York: Scribner & Welford. [1883]. [98] pp. il.   *OXB*

ELLIS, Frederick E. Possibly Frederick Edmund Ellis (1853–19) son of Frederick C. Ellis of Mortlake, Surrey. Educated at Westminster School, and Trinity College, Cambridge. Worked in the Foreign Office from 1872 until retirement in 1913. Re-appointed as a temporary clerk in 1917.

Sir Kenneth's wanderings: a poem; by Frederick E. Ellis. London: Digby, Long & Co. [1895]. 72 pp.   *OXB*

ELLIS, Frederick Startridge (1830–1901). Started a bookselling business in Covent Garden, 1860, moving to New Bond Street, 1872. Official buyer for the British Museum. Friend and publisher of William Morris, Rossetti and Ruskin. He edited the Huth library catalogue of books, 1880; compiled a concordance to the works of Shelley.

The history of Reynard the fox, his family, friends and associates, with glossarial notes in vulpine verse and an index-summary of chief matters contained in the story; written by F.S. Ellis. Devices by Walter Crane. London: David Nutt. 1894. x, 347 pp. il.

Spine-title is *Reynard the fox. OXB*

The history of Reynard the fox: his friends and his enemies, his crimes, hair-breadth escapes and final triumph: a metrical version of the old English translation, with glossarial notes in verse; by F.S. Ellis. With devices by Walter Crane. [New ed.]. London: David Nutt. 1897. xii, 290 pp. il. *OXB*

ELLIS, Lilith. Novelist.
Life echoes: poems; by Lilith Ellis. London: Thomas Murby. 1889. 91 pp. *UCD*

ELMY, Elizabeth Wolstenholme- *see* **WOLSTENHOLME-ELMY, Elizabeth**, (Ellis Ethelmer, pseud.)

ELPHINSTONE-DALRYMPLE, Charles (1817–91). Son of Sir Robert H. Elphinstone-Dalrymple of Logie-Elphinstone, Aberdeenshire. As a young man he served in a Guards regiment. Owned the estate of Glascoego, near Aberdeen, together with Kinnellar Lodge, where he lived. JP and deputy lieutenant, Aberdeenshire.
Lays, highland and lowland; by C. Elphinstone-Dalrymple. Aberdeen: John Rae Smith. 1885. [viii], 48 pp. *UCD*

ELSON, F. Clergyman.
Poems; by F. Elson. London: London Literary Society. [1885]. [vi], 56 pp. *OXB*

ELVYNDD *see* **KENWARD, Charles**, (Elvyndd)

EMERALD ISLE, pseud. *see* **HEPBURN, Duncan Dewar**, (Emerald Isle, pseud.)

EMERITUS, pseud.
Whims and fantasies: [poems]; by Emeritus. London: Remington & Co. 1887. 107 pp. *OXB*

EMERY, Alfred (1865–). Lobby correspondent, Press Association. Writer on chess, draughts and billiards. Lived at 43 Glenwood Avenue, Westcliff.
Orpheus, and other poems; by Alfred Emery. London: T. Fisher Unwin. 1885. viii, 116 pp. *UCD*

EMMA, Sister. Nun of the Community of Saint John the Baptist.
Lanterns unto our feet; and, Lights unto our path; by Sister Emma. With a preface by Florence Wilford. London: J. Masters & Co. 1891. 48 pp.   *OXB*

EMMOTT, James
A working man's verses; by James Emmott. London: Elliot Stock. 1896. 64 pp.   *OXB*

EMRA, Frances (1808–88). b. St George's, Gloucestershire, daughter of the vicar of Westbury, Somerset. She worked for the poor in the parish, and was known for her talented painting and fine needlework.
[Poems]; [by] Frances Emra, "a succourer of many". [Bristol?]. 1890. 43 pp. Printed for private circulation.   *BL*

EMSLEY, John. A Yorkshire village blacksmith.
Rural musings: [poems]; by John Emsley. Printed Skipton: Edmondson & Co. [1883]. xii, 152 pp. por.   *UCD*

EMSLEY, William, (Lionel Vulcan, pseud.). Lived at 2 Banstead Street, Roundhay, Leeds.
Avilantus, and other poems; by William Emsley (Lionel Vulcan). Printed Bradford: Thornton & Pearson. [1893]. 144 pp.   *LEP*

EMSLIE, John Philipps
New Canterbury tales: [poems]; by John Philipps Emslie. London: Griffith, Farran, Okeden, & Welsh. [1887]. [vi], 139 pp. il.   *OXB*

ENGLISHMAN, pseud.
English work and song, amid the forests of the south: being representations of old English patriotism and Roman domestic life, with other poems; by an Englishman. London: Sampson Low, Marston, Searle, & Rivington. 1882. xii, 280 pp.   *OXB*

ENGSTROM, H.S.
The steps of a good man, and other poems; by H.S. Engstrom. London: William Hunt & Co. 1886. 96 pp.   *OXB*

EPHZIBA, pseud. *see* **HOWELL, Annie**, (Ephziba, pseud.)

ERNEST, Count, pseud. *see* **THURSTAN, Frederick William**, (Count Ernest, pseud.)

ERRO, pseud.
The vale of Hermanli, and other poems; by Erro. London: Newman & Co. 1881. [iv], 90 pp.   *OXB*

ERSKINE, Francis Robert St Clair, Lord Rosslyn (1833–90). b. Dysart House, Fife, son of the 3rd Earl of Rosslyn. Educated at Eton College, and Merton College, Oxford. Styled Lord Loughborough, 1851–56. He joined the Coldstream Guards as an itinerant, going with them to Constantinople in 1854. Succeeded his father as 4th Earl in 1859, when he devoted his time to hunting, and formed a breeding stud at Easton Lodge.

Love that lasts forever: a jubilee lyric, dedicated by permission to the Queen on the fiftieth anniversary of her accession; by the Earl of Rosslyn. Edinburgh: William Blackwood & Sons. 1887. 20 pp.   *OXB*

Sonnets; by the Earl of Rosslyn. Edinburgh: William Blackwood. 1883. [vi], 116 pp.   *MPL*

Sonnets and poems; by the Earl of Rosslyn. London: Remington & Co. 1889. xviii, 314 pp.   *OXB*

Also 2nd ed. 1890.

ESCOTT, Hay Sweet (1818?–). Educated at Balliol College, Oxford; BA 1839, MA 1858. Headmaster of Somersetshire College, Bath. Rector, South Luffenham, Leicestershire, 1873–77, Kilve, Somerset, from 1877.

Poems of youth and age; by Hay Sweet Escott. Birmingham: C. Caswell; London: S.W. Partridge & Co. 1892. 89 pp.   *CU*

ESHER, Lord *see* **BRETT, Reginald Baliol**, Lord Esher

ESMONDE, Alice, pseud. *see* **RYAN, Margaret**, (Alice Esmonde, pseud.)

ESSDEE, pseud. *see* **DALE, Sarah**, (Essdee, pseud.)

ESTHER, pseud.

The hunted stag, and other poems; by 'Esther'. London: Robert Banks & Son. 1896. 160 pp.   *UCD*

ETA, pseud. *see* **BRIGGS, Edith M.**, (Eta, pseud.)

ETHEL, pseud.

The wandering angel, and other poems; by Ethel. Bedford: F. Hockliffe; London: Simpkin, Marshall, & Co. 1887. [ii], 58 pp.

Poetry and prose.   *OXB*

ETHELMER, Ellis, pseud. *see* **WOLSTENHOLME-ELMY, Elizabeth**, (Ellis Ethelmer, pseud.)

ETHYWIL MILLIWA, pseud. *see* **WHITLEY, William**, (Ethywil Milliwa, pseud.)

ETTRICK BARD *see* **PURDIE, David Walter**

EUGENIO, pseud.

The tale of the three tinkers; by Eugenio. With notes and a glossary. London: Remington & Co. 1880. 89 pp.   *OXB*

EUOE, pseud. *see* **MANSELL, Trevor, (Euoe,pseud.)**

EVANS, Margaret, (M.E.) (18 –93).
Dies dominica: being hymns and metrical meditations for each Sunday in the natural year; by Margaret Evans and Isabel Southall. London: Elliot Stock. 1897. viii, 112 pp.
　　Not joint authorship. *OXB*
Songs of Silura; to which is added, Fluvius lacrymarum; by M.E. and I.S. London: Elliot Stock; Birmingham: Cornish Bros. 1890. viii, 128 pp. *OXB*

EVANS, Mary Ann, (George Eliot, pseud.) (1819–80). b. Arbury Farm, near Nuneaton, Warwickshire, daughter of Robert Evans, a land agent. Her first twenty-one years were spent on the Arbury estate. Educated at schools in Attleboro, Nuneaton and Coventry, she showed early intellectual powers. After her father's death in 1849 she moved in with the freethinker Charles Bray and his wife Caroline. In 1851 she went to London to become editor of the *Westminster Review*. There she met Herbert Spencer and George Henry Lewes, and lived with Lewes from 1854 until his death in 1878. She married an old friend, John Cross, in 1880 but died in December of that year. A major novelist, the great popularity of whose books made her financially secure.
Complete poems; by George Eliot. With introductory notice by Matthew Browne. Special limited ed. With illustrations on Japan paper. Boston, [Mass.]: Estes & Lauriat. [1888]. 442 pp. il.
　　A limited ed. of 200 numbered copies. *BL*
The complete poetical works of George Eliot. Family ed. Fully illustrated with new wood-engravings. With border by J.D. Woodward. New York: Frederick A. Stokes & Brother. 1888. 272 pp. il., por. ("Family" poets, 3). *BL*

EVANS, William (1847–1918). Son of James Evans of Merthyr Tydfil, Glamorgan. Educated at Jesus College, Oxford. Student of Inner Temple, called to the Bar, 1874; member of the South Wales and Chester circuit.
Ballads of Wales, and other poems; by William Evans. London: C.F. Roworth. 1895. iv, 104 pp. *NLW*
Caesar Borgia: a tragedy, and other poems; by W. Evans. London: Maxwell & Son. 1888. viii, 223 pp. *OXB*
Caesar Borgia: a tragedy, and other poems; by William Evans. 2nd ed. Printed London: C.F. Roworth. 1890. viii, 223 pp.
　　Printed for the author. *NLW*

EVANUS THE SONG-SMITH, pseud.
Rhymes from a rhyming forge; by Evanus the song-smith. Birmingham: Cornish Bros. 1897. viii, 163 pp. *OXB*

EVENINGS WITH THE YOUNG: [poems]. London: G. Morrish. [1889]. 45 pp. il. *OXB*

EVERED POOLE, Eva L. Née Travers. Of Enfield House and Rockholme, Southampton.

Left alone with Jesus, and other poems; by Eva Travers Evered Poole. London: James Nisbet & Co. 1890. viii, 115 pp. *OXB*

"Lonely? No, not lonely", and other poems; by Eva L. Travers (Mrs. Evered Poole). 2nd ed. London: James Nisbet & Co. 1881. 133 pp. *OXB*
   Also 3rd ed. 1882.

EVEREST, John Payne. lived at 61 Grosvenor Road, London SW.

Poems on several occasions; by John Payne Everest. London: Author. [1893]. 72 pp.
   Cover-title is *Poems*. *BL*

EWEN, Robert. Kept a tweed clothing shop in Dennistoun, Glasgow. He became provost of Hawick, and a director of Hawick Savings Bank. Lived at 591 Alexander Parade, Glasgow.

A modern ballad on the reign of mammon and social and economical reform and people's thanks, with a glimpse into the coming century; by Robert Ewen. Glasgow: Wm. Love, W. & R. Holmes; W. Porteous & Co.; London: Houlston & Sons; Hawick: J.C. Goodfellow. 1894. 32 pp. *OXB*

EWING, Juliana Horatia (1841–85). b. Ecclesfield, Yorkshire, where her father, Dr Alfred Gatty, was vicar. In 1866 her mother, Margaret Gatty, started *Aunt Judy's Magazine*, in which many of her stories appeared. She married Major Alexander Ewing of the Army Pay Department in 1867, travelling around the world with him. On her mother's death in 1873 she helped to edit the magazine but eventually confined herself to her own story-writing. Her best known work is *Jackanapes*.

Blue red: or, the discontented lobster: his history related in verse; by Juliana Horatia Ewing. Pained in colours by R. Andre. London: Society for Promoting Christian Knowledge; New York: E. & J.B. Young. [1883]. 32 pp col. il. *BL*

Verses for children and songs for music; by Juliana Horatia Ewing. London: Society for Promoting Christian Knowledge; New York: E. & J.B. Young & Co. [1895]. 202 pp. il. *MPL*

EWING, T. Stirling. Writer on labour and socialism.

Rhymes of my youth; by T. Stirling Ewing. Manchester: John Heywood. 1888. 44 pp. *MPL*

EWING, William (1840–   ). b. Gardenside, Bridgeton, Glasgow. An engineer and boilermaker, he lost his sight in an accident at work.

Poems and songs; by William Ewing. Printed Glasgow: Robert Dawson. 1892. 32 pp. *OXB*

EX-MATERIALIST, pseud. *see* **BAKER, Charles**, (Ex-Materialist, pseud.)

EXUL, pseud. *see* **LE GALLIENNE, Richard,** (Exul, pseud.)

EYLES, Richard. Lived at 90 Elderfield Road, Clapton, London E.
A jubilee ode, and other poems; by Richard Eyles. London: [Author]. 1897. ii, 32
pp. *OXB*

EYRE, George (1862–   ). b. Govan, Renfrewshire. Educated at Glasgow
High School.
The lady of Ranza, and other poems; by George Eyre. Paisley: Alexander
Gardner. 1884. 101 pp. *OXB*
The sage of Thebes; by George Eyre. London: Elliot Stock. 1885. 57
pp. *OXB*

F

F., A. Of Harrogate, Yorkshire?
Poems; by A.F. Printed Harrogate: W. Dothie Dobson. 1891. iv, 48
pp. *LEP*

F., A.P.
The conceited sparrow of Neemuch: a conceit in four flights of fancy; by A.P.F.
London: Remington & Co. 1880. [iv], 72 pp. *OXB*

F., G.W.
"Day Dawn" praises: hymns and poems; by G.W.F. London: G. Morrish;
Edinburgh: J.S. Robertson; Dublin: Tract Depot. [1885]. xii, 175 pp. *OXB*
Midnight praises: being hymns and poems; by G.W.F. London: G. Morrish.
[1884?]. xii, 144 pp. *OXB*

F., H.M. *see* **FRERE, Helen M.,** (H.M.F.)

F., M.W. *see* **FAIRBURN, M.W.,** (M.W.F.)

F., S.
The Wesleyan Methodist class meeting; by S.F. London: E.W. Allen. 1882. iv, 51
pp. *OXB*

F., S.F.
Needless worries and needful strength: thoughts on Christian life and service:
[poems]; by S.F.F. With preface by H.C.G. Moule. London: Marshall Bros.
[1899]. [viii], 92 pp. *OXB*

F., W.
Fitzwilliam Square: a lawn tennis lay; [by] W.F. Dublin: Hodges, Figgis & Co.;
London: Simpkin, Marshall & Co. [1885]. [24] pp. il. (by Orpen).
Title from cover. Printed on one side of leaf only. *BL*

F., W.J. *see* **FERRAR, William John**. (W.J.F.)

FAED, pseud. *see* **WILSON, Arthur James**, (Faed, pseud.)

FAHY, Francis Arthur (1854–1935) b. Kinvara, County Galway. In 1873 he
went to London to work for the civil service. Founded two literary clubs in
Clapham which led to the formation of the London Irish Literary Society. A
native Irish speaker, he was president of the London Gaelic League.
Irish songs and poems; by Francis A. Fahy. Dublin: M. H. Gill & Son. 1887. iv,
126 pp. *OXB*

FAIRBURN, Margaret Waters, (M.W.F.) (1825–   ). b. Selkirk, née Waters.
Her father worked for the Duke of Buccleuch at Bowhill. In 1844 she married
a Mr Fairburn, who was successively a factory worker in Selkirk, a baker in
Edinburgh, and in the railway service in Perthshire. Eventually they separated
and she returned to the paternal home with her children. Her father was then
keeper of Melrose Abbey, and she became his assistant, appointed keeper on
his death in 1882.
"Songs in the night"; by M.W.F. London: Thomas Bosworth ; Edinburgh:
John Menzies & Co. 1885. viii, 195 pp. *BL*

FAIRCLOUGH, T.S. Of Patricroft, Lancashire.
Squibs and crackers, in verse or worse (partly in the Lancashire dialect); by T.S.
Fairclough. Patricroft: Author. 1895. 96 pp. *OXB*

FAIRLEY, Cessford Ramsay Sawyers (1868–   ). b. Leith, Midlothian.
Received a general education at Links Place School. He entered the postal
service as a telegraph messenger, eventually becoming a postman in Edinburgh. Had connections with several volunteer corps, attaining the rank of
sergeant. Known as 'The Postman Bard'. Lived at 9 Henderson Street, Leith.
Poems and songs; by Cessford R.S. Fairley. Printed Leith: Gardner Bros. 1890.
76 pp. por.
Printed for the author. *OXB*

FAIRLEY, Robert. Lived at Dovemount Place, then at 29 Dickson Street, Hawick, Roxburghshire. Sometimes wrote in Shetland dialect.
Poems and songs; by Robert Fairley. Printed Hawick: R. Deans & Co. 1881. [vi], 141 pp. *BL*
Teviotside musings: being 2nd ed. of Poems and songs; by Robert Fairley. Printed Hawick: R. Deans & Co. 1892. 176 pp. por.
Poetry and prose. *BL*

FAIRLIE, Marcus
Flicks and flings at men and things, [and other poems]; by Marcus Fairlie. [1889]. 16 pp. *OXB*

FAIRMAN, Edward Saint John. Miscellaneous writer. MRAS. Lived at 31 Bryanston Street, Portman Square, London W.
Philanthropy in 1886: a word of warning to the truly benevolent: four poems . . . ; by Edward Saint John Fairman. London: Author. 1886. 32 pp.
Title from cover. *BL*

The **FAIRY BALLAD BOOK**. London: George Bell & Sons. 1891. [x], 92 pp. *OXB*

FALCONER, Alexander. b. Glasgow but spent his early childhood on Bute. In his thirteenth year he became an assistant in an apothecary's shop, leaving to become involved with reformatory and industrial schools. After working in Ireland and England he returned to Glasgow in 1879 to become head of Mossbank Industrial School, the largest of its kind in Scotland.
Scottish pastorals and ballads, and other poems; by Alexander Falconer. Glasgow: William Hodge & Co. 1894. viii, 114 pp. *OXB*

FALKNER, Robert Henry. Educated at Trinity College, Dublin; BA 1851, MA 1867. Curate, Loose, Kent; rural dean, New Chapel, Cashel, County Tipperary; rector, Woodham Walter, Maldon, Essex, from 1875.
Fancies on facts, and other poems; by R.H. Falkner. London: Eden, Remington & Co. 1891. [viii], 324 pp. *OXB*

FANCHON, pseud.
Work-a-day poems; by Fanchon. London: Reveirs Bros. 1895. 119 pp. **UCD*

FANE, Violet, pseud. *see* **CURRIE, Mary Montgomerie**, Lady, Violet Fane, pseud.)

FANSHAWE, Reginald (1855–19   ). b. Lanchester, County Durham, son of Rev. John Fanshawe. Educated at Repton School, and New College, Oxford (scholar); BA 1877, MA 1878. Fellow of New College, 1877–80. Professor of classics, University College, Bristol, 1879–1902. Lived latterly at Boars Hill House, Boars Hill, Oxford.
Two lives: a poem; by Reginald Fanshawe. London: George Bell & Sons. 1894. xxxii, 180 pp. *OXB*

FARGUS, Frederick John, (Hugh Conway, pseud.) (1847-85). b. Bristol, son of an auctioneer. He was partly educated in the school frigate *Conway* with a view to a career at sea but family pressure directed him to accountancy. In 1868 he took over the family business on the death of his father. A novelist, his novel *Called Back* became a world-wide success. He valued and catalogued the Strawberry Hill collection, Twickenham.

Lays and lyrics; by Hugh Conway. London: Patey & Willis; Hamilton, Adams, & Co. [1887]. 53 pp. *UCD

FARMER, J.W.

The crucifixion of Our Lord Jesus Christ: being a detailed account of all that might have taken place, from the arrest of Christ until He was laid in the sepulchre, also a history of the creation and the fall of man and why man was ordained to fall; the result thereof being, a complete revelation of the attributes of God: a poem; by J.W. Farmer. London: Digby, Long & Co. [1892]. xxxii, 269 pp. il. OXB

FARQUHAR, Sir Robert Townsend- *see* **TOWNSEND-FARQUHAR, Sir Robert**

FARRER, Georgiana

Miscellaneous poems; by Georgiana Farrer. London: S.W. Partridge & Co. 1883. xii, 356 pp. BL

FARRIE, Hugh. Son of James Farrie of Liverpool. A journalist, he trained at the *Daily Post*, becoming chief leader writer; he resigned to purchase and manage the *Porcupine* and the *Citizen*. An active and influential Liberal worker, he was chairman of the Junior Reform Club. He published several novels and an inquiry into the conditions of the poor in Liverpool.

Imperia, and other prolusions in verse; by Hugh Farrie. Liverpool: Henry Young & Sons. 1899. viii, 88 pp. NLW

FARROW, George Edward. Writer of stories for children.

The king's gardens: an allegory; by G.E. Farrow. Illustrations by A.L. Bowley. London: Hutchinson & Co. 1896. 43 pp. OXB

FAUSTINETTI, Homer Michael, pseud. *see* **BENNETT, Samuel Rowe**, (Homer Michael Faustinetti, pseud.)

FAUVETTE, pseud. *see* **DEAS, Elizabeth Ann**, (Fauvette, pseud.)

FAWCETT, Caroline Elizabeth

Peace, and other poems; by Caroline Elizabeth Fawcett. Printed Edinburgh: Robert R. Sutherland. 1894. 95 pp. por. *UCD

FAWCETT, Edward Douglas (1866–1960). b. Hove, Sussex, son of E. Boyd Fawcett. Educated at Newton College, South Devon, and Westminster School. Interested in mountaineering and winter sports, he made the only recorded ascent to the Mer de Glace from Chamonix up the mule path in a motor car.

The curse of Edelbrock: or, the Viking's doom: a Norse legend of Viking tradition and adventure, in two cantos; by E.D. Fawcett. London: National Publishing Co. [1895?]. 59 pp.   **UCD*

The wrath of Ana: a poem, written during school days; [by] E.D. Fawcett. London: Hamilton, Adams & Co.; Teignmouth: Geo. Bull, [1880]. 54 pp.   *OXB*

FAY, Gerda, pseud. *see* **GEMMER, Caroline M.**, (Gerda Fay, pseud.)

FEARNLEY, Harriet Ann
Crumbs from the Master's table: [poems]; by Rachel Jane and Harriet Ann Fearnley. Printed Bradford: T. Brear & Co., Ltd. 1899. 92 pp.
   Not joint authorship.   *OXB*

FEARNLEY, Rachel Jane
Crumbs from the Master's table: [poems]; by Rachel Jane and Harriet Ann Fearnley. Printed Bradford: T. Brear & Co., Ltd. 1899. 92 pp.
   Not joint authorship.   *OXB*

FELIX THE OUTCAST, pseud.
Smoke clouds: a "medley of fancies": [poems]; by Felix the outcast & Horace the rustic. Edited by Horace. Leicester: W.H. Lead. 1883. [32] pp.
   Not joint authorship.   *OXB*

FELLOWS, Frank P. Writer on the metric system of weights and measures. FSA, FSS. Knight of Grace of the Order of Saint John of Jerusalem.
Poems: In memoriam, &c.; The Knights Hospitalers of Saint John of Jerusalem . . .; by Frank P. Fellows. Composed, designed, etched, lithographed and printed by F.P. Fellows for private circulation. [c. 1885]. viii, 214 pp. il., por.
   A few copies only, printed for friends.   *OXB*
Poems: In memoriam &c.; The Knights Hospitalers of of[sic] Saint John of Jerusalem; Acre; Cyprus; Rhodes & Malta . . .; by Frank P. Fellows. Composed, designed, etched, lithographed and printed by F.P. Fellows for private circulation. [1890?]. [464] pp. il., por.
   Printed mainly in facsim. of author's handwriting.   *BL*

FENTON, Charles O'Connor
The legend of the alchemist, and other poems; by Charles O'Connor Fenton. Printed Newcastle, Staffs.: B.J. Skerratt. 1897. 61 pp.
   A limited ed. of 100 copies.   **UCD*

FENTON, George Livingston (1813–). b. Cumberland. Educated at Trinity College, Dublin; BA 1835, MA 1869. Ordained 1837; curate, Cheadle, Staffordshire, 1837; curate, then vicar, Lilleshall, Shropshire, 1837–47; chaplain on the Bombay Ecclesiastical Establishment, 1847–66; chaplain, San Remo, Italy, 1869–85.

The canary, and other poems; by George Livingstone Fenton. Derby: Frank Murray; London: S.E. Stanesby. 1891. [xii], 66 pp.
    A limited small paper ed. of 140 copies, 130 of which are for sale. *OXB*

FENTON, K.

An Easter memory; [by K. Fenton]. Printed London: Edmund Evans. [1889]. [18] pp.
    Printed on one side of leaf only. *OXB*
An Easter memory; by K. Fenton. 2nd ed. London: Elliot Stock. 1892. [21] pp.
    Printed on one side of leaf only. *OXB*
Old memories of passing clouds: [poems]; by K. Fenton. London: Elliot Stock. 1891. [47] pp.
    Printed on one side of leaf only. *OXB*

FERGUSON, George

Our earth-night to twilight; by George Ferguson. London: T. Fisher Unwin. 1892. 2 vols. *OXB*
Our earth-night to twilight; by George Ferguson. 2nd ed. London: Simpkin, Marshall, Hamilton, Kent & Co., Ltd. [1899]. xx, 407 pp. *OXB*

FERGUSON, Robert (1817–98). Son of Joseph Ferguson, MP for Carlisle, 1852–57. A partner in the firm of Ferguson Bros, cotton manufacturers of Carlisle. Major, 1st battalion, Cumberland Rifle Volunteers, 1868–72. Twice mayor of Carlisle, and MP for Carlisle, 1874–86. He presented his collection of five hundred items relating to Cumberland and Westmorland to the museum in Tullie House. Lived at Morton House, Cummersdale. FSA

Dulcissima! Dilectissima!: a passage in the life of an antiquary, with some other subjects in prose and verse; by Robert Ferguson. With frontispiece by Margaret Dicksee. London: Elliot Stock. 1898. xii, 107 pp. il. *MPL*

FERGUSON, Sir Samuel (1810–86). b. Belfast of parents of Scottish extraction. Educated at the Academical Institution, Belfast, and Trinity College, Dublin, but never graduated. Called to the Irish Bar, 1838, and practised with success, becoming a QC, 1859. He was appointed deputy keeper of the newly created Irish Records Office, 1867; knighted, 1878. President, Royal Irish Academy, 1882.

The forging of the anchor: a poem; by Sir Samuel Ferguson. Illustrated by A. Barraud [and others]. London: Cassell & Co., Ltd. 1883. [50] pp. il.
    Printed on one side of leaf only. *TCD*
Lays of the red branch; by Sir Samuel Ferguson. With an introduction by Lady Ferguson. London: T. Fisher Unwin; Dublin: Sealy, Bryers & Walker. 1897. xxviii, 161 pp. (New Irish library). *OXB*

Poems; by Sir Samuel Ferguson. Dublin: William McGee; London: George Bell & Sons. 1880. [x], 168 pp.   *OXB*

FERGUSON, Thomas Owens (Tom). A relative of Sir Samuel Ferguson.
Ballads and dreams; by Tom Ferguson. London: Kegan Paul, Trench & Co. 1885. x, 168 pp.   *OXB*

FERGUSON, Tom *see* **FERGUSON, Thomas Owens** (Tom)

FERGUSSON, Isa Gillon
Parables in song, and other pieces; by Isa Gillon Fergusson. London: James Nisbet & Co. 1889. 126 pp.   *OXB*

FERGUSSON, Robert Menzies (1859–   ). Son of Rev. Samuel Fergusson, minister of Fortingall, Perthshire. Educated at the public school at Stanley, Edinburgh University, and St Mary's College, St Andrews. Contributed to the *Fifeshire Journal* and other periodicals.
The Viking's bride, and other poems; by R. Menzies Fergusson. Paisley: Alexander Gardner. 1896. 103 pp.   *OXB*
A village poet; by R. Menzies Fergusson. Paisley: Alexander Gardner. 1897. 185 pp. il.
   Poetry and prose.   *OXB*

FERGUSSON, Thomas. Of Dumbarton.
Walter Graeme: or, a home among the hills, and other poems; by Thomas Fergusson. Paisley: J. & R. Parlane; Edinburgh: John Menzies & Co.; London: Houlston & Sons. 1898. 191 pp.   *OXB*

FERNIE, John
In Ashover valley: a volume of verse; by John Fernie. Printed Derby: Frank Murray. 1899. [viii], 96 pp.
   Privately printed for the author.   *OXB*

FERNLEAF, pseud.
Gleanings; from, Thoughtland: [poems]; by 'Fernleaf'. London: Digby, Long & Co. 1893. viii, 192 pp.   *OXB*

FERRAR, William John, (W.J.F.) (1868–   ). b. Navestock, Essex, son of William G. Ferrar. Educated at Brentwood School, and Hertford College, Oxford (scholar); Newdigate prizewinner, 1891.
Fritillaries: a book of verse; by W.J.F. Oxford: B.H. Blackwell; London: Simpkin, Marshall & Co. 1892. 57 pp.   *OXB*

FEWKES, Charlotte Louisa
The royal album of great names: a jubilee offering to her most gracious majesty Queen Victoria: [poems]; by Charlotte Louisa Fewkes. Printed London: Eyre & Spottiswoode. [1889]. 48 pp. por.   *BL*

FFOULKES, L. Florence. Mrs Ffoulkes, née Wynne.
Short poems in sunlight and shade; by L. Florence Ffoulkes. London: Field & Tuer; Simpkin, Marshall & Co.; Hamilton, Adams & Co.; New York: Scribner & Welford. [1887]. 117 pp. *OXB*

FIELD, Michael, pseud. *see* **BRADLEY, Katherine Harris**, & **COOPER, Edith Emma**, (Michael Field, pseud.).

FIFE PAGANINI *see* **BURGESS, Alexander**, (Poute, pseud.)

FIFE-COOKSON, John Cookson (1844–1911). Son of William H. Fife of Wark, Northumberland. He adopted the additional name Cookson on succeeding to the estate of his grandfather, John Cookson. Educated privately, and at Sandhurst, entering the army in 1864; served in New Zealand, 1865; military attaché at Constantinople, 1877; accompanied the Turkish armies in the Balkan campaign; resigned 1879 with rank of lieutenant-colonel. JP and deputy lieutenant for County Durham, he contested the parliamentary seat of Scarborough for the Conservatives, 1880. Lived at Lee Hall, Wark.
A dream of other days: a romantic poem; by Lieut.-Colonel Fife-Cookson. London: Kegan Paul, Trench, Trübner, & Co., Ltd. 1891. [viii], 95 pp. *OXB*
The empire of man: an essay in verse, together with other poems; by Lieut.-Colonel Fife Cookson. London: Kegan Paul, Trench & Co. 1889. vi, 62 pp. *OXB*
Man and the deity: (an essay in verse), together with other poems; by Lieut.-Colonel Fife Cookson. London: Kegan Paul, Trench, Trübner & Co., Ltd. 1890. 46 pp. *OXB*

FINCH, Constance
The vision of a beginner, and other poems; by Constance Finch. London: Digby, Long & Co. 1892. viii, 88 pp. *OXB*

FINDLATER, Mary Williamina (1865–1963). b. Lochearnhead, Perthshire, daughter of Rev. Eric J. Findlater, and sister of Jane Helen. Educated privately, neither sister married; they set up home together at The Roundel Gate, Rye, Sussex. A novelist, Mary lived latterly at Four Hollies, Comrie, Perthshire.
Sonnets and songs; by M.W. Findlater. London: David Nutt. 1895. 57 pp. *OXB*

FINDLAY, John Haddow (1849–95). b. Kilmarnock, Ayrshire, and educated there at Mr Gunion's school. Aged thirteen he was apprenticed to the ironmongery trade, then worked as a commercial traveller for his father, a biscuit maker. He transferred to Messrs Gray, Dunn & Co., one of the oldest firms in the biscuit trade, working in south-west Scotland. Lived at Clyde Villa, Kilmarnock.
Prose and poetry; by the late John Haddow Findlay. Kilmarnock: J. Scott. 1899. xiv, 168 pp. por. *NLS*

FINLAYSON, John, (J.F. Layson, pseud.). Of Newcastle upon Tyne.
The haunted library; a Novocastrian reminiscence; by J.F. Layson. With illustrations by Thos. Mackay. Newcastle-on-Tyne: Tyne Publishing Co., Ltd; Mawson, Swan, & Morgan. 1880. 42 pp. il.
 Printed on one side of leaf only.   *NPL*

FISHER, Ada Gertrude
A tribute of praise: selected poems; by Ada Gertrude Fisher. London: James Nisbet & Co., Ltd. 1898. viii, 87 pp.   *OXB*

FISHER, Fanny. b. North of Ireland, née Lindsay. Married a Dr Fisher of Limerick. A novelist, she lived in Chelsea, London, for some years.
Poems; by Fanny Fisher. London: T. Fisher Unwin. 1889. xvi, 563 pp.   *TCD*
Poems and notes descriptive of Killarney, with dedication; by Fanny Fisher. London: T. Fisher Unwin. 1890. 64 pp.   *TCD*

FISHER, Francis H. Of West Kensington, London.
The burglars; by Francis H. Fisher. Printed West Kensington: F.L. Elson. [1892]. 16 pp.   *OXB*

FISHER, Lala (1872–1929)
A twilight teaching, and other poems; by Lala Fisher. London: T. Fisher Unwin. 1898. x, 176 pp.   *OXB*

FISHER, Richard Trott (1805–85). Son of Rev. Edmund Fisher, vicar of Linton, Cambridgeshire. Educated at Felstead School, and Pembroke College, Cambridge. Fellow of Pembroke College, 1829–37. Called to the Bar, Lincoln's Inn, 1829.
The work of Richard Trott Fisher, uniformly printed in four volumes. London: Pickering & Co. 1881. 4 vols.   *OXB*

FISHER, Robert *see* **FISHER, Robert M'Kenzie**

FISHER, Robert M'Kenzie (1840–). b. Prestwick, Ayrshire, son of a handloom weaver. He attended school at Maybole and Prestwick. Aged eleven he entered the weaving trade, then hired himself to a farmer. He went out to Africa as a wheelwright's apprentice, returning home to work in Govan and Renfrew, eventually becoming a bookseller in Friars' Vennel, Dumfries. A noted antiquarian.
Poems, songs, and sketches; by R. M'Kenzie Fisher. 3rd ed. Ayr: Ayrshire Post, Ltd; Author. 1898. [viii], 210 pp. por.
 Cover-title is *Poems and sketches*.   *OXB*
Poetical sparks; by Robert Fisher. Glasgow: Menzies & Co.; Dumfries: Author. 1881. 152 pp.   *EPL*
 Also 2nd ed. 1881.

FITCH, Walter. Botanical illustrator. Of Great Yarmouth, Norfolk.
Poems in spare moments; by Walter Fitch. Great Yarmouth: Author. 1892. 280 pp. *UCD

FITZACHARY, John Christopher (1840–1902). b. Duncannon, County Wexford. An auctioneer by profession, and self-styled 'Professor of Poetry', he contributed to many Irish periodicals. Lived at Rathgar, Dublin.
The bridal of Drimna, and other poems, legendary, patriotic, sentimental, and humorous; by John Christopher Fitzachary. Author's complete ed. Dublin: Sealy, Bryers & Walker. 1883. viii, 191 pp. *OXB*
The bridal of Drimna, and other poems; to which is added, The fall of Mustapha: an oriental romaunt; by John Christopher Fitzachary. New and complete [2nd] ed., revised and enlarged. Dublin: James Duffy & Sons. 1884. xii, 200 pp. *BL*
Legends, lays and lyrics: national and miscellaneous; by John Christopher Fitzachary. Author's complete ed. Dublin: Sealy, Bryers & Walker. 1887. [2], x, 272 pp. *OXB*

FITZ GERALD, Caroline. Afterwards Filippi.
Venetia victrix, and other poems; by Caroline Fitz Gerald. London: Macmillan & Co. 1889. [viii], 73 pp. *BL*

FITZGERALD, Edward (1809–83). b. Bradfield House, near Woodbridge, Suffolk, of Irish parents. Educated at King Edward VI School, Bury St Edwards, and Trinity College, Cambridge. At Trinity he formed lifelong friendships with Tennyson and Thackeray. A scholar of means with an interest in oriental poetry, he made fine translations from the Greek, Spanish and Persian. He lived a quiet life in various parts of Sussex.
Letters and literary remains of Edward Fitzgerald. Edited by William Aldis Wright. In three vols. London: Macmillan & Co. 1889. 3 vols. il., por.
Vol. I contains only prose. *OXB*
Occasional verses; by Edward Fitzgerald. Privately printed. 1891.

FITZGERALD, R.F. b. near Waterford, Ireland. He became a Christian Brother, making his novitiate in Preston, Lancashire; taught for many years at Francis Street, Dublin.
Roderick and Eva: a ballad romance of the cloister; by R.F. Fitzgerald and J. Manning. London: J. Manning. 1892. 32 pp. *BL*

FITZ-GERALD, Shafto Justin Adair (1859–19). b. Clifton, Bristol, of Irish parents, his father being Captain Thomas J. Fitz-Gerald. Educated privately. A novelist, dramatist and song writer, he wrote several pantomimes and children's plays; a prolific contributor to the press, writing for nearly every London daily newspaper. Member of the Playgoers' Club. Lived latterly at 8 Lancaster Gate, Bowes Park, London N.
Ballads of a Bohemian; by S.J. Adair Fitz-Gerald. London: Alfred Boot & Son. [1893]. xii, 194 pp. *OXB*

FITZPATRICK, John (1859–1929). Roman Catholic priest. Writer on religious topics.

Virgo praedicanda: verses in Our Lady's praise; by John Fitzpatrick. Dublin: Gill. 1898. 41 pp. *UCD*

FITZPATRICK, R.H. A merchant tailor with a business in Dame Street, Dublin, for a time. He moved to England, living at Stratford-upon-Avon, Warwickshire, where he edited *The Shrine*.

Lyrics; by R.H. Fitzpatrick. London: W. Stewart & Co. [1895]. 88 pp. *UCD*

FLAMMAN, Alere, pseud. *see* **ALERE FLAMMAN**, pseud.

FLANAGAN, Edward. A farmer near Enniskillen, County Fermanagh. Known as 'The Poet of the Moy'.

The poems of the late Edward Flanagan. Edited by Peter Magennis. Printed Enniskillen: Wm. Trimble. 1884. 64 pp.
    Includes poems by the editor. *OXB*

FLANAGAN, Jonathan. Lived at 3 Langdale Street, Liverpool.

Weavings in leisure hours: [poems]; by Jonathan Flanagan. Liverpool: [Author]. 1886. 120 pp. *OXB*

FLETCHER, Joseph Smith (1863–1935). b. Halifax, Yorkshire, son of Rev. John Fletcher of Hurstbourne. Educated privately. He worked as a journalist in London before becoming leader writer for the *Leeds Mercury*. A prolific general writer, particularly on Yorkshire matters, he wrote novels, adventure stories for boys, and contributed to leading magazines.

Anima Christi; by J.S. Fletcher. Bradford: J.S. Fletcher & Co. 1884. [vi], 123 pp. *OXB*

Anima Christi; by J.S. Fletcher. New ed. London: Robert Washbourne. 1887. [vi], 109 pp. *OXB*

Ballads of revolt; by J.S. Fletcher. London: John Lane, The Bodley Head. 1897. [vi], 44 pp. *OXB*

Deus homo, [and other poems]; by J.S. Fletcher. London: Robert Washbourne. 1887. xvi, 59 pp. *OXB*

Early poems; by Joseph Smith Fletcher. London: William Poole. 1882. viii, 72 pp. *CU*

Early poems; by J.S. Fletcher. New ed. Leeds: Author. 1885. viii, 71 pp. *NUC*

One of his little ones, and other tales in prose and verse; by J.S. Fletcher. London: Robert Washbourne. 1888. *EC*

Poems, chiefly against pessimism; by J.S. Fletcher. London: Ward & Downey. 1893. 56 pp. *OXB*

Songs after sunset; by Joseph S. Fletcher. London: William Poole. 1881. 62 pp.   *OXB*

FLETCHER, Walter (18 –85)
Occasional verses; by Walter Fletcher. Printed London: Richard Clay & Sons. 1885. [iv], 135 pp.   *OXB*

FLEUR L'EPINE, pseud.
Prometheus, and other poems; by Fleur L'Epine. 7th ed. Printed Birmingham: Oliver J. Packman. 1896. 54 pp.   *BL*

FLINT, Violet, pseud. *see* **THOMSON, J.E.**, (Violet Flint, pseud.)

FLITTON, James
Ellen of the isle: a new poem; by James Flitton. London: Thomas Laurie. 1890. 384 pp.   *OXB*

FLYNN, J.A., (Successor of Man, pseud.)
The last Christian: an epic poem; by a successor of man. Dover: W.A. Smeeth. [1883]. [iv], 36 pp.
    Printed and published for the author.   *BL*

FOLLIOTT, Thomas. Of Holford, Somerset.
The temple of man: [poems]; by Thomas Folliott. London: Elliot Stock. 1892. [viii], 121 pp.   *OXB*
The vision of a passion, and other poems; by Thomas Folliott. London: Wyman & Sons. 1887. [vi], 110 pp.   *OXB*

The FOLLY OF KING CANDAULES: A LAY OF THE ANCIENT WORLD. Kingston-upon-Hull: Leng & Co. [1880?]. 15 pp.   *BL*

FONBLANQUE, Ethel Maud De *see* **DE FONBLANQUE, Ethel Maud**

FOOTT, Mary Hannay (1846–1918). b. Scotland. She spent some time in Australia. Mrs Foott.
Morna Lee, and other poems; by Mary Hannay Foott. 2nd ed. London: Gordon & Gotch. 1890. [viii], 72 pp.   *TCD*

FORBES, Lavinia C.M. Scottish novelist.
The Harringtons; and, Select poetry; by Lavinia C.M. Forbes. Printed Glasgow: Pickering & Inglis. 1894. [ii], 171 pp.   *BL*

FORD, Ford Madox, (Fenil Haig, pseud.) (1873–1939). Born Ford Madox Hueffer, son of music critic Dr Francis Hueffer, and grandson of the artist Ford Madox Brown. Educated at University College School, London. Author and critic, he founded the *English Review*, 1908, and the *Transatlantic Review*, 1924. He served in France in the First World War. Changed his name in 1919. Afterwards he was a member of the literary circle that included Ernest Hemingway and Ezra Pound.
The questions at the well, with sundry other verses for notes of music; by Fenil Haig. London: Digby, Long & Co. 1893. viii, 69 pp.   *OXB*

FORDE, Gertrude. Novelist.
 Stray thoughts in verse; by Gertrude Forde. Cheltenham: J.J. Banks. 1895. [ii],
128 pp.   *OXB*

FOREMAN, Stephen R. Novelist, and contributor of verse to periodicals.
Lived at 3 Redclyffe, Western Road, Cork.
 The city of crimson walls, and other poems; by Stephen Foreman. London: Kegan
Paul, Trench, Trübner & Co., Ltd. 1895. [vi] 156 pp.   *OXB*
 A vision of the orient; by S.R. Foreman. London: Digby & Long. [1889]. vi,
282 pp.   *OXB*

FORMAN, Alfred (1840–1925). Brother of the writer Harry Buxton
Forman. A man of letters, he translated Wagner's operas, and Victor Hugo's
plays. Lived at 49 Comeragh Road, West Kensington, London W.
 Sonnets; by Alfred Forman. Printed London: Chiswick Press. 1886. [viii], 50
pp.
    A limited ed. of 50 numbered copies printed for private circulation
only.   *OXB*

FORSHAW, Charles Frederick (1863–19). b. Bilston, Staffordshire, but
lived in Bradford, Yorkshire, from childhood. He qualified as a dentist and
was soon established as a senior partner in a well-known practice; senior dental
surgeon to Bradford Dental Hospital, he also held other consultancies.
President of the West Riding Literary Society, and a Fellow of several learned
societies. He collected a large library of Yorkshire poetry.
 A legend of St. Bees, and other poems; by Chas. F. Forshaw. London: Simpkin,
Marshall, Hamilton, Kent & Co.; Bradford: Thornton & Pearson; G.B.
Russell; Enniskillen: Trimble; Saint Bees: R.W. Broomfield; Malton: G.J.
Jones. 1891. 245 pp.   *LEP*
 Poems; by Chas. F. Forshaw. Bradford: Percy Lund & Co.; G.B. Russell;
London: Trübner & Co.; Manchester: John Heywood. [1889]. 304 pp.   *OXB*
 Poems; by Chas. F. Forshaw. Bradford: Percy Lund & Co.; County Press;
G.B. Russell; London: Trübner & Co.; Manchester: John Heywood. [1899].
304 pp.   *LEP*
 Seaside sonnets; by Chas. F. Forshaw. Printed Bradford: Thornton & Pearson.
1893. [18] pp. il.   *LEP*
    Also small paper ed. 1893.
 Thoughts in the gloaming: a collection of poems; composed by Chas. F. Forshaw.
Printed Bradford: T. Brown. 1887. 56 pp. por.   *BL*
 Wanderings of imagery: a collection of original poems; by Charles Frederick
Forshaw. Printed Bradford: J. Woodhead. 1886. 72 pp. por.   *BL*

FORSITH, Nat. Editor of *Everybody's Christmas Annual*.
 Jingo jottings; and, "The last round"; by Nat Forsith. London: Literary
Production Committee. [1880?]. [32] pp. il.   *OXB*

FORSTER, William (1818–82). b. Madras, India. He went to Australia, became a 'squatter' but subsequently entered political life. A member of several administrations, in 1876 he was appointed agent-general in London for New South Wales.

Midas; by the late William Forster. London: Kegan Paul, Trench & Co. 1884. [vi], 205 pp. *UCD*

FORSYTH, Robert

Fledgling flights: [poems]; by Robert Forsyth. Glasgow: Morison Bros. 1887. viii, 120 pp. *UCD*

FORSYTH, William, (William o' ye West, pseud.) (1818–89). b. Earlston, Berwickshire, he became a pupil-teacher at his local school. When his parents moved to Galashiels, Selkirkshire, he entered one of the woollen mills as a spinner. He left to become a hotel-keeper in Edinburgh, then moved to Aberdeen to establish Forsyth's Hotel; in 1863 settled in the Cobden Hotel, Glasgow. For many years he enjoyed a wide circle of artistic and literary friends.

A lay of Lochleven; by William o' ye West. Glasgow: Robert Forrester. 1887. 108 pp. il., por. *UCD*

FORTUNE, Alexander A. (1867–82). Of Muircambus, Fife.

Fragments: [poems]; by Alexander A. Fortune. Printed Anstruther: Lewis Russell. 1882. 24 pp.
    Printed for private circulation. *OXB*

FOSKETT, Edward. Editor of *The Readers' Monthly*. Of London.

Hugh Trebarwith: a Cornish romance; by Edward Foskett. Illustrated. London: T. Fisher Unwin. [1899]. 57 pp. il. *OXB*

Poems; by Edward Foskett. London: Kegan Paul, Trench & Co. 1886. xii, 306 pp. *OXB*

The window in the rock: a Cornish tale in verse; by Edward Foskett. London: Simpkin, Marshall & Co. 1888. 22 pp. *OXB*

FOSTER, Eleanor. Irish, of a Queen's County family.

With the tide, and other poems; by Eleanor Foster. London: Gay & Bird. 1896. x, 96 pp. *OXB*

FOSTER, Mrs John *see* **FOSTER, R.**

FOSTER, R. Wife of John Foster of Selby, Yorkshire.

Spirit footprints, [and other poems]; by Mrs. John Foster. London: James Nisbet & Co. 1884. xiv, 232 pp. *OXB*

FOSTER, Will

The fallen city, and other poems; by Will Foster. Edinburgh: William Blackwood & Sons. 1892. xii, 215 pp. *OXB*

The legend of Lohengrin, and other poems; by Will Foster. London: T. Fisher Unwin. 1894. 159 pp. *OXB*

FOTHERGILL, G.M.M. Wharton

Birds of the Bible: a daily text-book; by G.M.M. Wharton Fothergill. London: Digby, Long & Co. 1893. [viii], 48 pp.
> Poetry and prose.   *OXB*
> Also 2nd ed. 1898.

'FOURSQUARE': OR, THE CITY OF OUR KING: [poems]. London: James Nisbet & Co. 1884. 120 pp.   *OXB*

FOWLER, Ellen Thorneycroft (1860–1929). b. Wolverhampton, Staffordshire, daughter of Henry Hartley Fowler who became the 1st Viscount Wolverhampton. Educated at Fox How School. Her stories were first published in magazines but she progressed to become a popular novelist, some of her works selling more than 25,000 copies. In 1903 she married A.L. Felkin, an inspector of schools.

Songs and sonnets; by Ellen Thorneycroft Fowler. Printed Edinburgh: Ballantyne, Hanson & Co. 1888. iv, 83 pp.
> Printed for private circulation.   *OXB*

Verses grave and gay; by Ellen Thorneycroft Fowler. London: Cassell & Co., Ltd. 1891. [ii], 148 pp.   *OXB*

Verses wise or otherwise; by Ellen Thorneycroft Fowler. London: Cassell & Co., Ltd. 1895. 140 pp.   *OXB*

FOX, Alfred. Of Leeds.

Poetical waifs and strays: the offspring of leisure moments; by Alfred Fox. [Leeds]. 1894. x, 148 pp. por.   *LEP*

FOX, Charles see FOX, Charles Armstrong

FOX, Charles Armstrong (1836–1900). Educated at St John's College, Cambridge; BA 1858. Ordained, 1872; curate, St Paul's, West Exe, Devon, 1871–73, St Jude's, Islington, London, 1873–75; perpetual curate, Eaton Chapel, Eaton Square, London, from 1875, living at 25 Eaton Terrace. Died at Dorking, Surrey.

Alpine summits: verses; by Chas. Fox. Sepia drawings by E.L. from sketches by E. St. B.H. [London]: E. St. B. Holland; J.E. Hawkins. [1890]. [16] pp. il.
> Printed on card.   *OXB*

Flashes of wild beauty: [poems]; by Charles A. Fox. London: S.W. Partridge & Co. 1897. 112 pp.   *OXB*

Lyrics from the hills; by Charles Armstrong Fox. London: Elliot Stock. 1891. xvi, 366 pp.   *BL*
> Also Cheaper ed. 1892.

Mountain waterbrooks, and other poems; by Charles A. Fox. London: S.W. Partridge & Co. [1885]. [viii], 143 pp.   *OXB*

A satchel of song: [poems]; by Charles A. Fox. London: S.W. Partridge & Co. [1888]. viii, 118 pp.   *OXB*

Summer voices: [poems]; by Charles A. Fox. London: S.W. Partridge & Co. [1887]. [iv], 74 pp.   *OXB*

FOXALL, Jane. Of Belbroughton, Worcestershire.
Poems; by Jane Foxall. Birmingham: Cornish Bros; Stourbridge: Mark & Moody. 1895. 120 pp. *OXB*

FOYSTER, E.L.
Feathered fancies: [poems]; by E.L. Foyster. London: Simpkin, Marshall, Hamilton, Kent & Co., Ltd; Brighton: John Beal & Sons; Carlisle: Charles Thurnam & Sons. [1895]. 60 pp. *OXB*

FRANCIS, Samuel Trevor
Gems from the Revised Version, with poems; by S. Trevor Francis. London: S.W. Partridge & Co. [1891]. 48 pp. *BL*
Whence-whither, and other poems; by S. Trevor Francis. London: Morgan & Scott. [1898]. xviii, 203 pp. *OXB*

FRANK, Somerset
Rough rhymes; by Somerset Frank. London: Samuel French. [1887]. 48 pp. *OXB*

FRASER, Gordon (1836–91). b. Wigtown, son of a bailie of the burgh. All his life was spent in the town, where he conducted the trades of chemist and druggist, printer and bookseller. He acted as shorthand writer to the law courts, and was a local historian, and correspondent to local newspapers.
Poems; by Gordon Fraser. Wigtown: Author. 1885. 240 pp. por. *OXB*

FRASER-TYTLER, Christina Catherine. Daughter of C.E. Fraser-Tytler. In 1871 she married Rev. Edward Liddell, hon. canon of Durham, who was successively rector at Wimpole, Cambridgeshire, at Jarrow-on-Tyne, then vicar, Welton, Northamptonshire. Lived latterly at Birdshanger, Puttenham, Surrey.
Songs in minor keys; by C.C. Fraser-Tytler (Mrs. Edward Liddell). London: Macmillan & Co. 1881. viii, 220 pp. *OXB*
　　Also 2nd ed. 1884.

FREE LANCE, pseud. *see* **GRAY, Miss**, (Free Lance, pseud.)

FREE-LANCE, pseud. *see* **RICHARDSON, Alexander, (Free-Lance, pseud.)**

FREELAND, William (1828–). b. Kirkintilloch, Dumbartonshire. He received a basic education but, showing signs of artistic talent, was apprenticed to one of the finer branches of calico printing. Moved to Glasgow in early youth, attending classes at the Athenaeum and other institutions. In 1858 he was appointed sub-editor at the *Weekly Citizen*, and in 1866 joined the staff of the *Glasgow Herald*. A close friend of the poet David Gray.
A birth song, and other poems; by William Freeland. Glasgow: James Maclehose & Sons. 1882. viii, 223 pp. *BL*

FREEMAN, Gage Earle (1820–1903). Educated at St John's College, Cambridge. Ordained, 1846; chaplain to the Earl of Lonsdale; vicar, Macclesfield Forest, 1856–89, Askham, Westmorland, 1889–1903. An expert and writer on falconry.

The broad and the narrow way: the Seatonian prize poem for 1894; by Gage Earle Freeman. Cambridge: Deighton, Bell, & Co.; London: George Bell & Sons. 1895. 22 pp.   *BL*

Damascus: the Seatonian prize poem for 1893; by Gage Earle Freeman. Cambridge: Deighton, Bell, & Co.; London: George Bell & Sons. 1894. 18 pp.   *OXB*

Jericho: the Seatonian prize poem for 1888; by Gage Earle Freeman. Cambridge: Deighton, Bell & Co.; London: George Bell & Sons. 1889. 16 pp.   *OXB*

Jordan: a poem written for the Seatonian prize of 1883; by Gage Earle Freeman. Printed Cambridge: J. & C.F. Clay, at the University Press. [1884]. 19 pp.
   Printed for private circulation.   *OXB*

The transfiguration: the Seatonian prize poem for 1882; by Gage Earle Freeman. Cambridge: Deighton, Bell, & Co.; London: George Bell & Sons. 1883. 16 pp.   *OXB*

FREEMAN, Hollis

An illusive quest, and other poems; by Hollis Freeman. London: Digby, Long & Co. 1893. viii, 135 pp.   *OXB*

FRENCH, Percy *see* **FRENCH, William Percy**

FRENCH, William *see* **FRENCH, William Percy**

FRENCH, William Percy (1854–1920). b. Clooneyquin, County Roscommon. Educated in England, and at Trinity College, Dublin. He practised as a civil engineer for six years then became editor of the comic paper *The Jarvey*. A librettist, he made stage appearances singing his own songs, many of which have become Irish folk music.

Racquety rhymes; by W. French and R. Orpen. Dublin: Mecredy & Kyle. 1888. [25] pp. il. (by R.S. Orpen).   *NLI*

FRERE, Helen M., (H.M.F.)

Divots: [poems]; by H.M.F. [1898]. 20 pp.   *BL*

FRIENDE, pseud.

Thee and me; bye a friende. London: Bros Headley. 1899. [20] pp. il.
   Published for the author.   *OXB*

FRIESE-GREENE *see* **FRIESE-GREENE, William**

FRIESE-GREENE, William (1855–1921). b. Bristol. He began his working life as a travelling photographer. Experimented with J.A.R. Rudge on the reproduction, by camera and projector, of the synthesis of motion, 1882–84, thus claimed by some as the English inventor of cinematography. He established a photographic business in London at 92 Piccadilly. Patented his devices for stereoscopic cinematography, 1893, and for colour films, 1898.

"Nonsense": [poems]; by Friese-Greene. Printed London: A.W. Morris & Co., Ltd. 1888. viii, 104 pp.   *OXB*

FROM A YACHT: KING ARTHUR & MORGAN LE FAY; THE CAPTIVE BRIDE; THE CARAVAN, AND OTHER VERSES. London: Leadenhall Press, Ltd; Simpkin, Marshall, Hamilton, Kent & Co., Ltd. [1894]. 60 pp.   *OXB*

FROM HEART TO HEART: [poems]. London: Kegan Paul, Trench, Trübner & Co. 1892. viii, 100 pp.   *OXB*

FRONDE, Mrs

Poems and tales in verse; by Mrs. Fronde. London: Griffith, Farran, Okeden & Welsh. 1889. [ii], 133 pp.   *OXB*

FROST, Arnold, pseud. *see* **HEMSLEY, G.T.**, (Arnold Frost, pseud.)

FROST, J.G.

Fourteen new and original poems; by J.G. Frost. Printed Lincoln: Keyworth & Sons. 1899. 24 pp.

Title from cover.   *OXB*

FRY, Matilda (1808–88). Née Penrose. She married Francis Fry, grandson of the founder of J.S. Fry, chocolate manufacturers of Bristol. Lived at Cotham, Bristol.

Historic memories, and other poems; by Matilda Fry. Printed London: Barclay & Fry. 1890. xii, 258 pp.

Not published.   *OXB*

FULFORD, John. Novelist.

A look around, and other poems; by John Fulford. London: Elliot Stock. 1893. [2], viii, 106 pp.   *OXB*

FULLARTON, Ralph Macleod (1833–96). Son of Archbishop Fullarton of Glasgow. Educated in Edinburgh, France, Germany, and at Trinity Hall and Queen's College, Cambridge; BA 1862. Barrister, Inner Temple, 1865; practised chiefly before the Privy Council; QC, 1891. He contested Scottish seats in four elections from 1886 to 1895. Lived at 1 Holland Park Avenue, Kensington, London W.

Lallan sangs and German lyrics; by Ralph Macleod Fullarton. Edinburgh: William Blackwood & Sons. 1894. xii, 112 pp.   *OXB*

FULLER, James Franklin, (Ignotus, pseud.) (1835–1924). Fellow of the Royal Institute of Architects of Ireland, FRIBA, FSA. Architect to the Church Representative Body, and the National Board of Education, he built churches and mansions in several Irish counties; his practice was based in Great Brunswick Street, Dublin. A frequent contributor to genealogical and heraldic publications. Lived at Eglinton Road, Dublin, and Glashnacree, Kenmare, County Kerry.

Miscellaneous scraps in verse; by Ignotus. Presentation copy. London. 1880. vi, 130 pp.
    Cover-title is *Lines by Ignotus*.   BL
Mornings with the muse: sonnets, descriptive and miscellaneous; by Ignotus. London: Elliot Stock. [1886]. x, 66 pp.   OXB

FULLER-MAITLAND, Ella. Daughter of Harry Chester. She married Robert Fuller-Maitland of Stanstead, Essex. Contributed verse to *St James's Gazette*. Lived at The Grove, Sidmouth, Devon.

Parva: [poems]; by E. Fuller-Maitland, (E.F.M.). Edinburgh: William Blackwood & Sons. 1886. viii, 80 pp.   BL
The song-book of Bethia Hardacre; by Ella Fuller-Maitland. London: Chapman & Hall, Ltd. 1897. 138 pp.   BL
Verse: rustic and elegiac; by Ella Fuller-Maitland. 2nd ed. Printed London: Richard Clay & Sons, Ltd. 1890. [ii], 17 pp.   BL

FURLONG, Alice (1875–1946). b. Tallaght, County Dublin. One of a group of Catholic writers contributing verse and prose to *The Irish Monthly* and other journals. She sometimes wrote in the Gaelic, and published a volume of Irish fairy tales.

Roses and rue: [poems]; by Alice Furlong. London: Elkin Mathews. 1899. viii, 64 pp.   BL

FURLONG, Atherton

Echoes of memory: [poems]; by Atherton Furlong. With etchings by Tristram J. Ellis. London: Field & Tuer; Simpkin, Marshall & Co.; Hamilton Adams & Co; New York: Scribner & Welford. [1884]. [iv], 76 pp.il.   OXB

FURSE, Allen

Heart echoes: [poems]; by Allen Furse. London: Digby, Long & Co. [1896]. [ii], 92 pp.   OXB

FYNE, Neal, pseud.

In the middle watch: a tale of the sea; by Neal Fyne. London: Smith & Botwright. [189–]. 15 pp.   OXB

G

G., A. *see* **GODLEY, Alfred Denis**, (A.G.)

G., A.S.O.
Luther: a poem; by A.S.O.G. Manchester: Tubbs, Brook, & Chrystal. [1883]. 40 pp. *MPL*

G., A.T.
Lammermoor leaves; [poems]; [by] A.T.G. Printed Galashiels: D. Craighead. [1898]. [viii], 100 pp. *OXB*

G., A.W.
Dissolution of parliament: a statesman's adventures in search of a majority: a political squib; [by] A.W.G. Edinburgh: E. & S. Livingstone; Glasgow: William Porteous & Co.; Manchester: Abel Heywood & Son. [1880?]. 37 pp. *BL*

G., E. Of Bournemouth, Hampshire.
Memories: [poems]; by E.G. [Bournemouth?]: [Author]. 1893. 48 pp. Privately printed. *BL*

G., E.A.
Cheering songs for wakeful hours; by E.A.G. London: Griffith & Farran; Campbell & Tudhope; Lincoln: Charles Akrill. [c. 1880]. [ii], 144 pp.
 Half-title is *Cheering songs for waking hours*. *BL*
Cheering songs for waking hours; by E.A.G. [1880?]. [144] pp.
 Cover-title is *Cheering songs for wakeful hours*. Sections printed on different coloured paper. *BL*

G., E.H.
The cup of life, and other poems; by E.H.G. Blandford: Henry Shipp. 1892. 46 pp. *★UCD*

G., H.J.L. *see* **GRAHAM, Sir Henry John Lowndes**, (H.J.L.G.)

G., I.
The fatal gift: a transformation piece; by I.G. Illustrated by K.J.G. London: Wyman & Sons. 1884. 40 pp. il. *OXB*

G., J.
French gems, with English reflections in verse: a French–English souvenir; by J.G.
London: Elliot Stock. 1895. 80 pp.
   'Profits of this edition will be devoted to the mission to French-speaking
foreigners in Great Britain, in Bayswater'.   *UCD*

G., J.E. *see* **GORDON, Julia Emily**, (J.E.G.)

G., J.E.D.
   Wandering echoes, in four parts; [poems]; by J.E.D.G. London: Kegan Paul,
Trench & Co. 1884. xiv, 266 pp.   *UCD*

G., L.B. *see* **GURNEY, L.B.**, (L.B.G.)

G., M.E. *see* **GRANGER, Mary Ethel**, (M.E.G.)

G., C.O. *see* **GRIDLEY, Charles Oscar**, (C.O.G.)

G., R.H.
   The Church's seasons; by R.H.G. London: Skeffington & Son. [1891]. 16
pp.   *OXB*

G., W.E.
   "They are five", and other humorous reminiscences in verse; by W.E.G. Edited by
the author of 'The scarecrow', [etc.]. London: David Bogue. 1880. 32
pp.   *OXB*

G., W.L. *see* **GREENSTREET, William Lees**, (W.L.G.)

GABBITASS, Peter (1822–   ) b. Worksop, Nottinghamshire. Educated
largely at a Wesleyan Sunday school. He was apprenticed to the carpentry
trade, moving to Bristol to find work. Lived at 2 Short Grove. Known as 'The
Clifton Poet'.
   Cook's Folly: a legendary ballad of St. Vincent's Rocks, Clifton, and written there;
by P. Gabbitass. 3rd ed. Clifton, Bristol: [Author]. 1882. 42 pp. il.   *BL*
   *Excelsior!: a day dream in autumn on St. Vincent's Rocks, with other poems suitable
for readings and recitations*; by P. Gabbitass. Clifton: [Author]. [1880?]. 42 pp.
il.   *BL*
   Heart melodies for storm and sunshine, from Cliftonia the beautiful: [poems]; by P.
Gabbitass. Clifton, Bristol: [Author?]. 1885. lvi, 390 pp. il., por.   *UCD*

GAELYN, Henry, pseud. *see* **NAEGELY, Henry**, (Henry Gaelyn, pseud.)

GALE, Norman *see* **GALE, Norman Rowland**

GALE, Norman Rowland (1862–1942). b. Kew, Surrey, son of William F. Gale, gentleman. Educated at Exeter College, Oxford; BA 1884. He was a schoolmaster for ten years then divided his time between tutoring, journalism, and original literary work; a frequent writer of reviews. Friend of Alfred Hayes and Richard Le Gallienne. Lived at Oakfield Cottage, Rugby, Warwickshire, and latterly at Bexhill, Sussex.

Anemones: a collection of simple songs from, Unleavened bread, Primulas and pansies, Marsh marigolds . . .; [by Norman Rowland Gale]. Rugby: George E. Over. 1889. [45] pp.

A limited ed. of 60 copies. (Pencil note in BL copy). *BL*

The candid cuckoo, [and other poems]; by Norman Gale. Printed [Rugby]: George E. Over. [1891]. [iv], 56 pp.

A limited ed. of 100 copies published at the village of Old Bilton. *BL*

A country muse: [poems]; by Norman R. Gale. London: David Nutt. 1892. [vi], 112 pp. *OXB*

A country muse, new series: [poems]; by Norman R. Gale. London: David Nutt. 1893. viii, 111 pp.

A limited ed. of 1,000 copies on laid paper and 75 copies on demy 8vo Dutch hand-made paper. *JRL*

A country muse: [poems]; by Norman Gale. First series. Westminster: Archibald Constable & Co. 1894. xii, 147 pp.

Contains six poems not in 1892 ed. published by David Nutt. *TCD*

A country muse: [poems]; by Norman Gale. Second series. Westminster: Archibald Constable & Co. 1895. viii, 124 pp.

Contains fifteen poems not in 1893 ed. published by David Nutt. *TCD*

Cricket songs; by Norman Gale. London: Methuen & Co. 1894. xii, 68 pp. *MPL*

Also limited ed. of 15 copies printed on Japanese vellum.

Gorillas; [by Norman Rowland Gale]. Printed Rugby: George E. Over. [1891]. 15 pp.

A limited ed. of 60 copies. *BL*

Here be blue and white violets from the garden wherein grew meadowsweet: [poems]; [by Norman Rowland Gale]. Printed Rugby: George E. Over at the Rugby Press. [1891]. [95] pp. il.

Cover-title is *Violets*. A limited ed. of 25 numbered copies in a large paper ed. signed by the author. *MPL*

Marsh marigolds: [poems]; by Norman Gale. Rugby: George E. Over. 1888. [40] pp.

A limited ed. of 60 copies. *BL*

On two strings: [poems]; by Norman Gale and Robinson Kay Leather. Printed Rugby: George E. Over. 1894. [viii], 72 pp.

Privately printed. Not joint authorship. *BL*

Orchard songs; by Norman Gale. London: Elkin Mathews & John Lane; New York: G.P. Putnam's Sons. 1893. xii, 112 pp. *MPL*

Primulas and pansies: simple verses; by [Norman Rowland Gale]. Boston: Dingwall & Wilson. 1886. 103 pp. *BL*

Songs for little people; by Norman Gale. Westminster: Archibald Constable & Co. 1896. viii, 111 pp. il.   *MPL*

A verdant county: [poems]; by Norman Gale. Rugby: George E. Over; London: Elkin Mathews & John Lane. 1893. [iv], 33 pp.   *BL*

GALES, Richard Lawson (1862–). b. Littlehampton, Sussex, son of Richard S. Gales, shipowner. Educated at Lincoln College, Oxford; BA 1887. Ordained, 1888; curate, St John's, Stanwick, Yorkshire, 1888. Lived at Foxgarth, Ravensworth, near Richmond.

Savonarola: Newdigate prize poem, recited in the Sheldonian Theatre, Oxford, 30 June 1886; by R.L. Gales. Oxford; A. Thomas Shrimpton & Son; London: Simpkin Marshall & Co. 1886. 20 pp.   *OXB*

GALLIENNE, Richard Le *see* **LE GALLIENNE, Richard**

GALLOWAY, Mrs F.C. *see* **GALLOWAY, Lillie**

GALLOWAY, Lillie. Mrs F.C. Galloway of Bradford, Yorkshire.

Twilight musings: a volume of poems; by Mrs. F.C. Galloway. Bradford: Author. 1893. 88 pp. il., por.   *BL*

GALWAY, Lady *see* **MONCKTON-ARUNDELL, Vere, Lady Galway**

GAMA, pseud. *see* **CLELAND, William**, (Gama, pseud.)

GAMES, Stephen Herbert Wynne Hughes- *see* **HUGHES-GAMES, Stephen Herbert Wynne**

GAMWELL, S.C.

Some "Pierre Claire" poems; by S.C. Gamwell. Edited with critical and biographical memoir of the author by James Brown. Swansea: The Cambrian Office. 1897. 160 pp.   *★UCD*

GANYMEDE, pseud. *see* **COUPLAND, John Arthur**, (Ganymede, pseud.)

GARDEN, William (1848–). b. Auchanacie, Banffshire, son of a crofter. He attended school in winter but worked in summer as a herdsman. Went to learn the bakery trade in Keith, where he joined a literary society. After working some time in Edinburgh he started his own business at Archiestown, Craigellachie.

Sonnets and poems; by William Garden. London: Gall & Inglis. 1890. viii, 239 pp.   *OXB*

GARDNER, Herbert, Lord Burghclere (1846–1921). Educated at Harrow School, and Trinity College, Cambridge; BA 1869, MA 1872; member and eventually manager of the amateur dramatic society. He acted with the Canterbury Old Stagers. MP for Saffron Walden, Essex, 1885–95. President, Board of Agriculture, 1892–95. Director of P. & O. Steamship Co. He was created Baron Burghclere of Walden. Chairman of the Royal Commission on historic monuments. Novelist and playwright.

Leolyn, and other verses; by Herbert Gardner. London: Remington & Co. 1882. 127 pp.   *OXB*

GARDNER, William M.

Wheels and wings, and other poems; by William M. Gardner. London: Digby, Long & Co. [1892]. [iv], 78 pp.   *OXB*

GARDYNE, Amelia Anne Greenhill (1836–19). Daughter of the 7th viscount Strathallan. In 1858 she married Lieutenant-Colonel Charles Green-hill, Coldstream Guards, who assumed the name Gardyne in 1864. Lived at Finavon, Forfarshire, and Glenforsa, Isle of Mull.

Earl Beardie: a ballad of Finavon; by the Hon. Mrs Greenhill Gardyne. Edinburgh: William Brown. 1899. 40 pp.

A limited ed. of 120 copies.   *OXB*

Hakon the Good, and other verses; by the Hon. Mrs Greenhill Gardyne. With illustrations by M. Irwin. Edinburgh: William Brown. 1890. x, 95 pp.   *BL*

GARDYNE, Mrs Greenhill *see* **GARDYNE, Amelia Anne Greenhill**

GARLAND, Alison L. Novelist and dramatist.

Eternity!; by Alison L. Garland. Birmingham: C. Caswell. [1887]. 16 pp.   *CU*

GARLAND, Nathaniel Arthur (1816?–). Son of Nathaniel Garland of Harley Street, London. Educated at Eton College, and Christ Church, Oxford; BA 1838, MA 1856. He held various curacies, 1840–51; vicar, Silbertswold with Coldred, Kent, 1851–53; rector, Deal, Kent, 1853–56; vicar, St Matthew's Brixton, 1856–98. Lived latterly at 49 Frant Road, Tunbridge Wells, Kent.

Prayer-thoughts: some names and titles of Christ, devotionally considered: [poems]; by N.A. Garland. London: Elliot Stock. 1892. [iv], 100 pp.   *OXB*

GARNETT, Richard (1835–1906). b. Lichfield, Staffordshire, son of a keeper of books in the British Museum. Educated privately. He entered the British Museum as an assistant in 1851, working his way up to become keeper of printed books, 1890-99. President of the Library Association, 1892–93. A critic and biographer, he was an anti-Christian and a practising astrologer.

Poems; by Richard Garnett. London: Elkin Mathews; Boston, [Mass.]: Copeland & Day. 1893. xii, 173 pp.

'Of this ed, 350 copies have been printed for England'.   *MPL*

GARRICK, H.B.W. Assistant archaeologist to the Government of India. He published accounts of his tours of duty throughout India.

   India: a descriptive poem; by H.B.W. Garrick. London: Trübner & Co. 1889. xvi, 138 pp.   OXB

GARTH, Philip, pseud.   *see* **SINCLAIR, Francis**, (Philip Garth, pseud.)

GASCOIGNE, Mrs *see* **GASCOIGNE, Caroline Leigh**

GASCOIGNE, Caroline Leigh (1813–83?). Daughter of John Smith, MP, of Dale Park. In 1834 she married General Ernest Gascoigne, Grenadier Guards, who became MP for Liverpool. A novelist and writer for children, she lived at 14 Lowndes Square, London SW.

   Poems; by Mrs Gascoigne. London: Wyman & Sons. 1884. iv, 159 pp.
     Cover-title is *Memorial poems*.   UCD

GASTER, Percy. Of London?

   The old and the new, and other poems; by Percy Gaster. Printed Peckham: Cooper & Budd. [1896]. 22 pp.   BL

GAVAN, John. Educated at St Mary's School, Hammersmith, Middlesex. He taught at St Mary's School, Isleworth.

   The sons of Usna, and other poems; by John Gavan. Hull: William Andrews & Co.; London: Simpkin, Marshall, Hamilton, Kent, & Co., Ltd. 1892. [xii], 70 pp.   OXB

GEDDES, James Young (1850–   ). b. Dundee, Angus. A tailor and clothier, his life was spent between Dundee and the Perthshire burgh of Alyth. Noted as a librettist.

   In the Valhalla, and other poems; by James Young Geddes. Dundee: John Leng & Co. 1891. 200 pp. il.   UCD

   The spectre clock of Alyth, and other selections; by James Young Geddes. Alyth: Thomas M'Murray. [1886]. 100 pp.
     Poetry and prose.   BL

GEMMEL, John. Rev. Gemmel, senior minister of the Free Church at Fairlie, Ayrshire. Writer on the gospels.

   The Tiberiad: or, the art of hebrew accentuation: a didactic poem, in three books; by John Gemmel. Glasgow: James Maclehose. 1880. xvi, 83 pp.   CU

GEMMELL, Robert (1821–87). b. Irvine, Ayrshire. On leaving school he was apprenticed to the shipbuilding trade but before completing his term he enlisted in the 30th Regiment of Foot. After a brief military service he purchased his discharge, becoming a clerk with a railway contractor. He worked as a stationmaster for the Glasgow & South Western Railway Co., then moved to work in the goods department of the Glasgow & Paisley Railway Co.

   The village beauty, and other poems; by Robert Gemmell. Glasgow: Porteous Bros; Edinburgh: Andrew Elliott; London: Simpkin, Marshall & Co. 1886. 204 pp.   UCD

GEMMER, Caroline M., (Gerda Fay, pseud.). Mrs Walter Gemmer. Lived at 293 Unthank Road, Norwich, Norfolk.
Fidelis, and other poems; by C.M. Gemmer. Westminster: Archibald Constable. 1897. xii, 99 pp. *OXB*

GENTLEMAN OF THE UNIVERSITY OF CAMBRIDGE, pseud. *see* **CROWLEY, Edward Alexander (Aleister)**, (Gentleman of the University of Cambridge, pseud.)

GEORGEHILL, Roland, pseud. *see* **HILL, Roland George**, (Roland Georgehill, pseud.).

GERARD, Helen Jane (18 –84?). Daughter of Dr Gilbert Gerard, minister of the Scottish Church in Amsterdam, and one of three sisters. A competent musician, the harp was her favourite instrument. Lived at 6 Chanonry, Old Aberdeen.
Selections from "Pensées fugitives" of the late Helen Jane Gerard: [poems]. In memoriam. Aberdeen: A. & R. Milne; London: Hamilton, Adams & Co.; Edinburgh: John Menzies & Co. 1884. xvi, 111 pp. por. *OXB*

GERARD, William. Dramatist, and writer on Lord Byron.
The vision, and other poems; by William Gerard. London: F.V. White & Co. [1886], [vi], 100 pp. *OXB*

GIBBONS, Sarah Ann. Lived at The Villa, Shareshill, near Wolverhampton, Staffordshire.
Presented to her most gracious majesty, the Queen, at the close of the jubilee year of her ever memorable and glorious reign: [poems]; by her faithful, devoted, and humble subject, Sarah Ann Gibbons. Printed Wolverhampton: William Gibbons. 1887. 28 pp. *BL*

GIBBS, William Alfred
Fifty years in fifty minutes: a rapid review of the past half century: an author's tribute to the Queen-Empress; by William Alfred Gibbs. London: Rydal & Co. [1887]. [x], 118 pp.
    Printed on one side of leaf only. *UCD*
Home rule!: "to be? or not to be? that's the question!"; by William Alfred Gibbs. Popular ed. London: Sampson Low, Marston & Co., Ltd. 1892. 27 pp. *OXB*
A prelude to the idylls of the Queen; by William Alfred Gibbs. London: Sampson Low, Marston, & Co., Ltd. 1892. 28 pp. *UCD*
What next?: or, the power of gold: a glimpse of the world as it will be; by William Alfred Gibbs. London: J. Boulton & Co., Ltd; Simpkin, Marshall, Hamilton, Adams & Co. [1891]. [8], vi, 133 pp. *OXB*

GIBERNE, Agnes (1845–1939). b. Belgaum, India, daughter of Major Charles Giberne. Educated at home, she was a popular and prolific writer of books for children, and a contributor to periodicals. Lived at Eastbourne, Sussex.

Twilight verses; by Agnes Giberne. London: James Nisbet & Co. 1888. iv, 73 pp.   *OXB*

GIDLEY, Lewis (1822–89). Son of Lewis Gidley of Honiton, Devon. Educated at Ottery Grammar School, and Exeter College, Oxford; BA 1843, MA 1845. Ordained, 1845; curate, Combe Raleigh, Devon, 1845–50, Gillingham, Dorset, 1850–51, Otterton, Gittisham, and Branscombe successively 1851–68, all in Devon; chaplain, St Nicholas Hospital, Salisbury, Wiltshire, 1868–88.

Poems; by Lewis Gidley. 2nd ed. Oxford: Parker & Co.; Exeter: Henry S. Eland. 1884. viii, 148 pp.   *OXB*

GIFFORD, Elizabeth

Poems; by Elizabeth Gifford. London: Eden Fisher & Co. 1897. viii, 100 pp.   *BL*

GILBART-SMITH, James William (1856?–   ). Son of Denham Smith of Kingstown, near Dublin. Educated at Christ Church, Oxford; BA 1880, MA 1882. Student of New Temple, 1880.

The log o' the "Norseman"; by J.W. Gilbart-Smith. London: Kegan Paul, Trench & Co. 1884. viii, 136 pp.   *OXB*

The loves of Vandyck: a tale of Genoa; by J.W. Gilbart-Smith. London: Kegan Paul, Trench & Co. 1883. vi, 44 pp.   *OXB*

Poems; by J.W. Gilbart-Smith. London: Field & Tuer. 1881. 73 pp.

Cover-title is *My ladye & others*.   *OXB*

Serbelloni: [poems]; by J.W. Gilbart-Smith. London: Kegan Paul, Trench & Co. 1887. xvi, 189 pp.   *OXB*

GILBERT, Lady *see* **MULHOLLAND, Rosa, Lady Gilbert**

GILBERT, Sir William Schwenk (1836–1911). b. London, son of William Gilbert. Educated in London, graduating from King's College. Worked as a clerk in the Privy Council office, 1857–62. Called to the Bar, Inner Temple, 1863; practised law in London and on the Northern circuit, 1864–68. He began writing for the stage, producing a long series of comedies, burlesques and operettas. The light operas, combined with the tuneful music of Sir Arthur Sullivan, appealed to large sections of the public.

The Bab ballads, with which are included, Songs of a Savoyard; by W.S. Gilbert. With 350 illustrations by the author. London: George Routledge & Sons, Ltd. 1898. xii, 554 pp. il., por.   *OXB*

Songs of a Savoyard; by W.S. Gilbert. Illustrated by the author. London: Routledge & Sons, Ltd. [1890]. 142 pp. il.   *MPL*

GILES, James
  Poems: domestic and miscellaneous; by James Giles. London: W.B. Whittingham & Co. 1881. xvi, 224 pp.   OXB

GILKISON, John (1851–95). b. Gorbals, Glasgow, son of a working man. Of delicate physique, he was sent to live with his maternal grandfather, a tenant farmer in the north of Ireland. He attended school there until nearly sixteen. Writer of comic and satirical papers, pantomimes, and children's toy story books. He lived in Dumbarton, where he went into retail shopkeeping on his own account. Friend of the artist George Ewing. An active member of Glasgow Ballad Club.
  The minister's fiddle: a book of verse, humorous and otherwise; by John Gilkison. Glasgow: A. Bryson & Co. 1888. 200 pp.   BL

GILLEN, Alma. Lived at 45 Longridge Road, Earls Court, London SW.
  Love's depths: [poems]; by Alma Gillen. London: Sold by W. Isacke. [c. 1899]. [viii], 66 pp.   BL
  The passion of passions: [poems]; by Alma Gillen. London: Simpkin, Marshall, Hamilton, Kent & Co. Ltd. 1896. 125 pp.   OXB
  Passionate passions: [poems]; by Alma Gillen. London: Osgood, McIlvaine & Co. 1895. viii, 87 pp.   OXB

GILLETT, Ellen Elizabeth.
  A Christmas tale, and other poems; by Ellen Elizabeth Gillett. Collected and edited by her sons. London: Elliot Stock. 1894. [iv], 58 pp.   BL

GILLINGTON, Alice Elizabeth (1862–19). b. Audlem, Cheshire, daughter of Rev. John M. Gillington, and sister of Mary Clarissa Gillington. She attended the Slade School of Art. Writer on singing games and on Christmas carols. Lived at Newlyn, Balmoral Road, Parkstone, Dorset.
  Poems; by M.C. Gillington and A.E. Gillington. London: Elliot Stock. 1892. xii, 99 pp.   OXB

GILLINGTON, Mary Clarissa (May Byron). (1861–1917). b. Audlem, Cheshire, daughter of Rev. John M. Gillington, and sister of Alice Elizabeth Gillington. A prolific writer of stories for children, including infants. She married George F. Byron and settled in London, writing as May Byron.
  Poems; by M.C. Gillington and A.E. Gillington. London: Elliot Stock. 1892. xii, 99 pp.   OXB

GILSTRAP, Elizabeth Haigh, Lady Gilstrap (1822–91). b. Colne Bridge House, Huddersfield, Yorkshire, daughter of Thomas Haigh. In 1847 she married William Gilstrap of Fornham Park, Bury St Edmund, Suffolk, and of Newark, Nottinghamshire, who was created 1st Bart in 1887. She completed two Eastern tours accompanying her husband.
  The harp of Colne: [poems]; by Elizabeth Haigh Gilstrap. Illustrated and revised ed. Printed London: Ilkeston Pioneer Printing Co., Ltd. 1894. [xvi], 160 pp. il., por.
  Printed for private circulation.   BL

GINGOLD, Hélène E.A. Granddaughter of Chevalier Sulzer, singer and songwriter; her mother was prima donna at the Imperial Opera House, Vienna. A novelist and songwriter, she was married to Laurence Cowen. Lived at Regent's Court, Regent's Park, London NW.

A cycle of verse; by Hélène E.A. Gingold. With portrait of the author. London: Remington & Co. 1889. xii, 160 pp. por. *UCD*
    Also 2nd ed. 1889; 3rd ed. 1889.

GINNER, Isaac B.
    The death of Otto, and other poems; by Isaac B. Ginner. London: Kegan Paul, Trench & Co. 1884. viii, 230 pp. *OXB*

GIPPS, L.M.
    Jael, and other poems; by L.M. Gipps. London: David Stott. 1892. iv, 169 pp. *OXB*

GLAD TIDINGS IN THE STARS, [and other poems]. London: Terry & Co. 1894. [32] pp. il. *OXB*

GLAZEBROOK, Harriet A. Mrs Beavan. Temperance reformer.
    The brooklet reciter, for temperance societies and Bands of Hope: [poems]; by Harriet Glazebrook. London: National Temperance Publication Depot. [1883]. [iv], 176 pp. il. *OXB*
    Readings in rhyme, from the drama of drink; by Harriet A. Glazebrook (Mrs. Beavan). New & enlarged ed. London: Marshall Bros. [1892]. [viii], 223 pp. il. *BL*

GLENDINING, Elizabeth (1808?–). Lived at 1 Mount Pleasant, Great Francis Street, Birmingham.
    Widow Glendining's book of loyal poems, with introduction. Printed Birmingham: R. Priddy. [1886]. 31 pp. *OXB*

GLENESSA, pseud.
    The discovery, and other poems; by Glenessa. London: National Publishing Co. 1886. 207 pp. *★UCD*

GLENLYON, pseud.
    Original poetry; by Glenlyon. Sandown, Isle of Wight: W. Beavan Martin. 1892. 16 pp. *OXB*

GLOVER, Richard H., (Cotswold Isys, pseud.). Rev. Glover of Wootton Rectory, Dorking, Surrey. Hon. member of the Fly-Fishers' Club.
    An angler's strange experiences: a whimsical medley, and an of-fish-all record without a-bridge-ment: [poems]; by Cotswold Isys. Profusely illustrated in a style never before app-roach-ed in these days after drawings in water-colours. London: Sampson Low, Marston, Searle, & Rivington. 1883. xvi, 100 pp. il. *OXB*
    Lyra piscatoria: original lyrics on fish, flies, fishing and fishermen, including poems on all the British freshwater fish; by Cotswold Isys. London: Horace Cox. 1895. xvi, 173 pp. *OXB*

GLUBB, Peter Southmead (1819–92?). b. Liskeard, Cornwall, son of Peter Glubb, barrister. Educated at Liskeard Grammar School, and Sidney Sussex College, Cambridge; BD 1857. Curate, Saltash, Cornwall, 1848–58; vicar, St Kew, St Anthony-in-Meneage, 1858–85. Lived latterly at Kevor House, Falmouth.

The Empress Charlotte, and other poems; by Peter Southmead Glubb. 2nd ed. London: Hamilton, Adams, & Co. 1881. 304 pp. il. *BL*

GLYNFERCH *see* **GRIFFITHS, Maggie**, (Glynferch)

GODLEY, Alfred Denis, (A.G.) (1856–1925). b. Ashfield, County Cavan. Educated at Harrow School, and Balliol College, Oxford. Tutor and Fellow, Magdalen College, 1883–1912; public orator, 1910–25. A classical scholar, he translated Horace, Tacitius and Herodotus; joint editor of the *Classical Review*, 1910–20. Died after contracting a malignant fever during a tour of the Levant.

Lyra frivola; by A.D. Godley. London: Methuen & Co. 1899. viii, 100 pp. *OXB*

Verses to order; by A.G. London: Methuen & Co. 1892. 71 pp. *CU*

GODSON, John. Graduated from Queen's College, Birmingham, 1857. Ordained, 1859; curate, St Michael's with St Olave's, Chester, from 1880.

Eirene: or, peace on earth; by John Godson. Chester: Phillipson & Golder. 1884. 188 pp. *OXB*

GOLDEN, John. Irish priest attached for some years to St George's Cathedral, Southwark, London. He had previously lived in New Zealand.

St Columba, and other poems; by J. Golden. London: Burns & Oates, Ltd. [1886], xvi, 152 pp. *OXB*

GOLDIE, Janet C. Of Beith, Ayrshire. Educated at Beith Industrial School. Wife of a working man and mother of five children.

Poems and songs: by Janet C. Goldie. Printed Ardrossan: Arthur Guthrie & Sons. [1895?]. xii, 1112 pp.

Printed for the author. *UCD*

GOLDING-BIRD, Robert James. Trained for the ministry at St Aidan's; curate in Kent, at Bexley, 1859–60, at St Clement's, Sandwich, 1860–61, St Philip's, Islington, London, 1861–62, St James's Southampton, 1862–63; vicar, St Bartholomew's, Gray's Inn Road, London, from 1863.

Fugitive verses; by Robert J. Golding-Bird. London: Elliot Stock. 1899. viii, 294 pp. *OXB*

GOODCHILD, John Arthur (1851–   ). b. Ealing, Middlesex. He trained for the medical profession at London University, and St George's Hospital; MRCS 1872, LRCP 1873; went into practice in Hampstead. Member of the Irish Literary Society. Writer on the watering places of France and Italy. Lived latterly at the Hotel Belvedere, Bordighera, Italy.

The book of Tephi; by J.A. Goodchild. London: Kegan Paul. Trench, Trübner & Co. Ltd 1897. viii, 260 pp. *OXB*

Lyrics; by J.A. Goodchild. London: Horace Cox. 1893. xii, 213 pp.   *OXB*

Somnia medici: [poems]; by John A. Goodchild. London: Kegan Paul, Trench, & Co. 1884. x, 219 pp.   *OXB*

Somnia medici: [poems]; by John A. Goodchild. Second series. London: Kegan Paul, Trench & Co. 1886. x, 258 pp.   *OXB*

    Also 2nd ed. 1892.

Somnia medici: [poems]; by John A. Goodchild. Third series. London: Kegan Paul, Trench & Co. 1887. vi, 247 pp.   *OXB*

Tales in verse; by J.A. Goodchild. London: Horace Cox. [1893]. [viii], 260 pp.   *OXB*

The two thrones: [play] etc., [and poems]; by John A. Goodchild. London: Kegan Paul, Trench, Trübner & Co., Ltd. 1895. x, 256 pp.   *OXB*

GOODFELLOW, John Cumming. Of Hawick, Roxburghshire. Writer on archaeology.

Occasional poems and verses; by J. Cumming Goodfellow. Hawick: Author. 1893. viii, 135 pp.

    A limited ed. of 250 numbered copies. Cover-title is *Poems and verses*.   *OXB*

GOOSESTEP, pseud. Member of Lloyd's of London.

Bric-a-brac ballads; by Goosestep. London: Leadenhall Press, Ltd; Simpkin, Marshall, Hamilton, Kent & Co., Ltd; New York: Charles Scribner's Sons. 1892. 94 pp.   *BL*

Rustling reeds: [poems]; stirred by Goosestep. London: Leadenhall Press, Ltd; Simpkin, Marshall, Hamilton, Kent & Co., Ltd; New York: Charles Scribner's Sons. 1894. 127 pp. (Funnynym series, no. 1).   *OXB*

Splay-feet splashings, in divers places: [poems]; by Goosestep. London: Leadenhall Press; Simpkin, Marshall, Hamilton, Kent & Co., Ltd; New York: Scribner & Welford. [1891]. viii, 123 pp.   *OXB*

GORDON, Mrs D.H., (Violet, pseud.). Of Dumfermline, Fife. An invalid for many years, she died pre-1890.

Poems; by "Violet" (Mrs D.H. Gordon). Printed Dunfermline: A. Romanes, 'Press' Office. 1890. viii, 147 pp. por.   *BL*

GORDON, Ella Mary. Daughter of William Paul of Waltham House, Hertfordshire, horticulturalist. She married William Gordon, town clerk of Aberdeen. Known as 'The Queen's Poetess'. Lived at The Hall, 26 Rubislaw Terrace, Aberdeen.

Golden rain: [poems]; by Ella Mary Gordon. Printed Aberdeen: G. Cornwall & Sons. [1897]. iv, 62 pp. por.   *NLS*

    Also 2nd ed. [1899?]

Poems; by Ella Mary Gordon. Illustrated by Florence Paul. [1898]. 104 pp. il.   *★UCD*

GORDON, Lord Granville (1856–1907). Sixth son of the 10th Marquess of

Huntly. He married Charlotte D'Olier Roe in 1878. A member of the Turf Club, and writer on horse-racing.

The legend of Birse, and other poems; by Granville Gordon. London: Bliss, Sands, & Foster. 1894. vi, 141 pp. *OXB*

Odd half-hours on odd half-sheets: [poems]; by Granville Gordon. London: Veale Chifferiel & Co. 1885. iv, 75 pp. *OXB*

GORDON, John. Qualified as a teacher; aged twenty he was appointed a master at the Royal Grammar School, Newcastle upon Tyne; also taught in the Mechanics' Institute. Principal of Bath House School, Hartlepool, for eight years. He moved south to Clifton to establish Salisbury House School, then returned to Newcastle to found Jesmond College, a school for 'the sons of gentlemen'.

The Northumbrian harp: or, melodies by Tyneside; by John Gordon. Newcastle-on-Tyne: Alexander M'Callum. 1897. 166 pp. por. *NPL*

The story of a death certificate, and other poems; by John Gordon. London: 376 Strand. [1886?]. 96 pp. **UCD*

GORDON, Julia Emily, (J.E.G.)

Songs and etchings in shade and sunshine; by J.E.G. London: Sampson Low, Marston, Searle, & Rivington. 1880. [2], viii, 159 pp. il. *UCD*

GORE-BOOTH, Eva (1870–1926). b. Lissadell, County Sligo, third child of Sir Henry Gore-Booth. A delicate child, she was educated privately. From 1897 she lived in Manchester, becoming involved in the women's suffrage movement, and helping to form the Women Textile Workers' Union. The climate affected her health adversely, and after an illness in 1913 she had to move south. Her last years were spent in Hampstead, saddened by the outcome of the 1916 Easter Rebellion in which her sister Constance, Countess Markiewicz, was implicated.

Poems; by Eva Gore-Booth. London: Longmans, Green, & Co. 1898. x, 128 pp. *MPL*

GORNALL, James Alfred (18 –99). Of Bury, Lancashire. A regular contributor to the *East Lancashire Review*.

Catherine, and other poems; by James Alfred Gornall. London: Robert Davies; Radcliffe: Thomas Gornall. 1885 viii, 78 pp. *JRL*

GOSSE, Sir Edmund (1849–1928). b. London, son of Philip Gosse, eminent zoologist. Educated in Devon. In 1867 he was appointed assistant librarian at the British Museum; translator to the Board of Trade, 1875. Clark lecturer in English Literature, Trinity College, Cambridge, 1885–90. Librarian to the House of Lords, 1904–14. Critic, biographer and scholar, he contributed weekly literary articles to the *Sunday Times*, 1918–28.

Firdausi in exile, and other poems; by Edmund Gosse. London: Kegan Paul, Trench & Co. 1885. x, 225 pp. il. *MPL*

In russet & silver, [and other poems]; by Edmund Gosse. London: William Heinemann. 1894. xiv, 158 pp. *MPL*

Also [3rd ed.] 1896.

GOULD, Sabine Baring- *see* **BARING-GOULD, Sabine**

GOVAN, William J. Of Thorntonhall, near Glasgow.
In His presence: verses of the Christian life; by William J. Govan. London:
Marshall Bros; Glasgow: R.L. Allan & Son. [1893]. x, 98 pp.   *OXB*

GOWENLOCK, George. Of Oldham, Lancashire.
*Selections from the writings of George Gowenlock. Printed Oldham: W.E. Clegg.
1891. 34 pp.*
    Poetry and prose.   *MPL*

GOWING, Mrs Aylmer *see* **GOWING, Emilia Aylmer**

GOWING, Emilia Aylmer (1846–1905). b. Bath, daughter of Mr Blake,
QC, a distinguished Dublin lawyer. She received a classical education under
her mother's tuition in Brighton and Paris. A dramatist and novelist, she
became known as a poet and reciter in French. In 1877 she married the actor
William Gowing, who assumed the additional surname of Aylmer.
    Ballads and poems for recitation; by Emilia Aylmer Blake (Mrs. Aylmer
Gowing). London: John & Robert Maxwell. [1884]. viii, 120 pp.   *OXB*
    Ballads of the Tower, and other poems, mostly adapted for recitation; by Mrs
Aylmer Gowing (Emilia Aylmer Blake). London: Griffith, Farran, Okeden &
Welsh. 1891. viii, 152 pp.   *OXB*
    Boadicea: a play in four acts; Poems for recitation, etc.; by Mrs. Aylmer Gowing
(Emilia Aylmer Blake). London: Kegan Paul, Trench, Trübner & Co. Ltd.
1899. [viii], 122 pp.   *MPL*
    The cithern: poems for recitation, etc.; by Emilia Aylmer Blake (Mrs. Aylmer
Gowing). London: John & Robert Maxwell. [1886]. viii, 134 pp.   *OXB*
    Sita, and other poems, mostly adapted for recitation; by Mrs. Aylmer Gowing
(Emilia Aylmer Blake). London: Elliot Stock. 1895. viii, 104 pp.   *OXB*

GRACE, C.W. Lived for a time in New Zealand.
    Songs and poems; by C.W. Grace. London: Authors' Cooperative Publishing
Co., Ltd. [1890]. viii, 88 pp.   *OXB*

GRACEY, Hugh Kirkwood (1868–1929). b. Camberwell, Surrey, son of
David Gracey, Baptist minister. Educated at St Catharine's College, Cam-
bridge. He entered the Indian Civil Service in 1887, serving in the North West
Province and in Oudh as a magistrate; deputy commissioner, 1896; magistrate
and collector, 1901; settlement officer, Cawnpore, 1903–06; commissioner,
Gorakhpore Division, 1916–20, then commissioner, Kumaon, United Prov-
inces; retired 1924. Lived latterly at La Roque, Jersey.
    Rhyming legends of Ind; by H. Kirkwood Gracey. Calcutta: Thacker, Spink &
Co.; London: W. Thacker & Co. 1892. [viii], 154 pp.   *OXB*

GRAHAM, Harry Joscelyn Clive, (Col. D. Streamer, pseud.) (1874–1936). Educated at Eton College, and Sandhurst Royal Military Academy. He was commissioned in the Coldstream Guards, serving in the Boer War and the First World War. A contributor to *Punch*, he also wrote scripts of West End farces, and composed librettos of operettas.

Ruthless rhymes for heartless homes. Words by Col. D. Streamer. Illustrations by G.H. London: Edward Arnold. [1899]. 60 pp. ★

GRAHAM, Sir Henry John Lowndes, (H.J.L.G.) (1842–1930). Son of William L. Graham of Gilmour Hill, near Glasgow. Educated at Balliol College, Oxford; BA 1865, MA 1867. Barrister, Inner Temple, 1868. Principal secretary to Lord Chancellor Cairns, 1874–80; Master of Lunacy, 1880–85; Clerk of Parliaments, 1885–1917. Lived latterly at 4 Cadogan Gardens, London SW.

Medleys, and songs without music: [poems]; by H.J.L.G. London: W.H. Allen & Co., 1891. [vi], 112 pp. *UCD*

GRAHAM, Jean Carlyle (1846–   ). A Scot, she married J.C.G. Speakman. Contributed on a variety of subjects to English and foreign periodicals. Lived at La Casa Graham Hamilton, Alassio, Italy.

The child of the bondwoman, and other verses; by Jean Carlyle Graham. London: David Nutt. 1897. viii, 66 pp. *BL*

Songs, measures, metrical lines; by Jean Carlyle Graham. London: Kegan Paul, Trench, Trübner & Co., Ltd. 1893. xii, 124 pp. *BL*

GRAHAM, William. Novelist.

Two fancies, and other poems; by William Graham. London: Kegan Paul, Trench & Co. 1883. x, 120 pp. *OXB*

GRAMMAR SCHOOL USHER, pseud.

Rhymes; by a grammar school usher. Printed Broadway, Stratford: Wilson & Whitworth. 1884. 92 pp. ★*UCD*

GRAMSHAW, Henry (1828–90). Trained for a medical career at University College, London; LRCP, MRCS. Admiralty surgeon and agent; medical officer of health, Walton-on-the-Naze and Tendring, Essex. He contributed medical papers to the *British Medical Journal* and other professional periodicals. Lived at Raglan House, Walton-on-the-Naze.

Sketches in verse; by Henry Gramshaw. Illustrated. Lowestoft: Arthur Stebbings; London: Jarrold & Sons. [1880]. 240 pp. il. *BL*

GRAND-PERE EDMOND, pseud. Of Edgbaston, Birmingham.

Reliquiae: [poems]; by Grand-Père Edmond. London: Elliot Stock. 1887. [58] pp. *OXB*

GRANGER, Mary Ethel, (M.E.G.) Roman Catholic writer.
Light after darkness; by M.E.G. With illustrations. London: James Nisbet & Co. 1885. [31] pp. il.   *OXB*
Peace: a thanksgiving after Holy Communion; by Mary Ethel Granger. With illustrations by N.K.D.S. With preface by George Body. London: Swan Sonnenschein, Lowrey & Co. 1886. 31 pp. il.   *OXB*

GRANNY, pseud. *see* **BODMER, Friederica**, (Granny, pseud.)

GRANT, Cecilia Havergal. Mrs Grant, née Havergal. Translator of Frédéric Mistral's *Mireio* from the original Provençal.
The Master's smile, and other poems; by Cecilia Havergal Grant. London: James Nisbet & Co. 1889. viii, 141 pp.   *OXB*

GRANT, Charles William. Colonel, Royal Engineers. Served in India, writing on the railways and civil engineering projects there. Lived latterly in Bath.
Judas Iscariot: a poem; [by Charles William Grant]. Printed Bath: E.R. Blackett. 1885. [ii], 41 pp.   *TAU*

GRANT, David (1823–86). b. Upper Banchory, Kincardineshire. Educated at Aberdeen University. Schoolmaster at Elgin; French master, Oundle Grammar School, 1861; assistant master, Eccleshall College, near Sheffield, 1865. He started a day school in Sheffield but became bankrupt. Private tutor in Edinburgh from 1880. FEIS
Lays and legends of the north, and other poems and songs, humorous and grave, original and translated; by David Grant. Edinburgh: Oliphant, Anderson, & Ferrier; Andrew Elliot. 1884. xii, 280 pp.   *OXB*
Metrical tales, and other poems; by David Grant. Edited by Mrs. Leith-Adams. First series complete. Printed Sheffield: W. C. Leng & Co. 1880. xvi, 304 pp.   *OXB*
Metrical tales, and other poems; by David Grant. Second issue. First series complete 1882. Sheffield: Thomas Widdison. [1886]. xvi, 304 pp.   *OXB*

GRANT, Eleanor
Crown blessings: a selection of poems; by Eleanor Grant. London: James E. Hawkings; Toronto: S.R. Briggs. [1888]. [24] pp. il.   *BL*

GRANT, John. Of The Manse, Croy, Inverness.
Poems of my youth, and other pieces, written on the banks of the Aven, the Conlass, the Livet, and the Spey; by John Grant. Edinburgh: James Gemmell; Nairn: John Fraser. 1888. 77 pp.   *OXB*

GRANT, John Cameron (1857–). b. Cuddalore, Madras, son of Patrick Grant of the Indian Civil Service. His early childhood was spent in the Scottish Highlands. Educated at Rugby School, and Christ Church, Oxford. After graduation he went to India for two years. He was connected with extensive engineering and industrial works abroad.

Bits of Brazil; The legend of Lilith, and other poems; by John Cameron Grant. London: Longmans, Green, & Co. 1885. [x], 82 pp. *OXB*

New verse in old vesture; by John Cameron Grant. With an introductory preface by Gleeson White. London: E.W. Allen. 1889. xxviii, 86 pp. *OXB*

Poems in petroleum; by John Cameron Grant. London: E.W. Allen. 1892. [viii], 149 pp. *MPL*

Prairie pictures; Lilith, and other poems; by John Cameron Grant. London: Longmans, Green, & Co. 1884. xviii, 93 pp. *OXB*

Songs from the sunny south; by John Cameron Grant. London: Longmans, Green, & Co. 1882. xii, 280 pp. *OXB*

Songs in spring-time; The passing of Lilith, and other poems, including, Intercepted letters, & Saint Augustine; by John Cameron Grant. 2nd ed. London: E.W. Allen. 1893. [viii]. 91 pp. *OXB*

Vauclin, and other verses; by John Cameron Grant. London: E.W. Allen. 1887. 50 pp. *OXB*

A year of life; The price of the bishop, and other poems; by John Cameron Grant. London: Longmans, Green, & Co. 1883. xvi, 251 pp. *OXB*

GRANT, Lewis Morris- *see* **MORRIS-GRANT, Lewis**

GRANT, Mary. b. Fraserburgh, Aberdeenshire. The family moved to Aberdeen in her infancy. She was educated to become a governess. Contributed verse, essays, stories and plays to many newspapers and magazines.

Selected poems; by Mary Grant. 3rd ed. Aberdeen: Lewis Smith & Son; London: Walter Scott; Edinburgh: John Menzies & Co. 1886. 190 pp. *★UCD*

GRANT-DUFF, Anna Julia, Lady, (A.J.G.D.). Daughter of Edward Webster. She married Sir Mountstuart Grant-Duff, barrister, statesman, and Liberal MP for the Elgin Boroughs.

Verses; by A.J.G.D. Printed Edinburgh: Edinburgh University Press, T. & A. Constable. 1882. [ix], 49 pp. *BL*

GRAVENER, George

Victoria regina, (A.D. 1881), and other verse and prose, grave and gay; by George Gravener. London: Harrison & Sons. 1881. xii, 190 pp.
Published for the author. *OXB*

GRAVES, Alfred Perceval (1846–1932). b. Dublin, son of the Protestant Bishop of Limerick. Educated in England, and at Trinity College, Dublin. Home Office clerk, 1869–75. Inspector of schools, 1875–1910, for many years in Taunton, Somerset, and from 1895 in Southwark, London. Published critical studies and edited various educational series. Much of his verse was set to Irish airs, his most famous piece being 'Father O'Flynn'. Father of the poet and novelist Robert Graves.

Father O'Flynn, and other Irish lyrics; by Alfred Perceval Graves. London: Swan Sonnenschein & Co. 1889. 128 pp. *MPL*

Irish songs and ballads; by Alfred Perceval Graves. Manchester: Alexander Ireland and Co. 1880. x, 276 pp.   *MPL*

GRAVES, Charles Larcom (1856–1944). Son of Charles Graves, Bishop of Limerick, and brother of Alfred Perceval Graves. Journalist on staff of *Spectator*, 1899–1917, *Punch*, 1902–36. He collaborated with Rudyard Kipling on an English version of the odes of Horace.
  The Blarney ballads; by Charles L. Graves. With illustrations by G.R. Halkett. 2nd ed. London: Swan Sonnenschein & Co. 1888. viii, 87 pp. il.   *MPL*
    Also 3rd ed. 1888; 4th ed. 1893.
  The green above the red: more Blarney ballads; by Charles L. Graves. With illustrations by Linley Sambourne. London: Swan Sonnenschein & Co. 1889. viii, 93 pp. il.   *MPL*
  The Hawarden Horace: [poems]; by Charles L. Graves. London: Smith, Elder, & Co. 1894. [viii], 91 pp.
    In English and Latin.   *OXB*
    Also 2nd ed. 1894; 3rd ed. 1895.
  More Hawarden Horace: [poems]; by Charles L. Graves. With an introduction by T.E. Page. London: Smith, Elder, & Co. 1896. xviii, 98 pp.   *MPL*

GRAY, Alfred Horatio. Educated at Trinity College, Dublin; BA 1870. Ordained 1872; curate, Gorey, County Wexford, 1872–79, Dalton-in-Furness, Lancashire, 1879–80; rector, St John's, Malone, Belfast, from 1880.
  Golden chimes, and other poems; by Alfred Horatio Gray. London: Elliot Stock. 1896. [vi], 58 pp.   *OXB*

GRAY, David (1836–88). b. Edinburgh, son of a stationer. The family emigrated to America in 1849. Lived in Wisconsin, 1849-56, then in Buffalo, New York State. He became a journalist with the *Buffalo Daily Courier*.
  Letters, poems and selected prose writings; by David Gray. Edited, with a biographical memoir by J.N. Larned. Printed Buffalo: Courier Co. 1888. 2 vols. por.
    Vol. 1. Life, letters, poems, etc. Vol. 2. Letters of travel.   *BL*

GRAY, John (1866–1934). b. Woolwich, Kent, son of working-class Nonconformist parents. Employed as a librarian in the Foreign Office, c. 1890. He was ordained a Roman Catholic priest in 1901; rector, St Peter's, Edinburgh, for many years. Friend of Aubrey Beardsley and of Oscar Wilde, who encouraged his progress as a poet.
  The blue calendar 1896: twelve sundry carols; invented by John Gray. London; [Author]. 1895. 35 pp.
    'Privately printed and not for general distribution'.   *BL*
  Silverpoints: [poems]; by John Gray. London: Elkin Mathews; John Lane at the sign of The Bodley Head. 1893. xxxix pp.
    A limited ed. of 250 numbered copies.   *MPL*

GRAY, Mary (1853–   ). b. Huntly, Aberdeenshire. She earned her living as a telegraph clerk in Huntly and later in England. Studied for the teaching profession and in 1882 received a qualification from St Andrews University. She went abroad in 1876, first to Hanover for study, then to Mecklenburg where she was engaged in teaching until 1880. Translator from the German.
Lyrics and epigrams, after Goethe and other German authors; by M. Gray. Edinburgh: David Douglas. 1890. xii, 120 pp.   *BL*

GRAY, Maxwell, pseud. *see* **TUTTIETT, Mary Gleed, (Maxwell Gray, pseud.)**

GRAY, Miss, (Free Lance, pseud.). Of Lilliesleaf, Roxburghshire.
Border rhymes; by Free Lance. Hawick: James Edgar. 1899. xvi, 374 pp.   *BL*

The GREAT INTERCESSION: A WHITSUN EUCHARIST IN THE HIGHLANDS OF AFRICA. Oxford: A.R. Mowbray & Co. [1899]. 31 pp.   *OXB*

GREATOREX, Edward (1823–1900). Son of Thomas Greatorex, organist of Westminster Abbey. Educated at Pembroke College, Oxford, and Durham University. Ordained 1848; curate, Egginton, Staffordshire, 1847–49; secretary, Society of the Sons of the Clergy, 1850–55; sacrist, Durham Cathedral, 1849–62, minor canon from 1849, precentor, 1862–72; librarian, Bishop Cosin's Library, Durham, 1855–81; rector, Croxdale, near Durham, from 1872.
The vision of S. John in Patmos: version by Edward Greatorex. London: J. Masters & Co. 1893. [vi], 61 pp.   *OXB*

GREATREX, Charles Butler, (Lindon Meadows, pseud.) (1832–98). Son of Charles B. Greatrex of Sutton Coldfield, near Birmingham. Educated at King's College, London. Ordained 1856; curate, Loppington, Shropshire, 1856–64, Halberton, Devon, 1864–69, Montgomery, 1869–74, Faccombe, Hampshire, 1874–78, West Camel, Somerset, 1880–81; rector, Hope Bagot, Shropshire, 1881–97.
Bagatelles: [poems]; by Lindon Meadows. London: W. Ridgway. [1887]. 45 pp.   *OXB*
Buffalo Bill on the war-path: a poem; by Lindon Meadows. London: W. Ridgway. [1893]. 22 pp.   *OXB*
Lawyers and their victims: a satire; by Lindon Meadows. 2nd ed. London: W. Ridgway. [1885]. [iv], 24 pp.   *OXB*
A world in white, and other poems; by Lindon Meadows (Chas. B. Greatrex). Third series. London: W. Ridgway, [1889]. 92 pp.   *OXB*
A world in white, and other poems; by Lindon Meadows (Chas. B. Greatrex). Third series. London: Roxburghe Press. [1896]. 92 pp.   *OXB*

GREEN, George Francis. Possibly George Francis Green (1846–). b. Morton, near Bingley, Yorkshire, son of George C. Green, papermaker. Educated at City of London School, leaving aged fourteen owing to ill-health. Established himself in London in the wood-pulp industry, becoming a member of London Chamber of Commerce.

The truth of God: or, the psalm of a Christian; an original poem; by George Francis Green. London: Digby, Long & Co. [1896]. 52 pp.   *OXB*

GREEN, James. Curate, St. John's-in-Weardale, Stanhope, County Durham, 1830–65; vicar of Weardale from 1865.

Poems and sonnets on Weardale and Teesdale; by James Green. Weardale: Nathan M. Egglestone. 1885. 32 pp.   *OXB*

GREEN, John. Of Sunderland, County Durham. Sometimes wrote in Wearside dialect.

Tales & ballads of Wearside; by John Green. Printed Sunderland: E. Thompson. 1882. [iv], 79 pp.   *CU*

Also 1st ed. 1880; 3rd ed. 1882.

Tales and ballads of Wearside; by John Green. 4th ed. London: Walter Scott. 1885. 330 pp.   *TCD*

Also 5th ed. 1897.

GREEN, Kathleen Haydn. Lived at 8 Maitland Park Road, London NW. One-time Lady Mayoress of London.

Poems; by Kathleen Haydn Green. London: Dean & Son, Ltd. 1899. xii, 138 pp.   *OXB*

The poet's corner, and other verses; by Kathleen Haydn Green. [London]: [Author]. 1895. 54 pp.

Printed by the author for private circulation.   *OXB*

GREEN, M. Mrs F. Gwinnett Green. Lived at St Lawrence, Thanet, Kent.

Love's romance: or, Jessie Gray: a poem; by Mrs F. Gwinnett Green. London: Elliot Stock. [1885]. 15 pp.

Published in aid of the Organ Fund, St Margaret's Church, Westminster.   *OXB*

GREEN, Septimus G.

Jennifred, and other verses; by Septimus G. Green. London: Elliot Stock. 1897. xii, 206 pp.   *BL*

Also Cheap ed. 1899.

GREENE, Friese *see* **FRIESE-GREENE, William**

GREENHOW, Edward Headlam (1814–88). b. North Shields, County Durham, son of Dr E. Greenhow. Studied medicine at Edinburgh and Montpelier. Practised for eighteen years with his father in North Shields and Tynemouth. Moved to London in 1853, where he held senior appointments at St Thomas's Hospital and the Middlesex Hospital. Served on several royal commissions, and reported on epidemics and questions of public health.

Recitations and poems; by Edward H. Greenhow. Printed North Shields: T. Todd. [1897?]. 16 pp.   *NPL*

GREENLAND, Alfred. Of Middle Temple.
Lunatic lyrics: [poems]; by Alfred Greenland, Junior. London: Tinsley Bros. 1882. xii, 186 pp.   *MPL*

GREENSTREET, William Lees, (W.L.G.) Commissioned in Royal Engineers, 1863; posted to India, 1870, serving in North West Province; in Bombay command, 1895. Returned to Europe, 1899, retiring in 1900 with rank of colonel.
The flower of Nepal; by W.L. Greenstreet. London: Samuel Tinsley & Co. 1880. [iv], 99 pp.   *OXB*
Lalu, the child widow: a poem; by W.L.G. Calcutta; Thacker, Spink & Co. 1893. [vi], 113 pp.   *BL*

GREENWELL, Dora (1821–82). b. Greenwell Ford, near Lanchester, County Durham, daughter of a country gentleman and magistrate who became impoverished. Her brother was William Greenwell the archaeologist. After the family home was sold in 1848 she lived in Durham City, later moving to London. A poet, prose-writer and hymn-writer, she wrote essays on social and medical topics.
Poems; by Dora Greenwell. (Selected), with a biographical introduction by William Dorling. London: Walter Scott; New York: Thomas Whittaker; Toronto: W.J. Gage & Co. 1889. xxii, 248 pp.(The Canterbury poets).   *BL*

GREER, Maria. Mrs S. Greer, novelist and dramatist.
A vision's voice, and other poems; by Maria Greer. London: Digby Long & Co. [1897]. 63 pp.   *OXB*

GREGORY, John
Murmurs and melodies: [poems]; by John Gregory. With portrait of the author. Bristol: J.W. Arrowsmith; London: Simpkin, Marshall & Co. [1885]. viii, 214 pp. por.   *OXB*

GREIG, David Lundie (1837–   ). b. Edinburgh, where his father was a gentleman's servant. In 1838 the family moved to Arbroath. One of many children, he received a scant education, at the age of eleven working in a yarn loft, at sixteen apprenticed to the trade of blacksmith. After serving his time he moved to Dundee in the employment of Baxter Bros & Co. A Sunday school teacher for many years.
Pastimes musings: [poems]; by David L. Greig. With supplementary contributions by John Paul & David Tasker. Printed Arbroath Herald Office, Brodie & Salmond. 1892. 168 pp.   *BL*

GREIG, James (1861–1941). b. Arbroath, Angus, son of Alexander Greig. Educated at a dame's school, and the Abbey School, he was apprenticed to the flax dressing trade, which adversely affected his health. He possessed a talent for painting, and in 1895 went to London, where he was art critic of the *Morning Post* for many years. Wrote biographies of Raeburn and Gainsborough. Member of the Savage Club.

Poems and songs from the hackle-shop; by James Greig. Arbroath: Thomas Buncle. 1887. viii, 106 pp.   *OXB*

GRETTON, John George. Member of the Society of Jesus.

The holy hill: a toiler's song; by John George Gretton. Roehampton: Manresa Press. 1892. 52 pp. il.   *OXB*

GREVILLE, M.E., pseud. *see* **MATHESON, Greville Ewing**, (M.E. Greville, pseud.)

GREVILLE-NUGENT, Ermengarda. Daughter of Augustus G. Ogilvy of Cove, Scotland. In 1882 she married the Hon. Patrick E.J. Greville-Nugent, son of 1st Baron Greville, and founder and president of the Society of King Charles the Martyr. Lived at Clonyn Castle, County Westmeath.

The rueing of Gudrun, and other poems; by the Hon. Mrs. Greville-Nugent. London: David Bogue. 1884. viii, 109 pp.   *BL*

GREY, Christina *see* **WILSON, Lisa**

GREY, Oliver, pseud. *see* **BROWN, Henry Rowland**, (Oliver Grey, pseud.)

GRIDLEY, Charles Oscar, (C.O.G.)

Ivy leaves, [and other poems]; by C.O.G. Printed London: Spottiswoode & Co. Collected 1890. viii, 104 pp.

Printed for private circulation.   *OXB*

GRIFFITH, George Chetwynd, (Lara, pseud.) (18 – 1906). Son of a country clergyman, he had little formal education but wandered about the world as sea-apprentice, sailor, stock-rider, butcher, schoolmaster, journalist, story writer. Settled at Norfolk Cottage, Littlehampton, Sussex.

Poems: general, secular, and satirical; by Lara. London: W. Stewart & Co.; Edinburgh: J. Menzies & Co. [1883]. 72 pp.   *OXB*

GRIFFITH, William G.

Sonnets and other poems; by William G. Griffith. London: Digby & Long. 1887. viii, 115 pp.   *OXB*

GRIFFITHS, Maggie, (Glynferch)

"Flow'rs of the vale" (Blodau'r glyn): poems; by Maggie Griffiths (Glynferch). Printed Cardiff: Daniel Owen & Co., Ltd. 1894. 61 pp.   *BL*

GRINDROD, Charles. Son of Dr Ralph B. Grindrod, MD. Novelist and dramatist.
   The stranger's story; and his poem, The lament of love: an episode of the Malvern hills; edited [i.e. written] by Charles Grindrod. London: Kegan Paul, Trench & Co. 1883. [viii], 87 pp. il.   *OXB*

GRINS AND GROANS, SOCIAL AND POLITICAL: [poems]. [London]: Swan Sonnenschein & Co. [1882]. [32] pp. il.
   Title from cover.   *OXB*

GRONOW, Bessie Marion. Daughter of William L. Gronow of Ash Hall, Glamorgan. In 1889 she married Louis M. Bassinet of Chambery, France.
   The angel with the censer, and other poems; by B.M. Gronow. London: Remington & Co. 1883. [iv], 78 pp.   *OXB*

GROSART, Alexander Balloch (1827–99). b. Stirling. Educated at Edinburgh University. Studied for the Presbyterian ministry; minister at Kinross, 1856–65, Princess Park, Liverpool, 1865–68; St George's, Blackburn, 1868–92. Literary critic, hymnist, editor of rare Elizabethan and Jacobean texts.
   Songs of the day and night: or, three centuries of original hymns for public and private praise and reading; The life-story of Jesus Christ – a cantata, with other sacred poems; by Alexander B. Grosart. Printed Edinburgh: Turnbull & Spears. 1890 [i.e. 1889]. xl, 510 pp.
   Printed for private circulation only. Spine-title is *Three centuries of hymns*.   *BL*
   Songs of the day and night: or, original hymns for public and private praise and reading; The life of Jesus Christ – a cantata, with other sacred poems; by Alexander B. Grosart. Blackburn: D.E. Rothwell; London: Elliot Stock. 1891. xxii, 282 pp.   *BL*

GROSART, James. Of Peebles.
   Poems; by James Grosart. Printed Innerleithen: Robert Smail. 1884. [ii], 102 pp.   *NLS*

GROSER, Horace George (1863–   ). b. London, son of William H. Groser, secretary of the London Sunday School Union. Employed in literary work as editor and author, contributing to the *Sunday Magazine, Girls' Own Paper*, etc. A member of the Congregational denomination, and author of several hymns.
   Atlantis, and other poems; by Horace G. Groser. London: Hutchinson & Co. [1891]. viii, 160 pp.   *OXB*
   Little folks' land: a book of verses; by Horace G. Groser. [London]: A. Melrose. [1895]. 76 pp. il.   *OXB*
   The log book: [poems]; by H.G. Groser & E. Dawson. Illustrated by A. Wilde Parsons. London: Ernest Nister. [1897]. [16] pp. col. il.
   Not joint authorship. Printed on card.   *BL*

GROTE, Augustus Radcliffe (1841–1900). English–American entomologist.

Rip Van Winkle: a sun myth, and other poems; by Augustus Radcliffe Grote. London: Kegan Paul, Trench, & Co. 1882. [vi], 43 pp.

A limited ed. of 500 copies printed at the Chiswick Press.   OXB

GROVE, George Bassford. Lived at Acock's Green, Birmingham.

Poems, sketches, and verses; by George Bassford Grove. Birmingham: William Downing. 1899. [iv], 139 pp. (Chaucer's Head Library).

For private circulation.   BIP

GRUBBE, Edmund Alexander. b. Southwold, Suffolk, son of John E. Grubbe. Educated at Eton College. Served in the Connaught Rangers Regiment. Lived latterly at Kingsley, Southwold.

Lays of the better land; by E.A. Grubbe. Lincoln: Akrill, Ruddock & Keyworth. 1886. 144 pp.   *UCD

GRUCHY, Augusta De see **DE GRUCHY, Augusta**

GUINNESS, Henry Grattan (1835–1910). Member of the Guinness family of brewers, he was ordained as an evangelist, 1857. He preached in England, Ireland, America, and on the continent, 1857–72. In Dublin he helped in the 'conversion' of Dr Barnardo. Founded the East London Institute for training missionaries, 1873, Livingstone Inland Mission in the Congo, 1878, and other missions in South America and India. Published grammars of the Congo language.

The city of the seven hills; by H. Grattan Guinness. London: James Nisbet & Co.; Morgan & Scott. [1891]. xvi, 302 pp. il.

Poetry and prose.   OXB

GULLAND, Charles, (G.) (1840–) b. Falkland, Fife. Educated there at the parish school, and at Edinburgh Academy and Edinburgh University. After training in London, in 1865 he joined his father in business in Falkland as a solicitor and banker.

Poetical & dramatic selections; by Charles Gulland. Cupar-Fife: J. & G. Innes. 1895. viii, 906 pp.   NLS

Scottish ballads, and other poems; by G. Printed Cupar-Fife: Fifeshire Journal Office. 1881. [iv], 187 pp.   NLS

Also 2nd ed. 1881.

GULSTON, Alan Stepney (1844?–). Son of Alan J. Gulston of Llandilo, Carmenthenshire. Educated at Merton College, Oxford. JP of Dirleton & Derwydd, Carmarthenshire, and captain in the Carmarthen Militia.

Aphrodite, and other poems; by A. Stepney Gulston. London: Remington & Co. 1884. viii, 294 pp.   OXB

GUNN, John (1813–93). Irish Roman Catholic priest. Appointed Dean of Maynooth College, 1838, resigned 1852. Died at Kingstown, near Dublin.

A casket of Irish pearls: being subjects in prose and verse, relating chiefly to Ireland; by Dean Gunn. Dublin: M.H. Gill & Son; London: Burns & Oates (Ltd). 1890. viii, 109 pp.   *OXB*

GURDON, Lady Camilla (1858–94). b. Hurstbourn Park, Hampshire, daughter of 5th Earl of Portsmouth. In 1888 she married Sir William Brampton Gurdon, private secretary to William Ewart Gladstone. She contributed short stories and sketches to *The Leisure Hour*, 1882–85. Died at Grundisburgh Hall, Woodbridge, Suffolk.

Suffolk tales & other stories; Fairy legends; Poems; Miscellaneous articles; by the late Lady Camilla Gurdon. London: Longmans, Green, & Co. 1897. xii, 370 pp.   *MPL*

GURNEY, Alfred (1843–98). b. Lutterworth, Leicestershire, son of Rev. John H. Gurney, prebendary of St Paul's Cathedral. Educated at Exeter College, Oxford; BA 1866, MA 1869. Student, Inner Temple, 1867. Ordained 1875; curate, St Paul's, Brighton, 1873–79; vicar of St Barnabas, Pimlico, London, from 1879.

A Christmas faggot: [poems]; by Alfred Gurney. London: Kegan Paul, Trench, & Co. 1884. x, 79 pp. il.   *OXB*

Day-dreams: [poems]; by Alfred Gurney. London: Longmans, Green & Co. 1896. xii, 90 pp.   *OXB*

Love's fruition; by Alfred Gurney. London: Longmans, Green, & Co. 1897. xii, 27 pp.

     Poetry and prose.   *OXB*

The vision of the Eucharist, and other poems; by Alfred Gurney. London: Kegan Paul, Trench, & Co. 1882. xii, 217 pp.   *OXB*

Voices from the holy sepulchre, and other poems; by Alfred Gurney. London: Kegan Paul, Trench, & Co. 1889. xii, 124 pp.   *OXB*

GURNEY, L.B., (L.B.G.)

Poems; by L.B.G. Composed for the most part at Clevedon Court, Somerset. Printed London: William Brown & Co. 1883. vi, 97 pp.   *TAU*

GUTHRIE, James Cargill (1814–93). b. Airniefoul Farm, Glamis, Forfarshire, son of a tenant farmer. Educated at the parish school, Montrose Academy, and Edinburgh University. He studied for the ministry but went instead into the business world, settling in Dundee. In 1868 he was appointed principal librarian to Dundee Free Library, the first institution of its kind in Scotland.

Woodland echoes: poems and songs; by James Cargill Guthrie. Edinburgh: N.R. Mitchell. 1882. viii, 307 pp. il., por.   *UCD*

GUTHRIE, Thomas Anstey, (F. Anstey, pseud.) (1856–1934). Educated at King's College School, and Trinity College, Cambridge. Associated with *Punch* from 1886, developing a talent for parody and burlesque. Author of comic sketches, short stories and novels, the best known being *Vice Versa*.
  Burglar Bill, and other pieces: [poems] for the use of the young reciter, with introduction, remarks, and stage-directions; by F. Anstey. London: Bradbury, Agnew, & Co. [1889]. viii, 100 pp.
    Reprinted, with some alteration and revision, from *Punch*.   *OXB*
  Mr. Punch's young reciter: (Burgler Bill, and other pieces), with introductions, remarks, and stage-directions; by F. Anstey. Enlarged and illustrated ed. London: Bradbury, Agnew, & Co. Ltd. [1892]. viii, 128 pp. il.
    Poetry and prose.   *OXB*

GWENNY, pseud.
  Miscellaneous verses; by Gwenny. Weston-super-Mare: Robbins. [1890?]. 53 pp.   *TAU*

GWYER, Joseph (1835–). b. Redlynch, Downton, Wiltshire, son of a farmer. Educated at Downton School, and Downton Wesleyan Church. Aged seventeen he went to London, working in mills at Bermondsey; joined the Baptist Church there and taught Sunday school. He married in 1864 and moved to Penge, Surrey, where he was connected with the temperance movement at Penge Tabernacle. Known as 'The Penge Poet'.
  Poems and prose; by Joseph Gwyer. With a short autobiography, also anecdotes of and personal interviews with the late C.H. Spurgeon and others. London: Perraton & Co. for Joseph Gwyer. 1895. 252 pp. il, por.
    Spine-title is *Sketches in prose, and poems*.   *CU*

GWYNNE, Pryce
  Poems and ballads; by Pryce Gwynne. London: T. Fisher Unwin. 1883. 117 pp.   *OXB*

H

H., A., (Child of Mary, pseud.)
  Churchyard flowers: or, memories of the holy dead: [poems]; by a Child of Mary. London: Burns & Oates, Ltd. [1889]. 12 vols.   *OXB*
  Churchyard flowers: or, memories of the holy dead: [poems]; by a Child of Mary. With preface by Father Gallwey. London: Burns & Oates, Ltd. 1891. xii, 174 pp.   *OXB*

Poems; by A.H. and A.F.H. Printed [London]: H.K. Lewis. 1884. 110 pp. Privately printed. ⋆*UCD*

H., A.F.

Poems; by A.H. and A.F.H. Printed [London]: H.K. Lewis. 1884. 110 pp. Privately printed. ⋆*UCD*

H., E. A servant in a parsonage. She was placed in Stafford Lunatic Asylum for ten weeks in 1882.

A bitter cry from the ploughfield; by E.H., a ploughman's daughter. Printed Longton: Wright. [1885]. 41 pp. *BL*

H., E. *see* **HAGGARD, Ella, (E.H.)**

H., E.C.

The suicide at sea, and other poems; by E.C.H. London: Bliss, Sands & Foster. 1895. 64 pp. *OXB*

H., G.S.

Pot-pourri: or, merry and wise: a book of verse; by G.S.H. London: Digby, Long & Co. 1892. viii, 117 pp. *OXB*

H., H.

The islet o'er the sea, and other poems; by H.H. With introductory note by J. Murray Mitchell. 2nd ed., revised and enlarged. London: Elliot Stock. 1894. 63 pp. *OXB*

Sybilline leaves [poems]; [by H.H.]. Printed Chester: Phillipson & Golder. 1885. 57 pp.

Printed for the author. ⋆*UCD*

H., J.

A ransomed soul: or, the conversion of Horse-Shoe Ben: a Christmas tale of village life; by J.H. London: Skeffington & Son. 1885. [ii], 45 pp. *OXB*

H., J.C.

Leaflets: or, thoughts in verse; by J.C.H. Printed Haddington: Neill & Son. 1880. [iv], 84 pp. *OXB*

H., J.L.

The starless crown, and other poems; by J.L.H. London: Elliot Stock. 1897. x, 77 pp. *OXB*.

H., M.

Wanderings, affectionately dedicated to those we love and those who love us: [poems]; [by M.H.]. Printed Liverpool: Turner & Dunnett. [188–]. 37 pp. ⋆*UCD*.

H., M. I.

A wreath of autumn flowers: [poems]; by M.I.H. Printed Ormskirk: T. Hutton. 1880. xii, 112 pp. *BL*

H., R.S. b. Exeter, Devon. Articled to a solicitor. Suffering from a consumptive tendency, he took sea voyages to Canada and Spain, spending some time in Malaga. Died aged twenty-one on board ship, and buried at sea.
A poem without a title; by R.S.H. Edited by a friend. London: Hamilton, Adams, & Co.; Exeter: Henry S. Eland. 1880. iv, 46 pp.   *BL*

H., T.H.
Sanitas sanitorum omnia sanitas: a rural sanitary reminiscence; by T.H.H. Printed Leigh: "Chronicle" Printing & Bookbinding Works. [1888]. 18 pp.   *OXB*

H., V.C. *see* **HALKETT, Violet Craigie**, (V.C.H.)

H., W. *see* **HASTIE, William**, (W.H.)

H., W.G. *see* **HENDRIE, William Girvan**, (W.G.H.)

HABERSHON, Matthew Henry. Of Sheffield, Yorkshire.
The monk's grange: an archaeological poem; by M.H. Habershon. Printed Sheffield: Leader & Sons. 1888. 32 pp.   *BL*

HACON, Henry. Trained for the ministry; deacon, 1862; curate, Fairstead, 1862–63, West Thurrock, 1864–67; chaplain in India, 1867–76, serving successively at Indore, Assenhole, Ajmere, Rajputana, Arrah, Chinsurah, Midnapore; vicar, Willoughton, Lincolnshire, 1886–95, Searby with Owmby, from 1895.
The Incarnation, and other poems; by Henry Hacon. Brigg: Jackson & Sons; London: Simpkin, Marshall, Hamilton, Kent & Co., Ltd. 1898. [viii], 64 pp.   *OXB*

HADDOCK, Charles Marston. Of Bradford, Yorkshire?
"Idle hours": or, poems, songs and sonnets; by C. Marston Haddock. Printed Bradford: J.S. Toothill. 1896. 377 pp.   *OXB*

HADFIELD, James. Schoolmaster. Lived at 80 West Fleet Street, Salford, Lancashire.
Poems; by James Hadfield. Printed Salford: J. Roberts. [1880]. 16 pp.
   Title from cover.   *OXB*
Third book of poems; by James Hadfield. [Salford]: [Author]. [1883]. 16 pp.   *MPL*
Fourth book of poems; by James Hadfield. [Salford]: [Author]. 1885. 16 pp.   *MPL*

HAFED, pseud. Of India.
A dream, and other poems; by Hafed. Printed Madras: Srinivasa, Varadachari & Co. 1893. [iv], 34 pp.   *BL*

HAGGARD, Andrew Charles Parker (1854–1923). b. Bradenham Hall, Norfolk, son of William M. Rider Haggard, and elder brother of novelist Sir Henry Rider Haggard. Educated at Westminster School. Entered army in 1873, serving in King's Own Scottish Borderers in India and Aden; staff officer in Egypt, 1882; saw action in other parts of Africa; retired with rank of lieutenant-colonel. Wrote novels and works of historical interest.

Polyglot poems; by A.C.P. Haggard. London: A.P. Watt. 1888. 134 pp. ★*UCD*

A strange tale of a scarabaeus, and other poems; by A.C.P. Haggard. London: Kegan Paul, Trench, Trübner & Co., Ltd. 1891. xii, 200 pp. *OXB*

HAGGARD, Ella, (E.H.) (1819–89). Daughter of Bazett Doveton of the East Indian Civil Service. Much of her girlhood was spent in India. In 1844 she married William M. Rider Haggard of Bradenham Hall, Norfolk. Mother of ten children including Andrew Charles Parker Haggard and Sir Henry Rider Haggard. Lived latterly at Ditchingham House, Bungay, Suffolk.

Life and its author: an essay in verse; by E.H. London: Jarrold & Sons. [1885?]. 22pp. *BL*

Life and its author: an essay in verse; by Ella Haggard. With portrait, and a memoir by H. Rider Haggard. London: Longmans, Green, & Co. 1890. [vi], 38 pp. por. *OXB*

HAGGER, John. b. Cockermouth, Cumberland. FLS. Lived in Oxford.

Poems; by J. Hagger. Printed Derby: Bemrose & Sons. 1891. viii, 182 pp.
For private distribution only. *BL*

HAIG, Fenil, pseud. *see* **FORD, Ford Madox**, (Fenil Haig, pseud.)

HAILSTONE, Herbert (1850–96). Son of Rev. John Hailstone, vicar of Bottisham, Cambridgeshire. Educated at Eton College, and Peterhouse, Cambridge; BA 1873, MA 1879. Assistant master at Eton, 1873–76, afterwards a private tutor in London. Editor of the *Clergy List*, 1889–91, and translator of some classical authors. Committed suicide by cutting his throat; found dead in Regent's Park.

Fasciculus: a song-bundle: [poems]; by H. Hailstone. Manchester: J.E. Cornish; Cambridge: J. Palmer. 1888. x, 52 pp. *MPL*

Floris domique: [poems]; by H. Hailstone. Cambridge: J. Palmer; Stamford: Jenkinson & Son. 1887. viii, 52 pp. *BL*

Grantae imagines: thirty-six sonnets; by H. Hailstone. Cambridge: J. Palmer. 1886. [viii], 36 pp. MPL

Hesperia: western songs; by H. Hailstone. Cambridge: W. Tomlin. 1888. viii, 69 pp. *CHE*

Musae eoae: eastern songs; by H. Hailstone. Cambridge: W. Tomlin. 1889. viii, 58 pp. *OXB*

Novae arundines: or, new marsh-melodies, in XXXVI metres; by H. Hailstone. Cambridge: J. Palmer. 1885. [iv], 52 pp. *OXB*

Novae arundines: or, new marsh-melodies; by H. Hailstone. 2nd ed. Cambridge: Macmillan & Bowes. 1887. xii, 77 pp. *MPL*

Poems of nature; by Herbert Hailstone. Manchester: John Heywood. 1893. xii, 168 pp.   *MPL*

Sertum: a song-garland: [poems]; by H. Hailstone. Manchester: J.E. Cornish; Cambridge: J. Palmer. 1888. x, 54 pp.   *MPL*

Songs and psalms; by Herbert Hailstone. Cambridge: E. Johnson. 1894. viii, 84 pp.   *MPL*

Susurri: [poems]; by H. Hailstone. Cambridge: Jonathan Palmer. 1886. viii, 31 pp.   *MPL*

Verse and translation; by Herbert Hailstone. Cambridge: E. Johnson; London: Simpkin, Marshall, Hamilton, Kent & Co. 1895. viii, 94 pp.   *MPL*

HAKE, Thomas Gordon (1809–95). b. Leeds. Educated at Christ's Hospital. Studied medicine in Glasgow and Edinburgh and at St George's Hospital; practised successfully at Brighton, Bury St Edmunds and elsewhere; physician to the West London Hospital. Lived latterly in St John's Wood. Attended Dante Gabriel Rossetti during his last days. Known as 'The Parable Poet'.

Maiden ecstasy: [poems]; by Thomas Gordon Hake. London: Chatto & Windus. 1880. [viii], 128 pp.   *MPL*

The new day: sonnets; by Thomas Gordon Hake. Edited, with a preface, by W. Earl Hodgson. With a portrait of the author by Dante Gabriel Rossetti. London: Remington & Co. 1890. [8], xxviii, 93 pp. por. (Rosslyn series).   *OXB*

The poems of Thomas Gordon Hake. Selected with a prefatory note by Alice Meynell and a portrait by Dante Gabriel Rossetti. London: Elkin Mathews and John Lane; Chicago: Stone & Kimball. 1894. viii, 155 pp. por.
     A limited ed. of 500 copies printed for England.   *JRL*

HALEY, Alice, (Allison Hughes, pseud.) b. Leeds. Her grandfather, Thomas Inchbald, was a well-known publisher in the town. Her uncle was the artist John William Inchbold, friend of Tennyson, Ruskin and Swinburne. Latterly she lived abroad a great deal. A contributor to *Good Words, Citizen, Glasgow Weekly*, etc.

Reed music: poems; by Allison Hughes (Alice Haley). London: Kegan Paul, Trench & Co. 1888. viii, 126, [10] pp.   *BL*

HALIBURTON, Hugh, pseud. *see* **ROBERTSON, James Logie**, (Hugh Haliburton, pseud).

HALIFAX CHEESEMONGER, pseud. *see* **HANSON, Samuel**, (Halifax Cheesemonger, pseud.)

HALKETT, Violet Craigie, (V.C.H.). Daughter of Lieutenant-Colonel John C. Craigie Halkett of the 45th Regiment and a JP. Lived at Cramond, Midlothian.

A child's rhymes, written between the age of six and thirteen; by V.C.H. Printed Twickenham: C.M. Major. 1887. 44 pp.   *OXB*

HALL, Arthur Vine (1862-). b. Luddenden Foot, Yorkshire, son of Rev. Arthur Hall and a nephew of Newman Hall. Educated at Cheshunt College. Appointed to the pastorate of South Cliff Congregational Church, Scarborough, Yorkshire in 1887. Lived at 6 Prince of Wales Terrace, Scarborough.
Poems; by Arthur Vine Hall. London: Simpkin, Marshall, & Co.; Scarborough: John Hagyard. [1889]. [2], viii, 60 pp. *OXB*
"Table Mountain": pictures with pen and camera: being an attempt in verse; by Arthur Vine Hall. With illustrations. Cape Town: J.C. Juta & Co. [1886]. 24 pp. il., col. il. *OXB*

HALL, Harriet M.M.
Voices in verse: [poems]; by Harriet M.M. Hall. [London]: H.R. Allenson. 1898. viii, 104 pp. *OXB*

HALL, Joseph Castle
The astrologer's daughter (a Derbyshire legend), and other poems; also appendix in prose: Legends of the High Peak; by Joseph Castle Hall. London: General Publishing Co. Ltd. [c. 1890]. 72 pp. *★UCD*

HALL, Newman (1816–1902). b. Maidstone, Kent, son of John V. Hall. Educated at Totteridge, Highbury College, and London University. First pastor, Albion Congregational Church, Hull, Yorkshire, 1842–54; pastor, Surrey Chapel, London, 1854–76, Christ Church, Lambeth, 1876–92. A noted preacher, he became a general evangelist on retirement. Lived at Vine House, Hampstead Heath.
Lyrics of a long life; by Newman Hall. London: James Nisbet & Co. [1894]. [viii], 256 pp. *OXB*
　Also 2nd ed. [c. 1896].
Mountain-musings, and other poems; by Newman Hall. London: Hodder & Stoughton. [1887?]. 124 pp. *MPL*
Songs of earth and heaven; by Newman Hall London: Hodder & Stoughton. 1885. viii, 268 pp. *OXB*

HALL, Samuel Carter (1800–89). b. Waterford, son of an English officer. Settled in London, 1821; literary secretary to Ugo Fosculo, 1822; a reporter in the House of Lords, 1823. Founded and edited *The Amulet*, 1826–37, connected with *New Monthly Magazine*, 1830–36; edited *Art Union Monthly* (afterwards *Art Journal*), 1839–80.
Rhymes in council: aphorisms versified; by S.C. Hall. London: Griffith & Farran; New York: E.P. Dutton & Co. 1881. [x], 64 pp. *OXB*

HALL, William. Possibly William Hall (1872–1938). b. Edinburgh, son of Peter Hall, merchant of Torrisdale Castle, Kintyre. Educated at Rugby School, and Pembroke College, Oxford. Served in 4th Argyll & Sutherland Highlanders, attaining rank of major. JP and deputy lieutenant, Argyllshire.
The victory of defeat, and other poems, chiefly on Hebrew themes; by William Hall. London: Swan, Sonnenschein & Co., Ltd. 1896. [x], 199 pp. *OXB*
The way of the kingdom, and other poems; by William Hall. London: Swan, Sonnenschein & Co., Limd. 1899. [vi], 232 pp. *OXB*

HALL, Sir William Clarke. Educated at Christ Church, Oxford. Barrister-at-law. Writer on the law relating to children.

Songs in a minor key: a small volume of verse; by William C. Hall. Dublin: Sealy, Bryers & Walker. 1889. 66 pp.   *CU*

HALLARD, James Henry (1861?–   ). b. Edinburgh, son of Frederick Holland, gentleman. Educated at Edinburgh University, and Balliol College, Oxford; BA 1884, MA 1889.

Carmina: a volume of verse; by J.H. Hallard. London: Rivingtons. 1899. [viii], 65 pp.   *OXB*

HALSE, George (1826–95). Son of John Halse, state page at St James's Palace. Educated at St Paul's School. A sculptor in London, 1855–88, exhibiting at the Royal Academy and elsewhere. A novelist, and writer on sculpture, he lived at 15 Clarendon Road, Notting Hill, London.

The legend of Sir Juvenis; by George Halse. With illustrations by Gordon Browne. London: Hamilton, Adams & Co. 1886. [ii], 46 pp. il.   *OXB*

A salad of stray leaves; by George Halse. With a frontispiece by the late Hablot K. Browne. London: Longmans, Green, Co. 1882. viii, 444 pp, il.

Poetry and prose.   *BL*

HAMBLY, Richard. Of Hayle, Cornwall.

Down in a mine, and other sketches in verse; by R. Hambly. Truro: Heard & Sons. 1883. 64 pp.   **UCD*

Down in a mine, and poems of west Cornwall, & c.; by R. Hambly. Printed Penzance: F. Rodda. 1897. 94 pp.   *BL*

HAMILTON, Annie Lee- *see* **LEE-HAMILTON, Annie**

HAMILTON, Edwin (1849–1919). b. Dublin, son of Rev. Hugh Hamilton. Educated at Durham Grammar School, and Trinity College, Dublin; BA 1874, MA 1877. He was called to the Irish Bar but made writing his profession, becoming well known for humorous and satirical prose. Edited several Dublin weekly papers, and contributed to many London journals. Member of the Royal Irish Academy, 1879. Lived latterly at Donaghadee, County Down.

The moderate man, and other verses; by Edwin Hamilton. With twelve original illustrations by Harry Furniss. London: Ward & Downey. [1888]. 108 pp. il.   *OXB*

HAMILTON Eugene Lee- *see* **LEE-HAMILTON, Eugene**

HAMILTON, Sir Ian (1853–1947). Educated at Wellington College, and Sandhurst. Served in 2nd Afghan War, 1878–80; South African revolt, 1881; Nile expedition, 1884–85; 3rd Burmese War, 1886–87; Tirah campaign, 1897–98; Boer War, 1899–1901. Chief of staff to Lord Kitchener, 1901–02; quartermaster general, 1903–04; promoted general, 1914. Commanded Mediterranean expeditionary force in vain attempts to land troops at Gallipoli, 1915.

The ballad of Hadji, and other poems; by Ian Hamilton. London: Kegan Paul, Trench, & Co. 1887. vi, 73 pp. il. *OXB*

The ballad of Hadji, and other poems; by Ian Hamilton. With etched frontispiece by William Strang, and head and tail pieces by J.B. Clark. London: Elkin Mathews & John Lane. 1892. [2], vi, 73 pp. il.

A limited ed. of 550 copies. *BL*

HAMLEY, Sir Edward Bruce (1824–93). b. Bodmin, Cornwall, son of an admiral. Studied at the Royal Military Academy, Woolwich, entering the Royal Artillery in 1843; adjutant in the Crimea; lieutenant-colonel, 1864; member of the Council of Military Education, 1866–70; commandant, Staff College, 1870–77; promoted major-general, 1877; served in Armenia, Bulgaria, Greece and Egypt, 1879–82. Elected Conservative MP for Birkenhead, 1885. Writer on wars and campaigns, and on Voltaire. Contributed to *Blackwood's Magazine* and *Frazer's Magazine*.

Leaves of summer and autumn: [poems]; by Edward Bruce Hamley. Printed Edinburgh: William Blackwood & Sons. 1893. vi, 95 pp.

For private circulation only. *OXB*

HAMMOND, Charles Eaton. Of Newmarket, Suffolk.

Poems; by Charles Eaton Hammond. Printed Newmarket: Tindall & Co. [1899?]. [viii], 372 pp. *OXB*

HAMMOND, Daphne, pseud. *see* **SMITH, Jennie M.**, (Daphne Hammond, pseud.)

HAMMOND, Thomas B.

Poems and lyrics; by Thomas B. Hammond. London: Digby, Long, & Co. 1896. 79 pp. *OXB*

HANBURY, Ernest Osgood. Of London.

On nature, and other verse; by Ernest Osgood Hanbury. London: Simpkin, Marshall, Hamilton, Kent & Co., Ltd. 1892. xii, 214 pp. *OXB*

HANCOCK, Augusta. Lived at Monk Wearmouth, County Durham, a relative of Rev. James H. Hancock, vicar of Venerable Bede Church.

Poems and prose idylls; by Augusta Hancock. Newcastle-on-Tyne: Mawson, Swan, & Morgan. 1893. [xiv], 149 pp. *NPL*

HANKIN, Mary L.

Year by year: [poems]; by Mary L. Hankin. London: T. Fisher Unwin. 1892. 64 pp. *BL*

HANSON, Samuel, (Halifax Cheesemonger, pseud.). Lived at 1 Winn Street, Halifax, Yorkshire.

A parcel of original poems; by a Halifax cheesemonger. Printed Halifax: Alexr. Priestley. 1885. [15] pp. *OXB*

HARDEN, Sidney
  The night and day of a soul, and other poems; by Sidney Harden. London: "Labour News" Publishing Offices. 1892. viii, 94 pp.   *OXB*

HARDING, Edward (1849–   ). b. Dublin. He married the daughter of J.F. Maguire, MP. Settled in Cork where he was a merchant, and a JP of the county from 1885. A noted amateur athlete.
  Sonnets, and other verses; by Edward Harding. London: Elliott Stock. 1894. viii, 59 pp.   *OXB*

HARDINGHAM, Edward. Novelist, and writer on the forests of Essex.
  The romance of Rahere, and other poems; by Edward Hardingham. London: Elliott Stock. 1896. [viii], 262 pp.   *MPL*

HARDY, Charles
  My boy's request, and other poems; by Charles Hardy. London: Remington & Co. 1889. [vi], 84 pp.   *OXB*

HARDY, Thomas (1840–1928). b. Upper Bockhampton, Dorset, son of a builder. Educated at local schools and privately, he trained as an architect in Dorchester. Employed in London by Sir Arthur W. Blomfield, 1862–67, he gave up architecture to become a novelist, only turning to poetry seriously in 1898. Lived at Max Gate, Dorchester, from 1886.
  Wessex poems, and other verses; by Thomas Hardy. With thirty illustrations by the author. London: Harper & Bros. 1898. xii, 228 pp. il.   *MPL*

HARDY, Thomas John (1868–1944). b. Oldham, Lancashire, son of Rev. Thomas Hardy. Educated at The Magnus School, and Queen's College, Cambridge. Ordained 1893; curate, Holy Trinity, Darwen, Lancashire, 1892–94, St Alban's, Rochdale, 1894–97; chaplain, Malacca, Strait Settlements, 1897–98; curate at Chichester, Frensham, Camden Town, Bournemouth, successively 1899–1917; warden, St Mary's House of Retreat, London, 1917–25; vicar, St Peter's, Upton, Nottinghamshire, 1938–39. Received into the Roman Catholic Church, 1939.
  Asdrufel: a soul's episode; by T.J. Hardy. London: Griffith, Farran & Co., Ltd. 1892. [viii], 56 pp.   *OXB*

HARE, Arthur
  Fragments of fancy, in verse; by Arthur and Leopold Hare. London: Remington & Co. 1890. xii, 196 pp.   *OXB*

HARE, Leopold
  Fragments of fancy, in verse; by Arthur and Leopold Hare. London: Remington & Co. 1890. xii, 196 pp.   *OXB*

HARFORD, Frederick Kill (1832?–1906). Son of Henry C. Harford of Clifton, near Bristol. Educated at Rugby School, and Christ Church and New Inn Hall, Oxford: BA 1855, MA 1858. Curate, Croydon, Surrey, 1856–58; chaplain to Bishop of Gibraltar, 1858–61; minor canon, Westminster Abbey, from 1861.

Epigrammatica: serious, semi-serious, and divertive: [poems]; by Frederick Kill Harford. London: Henry Sotheran. 1890. [4], iv, 108 pp.   *OXB*

HARGRAVE, Hugh Dunbar (1854–83). b. Parkhead, near Glasgow, son of a yarn dyer. After acquiring only an elementary education he left school at age of ten to work at Springfield Dye Works. At sixteen he was apprenticed as a bricklayer, following the trade throughout his life.

Poems, songs, and essays; by Hugh Dunbar Hargrave. With a sketch of the author. Glasgow: T.W. Farrell & Co.; T. Hargrave. 1886. 164 pp.   *BL*

HARLEY, Timothy (fl. 1865–85). Rev. Miscellaneous writer.

The pleasures of love, in four parts; by Timothy Harley. London: James Nisbet. 1882. 64 pp.   *BL*

HARRADEN, Gertrude. Of Glastonbury, Somerset?

Saint Hildred: a romaunt in verse; by Gertrude Harraden. Illustrated by J. Bernard Partridge. London: T. Fisher Unwin. 1887. viii, 56 pp. il.   *BL*

HARRINGTON, Jane Maria Elizabeth. Of Ryde, Isle of Wight.

Thoughts in prose and verse; by Jane Maria Elizabeth Harrington. Ryde, Isle of Wight: Author. 1892. 2 vols.

Printed for private circulation.   *UCD*

HARRIS, Alleyne

Solitary song: [poems]; by Alleyne Harris. London: Elliot Stock. 1891. x, 227 pp.   *OXB*

HARRIS, David George. Novelist.

Essays in verse; by D.G. Harris. London: Horace Cox. 1890. viii, 200 pp.   *OXB*

HARRIS, Emily Marion (1844?–1900). b. London of Jewish descent and faith, daughter of Aaron L. Harris. She worked earnestly for charitable organizations; president of West Central Girls' Club. Novelist, essayist, and short story writer. Died at 14 Tavistock Square, London.

Verses; by Emily Marion Harris. London: George Bell & Sons. 1881 [i.e. 1880]. viii, 151 pp.   *BL*

HARRIS, John (1824–84). b. Camborne, Cornwall, son of a copper miner. He joined his father in the mine at age of ten, working there for about twenty years, living in the village of Troon then later in Falmouth. Wrote for many magazines, including a series of articles on the land question. In 1879 he became a Quaker. Received several grants from the Royal Literary Fund and the Royal Bounty Fund.

John Harris, the Cornish poet: a lecture on his life and works; by John Gill.
Falmouth: Alfred Harris; Penryn: J. Gill & Son. [1891]. 40 pp.
  Consists largely of Harris's poems.   OXB
Linto and Laneer, [and other poems]; by John Harris. London: Hamilton,
Adams, & Co.; Falmouth: Author. 1881. viii, 174 pp. il.   OXB
My autobiography; by John Harris. With a photographic portrait of the author.
London: Hamilton, Adams, & Co.; Falmouth: Author; Penryn: John Gill &
Son; Exeter: F. Clapp. 1882. x, 124 pp. il., por.
  Contains author's *Unpublished poems.*   BL

HARRIS, Richard Julian (1861–   ). b. Plymouth, Devon, son of John O.
Harris. Educated at Merton College, Oxford.
  Life through the lotos: a romance in poetry; by Richard Julian Harris. London:
James Cornish. 1883. [iv], 77 pp.   OXB

HARRIS, Robert Alleyne- *see* **ALLEYNE-HARRIS, Robert**

HARRIS-BURLAND, John Burland (1870–   ). b. Aldershot, Hampshire,
son of Major-General William B. Harris-Burland. Educated at Sherborne
School, and Exeter College, Oxford.
  Amy Robsart: the Newdigate poem, 1893; by J.B. Harris Burland. Oxford: A.
Thos. Shrimpton & Son; London: Simpkin, Marshall, Hamilton, Kent & Co.
[1893]. 22 pp.   OXB

HARRISON, Clifford (1857–   ). b. Henley, Oxfordshire, son of William
Harrison, celebrated tenor and manager of the English Opera Co. He went on
the provincial stage as an actor at age of nineteen, discovering a particular
talent for recitation, and performing to enthusiastic audiences in public halls.
An artist in black and white, he held an exhibition of his drawings in 1898. A
close friend of Charles Kingsley.
  In hours of leisure: [poems]; by Clifford Harrison. London: Kegan Paul,
Trench & Co. 1887. viii, 183 pp.   OXB
    Also 3rd ed. 1896.
  Lines in pleasant places: [poems]; written and drawn by Clifford Harrison.
London: Kegan Paul, Trench, Trübner & Co., Ltd. 1895. 119 pp. il.   OXB
  On the common chords: verses; by Clifford Harrison. London: A.D. Innes &
Co. 1895. 111 pp.   OXB

HARRISON, Harry (1870–19   ). b. Wyther, Yorkshire. Educated at Repton
School, and the Royal Horticultural College, Cirencester. Lived latterly at
The Red House, Knaresborough, Yorkshire.
  Poems; by Harry Harrison. Clapham: Author. 1887. 152 pp.   OXB

HARRISON, James Bower (1814–90). Trained for medicine at St Andrews.
Practised in Manchester; surgeon, Ardwick & Ancoats Dispensary; physician,
Manchester Royal Infirmary. Writer on children's diseases and other medical
topics. Lived latterly at The Mount, Higher Broughton, Salford.
  A vision of Asmodeus, and the reflections of Dr. Anselmo; by James Bower
Harrison. Manchester: A. Heywood & Sons. 1880.   ★NUC

HARRISON, John (18 –92). Doctor of Berkeley Square, Bristol.
Ixora: a mystery; [by John Harrison]. London: Kegan Paul, Trench & Co.
1888. viii, 236 pp.
Poetry and prose. *OXB*

HARRISON, John Henry, (Alexander Lind, pseud.) (1829–1900). Educated
at King's College, London. Tutor to the sons of Sir Andrew Buchanan,
ambassador at St Petersburg, 1864; English tutor in the Imperial naval school
there, serving in that and similar establishments; became a councillor of state
with a government pension. Translator from the Russian and French. Died at
St Petersburg c. 6 February 1900.
A dream of the sea, and other poems; by Alexander Lind. London; Simpkin,
Marshall, Hamilton, Kent & Co. Ltd. 1894. vi, 134 pp. *MPL*

HARRISON, Matilda. Of Accrington, Lancashire.
The poet's wreath, being a selection of poems; by Matilda Harrison. Blackburn:
"Express and Standard" General Printing Works. 1890. 147, ii pp. *MPL*

HARTLEY, John (1839–1915). b. Halifax, Yorkshire. Educated there at Park
Place Academy. At an early age he entered the well-known house of James
Ackroyd & Sons, remaining as a designer of worsted goods for many years. In
1866 he began publication of the *Clock Almanac*, circulation exceeding 100,000
annually. Removed to America in 1872.
A sheaf from the moorland: poems; by John Hartley. Wakefield: William
Nicholson & Sons; London: Simpkin, Marshall & Co.; W. Tegg & Co; S.D.
Ewins & Co. [1881]. 184 pp. *OXB*
*Yorkshire lyrics: poems written in the dialect as spoken in the West Riding of
Yorkshire; to which is added a selection of fugitive verses not in the dialect*; by John
Hartley. London: William Nicholson & Sons Ltd. [1898]. 352 pp. por. *UCD*

HARTLEY, Thomas F. Of London.
A few little poems, with short prose introductions; by Thomas F. Hartley. Printed
London: R. Folkard & Son. 1890. [vi], 58 pp.
Cover-title is *Little poems*. *OXB*

HARVEY, Julian (1853–1938?). b. Winchcombe, Gloucestershire, son of
Rev. John R. Harvey. Educated privately, and at Jesus College, Cambridge;
BA 1876, MA 1893. Ordained 1879; curate, St Giles in the Fields, London,
1878–80, Christ Church, Brixton, 1880–83; secretary, London Jews' Society,
1883–86; curate, Christ Church, Warley, Essex, 1886–88, St Andrew's,
Plymouth, 1888–93; St John's, Weymouth, 1893–97, St Luke's, Cheltenham,
1897–1902; vicar, North Rode, Cheshire, 1902–38.
The man of sorrows: a metrical paraphase on Isaiah lii, 13, and liii; by Julian
Harvey. London: Simpkin, Marshall, Hamilton, Kent & Co.; Plymouth:
W.F. Westcott. [1892]. 32 pp. *OXB*

HARVEY, Laura
Thoughts in verse; by Laura Harvey. Printed Birmingham: Charles Caswell.
1884. 68 pp. *UCD*

HASTIE, William, (W.H.). (1842–1903). Educated at Edinburgh University; BD 1869; thereafter studied in Germany, Holland and Switzerland. Principal of the Church of Scotland College, Calcutta, 1878–83; professor of divinity, Glasgow University, from 1895. Writer on theology and philosophy, and translator of many theological works.
   La vita mia: a sonnet chain, in links of life and thought; by W.H. Printed Edinburgh: Miller & Son. 1896. [x], 72 pp.
      Printed for private circulation.   *OXB*

HATCH, Edwin (1835–89). Educated at Pembroke College, Oxford. Professor of classics, Toronto University, 1859–62; rector, Quebec High School, 1862–67; vice-principal, St Mary Hall, Oxford, 1867–85. Appointed first editor of the *Univesity Gazette*, 1870. Theologian and writer on church history.
   Towards fields of light: sacred poems; by the late Edwin Hatch. London: Hodder & Stoughton. 1890. 55 pp.   *UCD*

HATCH, James J.
   Mathias, and other poems; by James J. Hatch. London: Remington & Co. 1886. viii, 96 pp.   *OXB*

HATTON, Joshua, (Guy Roslyn, pseud.) (1850–   ). b. Chesterfield, Derbyshire, son of F.A. Hatton. He finished school at age of twelve, became a compositor on the *Lincolnshire Chronicle*, then a reporter on several daily and weekly newspapers. Aged twenty-three he became editor of the *Western Daily Mercury*, then leader writer on the *Sheffield Independent*; in 1879 he was appointed editor of *Colburn's New Monthly*.
   Throughout the year: poems old and new; by Guy Roslyn. London: W.B. Whittingham & Co. 1886. 225 pp.   *★UCD*

HAVILAND, Cyril
   Voices from Australia; [poems]; by Philip Dale and Cyril Haviland. London: Swan Sonnenschein & Co. 1892. iv, 288 pp.
      Not joint authorship.   *TCD*

HAWEIS, John Oliver Willyams (1806–   ). Son of Thomas Haweis of Bath. Educated at Queen's College, Oxford: BA 1828, MA 1831. Ordained 1830; curate, Prittlewell, Essex, 1829–31, St Mary-de-Lode, Gloucestershire, from 1835; chaplain, Magdalen Hospital, from 1846; rector, Slaugham, Sussex, 1874–86; prebendary of Chichester from 1883.
   Remnants: [poems]; by J.O.W. Haweis. Haywards Heath: C. Clarke. 1881. 28pp.   *★UCD*

HAWKES, Henry. Of Waterloo.
   The man of Nazareth: a true life; [by Henry Hawkes]. London: Kegan Paul, Trench & Co. 1889. [vi], 67 pp.   *OXB*

HAWKES, William, (Loyal Irishman, pseud.) Of Seacombe, Birkenhead, Cheshire.

The grand old man: a random rhyme; by William Hawkes. [1884]. 15 pp.   *OXB*
   Also 2nd ed. [1884?].

The grand old man: a political random rhyme; by a loyal Irishman. 4th ed. Printed Liverpool: Matthews Bros. [1889]. 16 pp.   *BL*

HAWKEY, Charlotte. Of Taunton, Somerset?

The Shakespeare tapestry, woven in verse; by C. Hawkey. Edinburgh: Blackwood & Sons. 1881. [vi], 209 pp.   *UCD*
   Also New ed. 1881.

HAWKINS, Hope Josephine. Lived at Buckingham House, 359 Liverpool Road, London N.

Ivy leaves; by Mrs. H.J. Hawkins. London: Author; William Colmer. 1881. 78 pp.
   Poetry and prose.   *OXB*

HAWLEY, John Hugh (fl. 1865–85). Writer of school texts.

In memoriam Louis Eugène Napoléon; in five parts . . . ; by John Hugh Hawley. London: John Mitchell; Leamington: Thos. Simmons; Henry Wippell. 1880. 20 pp.   *OXB*

HAWORTH, John. Of Bury St Edmunds, Suffolk.

At honour's cost; by John Haworth. Manchester: John Heywood. [1893]. 16 pp. (John Heywood's books of recitations by well known authors).
   Poetry and prose.   *BL*

The besieged city, [and other poems]; by John Haworth. Manchester: John Heywood. [1893]. 16 pp. (John Heywood's books of recitations by well known authors).   *BL*

The warning light, [and other poems]; by John Haworth. Manchester: John Heywood. [1895]. 16 pp. (John Heywood's books of recitations by well known authors).   *BL*

HAWTHORN, Joseph. Lived at Gold Street, Kettering, Northamptonshire.

Poems; by Joseph Hawthorn. Printed Kettering: Goss Bros. 1882. 100 pp.   *UCD*

HAYCRAFT, Margaret Scott. Née MacRitchie. Mrs Haycraft of Epsom, Surrey. She was secretary of a Band of Hope.

By the Sea of Galilee: a poem; by M.S. MacRitchie. With illustrations by H.I.A. Miles. London: Wells Gardner, Darton, & Co. [1881]. [22] pp. il.   *BL*
   Also 2nd ed. [1882].

Drift leaves: [poems]; by Margaret Scott MacRitchie (Mrs Haycraft). London: James Nisbet. 1884. 126 pp.   *OXB*

Guiding lights: [poems]; by Margaret Haycraft. Monotints by W.H.S. Thompson. London: George Routledge & Sons. [1888]. [16] pp. il.   *BL*

Songs of peace; by Margaret Haycraft. London: James Nisbet. 1883. 112 pp.   *OXB*

The springtide reciter: temperance recitations for young speakers; by Margaret Haycraft. London: Charles H. Kelly. 1890. viii, 103 pp.   *OXB*

Waters of quietness: being daily messages for invalids: [poems]; by Margaret Scott MacRitchie. London: James Nisbet & Co. 1881. 96 pp.   *OXB*

Wayside chimes: [poems]; by Margaret Scott Haycraft. London: James Nisbet & Co. 1886. 144 pp.   *BL*

HAYDEN, John J. (1859–   ). Son of Dr Thomas Hayden, Dublin physician. Barrister, Gray's Inn, he eventually emigrated to Vancouver, Canada.

Chequy: sonnets original and translated; by John J. Hayden. Printed Halifax: Ashworth & Birkhead. 1898. 82 pp.   *UCD*

Foam-bells: rhythmical trifles; by John J. Hayden. Printed Dublin: Cahill. 1889. 32 pp.
> Printed for private circulation.   *BL*

HAYES, Alfred (1857–1936). b. Wolverhampton, Staffordshire, son of Edwin J. Hayes, town clerk of Wolverhampton. Educated at King Edward's School, Birmingham, and New College, Oxford; BA 1881, MA 1885. Studied for the Bar, Inner Temple, but abandoned law for teaching. Held successive masterships at Felstead School, Essex, Brewood School, Staffordshire, and King Edward's School, Birmingham. Elected secretary, Birmingham & Midland Institute, 1889.

David Westren; by Alfred Hayes. Birmingham: Cornish Bros; London: Simpkin, Marshall, & Co. 1888. [vi], 124 pp.   *UCD*
> Also 2nd ed. 1888

From midland meadows: [poems]; by Alfred Hayes. Rugby: George E. Over; London: Elkin Mathews & John Lane. 1893. [iv], 31 pp.   *BL*

The last crusade, and other poems; by Alfred Hayes. Birmingham: Cornish Bros; London: Simpkin, Marshall, & Co. 1887. [viii], 150 pp.   *OXB*
> Also 2nd ed. 1887.

The march of man, and other poems; by Alfred Hayes. London: Macmillan & Co. 1891. viii, 178 pp.   *JRL*
> Also 2nd ed. 1892.

The Vale of Arden, and other poems; by Alfred Hayes. London: John Lane at The Bodley Head. 1895. 92 pp.
> A limited ed. of 550 copies.   *OXB*

The Vale of Arden; by Alfred Hayes. With illustrations by Oliver Baker. Birmingham: Cornish Bros. 1897. 33 pp. il., por.   *OXB*
> Also 'A limited ed. of 75 numbered copies' – author's MS. note in BL copy, 1897.

HAYES, Cornelius (Con.) F.

Ida: a monodrama; by Con. F. Hayes. London: Remington & Co. 1882. 61 pp.   *OXB*

HAYES, Thomas J.

Verse ventures; by Thomas J. Hayes. Leeds: Goodall & Suddick. 1895. vi, 112 pp.   *LEP*

HAYLEY, Harriet
   Saint Bernard, and other poems; by Harriet Hayley. London: Hatchards. 1888.
[iv], 83 pp.
'Any profits to be given to Bishop Caldwell's Victoria Institution for High-
Class Hindu Girls at Tuticorin'.   *OXB*

HAYLLAR, Florence H. (1869–   ). Lived at 41 Marlborough Place,
Brighton, Sussex.
   Camilla and Gertrude, and other poems; by Florence H. Hayllar. London: F.V.
White & Co. 1884. [2], iv, 106 pp.   *OXB*
   First efforts: [poems]; by Florence H. Hayllar. Printed Brighton: J.G. Bishop,
"Herald" Office. 1881. [vi], 48 pp.
   Published in aid of the funds of the Royal Alexandra Hospital.   *BL*

HAYWARD, Abraham (1801–84). b. Wilton, Wiltshire, son of Joseph
Hayward. Educated at Tiverton Grammar Schol. Articled to a solicitor;
studied law at Middle Temple, called to the Bar, 1830; QC 1845. Founded *Law
Magazine* which he edited, 1828–44. He had a small legal practice but was
known chiefly as a raconteur and literary man, contributing to *The Times*,
Saturday Review, *Quarterly Review*, etc. Published many legal texts.
   Verses of other days; by A. Hayward. (Reprinted, with additions, for friends).
Printed Edinburgh: Ballantyne, Hanson & Co. 1882. iv, 63 pp.   *UCD*

HAYWOOD, Annie Winsor (1866–   ). b. Folkestone, Kent, but lived in
Scotland from early girlhood. She studied for the teaching profession at
Edinburgh Church of Scotland Training College. Taught at a school in Leslie,
Fife. Contributed verse and prose to many Scottish magazines and
newspapers.
   Shepherd's tartan, and other poems; by Annie Winsor Haywood. Cupar-Fife; A.
Westwood & Son; Kirkcaldy: J. & R. Burt. [1895]. 144 pp.   *BL*

HAZLEHURST, Thomas. Of Runcorn, Cheshire?
   Readings, recitations, & c.; by Thomas Hazlehurst. Printed Runcorn: J.W.
Woodland. 1889. 96 pp.
   Poetry and prose.   *CPL*

HAZLITT, William Carew (1834–1913). Grandson of William Hazlitt,
essayist and critic. Educated at Merchant Taylors' School. Called to the Bar,
Inner Temple, 1861. Bibliographer and miscellaneous writer, he edited the
letters of William Hazlitt and Charles Lamb.
   Leisure intervals: [poems]; by W. Carew Hazlitt. London: George Redway.
1897. viii, 246 pp.   *OXB*

HEAD, N.
   Mabel: a tale of filial love; by N. Head. London: Ward, Lock, Bowden, & Co.
1893. [iv], 120 pp.   *OXB*

HEALD, W. Chandler
The stories of the 30th January, 1649, and the 29th May, 1660, told in rhyme; [by W. Chandler Heald]. London: J.T. Hayes. 1880. 42 pp.   *OXB*

HEARN, John Newton
Saul, and other poems; by J.N. Hearn. London: Thomas Le Mesurier. 1887. 31 pp. (Pen and ink series, IX).   *BL*

HEARTSEASE, pseud
God's garden: [poems]; by Heartsease. London: James Nisbet & Co. 1887. [iv], 155 pp.   *OXB*

HEATHORN, Thomas Bridges (1830–   ). Son of Joseph L. Heathorn, member of Trinity House. Educated at Putney College. Joined the army, leaving for India in 1850; attained rank of captain, Royal Artillery; in the Crimean War he served on the staff of the Turkish contingent; returned to India to join the Rajputana Field Force; involved in several military engagements, he was invalided home suffering from fever. Associated with many scientific enterprises, he became a director of Mason & Barry, Ltd. Lived latterly at 10 Wilton Place, London SW.
Light refreshment of different sorts; by T.B. Heathorn. London: Remington & Co. 1881. iv, 180 pp.
     Poetry and prose.   *OXB*

HEATON, Arthur Frederick (1841?–1911). Son of Rev. George Heaton of Cheltenham. Educated at Oakham School, and Clare College, Cambridge (scholar); BA 1865. Ordained 1866; curate, Axminster, Devon, 1865–68, St Ninian's, Castle Douglas, 1868–70, Sunninghill, Berkshire, 1871–73, Malpas, Cheshire, 1873–75, Rayleigh, Essex, 1877–80; Worksop, Nottinghamshire, 1880–83; chaplain at Christiania, Norway, 1883–99; rector, Covington, Huntingdonshire, 1892–1910, Waddesdon, Buckinghamshire, from 1910.
Now and then: [poems]; by A.F. Heaton. London: Elliot Stock. 1889. 61 pp.   *OXB*

HECKETHORN, Charles William. Writer on secret societies throughout the world.
Roses and thorns: poems; by Charles William Heckethorn. London: City of London Publishing Co. 1887. vi, 192 pp. il.   *UCD*

HEDDERWICK, James (1814–97). b. Glasgow, son of James Hedderwick, Queen's printer. Assistant editor of *The Scotsman*, 1837–42; editor and part owner of *Glasgow Citizen*, 1842–64; started *Glasgow Evening Citizen*. A founder of Glasgow Burns Club, twice chairman. Honorary LL.D, Glasgow University, 1878.
The villa by the sea, and other poems; by James Hedderwick. Glasgow: James Maclehose. 1881. xii, 239 pp.   *OXB*

HEDLEY, George Roberts (1833–   ). b. Ovington, Northumberland, into a farming family. Farmed all his life in the Newcastle upon Tyne area.
Ballads, and other poems; by George Roberts Hedley. London: Walter Scott. 1885. 148 pp. por.   *NPL*

HEFFERNAN, E.A. Topographical writer.
Songs in the nights: "Until the day dawn", and other poems; by E.A. Heffernan. London: L. Lloyd. 1899. 43 pp.   *OXB*

HEINEKEY, E.F. A woman. Lived at 26 Christchurch Avenue, Brondes-bury, London NW.
Bells of gold, and other poems; by E.F. Heinekey. Printed London: Wertheimer, Lea & Co. [1893]. 96 pp.   *OXB*

HELLON, Henry George. Member of the Authors' Club, London SW.
Daphnis: a Sicilian pastoral, and other poems; by Henry George Hellon. London: Kegan Paul, Trench & Co. 1881. viii, 122 pp.   *OXB*

HEMINGWAY, Percy, pseud. *see* **ADDLESHAW, William Percy**, (Percy Hemingway, pseud).

HEMSLEY, G.T., (Arnold Frost, pseud.). Of Lincoln.
The ballad of the wind, the devil, and Lincoln Minster: a Lincolnshire legend; [by] Arnold Frost. 2nd ed., enlarged. Printed Lincoln: Keyworth & Sons. 1897. 16 pp.   *OXB*
    1st ed. 12 pp., 1897.
The ballad of the wind, the devil and Lincoln Minster: a Lincolnshire legend; [by] Arnold Frost. 3rd ed. improved. Lincoln: Boots Ltd. 1898. 16 pp. il.   *OXB*

HENDERSON, Mrs David
Highland Flora, and other poems; by Mrs. David Henderson. Edinburgh: David Douglas. 1889. [vi], 108 pp.   *BL*

HENDERSON, Fred (1867–19   ). b. Norwich, son of J.A. Henderson. Senior member of Norwich City Council from 1902, alderman from 1923. Socialist and parliamentary candidate for East Norfolk. Writer on economic topics, his books appeared in many foreign translations. Lived at Earlham Rise, Norwich.
Alice, and other poems; by Fred Henderson. London: Jarrold & Sons. [1884]. 72 pp.   *BL*
By the sea, and other poems; by Fred Henderson. London: T. Fisher Unwin. 1891. [iv], 48 pp.   *OXB*
    Also 2nd ed. 1892.
Echoes of the coming day: socialist songs and rhymes; by Fred Henderson. London: Office of "The Commonweal". 1887. 16 pp.   *BL*
Love triumphant: a series of sonnets; by Fred Henderson. London: Jarrold & Sons. 1888. 32 pp.   *BL*

HENDERSON, James (1824–). b. Stirling. Orphaned when very young, aged twelve he went to Glasgow where he worked for a distant relative who was a councillor in the city. In 1849 he travelled to India, residing for some time in Calcutta before returning to Glasgow.

Glimpses of the beautiful, in verse; by James Henderson. Glasgow: Henderson & Co. 1890. viii, 353 pp. *BL*

Also 2nd ed. 1890.

HENDERSON, James C. (1858–81). b. Glasgow, son of the artist Joseph Henderson. Studied art at Glasgow Haldane Academy, and at the Royal Scottish Academy, Edinburgh. His paintings were exhibited at the Scottish Academy and at the Glasgow Institute. Died suddenly of rheumatic fever on 12 July 1881.

Poems; by James C. Henderson. Printed Glasgow: Robert Anderson. 1882. [iv], 84 pp. por.

Printed for private circulation. *OXB*

HENDERSON, Margaret (1843–93). b. Wick, Caithness, youngest daughter of John Henderson. Lived at Ormlie Lodge, Thurso.

My garden, and other poems; by Margaret Henderson. Edinburgh: David Douglas. 1896. xii, 108 pp. por. *BL*

HENDERSON, William (1831–91). b. Biggar, Lanarkshire. The family moved to Edinburgh, where he became an office boy. At age fourteen he was apprenticed as a compositor to the printers Thomas Constable. In 1856 he left for London, where he worked as a journeyman compositor for Novello's and other firms. In 1861 he went into partnership with J.C. Rait; the firm Henderson, Rait & Spalding was celebrated for its highly artistic work, music being its speciality. He himself was a composer of some ability.

Songs and poems; by William Henderson. Glasgow: Murray & Gilchrist. 1899. 51 pp. *★UCD*

Who wrote Shakespeare? "Aye, there's the rub"; by William Henderson. With pen and ink sketches by Charles Lyall. London: David Stott. 1887. 52 pp. il. *OXB*

HENDRIE, William Girvan, (W.G.H.) (1841–98). b. Galston, Ayrshire, son of a banker. Attended Glasgow University. He went into business, first in Brazil, then in West Africa, where his health was adversely affected by fever. Returned to Scotland, joined a Glasgow business partnership, working in Ireland for a time.

Poems; by W.G.H. Paisley: Alexander Gardner. 1899. [ii], 62 pp. *OXB*

HENDRY, Hamish. Of Alloa, Clackmannanshire.

Burns from heaven, with some other poems; by Hamish Hendry. Glasgow: David Bryce & Son. 1897. 96 pp.

A limited ed. of 260 numbered copies. *OXB*

HENLEY, William Ernest (1849–1903). b. Gloucester. Educated at Crypt Grammar School there, where he was a pupil of T.E. Brown, the Manx poet. A cripple from boyhood, he spent some time in an Edinburgh infirmary treated by Joseph Lister. On staff of the *Encyclopaedia Britannica* in Edinburgh, 1875, then moved to London, becoming an active contributor to well-known journals; helped to found *London*, of which he was editor, 1876–78; edited the *Magazine of Art*, 1882–86, *Scots Observer*, 1889–94, *News Review*, 1894–98. A friend of Robert Louis Stevenson, with whom he collaborated in a series of plays.

A book of verses; by William Ernest Henley. London: David Nutt. 1888. xii, 167 pp. *JRL*

Also 2nd ed. 1889; 3rd ed. 1891; 5th ed. 1897.

London types; by William Nicholson. London: William Heinemann. 1898. [40] pp. col. il.

Includes *Quatorzains*; by William Ernest Henley. *TCD*

London voluntaries; The song of the sword, and other verses; by W.E. Henley. London: David Nutt. 1893. x, 131 pp. *OXB*

Also 2nd ed. 1893.

Poems; by William Ernest Henley. London: David Nutt. 1898. xiv, 256 pp. por. *MPL*

Also 2nd ed. 1898.

The song of the sword, and other verses; by W.E. Henley. London: David Nutt. 1892. xii, 102 pp. *MPL*

Also a limited ed. of 20 copies printed on Japanese paper and signed by the publisher, 1892.

HENRY, Eliza. Mrs Henry. Lived at the Free Church Manse, Humbie, East Lothian.

Cherished memories of by-gone days: [poems]; by Mrs Henry. Portobello: T. Adams. 1888. [6], vi, 168 pp.

Spine-title is *Poems*. *BL*

HENRY, Mrs *see* **HENRY, Eliza**

HEONE, pseud. *see* **CLARK, Hugh**, (Heone, pseud.)

HEPBURN, Duncan Dewar, (Emerald Isle, pseud.)

Stray rhymes; by Duncan D. Hepburn "Emerald Isle". 2nd ed. revised and enlarged. With illustratons by Hume Nisbet. London: W.H. Allen. 1886. xvi, 112 pp. il. *OXB*

HEPBURN, Thomas Nicoll, (Gabriel Setoun, pseud.) (1861–1930). b. West Wemyss, Fife, son of Alexander Hepburn, merchant tailor. Educated at Moray House, Edinburgh, and St Andrews University. Headmaster, Milton House Public School, Edinburgh. President, Assistant Teachers' Association (Edinburgh branch), 1895–96 and 1901–02.

The child world: [poems]; by Gabriel Setoun. Illustrated by Charles Robinson. London: John Lane The Bodley Head. 1896. 175 pp. il. *JRL*

HERBERT, Auberon (1838–1906). Son of 3rd Earl of Caernarvon. Educated at Eton College, and St John's College, Oxford; Fellow of St John's, 1855–69. Served in 7th Dragoons, 1858–62. DCL 1865. Private secretary to Sir Stafford Northcote, 1866–68; abandoning Conservative views, he was elected Liberal MP for Nottingham, 1870–74. Farmed in the New Forest from 1874. Lived at Old House, Ringwood, Hampshire.

Windfall and waterdrift: [poems]; by Auberon Herbert. London: Williams & Norgate; New York: G.P. Putnam's Sons. 1894. xvi, 194 pp.   *UCD*

HERBISON, David (1800–80). b. Ballymena, County Antrim, son of an innkeeper. He lost his sight at the age of three but regained it later. Put to work at linen weaving aged fourteen. He emigrated to Canada, going to Quebec after surviving a shipwreck. Returned to Ireland in 1830, settling down in Ballymena as a weaver. Wrote for Ulster periodicals. Known as 'The Bard of Dunclug'.

The select works of David Herbison. With life of the author by David M'Meekin. Belfast: William Mullan & Son; Ballymena: John Wier & Moses Erwin; Londonderry: John Hempton. [1883?]. xxiv, 312 pp. il.

Spine-title is *Poetical works*.   *BL*

HERCUS, James Logie (1847–85). b. Kirkwall, Orkney. Educated at Kirkwall Grammar School. Engaged in business, first in Kirkwall, next in Edinburgh, finally in Glasgow.

Songs of the borderland, and other verses; by James L. Hercus. With a preface by W.A. Clouston. Kelso: J. & J.H. Rutherford; Kirkwall: William Peace & Son. [1888]. xiv, 140 pp.   *UCD*

HERFORD, Oliver (1836–1935) b. England. Writer of whimsical books which he illustrated himself.

Artful anticks: [poems]; by Oliver Herford. London: Gay & Bird. 1894. xii, 100 pp. il. (by the author).   *OXB*

Also American ed. published New York: Century Co., 1894.

The bashful earthquake, and other fables and verses; by Oliver Herford. With many pictures by the author. London: Downey & Co. Ltd. 1899. x, 126 pp. il. *OXB*

HERNAMAN, Claudia Frances (1838–98). b. Addlestone, Surrey, daughter of Rev. W.H. Ibotson, sometime vicar of Edwinstowe, Nottinghamshire. In 1858 she married Rev. J.W.D. Hernaman, an inspector of schools. She composed more than one hundred and fifty hymns, many for children.

The crown of life: verses for holy seasons; by Claudia Frances Hernaman. London: Griffith, Farran, Okeden & Welsh; New York: E.P. Dutton & Co. 1886. 260 pp.   *OXB*

HERON-ALLEN, Edward (1861–1943). b. London, son of George Allen and Catherine Heron. Educated at Harrow School. Admitted solicitor, Supreme Court of Judicature, 1884; held several governmental and municipal appointments in London; National Service Commissioner, 1916–17; attached to Staff Intelligence, War Office, 1918. Translator from the Persian, he also wrote novels, books on the violin, and on cheirosophy. Lived latterly at Large Acres, Selsey Bill, Sussex.

The ballades of a blasé man; to which are added some rondeaux of his rejuvenescence, laboriously constructed by the necromancer to the Sette of Odd Volumes [by Edward Heron-Allen]. Printed London: Charles Whittingham. 1891. 72 pp. (Privately printed opuscula, issued to members of the Sette of Odd Volumes, no. XXVIII). *BL*

The love-letters of a vagabond: [poems]; by Edward Heron-Allen. London: Henry J. Drane. 1889. [viii], 87 pp. *OXB*

HESTER, George Norman. Writer on Ancient Greece.

The annals of England, in verse and rhyme; by George Norman Hester. London: Chapman & Hall, Ld. 1897. viii, 184 pp. *UCD*

HEWITT, Edgar (1868–19). Son of William H. Hewitt, solicitor of Manchester. He qualified as a solicitor, entering his father's firm in 1890, retiring c. 1938. Lived at Ormonville, 394 Great Clowes Street, Higher Broughton, Salford.

Poems; by Edgar Hewitt. London: Wyman & Sons. 1887. vi, 66 pp. *MPL*

HEWITT, J.A.

Summer songs, and other poems; by J.A. Hewitt. London: Remington & Co. 1882. x, 294 pp. *OXB*

HEWITT, Susan (1821–). Hon. Susan Hewitt, daughter of James Hewitt, 3rd Viscount Lifford.

Songs of coming day; [by Susan Hewitt]. London: Kegan Paul, Trench & Co. 1885. viii, 152 pp. *OXB*

HEWLETT, Henry Gay (1832–97). Keeper of Land Revenue Records, 1865–96. Writer on English and European history. Lived at Shaw Hill, Addington, Kent. Father of Maurice Hewlett.

A wayfarer's wallet; Dominus redivivus, [and other poems]; by Henry G. Hewlett. London: George Redway. 1888. viii, 120 pp. *OXB*

HEWLETT, Maurice (1861–1923). b. Weybridge, Surrey, son of Henry Gay Hewlett. Educated at Sevenoaks Grammar School, and Isleworth International College. Called to the Bar, 1891, but never practised. Succeeded his father as Keeper of Land Revenue Records, 1897–1900. Made his name by popular romantic fiction. Lived at Broad Chalke, Wiltshire.

Songs and meditations; by Maurice Hewlett. Westminster: Archibald Constable. 1896. xii, 136 pp. *OXB*

HEWSON, J. James. Short story writer.

Rank doggerel: being a little laughter with a sediment of sentiment; by James J. Hewson. Illustrated by R. Talbot Kelly. London: Simpkin, Marshall, Hamilton, Kent, & Co., Ltd. 1892. 64 pp. il. *UCD*

Also 2nd ed. 1892.

HICKEY, Emily Henrietta (1845–1924). b. Ireland, daughter of Rev. Canon Hickey. Educated at her home, Macmine Castle, and at private school. She lived in London, attending lectures at University College, and subscribed to Cambridge correspondence classes. Co-founder, with Dr Furnival, of the Browning Society. Contributed to many English and American magazines.

Ancilla domini: thoughts in verse on the life of the Blessed Virgin Mary; by Emily Hickey. London: Author. [1898]. 38 pp.   *BL*

Michael Villiers, idealist, and other poems; by E.H. Hickey. London: Smith Elder, & Co. 1891. vi, 192 pp.   *OXB*

Poems; by Emily Hickey. London: Elkin Mathews. 1896. [viii], 63 pp. il.   *OXB*

A sculptor, and other poems; by E.H. Hickey. London: Kegan Paul, Trench, & Co. 1881. viii, 176 pp.   *BL*

Verse-tales, lyrics, and translations; by Emily H. Hickey. Liverpool: W. & J. Arnold. 1889. [2], viii, 120 pp.   *OXB*

'Also a limited ed. of 50 large paper numbered copies ' – handwritten note in BL copy.

HICKLING, George, (Rusticus, pseud.). Of Cotgrave, Nottinghamshire. Educated in the village school.

Echoes from the woodlands: [poems]; by George Hickling ("Rusticus"). Nottingham: Thomas Forman & Sons. 1892. xvi, 288 pp. por.   *UCD*

HICKS, Maude Robertson- *see* **ROBERTSON-HICKS, Maude.**

HILL, A.E., (Blancor Dash, pseud.)

Dreaming, [and other poems]; by Blancor Dash. London: Kegan Paul, Trench, Trübner, & Co. Ltd. 1890. viii, 152 pp.   *OXB*

Tales of a tennis party; [poems]; by Blancor Dash. London: Kegan Paul, Trench & Co. Ltd. 1889. [vi], 166 pp.   *OXB*

HILL, Alsager Hay (1839–1906). Educated at Trinity Hall, Cambridge; LL.B 1862. Called to the Bar, 1864. Social reformer concerned with pauperism, labour and employment; established a labour exchange in London, 1871; edited *Labour News*, journal of communication between masters and men seeking work. Vice-president of National Sunday League, 1876–90. Lived at 15 Russell Street, Covent Garden, London.

A household queen, sonnets, and other poems; by Alsager Hay Hill. London: "Labour News" Publishing Offices. 1881. xvi, 144 pp.   *OXB*

HILL, E.S. A man of Burton-upon-Trent, Staffordshire.

A tale of ancient times, and miscellaneous poems; by E.S. Hill. Printed Burton-upon-Trent: "Standard" Office. 1881. 104 pp.   *BL*

HILL, J. Graham

Under her window: [poems]; by J. Graham Hill. London: Griffith, Farran, Okeden & Welsh. 1888. 78 pp.   *OXB*

HILL, James N. Rev. Hill, minister of Prinlaws, Fife.
The cycle of life, and other poems; by James N. Hill. Edinburgh: John Menzies & Co; Cupar-Fife: A. Westwood & Son; Kirkcaldy: James Burt; Leslie: P. Jollie & Son. 1893. 64 pp. *OXB*

HILL, John (18 –1904). Irish novelist. Lived some years in the Isle of Wight, then afterwards in Brussels.
Songs; by John Hill. London: Remington & Co. [iv], 60 pp. *OXB*

HILL, Roland George, (Roland Georgehill, pseud.)
Voices in solitude: [poems]; by Roland Georgehill. First series. London: Samuel Tinsley & Co. 1880. iv, 140 pp. *OXB*

HILLS, A.E.
Elfinn's luck, and other poems; by A.E. Hills. London: A.D. Innes. 1897. viii, 120 pp. *OXB*

HIME, Mrs Maurice Charles *see* **HIME, Rebecca**

HIME, Rebecca (1841–). Youngest daughter of John Apjohn, professor of chemistry, Trinity College, Dublin. In 1887 she married Dr Maurice C. Hime, eminent educationist of Foyle College, Londonderry.
Brian Boru and the battle of Clontarf: a ballad; by Mrs. M.C. Hime. London: Simpkin, Marshall, & Co.; Dublin: Sullivan Bros. 1889. 48 pp. il. *OXB*

HIND, William Lewis. Of Sutton, Surrey.
Poems; by William Lewis Hind. Sutton, Surrey: Author. 1897. 31 pp. *BL*

HINE, Maude Egerton (1872?–). Her poems, published in 1885, were written when she was less than eight years old.
Poems; by Maude Egerton Hine. Privately printed. 1885. x, 84 pp. *BL*

HINKSON, Katharine Tynan *see* **TYNAN, Katharine**

HINSCLIFF, Matthew W.
King John and the abbot of Canterbury: an old English ballad herein set forth in new fashion; by M.W. Hinscliff. London: George Routledge & Sons. [1886]. 31 pp. il.
    Printed on one side of leaf only. *OXB*

HINSHELWOOD, A. Ernest
Through starlight to dawn; [poems]; by A. Ernest Hinshelwood. London: Gay & Bird. 1893. [viii], 103 pp. *OXB*
Wedded in death, and other poems; by A.E. Hinshelwood. London: Eden, Remington & Co. 1890. xii, 170 pp. *OXB*

HINTON, James, pseud. *see* **BARLOW, George**, (James Hinton, pseud.)

HIPSLEY, William (1807?–91). Of York.
Undine: the spirit of the waters: a poem, containing a version of the narrative by Baron De La Motte Fouqúe; by William Hipsley. London: Elliot Stock. 1886. xiv, 184 pp. *OXB*

HITCHCOCK, George Stewart (1866–   ). b. Dublin, son of George R. Hitchcock. Educated at Adelaide Hall, Dublin, Eliot Park School, Blackheath, Trinity College, Dublin, and in Rome. Anglican chaplain of Medway Union, afterwards Unitarian minister of Chatham, Kent. In 1903 he became a Roman Catholic, was subsequently ordained, acting as assistant priest at Eastbourne from 1910. Held classes in metaphysics, logic, and the classics for working men. An ardent advocate of women's suffrage, and home rule for Ireland.

In rebel moods: poems; by George Stewart Hitchcock. London: Simpkin, Marshall, Hamilton, Kent & Co., Ltd. 1899. [vi], 116 pp.   *OXB*

The King of the Jews: a poem; by George Stewart Hitchcock. Chatham: W. Hutchinson. 1898. 162 pp.   *OXB*

HIVES, E.M.

Verses and epigrams; by E.M. Hives. Printed London: Richard Clay & Sons, Ltd. [c. 1898]. 84 pp.   **UCD*

HOARE, Bernard George. Of Inverness?

The joys of home, and other poems; by Bernard George Hoare. Printed Inverness: Courier Office. 1894. [2], vi, 208 pp.   *OXB*

HOCKIN, William (1798–1886). Son of William L. Hockin of Dartmouth, Devon, gentleman. Educated at St Paul's School, and Exeter College, Oxford: BA 1820, MA 1862. Ordained 1822; vicar, Blackawton, Devon, 1834–41; chaplain, Devon & Exeter Hospital, 1841–86; he and his wife, Mary, celebrated their golden wedding in May 1873 and were presented with a gift of £600.

Warning notes; by W. Hockin. London: Hamilton, Adams & Co.; Exeter: Eland. [1883]. 28 pp.   *OXB*

HODGE, John Barwick (1863–   ). b. London, son of William B. Hodge. Educated at Westminster School, and Christ Church, Oxford (scholar); BA 1886.

West Somerset ballads; [by John Barwick Hodge]. Printed [London]: J. Swain & Son. [1895]. 32 pp.   *OXB*

HODGSON, Henry John (1816–92). b. London, son of John Hodge, barrister. Educated at Shrewsbury School, and Trinity College, Cambridge; Fellow of Trinity, 1840–48. Barrister, Lincoln's Inn, 1842; lecturer on common law at Incorporated Law Society, 1850–52; recorder of Ludlow, Shropshire, 1851–72; master of court of Queen's Bench, 1857, and of supreme court of judicature, 1879–88. Author of several legal works. Lived at 85 Onslow Gardens, London.

Lusus intercisi: verses, translated and original; by Henry John Hodgson. London: George Bell & Sons; Cambridge: Deighton, Bell, & Co. 1883. [vi], 108 pp.   *BL*

HODGSON, S.M., (Two Tramps, pseud. with James Jones)
Low down: wayside thoughts in ballad, and other verse; by two tramps. London: George Redway. 1886. viii, 98 pp.
Title from cover. *MPL*

HOEY, John O'Reilly
Sir Hervey's bride, and other poems; by J. O'Reilly Hoey. London: Marcus Ward & Co. 1882. 200 pp. *OXB*

HOGAN, Michael (1832–99). b. Thomond Gate, County Limerick. He was employed by Limerick Corporation as governor of the King's Island Bank at £1 per week. Much of his verse was published in the *Nation*. He produced many poetry pamphlets in small eds, most of them quite rare. Known as 'The Bard of Thomond'.
Lays and legends of Thomond, with historical and traditional notes; by Michael Hogan. New, select, and complete ed. Dublin: M.H. Gill & Son. 1880. 449 pp. *UCD*

HOGBEN, William Smith. Of the Hebrides?
The grave of a hamlet, and other poems, chiefly of the Hebrides; by William S. Hogben. Selected, with an introduction, by his son, John Hogben. Edinburgh: Darien Press. 1895. 77 pp. *OXB*

HOGG, William (1822–89). b. Cambusnethan, Wishaw, Lanarkshire. Attended school until age of eight, when he was employed as a cowherd. He eventually became a butcher, trading in the village of Bellshill, near Glasgow. President of the local Burns Club.
That Hielan' coo, and other poems; by William Hogg. Glasgow: David Bryce & Son. 1892. xii, 175 pp. il., por. *OXB*

HOGG, William T. Munro, (J.F. Lysander, pseud.) (1842–). b. Haddington, East Lothian, where his father was teacher at the parish school of Whitekirk. The family moved to Gullane, where he was educated, then to Edinburgh. Aged fourteen he was apprenticed to a grocer but after four years decided to study for the ministry. Entered college in his twenty-seventh year, then became a successful teacher of shorthand.
Gullane: a poem; by J.F. Lysander. Edinburgh: John Robertson. 1887. 39 pp. il. *OXB*

HOGGARTH, James (1834–). b. Ambleside, Westmorland, son of a small farmer at Troutbeck. Self-educated, in 1850 he was apprenticed to a bobbin manufacturer near Kendal. He lost an eye from glaucoma in 1888, thereafter unable to work. Lived latterly at Stricklandgate, Kendal.
Echoes from years gone by: [poems]; by James Hoggarth. With a sketch of the author's life. Kendal: Thompson Bros. 1892. xx, 168 pp.
Cover-title is *Echoes*. *OXB*
Evening strains and parlour pastimes: [poems]; by James Hoggarth. Printed Kendal: Thompson Bros. 1880. [8], viii, 178 pp. por. *OXB*
Outlets from the hills: [poems]; by James Hoggarth. Kendal: Thompson Bros. 1896. viii, 184 pp. il. *BL*

HOLE, W.G. Contributed to *Fortnightly Review, Spectator*, etc. Member of
PEN Club. Lived at 49 Earls Court Square, London SW.
Amoris imago: [poems]; by W.G. Hole. London: Kegan Paul, Trench,
Trübner & Co., Ltd. 1891. [viii], 142 pp.   *OXB*
Procris, and other poems; by W.G. Hole. London: Kegan Paul, Trench, & Co.
1886. [x], 118 pp.   *OXB*

HOLIDAY, Erasmus
Parson Dash: or, a rap at ritualism in hudibrastic verse; by Erasmus Holiday.
London: George Redway. 1899. vi, 127 pp.   *OXB*

HOLLAND, Frederick, (F.H.)
Verses miscellaneous & grave; by F.H. Printed Edinburgh: R. & R. Clark. 1881.
48 pp.
    Privately printed.   *BL*

HOLLAND, Maud, (Maud Walpole). Mrs Holland. Translator from the
Italian. A contributor to *National Review, Spectator*, etc.
Verses; by Maud Holland (Maud Walpole). London: Edward Arnold. [1898].
viii, 66 pp.   *BL*

HOLLAND, Thomas Agar (1803–88). Educated at Worcester College,
Oxford; MA 1828. Rector, Poynings, Sussex, 1846–88.
    Dryburgh Abbey, and other poems; by Thomas Agar Holland. New ed.
London: Hatchards; Brighton: H. & C. Treacher; Edinburgh: W. Paterson.
1884. viii, 236 pp.   *OXB*

HOLLINS, Dorothea
    The veiled figure, and other poems; [by Dorothea Hollins]. London: Williams &
Norgate. 1895. 87 pp.   *OXB*

HOLLOWAY, William (1828–93). Son of William Holloway of Wanstead,
Essex.
    Leaves from a lawyer's diary; by William Holloway. London: Digby, Long &
Co. [1895]. 90 pp.
    Poetry and prose.   *OXB*

HOLME, James Wilson, (Philip Acton, pseud.) (1830?–   ). Son of Samuel
Holme of Liverpool, gentleman. Educated at Wadham College, Oxford; BA
1851, MA 1857.
Songs and sonnets; by Philip Acton. New ed. Longmans, Green & Co. 1889. x,
140 pp.   *OXB*

HOLMES, Edmond (1850–1936). b. Watersown, County Westmeath, son of
Robert Holmes, noted racehorse breeder. Went to England, 1861; educated at
Merchant Taylors' School, and St John's College, Oxford: BA 1874, MA
1876. Appointed inspector of schools in 1875, retiring in 1911.
    The silence of love: [poems]; by Edmond Holmes. London: John Lane. 1899
[i.e. 1898]. [61] pp.   *BL*
    Also [2nd ed.] 1899.

HOLMES, Fred (1865–   ). b. Northallerton, Yorkshire. Educated at North-allerton Grammar School. Apprenticed to the printing trade in 1880.
 Two Christmas eves, and other poems; by Fred Holmes. [Northallerton]: [Author]. 1886. ★

HOLT, Catherine D.
 A season of rest, and other verse; by Catherine D. Holt. Liverpool: Henry Young & Sons. 1898. 47 pp.   *UCD*

HOLTHAM, Thomas Edwin. Educated at Byculla School, Bombay.
 Lyric chimes: a miscellany of minor poems; by Thomas E. Holtham. Printed Bombay: Times of India Steam Press. 1881. [iv], 26 pp.   *BL*
 On Yarra banks; Lyric chimes, and other poems; by Thomas Edwin Holtham. Melbourne: McCarron, Bird & Co. 1894. vi, 82 pp.   *BL*

The HOLY ISLE. London: Leadenhall Press, Ltd; Simpkin, Marshall, Hamilton, Kent & Co., Ltd; New York: Charles Scribner's Sons. 1896. 116 pp. il. (Lays of the bards, I).   *OXB*

HOLYOAKE, George Jacob, (Ion, pseud.) (1817–1906). A tinsmith and whitesmith in Birmingham, he joined Birmingham Reform League in 1831, then became a Chartist, being present at the Birmingham Chartist riots in 1839. He became a rationalist and a foremost exponent of secularism. In 1842 he was sentenced at Gloucester to six months' imprisonment for blasphemy. Writer on co-operation, and biographer of Tom Paine, Robert Owen and John Stuart Mill.
 Blasts from Bradlaugh's own trumpet: ballads, extracts, cartoons; versified, selected, and sketched by "Ion". With 13 illustrations. London: Houlston & Sons. [1882]. 30 pp. il.   *OXB*
 Songs of love & sorrow; by Ion. Manchester: George Falkner; John Heywood; London: Simpkin, Marshall, & Co. [1887]. [ii], 57 pp. il.   *MPL*

HOME, Cecil, pseud. *see* **WEBSTER, Augusta,** (Cecil Home, pseud.)

HOME, F. Wyville (1851–   ). b. Edinburgh.
 Lay canticles, and other poems; by F. Wyville Home. London: Pickering & Co. 1883. viii, 171 pp.   *UCD*
 The wrath of the fay; by F. Wyville Home. London: Gardner, Darton, & Co. [1887]. [iv], 51 pp. il.   *OXB*

HOME, Julian, pseud. *see* **CHRISTIE, Edward Richard,** (Julian Home, pseud.)

HOMELY, Josias, pseud. *see* **BRADFORD, John,** (Josias Homely pseud.)

HOMFRAY, Francis Alexander (1854?–19   ). Son of Rev. Kenyon Homfray, of Llangoven, Monmouthshire. Educated at New College, Oxford (scholar); BA 1876. Curate, Christ Church, Cheltenham, 1878–80; assistant chaplain, Tyntesfield, 1880–87; curate, Westbury-on-Trym, Gloucestershire, 1887–89. Lived latterly at Mendip House, Cheddar.
Idyls of thought; and, Lyrical pieces; by F.A. Homfray. London: George Allen. 1898. vi, 88 pp.   OXB

HONEST, E.G. Of Hampstead, London.
Under the cedars: verses; letters to some eminent members of the C.L.C.; [by E.G. Honest]. Hampstead: [Author?]. 1891. [x], 89 pp. il., por.   OXB

HONEYWOOD, Patty, pseud. *see* **JACKSON, Ann Olivia**, (Patty Honeywood, pseud.)

HOOD, Arthur
Smiles & tears, [and other poems]; by Arthur Hood. London: Record Press, Ltd. [1893]. 40 pp.   OXB

HOOLE, Charles Holland (1837–   ). b. Clerkenwell, London, son of Elias Hoole, gentleman. Educated at Islington School, and at Magdalen Hall, Oxford: BA 1859, MA 1862. Tutor, Christ Church, 1863–68.
Poems; by Charles H. Hoole. New ed. Oxford; Parker & Co. 1882. viii, 264 pp.   CU
New ed. of *Poems and translations*, 1875.

HOOPER, Charles E. Dramatist.
The Mexicans: a romance; by Charles E. Hooper. London: Remington & Co. 1883. [ii], 87 pp.   OXB

HOOPER, H.G. Of Cheltenham, Gloucestershire.
A poetical sketch of the Thames, from the Seven Springs to the Nore; by H.G. Hooper. Printed Cheltenham: Thomas Hailing. [1885]. 19 pp.   OXB
Wellington: in memoriam; by H.G. Hooper. Printed Cheltenham: G.H. Devereux. [1885]. [ii], 18 pp.   BL

HOPE, Laurence, pseud. *see* **NICOLSON, Adela Florence**, (Laurence Hope, pseud.)

HOPKINS, Ellice (1836–1904). b. Cambridge, daughter of William Hopkins, mathematician. As a social reformer she worked among the navvies in Cambridge. After her father's death she moved to Brighton, coming into contact with the work done among prostitutes, and was soon a leader in rescue work. She organized a campaign to reform the law concerning women and children, and also supported female suffrage.
Autumn swallows: a book of lyrics; by Ellice Hopkins. London: Macmillan & Co. 1883. viii, 283 pp.   MPL

HOPKINS, Gerard Manley (1844–89). b. Stratford, Essex, son of Manley Hopkins, consul for Hawaii. Educated at Cholmondeley School, Highgate, and Balliol College, Oxford, where he was tutored by Walter Pater. In 1866 he became a Roman Catholic, and in 1877 was ordained a Jesuit priest. He served in missions in London, Oxford, Liverpool and Glasgow; classics teacher, Stonyhurst College, 1882–83; professor of Greek, University College, Dublin, 1884–89. He was a major poet, original and innovative in his poetic language, but his work was not published in book form until 1918.

BIBLIOGRAPHY: **DUNNE, Tom**. *Hopkins: a comprehensive bibliography*. Oxford: Clarendon Press. 1976.

HOPKINS, Manley (1817?–97). Average adjustor and arbitrator, City of London, 1844–97. Consul-general in London for Hawaiian Islands, 1856–97. Writer on marine insurance and other topics. Father of Gerard Manley Hopkins. Lived latterly at The Garth, Haslemere, Surrey.

Spicilegium poeticum: a gathering of verses; by Manley Hopkins. London: Leadenhall Press. [1892]. 182 pp. il.

Printed for private circulation. *OXB*

HOPPER, Nora (1871–1906). b. Exeter, Devon, daughter of an Irishman, Captain Harman B. Hopper of the 31st Bengal Infantry. Her father died in her early childhood, and she was educated in London. In 1901 she married Wilfrid Hugh Chesson, novelist and critic. Lived latterly at 337 Sandycombe Road, Kew, London SW.

Under the quicken boughs: [poems]; by Nora Hopper. London: John Lane The Bodley Head; New York: George Richmond & Co. 1896. [viii], 152 pp. *OXB*

HOPPS, John Page (1834–1911). b. London. Educated at the Baptist College, Leicester. Baptist minister and co-pastor at Birmingham, 1857. Joined the Unitarians, 1860; minister successively at Sheffield, Dukinfield, Glasgow, Leicester and Croydon. In 1866 he contested the South Paddington parliamentary seat. Proprietor and editor of *The Coming Day* from 1891. Founder of Our Father's Church, 1892. Lived latterly at The Roserie, Shepperton-on-Thames.

Pilgrim songs, with other poems, written during forty years; by J. Page Hopps. London: Williams & Norgate. [1891]. [viii], 90 pp. por. *OXB*

HORACE THE RUSTIC, pseud.

Smoke clouds: a "medley of fancies": [poems]; by Felix the outcast & Horace the rustic. Edited by Horace. Leicester: W.H. Lead. 1883. [32] pp.

Not joint authorship. *OXB*

HORGAN, Michael P. (1846–). b. Bristol of Irish parents. Parish priest at Hainton, Lincolnshire.

Cork and the river Lee, and other historical verses; by Michael P. Horgan. Printed Louth: J.W. Goulding. 1890. 48 pp. *UCD*

Legends of English saints, and other legends and verses; by Michael P. Horgan. Printed Louth: J.W. Goulding. 1890. 105 pp. *OXB*

The life and labours of Saint Wilfrid, Bishop of York, born A.D. 634, died A.D. 709; by Michael P. Horgan. Printed Louth: J. W. Goulding. 1889. 68 pp.   *BL*
Reason and unbelief: a story of a conversion founded on fact, and other verses; by Michael P. Horgan. Printed Louth: J. W. Goulding. 1891. 112 pp.
    Cover-title is *Faith of our fathers*.   *OXB*
Sketches of Lindisfarne: [poems]; by M.P. Horgan. London: Art & Book Co. 1896. [iv], 66 pp.   *NPL*

HORNE, Herbert Percy (1864–1916). Architect, writer and connoisseur. He built the Church of the Redeemer, Bayswater, the baptistry, St Luke's, Camberwell, other public buildings and various private houses. Editor of *Hobby Horse*, 1887–91, he contributed to *Burlington Magazine, Fortnightly Review*, etc. Lived latterly at Palazzo Proprio, 6 Via de Benci, Florence.
Diversi colores: [poems]; [by Herbert Percy Horne]. London: Published by the author at the Chiswick Press. 1891. 48 pp.   *MPL*

HORSLEY, James (1828–91). b. near Alnwick, Northumberland, son of a farmer who set up a business in Newcastle upon Tyne. Orphaned at an early age, he took a variety of jobs, becoming cabin boy, messenger, stable boy. In 1850 he worked for *Ward's Directory*, then in 1859 for the *Railway Guide*. An occasional contributor to *North of England Advertiser* and other journals.
Lays of Jesmond, and Tyneside songs and poems; by the late James Horsley. Newcastle-on-Tyne: Andrew Reid; Allan. 1891. xvi, 174 pp. por.   *OXB*

HORSLEY, John (1817–93). Of Darlington, County Durham.
The royal rose, and other poems; by J. Horsley. Printed Darlington: W. Stairmand. 1881. xii, 136 pp. il., por.
    Cover-title is *Poems*.   *OXB*
    Also 2nd ed. 1881.
The sailor's bride, and other poems; by J. Horsley. Printed Darlington: W. Stairmand. 1889. viii, 144 pp. por.
    Cover-title is *Poems*.   *UCD*

HOSKEN, James Dryden (1861–19). b. Helston, Cornwall, son of Henry Hosken, iron-founder. Educated at Helston national school, his father died when he was nine. In 1880 he went to London to find work, becoming an extra outdoor officer in H.M. Customs stationed at Royal Albert Docks. His health broke down and he took a series of temporary jobs before returning to Helston in 1899. Employed as an auxiliary postman.
Christopher Marlowe; and, Belphegor; by James Dryden Hosken. London: H. Henry & Co. Ltd. 1896. [vi], 166 pp.   *OXB*
A monk's love, and other poems; by James Dryden Hosken. [London]: 29 Denmark Road, Ealing. [1895?]. [iv], 81 pp.   *UCD*
Phaon and Sappho: a play; with, Selection of poems; by J.D. Hosken. Printed Penzance: F. Rodda. 1891. [iv], 116 pp.   *OXB*
Verses by the way; [by] J.D. Hosken. London: Methuen & Co. [1893]. xxxii, 83 pp.   *MPL*

HOUGHTON, Lord *see* **MILNES, Robert Offley Ashburton, Lord Houghton**

HOULDING, Henry (18 –1901). b. Burnley, Lancashire. He began his working life in a factory. Editor of *Burnley Gazette* for twenty-eight years. Member of Burnley Literary & Scientific Club from its formation, president for four years.

Rhymes and dreams: legends of Pendle Forest, and other poems; by Henry Houlding. Burnley: B. Moore for the Joint Committee of the Literary and Scientific Club and the Literary and Philosophical Society. 1895. xvi, 336 pp. il., por. *MPL*

HOUSMAN, Alfred Edward (1859–1936) b. Fockbury, Worcestershire, brother of Laurence Housman. Educated at Bromsgrove School, and St John's College, Oxford. He failed his finals but then pursued his own studies and was awarded MA. Clerk in the Patent Office, London, 1882–92. Professor of Latin, University College, London, 1892–1922; Kennedy Professor of Latin, Cambridge University, and Fellow of Trinity College, 1911–36. Critic and classical scholar.

A Shropshire lad; by A.E. Housman. London: Kegan Paul, Trench, Trübner, & Co. Ltd. 1896. viii, 96 pp. *OXB*

A Shropshire lad; by A.E. Housman. London: Grant Richards. 1898. viii, 96 pp. *OXB*

HOUSMAN, Laurence (1865–1959). b. Bromsgrove, Worcestershire, a younger brother of A.E. Housman. Educated at Bromsgrove School, then studied art in London. Art critic of *Manchester Guardian*, 1895–1911; playwright, novelist, and miscellaneous writer. A socialist, pacifist and feminist.

All-fellows: seven legends of lower redemption, with insets in verse; by Laurence Housman. London: Kegan Paul, Trench, Trübner & Co. 1896. x, 138 pp. il. *OXB*

Green arras: [poems]; by Laurence Housman. London: John Lane, The Bodley Head; Chicago: Way & Williams. 1896. viii, 92 pp. *OXB*

The little land, with songs from its four rivers; by Laurence Housman. London: Grant Richards. 1899. viii, 100 pp. *MPL*

Rue: [poems]; by Laurence Housman. London: At the sign of the Unicorn. 1899. x, 96 pp. *OXB*

Spikenard: a book of devotional love-poems; by Laurence Housman. London: Grant Richards; Boston, [Mass.]: Richard G. Badger & Co. 1898. [viii], 54 pp. *MPL*

HOW, William Walsham (1823–97). Educated at Wadham College, Oxford. Ordained 1847; appointed rural dean of Oswestry, 1854; hon. canon of St Asaph, 1860; bishop of Bedford, 1879, and prebendary, St Paul's Cathedral; first bishop of Wakefield, 1888. Well known for his work with the poor in the East End of London.

Poems; by William Walsham How. 2nd ed. London: Wells Gardner, Darton, & Co. [1886]. viii, 271 pp. *TCD*

Also New and enlarged ed. [1886]; 4th ed. [1887].

A sermon in a children's ward in a hospital; by the Bishop of Wakefield: (suggested by "The sermon in the hospital" from The Disciples by Mrs. Hamilton King). London: Society for Promoting Christian Knowledge; New York: E. & J.B. Young & Co. 1896. 16 pp.   *OXB*

"Was lost and is found": a tale of the London Mission of 1874; by W. Walsham How. London: Wells Gardner, Darton, & Co. [1886]. 29 pp. il.   *OXB*

HOWARD, Henry C.

Christabel (concluded), with other poems; by Henry C. Howard. London: Kegan Paul, Trench, Trübner & Co., Ltd. 1893. viii, 108 pp.   *MPL*

HOWARD, Henry Newman (1861–1929). b. King's Langley, Hertfordshire, son of William L. Howard. Educated privately. He entered business life aged thirteen; practised as a chartered accountant, 1882–95. Writer and dramatist, he lived latterly at The Wainholm, Watcombe, Torquay, Devon.

Footsteps of Proserpine, and other verses and interludes; by Henry Newman Howard. London: Elliot Stock. 1897. viii, 121 pp.   *OXB*

HOWARD, Leslie

College days: recorded in blank verse; [by Leslie Howard]. London: T. Fisher Unwin. 1883. [iv], 152 pp.   *OXB*

HOWELL, Agnes Rous. Relative of Rev. Hinds Howell, rector of Drayton with Hellesdon, Norwich.

Fifty years after: a tale in verse; by Agnes R. Howell. Norwich: G.S. Hanchett. 1880. xii, 87 pp.   *BL*

HOWELL, Annie, (Ephziba, pseud.). Mrs Howell of Harrogate, Yorkshire.

Elim: or, Harrogate in prose and verse; by Mrs. Annie Howell (Ephziba). Printed Harrogate: R. Ackrill, "Herald" Printing Works. 1892. xvi, 127 pp.   *BL*

HOWELL, Hiram. Of Shrewsbury, Shropshire.

The Wrekin legend: or, the cobbler, and the devil, and the mayor: an ancient tale in modern verse; by Hiram Howell. With poems, songs and ballads by the same author. Printed Shrewsbury: L. Wilding. [1894]. [vi], 64 pp.   *OXB*

HOWITT, Mary (1799–1888). b. Coleford, Gloucestershire, daughter of Samuel Botham, a prosperous Quaker. She was brought up in Uttoxeter, Staffordshire, and was educated at home. In 1821 she married the writer William Howitt. They settled in Nottingham, where he kept a chemist's shop, then moved to Esher, Surrey. She collaborated with her husband in many literary works but also published children's books; taught herself Danish and Swedish, making English translations. An active participant in the anti-slavery movement. A Quaker most of her life, she converted to Roman Catholicism in 1882.

With the birds: poems; by Mary Howitt. With ninety illustrations by Giacomelli. London: Thomas Nelson & Sons. [c. 1880]. 128 pp. 128 pp. il.   *UCD*

With the flowers: poems; by Mary Howitt. With one hundred illustrations by Giacomelli. London: Thomas Nelson & Sons. [c. 1880]. 128 pp. il.   *UCD*

HOYLE, William (1831–86). b. Vale of Rossendale, Lancashire. A cotton spinner with his father at Brookbottom, near Bury, 1851–59, then at Tottington, from 1859 to his death. A temperance reformer, Good Templar, and a vegetarian. Unsuccessfully contested the Dewsbury constituency, Yorkshire, 1880. Died at Southport, Lancashire.
Daisy ballads and recitations; by William Hoyle. London: S.W. Partridge & Co.; Manchester: "Onward" Publishing Office; John Heywood. [1891]. 160 pp. il., por. ("Onward" series).   *OXB*

HUDSON, John (1860–1923). Educated at Peterhouse, Cambridge; (classical scholar and prizeman). Curate of Histon, near Cambridge, then of Chillingham, Northumberland. Assistant master, Denstone College, Staffordshire.
The dream of Pilate's wife: a poem suggested by Doré's famous picture; by John Hudson. London: Kegan Paul, Trench, Trübner, & Co., Ltd. 1890. 43 pp.   *OXB*

HUES, Ivan
"Heart to heart": the song of two nations, with aftertones and other pieces; by Ivan Hues. London: Kegan Paul, Trench & Co. 1889. [viii], 221 pp.   *OXB*

HUGGARD, J.J. Rev. Huggard, Roman Catholic priest.
The Christian armed, in verse; by J.J. Huggard. London: Burns & Oates; New York: Catholic Publication Society Co. [1887]. 96 pp.   *OXB*

HUGHES, Allison, pseud. *see* **HALEY, Alice**, (Allison Hughes, pseud.)

HUGHES, John
Tristiora: or, songs in the night; by John Hughes. London: James Nisbet & Co. 1896. [viii], 194 pp.   *BLD*

HUGHES, Walter. Of Manchester?
Lyra Mancuniensis; by Walter Hughes. London: Kegan Paul, Trench, Trübner & Co., Ltd. 1890. viii, 48 pp.   *MPL*

HUGHES-GAMES, Stephen Herbert Wynne (1862–   ). b. Liverpool, son of Archdeacon Joshua Hughes-Games of the Isle of Man. Educated at King William's College, and Worcester College, Oxford. Domestic chaplain to bishop of Sodor & Man, 1888–89; curate, St Giles's, Cripplegate, London, from 1890.
Ruth: the poem which obtained the 'Triennial prize for a poem on a sacred subject' in the University of Oxford 1893; by S.H.W. Hughes-Games. Oxford: B.H. Blackwell; London: Simpkin, Marshall, Hamilton, Kent & Co. 1893. 24 pp.   *OXB*

HULL, Amelia Matilda (1825–82). b. Marpool Hall, Exmouth, Devon, daughter of William T. Hall. A hymnist, she contributed to *Pleasant Hymns for Boys and Girls*, 1860, and to *The Enlarged London Hymn Book*, 1873. She worked in the East End of London at the Rowley Home for young women in business.

Royal musings, concerning the King and his work; [poems]; by the late A.M. Hull. London: James E. Hawkins; S.W. Partridge & Co. [1884]. 175 pp. il., por.   *UCD*

HULL, George (1863–1933). b. Blackburn, Lancashire. He lived in the country as a child, at Hoghton, then at Croston, where he was sent to a dame school. Educated at St Ann's and St Mary's Schools, Blackburn. Worked as a clerk to a solicitor, a brass founder, and a builder before joining his father's coal merchant business.

The heroes of the heart, and other lyrical poems; by George Hull. Preston: J. & H. Platt; London: Simpkin, Marshall, Hamilton, Kent & Co., Ltd. 1894. [2], vi, 118 pp.   *UCD*

HUNKY LARRY, pseud. *see* **LARRY, Hunky**, pseud.

HUNT, Horatio. Lived at 6 Ladbroke Crescent, Ladbroke Grove, Notting Hill, London W.

Nero: or, the trials, battles and adventures of the sixth emperor of Rome, during a period of nearly two thousand years in darkest Hades!: a poem in twelve books; by Horatio Hunt. Book I. London: James Burns. 1893. 39 pp.   *OXB*

Nero: or, the trials, battles and adventures of the sixth emperor of Rome in darkest Hades: an allegory, a satire, and a moral (in blank verse), revised, corrected, and complete in nine books; by Horatio Hunt. London: Downey & Co. Ltd. 1899. [vi], 130 pp. por.   *OXB*

HUNT, Matthew

The king's daughter, and other poems; by Matthew Hunt. London: Elliot Stock. 1895. vi, 66 pp.   *CHE*

HUNT, William

The dream to come and other poems; by William Hunt. With seven illustrations. London: Sampson Low, Marston, Searle, & Rivington. 1885. 160 pp. il.   *UCD*

HUNT, William Jones. Of Bath, Somerset.

Jubilee poems to the Empress Queen, Victoria the first, June 20, 1887; by William Jones Hunt. London: Isaac Pitman & Sons. [1887]. 32 pp.   *JRL*

HUNTER, James (1847–19). b. Yett, Dumfriesshire, son of James Hunter, a magistrate. He started in business as a grocer and wine merchant in Glasgow, 1871, and with his brother as partner opened branches in various parts of the city. A commissioner for Govanhill, then provost for six years. Joined Glasgow town council, 1891, elected bailie, 1904. JP for Glasgow and for Renfrewshire. A director of Glasgow Dumfriesshire Society.

Poems and sketches; by James Hunter. Glasgow: William M. Stuart. 1884. 52 pp.   *UCD*

HUNTON, Thomas, (T.H.) (1818–99). b. Yarmouth, Isle of Wight. Educated at Rochester and Ackworth Schools, and London University, where he was the first Quaker to receive a BA. For some years a private tutor, he became superintendent of Grove House School, Tottenham, London, 1849–60. Lived latterly in Torquay, Devon.
Scenes from the past, and other poems; by T.H. London: E. Hicks. 1890. vi, 132 pp.   *UCD*
Scenes from the past, and other poems; by Thomas Hunton. Part second. London: E. Hicks. 1894. [vi], 108 pp.   *UCD*

HURRELL, John Waymouth (1850–19   ). b. Burslem, Staffordshire, a descendant of the ancient Hurrell family of Devon. Educated in private schools, and in France. He received architectural training in the office of Thomas Lewis, Newcastle-under-Lyme: a quantity surveyor in Manchester, 1876–79; in partnership with Thomas W. Taylor as quantity surveyors in Manchester and Liverpool.
Poems; [by John Waymouth Hurrell]. Manchester: John Heywood. [1892]. 24 pp.   *OXB*

HURRELL, William
Poems: lyric, dramatic and heroic; by William Hurrell. London: Simpkin, Marshall, Hamilton, Kent & Co., Ltd. 1898. [ii], 80 pp.   *OXB*
Pygmalion, and some sonnets, and drama; by William Hurrell. London: Simpkin, Marshall, Hamilton, Kent & Co., Ltd. 1898. 45 pp.   *OXB*

HUTCHINSON, James. Of Wath-upon-Dearne, Yorkshire.
Wensleydale, and other poems; by James Hutchinson. Leeds: Rhodes & North. 1894. [iv], 94 pp.   *UCD*

HUTCHINSON, John, (Ladylift, pseud.) (18   –1916). b. Ballingham, Herefordshire, son of George Hutchinson, brother-in-law of Willam Words-worth. Educated at home, in Chelsea under Rev. Derwent Coleridge, and in Paris. In 1855 he was appointed a master at Harrow School; subsequently vice-principal, Hereford Proprietory College, then a master at Doncaster Gram-mar School; in 1879, after establishing Llandrindod College, Radnorshire, he left educational work. Appointed librarian, Middle Temple, London, 1880.
Llandrindod legends & lyrics, including the languishing lay of, The lady of the lake; [poems]; by Ladylift. With views of Llandrindod scenery. Printed Brecon: Edwin Davies & Bell. [1895]. [viii], 57 pp. il.   *OXB*

HUTCHINSON, Thomas. Lived at Pegswood, Morpeth, Northumberland.
Ballades, and other rhymes of a country bookworm; by Thomas Hutchinson. London: Stanesby & Co.; Derby: Frank Murray. 1888. [1], viii, 88 pp.
   A limited small paper ed. of 140 copies, of which 120 were for sale.   *UCD*
   Also a limited large paper ed. of 60 numbered and signed copies, 50 of which were for sale, 1888.

Jolts and jingles: a book of poems for young people; by Thomas Hutchinson. London: Stanesby & Co.; Derby: Frank Murray. 1889. [1], viii, 82 pp.

A limited ed. of 130 copies, 120 of which were for sale.   *OXB*

Also a limited large paper ed. of 60 numbered and signed copies, 52 of which were for sale, 1889. OXB has the only single copy printed on vellum.

HUTTON, John

Poems; by John Hutton. Printed London: Wyman & Sons, Ltd. [1896]. viii, 126 pp.

Printed for private circulation.   *OXB*

HUXLEY, Henrietta (18 –1915). Née Heathorn. Wife of Thomas Henry Huxley whom she met in Sydney, Australia, whence he had sailed on the frigate *Rattlesnake* as assistant surgeon. She came to England in 1855 to be married. It was an intensely happy marriage; they had five daughters and three sons.

Poems of Henrietta Huxley; with three of Thomas Henry Huxley. [Eastbourne]. 1899. x, 181 pp.

Privately printed.   *OXB*

HUXLEY, Thomas Henry (1825–95). b. Ealing, Middlesex, son of a schoolmaster. Studied medicine at Charing Cross Hospital, and London University; MB 1845. In 1846 he entered the Royal Navy as assistant surgeon on *Rattlesnake*; professor of natural history, Royal School of Mines, 1855; professor of physiology, Royal Institution, 1855; professor of comparative anatomy, Royal College of Surgeons, 1863–70; elected lord rector, Aberdeen University, 1872; president of the Royal Society, 1883. A strong supporter of the Darwinian theory. Prolific author of scientific works, and contributor to the leading scientific journals.

Poems of Henrietta Huxley; with three of Thomas Henry Huxley. [Eastbourne]. 1899. x, 181 pp.

Privately printed.   *OXB*

HYDE, Douglas (1860–1949). b. Frenchpark, County Roscommon, son of a clergyman. Educated at Trinity College, Dublin; took a law degree but never practised. Professor of modern languages at New Brunswick, 1891, then returned to Ireland; president, Gaelic League, 1893–1915; professor of modern Irish, University College, Dublin, 1908–32; first president of Eire, 1937–45. Edited many Irish texts and translated medieval tales from the Irish. A founder of the Abbey Theatre, Dublin.

The three sorrows of story-telling: [poems]; and, Ballads of St. Columkille; by Douglas Hyde. London: T. Fisher Unwin. 1895. viii, 166 pp.   *TCD*

HYDE, Mabel C.

Pansies: [poems]; by Mabel C. Hyde. London: Swan Sonnenschein. 1897. 64 pp.   *OXB*

HYDE, Mary Newton

Early poems; by Mary Newton Hyde. Manchester: John Heywood. 1880. 72 pp. *★UCD*

HYDREF, Mair, pseud.

Autumn leaves: [poems]; Mair Hydref. Rhyl: J. Morris. [1880?]. 88 pp. *★NUC*

Autumn leaves: [poems]; by Mair Hydref. 3rd ed. Printed Liverpool: Baskerville Printing Co., Ltd. 1883. 120 pp.

Printed for the authoress. *★UCD*

Autumn leaves: [poems]; by Mair Hydref. 4th ed. Printed Wrexham: Hughes & Son. 1889. 132 pp.

Printed for the authoress. *BL*

HYSLOP, John (1837–92). b. Kirkland, Dumfriesshire. His father's ill-health caused the family to move to Thornhill. He received less than two years' education, working on the land at eleven. When the family moved to Kilmarnock he completed an engineering apprenticeship but eventually became one of the town's letter carriers, serving until retirement in 1891. Known as 'The Postman Poet'.

The dream of a masque, and other poems; by John Hyslop. Printed Kilmarnock: James M'Kie. [1882]. xii, 192 pp.

Spine-title is *Poems*. *BL*

Memorial volume of John Hyslop, the postman poet. Edited by William Johnston. Kilmarnock: J.C. Motson. 1895. xvi, 295 pp. *NLS*

I

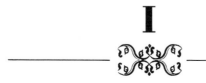

I., A.E. *see* **IRELAND, Annie Elizabeth**, (A.E.I.)

I., C.H. *see* **INGLIS, Catherine Hartland**, (C.H.I.)

IBBETT, William Joseph, (Antaeus, pseud.) (1858–   ). Of Cann, Shaftesbury, Dorset. Lived latterly at Epsom, Surrey.

The backslider, and other poems; by Antaeus. Printed London: Chiswick Press. 1890. [viii], 30 pp.

A limited ed. of 100 copies. Printed for the author. *OXB*

Ibbett's best: [poems]; [by William Joseph Ibbett]. Printed London: Chiswick Press. 1899. viii, 56 pp.

A limited ed. of 150 copies. *OXB*

Little poems: a poeticule; by Antaeus. Printed London: Chiswick Press. 1893. [vi], 36 pp. *OXB*

Poems; by Antaeus. [Epsom]. 1889. [viii], 136 pp.   *OXB*
Poems; by Antaeus. London: Swan Sonnenschein & Co. 1889. 96 pp.   *OXB*
Rosamunda: a poem; by Antaeus. Printed Epsom: H. Buxton Forman. 1890.
[23] pp.
    A limited ed. of 12 copies. Printed on one side of leaf only.   *OXB*
Three letters from W.J. Ibbett to his friend H. Buxton Forman in praise of Venus:
[poems]. Printed London: Chiswick Press. 1894. [vi], 42 pp.   *OXB*
A west Sussex garland: [poems]; by W.J. Ibbett. Printed London: Chiswick
Press. 1897. 20 pp.   *BL*

IDLE, William George. Lived at The Hollies, Ryton, Dorrington,
Shropshire.
    Verses on old and modern subjects, being a collection of poems, rhymes, parodies, & c.;
by George William Idle. Printed Ormskirk: "The Advertiser" Office. [1896].
viii, 80 pp. por.   *OXB*

IDLE SINGER, pseud.
    The simple songs of an idle singer. Vol. I. Printed London: J.W. Wakeham. 1891.
48 pp.   *OXB*

IDLETHORNE, Otto. Lived at 53 Quai de Bourbon, Paris.
    Great Tom: the curfew bell of Oxford: an historical ballad; by Otto Idlethorne.
Paris: Librairie Européenne de Baudry. 1885. 31 pp.   *OXB*

IGNOTUS, pseud. *see* **FULLER, James Franklin**, (Ignotus, pseud.)

IMAGE, Selwyn (1849–1930). Educated at New College, Oxford. Ordained
1872. A disciple of John Ruskin, he was Slade professor of fine art at Oxford,
1910–16. Best known by his designs for stained glass, he was a talented and
versatile artist producing landscape drawings, water-colours, designs for
decorative title-pages, etc.
    Poems & carols; [by Selwyn Image]. London: Elkin Mathews. 1894. 48
pp.   *BL*

IN BLACK AND GOLD: IMPRESSIONS IN VERSE. London: Digby,
Long & Co. 1893. 16 pp.   *OXB*

INCE, Thomas (1850–1902). b. Bingley, Yorkshire, son of a soldier.
Educated at Wigan Union Workhouse. Apprenticed to coal mining, he
studied medical botany and became a herbalist. Lived latterly at Blackburn,
Lancashire.
    Beggar manuscripts: an original miscellany in verse and prose; by Thomas Ince.
Subscription ed. Blackburn: North-East Lancashire Printing & Publishing
Co., Ltd. 1888. [2], x, 143 pp.   *UCD*

INGELOW, Jean (1820–97). b. Boston, Lincolnshire, eldest child of William Ingelow, banker. Her early life was spent in Lincolnshire but she also lived in Ipswich, Suffolk, before going to London c. 1863. She became acquainted with Tennyson, Ruskin, Froude, Christina Rossetti, and with most of the poets, painters and writers of the time. Published novels, and stories for children, but is best known for her poetry. Died in Kensington and is buried at Brompton Cemetery.

BIBLIOGRAPHY: **PETERS, Maureen**. *Jean Ingelow, Victorian poetess*. Ipswich: Boydell Press. 1972.

INGHAM, Jane Sarson Cooper, (Sarson C.J. Ingham, pseud.)
Caedmon's vision, and other poems; by Sarson C.J. Ingham. London: Kegan Paul, Trench & Co. 1882. xiv, 252 pp. *OXB*

INGHAM, Sarson C.J., pseud. *see* **INGHAM, Jane Sarson Cooper**, (Sarson C.J. Ingham, pseud.)

INGLIS, Catherine Hartland, (C.H.I.) (1815–). b. Roscommon, daughter of Rev. A. Mahon. In 1844 she married a Captain Inglis.
One hundred songs in sorrow and in joy; by C.H.I. Edinburgh: James Taylor. 1880. 188 pp.
Cover-title is *Songs in sorrow*. *BL*

INGLIS, Robert Stirling (1835–86). b. Heriot, Midlothian, son of a shepherd. The family moved to Temple, where he was educated in the parish school. He left home at the age of twelve to work as a shepherd at various places in Scotland, eventually settling near Falkland, Fife. Married with six children, he was ill and unable to work for some time before his death.
Whisperings from the hillside: [poems]; by Robert S. Inglis. With prefatory note by James Bell. Edinburgh: Andrew Elliot. 1886. xii, 135 pp. *NLS*
Also 2nd ed. 1888.

INGLISFIELD, Walter. Dramatist.
Poems: allegorical, lyrical, and narrative; by Walter Inglisfield. London: Swan Sonnenschein & Co. 1895. [viii], 150 pp. *OXB*

INGHAM, Arthur Winnington- *see* **WINNINGTON-INGRAM, Arthur**

ION, pseud. *see* **HOLYOAKE, George Jacob**, (Ion, pseud.)

IRELAND, Annie Elizabeth (A.E.I.) Daughter of Dr John Nicholson. Educated at a London boarding school. In 1865 she married Alexander Ireland, manager of the *Manchester Examiner*. Lived at Bowdon, Cheshire, where she and her husband entertained many notables in the world of art and literature, e.g. Ralph Waldo Emerson, Anthony Trollope, Ford Madox Brown, Charles Calvert. She wrote a biography of Jane Welsh Carlyle, and contributed biographical sketches of local people to the Manchester press.
Tales, sketches, and verses; by A.E.I. Manchester: Richard Gill; London: Simpkin, Marshall, & Co. 1883. [viii], 285 pp. *UCD*

IRELAND, Arthur Joseph (1874–1931). b. Loughrea, County Galway, son of Arthur J. Ireland, staff-surgeon, Royal Navy. Educated at Corrig School, Royal Naval School, and Fir Lodge College. A schoolmaster in London and Lausanne, then professor of English, Académie de Lausanne. On the editorial staff of several newspaper groups; founder and editor of *Swiss Anglo-Saxon Magazine*; founder of the Press Photographic Bureau and of the Universal Press Service. Lived latterly at Brighton, Sussex.

Hours of leisure: [poems]; by Arthur J. Ireland. London: A. G. Taylor. 1895. 63 pp.

A limited ed. of 200 numbered copies.   *OXB*

IRISH PEASANT POET *see* **O'CONOR, Charles Patrick**

IRROY, R.E.
Verses of love and life; by R.E. Irroy. London: Reeves & Turner. 1892. 64 pp.   *OXB*

IRVINE, Andrew Alexander, (Subaltern, pseud.). Co-editor of the *Cawnpore Fortnightly Foghorn*; contributed verse to several journals published in India.

Lays of a subaltern; by "The Subaltern". Lahore: Civil & Military Gazette Press. 1895. [6], ii, 42 pp.   *BL*

IRWIN, Anne. Educated in a village school, she was a working-class woman, a servant in several households, including Neva House, Ilfracombe, Devon.

Autumn berries: poems; by Anne Irwin. Ilfracombe: "Ilfracombe Chronicle & Visitors' List". [1889]. 31 pp.   *UCD*

IRWIN, Henry Crossley (1848?–19   ). Son of Henry Irwin of Banda, India, gentleman. Educated at St Edmund Hall, and Queen's College, Oxford (scholar); BA 1870. Entered the Indian Civil Service, serving in the North West Province and Oudh in various posts. Writer on Indian history and affairs.

Rhymes and renderings; by H.C. Irwin. London: David Stott. 1886. [2], vi, 144 pp.   *UCD*

IRWIN, Thomas Caulfield (1823–92). b. Warren Point, County Down, into a wealthy family. Educated privately. He lost his inheritance and became a journalist. A prolific contributor to the *Nation* and other Irish periodicals, he wrote stories and sketches. Died insane at Rathmines, Dublin.

Pictures and songs; by Thomas Caulfield Irwin. Dublin: M.H. Gill & Son; London: Simpkin, Marshall & Co. 1880. viii, 240 pp.   *BL*

Poems, sketches and songs; by Thomas Caulfield Irwin. Dublin: M.H. Gill & Son. 1889. vi, 248 pp.   *BL*

Sonnets on the poetry and problems of life; by Thomas Caulfield Irwin. Dublin: M.H. Gill & Son; London: Simpkin, Marshall & Co. 1881. [iv], 104 pp.   *NLI*

Versicles; by Thomas Caulfield Irwin. Dublin: Gill & Son; London: Simpkin, Marshall & Co. 1882. [x], 168 pp.   *TCD*

ISA, pseud. *see* **COWAN, Isa**, (Isa, pseud.)

ISHAM, Sir Charles Edward (1819–1903). b. Lamport, Northamptonshire, second son of the 8th Bart. Educated at Rugby School, and Brasenose College, Oxford. He succeeded his brother as 10th Bart, 1846. Over a period of fifty years he constructed the famous rock garden at Lamport Hall, home of the Isham family from 1560. Lived latterly at Horsham, Sussex.
The tyrant of the Cuchullin Hills; [by Sir Charles Edward Isham]. [Lamport]: [Author]. [1880]. [16] pp. il.   *OXB*

ISLA, pseud. *see* **COOPER, Edith Emma**, (Isla, pseud.)

ISRAEL, I., (Luscombe Searelle, pseud.). FRGS. Of London.
The dawn of death; by Luscombe Searelle. London: Trübner & Co. 1889. viii, 148 pp.   *BL*

ITHURIEL, pseud.
Poems; by "Ithuriel". London: John Heywood. 1883. viii, 102 pp.   *BL*

IVERSON, Winifred A.
God's touch, and other poems; by Winifred A. Iverson. With introduction by F.B. Meyer. London: Marshall Bros. [1891]. 95 pp.   *OXB*
Whispers from the throne, and other verses; by Winifred A. Iverson. London: Elliot Stock. 1894. vi, 156 pp.   *OXB*

J

J., H.A.R. *see* **JOY, Henry Archibald Robert**, (H.A.R.J.)

J., L.
Occasional poems; by L.J. London: Elliot Stock. [1887]. [viii], 136 pp.   *OXB*

JACK, Thomas Godfrey (1849–). Son of Charles Jack of Ealing, Middlesex, gentleman. Brought up in Guildford, Surrey. Educated at Guildford Royal Grammar School, and Queen's College, Oxford.
My soul and her saviour; by Thomas Godfrey Jack. London: Houlston & Sons. [1891]. 69 pp.   *OXB*
To the friends of long ago; by Thomas Godfrey Jack. London: Houlston & Co. [1891]. 47 pp. il.   *OXB*

"JACK PAY-FOR-ALL ON THE REVOLUTION IN THE FARMER'S WORLD": THE SITUATION NEW YEAR'S EVE, 1861, NEW YEAR'S EVE, 1881, IN VERSE. Manchester: John Heywood. 1882. 22 pp. *BL*

JACKMAN, John A. (1842–). b. Carrick-on-Suir, Tipperary. He joined the Irish Franciscan Province at age of sixteen, going to St Isidore's, Rome, for training; ordained in Waterford. He was elected Minister Provincial in 1882 and re-elected in 1885. Lived chiefly in Dublin.
The seraph of Assisi; by John A. Jackman. Books I–IX. Dublin: James Duffy & Co., Ltd. 1898–99. 2 vols. *OXB*
Via crucis, and other poems; by John A. Jackman. Dublin: M.H. Gill & Son. 1884. viii, 197 pp. *OXB*

JACKSON, Ann Olivia, (Patty Honeywood, pseud.) (1856–). b. Leeds, older sister of Florence Jackson. She scribbled rhymes from early childhood. Her verse was well known to readers in the West Riding of Yorkshire, then later to readers on a national scale. She contributed to *Leeds Mercury, Yorkshire Post*, etc.
Poems; by Patty Honeywood. London: Kegan Paul, Trench & Co. 1883. viii, 99 pp. *OXB*

JACKSON, C., (C.J.), (Owner of the Drunken Dog, pseud.). Lived at Clegg Street, Oldham, Lancashire.
Five popular hobbies, with several original facts and fables in prose and poetry; by the owner of the drunken dog, C.J. London: Simpkin, Marshall, & Co.; John Heywood; Oldham: W.E. Clegg. 1880. viii, 48 pp. *OXB*

JACKSON, Mrs Clement Nugent, (Jim's wife, pseud.). Married Clement Nugent Jackson, Fellow of Hertford College, Oxford.
Gordon League ballads, for working men and women; by Jim's wife (Mrs. Clement Nugent Jackson). First series. London: Skeffington & Son. [1897]. xviii, 165 pp. *TCD*
Also 2nd ed. 1898; 3rd ed. 1899.

JACKSON, Edgar Stanway. Ordained, 1880; curate, Buckhurst Hill, Essex, 1880–89, Hitchin, Hertfordshire, 1889–93, St Augustine's, Croydon, Surrey, 1894–95, St Giles's, Camberwell, from 1898.
Ballads of home and life, with poems and sonnets; by E. Stanway Jackson. London: Wells Gardner, Darton & Co. [1887]. viii, 120 pp. il. *BL*
Also a limited ed. of numbered copies, [1887].

JACKSON, Florence (Flo). b. Leeds, younger sister of Ann Olivia Jackson. She often wrote as Flo Jackson in Yorkshire dialect.
Sea dreams: [poems]; by Flo. Jackson. Hull: William Andrews & Co.; Leeds: James Milnes; London: Simpkin, Marshall, Hamilton, Kent, & Co., Ltd. 1893. [iv], 24 pp. *OXB*

JACKSON, G. Hunt

The demon of the wind, and other poems; by G. Hunt Jackson. London: John Long. 1898. 135 pp. *OXB*

In memoriam Thomas Carlyle and other lights obscured but not gone out: [poems]; by G. Hunt Jackson. London: Office of the 'Christian Age'. 1881. 59 pp. *BL*

Modern song from classic story: verse suggested by some of the most interesting and instructive characters and events of mythology and classical history; by G. Hunt Jackson. Printed London: Spottiswoode & Co. 1895. viii, 134 pp. il. *JRL*

JACKSON, Henry. Lived at 54 Waller Street, Byker, Newcastle upon Tyne.

Flora's levee, and other poems; by Henry Jackson. Newcastle-upon-Tyne: Andrew Reid & Co., Ltd. 1897. viii, 152 pp. por. *OXB*

JACKSON, James Shade

Biographical and miscellaneous sonnets (written in 1880–82); [by James Shade Jackson]. London. 1883. 40 pp. *BL*

Sonnets; [by James Shade Jackson]. London. 1884. 36 pp. *BL*

JACKSON, Richard Charles. Educated at Keble College, Oxford. FSA. Lived at Grosvenor Park, Camberwell, Surrey.

The golden city: sonnets and other poems, written at Keble College, Oxford, with a sonnet "In memoriam" of Dr. E.B. Pusey; by Richard C. Jackson. Oxford: B.H. Blackwell. 1883. [viii], 26 pp.

Half-title is *Keble College poems*. *OXB*

His presence: spiritual hymns and poems of the blessed sacrament of the altar, for devotional use at holy communion; by Richard C. Jackson. London: James Westell. 1886. 101 pp. *OXB*

His presence: spiritual hymns and poems of the blessed sacrament of the altar, for devotional use at holy communion; by Richard C. Jackson. 2nd ed., with new hymns. London: Church of England Text Society. 1887. [xii], 92 pp. il. *BL*

His presence: hymns & poems of the blessed sacrament of the altar; by Richard C. Jackson. 3rd ed. London: R. Elkins & Co. [1889]. [xii], 92 pp. il. *BL*

Also 4th ed. 1891.

In the wake of spring: love songs and lyrics; by Richard C. Jackson. London: Bowyer Press. 1898. 80 pp. il. *OXB*

Ye purple yeast: a poem written in vindication of old England's honour; by Richard C. Jackson. London: Bowyer Press. 1896. vi, 21 pp. il. *OXB*

The risen life; by [Richard Charles Jackson]. London: Hamilton, Adams & Co.; Bristol: W.C. Hemmons. [1882]. [iv], 71 pp.

Poetry and prose. *OXB*

The risen life: hymns and poems for the Christian year, Easter to Advent; by Richard C. Jackson. London: J. Masters & Co. 1883. viii, 55 pp. *BL*

The risen life: hymns and poems for the Christian year (Easter to Advent); by Richard C. Jackson. New ed. with miniatures in gold and colours. London: James Westell. 1886. viii, 55 pp. col. il. *BL*

The risen life: hymns and poems for days and seasons of the Christian year (Easter to Advent); by Richard C. Jackson. 3rd ed., illustrated by Dante Gabriel Rossetti, and others. London: R. Elkins & Co. 1889. viii, 55 pp. col. il. *BL*

JACOBS, Henry (1824–1901). b . Chale, Isle of Wight, son of William H. Jacobs, gentleman. Educated at Charterhouse, and Queen's College, Oxford (scholar); BA 1845, MA 1848, DD 1880. Fellow of Queen's College, 1848–51. Headmaster, St Nicholas College, Shoreham, 1848–49, Christchurch Grammar School, New Zealand, 1852–63. Dean of Christchurch, 1866–96. Edited *The New Zealand Church News*.

A lay of the Southern Cross, and other poems; by Henry Jacobs. London: Skeffington & Son; Christchurch, New Zealand: A. White. 1893. x, 147 pp.   *OXB*

JACOBUS, pseud.
"A drug in the market": being some of the songs of Zion that are not wanted; written by Jacobus. London: Passmore & Alabaster. [1884]. [2], viii, 96 pp.   *OXB*
Songs at sunset: or, leisure lays of a business man; written by Jacobus. London: Passmore & Alabaster. [1886]. [2], viii, 96 pp.   *OXB*

JACQUE, George (1806–92). b. Douglas, Lanarkshire. Minister of the United Presbyterian Church, Auchterarder, Perthshire, for fifty-seven years. At the time of his death was probably the oldest member of the denomination. He wrote many hymns and songs, and was an accomplished violinist.

The crofter's wedding jubilee; [by George Jacque]. Edinburgh: Oliphant, Anderson, & Ferrier. 1882. 30 pp.   *OXB*

JACSON, Charles Roger. Of Barton in Amounderness. JP and deputy lieutenant for Lancashire.

Reliquiae rerum; [poems]; by C.R. Jacson. Printed Edinburgh: R. & R. Clark. 1890. xii, 176 pp.
     Privately printed.   *NLS*

JAMES, Arthur *see* **JAMES, Arthur Coleridge**

JAMES, Arthur Coleridge (1842?–1921). b. Alton, Hampshire, son of Rev. Edward James, Canon of Westminster. Educated at Eton College, and King's College, Cambridge (scholar): BA 1864, MA 1867. Fellow of King's College, 1863–70. Assistant master at Eton, 1864–99, he subsequently lived at Paignton, Devon. Skilled in wood-carving, some of his work can be seen at Wortham Church, Suffolk. Twice married, his first wife was a daughter of Isambard K. Brunel, civil engineer.

Deucalionea: or, autumn episodes of Eton, 1894; by Arthur James. With illustrations by the old masters. Printed Eton: George New. 1895. [24] pp. il.   *OXB*

Songs of sixpenny; and, Pupilroom rippings, etc.; by Arthur C. James. [Eton]: R. Ingalton Drake, Eton College Press. 1899. [iv], 88 pp. il.   *OXB*

JAMES, Charles
Poems and fragments; by Charles James. Paisley: Alex. Gardner. [1884]. 125 pp.   *OXB*

JAMES, Charles Wilford (1874-19). b. Coatham, Yorkshire, son of Thomas James, iron master. Educated at Rossall School, and Lincoln College, Oxford. Ordained 1900; appointed curate, Middlesbrough, 1900; rector, Westerdale, 1909; vicar, Sherburn, 1915; chaplain to the forces, 1917–18; vicar, Shipton, 1921.

Leisure hour lyrics; by C.W. James. Oxford: B.H. Blackwell; London: Simpkin, Marshall, Hamilton, Kent & Co. 1897. 25 pp. *OXB*

"JAMMED", AND OTHER VERSE. London: Bickers & Son. 1880. 94 pp. *OXB*

JAPP, Alexander Hay, (A.N. Mount Rose, pseud.), (A.F. Scot, pseud.). (1837–1905). Began work as a tailor's book-keeper in Edinburgh. Attended classes at Edinburgh University, 1860–61. Literary adviser in London to Isbister & Co.; assisted in editing *Good Words, Sunday Magazine*, and *Contemporary Review*. Wrote studies of Hawthorne, Thoreau, R.L. Stevenson, and De Quincey. LL.D Glasgow 1879.

The circle of the year: a sonnet-sequence, with proem and envoi; by Alexander H. Japp. Printed London: Hazell, Watson, & Viney, Ltd. 1893. 77 pp.

Printed for the author. Spine-title is *Sonnets, lyrics, etc. BL*

Dramatic pictures; English rispetti; Sonnets, and other verses; by Alexander H. Japp. London: Chatto & Windus. 1894. viii, 152 pp. *OXB*

Facts and fancies, from the Koran, the doctors, and the rabbis, & c.; [poems]; by A.N. Mount Rose. London: Thomas Burleigh. 1899. 85 pp. *OXB*

Lilith and Adam: a poem in four parts; by A.F. Scot. London: Thomas Burleigh. 1899. 91 pp. *OXB*

JARVIS, Mary Rowles. Wrote for *The Girl's Own Paper*.

Sunshine and calm: songs by the way; by Mary Rowles Jarvis. 2nd ed. London: Religious Tract Society. [1896]. 128 pp. *TCD*

JAY, Kay, pseud.

Rose; a romance of 192-; by Kay Jay. Bristol: J.W. Arrowsmith; London: Simpkin, Marshall, Hamilton, Kent & Co. Ltd. [1898]. 126 pp. *OXB*

JAY, P. Of Newcastle upon Tyne?

The water bailey: a tale of the coquet, being a cheerful chant in the common tongue, descriptive of some events which happened on the night when the bailey went to town, with sundry matters thereto appertaining; by P. Jay. Newcastle-on-Tyne: Mawson, Swan, & Morgan. 1897. 62 pp. *OXB*

JEFFERSON, Samuel (1840–19). b. Leeds, son of William Jefferson. Educated in Leeds, and at St Mark's College, Chelsea, under Derwent Coleridge. Professor of natural science at schools and colleges in Harrogate, Ilkley and Scarborough. Public lecturer to mechanics' institutes and other societies. Secretary to Yorkshire Board of Education, 1866–70. FRAS.

Columbus: an epic poem, giving an accurate history of the great discovery in rhymed heroic verse; by Samuel Jefferson. Chicago: S.C. Griggs & Co. 1892. 239 pp. por. *BL*

The invincible Armada: the story of England's great deliverance, told in heroic verse, at the tercentenary celebration; by S. Jefferson. London: Simpkin, Marshall & Co.; Edinburgh: John Menzies & Co.; Plymouth: W.H. Luke. [1888]. 159 pp.   *OXB*

An ode for Victoria Day, June 20, 1897; by Samuel Jefferson. London: George Blackie & Son; Leeds: Fred. R. Spark & Son. [1897]. 48 pp.   *OXB*

An ode for Victoria Day, June 20th 1897; by Samuel Jefferson. Cheap ed. Leeds: Pedley & Sons; London: Simpkin, Marshall, & Co. [1897]. 16 pp.   *OXB*

Sonnets on nature & science; by S. Jefferson. London: T. Fisher Unwin. [1886]. 96 pp.   *OXB*

Urania; Night, and other astronomical poems; by S. Jefferson. London: Elliot Stock. 1896. x, 96 pp.   *OXB*

JENKINS, Robert Charles (1815–96). Educated at Trinity College, Cambridge; BA 1841, MA 1844. Ordained, 1842; curate, Willesden, 1841–43; perpetual curate, Christ Church, Turnham Green, 1843–54; rector, Lyminge, Kent, 1854–96; hon. canon, Canterbury Cathedral, 1869–96. Hon. curator, Lambeth Palace Library, 1881–96.

Ballads of high and humble life, with some occasional verses; by Robert C. Jenkins. Printed Folkestone: T. Kentfield. [1893]. [ii], 100 pp.   *BL*

JENNINGS, James George. Educated at Lincoln College, Oxford. Professor of English literature and logic, Queen's College, Benares, 1892, then Allahabad, 1895; inspector of schools, United Provinces, 1905; principal, Muir Central College, Allahabad, 1906; temporary director of education, Bihar and Orissa, 1914; vice-chancellor, Patna University, 1917; director of education, Bihar and Orissa, 1920; retired 1921.

From an Indian college; [poems]; by James George Jennings. London: Kegan Paul, Trench, Trübner & Co. Ltd. 1898. 119 pp.   *OXB*

JENNINGS, John Andrew. Educated at Trinity College, Dublin; BA 1880, MA 1883. Incumbant, Portnashangan, 1881–82, Donaghpatrick, County Meath, 1882–96, St Matthew's, Dublin, 1896–1901; chaplain, Mount Grove Cemetery, 1904.

Wayside restings: [poems]; by John A. Jennings. Dublin: Carson Bros; London: Simpkin, Marshall, & Co. [1882]. 112 pp.   *OXB*

JERDON, Gertrude. Story writer.

Flowering thorns; by Gertrude Jerdon. London: James Nisbet. 1886. 64 pp.   *OXB*

JESHARELAH, pseud.

A lay of two cities; by Jesharelah. London: Passmore & Alabaster. 1888. 96 pp.   *OXB*

JESSOP, Mary K. Irish. God-daughter of the Hon. Mrs King-Harman. Lived at Doory Hall.

Patchwork: a collection of poems, etc.; by M.K. Jessop. [1882]. [x], 89 pp.
     Printed for private circulation only.   *BL*

JESSOPP, C.S. Of Norwich.
Two dreams: I. Jael; II. Bathsheba; by C.S. Jessopp. Norwich: A.H. Goose & Co. 1882. [viii], 69 pp.
For private circulation. *OXB*

JEVONS, William
The monastery's tale, and other poems; by William Jevons. London: Swan Sonnenschein & Co., Ltd. 1896. 94 pp. *OXB*

JEWITT, William Henry (1842–).b. Headington, Oxford, nephew of Orlando Jewitt, engraver. An architect and artist by profession, he wrote several hymns of more than usual merit.
The romance of love: a garland of verse; by W.H. Jewitt. London: Elliot Stock. [1886]. [viii], 88 pp. *OXB*

JIM, pseud. *see* **EDWARDS, James H.**, (Jim. pseud.)

JIM's WIFE, pseud. *see* **JACKSON, Mrs Clement Nugent**, (Jim's Wife, pseud.)

JOHN, Paul, pseud. *see* **KAY, Samuel Walton, (Paul John, pseud.)**

JOHNS, Edward, pseud. *see* **EDWARDS, Robert John**, (Edward Johns, pseud.)

JOHNSON, Ernle Sacheverell Wilberforce (1859?–). Son of George H. Johnson, Dean of Wells. Educated at Christ Church, Oxford; BA 1881.
Ilaria, and other poems; by Ernle S.W. Johnson. London: Kegan Paul, Trench & Co. 1884. [viii], 127 pp. OXB

JOHNSON, George
Breezes of song from Mount Pleasant: a series of sacred and secular poems; by Geo. Johnson. London: W. Poole. 1880. viii, 133 pp. *OXB*

JOHNSON, J.L.
Church and state: or, the corruptions of politics and religion: a satire (in verse); by J.L. Johnson. Manchester: John Heywood. [1885?]. 16 pp. *MPL*

JOHNSON, J.R.
The parachute & the bad shot, [and other poems]; written by J.R. Johnson. Pictured by C.E. Brock. [London]: George Routledge & Sons, Ltd. [1891]. [v], 51 pp. il. *BL*

JOHNSON, Lionel (1867–1902). b. Broadstairs, Kent. Educated at Winchester College, and New College, Oxford, where he came under the influence of Walter Pater; BA 1890. Converted to Roman Catholicism in 1891. He settled in London, making a living by writing critical reviews and articles for *Academy, Pall Mall Gazette*, etc. Interested in Irish politics and the literary revival. He died from a fractured skull after a fall.

Ireland, with other poems; by Lionel Johnson. London: Elkin Mathews; Boston; Copeland & Day. 1897. xii, 128 pp.   *BL*

Poems; by Lionel Johnson. London: Elkin Mathews; Boston: Copeland & Day. 1895. xii, 116 pp.

A limited ed. of 750 copies for England and America.   *MPL*

JOHNSON, Paul (1789–1883). Educated at St John's College, Cambridge. Rector of Sidestrand and Overstrand, Norfolk, 1834–72. Died at Kirmington, Lincolnshire.

An epitome in verse of the life of his royal highness the late Prince Consort; by Paul Johnson. London: James Nisbet & Co.; Norwich: Jarrold & Sons. 1883. 120 pp.

Spine-title is *The Prince Consort*.   *OXB*

JOHNSON, Reginald Brimley (1867–1932). Son of William H.F. Johnson, schoolmaster of Cambridge. Educated in Cambridge, Crawford College, and Corpus Christi College, Cambridge. He established a small publishing business in London and Edinburgh in 1900. Founded and edited *The Gownsman*. Wrote critical studies of Jane Austen and other women novelists.

Verse essays; by Reginald Brimley Johnson. London: Stanesby & Co.; Derby; Frank Murray. 1890. [4], viii. 87 pp. (Moray library).

A limited small paper ed. of 140 copies, 130 of which were for sale.   *TCD*

BL has the only copy printed on Japanese vellum.

JOHNSON, William Knox (1868–1906). b. Monkstown, County Dublin, son of Canon Johnson of Carbery, County Kildare. Educated at home, at Parsonstown, and Merton College, Oxford; BA 1891. He entered the Indian Civil Service, and was based at Benares. Died in India.

Terra tenebrarum; Love's jestbook, and other verses; by William Knox Johnson. London: Kegan Paul, Trench, Trübner & Co. Ltd. 1898. xii, 155 pp.   *UCD*

JOHNSON-BROWN, Annie. Educated at Cheltenham Ladies' College.

Myths of the dawn: poems; by Annie Johnson-Brown and other members of the Daisy Guild. London: Kegan Paul, Trench, & Co. 1885. 123 pp.

Cover-title is *Poems by the Daisy Guild*. Most are by Annie Johnson-Brown.   *BL*

Rejected of men, and other poems; by A. Johnson-Brown. London: Sampson Low, Marston, Searle & Rivington Ltd. 1890. iv, 88 pp.   *OXB*

The JOHNSONIANS: [poems]. Second series. London: Burns & Oates, Ltd. [1887]. [67] pp.

Printed on one side of leaf only.   *OXB*

JOHNSTON, David. Possibly David Johnston (1836–99). Son of Charles Johnston of Monkwearmouth, County Durham. Educated at St Andrews and Glasgow Universities, and St Mary Hall, Oxford. Church of Scotland minister, Unst, Shetland, 1865–68, Harray and Bursay, Orkney, 1868–93. Professor of divinity & biblical criticism, Aberdeen University, 1893–99.

The school of Christ: a song to Christ the Lord: a metrical rime; [by David Johnston]. Edinburgh: James Gemmell. 1887. lxxx, 144 pp.   *UCD*

JOHNSTON, James M. A Belfast working man.

Jottings in verse; by James M. Johnston. Printed Belfast: M'Caw, Stevenson & Orr. 1887. 80 pp.   *NLI*

JOHNSTON, John (1852–1927). b. Annan, Dumfriesshire. Educated at Annan Academy, and Edinburgh University; MD. Appointed house surgeon to West Bromwich District Hospital, 1874; afterwards resident medical officer to Birmingham & Midland Hospital for Sick Children. In 1876 he established himself as a general practitioner in Bolton, Lancashire; hon. surgeon to Bolton Infirmary, and medical officer for Bolton. Vice-president of Bolton & District Medical Society.

Musa medica: a sheaf of song and verse; by J. Johnston. London: Savoy Press, Ltd. 1897. 152 pp. por.   *OXB*

JOHNSTON-SMITH, Frederick James. Of Portsmouth.

The captain of the "Dolphin", and other poems of the sea; by Frederick J. Johnston-Smith. London: Digby, Long & Co. [1897]. 224 pp.   *OXB*

JOHNSTONE, Charles Edward (1865–1923). b. Wareham, Kent, son of Edward Johnstone. Educated at Radley College, and Keble College, Oxford; BA 1888. Became a preparatory schoolmaster. Died at Ashford, Kent.

Ballads of boy and beak; by C.E. Johnstone. London: John Lane The Bodley Head. 1895. vi, 62 pp.   *OXB*

JOHNSTONE, Eros M.

Merry mischief May: an allegory of a nineteenth century fairy; by Eros M. Johnstone. In three parts. Edinburgh: R. Grant & Son. 1891. 16 pp. il.   *OXB*

JOHNSTONE, James. Lived at 12 Factory Street, Inverness.

A few words: James Johnstone's book: [poems]. [Inverness]: [Author]. [1896?]. 21 pp.

   Title from cover. Printed on one side of leaf only.   *OXB*

James Johnstone's book of remarks: [poems]. [Inverness]: [Author]. [1897]. [37] pp.

   Title from cover. Printed on one side of leaf only.   *BL*

James Johnstone's new original works: [poems]. [Inverness]: Author. [1896]. [27] pp.

   Title from cover. Printed on one side of leaf only. Previously published as separate broadsides.   *OXB*

James Johnstone's work of new dictation: the standard of the world: [poems]. [Inverness]: Author. [1899]. [69] pp.

Title from cover. Printed on one side of leaf only. Previously published as separate broadsides. *OXB*

JOHNSTONE, John (1839–). b. Lochwood, Dumfriesshire. He worked as a pupil-teacher at the village school, then attended Edinburgh and Glasgow Universities, 1857–62. Appointed a master at the High School, Auckland, New Zealand, in 1862. At the outbreak of the Maori war he joined the volunteers, his company holding the redoubt at Wairoa for six weeks. Returned to teaching in Auckland, then taught in Melbourne, and Braidwood, New South Wales. He left for home in 1862, holding teaching posts in Stalybridge and Stockport, Cheshire, in his spare time preparing entrants for Oxford and Cambridge.

Nugae poeticae: or, a wheen rhymes, setting forth fragments of an old man's story, and other matters; by J. Johnstone. Paisley: Alexander Gardner. 1881. [ii], 172 pp. *NLS*

JOLLY, Ellen E. Mrs Jolly of Bath, Somerset.

Verses; by Ellen E. Jolly. Printed Bath: Herald Office. [1898]. 23 pp.

Title from cover. *TAU*

JOLY, John Swift (1818–87). b. Dublin. Educated at Trinity College, Dublin; BA 1839, MA 1852. Rector, Tullamore, Meath, 1863–69; rector and vicar, Athlone, 1869–87. He left a large quantity of unpublished poetry.

Earth's Christmas ode; by John S. Joly. Dublin: George Herbert. 1886. 32 pp. *OXB*

JONES, A.

Ballads and poems; by A. Jones. Printed Canterbury: H.J. Goulden. 1881. 104 pp. *BL*

JONES, A. Mrs Jones of Ash Grove, Ashton-on-Ribble, near Preston, Lancashire.

Poems and songs, written in spare moments; by Mrs. A. Jones. Printed Preston: R. Parkinson & Co. [1890]. [viii], 103 pp. *OXB*

JONES, Hannah Watts- *see* **WATTS-JONES**, Hannah, (British Matron, pseud.)

JONES, Isabel Mary. Novelist.

The Christmas bells, and other verses; by Isabel Mary Jones. Oxford: A.R. Mowbray & Co. [1898]. 40 pp. *OXB*

JONES, James, (Two tramps, pseud. with S.M. Hodgson). Forty-five years pastor of The Strict Baptist Church, Shovers Green, Wadhurst, Sussex.

A brief memoir of James Jones . . . With a sermon preached September 11th, 1836, together with various writings, letters, poems, and hymns; written by himself. Wadhurst, Sussex: Miss Betts; Hastings: R. Betts. [1889]. 267 pp. *★UCD*

Low down: wayside thoughts in ballad, and other verse; by two tramps [S.M. Hodgson and James Jones]. London: George Redway. 1886. viii, 98 pp.

Title from cover. *MPL*

JONES, James Pickering, (Raimonde Bell, pseud.). Of Liverpool.
A little book of verse, wherein is set forth the pleasant occupation of many hours perhaps thus employed less profitably than they might have been; by Raimonde Bell. London: Offices of 'Poetry and Prose'. 1893. [viii], 91 pp.   *MPL*

JONES, John, (Joannes Towy). Curate, Morriston, Swansea.
Newport Castle, and other short poems, descriptive and elegiac; by John Jones (Joannes Towy). Printed Carmarthen: William Spurrell. 1886. 47 pp.   *NLW*

JONES, Margaret Lawrence. Married Paul Blaise.
A decade of verse; by Margaret Lawrence Jones. London: Remington & Co. 1881. 143 pp.   **UCD*

JONES, Robert *see* **DERFEL, Robert Jones**

JONES, Thomas, (T.J. Powys, pseud.). Of Llanerchrogog, near Ruabon, Denbighshire.
Poems; by T.J. Powys. London: Kegan Paul, Trench, Trübner & Co., Ltd. 1891. [xvi], 156 pp. por., facsim.   *UCD*

JOSEPH, Rosabelle. Of Swansea, Glamorgan.
Acrostics and stray verses; [by Rosabelle Joseph]. Swansea: [Author]. [1898]. [ii], 33 pp. por.
    Cover-title is *Album of acrostics and stray verses*. Printed expressly for the "Jewish Chronicle" stall of the Press Bazaar, in aid of the London Hospital.   *BL*

JOURDAIN, W.E. Of Worcester.
The tale of Worcester fight, and other poems; by W.E. Jourdain. London: London Literary Society. [1881?]. 79 pp.   *OXB*

JOY, Henry Archibald Robert, (H.A.R.J.) (1870–19). b. Bampton, Oxfordshire, son of Henry Joy, DD. Educated at Worthing School, and Worcester College, Oxford; BA 1891.
Poems, and other verses; by H.A.R.J. London: T. Fisher Unwin. 1896. viii, 200 pp.   *TCD*

JOY AND HEALTH. London: S.W. Partridge & Co. [1891]. 32 pp.   *OXB*

JOYCE, A.J.
A Roman anti-Christ: a narrative in rhyme; by A.J. Joyce. London: Digby, Long & Co. 1899. [viii], 81 pp.   *OXB*

JOYNES, Bessie
Out of the darkness; by Bessie Joynes. Manchester: Labour Press Society Ltd. [189-]. 31 pp.
    Poetry and prose.   **NUC*

JOYNES, James Leigh (1853–93). Son of Rev. James Leigh Joynes. Educated at Eton College, and King's College, Cambridge (scholar). Assistant master at Eton, 1876–82. Entered Middlesex Hospital as a medical student but his health broke down. Author of *The Adventures of a Tourist in Ireland*, publication of which resulted in a government apology to Henry George, American journalist. He was forced to resign his Eton mastership. Lived latterly at West Hoathly, Sussex.

On lonely shores, and other rhymes; by James Leigh Joynes. Printed London: Chiswich Press. 1892. x, 143 pp.

Printed for the author.   *OXB*

Socialist rhymes; by J.L. Joynes. London: Modern Press. 1885. 16 pp.

Title from cover.   *WCM*

JULIO, pseud. *see* SYKES, Joseph, (Julio, pseud.)

JUNDA, pseud.

Echoes from Klingrahool: [poems]; by "Junda". Lerwick: Johnson & Greig. [1898]. 52 pp. (Old rock series).   *OXB*

JUSTIN: A MARTYR, AND OTHER POEMS. London: Simpkin, Marshall & Co. 1880. [iv], 108 pp. il.   *OXB*

The **JUVENILE GALLERY, ILLUSTRATING THE JOYS AND CARES OF CHILDHOOD: TWELVE SCENES PHOTOGRAPHED FROM LIFE, WITH APPROPRIATE VERSES.** London: Fred. Bruckmann. [1880]. [ii], 28 pp. il.   *OXB*

K

K *see* **KELLETT, Ernest Edward**, (K)

K., A.S. *see* **STANSFIELD, Abraham**, (A.S.K.)

K., M. *see* **MILLICAN, Kenneth William**, (M.K.)

KALGA, pseud.

The house that Bull built; by Kalga. London: Chas. J. Clark. 1894. 32 pp.   *OXB*

KANE, Edward pseud. *see* **KNOX, Kathleen**, (Edward Kane, pseud.)

KANTZOW, Theodosia De *see* **DE KANTZOW**, Theodosia

KAPPA, pseud *see* **PERCEVAL, C.**, (Kappa, pseud.)

KAPPEY, Ferdinand E. Translator from the German.
Sonnets & lyrics; by Ferdinand E. Kappey. London: Simpkin, Marshall, Hamilton, Kent & Co., Ltd. 1899. [x], 116 pp.   *OXB*

KATIE, AND OTHER POEMS. London: Wyman & Sons. 1885. [2], vi, 148 pp.   *OXB*

KAY, Samuel Walton, (Paul John, pseud.)
[Poems]; by Paul John. Oxford: Mowbray & Co. 1896–97. 2 vols.
    Vol. I. Poems; and, Kerdos, the miser. Vol. II. Saul: a tragedy, and other poems.   *OXB*

KAY, Thomas (1841–1914). b. Heywood, Lancashire. Educated at Bury Grammar School. Apprenticed to James Greenhalgh, chemist of Heywood. In 1866 he went into business with his brother Samuel as manufacturing chemists in Stockport, Cheshire. He took an active part in the public life of the town. A Liberal, he was president of Stockport Liberal Association.
In the clouds; a sportive & sporting sketch, from papers read before Manchester and Stockport Literary Clubs; by Thomas Kay. Printed Manchester: John Heywood. [1899]. 164 pp. il.
    Poetry and prose. Reprinted for private circulation.   *HPL*
Sporting songs; [by] Thomas Kay. To illustrate a paper read before the Manchester Literary Club, Dec. 1897. [1897]. [21] pp.
    Printed on one side of leaf only.   *OXB*

KAY, W.H. (1865–1900). Engraver and stamp maker of 66 Mawson Street, Ardwick Green, Manchester.
Light and shade: a poem; by W.H. Kay. Printed [Manchester]: [Cuthbertson & Black]. [1883]. 20 pp.   *MPL*

KAY, William C., (Arnica, pseud.). Of Moston Priory, Manchester.
Snatches of song and prosaic musings; by Arnica. Manchester: Author. 1885. 24 pp.   *MPL*

KEAN, Edward Ashtonius
St. Valentine's gift: a poem, including Cupid's 'Romance of earth's history'; by Edward Ashtonius Kean. London: Digby & Long. 1890. [iv], 61 pp.   *OXB*

KEANE, Evan T.
A moorland brook, and other poems; by Evan T. Keane. London: Digby, Long & Co. [1897]. xii, 88 pp.   *OXB*

KEAY, William Isaac. Educated at St Andrews University. Ordained 1878; curate at the Cathedral, Trinidad, 1877–80; chaplain, Convict Depot, Chaguanas, Trinidad, 1880–83; curate, St Paul's, Great Yarmouth, Norfolk, 1883–84, Normansfield Asylum, Hampton Wick, 1884–86; vicar of St Michael's and chaplain to the Leper Asylum, Trinidad, from 1887.

Iscariot: a poem; by William Isaac Keay. London: George Stoneman. 1893. [ii], 124 pp.   *OXB*

KEEN, Lucretius, pseud. *see* **VAN STRAALEN, Robert**, (Lucretius Keen, pseud.)

KEENE, Henry George (1825–1915). Son of Rev. Professor H.G. Keene. Educated at Rugby School, Oxford, and Haileybury. Entered the Bengal Civil Service, 1847; a magistrate and judge for thirty-five years. Lecturer on Indian history, Oxford University Extension, 1889. Lived latterly at Buckleigh, Westward Ho, Devon.

Hic et ubique: verses written in idleness; by H.G. Keene. Allahabad: [Pioneer Press]. 1899. [iv], 53 pp.   *BL*

Poems, original and translated; by H.G. Keene. Printed Calcutta: "Englishman" Press. 1882. [vi], 81 pp.   *BL*

Verses: translated and original; by H.G. Keene. London: W.H. Allen & Co.; New York: Appletons. 1886. viii, 112 pp.   *OXB*

KELLETT, Ernest Edward, (K) (1864–1950). b. Maidstone, Kent, son of Featherstone Kellett, Wesleyan minister. Educated at Kingswood School, and Wadham College, Oxford; BA 1886, MA 1889. Senior English master, The Leys School, Cambridge. Literary critic; editor of the *Book of Cambridge Verse*, 1911. Lived latterly at Lantern House, Meadvale, Redhill, Surrey.

Jetsam: occasional verses; by K (E.E. Kellett). Cambridge: E. Johnson. 1897. [viii], 144 pp.   *OXB*

KELLY, J.J. b. Galloway, Kirkcudbrightshire. Educated there, and at Glasgow College. Lived at Tarf Cottage, Glenogle, Edinburgh.

Poems; by J.J. Kelly. Subscription ed. Edinburgh. 1894. viii, 52 pp.   *OXB*

KELLY, James (1856–81). b. Airdrie, Lanarkshire. Employed as a bookkeeper in Glasgow. He returned to Airdrie, appointed to a responsible position with Messrs Thomas Goldie & Co.

Poems; by James Kelly. Glasgow: Aird & Coghill; Edinburgh: John Menzies & Co. 1888. 200 pp.   *NLS*

KELLY, Joan. b. Irvine, Ayrshire, daughter of a Manxman who was drowned before her birth. Her mother earned a living as a sick nurse. The two women always lived together, only separated by her mother's death at eighty-three. She became gravely ill two years later and was taken into the poorhouse, a permanent invalid.

Miscellaneous poems; by Joan Kelly. [Irvine]: Mr Murchland. 1884. v, 127 pp.   *BL*

KELLY, John Kelso (1864–   ). b. Portwilliam, Wigtownshire. Apprenticed as a pupil-teacher, he eventually became a teacher in Edinburgh.

A home of heroes: or, a lay of liberty: being a poem, chiefly historical, to which is added a prose essay "A foray into Galloway song-land"; by John Kelso Kelly. Edinburgh: Darien Press. 1895. xxviii, 107 pp. il.

A limited ed. of 250 numbered copies signed by the author.   *EPL*

Pebbles from the brook: being miscellaneous poems; by John Kelso Kelly. With notes. Edinburgh: Brydone & Luke. 1888. [vi], 63 pp. por., facsim.   *NLS*

KELLY, Mrs Tom. Wrote a history of the Crimean War.

Meadowsweet; by Mrs Tom Kelly. Illustrated by Tom Kelly. London: Von Portheim & Co. [1891]. [22] pp. il.   *OXB*

Those were the days: poem; by Mrs Tom Kelly. Illustrations by Tom Kelly. London: Dean & Son. [1891]. [47] pp. il.

Printed on one side of leaf only.   *OXB*

KEMBLE, Frances Anne (Fanny) (1809–93). Actress daughter of the actor Charles Kemble, and a niece of Sarah Siddons. She made her first stage appearance at Covent Garden in 1829, and went on to play many leading roles. In 1833 she visited the United States, met and married a Georgia planter, Pierce Butler, but divorced him in 1848. She gave Shakespearian readings for over twenty years, living in America part of the time. She died at Gloucester Place, London, and is buried at Kensal Green.

Poems; by Frances Anne Kemble. London: Richard Bentley & Son. 1883. xii, 340 pp.   *MPL*

KEMP, Francis S.

The fogs, and other poems; by Francis S. Kemp. London: Digby, Long & Co. 1894. viii, 64 pp.   *OXB*

The masque of Civilisa, [and other poems]; by Francis S. Kemp. London: Digby, Long & Co. [1892]. 77 pp.   *OXB*

KENDALL, Harriet. Educated at the Royal Academy of Music, and King's College, London. Teacher of elocution, recitation and voice-production, she taught at King's College from 1893. Composer of songs and piano pieces. Lived at East Twickenham, Middlesex.

A Lakeland story; by Harriet Kendall. With illustrations by Alfred Woodruff and Tom Taylor. London: John Walker & Co. [1888]. [32] pp. il.   *BL*

Synariss, and other poems for recitation; by Harriet Kendall. London: Simpkin, Marshall, Hamilton, Kent & Co. 1894. 168 pp.   *OXB*

KENDALL, May (1861–19   ). b. Bridlington, Yorkshire, and lived there. She wrote novels and short stories, and collaborated with B.S. Rowntree in writing *How the Labourer Lives*.

Dreams to sell: [poems]; by May Kendall. London: Longmans, Green, & Co. 1887. x, 150 pp.   *OXB*

Songs from dreamland; by May Kendall. London: Longmans, Green, & Co. 1894. viii, 136 pp.   *BL*

KENDREW, Mary E. Temperance writer.

'*Lyra sacra*': [poems]; by Mary Kendrew. London: Elliot Stock. 1894. viii, 71 pp. *OXB*

KENNEDY, Alexander William Maxwell Clark (1851–94). b. Knockgray, Galloway, Kirkcudbrightshire, son of Colonel John C. Kennedy, commandant of the Royal Military Train. Educated at Eton College, where he published a work on ornithology at age sixteen. Commissioned in Coldstream Guards, 1870, resigning as captain, 1874; left army because of ill-health due to overseas service. Fellow of several learned societies, he was devoted to every kind of field sport. Lived at Knockgray, and at Henbury, Wimborne, Dorset.

Robert the Bruce: a poem, historical and romantic; by Alexander W.M. Clark Kennedy. Illustrated by James Faed, junr. London: Kegan Paul, Trench, & Co. 1884. x, 295 pp. il. *MPL*

KENNEDY, Arthur Clark. Translator from the French, German and Arabic.

Avenged, and other verses; by Arthur Clark Kennedy. London: Gay & Bird. 1899. 47 pp.

'Any profits will be divided between the fund of the Gordon Memorial College at Khartoum and orphans of soldiers killed during the present fighting in South Africa'. *OXB*

Erotica: [poems]; by Arthur Clark Kennedy. London: Gay & Bird. 1894. [viii], 72 pp. il.

A limited ed. of 250 numbered copies. *OXB*

Pictures in rhyme; by Arthur Clark Kennedy. Illustrated by Maurice Greiffenhagen. London: Longmans, Green, & Co. 1891. [viii], 83 pp. il. *OXB*

Two princes; by Arthur Clark Kennedy. Printed London: Chiswick Press. 1884. [15] pp.

Printed on one side of leaf only. *BL*

KENNEDY, Bass. Of Glasgow.

Songs and poems; by Bass Kennedy. Glasgow: Andrew Cochrane. 1888. 128 pp. por. *BL*

KENNEDY, James Christopher (1844–). b. Ireland, his father a native of Ayrshire. Educated at Elgin Academy.

Thoughts in verse; by James Christopher Kennedy. Edinburgh: Andrew Elliot. 1895. viii, 266 pp.

Printed for private circulation. *BL*

KENNEDY, Thomas (1823–). b. Cowgate, Galashiels, Selkirkshire. At age of eight he worked eleven hours a day in a local woollen factory. Apprenticed to the weaving trade, he was eventually employed in the pattern department of Sanderson's Tweed Mill, Galashiels. Member of Galashiels Burns Club.

Poems; by Thomas Kennedy. Illustrated by Geo. Tait. Galashiels: John M'Queen. [1889]. [iv], 235 pp. il. *BL*

KENTISH RAG, pseud. *see* **WARD, Bernard Rowland**, (Kentish Rag, pseud.)

KENWORTHY, John Coleman (1861–19   ). Ph.D. Writer on Tolstoy. Lived at The Grey House, Purleigh, near Maldon, Essex.
Amgiad and the fair lady, and other poems; by John C. Kenworthy. London: Swan Sonnenschein & Co. 1893. 38 pp. *OXB*
The judgment of the city, and other poems, and verses; [by John Coleman Kenworthy]. London: Swan Sonnenschein & Co. 1889. 73 pp. *OXB*

KERR, John. Book agent of Laurencekirk, Kincardineshire.
Reminiscences of a wanderer, and comical curiosities of country life, chiefly collected in the north-eastern counties of Scotland: [poems]; by John Kerr. Part first. Printed Dundee: John Leng & Co. 1890. 108 pp.
Printed for the author. *OXB*

KERSLEY, George Herbert. Dramatist.
Early flight, and other poems; by George Herbert Kersley. With an illustration and designs by the author. London: Bickers & Son. 1885. xii, 183 pp. il. *OXB*
A little book: poems; by George Herbert Kennedy. London: Bickers & Son. 1890. [vi], 92 pp.
Cover-title is *Poems*. *OXB*
Lorenzo (Il Pittore); and, Love sonnets; by Geo. Herbert Kersley. London: Bickers & Son. 1892. [viii], 152 pp. *OXB*
Nature worship, and other poems; by George Herbert Kersley. London: Bickers & Son. 1897. viii, 80 pp. *OXB*
A play & XV sonnets; by Geo. Herbert Kersley. London: Bickers & Son. 1890. [vi], 60 pp. *OXB*

KETTLE, Rosa MacKenzie (18   –1895). b. Overseale, Leicestershire. A prolific novelist, she lived at Heathside, Parkstone, Dorset.
Autumn leaves from the Leny Pass; by Rosa Mackenzie Kettle. London: James Weir. 1882. [viii], 47 pp.
Poetry and prose. *CU*
Christmas berries and summer roses; by Rosa MacKenzie Kettle. London: James Weir. 1881. [viii], 135 pp.
Poetry and prose. *CU*
Furse blossoms: stories and poems for all seasons; by Rosa Mackenzie Kettle. London: T. Fisher Unwin. [1891]. iv, 316 pp. *CU*

KIDSON, Eastwood. Novelist.
Told in a city garden: tales and lyrics; by Eastwood Kidson. London: Elliot Stock. 1889. [iv], 143 pp. *OXB*

KING, Clifford, (Rhyd-y-Godor). Anglo-Welsh bard.

Poems; by Clifford King. London: Digby, Long & Co. 1899. [viii], 282 pp.   *OXB*

"The royal pearl", and other poems; by Clifford King, ("Rhyd-y-Godor"). Hereford: Jakeman & Carver. [1894]. [2], ii, 63 pp.   *BL*

KING, Daniel (1844–92?). b. Glasgow. Both parents died of cholera when he was four. He worked on the land in Arran and West Kilbride, Ayrshire, then moved to Govan, where he worked in a shipyard as foreman riveter. A member of Newark Free Church, Port Glasgow, he was an ardent Freemason.

The Auchmountain warbler: songs, poems, & c.; by the late Daniel King. With portrait and biographical sketch. Paisley: J. & R. Parlane; Edinburgh: John Menzies & Co.; London: Houlston & Sons. 1893. [iv], 221 pp. por.   *BL*

KING, Harriet Eleanor Hamilton, (Maria Monica, pseud.) (1840–1920). b. Edinburgh, daughter of Admiral W.A. Baillie Hamilton and Lady Harriet Hamilton, sister of the Duke of Abercorn. In 1864 she married Henry S. King, banker and publisher. She had a sympathetic interest in the cause of Italian republicanism, and wrote a biography of Giuseppe Mazzini. Lived at the Manor House, Chigwell, Essex, all her married life.

Ballads of the north, and other poems; by Harriet Eleanor Hamilton King. London: Kegan Paul, Trench, & Co. 1889. vi, 158 pp.   *MPL*

A book of dreams; [poems]; by Harriet Eleanor Hamilton King. London: Kegan Paul, Trench, & Co. 1883. [vi], 93 pp.   *OXB*

   Also 3rd ed. 1888.

The desolate soul: poems for holy week; by Maria Monica. London: Society for Promoting Christian Knowledge. 1897. 80 pp.   *OXB*

The prophecy of Westminster, and other poems in honour of Henry Edward, Cardinal Manning; by Harriet Eleanor Hamilton King. London: W.B. Whittingham & Co., Ltd. 1895. 63pp.   *BL*

KING, J. Percy

As the wind blows: stray songs in many moods; by J. Percy King. London: Leadenhall Press; Simpkin, Marshall, Hamilton, Kent & Co., Ltd.; New York: Scribner & Welford. [1891]. viii, 185 pp.   *OXB*

KING, John Myers (1804–87). Son of Edward King of Askham, Westmorland. Educated at Balliol College, Oxford: BA 1824, MA 1827. Ordained 1827. Vicar of Cutcombe, Somerset, from 1832. Translator of Virgil into English verse.

Consolations of age; [poems]; by the late J.M. King. Clifton: E. Austin & Son. 1889. 104 pp.   ★*UCD*

KING, Maude Egerton. Mrs Joseph King. Editor of *The Country Heart*. Lived at Hill Farm, Camelsdale, Haslemere, Surrey.

My book of songs and sonnets; by Maude Egerton King. London: Percival & Co. [1893]. viii, 115 pp.   *OXB*

KINGSFORD, Anna Bonus (1846–88). Née Bonus. In 1867 she married Algernon G. Kingsford, vicar of Atcham, Shropshire. Contributed stories to *Penny Post*, 1868–72; purchased *Lady's Own Paper*, 1872, editing it, 1872–73. She studied medicine in Paris, 1874, qualified in 1880, and practised in London. President of the Theosophical Society, 1883. Founded the Hermetic Society, 1884.

The ideal in diet: selections from the writings of Anna Bonus Kingsford. London: Ideal Publishing Union, Ltd. 1898. 176 pp. (Vegetarian jubilee library, IX).

Stories, essays, lectures, and verse.   ★*UCD*

KINGSTON, Frederick William (1855–1933?) .b. Oundle, Northampton-shire, son of William Kingston, schoolmaster. Educated at Pembroke College, Cambridge: BA 1879, MA 1887, BD 1929. Ordained 1884; curate, South Hill with Callington, Cornwall, 1883–86, Thornby, Northampton-shire, 1886–91; Marston-Trussell, 1895–1900. Headmaster, Guilsborough Grammar School, 1886–1910. Curate, Elmton, Derbyshire, 1910–12, Beigh-ton, 1912–13; vicar, Willington, Bedfordshire, 1913–32.

Julian's vision, and other poems; by F.W. Kingston. London: T. Fisher Unwin. 1896. [vi], 103 pp.   *OXB*

KINGSTON, William Beatty- *see* **BEATTY-KINGSTON, William**

KINGSTONE, K.

Scattered roses: [poems]; by K. Kingstone. Printed Grantchester, Cambridge: S.P. Widnall at his private press. 1890. 161 pp.   ★*UCD*

KINLOCH, Marjory G.J. Daughter of Sir John Kinloch of Kinloch House, Perthshire. An historian, she wrote *Scottish Ecclesiastical History*, and a biography of St Catherine of Siena. A Roman Catholic.

A song-book of the soul: [poems]; by Marjory G.J. Kinloch. London: Kegan Paul, Trench, Trübner & Co. Ltd. 1892. xii, 252 pp.   *OXB*

KINNEAR, Benjamin Gott. Shakespearian scholar.

Versus: a Roman story; by Benjamin Gott Kinnear. London: Elliot Stock. 1885. [ii], 47 pp.   *OXB*

KIPLING, Rudyard (1865–1936). b. Bombay, India, where his father, John L. Kipling, was principal of a new art school. Educated at the United Services College, Devon, he returned to India to become assistant editor, *Civil and Military Gazette*, Lahore, 1882–87; editor, *Week's News*, Allahabad, 1887–89. He settled in England as a full-time writer, in London from 1889, then in Burwash, Sussex. Major writer of short stories and verse of the British Empire period, he was awarded the Nobel prize for literature in 1907.

BIBLIOGRAPHY: **STEWART, James McG.** *Rudyard Kipling: a bibliographical catalogue*. Edited by A.W. Yeats. Toronto: Dalhousie University Press & University of Toronto Press. 1959.

KIRBY-TURNER, Maud E.
"Dream love", and other poems; by Maud E. Kirby-Turner. Printed Walsall: W. Henry Robinson. 1895. 49 pp.   *BL*

KIRK, William Boyton. Studied for the ministry at St Aidan's; curate, Burslem, Staffordshire, 1860; chaplain to seamen; curate, Cotham, Nottinghamshire, 1871–72, St Nicholas's, Clifton, Bristol, 1872–75; vicar, Two-Mile-Hill, Bristol, 1875–77, Holy Trinity, Birkenhead, Cheshire, 1877–82, St Peter's, Ashton-under-Lyne, Lancashire, from 1882.
Poems on St. Peter's Church and parish, Ashton-under-Lyne, the antiquities of Ashton and neighbourhood, and the ancient customs of the black lad, & Wakes; by W.B. Kirk. Manchester: John Heywood. 1883. 64 pp.
   Cover-title is *Poems on Ashton and neighbourhood.*   *TAM*

KITCHING, George. Lived at Allenby House, Derby.
Dick Knap and his master; by George Kitching. London: Simpkin, Marshall, & Co. 1899. viii, 135 pp.   *OXB*
Poems and tales; by George Kitching. London: Simpkin, Marshall & Co.; Derby: Francis Carter. 1884. [viii], 116 pp.   *OXB*

KITCHING, William (1837–   ). b. Gainsborough, Lincolnshire, son of William Kitching, Quaker. Educated at Ackworth and Bootham Schools. Became a junior teacher at York, continuing his studies at the Flounders Institute; taught at Sidcot for two years, followed by eighteen years at Ackworth as a senior master. Became a Quaker minister in 1872. In 1880 he moved to Southport, Lancashire, where he established Ackworth Lodge, a successful private school.
Verses for my friends; by William Kitching. London: Edward Hicks, Jun. [c. 1891]. 136 pp.   *★UCD*

KITTERMASTER, Frederick Wilson (1820–1906?). Son of Dr James Kittermaster of Meriden, Warwickshire. Educated at Ruabon School, and Pembroke College, Oxford; MA 1849. Ordained 1849; curate, Bangor, 1848–51, St James's, Ratcliffe, London, 1851–53, St Paul's, Lisson Grove, 1853–56, St Chad's, Shrewsbury, 1856–65; vicar, Edgton, Shropshire, 1865–69, All Saints, Coventry, 1869–79, Bayston Hill, Shropshire, 1879–1906.
Rhuddlan Castle, and other poems; by Fred. W. Kittermaster. Coventry: Curtis & Beamish. 1890. viii, 120 pp.   *CU*

KNIGHT, H. Of Bradford, Yorkshire.
Local lyrics; by H. Knight. Bradford: "Yorkshireman" Newspaper Co. Ltd. [c. 1886]. 60 pp.   *BL*

KNIGHT, Olivia. (Thomasine, pseud.) (1830?–   ). b. Castlebar, County Mayo, daughter of Patrick Knight, engineer, who died early. She became a teacher to support her family, teaching at Gainstown, County Westmeath. Emigrated to Queensland in 1860, working in Brisbane Normal School. In 1869 she married Mr Hope Connolly, but was soon widowed. Moved to a country school near Warwick on the Darling Downs. She published stories, verse, and translations from the French.

Wild flowers from the wayside: Thomasine's poems. With an introduction by Sir Chas. Gavan Duffy. Dublin: James Duffy & Sons. [1883]. xxiv, 130 pp. *TCD*

KNOX, Kathleen, (Edward Kane, pseud.) Wrote novels, stories for children, and other works. Lived at Howth, County Dublin.
The islanders: a poem, in seven cantos; by Edward Kane. London: Elliot Stock. 1888. [viii], 232 pp. *OXB*

KNOX, Lucy (1845–84). Daughter of Stephen E. Spring-Rice. Her grand-father, Thomas Spring-Rice, was the 1st Baron Monteagle of Brandon in Kerry, and Chancellor of the Exchequer, 1835–39. Her brother succeeded to the title. In 1866 she married Octavius Newry Knox.
Four pictures from a life, and other poems; by the Hon. Mrs. O.N. Knox. London: Kegan Paul, Trench & Co. 1884. x, 103 pp. *OXB*

KYD, Jean, (Deborah, pseud.) (1858–). b. Dundee. Educated in Dundee, living there until her marriage at the age of nineteen. By twenty-one she was widowed so returned to her father's house. She remarried, living a few years in Kenilworth, Warwickshire, and London, until in 1886 she returned to Dundee, widowed again and her two children dead.
Poems of the hearth; by Jean Kyd, "Deborah". Printed Dundee: John Leng & Co. 1889. 195 pp. *OXB*

KYLE, Robert. Of Alva, Clackmannanshire.
Musings among the Ochils, and other poems; by Robert Kyle. Alva: [Author?]. [c. 1880]. 34 pp.
Printed for private circulation. *OXB*

KYRIOS = THE LORD: AN AUTOBIOGRAPHICAL SCRIPTURE POEM. Printed Wellington College Station: George Bishop. [1895]. 40 pp. *BL*

L

L., pseud *see* **SHORE, Louisa,** (L., pseud.)

L., A.C.
Verses written in India; [by] A.C.L. [c. 1885]. [iv], 71 pp. *BL*

L., C., *see* **LUCY, C.**, (C.L.)

L., E.
Wild flowers: [poems]; by E.L. London: Henry J. Glaisher. [1899]. 178 pp. *UCD

L., E. *see* **LAWLESS, Emily**

L., E. *see* **LINCOLN, Emily**, (E.L.)

L., E.A.M. *see* **LEWIS, Estelle Alice M.**, (E.A.M.L.)

L., E.V. *see* **LUCAS, Edward Verrall**, (E.V.L.)

L., H.
Odin sagas, and other poems; [by H.L.]. Manchester: J.E. Cornish. 1882. 44 pp.
    Printed for private circulation.   *OXB*

L., J.
Dotty, and other poems; by J.L. Glasgow: James Maclehose. 1880. viii, 127 pp.   *OXB*

L., L.M. *see* **LUSHINGTON, Lucy Maria**, (L.M.L.)

L., S.
England and Egypt: the latest poetical intelligence: a tale; by S.L. London: Pickering & Co. 1885. [viii], 46 pp.
    Poetry and prose.   *OXB*

L., S.A.
Isola: a poem; by S.A.L. Printed Evesham: W. & H. Smith. 1891. 67 pp.   *BL*

L., W.M. *see* **LUCAS, Winifred M.**, (W.M.L.)

A LADDER OF HEAVEN: AN ALLEGORY IN VERSE. With preface by the Lord Bishop of Lincoln. London: Longmans, Green, & Co. 1891. [xiv], 55 pp.   *OXB*

LADDIE BARD *see* **M'LAREN, John Wilson**

The LADY AND THE CAVALIER; THE MISTLETOE BOUGH, AND OTHER POEMS. Illustrated by J. Willis Grey. London: Raphael Tuck & Sons. [1891]. [24] pp. il.
    Printed on card.   *OXB*

LADYLIFT, pseud. *see* **HUTCHINSON, John**, (Ladylift, pseud.)

LAFFAN, Bertha (18 –1912). Daughter of Frederick Grundy, solicitor of Mottram-in-Longdendale, Cheshire. Her first husband was Surgeon-General Andrew Leith-Adams, with whom she lived in New Brunswick, Canada, 1867–71. In 1883 she maried Rev. R.S. De Courcy Laffan, headmaster. A novelist, she was on the staff of *All the Year Round* from 1880. Lived latterly at 119 St. George's Road, London SW.

A song of jubilee, and other poems; by Mrs. R.S. De Courcy Laffan (Mrs. Leith-Adams). London: Kegan Paul, Trench, & Co. 1887. 78 pp. il.   *UCD*

LAGENIENSIS, pseud. *see* **O'HANLON, John**, (Lageniensis, pseud.)

LAICUS, pseud.
Psychothen: or, reflections in verse on some of the graver aspects of human life; by Laicus. London: George Bell & Sons. 1892. x, 115 pp.   *OXB*

LAING, Alexander. Of Glasgow. Often wrote in Scots dialect.
The true hero, and other poems; by Alexander Laing. Glasgow: Morison Bros. 1893. 164 pp.   *UCD*

LAING, John. Of Troon, Ayrshire.
Miscellaneous poems, chiefly Scottish; by John Laing. Irvine: Charles Murchland. 1894. 160 pp.   *OXB*

LAIRD-CLOWES, Sir William (1856–1905). b. Hampstead, London, son of a legal official. Educated at King's College, London, then trained as a lawyer. In 1879 he became a journalist; naval correspondent to *The Times*, 1890–95; wrote anonymous articles in the *Daily Graphic*, which influenced official government policy. Compiled The Royal Navy, 1897–1903, in 7 vols. Knighted in 1902.

Eclogues; by William Laird Clowes. London: Sampson Low, Marston & Co. Ltd. 1899. x, 192 pp. por.   *BL*

The lover's progress: poems; by W. Laird Clowes. London: Effingham Wilson. 1881. 117 pp. il.   *BL*

LAMONT, Duncan (1842–). b. Lochgilphead, Argyllshire, son of a joiner on the estate of Sir John Orde of Kilmory. In 1851 the family moved to Greenock, Renfrewshire, where he became a blacksmith.

Poems and songs; by Duncan Lamont. Greenock: James M'Kelvie & Sons. 1895. 146 pp.   *UCD*

LAMONT, J.K. A lawyer of Glasgow?
Poems; by J.K. Lamont. Paisley: Alexander Gardner. 1893. [62] pp.   *UCD*
St. Kentigern: the story of the bird and the tree; the bell, the fish, and the ring; by J.K. Lamont. Glasgow: William Hodge & Co. 1894. 55 pp.   *OXB*

LAMPLOUGH, Edward (1845–   ). b. Flamborough, Yorkshire. A teacher, he was much involved with the Sunday School movement. Contributed verse and prose to a number of provincial and London magazines; published temperance tracts, and works on Yorkshire history. A founder of Hull Literary Club. Lived at Spring Bank, Hull.

Hull and Yorkshire frescoes: a poetical year-book of "specimen days"; by Edward Lamplough. Hull: Charles Henry Barnwell. 1888. xvi, 384 pp.

Printed for private circulation.   *OXB*

The siege of Hull, and other poems; by Edward Lamplough. Hull: Charles Henry Barnwell. 1881. viii, 104 pp.   *LEP*

LAMPSON, Frederick Locker- *see* **LOCKER-LAMPSON**, Frederick

LANCASHIRE BURNS *see* **WAUGH, Edwin**

LANCASTER, George Eric, pseud. *see* **MACKAY, Eric**, (George Eric Lancaster, pseud.)

LANCASTER, William James. Educated at Worcester College, Oxford (commoner).

Theodoric the Goth in Italy: the Newdigate poem, 1896; by William J. Lancaster. Oxford: B.H. Blackwell; London: Simpkin, Marshall, Hamilton, Kent & Co. 1896. 21 pp.   *OXB*

LANDLUBBER, pseud. *see* **THOMPSON, William Mort**, (Landlubber, pseud.)

LANE, Geoffrey

A song for the season, and other poems; by Geoffrey Lane. London: Swan Sonnenschein & Co. 1893. 48 pp.   *OXB*

LANE, J. J. (1852–19   ). A Yorkshireman. Taught at Borough College, Brighouse. Member of Raistrick Local Board, and chairman of the Health Committee. FRSL. Lived latterly at Alma Terrace, Brighouse.

Wayside thoughts: miscellaneous poems; by J.J. Lane. Printed Manchester: Onward Publishing Office. [c. 1885]. 143 pp. il., por.   *UCD*

LANG, Andrew (1844–1912). b. Selkirk. Educated at Edinburgh Academy, St Andrews University, and Balliol College, Oxford. Fellow of Merton College, 1868–75. He chose a literary career, becoming one of the busiest writers in English journalism and letters, free-lancing after 1875; published essays, novels, and children's books. A founder of the Psychical Research Society.

Ballades and verses vain; by Andrew Lang. New York: Charles Scribner's Sons. 1884. viii, 166 pp.   *BL*

Ban and Arrière Ban: a rally of fugitive rhymes; by Andrew Lang. London: Longmans, Green & Co. 1894. xvi, 118 pp. il.   *MPL*

Also 2nd ed. 1894.

Grass of Parnassus: rhymes old and new; by Andrew Lang. London: Longmans, Green & Co. 1888. xiv, 128 pp.   *MPL*

Also 2nd ed. 1889.

Grass of Parnassus: first and last rhymes; by Andrew Lang. London: Longmans, Green, & Co. 1892. xvi, 190 pp.   *MPL*

Helen of Troy; by A. Lang. London: George Bell & Sons. 1882. [viii], 196 pp.   *BL*

Helen of Troy: her life and translation; done into rhyme from the Greek books; by Andrew Lang. The second time set forth. London: George Bell & Sons. 1883. [viii], 202 pp.   *OXB*

Rhymes à la mode; by A. Lang. London: Kegan Paul, Trench & Co. 1885. x, 140 pp. il.   *MPL*

Also [3rd ed.] 1887.

XXXII ballades in blue china; [by] A. Lang. London: Kegan Paul, Trench & Co. 1885. 112 pp.   *BL*

XXXII ballades in blue china; [by] A. Lang. London: Kegan Paul, Trench & Co. 1888. [i], 119 pp.

A limited ed. of 50 numbered copies printed on large paper.   *BL*

XXII ballades in blue china; [by] A. Lang. London: C. Kegan Paul & Co. 1880. 80 pp.   *MPL*

XXII and XXXII ballades in blue china; [by] A. Lang. London: C. Kegan Paul & Co. 1881. 112 pp. il.   *BL*

LANG, Andrew Miller (1857–   )

Poems and hymns; by Andrew Miller Lang. Glasgow: C.L. Wright; London: Nisbet & Co. 1887. 175 pp.   *BL*

The Prince of Omur, and other poems; by Andrew M. Lang. London: Houlston & Son; Edinburgh: J. Menzies & Co.; Glasgow: James M'Geachy. 1880. 142 pp.   *OXB*

LANGBRIDGE, Frederick (1849–1922). b. Birmingham, son of Henry C. Langbridge. Educated at King Edward VI School, Birmingham and at Merton College, Oxford. Curate, St George's Kendal, 1876–78; incumbent, Glen Alla, Derry, 1879–81; canon, St Munchin's, Limerick, 1881–82; rector, Newcastle West, 1882–83, St John's, Limerick, from 1883. Novelist, and a distinguished scholar, he was awarded a D.Litt. by Trinity College, Dublin, 1907.

Clear waters: [poems]; by Frederick Langbridge. London: Cassell & Co., Ltd. 1898. 62 pp. il. (by Zillah Taylor).   *OXB*

A cluster of quiet thoughts; [poems]; by Frederick Langbridge. [London]: Religious Tract Society. 1896. 47 pp.   *OXB*

Also 2nd–4th eds 1896.

Come ye to the waters: sacred poems; by Frederick Langbridge. Illustrated. [London]: Eyre & Spottiswoode. [1888]. [16] pp. il., col. il.

Printed on card.   *BL*

A cracked fiddle: being selections from the poems of Frederick Langbridge. Limerick: G. McKern & Sons. [189–]. 206 pp. por.   *NLI*

Gaslight and stars: a book of verse; by Frederick Langbridge. London: Marcus Ward & Co. 1880. 174 pp.   *OXB*

Little tapers: a day-book of verses; by Frederick Langbridge. [London]: Religious Tract Society. [1899]. 48 pp.   *OXB*

Poor folks' lives: ballads and stories in verse; by Frederick Langbridge. London: Simpkin, Marshall, & Co. 1887. 103 pp.   *OXB*

   Also Special ed. 1888.

The river of years: verses; by Frederick Langbridge. Illustrated with riverscapes and landscapes. London: Eyre & Spottiswoode; New York: E. & J.B. Young & Co. [1888]. [16] pp. il., col. il.   *BL*

The scales of heaven: poems, narrative, legendary, and meditative, with a few sonnets; by Frederick Langbridge. London: Elliot Stock. 1896. [viii], 194 pp.   *TCD*

Sent back by the angels, and other ballads of home and homely life; by Frederick Langbridge. Leeds: J.S. Fletcher & Co. 1885. xii, 126 pp.   *MPO*

   Also New ed. 1889 published by Cassell & Co., Ltd.

Sent back by the angels: ballads of home & homely life; by Frederick Langbridge. 4th ed., enlarged. London: Cassell & Co. Ltd. 1898. [6], ii, 206 pp. il., por.   *OXB*

Songs in sunshine: lyrics and rhymes about a beautiful world and a life worth living; by Frederick Langbridge. London: Eyre & Spottiswoode. 1882. 128 pp.   *OXB*

LANGFORD, John Alfred (1823–1903). b. Birmingham. Became a journalist, contributing to *Howitt's Journal*. He ran a printing business in Birmingham, 1852–55. Associated with *Birmingham Daily Press* and *Birmingham Daily Gazette*. An ardent Liberal, he helped in party organization. Joined the Unitarians under George Dawson. LL.D, FRHS.

Child Life, as learned from children: [poems]; by John Alfred Langford. London: Simpkin, Marshall, & Co. 1884. [2], viii, 96 pp.   *OXB*

Heroes and martyrs, and other poems; by John Alfred Langford. London: T. Fisher Unwin. 1890. viii, 132 pp.   *OXB*

The lily of the west, and other poems; by John Alfred Langford. Birmingham: Achilles Taylor; London: Simpkin, Marshall, Hamilton, Kent & Co., Ltd. [1898]. [viii], 134 pp.   *OXB*

On sea and shore: [poems]; by John Alfred Langford. London: Kegan Paul, Trench & Co. 1887. viii, 194 pp.   *OXB*

LANGHORNE, William Henry (1826?–1916). Son of Rev. Thomas Langhorne, of Musselburgh, Midlothian. Educated at Loretto, and Glasgow and Edinburgh Universities. Ordained 1855; curate, Alnwick, Northumberland, 1854–57, All Saints, Knightsbridge, London, 1858–61, St Paul's, Knightsbridge, 1862–68, St Gabriel's, Pimlico, 1869–72, St Augustine's, Stepney, 1872–79, vicar there, 1879–83; rector of Over Worton and vicar of Nether Worton, Oxfordshire, 1883–1909. Lived latterly at Sefton, Cheltenham, where he died aged ninety.

A season at Aix-la-Chapelle: humorous description, in blank verse, of that ancient city, and of the life at the Baths there; [by William Henry Langhorne]. Part I. London: J. Mardling. 1885. 115 pp.   *BL*

LANGSTON, Mrs C.B. Of London.

Poems; by Mrs C.B. Langston. London: F.V. White & Co. 1882. viii, 240 pp. *OXB*

LANGTON, William (1803–81). b. Farfield, West Riding, Yorkshire. Educated chiefly in Italy, Switzerland and Germany. In business in Liverpool, 1821–29, sometime agent for several mercantile firms in Russia. Held a position in Heywood's Bank, Manchester, 1829–54, then became managing director of the Manchester & Salford Bank. Member of the Chetham Society. Antiquarian, genealogist, philologist, and writer of English and Italian verse.

Sonnets: original and translations from the Italian; by William Langton. With portraits and a notice of his life. Manchester: J.E. Cornish. 1897. xii, 75 pp. por.

Printed for private circulation by one of his daughters. *MPL*

LARA, pseud. *see* **GRIFFITH, George Chetwynd**, (Lara, pseud.)

LARGE, J.R. Writer on physiology.

The dream of the undergrad, and other rhymes; by J.R. Large. London: Cromwell Press. [1898]. 16 pp. *BL*

LARMINIE, William (1849–1900). b. Castlebar, County Mayo. Educated at Trinity College, Dublin. He worked in the civil service for many years, retiring for reasons of health. He collected Irish folk tales and romances, and was associated with the literary revival. Died at Bray, County Wicklow.

Fand, and other poems; by William Larminie. Dublin: Hodges, Figgis, & Co., Ltd; London: Simpkin, Marshall, Hamilton, Kent, & Co., Ltd. 1892. [viii], 149 pp. *OXB*

Glanlua, and other poems; by William Larminie. London: Kegan Paul, Trench & Co. 1889. [vi], 85 pp. *OXB*

LARRY, Hunky, pseud. Of London.

The Tiklerusa ballads; by Hunky Larry. London: Gurney & Jackson. [1888]. [59] pp. *OXB*

LASCELLES, John (1841–19   ). b. Fryton, near Hovingham, Yorkshire, son of Robert M. Lascelles, surgeon of Slingsby. Educated at the Royal Military Academy, Sandhurst, and Clare College, Cambridge: BA 1864, MA 1877. Called to the Bar, Middle Temple, 1866; served for a time on the Northern circuit. Ordained, 1878; curate, Slingsby, 1877–80; vicar, Sheriff Hutton, 1880–1905.

Golden fetters, and other poems; by John Lascelles. London: Kegan Paul, Trench & Co. 1886. [viii], 96 pp. *OXB*

The great drama, and other poems; by John Lascelles. London: Leadenhall Press, Ltd; Simpkin, Marshall, Hamilton, Kent & Co., Ltd; New York: Charles Scribner's Sons. [1897]. [vi], 71 pp. (Sun and serpent series). *OXB*

X.Y.Z. and other poems; by John Lascelles. London: Leadenhall Press, Ltd; Simpkin, Marshall, Hamilton, Kent & Co., Ltd; New York: Charles Scribner's Sons. [1895]. [iv], 50 pp. *OXB*

LASH, Augustus Henry. A clergyman, he worked for the Church Missionary Society in India; at the mission in Tinnevelly, 1867–83; secretary of Female Normal School Society, 1883–88; at the mission in Pallam, Travancore, 1888–93; superintendent of Nilgiri Tamil mission, Madras, from 1893.

The children's picnic, and other tales in verse for young people; by A.H. Lash. London: Jarrold & Sons. [1883]. 119 pp. il.   *OXB*

LATTER, Thomas. Of St John's Wood, London.

The power of conscience: or, the monopolist, and other works: [poems]; by Thomas Latter. London: Simpkin, Marshall, Hamilton, Kent & Co., Ltd. 1891. viii, 502 pp.   *OXB*

LATTO, Thomas Carstairs (1818–   ). b. Kingsbarns, Fife, son of Alexander Latto, schoolmaster. Educated at St Andrews University. In 1838 he went to Edinburgh, employed as a lawyer's clerk, then became private secretary to William E. Aytoun, professor of logic. Later he started in business as a commission merchant in Glasgow. In 1851 he went to the United States as a founder and first editor of the *Scottish American Journal*, New York, afterwards entering the publishing house of Ivison & Co. Proprietor of an estate agency in Brooklyn.

Memorials of auld langsyne, containing, The school examination, The country sacrament, and other poems; by Thomas C. Latto. Paisley: Alexander Gardner. 1892. 116 pp.   *OXB*

LAUDER, Alexander

The leper of Chorazin; [by] Alex. Lauder. London: J. Akerman. 1889. 26 pp. il.   *OXB*

LAURENCE, Ernest J. Of Clifton, Bristol.

A few essays in poetry; [poems]; by Ernest J. Laurence. London: Remington & Co. 1880. [viii], 43 pp.   *OXB*

LAURIE, Catherine Ann (18   –95). Daughter of W. Hibburd of Berkshire. In 1861 she married Simon S. Laurie, educationist, of Edinburgh. Lived latterly in Duddington, Midlothian.

In memory of Catherine Ann Laurie, Nairne Lodge, Duddington, Midlothian, who departed this life on the 31st July 1895. Edited by her husband. Printed Edinburgh: T. & A. Constable. 1896. vi, 145 pp. por.

Poetry and prose. Privately printed for Mrs R.T. Hamilton Bruce of Edinburgh, the author's daughter.   *OXB*

LAVERACK, Alfred. Quartermaster-Sergeant with twenty-one years service in the 98th Prince of Wales Own Regiment, in India at one time. Lived latterly at 37 Albert Terrace, Hyde Park, Leeds.

The Leeds temperance reciter, No. 2; by A. Laverack. Leeds: Author. [1892]. 16 pp.

Title from cover.   *OXB*

LAW, James C. Customs officer at Leith, Midlothian. Lived latterly at 29 West Nicholson Street, Edinburgh.

For some purpose: [poems]; by J.C. Law. Printed Edinburgh: H. Armour & Co. 1893. [viii], 72 pp. il.

Printed for the author. *NLS*

Leaves from my portfolio: [poems]; by J.C. Law. Printed Edinburgh: H. Armour & Co. 1886. [ii], 78 pp. por., facsim. *NLS*

Saved from the wreck: a continuation of "Leaves from my portfolio": [poems]; by J.C. Law. Printed Edinburgh: H. Armour & Co. 1889. [ii], 78 pp. il.

Printed for the author. *NLS*

LAW, James Duff. Scot who emigrated to Camden, New Jersey, USA.

Dreams o' hame, and other Scotch poems, (with a few experiments in English verse); by James D. Law. Paisley: Alexander Gardner. 1893. xvi, 302 pp. por.

A limited ed. of 1,000 numbered copies. *CU*

LAWFORD, Mrs F.G.V., (Lillian, pseud.). Temperance writer.

Our Queen, and other poems; by Lillian. London: Digby, Long & Co. [1895]. viii, 136 pp. *OXB*

LAWLESS, Emily, (E.L.) (1845–1913). b. Lyons, County Kildare, daughter of the 3rd Baron Cloncurry. Privately educated by governesses. Most of her life was spent on the family estate in Ireland. Her father and two sisters committed suicide. A novelist, she also wrote historical studies, and a biography of Maria Edgeworth. Received D. Litt. from Trinity College, Dublin.

Atlantic rhymes and rhythms; by E.L. Printed London: Richard Clay & Sons, Ltd. 1898. 102 pp.

A few copies only, privately printed. Title-page states 'Printed by S.S. for herself and four others'. *BL*

LAWSON, Catherine Innes

Short poems; by Catherine Innes Lawson. Galashiels: D. Craighead. 1894. 80 pp. *NLS*

LAWSON, James Anthony (1817–87). b. Waterford. Educated at Trinity College, Dublin. Called to the Irish Bar, 1840; QC 1857; legal adviser to the crown in Ireland, 1858–59; Solicitor General for Ireland, 1861; Attorney-General, 1865; Privy Councillor, 1865. MP for Portarlington, 1865–68. Judge, Queen's Bench, 1882–87. Published his lectures on political economy.

Hymni usitati, Latine redditi, with other verses; by James Anthony Lawson. London: Kegan Paul, Trench & Co. 1883. xiv, 156 pp. *OXB*

LAWSON, William

Whittle Dene, and other poems; by William Lawson. With an introduction by William Fergusson. 2nd ed. Printed Newcastle-on-Tyne: Robinson, Mash & Co. 1893. 57 pp. *NPL*

LAX, Joshua (1835–   ). Of Shotley Bridge, County Durham.
Historical and descriptive poems by Joshua Lax. With numerous explanatory and other notes, and illustrated with portraits and local views. Durham: Geo. Neasham. 1884. xxxii, 197 pp. il, por.
Spine-title is *Poems*. *BL*

LAYARD, Nina Frances. Member of the British Association general committee. Contributed verse to *Harper's Magazine, Longman's Magazine*, and other periodicals.
I and myself, and other poems; by Nina Frances Layard. London: Simpkin, Marshall, Hamilton, Kent, & Co. (Ltd); Ipswich: Pawsey & Hayes. 1893. xii, 119 pp. *BL*
Poems; by Nina F. Layard. London: Longmans, Green, & Co. 1890. xii, 162 pp. *BL*
Songs in many moods; by Nina Frances Layard; [and], The wandering albatross, etc.: [poems]; by Annie Corder. London: Longmans, Green, & Co. 1897. viii, 126 pp. *BL*

LAYCOCK, Samuel (1826–93). b. near Huddersfield, Yorkshire. The family moved to Stalybridge, where he became a weaver, then a cloth-looker. In 1862 the Cotton Famine brought disaster to Lancashire, and he and thousands of others were thrown out of work. He found a job as hall-keeper and librarian of the Mechanics' Institute, Stalybridge, then became curator at the Whitworth Institute, Fleetwood. Latterly lived at Blackpool, where he ran a small business. Lancashire dialect poet.
Warblin's fro' an owd songster; by Samuel Laycock. With an introductory sketch by W. Trevor. Oldham: W. Clegg; London: Simpkin, Marshall, Hamilton, Kent & Co. Ltd; Manchester: John Heywood; Abel Heywood & Son. [1893]. xvi, 376 pp. il. por.
Poetry and prose. *BL*
Warblin's fro' an owd songster; by Samuel Laycock. With an introductory sketch by W. Trevor. 3rd ed., enlarged, containing a supplementary sketch by James Middleton . . . Oldham: W.E. Clegg. 1894. [2], xxxvi, 390 pp. il., por.
Poetry and prose. *BL*

LAYMAN, pseud.
Lays of a law-court; by a layman. With a preface by Coker Adams. London: James Parker & Co. [1882]. x, 17 pp.
Title from cover. 'Mostly reprinted from the *Church Times*'. *OXB*

LAYS OF THE LINKS: A SCORE OF PARODIES. Edinburgh: David Douglas. 1895. [vi], 68 pp. *OXB*

LAYSON, J.F., pseud. *see* **FINLAYSON, John**, (J.F. Layson, pseud.)

LAYTON, Bertha Temple *see* **TEMPLE LAYTON, Bertha**

LEADER, E.C.
Stray thoughts in verse; by E.C. Leader. London: Digby, Long & Co. [1892]. [vi], 24 pp. *OXB*

LEAKE, Robert (1824–1901). b. Manchester, son of a businessman. Educated at local schools. Aged sixteen he was apprenticed to a firm of engravers to calico printers; eventually a partner, and ultimately head of the firm Lockett, Leake & Co. President of Salford Liberal Association, he later helped re-organize the Liberals in Manchester. MP for Radcliffe-cum-Farnworth in 1885, 1886 and 1892. Lived at The Dales, Whitefield.
Piece work in the overtime of a business man; [by Robert Leake]. Manchester: Palmer, Howe, & Co. 1893. xiv, 450 pp. il.
Poetry and prose. Printed for private circulation. *UCD*

LEAN, William Scarnell (1833–1908). Son of William Lean, headmaster of the Quaker school at Camp Hill, who later opened a school at Edgbaston where W.S. Lean was educated. At seventeen he became a junior teacher at the Friends' School, York, then after training became a tutor at Darlington. In 1861 he moved to London, taking a degree in classics at University College. Appointed classics master at University College School; in 1870 made principal of the Flounders Institute, where he remained for twenty-nine years. Resigned to become a member of the Church of England; ordained curate in 1901 but left in 1907 and was re-admitted to the Society of Friends.
To my mother, and other home verses; by William Scarnell Lean. London: Kegan Paul, Trench, Trübner & Co., Ltd. 1898. viii, 132 pp. *OXB*

LEATHER, Robinson Kay. Educated at London University; MA.
On two strings: [poems]; by Norman Gale and Robinson Kay Leather. Printed Rugby: George E. Over. 1894. [viii], 72 pp.
Privately printed. Not joint authorship. *BL*
Verses; by R.K. Leather. [1890?]. 36 pp.
Title from cover. *BL*
Verses; by Robinson Kay Leather. London: T. Fisher Unwin. 1891. 88 pp. *OXB*

LEATHLEY, Mary Elizabeth Southwell. Mrs Leathley. Writer of Bible stories. Lived at Ladymead, Ascot, Berkshire.
Verses; by Mary E.S. Leathley. London. 1896. [ii], 102 pp.
Printed for private circulation. *BL*

LEATHWOOD, William H. Of Liverpool?
Reflections on the aesthetic principle; with, Tales and poems; by William H. Leathwood. Printed Liverpool: James Lynch. [1894]. [ii], 272 pp. por.
Printed for the author. *BL*

LEAVES FROM A SPIRITUAL DIARY: [poems]. London: Samuel Harris & Co. [1883]. 79 pp.   *OXB*

LECK, Jane. Eldest daughter of Henry Leck of Ayr, formerly of Glasgow. Educated in Glasgow, then spent a year and a half in Germany. Travel writer.
  Doon lyrics: [poems]; by Jane Leck. Printed Glasgow: James Maclehose & Sons. 1894. viii, 183 pp.
    Printed for the author.   *BL*

LECKY, William Edward Hartpole (1838–1903). b. Newtown Park, County Dublin. Educated at Cheltenham, and at Trinity College, Dublin; BA 1859, MA 1863. After a distinguished career in historical research he was elected MP for Dublin University, 1895–1903. Although a moderate he was opposed to Home Rule. Author of the multi-volume *History of England in the Eighteenth Century*, 1878–90.
  Poems; by William Edward Hartpole Lecky. London: Longmans, Green, & Co. 1891. x, 108 pp.   *MPO*
    Also a limited large paper ed. of 113 numbered copies.

LEE, Edmund. Of Bradford, Yorkshire.
  Hinemoa, and other poems; by Edmund Lee. London: James Clarke & Co. [1898]. xii, 126 pp.   *OXB*

LEE, Frederick George (1832–1902). b. Thame, Oxfordshire. Educated at St Edmund Hall, Oxford; Newdigate prizewinner, 1854. Vicar, All Saints, Lambeth, London, 1867–99. He founded and edited the *Union Review*, 1863–69; hon. secretary, Association for the Promotion of the Unity of Christendom, 1857–69; worked for union with the Church of Rome, and became a Roman Catholic in 1901.
  De profundis: various verses . . . ; by Frederick George Lee. Printed London: Mitchell & Hughes. 1899. 16 pp.
    Printed for private circulation.   *OXB*

LEE, Helen. Of Poulton-le-Fylde, Lancashire.
  Bit o' things: [poems]; by Helen Lee. Manchester: John Heywood. [1893]. xii, 280 pp. por.   *MPL*

LEE, Ida (1865–1943). b. Kelso, New South Wales, daughter of a grazier. On a visit to England in 1891 she married Charles J.B. Marriott, international rugby player. He was a housemaster at Highgate School, Hampstead, and she took an active part in the life of the school. Their only child was born in 1892. Trained as an historical geographer, she spent her spare time researching British records. Lived latterly at the Dower House, Sizewell, Suffolk.
  The bush fire, and other verses; by Ida Lee. London: Sampson Low, Marston & Co. 1897. viii, 62 pp.   *BL*
    Also 2nd ed. 1897.

LEE-HAMILTON, Annie. Née Holdsworth. In 1898 she married Eugene Lee-Hamilton, writer and diplomat. She and her husband lived at the Villa Benedettini, San Gervasio, Florence, which became a centre of intellectual society.

Forest notes: [poems]; by Eugene and Annie Lee-Hamilton. London: Grant Richards. 1899. xii, 93 pp. *OXB*

LEE-HAMILTON, Eugene (1845–1907). b. London, son of James F. Lee-Hamilton. Educated in France and Germany, and at Oriel College, Oxford. Entered the diplomatic service, holding minor posts in Paris and Lisbon. In 1873 he contracted a rare spinal complaint which disabled him until restored to health in 1897. His home in Florence became a centre of intellectual society.

Apollo and Marsyas, and other poems; by Eugene Lee-Hamilton. London: Elliot Stock. 1884. vi, 138 pp. *OXB*

Forest notes: [poems]; by Eugene and Annie Lee-Hamilton. London: Grant Richards. 1899. xii, 93 pp. *OXB*

Gods, saints, & men: [poems]; by Eugene Lee-Hamilton. With ten full-page illustrations designed by Enrico Mazzanti. London: W. Satchell & Co. 1880. viii, 129 pp. il. *OXB*

Imaginary sonnets; by Eugene Lee-Hamilton. London: Elliot Stock. 1888. x, 101 pp. *OXB*

The new Medusa, and other poems; by Eugene Lee-Hamilton. London: Elliot Stock. 1882. 120 pp. *OXB*

Sonnets of the wingless hours; by Eugene Lee-Hamilton. London: Elliot Stock. 1894. xii, 116 pp. *OXB*

LEECH, Thomas. Financial writer.

Life's pathway, and other poems; by Thomas Leech. Printed [Dublin]: Dublin Steam Printing Co. 1880. viii, 191 pp.

Cover-title is *Miscellaneous poems*; spine-title is *Poems*. *NLI*

LEES, Edwin (1800-87). b. Worcester. A botanist, one of the first to carry out research into the forms of brambles. A founder of the Worcestershire Natural History Society. *FLS*

Scenery and thought, in poetical pictures of various landscape scenes and incidents; by Edwin Lees. London: Henry Frowde. 1880. xii, 288 pp. *OXB*

LEFROY, Edward Cracroft (1855–91). Son of George B.A. Lefroy of London. Educated at Blackheath, and Keble College, Oxford; BA 1877, MA 1881. Ordained in 1878, he held curacies successively at Lambeth, Truro, and St John's, Woolwich, 1880–82. He relinquished church work for educational work. Died at his father's house, 42 Shooter's Hill Road, Blackheath.

Cytisus and Galongale: a series of sonnets; by Edward C. Lefroy. Blackheath: H. Burnside. [1883]. 32 pp.

Title from cover. *BL*

Echoes from Theocritus: a cycle of sonnets; by Edward C. Lefroy. Blackheath: H. Burnside. [1883]. [ii], 30 pp.

Title from cover. *BL*

Echoes from Theocritus, and other sonnets; by Edward Cracroft Lefroy. London: Elliot Stock. 1885. xii, [70] pp.   *OXB*

Edward Cracroft Lefroy: his life and poems including a reprint of Echoes from Theocritus; by Wilfred Austin Gill. With a critical estimate of the sonnets by the late John Addington Symonds. London: John Lane The Bodley Head. 1897. xiv, 200 pp. por.   *MPL*

Sketches and studies, and other sonnets; by [Edward Cracroft Lefroy]. Blackheath: H. Burnside. [1884]. 32 pp.

    Title from cover.   *BL*

Windows of the church, and other sonnets; by Edward C. Lefroy. Blackheath: H. Burnside. [1883]. 32 pp.

    Title from cover.   *BL*

LE GALLIENNE, Richard, (Exul, pseud.) (1866–1947). b. Liverpool, member of a Channel Islands family. Educated at Liverpool College. He trained as an accountant but disliked the work and made literature his career. In 1888 he moved to London, becoming a reader for Elkin Mathews and John Lane. One of the original members of the Rhymers' Club, he was adviser and contributor to the *Yellow Book*. A prominent figure in the literary movements of the 1890s, he wrote novels, essays and reviews. In 1901 he moved to the United States, later settling in Mentone, France.

English poems; by Richard Le Gallienne. Printed Edinburgh: T. & A. Constable. 1892. xii, 136 pp.

    A limited ed. of 25 copies privately printed on Japanese paper for Richard Le Gallienne, Elkin Mathews, John Lane, and their friends.   *BL*

English poems; by Richard Le Gallienne. London: Elkin Mathews & John Lane at The Bodley Head; New York: Cassell Publishing Co. 1892. xii, 132 pp.

    A limited ed. of 800 copies printed for England and America.   *GPR*

    Also a limited large paper ed. of 150 numbered copies printed for England and America.

    Also 2nd ed. 1892; 3rd ed. 1894.

English poems; by Richard Le Gallienne. [4th ed.]. London: John Lane, The Bodley Head; Boston [Mass.]: Copeland & Day. 1895. xii, 114 pp.   *OXB*

    Also 5th ed. 1895.

My ladies' sonnets, and other "vain and amatorious" verses, with some of graver mood; by Richard Le Gallienne. Printed Liverpool: W. & J. Arnold. 1887. [viii], 147 pp.

    Privately printed.   *OXB*

Nightingales: [poems]; by Richard Le Gallienne. Rugby: George E. Over; London: Elkin Mathews & John Lane. 1893. [iv], 32 pp.   *BL*

Robert Louis Stevenson: an elegy, and other poems mainly personal; by Richard Le Gallienne. London: John Lane; Boston [Mass.]: Copeland & Day. 1895. viii, 100 pp.   *OXB*

    Also 2nd ed. 1895.

Twilight and candle-shades; by 'Exul'. London: Kegan Paul, Trench & Co. 1888. x, 163 pp.

Poetry and prose. *OXB*

Volumes in folio; [poems]; by Richard Le Gallienne. London: C. Elkin Mathews. 1889. [xii], 90 pp.

A limited ed. of 250 copies. *OXB*

LEGGE, Arthur Edward John. Novelist and illustrator.

Sunshine and smoke: a book of verse; by Arthur E.J. Legge. London: Simpkin, Marshall & Co. 1895, iv, 96 pp. *OXB*

Wind on the harp-strings: poems; by Arthur E.J. Legge. London: Arthur L. Humphreys. 1896. [viii], 86 pp. *OXB*

LEGGE, Robert George. Possibly Robert George Legge (1864–1905). b. Leamington, Warwickshire, son of Hon. George B. Legge, and grandson of 4th Earl of Dartmouth. Educated at Haileybury, and Keble College, Oxford; BA 1887.

Player poems; by Robert George Legge. London: A.D. Innes. 1895. 75 pp. *OXB*

Songs of a strolling player; by Robert George Legge. London: A.D. Innes & Co. 1893. 60 pp. *OXB*

LEGH, Vivien

Dreamland: a book of sonnets; by Vivien Legh. London: David Bogue. 1884. viii, 100 pp. *OXB*

LEHMANN, Rudolph Chambers (1856–1929). b. near Sheffield, Yorkshire, of a German father and a Scottish mother. Educated at Highgate School, and Trinity College, Cambridge; president of the Union, 1876. Holding Liberal views, he stood for Parliament on several occasions. A journalist, he wrote for *Punch*, 1890–1917; appointed editor of the *Daily News*, 1901. Father of the writers Rosamund and John Lehmann.

The Billsbury election, and other papers from Punch; by R.C. Lehmann. With twenty-eight illustrations by Hal Hurst. London: Henry & Co. 1892. viii, 267 pp. il.

Poetry and prose. *OXB*

In Cambridge courts: studies of university life in prose and verse; by R.C. Lehmann. With illustrations by A.C. Payne. London: Henry & Co. [1892]. viii, 240 pp. il., por. (Whitefriars library of wit and humour). *MPL*

LEICESTER, Mary

Sung in the shadow: a collection of short poems; by Mary Leicester. London: E. Lloyd. 1899. 32 pp. *OXB*

LEIGH, Allesley Boughton. Of Brownsover Hall, near Rugby, Warwickshire.

Poems; by Allesley Boughton Leigh. London: Hatchards. 1885. [iv], 60 pp. *OXB*

LEIGH, Arran, pseud. *see* **BRADLEY, Katherine Harris**, (Arran Leigh, pseud.)

LEIGH, Henry Sambrook (1837–83). b. London, son of James Matthew Leigh, painter and writer. A dramatist, he translated and adapted French operas for the English stage. Lived in the Strand, London WC.
Strains from the Strand: trifles in verse: by Henry S. Leigh. London: Tinsley Bros. 1882. xii, 177 pp.   *OXB*

LEIGH, Isla, pseud. *see* **COOPER, Edith Emma**, (Isla Leigh, pseud.)

LEIGH, John (1813–87). b. Foxdenton Hall, Lancashire. Trained in medicine; MRCS 1837; resident medical officer, Manchester Infirmary, and lecturer there; medical officer of health, Manchester, 1868. Wrote on coal smoke nuisance and on the cholera epidemic in Manchester.
Lay and legends of Cheshire, with other poems and ballads; by John Leigh. Manchester: John Heywood. [1880]. 157 pp. il.   *MPL*

LEITH, Emily. b. Calcutta, India, daughter of John F. Leith, QC, a practising barrister in India, who had been MP for Aberdeen. She lived latterly in London, contributing verse to *Cassell's Magazine* and other journals.
Thoughts and remembrance: verses; by Emily Leith. Glasgow: David Bryce & Son. 1885. xii, 117 pp.   *BL*

LEITH, Mrs Disney *see* **LEITH, Mary Charlotte Julia**

LEITH, Mary Charlotte Julia (18 –1926). Mrs Disney Leith. Mother of six children.
Original verses and translations; by Mrs. Disney Leith. London: J. Masters & Co. 1895. viii, 152 pp.
   Cover-title is *Verses and translations*.   *BL*

LENANE, John Harrington. Emigrated to Australia in 1890, settling in Melbourne.
The hill of visions, and other poems; by John Harrington Lenane. London: Kegan Paul, Trench, Trübner & Co., Ltd. 1899. viii, 151 pp.   *OXB*

LENNARD, Horace, (Melancholy Jacques, pseud.)
Chirrups: [poems]; by Horace Lennard. London: Strand Publishing Co. 1883. viii, 110 pp.   *OXB*
Follies and fancies: a medley in metre . . . ; by Horace Lennard ("The Melancholy Jacques"). London: "Society" Office. [c. 1880]. 128 pp.   *★UCD*

LENNARD, J.E.
Humour and sentimentalism versified, dedicated to the Hon. Vincent Brown, Solicitor-General, Trinidad; by J.E. Lennard. Printed Port-of-Spain, Trinidad: "Creole" Office. [1894]. 37 pp.   *BL*

LENO, John Bedford (1820–94). b. Uxbridge, Middlesex. A printer and publisher at Drury Lane, London, 1860–70, at Holywell Street, 1870–80, and a second-hand bookseller, 1880–92. A Chartist. Member of the Clown lodge of Royal Antidiluvian Order of Buffaloes. An excellent public reader of verse, he wrote a series of poems for recitation. Buried at Uxbridge.

The aftermath, [and other poems]; with, Autobiography of the author, John Bedford Leno. London: Reeves & Turner. 1892. 3 vols in 1.   *OXB*

The last idler, and other poems; by John Bedford Leno. London: Reeves & Turner. 1889. 126 pp.   *BL*

LEONARD, Henry Charles (1836–98). b. Brislington, near Bristol, son of Robert Leonard. Educated at University College, London, and Regent's Park College; BA 1854, MA 1856. Baptist minister, Boxmoor, 1858, Boscombe, near Bournemouth, 1875–81, Clarence Street, Penzance, 1881–83, Bowdon, Cheshire, 1888–90. Member of the council, Baptist Union, for many years.

John the Baptist: an epic poem, in three books; by Henry C. Leonard. London: James Clarke & Co. 1880. 71 pp.   *OXB*

Sonnets on the parables of Our Lord, with a new classification and a new nomenclature; by Henry C. Leonard. London: James Clarke & Co. 1884. 112 pp.   *OXB*

The Spanish Armada: a ballad of old England: Lord Maccaulay's "Fragment", completed by another hand [Henry Charles Leonard]. Bristol: J.W. Arrowsmith; London: Simpkin, Marshall & Co. [1886]. 30 pp.   *OXB*

LESCRIBLEUR, V., pseud.

The great Anti-Crinoline League; by V. Lescribleur. London: Wyman & Sons. 1883. [iv], 89 pp.   *OXB*

LESLIE, Peter, (John Pindar, pseud.) (1836–   ). b. Glenvale, Fife, of humble origin. At the age of ten he began working in a coal mine. Learned to write when sixteen. Enlisted in the Army in 1858; served with the Fusiliers in India, Ireland, Gibraltar and Malta; promoted to corporal.

Random rhymes; by John Pindar. Edited by A.M. Houston. Cupar: J. & G. Innes. 1893. viii, 159 pp. por.   *BL*

LESTER, Hubert (1868–194   ). b. Hull, Yorkshire, son of Thomas Lester. Educated at Hull College, and Queen's College, Cambridge: BA 1891, MA 1895. Ordained 1893; curate, St Paul's, Lozells, Birmingham, 1892–95, Meanwood, Yorkshire, 1895–98, Keighley, 1898–1906; vicar, Edingley with Halam, Nottinghamshire, 1906–16; rector, St Elizabeth's, Reddish, Lancashire, 1916–19; vicar, Skipsea, Yorkshire, 1919–48.

Memories of Gloucester Cathedral, and other poems; by Hubert Lester. Hull: William Andrews & Co.; London: Simpkin, Marshall, Hamilton, Kent, & Co., Ltd. 1893. [viii], 40 pp.   *OXB*

LETTS, A.W.
"The angel hermit": (a legend); by A.W. Letts. Illustrated by W.F. Southcott. London: Simpkin, Marshall, Hamilton, Kent & Co., Ltd. 1898. 29 pp. il. *OXB*

LEVER, Sydney (1849–). Daughter of Charles Lever, Irish novelist, of 18 Upper Wimpole Street, London. She acted as a companion to her mother, was an extravagant spender, and had a talent for writing songs. In 1870 she married Edgar Crafton Smith, mill owner, paper manufacturer, and shipbuilder of Austria. They lived at Fiume, Croatia.
Fireflies: ballads and verses; by Sydney Lever. London: Remington & Co. 1883. xii, 133 pp. *OXB*

LEVETUS, Edward Lewis
Verse fancies; by Edward L. Levetus. With designs by Celia Levetus. London: Chapman & Hall. [1898]. 112 pp. il. *OXB*

LEVY, Amy (1861–89). b. Clapham, London, of Jewish parents, Lewis and Isabelle Levy. In 1876 the family moved to Brighton where she was educated before going up to Newnham College, Cambridge, the first Jewish girl to matriculate. A novelist as well as a poet, her work reflects her own melancholy nature. On 10 September 1889 she committed suicide by suffocating herself with charcoal fumes at her parents' house in Endsleigh Gardens, London.
A London plane tree, and other verse; by Amy Levy. London: T. Fisher Unwin. 1889. 95 pp. il. (Cameo series). *MPL*
A minor poet, and other verse; by Amy Levy. London: T. Fisher Unwin. 1884. viii, 96 pp. *OXB*
    Also 2nd ed. 1891.
Xantippe, and other verse; by Amy Levy. Cambridge: E. Johnson. 1881. [iv], 31 pp. *OXB*

LEVY, Mark
As Englishman, Jew and Christian: [poems]; by Mark Levy. London: S.W. Partridge & Co. [1898]. 95 pp. *OXB*

LEWIS, Estelle Alice M., (E.A.M.L.)
Margaret Ericson's choice, and other poems; by E.A.M.L. London: Jarrold & Sons. [c. 1880]. vii, 167 pp. *OXB*

LEWIS, Gerrard (1829?–1921). Son of Walter C. Lewis of Brompton, Middlesex. Educated at St Catherine's College, Cambridge; BA 1854, MA 1868. Ordained, 1855; curate, St Clement's, Liverpool, 1854–56, Epsom, 1857–60, St John the Baptist, Margate, Kent, 1860–63, Holy Trinity, Margate, 1864–73; vicar, St Paul's, Cliftonville, 1873–1915. Lived latterly at 29 Edgar Road, Margate. Died aged ninety.
Ballads of the Cid; by Gerrard Lewis. London: Sampson Low, Marston, Searle, & Rivington. 1883. [2], iv, 106 pp. *OXB*

LEWIS, Howell Elvet, (Elfed) (1860–1953). b. Conwil Elvet, Carmarthenshire. Educated at the Presbyterian College, Carmarthen; held Congregational pastorates at Buckley, Hull, Llanelly, Canonbury, and the Welsh Tabernacle, King's Cross, London. Poet and hymnwriter, winner of the Bardic crown and chair, National Eisteddfod of Wales, 1888; Arch-Druid of Wales, 1923–27. President, National Free Church Council, 1926–27; chairman, Congregational Union of England & Wales, 1933–34. Lived latterly at Erw'r Delyn, Penarth, Glamorgan.
My Christ, and other poems; by H. Elvet Lewis (Elfed). Hull: William Andrews & Co; London: Simpkin, Marshall, Hamilton, Kent, & Co., Ltd. 1891. [iv], 51 pp.   *OXB*

LEWIS, Landred
The proving of Gennad: a mythological romance; by Landred Lewis. London: Elliot Stock. 1890. iv, 142 pp.   *OXB*

LEWIS, Leonard
The merry ploughman: or, harvest home: a tale of shepherds; [by Leonard Lewis]. [1894]. 24 pp.   *OXB*

LEYTON, Frank, pseud. *see* **PEEK, Hedley,** (Frank Leyton, pseud.)

LEYTONSTONE. L.S. *see* **SHOREY, L.,** (L.S. Leytonstone)

LIBRA, pseud. Married woman of London.
Darkness and daylight: songs of the east; by Libra. London: Baldock & Co. 1888. viii, 118 pp.   *OXB*

LIDDELL, Mrs Edward *see* **FRASER-TYTLER, Christina Catherine**

LIDDELL, Robert (1808–88). Hon. Robert Liddell, son of 2nd Baron and 1st Earl Ravensworth. Educated at Charterhouse, and Christ Church, Oxford: BA 1829, MA 1834. Fellow of All Souls College, 1831–36. Ordained 1833; vicar, St Paul's, Knightsbridge, with St Barnabas, Pimlico, London, 1851–81; in 1855 he was taken to court for erecting crosses in both these churches, judgment against him confirmed in 1856.
The lay of the last angler, in four cantos; to which is added, Jack's dangers and deliverances; by the Hon. Robert Liddell. With illustration, from original etchings by the author. Kelso: J. & J.H. Rutherfurd. 1884. [iv], 211 pp. il, por.   *OXB*

LIFE AND TRUTH. Also a scripture chart, Life or death. London: Bible Christian Book Room. 1881. 58 pp.   *OXB*

LIFELONG THINKER AND WANDERER, pseud. *see* **CUST, Robert Needham**, (Lifelong Thinker and Wanderer, pseud.)

LIGGINS, J. Lived at 16 St John's Terrace, Queen Victoria Road, Coventry, Warwickshire.

The destiny machine: a glaub; [by J. Liggins]. Printed Coventry: Curtis & Beamish. [1894]. 16 pp.   *OXB*

LILLEY, Arthur

The athiest: an original poem; by Arthur Lilley. London: E.W. Allen. 1883. 64 pp.   *OXB*

LILLIAN, pseud. *see* **LAWFORD, Mrs F.G.V.**, (Lillian, pseud.)

LINCOLN, Emily, (E.L.)

Memories and hopes of E.L. Printed Dublin: R. Chapman. 1880. 32 pp.
Poetry and prose.   *NLI*

LIND, Alexander, pseud. *see* **HARRISON, John Henry**, (Alexander Lind, pseud.)

LINDSAY, Caroline Blanche Elizabeth, Lady (1844–1912). Only daughter and heir of the Right Hon. Henry Fitz-Roy. In 1864 she married Sir Coutts Lindsay, an army officer who was commandant of the British Italian Legion, and Deputy-Lieutenant of Fife. She was a novelist and short story writer, also writing books for children.

The apostle of the Ardennes; by Lady Lindsay. London: Kegan Paul, Trench, Trübner & Co., Ltd. 1899. 162 pp.   *OXB*

The flower seller, and other poems; by Lady Lindsay. London: Longmans, Green, & Co. 1896. viii, 188 pp.   *BL*

The king's last vigil, and other poems; by Lady Lindsay. London: Kegan Paul, Trench, Trübner, & Co. Ltd. 1894. viii, 203 pp.   *OXB*
    Also 2nd ed. 1895; 3rd ed. 1895.

Lyrics, and other poems; by Lady Lindsay. London: Kegan Paul, Trench, Trübner & Co., Ltd. 1890. xii, 170 pp.   *BL*

LINEHAM, Joseph. Bookseller of 41 Chetham Street, Rochdale, Lancashire.

The redeemer, and other poems; by Joseph Lineham. Manchester: John Heywood. [1884]. 191 pp.   *OXB*

LINGSTON, Rowe

John Chinaman: description versified by Rowe Lingston. London: Griffith, Farran, Okeden & Welsh, [1891]. 32 pp. col. il.   *OXB*

A sleeping beauty, and other tales; [poems]; by Rowe Lingston. London: Griffith Farran & Co. 1894. 90 pp.   *OXB*

Through misty veils: verses of the past and of day-dreamland; by Rowe Lingston. London: Griffith, Farran, Okeden & Welsh. [1891]. [vi], 84 pp.   *OXB*

Verses of country and town; by Rowe Lingston. London: Griffith, Farran, Okeden & Welsh; New York: E.P. Dutton & Co. 1886. [iv], 76 pp.   *BL*

Woodland and dreamland: [poems]; by Rowe Lingston. London: Griffith, Farran, Okenden & Welsh. 1888. 82 pp.   *OXB*

LINTON, William James, (Abel Reid, pseud.) (1812–98). b. Stratford, London E. An eminent wood-engraver, he was an ardent Chartist, and committed to socialism and republicanism. Friend of the Italian patriot Giuseppe Mazzini. He founded a monthly journal *The English Republican*, and also established a private press. In 1867 he went to America, settling at New Haven, Connecticut, while his wife Eliza Lynn Linton remained in England pursuing her career as a novelist. He continued to be in great demand as a wood-engraver for London magazines.

Broadway ballads, collected for the centenniel commemoration of the Republic, 1876; by Abel Reid. [Hamden, Connecticut]. [1893]. [x], 126 pp.

Author's ed. of 50 copies. *OXB*

Love-lore: [poems]; [by] W.J. Linton. [Hamden, Conn.]: Appledore Private Press. 1887. [4], vi, 125 pp.

A limited ed. of 50 copies. *BL*

Love-lore, and other, early and late, poems; [by] W.J. Linton. Hamden, Conn., U.S.A.: Appledore Press. 1895. [4], viii, 256 pp.

A limited ed. of 100 numbered copies, signed by the author. *BL*

Poems and translations; by W.J. Linton. London: John C. Nimmo. 1889. x, 202 pp. por.

A limited ed. of 780 numbered copies printed for England and America. *MPL*

LISHMAN, Alfred (1854–) b. Leeds, son of a stonemason who became headmaster of Fockerby Grammar School. Educated at Durham University, and York Training College for Teachers. He succeeded his father as headmaster of Fockerby Grammar School; clerk to Adlingfleet School Board. Married the daughter of W.H. Monkman, solicitor of York.

Terje viken (from the Norsk of Henrik Ibsen), and other poems, grave and gay; by Alfred Lishman. Fockerby, Goole: Author. [1897]. 84 pp. *★UCD*

LISTER, David (1865–). b. Ceres, Fife. His father was a labourer, his mother a handloom weaver. At age of twelve he was apprenticed to a chemist in Cupar for five years. When qualified he spent two years in Edinburgh, then became manager of a chemist's shop in West Calder. He produced pieces suitable for recital, which he delivered in large public assemblies with some success. He contributed verse and prose sketches to many periodicals, also taught elocution.

Temperance poems for recital: dramatic and humorous; by David Lister. Edinburgh: Darien Press. 1888. 84 pp. *OXB*

LITTELRED, John

Cytheraea and Cynthia (Venus and Diana): a love poem; by John Littelred. Bonn on the Rhine: University Press. 1892. 25 pp. *BL*

LITTLE, Elizabeth Mary (Lizzie) (18 –1909). Daughter of a Roscommon landowner. Educated at Alexandra College, Dublin, where she distinguished herself. For a time she was employed as a teacher in north London. Died at Bray, County Wicklow.

Persephone, and other poems; by Lizzie Mary Little. Dublin: William McGee; London: Simpkin, Marshall, & Co. 1884, 115 pp. *OXB*

Wild myrtle: [poems]; by L.M. Little. London: J.M. Dent & Co. 1897. viii, 97 pp.
    A limited ed. of 500 copies. *OXB*

LITTLE, Lizzie Mary *see* **LITTLE, Elizabeth Mary (Lizzie)**

LITTLE, Thomas W. (1858–). b. Mickley, Northumberland, son of Samuel Little, grocer. Attended the village school, then the Royal Grammar School, Hexham. He joined his father's grocery business, which became a flourishing concern. Contributed verse to many local journals. Lived at Mickley Square, Stocksfield-on-Tyne.
    North country lyrics; by T.W. Little. London: Stanesby & Co.; Derby: Frank Murray. 1889. [3], viii, 93 pp. (Moray library).
    A limited small paper ed. of 140 copies, of which 130 were for sale. *OXB*
    Also a limited large paper ed. of 60 numbered copies signed by the author.
Ripples and breezes: [poems]; by T.W. Little. Hull: William Andrews & Co.; London: Simpkin, Marshall, Hamilton, Kent, & Co., Ltd. 1891. [vi], 62 pp. *OXB*

LITTLE NONY'S SISTER, pseud.
    "God is love", and other verses; by "Little Nony's" sister. London: James Nisbet & Co. 1887. 96 pp. *OXB*

The LITTLE PILGRIM. London: J.E. Hawkins. [1888]. 16 pp. (Life-words series, no. 9). *OXB*

The LITTLE PILGRIM. With illustrations by Emily Cook & E. Heatly. London: Ernest Nister; New York: E.P. Dutton & Co. [1898]. 40 pp. il., col. il. *OXB*

LITTLEWOOD, William Edensor (1831–86). Educated at Merchant Taylors' School, and Pembroke College, Cambridge; BA 1854. Ordained, 1857; vicar, St James's, Bath, 1872–81. Published theological and historical works.
    A garland from the parables; [poems]; by William Edensor Littlewood. 2nd ed., with corrections and additional poems. With portrait. London: William Mack. 1887. 144 pp. por. *OXB*

LLIENO, pseud.
    Pictures from a cathedral, and other poems; by Llieno. London: Literary Production Committee. [1880]. 75 pp. *OXB*

LLOLLANDLLAFF, Louis, pseud.
    The Llollandllaff legends: [poems]; by Louis Llollandllaff. London: Cassell & Co. Ltd. 1894. 160 pp. *OXB*

LLOYD, Arthur (1852–1911). b. Simla, India, son of Major Frederick Lloyd, Bengal Native Infantry. Educated at St John's College and Peterhouse, Cambridge (scholar); BA 1874, MA 1877. Fellow of Peterhouse. 1877–80; dean and librarian. Ordained 1876; curate, St Barnabas's, Liverpool, 1875–77, Great St Mary's, Cambridge, 1877–79; rector of Norton, Suffolk, 1879–84, and vicar of Hunston, 1881–84; missionary, Tokyo, Japan, 1884–90. Held academic posts in Canada, 1890–94, then returned to Japan; priest in Tokyo, 1894–1903, successively holding academic appointments at St Paul's College, Keiogijiku University, the Imperial Naval Academy, and the Imperial University. President, Asiatic Society of Japan, 1903–05.

Kenshin's vision: a poem of Japan; by A. Lloyd. Tokyo: Z.P. Maruya & Co.; Yokohama: Kelly & Walsh. 1894. [ii], 27 pp. il.   *BL*

LLOYD, Cecil

Angharad, and other verses; by Cecil Lloyd. Printed Woking: Gresham Press. 1896. [viii], 64 pp.

Privately printed.   *OXB*

LLOYD, Leonard. Editor of *The Poet's Magazine.*

A modern Babylon; by Leonard Lloyd. 2nd ed. London: Remington & Co. 1881. 94 pp.   *★UCD*

LOCAL LAY-MAN, pseud.

Blatchington ballads; by a "local lay"-man. Printed Deal: M. Adkins. [1896]. [ii], 34 pp.

Printed by request.   *OXB*

LOCHNELL, pseud. Of Comballaz.

Saxon lyrics & legends, after Aldhelm; by Lochnell. London: Field & Tuer; Simpkin, Marshall & Co.; Hamilton, Adams & Co.; New York: Scribner & Welford. [1885]. 114 pp.   *OXB*

LOCKER, Frederick *see* **LOCKER-LAMPSON, Frederick**

LOCKER-LAMPSON, Frederick (1821–95). b. Greenwich Hospital, son of Edward H. Locker, secretary & civil commissioner. Educated at private schools before becoming a junior clerk in a London broker's office. In 1841 he got a clerkship at Somerset House, then transferred to the Admirality, where he eventually became a précis reader. He left government service in 1850 owing to ill-health. Contributed reviews to *The Times*, and verse to *Punch, The Cornhill Magazine*, and other journals. In 1885, after the death of his second wife, he added her maiden name, Lampson, to his. Lived latterly at Rowfant, near East Grinstead, Sussex.

London rhymes, by Frederick Locker. 1882.

Revised ed of his *London lyrics*, first published 1857.*

The poems of Frederick Locker. New York: White, Stokes, & Allen. 1883. 244 pp.

'This is a pirated edition' – author's ms. note in BL copy.   *BL*

The poems of Frederick Locker. Authorized ed. New York: White, Stokes, & Allen. 1884. viii, 7–262 pp. por.   *BL*

LOCKHART, David, pseud. *see* **MACKENNA, Robert W.**, (David Lockhart, pseud.)

LOCKWOOD, Henry. Of Bournemouth, Hampshire.
Masaniello, and other poems; by Henry Lockwood. London: Kerby & Endean. 1883. viii, 198 pp.   *OXB*

LODGE, Arthur A.
Blots from a bad pen: [poems]; by Arthur A. Lodge. Huddersfield: Allan Parkin. 1894. 107 pp. il.   *★UCD*

LOFFT, Robert Emlyn (1830?–1900). Son of Robert E. Lofft of Bury St Edmunds, Suffolk. Educated there, and at Trinity College, Cambridge: BA 1854. Succeeded his elder brother at Troston Hall, 1866. He completely restored Troston Church at his own expense, and personally carved the oak benches.
Sonnets; by R.E. Lofft. London: Griffith, Farran, Okeden, & Welsh. [1890]. [ii], 80 pp.   *OXB*

LOGIE ROBERTSON, James, (Hugh Haliburton, pseud.) (1846–1922). b. Milnathort, Kinross. He became a pupil-teacher at Haddington before attending Edinburgh University. Taught at Edinburgh Ladies' College and other Edinburgh schools. Produced editions of the poetry of William Dunbar, Robert Burns, and other Scottish poets.
Ochil idylls, and other poems; by Hugh Haliburton. London: William Paterson & Co. 1891. 162 pp.   *OXB*
Orellana, and other poems; by J. Logie Robertson. Edinburgh: William Blackwood & Sons. 1881. x, 264 pp.   *OXB*
Our holiday among the hills: [poems]; by James and Janet Logie Robertson. Edinburgh: William Blackwood & Sons. 1882. xii, 124 pp.   *OXB*
Poems; by J. Logie Robertson. Printed Dundee: John Leng & Co. 1898. 200 pp.   *UCD*

LOGIE ROBERTSON, Janet (1860–   ). b. Pittenweem, Fife, daughter of an Edinburgh lawyer named Simpson. Educated at Edinburgh Educational Institution, achieving outstanding results in the Edinburgh University local examinations. In 1881 she married James Logie Robertson.
New songs of innocence; by Janet Logie Robertson. Edinburgh: Macniven & Wallace. 1889. viii, 111 pp.   *UCD*
Our holiday among the hills: [poems]; by James and Janet Logie Robertson. Edinburgh: William Blackwood & Sons. 1882. xii, 124 pp.   *OXB*

LOMAS, Elizabeth. b. Derbyshire, descended from farming stock on her mother's side. Lived latterly at The Hollies, Whalley Range, Manchester.
"One Christmas eve"; an o'er true tale; by Elizabeth Lomas. Manchester: Author. 1887. [16] pp.   *MPL*

LONDON HERMIT *see* **PARKE, Walter**

LONGFIELD, Lewis

Twilight to dawn: "Samaria", and other poems; by Lewis Longfield. London: T. Weston. [1899]. [vi], 72 pp. *OXB*

LONGRIGG, George H. Of Chester.

Sermons in timber and stone: historic legends of the city of Chester: [poems]; by George H. Longrigg. London: Elliot Stock. 1892. viii, 71 pp. *OXB*

The tongue of the bells, [and other poems]; by George H. Longrigg. With illustrations by the author. Chester: Phillipson & Golder; London: Simpkin, Marshall & Co. 1894. 83 pp. il. *OXB*

LONGSTAFF, Mrs Leam

Poems, 1894–98; by Mrs. Longstaff. London: Edward Stanford. 1898. [iv], 33 pp. *OXB*

LONGSTAFF, William (1849–). b. Soulby, Westmorland, son of a farm labourer who died early, leaving his young family in poverty. He attended school from five to twelve years of age, then became successively a railway 'nipper lad', gardener's boy, farm servant, navvy on the Settle & Carlisle railway. Eventually he was a signalman for the North Eastern Railway Co.

Her Majesty's royal jubilee, 1887: ode and song, the tribute of a working man; by W. Longstaff. Printed Newcastle-upon-Tyne: Stevenson & Dryden. 1887. 31 pp. **UCD*

LONGSTAFF, William Luther. Of Sunderland, County Durham.

Weeds and flowers: poems; written by William Luther Longstaff. London: Greening & Co. Ltd. 1899. viii, 152 pp. *TCD*

LONGSTAFFE, John Lawrance, (Peter Primrose, pseud.) (1834–). Lived at 3 Upper Westbourne Terrace, London W.

A pen'orth o' poetry for the poor; by Peter Primrose. London: Harrison & Sons. 1884. 123 pp. *OXB*

Poems for the poor; by Peter Primrose. London: Harrison & Sons. 1885. 123 pp. *OXB*

LORD, James (1814–). Son of Rev. H. Lord of Northiam, Sussex. Student, Lincoln's Inn, 1833; went to Inner Temple, 1837; called to Bar, 1837. He was married twice, to Eleanor Barton in 1842, then to Elizabeth M. Cox in 1847.

America: a poem; by James Lord. London: Hamilton, Adams & Co.; Brixton: W.C. Edmonds. [1888]. xvi, 76 pp. *BL*

LORNE, Marquess of *see* **CAMPBELL, John Douglas Sutherland, Duke of Argyll.**

LOTHIAN JUSTICE QUONDAM M.P., pseud. *see* **MACFIE, Robert A.**, (Lothian Justice Quondam M.P., pseud.)

LOVAINE, Henry Algernon George, Lord Warkworth (1871–1909). Son of the 7th Duke of Northumberland. Educated at Eton College, and Christ Church, Oxford; BA 1893. Contested Berwick-on-Tweed, 1895; MP for South Kensington, 1895–1909. Deputy Lieutenant for Northumberland. Under-Secretary of State for India, 1902–03. Trustee for the National Portrait Gallery.

   S. Francis of Assisi: the Newdigate poem, 1892; by Lord Warkworth. Oxford: B.H. Blackwell; London: Simpkin, Hamilton, Kent & Co. 1892. 15 pp.   *BL*
     Also a limited ed. of 50 copies printed on large paper.
     Also 2nd ed. 1892.

LOW, Charles Rathbone (1837–1918). b. Dublin, son of Major J.H. Low. Educated at Douglas College, Isle of Man. Joined the Indian Navy, 1853; served in the Indian and China seas, Persian Gulf, Red Sea, and east coast of Africa, in suppression of piracy and the slave trade. On retirement he became librarian of the Royal United Service Institute. Naval historian and biographer. Lived latterly at 27 Russell Road, Kensington, London W.

   Britannia's bulwarks: an historical poem, descriptive of the deeds of the British Navy; by Charles Rathbone Low. London: Horace Cox. 1895. viii, 430 pp.   *OXB*
   Cressy to Tel-el-Kebir: a narrative poem, descriptive of the deeds of the British Army; by Charles Rathbone Low. London: W. Mitchell & Co. 1892. viii, 343 pp.   *OXB*
   The epic of Olympus: a narrative poem descriptive of the deeds of the deities and heroes of Greek mythology; by Charles Rathbone Low. London: Digby, Long & Co. [1897]. viii, 245 pp.   *OXB*
   Old England's navy: an epic of the sea; by Charles Rathbone Low. London: Elliot Stock. 1891. [iv], 127 pp.   *OXB*

LOWE, David (1868–19). b. Leslie, Fife. Founded Dundee Labour Party, 1891; stood as the first parliamentary Labour candidate for Dundee, 1892. Manager and sub-editor of *Labour Leader*, 1894–1902. Took part in the miners' strike of 1894, and the engineer's strike of 1898. Intermediary between deportees and the government during the First World War. Lived latterly at Craigwood House, Blebo Craigs, Cupar, Fife.

   Gift of the night, and other poems; by David Lowe. With twelve page illustrations by Alec Webster. London: Frederick W. Wilson & Co. 1898. 106 pp. il.   *OXB*

LOWE, Robert, Lord Sherbrooke (1811–92). Educated at Winchester College, and University College, Oxford. Barrister, Lincoln's Inn, 1842. Went to Sydney, Australia, where he practised as a lawyer. In the Legislative Council for New South Wales, 1843–50. He returned to England in 1850, becoming leader-writer for *The Times*. MP for Kidderminster, 1852–59; joint secretary, Board of Control, 1852–55; vice-president, Board of Trade and Paymaster-General, 1855–58; Privy Councillor, 1855. MP for Calne, 1859–67; first MP for London University, 1868–80. Chancellor of the Exchequer, 1866–73;

Home Secretary, 1873. Created Viscount Sherbrooke of Sherbrooke in Surrey, 1880.

Poems of a life; by Lord Sherbrooke. London: Kegan Paul, Trench, & Co. 1885. vi, 109 pp.   *MPL*
>   Also 2nd ed. 1885

LOWNDES, Henry (1828–89). Son of William Lowndes, Liverpool county court judge. He nearly died trying to save his father who was drowned at Liverpool. Trained for a medical career; MRCS 1852. Practised in Liverpool; surgeon to the Northern Hospital to 1881, consulting surgeon, 1881–89. Lived at 1 Catherine Street, Liverpool.

Poems; by Henry Lowndes. London: Swan Sonnenschein & Co. 1892. viii, 88 pp.   *OXB*

Poems and translations; by Henry Lowndes. London: C. Kegan Paul & Co. 1880. xii, 245 pp.   *OXB*

LOYAL IRISHMAN, pseud. *see* **HAWKES, William** (Loyal Irishman, pseud.)

LUCAS, Edward Verrall, (E.V.L.) (1868–1938). Member of a Quaker family. Aged sixteen he was apprenticed to a bookseller. Became a reporter on the *Sussex Daily News*, 1889–92; assistant editor of *Punch*; joined staff of the *Globe*, 1893. Journalist, essayist and critic, he is perhaps best known as editor of the life, works, and letters of Charles and Mary Lamb.

Sparks from a flint: odd rhymes for odd times; by E.V.L. London: Howe & Co. [1890]. 95 pp. (Everybody's series).   *OXB*

LUCAS, Francis. b. Hitchin, Hertfordshire, son of William Lucas. Student, Middle Temple, called to the Bar, 1841. JP for Hertfordshire and Bedfordshire.

Sketches of rural life, and other poems; by Francis Lucas. London: Macmillan & Co. 1889. x, 157 pp.   *UCD*
>   Also 2nd ed. 1897.

LUCAS, John Templeton (1836–80). Son of John Lucas, portrait painter. A landscape painter, he exhibited at the Royal Academy, the British Institution, and the Suffolk Street Gallery, 1859–76. Published a farce and a volume of fairy tales.

Thoughts in rhyme; by J.T. Lucas. London: Frederick Warne & Co. 1888. viii, 55 pp.   *OXB*

LUCAS, Reginald. Lived at 207 Piccadilly, London and at Cirencester House, Cirencester, Gloucestershire.

Poems and verses, 1887–1897; by Reginald Lucas. Printed London: Spottiswoode & Co. 1897. [viii], 79 pp.
>   Privately printed.   *OXB*

Poems and verses; by Reginald Lucas. Printed London: Strangeways. 1898. [iv], 71 pp.
>   Privately printed.   *OXB*

Poems and verses; by Reginald Lucas. Printed London: Spottiswoode & Co. 1899. viii, 53 pp.
　　Privately printed.　*OXB*

LUCAS, Winifred *see* **LUCAS, Winifred M.**, (W.M.L.)

LUCAS, Winifred M., (W.M.L.). Mrs Louis H. Le Bailly. She contributed to various newspapers and magazines.
Fancies and fragments; [poems]; by Winifred M. Lucas. Printed for the author and sold by A. and F. Denny, London. 1893. 52 pp.　*BL*
Fugitives: [poems]; by Winifred Lucas. John Lane The Bodley Head. 1899. viii, 96 pp.　*BL*
Lana caprini: [poems]; [by W.M.L.]. Printed London: Diprose, Bateman & Co. 1888. viii, 31 pp.
　　Printed for private circulation only.　*BL*
Units, [and other poems]; by Winifred Lucas. London: John Lane The Bodley Head. 1896. x, 80 pp.　*OXB*
Verses; by Winifred Lucas. [London]: [Squire]. 1895. 58 pp.　*NUC

LUCIFER IN LONDON, AND HIS REFLECTIONS ON LIFE, MAN-NERS, AND THE PROSPECTS OF SOCIETY. London: Vizetelly & Co. 1885. 64 pp.　*OXB*

LUCIFER'S ORATION TO THE INFERNALS ON RELIGION AND MORALS: FAS EST ET AB HOSTE DOCERI. London: William Ridgway. 1887. 72 pp.　*JRL*

LUCUS A NON LUCENDO, pseud.
Rays from the starry host: [poems]; by "Lucas a non lucendo". Westminster: Roxburghe Press, Ltd. [1897]. [iv], 376 pp.　*OXB*

LUCY, Ernest. Writer on the Irish in America.
A loyal Whig's reflections, upon the late elections; with, Appendix on the history of Parties during the last two hundred years; by Ernest Lucy. Cambridge: J. Palmer. 1886. [iv], 42 pp.　*OXB*

LUFF, William
About Jesus: one hundred poems; by William Luff. Stirling, N.B: Drummond's Tract Depot; London: S.W. Partridge & Co. [1885]. 158 pp.　*OXB*
About our Father: one hundred & five poems, in large type; by William Luff. Stirling: Drummond's Tract Depot; London: S.W. Partridge & Co. [1886]. 156 pp.　*OXB*
Equally yoked: (a companion poem to "Unequally yoked"); by William Luff. Stirling: Drummond's Tract Depot; London: S.W. Partridge & Co. [1890]. 15 pp.　*OXB*
Unequally yoked: (a companion poem to "Equally yoked"); by William Luff. Stirling: Drummond's Tract Depot; London: S.W. Partridge & Co. [1890]. 15 pp.　*OXB*

LUIGI, pseud.

A legend of Lake Leman; by Luigi. Geneva: R. Burkhardt. 1885. 28 pp. il.   *BL*

LULWORTH, Eric

Sunshine and shower, and other poems; by Eric Lulworth. London: Kegan Paul, Trench & Co. 1889. vi, 110 pp.   *GPR*

LUMSDEN, James, (Samuel Mucklebackit, pseud.) (1839–1903). b. at the Abbey Mill, Haddington, East Lothian, son of the mill master. Aged thirteen he was apprenticed to a grocer at Prestonpans; his master became bankrupt, and he eventually found another place with a relative, a millwright. He left for Edinburgh, then spent some time wandering about Scotland and England, settling in London. After an unsuccessful period in farming, he went to America, staying only one year, after which illness compelled him to return to Haddington. He settled in East Linton, working in the potato trade, at the same time engaged in journalism.

The battles of Dunbar & Prestonpans, and other selected poems (new and old); by James Lumsden ("Samuel Mucklebackit"). Haddington: William Sinclair. 1896. [vi], 240 pp. por.   *OXB*

Edinburgh poems and songs; by James Lumsden (Samuel Mucklebackit). Haddington: Sinclair & Co. 1899. xvi, 328 pp.   *OXB*

Edinburgh poems and songs; by James Lumsden (Samuel Mucklebackit). 2nd and revised ed. Edinburgh: Thomas Allan. 1899. xiv, 328 pp.   *BL*

Lays and letters from Linton; by Samuel Mucklebacket [sic]. Haddington: William Sinclair; Edinburgh: John Menzies & Co. [1889]. xvi, 220 pp.   *BL*

Rural rhymes, and sketches in East Lothian; by Samuel Mucklebackit. Edinburgh: James Thin. [1886]. [viii], 256 pp.

Poetry and prose.   *BL*

Sheep-head and trotters: being savoury selections, poetic and prosaic, from the bulky literary remains of Samuel Mucklebackit and Thomas Pintail, late Parnassian hill and arable farmers in Lothian; prepared and presented by their sole living executor, James Lumsden. Haddington: William Sinclair. [1892]. [viii], 319 pp.   *BL*

LUNKAH, pseud.

Whiffs: Anglo-Indian & Indian; [poems]; by "Lunkah". Allahabad: A.H. Wheeler & Co. 1891. vi, 112 pp.   *OXB*

LUSCOMBE, Alfred, (Spes, pseud.). Lived at Alexandra Road, then at Crescent Road, Kingston Hill, Kingston-on-Thames, Surrey.

Additional wayside musings: [poems]; by A. Luscombe. Printed Kingston-on-Thames. 1894. 24 pp.   *BL*

Continuation of wayside musings: [poems]; by Spes. Printed Putney. [1893]. 28 pp.   *BL*

Wayside musings: [poems]; by Spes. Printed Kingston-on-Thames: G. Phillipson. 1891. [27] pp.   *BL*

Also New & enlarged ed. 1895.

LUSHINGTON, Vernon (1832–1912). Son of Stephen Lushington, MP. Educated at Trinity College, Cambridge (scholar); LL.B 1859, LL.M 1885. President of the Cambridge Union, 1854. Called to the Bar, Inner Temple, 1857; deputy judge advocate-general, 1864–69; QC, 1868; bencher, 1869; secretary to the Admirality, 1869–77; county court judge, Surrey and Berkshire, 1877–1900.

Positivist hymns: [poems]; by Vernon Lushington. Printed London: Chiswick Press. 1885. [iv], 60 pp.

Printed for private circulation. *OXB*

LUSIGNAN, Marie De, Princess *see* **DE LUSIGNAN, Marie**, Princess

LUSTED, Charles T.

The feast of Cotytto, and other poems; by Charles T. Lusted. London: Digby, Long & Co. 1893. xii, 146 pp. *OXB*

Semblance, and other poems; by Charles T. Lusted. London: Kegan Paul, Trench & Co. 1888. viii, 90 pp. *OXB*

LYALL, Sir Alfred (1835–1911). b. Coulston, Surrey, son of Alfred Lyall, philosopher. Educated at Eton College, and Haileybury for a career in India. Joined Indian Civil Service, 1856; actively served in the Mutiny, 1857–58; posted in West Berar, then in Rajputana before becoming lieutenant-governor, North-West Provinces, 1882–87; returned to England, 1887; appointed a member of the Indian Council in London, 1888–1902. Received hon. degrees from Oxford and Cambridge. A Liberal Unionist, free trader, and opponent of women's suffrage.

Verses written in India; by Sir Alfred Lyall. London: Kegan Paul, Trench & Co. 1889. vi, 140 pp. *MPL*

Also [2nd] ed. 1890; [4th] ed. 1896.

LYALL, John W. (1836–).b. Paisley, Renfrewshire, son of a weaver. His early working years were spent at sea; eventually he became an iron planer. Lived latterly at Port Glasgow.

Sun-gleams through the mist of toil: poems; songs, dialogues, recitations and sacred verses; by John W. Lyall. With autobiographical sketch and narrative of the author's experiences in America, &c. Brechin: Advertiser Office; Edinburgh: John Menzies & Co. 1885. 192 pp. *OXB*

LYDE, Lionel William (1863–19). b. Wigton, Cumberland, son of William Lyde. Educated at Sedbergh Grammar School, and Queen's College, Oxford (exhibitioner); BA 1886, MA 1889. An economist, he became professor of economic geography, University College, London. FRGS.

Moods of the moment: being verses collected from The Merchistonian, Time, The Academy, The Monthly Packet, & c.; by Lionel W. Lyde. Illustrated by G. Straton Ferrier. Edinburgh: H. & J. Pillans & Wilson. [1895]. 65 pp. il. *NLS*

LYME LYRICS. Lyme Regis: E. Locke. 1884. 206 pp. *BL*

LYNCH, Arthur (1861–1934). b. near Ballarat, Australia, son of a civil engineer. Educated in Ballarat, at Melbourne University, and in Paris, Berlin and London. Paris correspondent for the *Daily Mail*, 1898–99. Served as colonel in the Irish Brigade on the Boer side in the South African War. Elected MP for Galway City, 1901. In 1903 he was sentenced to death for high treason but was eventually pardoned. Qualified and practised medicine in north London, 1908–34; LRCP, MRCS. MP for West Clare, 1909–18. Colonel in British army in the First World War.

A Koran of love; The Caliph, and other poems; by Arthur Lynch. London: Remington & Co., Ltd. [1894]. [iv], 135 pp. *OXB*

Our poets!: [poems]; by Arthur Lynch. London: Remington & Co., Ltd. 1894. [viii], 92 pp. *OXB*

LYNCH, J.D.
Priest and poet, and other poems; by J.D. Lynch. Dublin: James Duffy & Sons. [1882?]. viii, 88 pp. *★NUC*

LYS, Francis John (1863–1947). b. Bere Regis, Dorset, son of Francis D. Lys, gentleman. Educated at Sherborne School, and Worcester College, Oxford (scholar); BA 1886, MA 1889. Assistant master at St Edward's School, Oxford, then at Radley College. Fellow and tutor, Worcester College, 1899. Ordained 1899. Provost, 1919; Vice-Chancellor, Oxford University, 1932–35.

A summer's poems; by F.J. Lys. London: Selley & Co. Ltd. 1893. 32 pp. *★UCD*

LYSANDER, J.F., pseud. *see* **HOGG, William T. Munro**, (J.F. Lysander, pseud.)

LYTTON, Edward Robert Bulwer-, Lord Lytton *see* **BULWER-LYTTON, Edward Robert, Lord Lytton**, (Owen Meredith, pseud.)

M

M. *see* **MARY**, (M.)

M., A.M.
Timothy's courtship; by [A.M.M.]. Printed Birmingham: Hudson & Son. 1883. 25 pp. *BL*

M., B. *see* **MACANDREW, Barbara**, (B.M.)

M., E.A.C. *see* **McCURDY, Edward Alexander C.**, (E.A.C.M.)

M., F.G.
  Our Lady of Light, and other verses; by F.G.M. Printed London: T. Kelly.
  [1884]. 28 pp.
    Not published.   *★BL*

M., J. *see* **MARSHALL, Jenner**, (J.M.)

M, J.M.
  Unfoldings of the word of life: or, pictures from the gospel of St. John; by J.M.M.
  London: James Nisbet & Co. [1881]. 64 pp.
    'Profits devoted to Foreign Missions'.   *OXB*

M., J.P. *see* **MUIRHEAD, James Patrick**, (J.P.M.)

M., J.S.
  Ballads, bagatelles, and kindergarten; by J.S.M. Printed London: Jas. Wade.
  [1880?]. 106 pp.   *BL*

M., M.
  Rest and hope; [poems]; by M.M. London: Kerby & Endean. 1881. 112
  pp.   *OXB*

M., N.
  Verses; by N. and R.M. [1899]. 50 pp.   *★UCD*

M.P. Author states in preface that he could be either a 'Member of Parliament'
or a 'Minor Poet'.
  The founding of St. Stephen's Golf Club; by an M.P. London: W. Ridgway.
  [1893]. 31 pp.   *OXB*

M., R. Of Leicester.
  Lines for the times: [poems]; by R.M. London: Wyman & Sons. 1888. 63
  pp.   *OXB*

M., R.
  Verses; by N. & R.M. [1899]. 50 pp.   *★UCD*

M., W. Scottish
  Verses and rhymes illustrated; [by]; W.M. Glasgow. 1880–90. 2 vols. il.   *NLS*

M., W.H. *see* **MALLETT, William Hurrell**, (W.H.M.)

MABON, Agnes Stuart (1841–). b. Lochtower Farm, Yetholm, Roxburghshire, daughter of a farm overseer. Her father died when she was two, and the family moved to Town Yetholm, where she attended the village school. They next settled in Jedburgh, where she worked in a mill until her marriage. The mother of several children, she was confined to bed for some years with a spinal complaint. Writer of prose sketches and tales published in various journals.

Homely rhymes, etc. from the banks of the Jed; by Agnes Stuart Mabon. Preface by Rev. James King. Paisley: J. & R. Parlane; Edinburgh: J. Menzies & Co.; Jedburgh: Thomas Small. 1887. [ii], 270 pp. *BL*

MABON, James. Scottish. A member of the Church of Scotland.

Rose and thorn: poems and songs; by James Mabon. Edinburgh: John Menzies & Co. [1895]. [2], xii, 180 pp. por. *OXB*

When west winds blow: [poems]; by James Mabon. Galashiels: A. Walker & Son. 1898. [viii], 68 pp. *OXB*

MAC, pseud. *see* **MacMANUS, Seumas**, (Mac, pseud.)

MACALPINE, Mary. Lived at Sea Bank House, Greenock, Renfrewshire.

The traitor lake, and other poems; by Mary Macalpine. Greenock: W. Hutchinson. 1895. [x], 106 pp. facsim. *OXB*

MACAN, Reginald Walter (1848–1941). b. Dublin, son of Judge John Macan. Educated at Charterhouse, Christ Church, and University College, Oxford (scholar); BA 1871. Fellow of University College, 1884; classics tutor and librarian, 1883–1900; university reader in ancient history; lecturer at Brasenose College; member of Hebdomadal Council, 1892. Lived at Broom Hill House, Boars Hill.

Hellenikon: a sheaf of sonnets after Herodotus, gathered by the giver; [by Reginald Walter Macan]. Printed Oxford: Sheppard. 1898. 16 pp.

A limited ed. of 125 numbered copies signed by the author. *OXB*

M'ANALLY, Henry. b. Castledawson, Londonderry. He left Ireland in 1859 for Dumbarton, where he was employed in a shipbuilding yard. Later worked in the Clyde Shipyard, living at Partick, Glasgow. He went to the United States, where he was employed by a railway company in Chicago. An Irish patriot.

Effusions after toil: a collection of poems and lyrics; by Henry M'Anally. Printed Glasgow: Cameron & Ferguson. 1884. viii, 200 pp. por. *EPL*

MACANDREW, Barbara, (B.M.). Née Miller.

Elijah, and other poems; by B.M. London: T. Nelson & Sons. 1880. 142 pp. *BL*

M'ARTHUR, Peter (1805–81). b. Barrhead, Renfrewshire. At the age of eight he was sent as assistant to a calico printer, then apprenticed to the trade. His employers noticed his talent for sketching, and proposed he enter a new apprenticeship to pattern designing. He made good progress, eventually transferring to a firm in Glasgow where he became a head of department. Lived at 327 Dalmarnock Road, Glasgow.

Amusements in minstrelsy: [poems]; by P. M'Arthur. Glasgow: Porteous Bros. 1880. viii, 176 pp. il.

Spine-title is *Poems*.   BL

MACARTNEY, Thomas J. Irishman and army officer.

A bid for the laureateship: [poems]; by Thomas J. Macartney. London: Simpkin, Marshall & Co.; Plymouth: W.H. Luke. [1889]. 153 pp. por.   OXB

MACAULAY, John (1854–   ). b. Port Glasgow into a poverty-stricken family. He became a blacksmith. His verse was published in the *Glasgow Weekly Mail*.

Poems and songs; by John Macaulay. Greenock: David Blair. 1895. viii, 240 pp.   BL

M'AUSLANE, William Thomson (1832–93). b. Glasgow. He was brought up at Strathblane, Stirlingshire, attending the village school; later he went to evening classes to learn French and elocution. In 1849 his family settled in Glasgow, where he worked as clerk and book-keeper for *North British Daily Mail*, later promoted to reporter. Worked as sub-editor and reporter for a succession of newspapers. In 1875 he was appointed secretary to the Association for the Relief of Incurables for Glasgow and West Scotland.

Follow me: or, the young preacher: life, character, and descriptive sketches, with "Songs in the night". Edited by William T. M'Auslane. Glasgow: David Bryce & Son. 1892. viii, 174 pp. por.

Biographical sketch and poems written after the death of author's son.   BL

Summer musings; and, Memories dear; by W.T. M'Auslane. Glasgow: Maclure, Macdonald & Co. 1889. 126 pp. por.

Poetry and prose.   BL

MACBETH, James, pseud. *see* **BAIN, James Leith Macbeth**, (James Macbeth, pseud.)

MACBREMEN, pseud. *see* **BREMNER, Joseph, (MacBremen**, pseud.)

McCAIG, Donald (1827–86). Educated at Glasgow University. He became a Church of Scotland minister, successively appointed to St Columba's, Glasgow, the parish of Killarrow, Isle of Islay, Watton, Caithness, and Mackairn, Argyllshire.

The last enemy, and other poems; by Donald McCaig. Paisley: J. & R. Parlane. 1899. [iv], 298 pp. por.   OXB

McCALL, Patrick Joseph (1861–1919). b. Dublin. Educated at the Catholic University. Well known in his time as a poet, song-writer, and translator from the Irish. Contributed poetry and prose to the popular press.

Irish nóiníns (daisies): being a collection of I – Historical poems and ballads, II – Translations from the Gaelic, III – Humorous and characteristic sketches, IV – Miscellaneous songs; by Patrick Joseph McCall (Cavellus). Dublin: Sealy, Bryers & Walker. 1894. viii, 128 pp.   *OXB*

Songs of Erinn; by P.J. McCall. London: Simpkin, Marshall & Co., Ltd; Dublin: M.H. Gill & Son; O'Donoghue. 1899. 150 pp.   *OXB*

MacCARTHY, Denis Florence (1817–82). b. Dublin. Educated at Maynooth, he was intended for the Catholic priesthood. At an early age he began to contribute verse to Dublin periodicals, including the *Nation*. Interested in the Young Ireland movement. An accomplished Spanish scholar, and translator of Calderón, he held the post of lecturer in English literature at the Catholic University. His health failed in 1864.

The centenary of Moore, May 28th, 1879: an ode; by Denis Florence MacCarthy. With a translation into Latin verse by Julius Maxwell Blacker. Printed London: J. Davy & Sons. 1880. 38 pp.
   Printed for private circulation.   *OXB*

Poems; by Denis Florence MacCarthy. Dublin: M.H. Gill & Son. 1882. xxii, 287 pp.   *MPL*
   Also 2nd ed. 1884.

McCARTHY, Justin Huntly (1860–1936). Son of Justin McCarthy, Irish politician and writer. Educated at University College School, and University College, London. He worked as a journalist for many years, and was also a novelist, playwright, historian, and translator of the *Rubaiyat* of Omar Khayyam. Nationalist MP for Athlone, 1884–85, then for Newry. Lived latterly at 10 Egliston Road, Putney, London SW.

Hafiz in London, [and other poems]; by Justin Huntly McCarthy. London: Chatto & Windus. 1886. viii, 91 pp.   *OXB*

Harlequinade: a book of verses; by Justin Huntly McCarthy. London: Chatto & Windus. 1890. xii, 170 pp.   *OXB*

Serapion, and other poems; by Justin H. McCarthy. London: Chatto & Windus. 1883. viii, 177 pp.   *OXB*

Songs for Cecilia; by Justin Huntly McCarthy. Printed New York: Lotus Press. 1895. 31 pp.
   A limited ed. of 100 numbered copies.   *BL*

MacCARTHY, Mary Stanislaus (1849–97). Daughter of the poet Denis Florence MacCarthy. Sister Mary Stanislaus of St Catherine's Dominican Convent, Sion Hall, Blackrock, County Dublin.

Songs of Sion; by Mary Stanislaus MacCarthy. Dublin: Browne & Nolan, Ltd. 1898. viii, 160 pp. il., por., facsim.   *OXB*

McCAUL, Joseph Benjamin (18 –92). Son of Alexander McCaul, DD. Educated at King's College, London. Ordained 1851. Assistant librarian at the British Museum, 1846–49, and engaged on the compilation of the catalogue, 1851–65. Divinity lecturer, King's College, 1852–54. Curate at a succession of London churches, 1851–65; chaplain at Amsterdam. 1877–79; rector, St Michael's, Bassishaw, and hon. canon of Rochester, from 1865.

The last great plague of Egypt; The German gladiators; Great King Herod, and other poems: a metrical medley of original pieces, written at various times, for the amusement of the author's children, and also for general readers; by Joseph B. McCaul. London: Longmans, Green, & Co. 1880. viii, 232 pp. *OXB*

MACCOLL, Dugald Sutherland (1859–1948). b. Glasgow, a son of the manse. Educated at Glasgow Academy, University College, London, and Lincoln College, Oxford. Studied art under Frederick Brown. Art critic successively on *Spectator, Saturday Review*, and *Weekend Review*; editor of *Architectural Review*, 1901–05. Keeper, Tate Gallery, 1906–11, Wallace Collection, 1911–24.

The fall of Carthage: Newdigate prize poem, recited in the Sheldonian Theatre, Oxford, June 14, 1882; by Dugald Sutherland Maccoll. Oxford: A. Thomas Shrimpton & Son. [1882]. [ii], 16 pp. *OXB*

McCOSH, John. A physician, he qualified at Edinburgh University; MD, FRGS. Writer on travel and medical topics. Member of the Junior United Service Club.

Grand tours in many lands: a poem in ten cantos; by John McCosh. London: Remington & Co. 1881. xii, 292 pp. *OXB*

Sketches in verse at home and abroad, and from the war of the Nile, in ten cantos; by John McCosh. London: James Blackwood & Co. [1882]. [iv], 220 pp. *MPL*

M'CULLAGH, Thomas (1821?–1908). He entered the Ordnance Survey when very young, then became a Wesleyan lay preacher. Ordained in 1849, he went to New Zealand in 1852, stayed a few years, and on his return settled in Liverpool. Hymnist and biographer, he was president of the Wesleyan Conference in 1883.

The first wedding, and other poems: sacred – domestic – playful; by Thomas M'Cullagh. London: Charles H. Kelly. 1899. 102 pp. por. *OXB*

M'CULLOCH, James Sloane (1855–). b. Burnfoot, Carsphairn, Galloway, son of a smallholder and stonedyke contractor. On leaving the village school he became a stonedyker, working in remote parts of the county with his father and three brothers.

Poems: local, lyric, and miscellaneous; by James S. M'Culloch. Edinburgh: James Gemmell. 1885. [2], x, 178 pp. *OXB*

McCURDY, Edward Alexander Coles, (E.A.C.M.) (1871–). b. Nottingham, son of Alexander McCurdy. Educated at Loughborough School, and Balliol College, Oxford.

Parve seges: [poems]; by E.A.C.M. Oxford: B.H. Blackwell; London: Simpkin, Marshall, Hamilton, Kent & Co. 1894. [ii], 39 pp. *OXB*

McDERMOTT, F. Of Southport, Lancashire.
Our Rip Van Winkle; Albert Victor, and other poems; by F. McDermott.
Southport: Robert Johnson & Co. Ltd. 1892. 18 pp. por. *OXB*

McDONAGH, Michael (1822–93). b. Greencastle, County Donegal. He
served his apprenticeship as a printer, becoming a compositor in the *Limerick
Reporter* office, following his trade for over thirty years. His three sons,
Michael, Frank and Duffy, all became journalists.
Lays of Erin, and other poems; by Michael McDonagh. Printed Limerick:
Author. 1882. [iv], 92 pp. *NLI*

MACDONALD, Donald (1846–). b. Thurso, Caithness. He attended the
parish school until twelve years old, then became apprentice clerk to John
Hay, factor for J.G.T. Sinclair of Ulster; afterwards clerk to Donald M'Kay of
Thurso. In 1867 he rejoined his family who had moved to Dundee; there he
was book-keeper and cashier to Charles Parker & Son of Ladybank Foundry;
after thirteen years he started in business as a mill furnisher and machinery
agent, later becoming a commission agent.
*Will o' the wisp flashes: a selection of stories, sketches, poems, & c., including,
Lectures by Old Blogg, and, Fellows I have known*; by Donald Macdonald.
Printed Dundee: John Leng & Co. 1890. 248 pp. *OXB*

MACDONALD, George (1824–1905). b. Huntly, Aberdeenshire, son of a
farmer. Educated at King's College, Aberdeen; MA 1845. In 1845 he moved
to London, where he worked as a tutor. Attended theological college,
becoming a Congregational minister at Arundel, Sussex. Lived in Manchester, 1853–60, preaching as a layman and supporting himself by writing. He
finally settled in London, becoming a friend of Browning, Ruskin, Carlyle,
William Morris, and Tennyson. Novelist and fantasy writer. His last years
were spent mainly at Bordighera, Italy.
A book of strife, in the form of the diary of an old soul; by George Macdonald.
Printed Chilworth: Unworth Bros. 1880. 267 pp.
    Printed for the author. Printed on one side of leaf only. *BL*
    Also re-issue, 1882.
A book of strife, in the form of the diary of an old soul; by George Macdonald. New
ed. London: Longmans, Green & Co. 1885. 267 pp.
    Printed on one side of leaf only. *LL*
Poems; by George Macdonald. London: Alexander Strachan. 1884. 3 vols.   ★
Poems; by George Macdonald. Selected by V.D.S. and C.F. New York: E. P.
Dutton & Co. 1887. xvi, 207 pp. por. *BL*
The poetical works of George Macdonald in two volumes. London: Chatto &
Windus. 1893. 2 vols. *MPL*
*Rampolli: growths from a long-planted root: being translations, new and old, chiefly
from the German; along with, A year's diary of an old soul*; by George Macdonald.
London: Longmans, Green, & Co. 1897. viii, 303 pp. *BL*

MACDONALD, James Cecil. Of Perth?
Verses on valour: by James Cecil Macdonald. Perth: James Barlas. 1898. 16
pp. *BL*

MACDONALD, Mosse (1856?–   ). Son of Thomas M. Macdonald of
Nottingham. Educated at King's School, Canterbury, and Brasenose College,
Oxford (scholar); BA 1879. Curate, St John's, Fulham, 1879–87, Perlethorpe,
Nottinghamshire, and chaplain to Earl Manvers, from 1887.
Poems; by Mosse Macdonald. [London]: A.D. Innes & Co. 1894. 112
pp. *JRL*

MACDONELL, Alice Clare
Lays of the heather: poems; by A.C. Macdonell. London: Elliot Stock. 1896.
viii, 204 pp. *OXB*

MACDOUGALL, William Brown (18 –1936). b. Glasgow, son of W.
Macdougall. Educated at Glasgow Academy; studied art at the Julian School,
Paris. A painter, etcher, wood-engraver, black-and-white artist, he exhibited
in London, Edinburgh, Munich and elsewhere. One of the early members of
the New English Art Club. He married Margaret Armour. Lived latterly at
The Cottage, Debden Green, Loughton, Essex.
Thames sonnets and semblances; by Margaret Armour and W.B. Macdougall.
London: Elkin Mathews. 1897. 64 pp. il.
   Not joint authorship. Printed on one side of leaf only. *OXB*

MACDOWALL, Cameron. Lived in India. Writer on medical topics.
Lady Margaret's sorrows: or, via dolorosa, and other poems; by Cameron
Macdowall. London: W.H. Beer & Co. 1883. 120 pp. *BL*

McDOWALL, William (1815–88). Journalist and antiquary. He was
appointed to editorial staff of the *Scottish Herald*, 1843; editor of the *Dumfries
and Galloway Standard*, 1846–88. A local historian, he published a history of
Dumfries, 1867. Lived at 17 Cresswell Terrace, Dumfries.
The man of the woods, and other poems; by William McDowall. 2nd ed., greatly
enlarged. Edinburgh: Adam & Charles Black. 1882. viii, 208 pp. *OXB*

MACDUFF, John Ross (1818–95). b. Bonhard, Perthshire, son of Alexander
Macduff. Educated at Edinburgh High School, and Edinburgh University.
Ordained 1843; minister, Kettins, Forfarshire, 1842–43, St Madoes, Perth-
shire, 1849–55; the first minister appointed to Sandyford, Glasgow, 1855–71.
He then retired to Chislehurst, Kent, devoting his time to writing. His books
had an immense circulation, particularly in Scotland.
*The anchor of hope: or, some of God's words of hope in the Old Testament: a
devotional text book for every morning*: [poems]; by [John Ross Macduff].
London: Marcus Ward & Co. [1881]. [41] pp. col. il.
   Bound with author's *The haven of peace*. *OXB*
*The haven of peace: or, some of Christ's words of peace in the New Testament: a
devotional text book for every evening*: [poems]; by [John Ross Macduff].
London: Marcus Ward & Co. [1881]. [41] pp. col il.

Bound with author's *The anchor of hope*.   *OXB*

Knocking; the words of Jesus at the door of the heart: a sacred monody; by J.R. Macduff. London: James Nisbet. 1884. 88 pp.   *OXB*

Matin and vesper bells: earlier and later collected poems (chiefly sacred); by J.R. Macduff. London: Cassell & Co., Ltd, 1898. 2 vols. il.   *OXB*

The story of Jesus, in verse; leading incidents in the great biography; by J.R. Macduff. London: Cassell & Co. Ltd. 1893. viii, 124 pp. il. (Bible biographies).   *OXB*

MACEY, Alfred. Of South Shields, County Durham.

The heart's love and feeling in poetic verses; by Alfred Macey. London: James Blackwood & Co. [1899]. 121 pp.   *OXB*

MacFADYEN, Dugald (1857–). b. Maryhill, Glasgow, of Donegal parents. Apprenticed to the drapery trade at thirteen, eventually working in one of Glasgow's leading drapery establishments. Wrote and published songs for music.

Songs from the city; by Dugald MacFadyen. London: Houlston & Sons; Edinburgh: J. Menzies & Co.; Dublin: M.H. Gill & Son. 1887. 217 pp.   *OXB*

M'FARLAN, James (1845–89). Son of James M'Farlan, Presbyterian minister. Educated at Edinburgh Academy, and Edinburgh University. Presbyterian minister at Ruthwell, Dumfriesshire, 1871–89.

[Selected writings]; [by] James M'Farlan. Printed Edinburgh: T. & A. Constable. 1892. [viii], 211 pp.

Poetry and prose. Privately printed.   *OXB*

M'FEE, Robert Cumming (1848–). b. Saltcoats, Ayrshire, son of a shipmaster. Educated at Stevenston, and Irvine Academy. He went to sea aged fourteen, apprenticed to George Smith & Sons of the City Line of sailing ships; became a master mariner at twenty-one. In 1870 he joined the Anchor Line; after commanding several steamers he was appointed shore superintendent. Lived at 37 St Vincent Crescent, Glasgow.

Norman: a legend of Mull: a poem, in five duans; by Robert C. M'Fee. Printed Glasgow: John Horn. 1893. [iv], 224 pp.   *BL*

Random rhymes; by Captain M'Fee. Printed Glasgow: Horn & Connell. 1888. 175 pp.   *NLS*

MACFIE, Robert Andrew, (Lothian Justice, Quondam M.P., pseud.) (1811–93). b. Dreghorn, Ayrshire. Educated in Leith and Edinburgh. Started in business as a sugar refiner in Edinburgh and Liverpool. Helped to form Liverpool Chamber of Commerce. MP for Leith Burghs, 1868–74. Writer on copyright and patents.

Brotherhood, fellowship, and acting together: further practical reflections in rhyme: a sequel to 'New covenant ordinances and order'; [by Robert Andrew Macfie]. London: Elliot Stock; Edinburgh: Macniven & Wallace. 1883. viii, 30 pp.

Title from cover.   *OXB*

Jubilee and other rhymings: patriotic and domestic, in English and Scotch; by a Lothian justice, quondam M.P. Edinburgh: Macniven & Wallace; London: Elliot Stock. 1887. 39 pp.   *OXB*

Also [2nd ed.] 1887.

Mottoes and motives: themes and apophthegms and other practical matter including a dialogue on the price of books in homely lines: [poems]; [by Robert Andrew Macfie]. London: Elliot Stock; Edinburgh: Macniven & Wallace. 1884. 39 pp.   *OXB*

New covenant ordinances and order: the word, sacraments, and prayer: practical reflections in rhyme; [by Robert Andrew Macfie]. London: Elliot Stock. 1882. [iv], 76 pp.   *OXB*

Also 3rd ed. enlarged, 1883.

Verities in verse: combining, Mottoes and motives; Brotherhood, fellowship, & acting together; New covenant ordinances and order: [poems]; [by Robert Andrew Macfie]. London: Elliot Stock; Edinburgh: Macniven & Wallace. 1885. 3 vols in 1.   *BL*

Also 2nd ed., 4 vols in 1, 1887–88.

MACFIE, Ronald Campbell (1867–1931). Educated at Aberdeen University: MA, MB. Travelled extensively, holding various medical appointments; Thomson lecturer, Aberdeen, 1929. Lived latterly at Hôtel des Dunes, Sables D'Or, France.

Granite dust: fifty poems; by Ronald Campbell Macfie. London: Kegan Paul, Trench, Trübner & Co., Ltd. 1892. viii, 106 pp.   *OXB*

McGIVNEY, John S. A native of County Louth.

The bringing home of bell and burial: a poem; by John S. McGivney. London: Digby, Long & Co. [1892]. 34 pp.   *OXB*

McGONAGALL, William (1830–1902). b. probably Edinburgh, son of an Irish cotton weaver. After a childhood spent in South Ronaldsay, Orkney, his family settled in Dundee, where he remained for the rest of his life, working as a handloom weaver. He became an amateur Shakespearian actor playing at the Theatre Royal, Dundee. Well known in Scotland for his public poetry readings, he visited London in 1880 and New York in 1887. A figure of fun in his day, he now has a reputation as the world's worst poet. Lived at 48 Step Row, Dundee.

Poetic gems, selected from the works of William McGonagall. With biographical sketch by the author, and portrait. Printed Dundee: Winter, Duncan & Co. 1890. 96 pp.

Printed for the author. Title from cover.   *NLS*

Poetic gems (second series): selected from the works of William McGonagall. With biographical reminiscences by the author, and portrait. Printed Dundee: Winter, Duncan & Co. 1891. 96 pp. por., facsim.   *NLS*

M'GREEVEY, James. Minister, St Peter's, Belfast.

Wreaths of roses: a tribute to Mary: [poems]; by James M'Greevey. Printed Belfast: D.T. Doherty. 1885. 131 pp.   *BL*

MACGREGOR, Duncan (1854–1923). b. Fort Augustus, Inverness, son of a schoolmaster. Entered Aberdeen University at age of fifteen. He went as a missionary to the Orkneys; afterwards appointed to the Gardenstown Mission Church, Banffshire; became pastor at Inverallochy, Aberdeenshire.

Clouds and sunlight: poems; by Duncan Macgregor. London: Kegan Paul, Trench & Co. 1884. viii, 199 pp. *OXB*

MACGREGOR, John, (Ralph, pseud.) (1848–1932). b. Stornoway, son of John Macgregor. Surgeon Lieutenant-Colonel, Indian Medical Service. Hon. Bard to the Clan Macgregor. Held office in several Gaelic societies. Member of the Highland Society of London, and the Scottish Club, Piccadilly. Lived latterly at Victoria House, 56 Promenade, Portobello, Midlothian.

The girdle of the globe: or, the voyage of Mister Mucklemouth: being a poem descriptive of toil and travel round the world, in ten cantos; by Ralph. London: Authors' Co-operative Publishing Co., Ltd. [1890]. xii, 359 pp. il. *OXB*

Victoria maxima; et, Victoria regina: two loyal poems in commemoration of Her Majesty Queen Victoria's two-fold jubilees; by John Macgregor. Printed [London]: J.A.K. Mackay. [1897]. [20] pp.

Parallel English and Gaelic texts. *BL*

MacHALE, M.J. (c. 1845–87). b. Enniscrone, County Sligo. After ordination as a priest he became curate in his home parish. Often wrote in Irish periodicals under the signature 'A Country Curate'.

Songs for freedom, and other poems; by M.J. MacHale. Dublin: M.H. Gill & Son. 1880. 299 pp. *TCD*

McHALE, Richard, (Ricardo, pseud.) (1862–   ). b. Liverpool. Educated at the Christian Brothers School, Westport, County Mayo, and St Jarlath's College, Tuam. A journalist, he wrote for the Liverpool press; left for the United States in 1882; contributed to *Irish World, Boston Pilot*, etc.

Poetical attempts; by Ricardo. 1880.★

McHARDY, James, (Calamo Currente, pseud.)

Half hours with an old golfer: [poems]; by "Calamo Currente". Illustrated by G.A. Laundy. London: George Bell & Sons. 1895. viii, 184 pp. il., col. il. *OXB*

MACINTOSH, John (1853–   ). b. Strath Cottage, Galston, Ayrshire, son of a papermaker. Educated at Galston parish school, and Kilmarnock Academy. He entered the office of Mr Railton, architect & civil engineer, Kilmarnock, later moving to an office in Ayr; eventually he practised as an architect in Newmilns, centre of the Scottish lace trade, designing several of the mills in the district. He also ran a photographic business. Antiquarian.

Historical review of Galston and Loudon parishes; and, Poems; by John Macintosh. Printed Newmilns: M. & W. Walker. 1890. [2], viii, 244 pp. il.

Printed for the author. *BL*

MACKAIL, John William (1859–1945). Educated at Ayr Academy, Edinburgh University, and Balliol College, Oxford; Fellow of Balliol, 1882.
Entered the Education Department, later the Board of Education, 1884;
assistant secretary, 1903–19; professor of poetry, Oxford University, 1906–
11. President, British Academy, 1932–36. Classicist, and biographer of
William Morris.
  Thermopylae: Newdigate verse, 1881; by J.W. Mackail. Oxford: B.H. Blackwell; London: Simpkin, Marshall, & Co. 1881. 16 pp.   *OXB*

MACKAY, Charles (1814–89). b. Perth, son of a former army officer. His
mother being dead, his first eight years were spent in the care of a nurse in a
lonely house on the Firth of Forth. Educated in London and Brussels,
acquiring a good knowledge of European languages. Worked as private
secretary to an ironmaster near Liège, contributing to Belgian newspapers.
Returned to London, 1834, and began a career as a journalist; worked for
several journals, becoming editor of the *Illustrated London News*, 1852;
founded the *London Review*, 1860; *The Times* correspondent in the American
Civil War. His songs attained world-wide popularity. He was semi-paralysed
in the last seven years of his life. Father of the novelist Marie Corelli. LL.D,
FSA.
  Gossamer and snowdrift: the posthumous poems of Charles Mackay. With an
introduction by his son, Eric Mackay. London: George Allen. 1890. xii, 287
pp.   *UCD*
  Interludes and undertones: or, music at twilight: [poems]; by Charles Mackay.
London: Chatto & Windus. 1884. xii, 179 pp.   *OXB*
  Selected poems and songs of Charles Mackay. With a commentary and critical
introduction by eminent writers. London: Whittaker & Co. 1888. xxx, 272
pp.
    Spine-title is *Poems*.   *OXB*

MACKAY, D.E. Served in 9th Queen's Royal Lancers. Lived latterly in
Hounslow, Middlesex.
  Notes from a soldier's diary: [poems]; by D.E. Mackay. [2nd ed.]. London:
Remington & Co. 1890. 35 pp.   *BL*

MACKAY, Eric, (George Eric Lancaster, pseud.) (Violinist, pseud.) (1851–
98). b. London, son of Charles Mackay, journalist. Educated in Scotland and
Italy, where he was known as Giorgio Arrigo Mackay; he started *The Roman
Times* in Rome, and *Il Paliglotta* in Venice, both of which failed. His recreation
was the violin; 35,000 copies of his *Love Letters of a Violinist* were sold.
Member of the Junior Athenaeum Club. He died from pneumonia at 47
Longridge Road, South Kensington, London.
  Ad reginam; by George Eric Lancaster. With notes. London: David Bogue.
1881. 18 pp.   *BL*
  Ad reginam: a loyal address to Her Majesty Queen Victoria; by George Eric
Lancaster. 2nd ed., with notes. London: David Bogue. 1881. 28 pp.   *OXB*

Arrows of song: [poems]; [by Eric Mackay]. London: Hutchinson & Co. 1895. 110 pp. *OXB*

Also 3rd ed. with newly added lyrics, 1896.

Gladys the singer, and other poems; by Eric Mackay. London: Reeves & Turner. 1887. 113 pp. *OXB*

The little gods of Grub Street: a satire; [by Eric Mackay]. London: H. & W. Brown. 1896. 90 pp. *OXB*

Love letters; by a violinist. London: Field & Tuer; Simpkin, Marshall & Co; Hamilton, Adams & Co; New York: Scribner & Welford. 1884. 127 pp. *OXB*

Love letters of a violinist, and other poems; by Eric Mackay. London: Walter Scott. 1886. xxx, 201 pp. (Canterbury poets). *MPL*

Also 4th ed. [1887].

Love letters of a violinist, and other poems; by Eric Mackay. Copyright ed. Leipzig: Bernhard Tauchnitz. 1891. 288 pp. *OXB*

Love letters of a violinist, and other poems; by Eric Mackay. Author's ed., with newly-added lyrics, being the 7th ed. of this work. London: Lamley & Co. 1893. x, 244 pp. *OXB*

A lover's litanies; [poems]; by Eric Mackay. London: Field & Tuer; Simpkin, Marshall & Co; Hamilton, Adams & Co.; New York: Scribner & Welford. 1888. 148 pp.

A limited ed. of 250 numbered copies. *OXB*

A lover's litanies, and other poems; by Eric Mackay. With portrait. London: Kegan Paul, Trench, Trübner, & Co., Ltd. 1890. 244 pp. por. (Lotus series). *TCD*

Also 3rd ed. 1895.

The lover's missal, [and other poems]; by Eric Mackay. London: Walter Scott, Ltd. 1897. 243 pp. (Canterbury poets).

A limited ed. of 6,000 [sic] copies. *OXB*

Pygmalion in Cyprus, and other poems; by George Eric Lancaster. Printed London: William Clowes & Sons, Ltd. 1880. xii, 155 pp. *UCD*

The royal marriage ode, for the nuptials of H.R.H. the Duke of York with the Princess Mary of Teck, July 6th, 1893; by Eric Mackay. London: Lamley & Co. 1893. 54 pp. *OXB*

The song of the flag: a national ode; by Eric Mackay. London: Lamley & Co. 1893. 26 pp. *OXB*

A song of the sea; My lady of dreams, and other poems; by Eric Mackay. London: Methuen & Co. 1895. 163 pp. *OXB*

Also 2nd ed. 1895.

The white rose of the crown: being an ode on the birth of the son of their royal highnesses the Duke and Duchess of York on Saturday, June the twenty-third, 1894; by Eric Mackay. London: Lamley & Co. 1894. 24 pp. *OXB*

MACKELLAR, Mary (1834–90). Née Cameron. Married John Mackellar, captain of a coasting vessel; obtained a judicial separation from him; settled in

Edinburgh. Translated into Gaelic the second series of Queen Victoria's *Leaves from Our Journal in the Highlands*. Mrs Bard to the Gaelic Society, Inverness.
  Poems and songs: Gaelic and English; by Mary Mackellar. Edinburgh: Maclaghlan & Stewart; Inverness: John Noble; Oban: J.W. Miller. 1880. viii, 140 pp. *OXB*

MACKENNA, Robert William, (David Lockhart, pseud.) (1874–1930). b. Dumfries, son of Rev. Robert Mackenna. Educated at Dumfries Academy, Edinburgh Royal High School, Edinburgh University, and in Vienna, Berlin, Paris and Copenhagen. Physician and specialist in dermatology, he held senior appointments in Edinburgh and Liverpool. He contributed numerous articles to medical journals. Lived latterly at 76 Rodney Street, Liverpool.
  Verses; by Robert W. Mackenna ("David Lockhart"). Edinburgh: William Bryce; London: Simpkin, Marshall, Hamilton, Kent & Co. Ltd. [1898]. 64 pp. *OXB*

MACKENZIE, Charles
  Poems; by Charles Mackenzie. Paisley: Alexander Gardner. 1892. 96 pp. *OXB*

MACKENZIE, G.L.
  Brimstone ballads, and other verse; by G.L. Mackenzie. With an introduction by G.W. Foote. London: R. Forder. 1899. viii, 192 pp. *BL*

MACKENZIE, George (1859–   ). b. Inverness. Educated at Farraline Park School. On leaving school he entered the postal telegraph service, eventually appointed a superintendent. President of Inverness Literary Society, he wrote prose and verse for various magazines. Lived at Seaforth Lodge, Ballifeary, Inverness.
  Highland day-dreams: poems and sonnets; by George Mackenzie. Printed Inverness: "Northern Chronicle". 1887. xii, 160 pp. *OXB*

MACKENZIE, William Andrew (1870–1942). b. Invergordon, Ross-shire, son of Andrew Mackenzie. Educated at Tain Royal Academy, and Aberdeen Grammar School. Studied medicine at Marischal College, Aberdeen, 1887–90. Afterwards engaged in journalism in London; contributed much anonymous work to *Pall Mall Gazette* and other periodicals; edited *Black and White*, 1897–1900; editor, Burns & Oates publishers, 1919. Secretary-General of the Save the Children International Union, Geneva, 1928–40. Lived latterly at Château d'Hermance, Geneva.
  Poems; by W.A. Mackenzie. Aberdeen: J. Johnston & Co. 1893. 56 pp. *OXB*

McKEON, James Felix (1858–   ). Son of Thomas McKeon of Annagharah, County Armagh, a farmer on the Caledon estate. Educated at Roscrea School. Became a supervisor in the Inland Revenue.
  Songs of the R.I.C.; by J.F. McKeon. Printed Worcester: Humphreys & Co. 1893. 64 pp. ★*UCD*

MACKERETH, James Allan (187 –). Lived at Stocka House, Cottingley, Bingley, Yorkshire.
Lays of love and liberty; by James A. Mackereth. London: Elliot Stock. 1897. viii, 97 pp. *OXB*

MACKIE, David (1841–). Spent the greater part of his early life at Whithorn, Galloway. Became a banker in Edinburgh.
Ayrshire village sketches; and, Poems; by David Mackie. Kilmarnock: Dunlop & Drennan; Edinburgh: John Menzies & Co. 1896. [viii], 152 pp. por. *OXB*

MACKIE, David Bruce. Of Brechin, Angus.
Chirps and chimes in various keys: [poems]; by D. Bruce Mackie. Brechin: Author; Edinburgh: John Menzies & Co. 1892. xxiv, 9–120 pp. *BL*

MACKIE, Gascoigne (1867–19). b. Cotham, Gloucestershire, son of Rev. John Mackie. Educated at Magdalen College School (chorister), Sedbergh School, and Keble College, Oxford; BA 1889. Ordained 1906; curate, Hordle, Brockenhurst, Hampshire, from 1905.
The ballad of pity, and other poems; by Gascoigne Mackie. Bristol: J.W. Arrowsmith; London: Simpkin, Marshall, Hamilton, Kent & Co., Ltd. [1892]. 92 pp. *OXB*
Charmides: or, 'Oxford twenty years ago': [poems]; by Gascoigne Mackie. Oxford: B.H. Blackwell. 1898. 71 pp.
  A limited ed. of 250 copies. *OXB*
Poems, dramatic and democratic; by Gascoigne Mackie. London: Elliot Stock; Clacton-on-Sea: Line Bros. 1893. viii, 170 pp. *OXB*
The reconciliation: a romance of fairy land, [and other poems]; by Gascoigne Mackie. Bristol: J.W. Arrowsmith; London: Simpkin, Marshall, Hamilton, Kent & Co., Ltd. 1894. 142 pp. *OXB*

McKIE, Thomas. Scottish advocate.
Lyrics and sonnets; by Thomas McKie. Edinburgh: David Douglas. 1893. viii, 107 pp. *OXB*

McKIM, Joseph. Native of County Sligo, probably of Collooney. Educated at Dublin University, where he was awarded the Vice-Chancellor's prize for English verse. Writer for children.
Poems; by Joseph McKim. London: Kegan Paul, Trench & Co. 1888. viii, 89 pp. *OXB*

M'LACHLAN, Tom. Lived at 168 Gallowgate, Glasgow.
Thoughts in rhyme; by Tom M'Lachlan. Glasgow: Porteous Bros; Author. 1884. 88 pp. *OXB*

M'LAREN, John Wilson (1861–). b. Grassmarket, Edinburgh, son of a seaman. His father died when he was three, so he had only five years of schooling. Employed as messenger boy to a bootmaker, then afterwards to a newsagent. He became a compositor with Ballantyne, Hanson & Co., Edinburgh. Regularly contributed to numerous papers and literary miscellanies. Lived at 177 Dalkeith Road, Edinburgh.

Rhymes frae the chimla-lug; by John W. M'Laren, "The Laddie Bard". Edinburgh: Author. 1881. 100 pp. *OXB*

Scots poems and ballants; by J. Wilson M'Laren. Edinburgh: Author. 1892. xii, 114 pp.
A limited ed. of 150 copies signed by the author. *OXB*

M'LATCHIE, John. Of Ayr?
Poems, songs &c.; by John M'Latchie. Printed Ayr: 'Ayr Advertiser' Office. 1897. 288 pp.
Spine-title is *Poetry*. *BL*

McLATCHIE, Laurie Lorimer
Stray thoughts: [poems]; by Laurie Lorimer McLatchie. London: Office of the "Christian Herald". [1882]. 58 pp. *★UCD*

M'LEAN, Alexander Thomson (18 –82). b. Glasgow, son of a warehouseman. His father died when he was a boy so he started work at a very young age. He attended evening classes and, helped by self-tuition, qualified as a schoolmaster. Studied for the ministry at Glasgow University. Minister of the United Presbyterian Church at Ballieston, Lanarkshire.

Memorial volume of the Rev. Alexander T. M'Lean. Including selections from his writings in poetry, prose, and sermons, with biographical sketch. Edited by his son. Airdrie: Baird & Hamilton. 1883. 320 pp. *★UCD*

M'LEISH, Alexander. Lived at 26 Glover Street, Perth.
Songs of St. Johnston; by Alexander M'Leish. Printed Perth: Wood & Son. 1899. [viii], 112 pp. *BL*

McLENNAN, Anne (1840–83). b. Resolis, Ross & Cromarty. When she was four the family moved to Killearnon. She worked as a domestic servant at a manse in Perth. Became a 'Bible-woman' in Lochgilphead, Argyllshire, devoting her life to visiting the poor.

Poems: sacred and secular; by Anne McLennan. Printed Edinburgh. 1884. 68 pp. por. *BL*

M'LEOD, Addison. Possibly Addison McLeod (1871–19). Son of Joseph A. McLeod of Craven Hill, Hyde Park, London. Educated at Eton College, and Trinity Hall, Cambridge (scholar); LL.B 1892. Called to the Bar, Inner Temple, 1896. In the First World War he was employed by the postal censorship. Wrote a history of the Palestine campaign.

A window in Lincoln's Inn, and what was seen within and without: [poems]; by Addison M'Leod. London: Kegan Paul, Trench, Trübner & Co. Ltd. 1897. vi, 88 pp. *OXB*

MACLEOD, Fiona, pseud. *see* **SHARP, William**, (Fiona Macleod, pseud.)

MACLEOD, Neil (1843–1913). b. Isle of Skye. Became a commercial traveller in Edinburgh. Writer of Gaelic songs.
Wallace: a poem; by Neil Macleod. London: Alexander Gardner. 1896. 97 pp.   *OXB*

MacMANUS, James *see* **MacMANUS, Seumas**

MacMANUS, Seumas, (Mac, pseud.) (1868–1960). b. James MacManus in County Donegal, son of a poor farmer. Taught in a national school from the age of eighteen, then worked as a journalist. Wrote novels and stories depicting Irish life, contributing to many Irish papers. He made several lecture tours in the United States, where his stories were extremely popular. Contributed to the Nationalist magazine *The Shan Van Vocht*, marrying one of its editors, the poet Anna Johnston (Ethna Carbery) in 1901. He died in New York City.
Shuilers from healthy hills; by Mac. Mountcharles, Donegal: G. Kirke. 1893. 102 pp.
     Poetry and prose.   *OXB*

McMILLAN, Alec (1845–1919). Son of John McMillan of Castramont, Kirkcudbrightshire. Educated at Aldenham School, and Brasenose and Merton Colleges, Oxford. Joined the Indian Civil Service, 1868; Under-Secretary, North West Province and Oudh, 1874–77; district judge in several locations, 1884–92. Barrister, Inner Temple, 1883. Professor of Indian jurisprudence & Indian history, King's College, London, 1899–1902. Consul for the Alpes Maritimes & Monaco, 1902–10.
Divers ditties, chiefly written in India, with appendices; by Alec McMillan. Westminister: Archibald Constable. 1895. viii, 146 pp.   *OXB*

M'MURDO, George (1843?–   ). b. Muirkirk, Ayrshire, son of a coal miner. After a rudimentary education at the Ironworks School, he went to work in the pit at the age of twelve.
Poems and miscellaneous pieces; by George M'Murdo. Ardrossan: Arthur Guthrie. [1882]. 119 pp.   *BL*

MacNAUGHTON, Samuel (fl. 1869–1912). b. Eureka, New Brunswick, Canada, son of Robert MacNaughton. Educated at Dalhousie University. Presbyterian pastor of a church at Moncton, he then did evangelical work in Scotland; assistant minister at Unst, Shetland, then successively at Avingdon, Liverpool, and the East End of London; he was licensed by Manchester Presbyterians in 1877, and had charge of the church at Preston. His wife was Elizabeth Ellen MacNaughton, writer of children's stories. Lived at 33 Barrow Road, Preston.
Lily and Leander: or, the secret of success in service; A poem of life, and other poems and hymns; by Samuel MacNaughton. Edinburgh: James Gemmell. 1890. 196 pp.   *UCD*

MacNICOL, Duncan (1851–   ). b. Luss, Dunbartonshire. Aged fourteen he was sent to Inchlonaig Island to teach the children of Sir James Colquhoun's gamekeeper to read. Afterwards he worked as a gardner and handyman. Settled at Rothesay, Buteshire, in the employment of a cab proprietor.
  Bute, and other poems; by Duncan MacNicol. Printed Glasgow: Aird & Coghill. 1897. 190 pp.   *BL*
  Glen Fruin, and other poems; by Duncan McNicol [sic]. Rothesay: George Higgie. [1885]. [viii], 94 pp.   *OXB*

MACPHERSON, A.C. Writer on religious topics. Of Bristol.
  The good ship "Matthew": or, four hundred years ago: a poem; by A.C. Macpherson. Bristol: J.W. Arrowsmith; London: Simpkin, Marshall, Hamilton, Kent & Co. Ltd. [1897]. 31 pp.   *BL*

MACRAE, Flora Maitland, Lady (18 –1921). Daughter of John Colquhoun of Edinburgh. Her grandmother was the poet Lady Colquhoun of Luss. In 1877 she married Sir Colin G. Macrae, a respected writer to the signet, and director of the Commercial Bank of Scotland. Lived at 45 Moray Place, Edinburgh, and Glenflora, Colinton, Midlothian.
  The private note-book opened: or, a broken heart bound up, and other pieces: [poems]; by F.M. Macrae. Stirling: Drummond's Tract Depot; London: S.W. Partridge & Co. [1888]. 159 pp.   *OXB*

MACRITCHIE, Margaret Scott *see* **HAYCRAFT, Margaret Scott**

MACTAGGART, John (1845–   ). b. Campbeltown, Argyllshire. Educated at the Free Grammar School there. He was engaged in commerce until 1878, chiefly in Glasgow. An active volunteer in the 19th Lanarkshire Rifles. Became hon. secretary of the Young Men's Christian Association. He moved to Edinburgh in 1879 on his appointment to the Waldensian Pastors' Fund commitee.
  Mackinnon and the bards: [poems]; by John Mactaggart. Edinburgh: Oliphant, Anderson & Ferrier. 1899. [x], 69 pp. por., facsim.   *OXB*
  Our land: sketches in verse; by John Mactaggart. London: James Nisbet & Co; Edinburgh: Religious Tract and Book Society: 1890. [x], 166 pp. il.   *NLS*

M'VITTIE, James (1833–   ). b. Langhorn, Dumfriesshire, son of a crofter and shepherd. Attended Broomhill Free School until age of nine when he was apprenticed as a cotton weaver; at sixteen he became a woollen spinner. Married at nineteen, he experienced a religious awakening in response to the American revivalist group which visited the town; he became a temperance reformer and an agent of the Scottish Temperance League.
  In memoriam, and songs of cheer from the cradle to the grave; by James M'Vittie. Glasgow: Scottish Temperance League Office. 1893. xvi, 216 pp.   *OXB*

M'WHIRTER, David. Of the Isle of Whithorn, Wigtownshire.
  A ploughboy's musings: being a selection of English and humorous Scotch poems; by David M'Whirter. Whithorn: R.D. Ballantine; Author. 1883. 152 pp.   *BL*
    Also 2nd ed. 1884.

MAGENNIS, Bernard (1833–1911). b. Ballybay, County Monaghan. He taught for a time in a national school, then moved to Dublin to edit *The Social Mirror and Temperance Advocate*. An energetic and successful lecturer and speaker, he lived and worked in New York for a period, and was also an occasional resident of Salford, Lancashire.

Lamh dearg: or, the red hand, and other national and miscellaneous poems; by B. Magennis. Dublin: Sealy, Bryers & Walker. 1887. viii, 300 pp.   *MPL*

   Also 2nd ed. 1887.

MAGENNIS, Peter (1817–1910). b. Knockmore, County Fermanagh, son of a farmer. He became a national schoolteacher. A novelist, he was known as 'The Bard of Lough Erne'.

Poems; by Peter Magennis. Enniskillen: Geo. B. White. [1888]. [iv], 93 pp.   *BL*

Poems; by Peter Magennis. London: Roper & Drowley; Enniskillen: Geo. B. White. 1889. [iv], 196 pp.   *OXB*

The poems of the late Edward Flanagan. Edited by Peter Magennis. Printed Enniskillen: Wm. Trimble. 1884. 64 pp.

   Includes poems by the editor.   *OXB*

MAGUIRE, Tom (1866?–95). b. Leeds of Irish Catholic parents. As a boy he sang in the Roman Catholic Cathedral choir. He earned his living as a photographer. Became a socialist, active in setting up trade unions in Leeds industries. His name appeared in the Socialist League manifesto with twenty-two others including William Morris. He contributed to many socialist periodicals.

Machine-room chants; by the late Tom Maguire. London: "Labour Leader". 1895. 32 pp.   *LEP*

Tom Maguire: a remembrance: being a selection from the prose and verse writings of a socialist pioneer. With memoirs. Manchester: Labour Press Society Ltd. 1895. [iv], 128 pp. por.   *LEP*

MAITLAND, Ella Fuller *see* **FULLER MAITLAND, Ella**

MAJOR, Albany Featherstonehough (1858–1925). Son of Charles M. Major of Cromwell House, Croydon, Surrey. Educated at Dulwich College. Appointed clerk in Admiralty, 1878, eventually promoted to principal in War Office, 1900. Married Margit Gron of Norway. Hon. secretary, Viking Club, 1894–1904. President, Croydon Natural History & Scientific Society, 1919–20. Lived at The Waldrons, Croydon.

Sagas and songs of the Norsemen; by Albany F. Major. London: David Nutt. 1894. viii, 134 pp.   *OXB*

MALCOLM, C.H. Novelist.

Poems; by C.H. Malcolm. Westminster: Roxburghe Press. [1898]. 92 pp. por.   *OXB*

MALINS, Joseph (1844–1926). b. Worcester. He was apprenticed to a decorative painter at nine years old, when the family moved to Birmingham. After two years in the United States he returned home to start his own business. A temperance advocate, he was founder and chairman of the National Temperance Federation; elected Grand Chief Templar, 1870–1912; International Chief Templar, 1880–85 and 1897–1905. JP and Worcestershire county councillor.

Popular temperance recitations; composed by Joseph Malins. With biographical sketch, portrait, and other illustrations. Printed Maidstone: G.H. Graham. [1890]. 24 pp. il., por.
     Title from cover.   *OXB*

MALLETT, John. Of Somerset.
At Culbone; The white lily of Corvei, and other poems; by John Mallett. Printed London: McCorquodale & Co., Ltd. 1888. 174 pp.   *TAU*
Grace Bell, and other poems; by John Mallett. London: McCorquodale & Co., Ltd. 1895. viii, 205 pp.   *OXB*

MALLETT, Josiah Reddie. Of Harlyn Bay.
A life's history, told in homely verse, and miscellaneous poems; by J. Reddie Mallett. London: Richard Bentley & Son. 1895. [viii], 156 pp. por.
     Spine-title is *Poems*.   *OXB*

MALLOCK, William Hurrell, (W.H.M.) (1849–1923). b. Cockington Court, Devon, son of Rev. Roger Mallock, and nephew of the historian J.A. Froude. Educated privately, and at Balliol College, Oxford. Novelist, and writer on philosophy and politics, best known as author of *The New Republic*, 1877.
Poems; by William Hurrell Mallock. London: Chatto & Windus. 1880. xii, 154 pp.   *MPL*
Verses; by W.H.M. Printed London: Spottiswoode & Co. [1885?]. 18 pp.
     For private circulation. Title from cover.   *OXB*
Verses; by W.H. Mallock. London: Hutchinson & Co. 1893. 159 pp.   *MPL*

MANNERS, Mary Emmeline (1858–1941). b. Penge, Surrey, daughter of George Manners, a member of the City of London Corporation. Educated at the Quaker school kept by E. & C. Sharp at Redhill. She lived the greater part of her life at Croydon. Wrote pieces for *The Christian World, The Family Circle*, and other magazines.
Aunt Agatha Ann, and other verses; by Mary Emmeline Manners. Illustrations by Ernold A. Mason and Louis Wain. London: James Clarke & Co. 1897. [x], 88 pp. il.   *BL*
The bishop and the caterpillar, (as recited by Mr. Brandram), and other pieces: [poems]; by Mary E. Manners. 2nd ed. London: James Clarke & Co. 1893. x, 92 pp.   *BL*

MANNING, Eliza F. Wrote children's picture books.
Delightful Thames: [poems]; by E.F. Manning. Engraved by I.D. Cooper. London: Sampson Low, Marston, Searle, & Rivington. [1886]. [53] pp. il. Printed on one side of leaf only. *OXB*

MANNING, J. Lived at 48 Huntley Street, Gordon Square, London.
Roderick and Eva: a ballad romance of the cloister; by R.F. Fitzgerald and J. Manning. London: J. Manning. 1892. 32 pp. *BL*

MANNING, Mrs R. Of Clonmel, County Tipperary.
In memoriam Very Rev. T.N. Burke, O.P., died July 2nd, 1883, dedicated to his brethren of the Order in Dublin who feel the bereavement of his loss most deeply; by Mrs. R. Manning. Printed Clonmel: "Chronicle" Steam-Printing Works. [1883]. 15 pp. *BL*

MANNING, William (18 –1905).
The glow-worm; by William Manning. Illustrated by Westley Horton, the cover designed by Charles Holme. London: Frank T. Sabin. 1896. [x], 63 pp. il. *OXB*

MANSELL, Trevor, (Euoe, pseud.)
Verses; written by Euoe. Abergavenny: E. Harrison. [1896]. 18 pp. *OXB*

MANSFIELD, Charlotte. FRGS. The first woman to lecture in Rhodesia. Member of the English Speaking Union, Writer's Club, and Sesame Club. Contributed to many periodicals; novelist.
Flowers of the wind: [poems]; [by] Charlotte Mansfield. London: Elkin Mathews. 1899. viii, 54 pp. *BL*

MANT, Frederick Woods (1809–93). b. Crawley, Hampshire, son of the Bishop of Down & Connor. Educated at New Inn Hall, Oxford; BA 1844. Ordained 1841; curate, Tottington, Norfolk, and vicar, Stanford, Norfolk, 1851–58; vicar, Woodmancote with Popham, Hampshire, 1858–70, Egham, Surrey, 1870–79. Lived latterly at Teddington, Middlesex.
Tales of mission work, in verse; by F.W. Mant. London: Society for Promoting Christian Knowledge; New York: E. & J.B. Young & Co. [1881]. 64 pp. il. *OXB*

MARCHANT, Robert M. Writer on Christian philosophy.
Fire of the altar, for "the time at hand!" . . . ; [by Robert M. Marchant]. London: Robert Banks & Son. [1894]. 24 pp. *BL*

MARCHBANK, Agnes. Mrs. Marshall. She contributed to many magazines on women's work in the home. Lived at 44 Cumlodden Drive, Maryhill, Glasgow.
Songs of labour, home, and country; by Agnes Marchbank. Auchterarder: Tovani & Co.; London: Simpkin, Marshall, Hamilton, Kent & Co., Ltd. [1893]. vi, 41 pp. *OXB*

MARGESSON, John James

    Early poems; Hastings 1844; by John James Margesson. Printed Red Hill, Surrey: Inmates of the Earlswood Asylum. [c. 1890]. [viii], 60 pp.   *OXB*

MARGESSON, Reginald Whitehall (1828?–   ). Son of William Margesson of Ockley, Surrey. Educated at Magdalen Hall and St Mary Hall, Oxford; BA 1857. Ordained 1859; curate, Mounfield, Sussex, 1860–72, Werrington, Cornwall, 1877; rector, Virginstowe, Cornwall, 1879–81, Blendworth, Hampshire from 1881.

    A poem; by Reginald Whitehall Margesson. New ed. Printed Red Hill, Surrey: Inmates of the Earlswood Asylum. 1892. [ii], 37 pp.   *OXB*

MARIA MONICA pseud. *see* **KING, Harriet Eleanor Hamilton**, (Maria Monica, pseud.)

MARK, Amy

    The sea king's daughter, and other poems; by Amy Mark. Decorated with designs by Bernard Sleigh, engraved by the designer and by L.A. Talbot. Birmingham: G. Napier & Co.; London: Tylston & Edwards and A.P. Marsden. 1895. [44] pp. il.

        Title-page at end of book.   *OXB*

        Also a limited ed. of 50 copies printed on large paper.

MARKLEY, John T. Of Eastbourne, Sussex.

    Songs of humanity and progress: a collection of lyrics, contributed to various publications; by John T. Markley. Eastbourne: H. Holloway. 1882. [86] pp.   *OXB*

MARKS, Mary A.M. Née Hoppus.

    The tree of knowledge; by Mary A.M. Marks. Printed Guildford: Billing & Sons. [1896]. [iv], 64 pp.   *BL*

MARMONT, J.B.

    Wild honey: poems; by J.B. Marmont. London: Passmore & Alabaster. [1896]. 64 pp.   *★UCD*

MARPLES, David (1796–1881). b. Baslow, Derbyshire. Educated at the village school, then apprenticed to the proprietor of the *Sheffield Mercury*. In 1820 he went to Liverpool where he built a successful printing business. A Liberal in politics, he was secretary of the Religious Tract Society, and was connected with the Seaman's Friend Society over many years.

    Sonnets and occasional verses; by David Marples. Printed Liverpool: D. Marples & Co. Ltd. 1882. x, 60 pp.   *OXB*

MARRIOTT WATSON, Rosamund, (Graham Rosamund Tomson, pseud.) (1863–1911). Essayist, and author of one novel, she was born in the United States. She married Henry Brereton Marriott Watson, an Australian-born journalist and writer settled in London. They lived latterly at Shere, Surrey.

The bird-bride: a volume of ballads and sonnets; by Graham R. Tomson. London: Longmans, Green, & Co. 1889, viii, 136 pp.   *OXB*

The patch work quilt; by Graham R. Tomson. London: Ernest Nister; New York: E.P. Dutton & Co. [1892]. [16] pp. col. il.   *OXB*

A summer night, and other poems; by Graham R. Tomson. With a frontispiece by A. Tomson. [London]: Methuen & Co. 1891. xii, 84 pp. il.   *OXB*

Tares: [poems]; [by Rosamund Marriott Watson]. London: Kegan Paul, Trench & Co. 1884. [vi], 29 pp.   *OXB*

Vespertilia, and other verses; by Rosamund Marriott Watson. London: John Lane The Bodley Head; Chicago: Way & Williams. 1895. xii, 112 pp.
A limited ed. of 650 copies printed for England and America.   *OXB*

MARSDEN, Elizabeth Anne Rogerson. b. Edinburgh. Brought up at Potwells Farm, Ackworth, Yorkshire.

Leisure musings of a busy life: or, poems of youth and age; by E.A. Rogerson Marsden. Printed Leeds: A. Megson & Sons. [1885]. [ii], 90 pp.   *BL*

MARSDEN, Janet Ousey

Poems (original) on various subjects; by Janet O. Marsden. Manchester: John Heywood. [1895]. [2], iv, 90 pp.   *MPL*

MARSDEN, Victor Emile. Translator from the Russian.

Songs of an exile; by V.E. Marsden. London: David Stott. 1892. viii, 88 pp.   *OXB*

MARSH, William (1826–   ). b. Bentley, West Riding of Yorkshire, son of a farmer and miller. He became acting United States consul at Altona for the Duchies of Schleswig-Holstein, and for the Elbe district of Hanover, 1862–76. In retirement he lived at 2 Bridge Terrace, Bentley Road, Doncaster, Yorkshire.

A jubilee collection of revised songs and poems; by William Marsh. Leeds: Richard Jackson. 1897. xii, 120 pp. por.
Spine-title is *Songs and poems*.   *BL*

MARSHALL, Emma (1830–99). b. Cromer, Norfolk, daughter of Simon Martin, banker of Norwich, and a Quaker mother. In 1849 she and her mother went to live in Clifton, Bristol. In 1852 she married Hugh G. Marshall, a banker, eventually moving to Exeter, then to Gloucester. After the collapse of the West of England Bank they endured financial hardship. They had nine children, and she became the breadwinner by publishing numerous novels and stories.

The eve of St. Michael and All Angels, and other verses; by Emma Marshall. Bristol: J.W. Arrowsmith; London: Simpkin, Marshall, Hamilton, Kent & Co. Ltd. [1893]. 48 pp.

'The profits will be given to St. Lucy's Free Hospital for Sick Children at Kingsholme, Gloucester'. *OXB*

MARSHALL, Frederick. Lived at Clifton, Biggleswade, Bedfordshire, then at Bexwell Road, Downham, Norfolk.
Meditations of the heart: poems; by Frederick Marshall. Oxford: J.C. Pembry; Biggleswade, Beds.: Author. 1884. xii, 196 pp. *OXB*
Transition; Ministering spirits, and other poems; by Frederick Marshall. London: Simpkin, Marshall, Hamilton, Kent & Co., Ltd. [1899]. 208 pp. *OXB*
Waking thoughts; The mystic river; Sandringham, and other poems; by Frederick Marshall. London: Jarrold & Sons. [1894]. x, 198 pp. *OXB*

MARSHALL, Jenner, (J.M.) (1817–1904). Son of Rev. Edward Marshall of Iffley, Oxford. Educated at Rugby School, and Worcester College, Oxford: BA 1839, MA 1843. After ordination he held various curacies in Oxfordshire. Lord of the manor of Westcott Barton, Oxfordshire.
Miscellaneous pieces in verse; by J.M. [1884]. [viii], 56 pp.
    Printed for private circulation. *OXB*

MARSHALL, William. Writer on the English language.
Rinalpho's dream: a poem in 5 cantos; by William Marshall. London: John Kensit. 1887. [iv], 88 pp. *OXB*

MARSHMAN, Mrs
Bible narratives in verse; by Mrs. Marshman. 2nd ed. London: John F. Shaw & Co. [188–]. 128 pp. *★UCD*

MARSTON, Philip Bourke (1850–87). b. London, son of John Westland Marston. At the age of four he received an injury to an eye that seriously affected his sight. He became engaged to Mary Nesbit, sister of Edith Nesbit, who died in 1871. Friend of Oliver Madox Brown, Rossetti, Swinburne and Watts–Dunton.
The collected poems of Philip Bourke Marston, comprising "Song-tide", "All in all", "Wind-voices", "A last harvest", and "Aftermath". With biographical sketch by Louise Chandler Moulton. London: Ward, Lock, Bowden & Co. 1892. xxxviii, 413 pp. por. *MPL*
A last harvest: lyrics and sonnets from the book of love; by Philip Bourke Marston. With biographical sketch by Louise Chandler Moulton. London: Elkin Mathews. 1891. [1], xii, 147 pp.
    A limited ed. of 50 large paper copies printed for England, numbered and signed by Louise Chandler Moulton. *JRL*
Wind-voices: [poems]; by Philip Bourke Marston. London: Elliot Stock. [1883]. x, 176 pp. *MPL*

MARTELLIUS, pseud. *see* **SHEPPARD, Henry Winter**, (Martellius, pseud.)

MARTIN, George Henry

A song for my son; by George Henry Martin. London: Watts & Co. 1890. 64 pp. *OXB*

MARTIN, Henry (1824–). b. Queenstown, County Cork, son of a customs officer. Established as a leather manufacturer and merchant in Birkenhead, Cheshire. A Freemason, he was secretary of Birkenhead District Lodge, 1845–60.

Thoughts by the wayside: some of the use of my leisure moments spreading over a quarter of a century: [poems]; by Henry Martin. Birkenhead: Willmer Bros & Co., Ltd. 1881. xvi, 184 pp. *WPL*

MARTIN, Robert Jasper. Well-known Irish sporting journalist from County Galway. He wrote for *The Sporting Times* under the signature 'Ballyhooley'. Songwriter for burlesque stage performance.

Days of the Land League, and other poems; By R.J. Martin. Dublin: Hodges, Figgis, & Co. 1884. 31 pp. *OXB*

MARTIN, William Wilsey (1833–). b. Reading, Berkshire. Employed by the civil service from 1854.

By Solent and Danube: poems and ballads; by W. Wilsey Martin. London: Trübner & Co. 1885. xii, 171 pp. *OXB*

Quatrains: Life's mystery, and other poems; by Wm. Wilsey Martin. London: Elkin Mathews. 1891. [x], 67 pp.

A limited ed. of 400 copies of which only 200 were for sale. *UCD*

MARY AGNES, Sister *see* **POVEY, J.M.**, (Sister Mary Agnes)

MARY FRANCIS CLARE, Sister *see* **CUSACK, Mary Frances**, (Sister Mary Francis Clare)

MARZIALS, Sir Frank Thomas (1840–1912). b. Lille, France, son of Rev. A.T. Marzials. Educated at his father's school. Entered the War Office during the Crimean War; accountant-general of the army, 1898–1904. Biographer of Charles Dickens and Victor Hugo. Lived at 9 Ladbroke Square, Notting Hill, London W.

Death's disguises, and other sonnets; by Frank T. Marzials. London: Walter Scott. 1889. 59 pp. *OXB*

MASKREY, Herbert. Of Hathersage, Derbyshire. A young person in the 1880s.

The castaway, and other poems; by Herbert Maskrey. Printed Sheffield: Leader & Sons. 1886. [iv], 76 pp. *OXB*

MASON, Eugene. Writer on French medieval romances. Contributor to the *Bookman, To-day,* and other periodicals. Lived at 33 Endymion Road, Finsbury Road, London.

The field floridus, and other poems; by Eugene Mason. London: Grant Richards. 1899. viii, 112 pp. *UCD*

Flamma vestalis, and other poems; by Eugene Mason. London: T. Fisher Unwin. 1895. 76 pp. il. (Cameo series). *UCD*

The ivory gates, [and other poems]; by Eugene Mason. Printed Cheltenham: "Looker-On" Office. [189–]. [29] pp.

    Title from cover. *UCD*

MASON, Marie (18 –81).

In memoriam: poems; by Marie Mason, died November 10, 1881. [1882?]. 126 pp. *BL*

MASSEY, Gerald (1828–1907). b. Gamble Wharf, near Tring, Hertfordshire, son of a canal boatman. Aged eight he went to work in a silk factory and as a straw-plaiter before becoming an errand boy in London at fifteen. He joined the Chartist movement and was associated with the Christian Socialists, writing for *The Spirit of Freedom,* which he ultimately edited. He became a popular lecturer on spiritualism and mesmerism, and on the origins of myths and mysteries. He is believed to have been the original of George Elliot's 'Felix Holt'. Lived for a time in Edinburgh, and from 1862–77 at Little Gaddesdon, Hertfordshire.

Carmen nuptiale: [poems]; by Gerald Massey. Printed [London]: Spottiswode & Co. [1880?]. 62 pp.

    Privately printed. *BL*

Home rule rhymes and labour lyrics; by Gerald Massey. Printed London: National Press Agency, Ltd. [1891]. 24 pp. *OXB*

My lyrical life: poems old and new: by Gerald Massey. First series. London: Kegan Paul, Trench & Co. 1889. xxxiv, 364 pp.

    Spine-title is *Poems*. *UCD*

    Also American ed. published by Colby & Rich in Boston.

My lyrical life: poems old and new; by Gerald Massey. First series, with additions. 2nd ed. London: Kegan Paul, Trench, Trübner & Co. 1890. xxxiv, 376 pp. *MPL*

My lyrical life: poems old and new; by Gerald Massey. Second series. London: Kegan Paul, Trench & Co. 1889. xii, 428 pp. *MPL*

    Also American ed. published by Colby & Rich in Boston.

MASSEY, Lucy. Née Fletcher. Writer of religious works for children.

Figures of the true: [poems]; by Mrs. Massey. London: Skeffington & Son. 1890. [viii], 70 pp. *UCD*

MASSEY, Mrs *see* **MASSEY, Lucy**

MATCHING GREEN: A LAY MADE ABOUT THE YEAR 1883, WITH APOLOGIES TO LORD MACAULAY. [1883?]. 15 pp. *OXB*

MATHER, James (1839–   ). b. Eaglesham, Renfrewshire, son of a farmer. Educated at Mearns School, Glasgow High School, and Glasgow University. Trained for the United Presbyterian Church in Edinburgh; ordained 1867; minister in Glasgow, Paisley, Greenock, and Dalry, Galloway.

Poems; by James Mather. Paisley: Alexander Gardner. 1892. 261 pp.   *UCD*

MATHESON, Annie (1853–1924). b. Blackheath, London, daughter of Rev. James Matheson, Congregational minister. Author of a number of children's books, a biography of Florence Nightingale, and introductions to the novels of George Eliot. Lived latterly at Honeysuckle Cottage, Maybury Hill, Woking, Surrey.

Love triumphant, and other new poems; by Annie Matheson. London: A.D. Innes & Co. Ltd. 1898. xiv, 114 pp. il.   *UCD*

Love's music, and other poems; by Annie Matheson. London: Sampson, Low, Marston & Co. 1894. viii, 96 pp.   *MPL*

"The religion of humanity", and other poems; by Annie Matheson. London: Percival & Co. 1890. xvi, 184 pp.   *OXB*

Selected poems old and new; by Annie Matheson. London: Henry Frowde. 1899. 152 pp.   *OXB*

MATHESON, George (1842–1906). Educated at Glasgow University; BA 1861, MA 1862. Became a Church of Scotland minister, 1866. Blind from boyhood, he was known as 'The Blind Preacher'. Minister, Innellan Church, 1868–86, St Bernard's, Edinburgh, 1886–99. Writer of theological and devotional works which were widely popular. DD, LL.D, FRS, Edinburgh.

Sacred songs; by George Matheson. Edinburgh: William Blackwood & Sons. 1890. x, 176 pp.   *OXB*

MATHESON, Greville Ewing, (M.E. Greville, pseud.) b. Soham, Cambridgeshire, son of Rev. D.L. Matheson of Wolverhampton. Educated privately, and at Tettenhall College, Staffordshire. From 1883 he was on the staff of Donald Currie & Co., managers of Union Castle Line. Hon. secretary of Anglo-African Writers Club, 1895. Contributed numerous articles and verses to various periodicals. Lived at 3 Fenchurch Street, London EC.

From veld & "street": rhymes more or less South African; by M.E. Greville. London: Effingham Wilson; Cape Town: J.C. Juta & Co. 1899. [iv], 64 pp.   *OXB*

Also [2nd ed.] 1899.

MATHEWS, Henry. Minister of Flanshaw, Wakefield, Yorkshire.

Miscellaneous poems; by Henry Mathews. Morley: S. Stead. 1896. 60 pp. Cover-title is *Poems*.   *LEP*

MATIN SONGS. London: Kegan Paul, Trench & Co. 1888. [vi], 63 pp.   *OXB*

MATSON, Jane C.

Home poems; by Jane C. Matson. Printed Portsmouth: Charpentier. [1882]. 87 pp.   *★UCD*

MATSON, William Tidd (1833–99). b. Kingsland, London. Secretary of European Freedom Committee, 1853. Studied at the Congregational Institute, 1857–58; pastor at Havant, Hampshire, 1858–62, Gosport, 1862–71, Sleaford, 1871, Rothwell, then Portsmouth to 1891, Sarisbury Green, 1891–97. President, Portsmouth Sunday School Union, 1880. He wrote many hymns, some of which are in more than forty different hymnals. Lived at 4 Mornington Terrace, London Road, Portsmouth.

Edderline, and other poems; by W. Tidd Matson. London: Elliot Stock; Portsmouth: J.F. Rayner; Gosport: Walford & Son. 1880. 20 pp.   *OXB*

Esther, the queen: a poetical drama in three acts, and other poems; by William Tidd Matson. London: Elliot Stock. 1890. 20 pp.

Printed and published for the author.   *JRL*

The inner life: a poem; by William Tidd Matson. 4th ed. Portsmouth: A.H. Stride. 1893. [viii], 108 pp.

Published for the author.   *OXB*

Lays of laud, life, and litany, including, The inner life; by William Tidd Matson. Southsea, Portsmouth: A.H. Stride; London: Elliot Stock. 1891. [viii], 107 pp.

Published for the author.   *OXB*

The poetical works of William Tidd Matson, now first collected and including a large number of pieces not before published. Southsea, Portsmouth: A.H. Stride; London: Elliot Stock. 1894. xii, 630 pp. por.   *JRL*

The priest in the village: four eclogues, illustrating the great advantage of an Established Church in providing for the work of the ministry "an educated gentleman(?) in every parish"; by W. Tidd Matson. Portsmouth: C. Annett & Sons; London: Elliot Stock. 1884. 38 pp.

Printed and published for the author.   *OXB*

The world redeemed: a poem; by William Tidd Matson. London: Elliot Stock. 1881. 28 pp.   *OXB*

MATTHEWS, William E. Lived at Sea View, Isle of Wight.

Gems of the isle: original poems; by William E. Matthews. Printed Ryde: Henry Wayland. 1884. viii, 68 pp.   *OXB*

MAURIER, George Du *see* **DU MAURIER, George**

MAVOR, William S.

In leisure time: a booklet of verse; by William S. Mavor. London: Elliot Stock. 1895. viii, 94 pp.   *OXB*

MAXWELL, James. Of Belfast.

Hymns and poems; by James Maxwell. Printed Belfast: Marcus Ward & Co., Ltd. 1891. 80 pp.   *OXB*

The transfer of the crown, and other poems; by James Maxwell. Printed Belfast: Marcus Ward & Co., Ltd. 1887. [ii], 62 pp.   *OXB*

MAY, pseud.

Mussoorie portraits, in rhyme, taken during the season; by "May". Mussoorie: Beacon Press. [1889]. [22] pp.   *BL*

MAY, George

George May's writings in rhyme. Portsmouth: Holbrook & Son, Ltd. [c. 1882]. *★UCD*

MAY, George Parker. Of Maldon, Essex.

Lays of leisure hours; by George Parker May. Printed Maldon: Richard Poole. 1881. 47 pp. *★UCD*

MAYHEW, T.

Easy rhymes in English history; by T. Mayhew. Manchester: John Heywood. [1882]. 16 pp. *BL*

MAYNE, Thomas Ekenhead (1866–99). b. Belfast, son of a bookseller. Short story writer.

Blackthorn blossoms: Irish verses; by Thomas E. Mayne. Belfast: R. Aickin. 1897. 91 pp. *★NUC*

MEAD, Thomas, pseud. *see* **PRESCOTT, Thomas**, (Thomas Mead, pseud.)

The MEADOW PALACE: A METRICAL SOUVENIR. Edinburgh: John B. Fairgrieve. 1887. 24 pp. il.

On the Intenational Exhibition, Edinburgh, 1886. *NLS*

MEADOWS, Alice Maud (18 –1913). b. London, daughter of John O. Meadows, solicitor. Educated at private schools and by home tutors. She began to write when very young.

Ethelwold: a idyl; by Alice Maud Meadows. London: H.M. Pollett & Co. [1885]. 26 pp. *OXB*

MEADOWS, Lindon, pseud. *see* **GREATREX, Charles Butler**, (Lindon Meadows, pseud.)

MEADOWS, Thomas, (Swithin Saint Swithaine, pseud.). Possibly Thomas Meadows (1832–19). b. Churchtown, North Meols, son of James Meadows, master miller. Educated at private schools in Liverpool, Wallasey, and Wavertree. He became a schoolmaster, teaching at Whitchurch, Birkenhead and Bowdon, 1852–59; private tutor to the Howards of Greystoke Castle, and to the Earl of Antrim. Attended Trinity College, Dublin; BA, MA, BD. Curate, All Souls, Liverpool, 1863–64, Holy Trinity, Runcorn, 1864–70; vicar, Thornton, Poulton-le-Fylde, from 1870.

A divan of the dales: Micah, and other poems; by Swithin Saint Swithaine. London: Digby, Long & Co. [1897]. xii, 177 pp. *OXB*

MEARS, Amelia Garland. b. Freshford, County Kilkenny but was taken to England at an early age. Daughter of John Garland, schoolmaster. In 1864 she married a Mr Mears, West Hartlepool merchant.
Idylls, legends and lyrics; by A. Garland Mears. London: Kegan Paul, Trench, Trübner, & Co. Ltd. 1890. viii, 279 pp.   *MPL*

MEDWIN, A. Of Folkstone, Kent.
The life and teaching of Jesus Christ, in verse, adapted to interest the young; and as an appendix, a selection from the parables, with their application; by A. Medwin. London: S.W. Partridge & Co. [1880]. 78 pp.
    Title from cover.   *OXB*

MEEK, Elizabeth. Mrs Meek. b. Manchester. Lived at 72 Deansgate c. 1842, then afterwards for many years at 141 Moss Lane East, Moss Side.
Poems; by Elizabeth Meek. Printed Farnworth: R. Cooke. 1895. [iv], 30 pp.
    Printed on one side of leaf only.   *MPL*

MEGAW, Arthur Stanley, (Arthur Stanley, pseud.) Possibly Arthur Stanley Megaw (–1961). Son of Robert Megaw of Holywood, County Down. Educated at Sullivan Upper School, Holywood, and Queen's University, Belfast. A solicitor, and silver medallist of Incorporated Law Society of Ireland. He was a frequent contributor to *The Times, Blackwood's Magazine*, etc. Lived latterly at Arden, Fortwilliam Drive, Belfast.
Poems; by Arthur Stanley. London: Digby & Long. 1889. [vi], 57 pp.   *OXB*

MELANCHOLY JACQUES, pseud. *see* **LENNARD, Horace**, (Melancholy Jacques, pseud.)

MELCA, Rue, pseud?
The work of the ocean, and other poems; by Rue Melca. London: London Literary Society. [1886]. viii, 103 pp.   *OXB*

MELLOR, J.
Day-dawn; Consolation and other poems; by J. Mellor. London: Elliot Stock. 1891. viii, 343 pp.   *OXB*

MEMBER OF THE DRESDEN "VICTORY" LODGE, pseud.
The banner of temperance: a collection of original verses; by a member of the Dresden "Victory" Lodge, I.O.G.T. Manchester: John Heywood. 1886. 94 pp.   *OXB*

MENNON, Robert (1797–1885). b. Ayton, Berwickshire. After a very elementary education he worked with his father, a slater, plasterer and glazier. In 1824 he sailed to London in a fishing boat. After twenty-five years in London he started business on his own account in Dunbar, East Lothian. He retired to the house of his birth at Ayton.
Poems: moral and religious; by Robert Mennon. Printed Edinburgh: A. Ritchie. [1885?]. xiv, 351 pp.   *OXB*

MEREDITH, George (1828–1909). b. Portsmouth, son of a tailor. Educated in Portsmouth and Southsea, and at a Moravian school in Germany. He was articled to a London solicitor in 1845 but soon turned to journalism. In 1849 he married Mary Ellen Nicolls, widowed daughter of Thomas Love Peacock, and settled in Weybridge, Surrey. He was co-editor of *The Monthly Observer*, 1848–49, contributed to *Chambers's Journal* and *Fraser's Magazine*, and was leader writer for the *Ipswich Journal* from 1860; literary adviser to publishers Chapman & Hall. Major novelist of the Victorian period.

Ballads and poems of tragic life; by George Meredith. London: Macmillan & Co. 1887. [vi], 160 pp. *OXB*

Also [2nd ed.] 1894.

Jump-to-glory Jane: a poem; by George Meredith. London. 1889. 15 pp.

Reprinted from *The Universal Review*, 15th October 1889. 'The present issue, privately printed for friends, consists of fifty copies only'. *OXB*

Jump to glory Jane; by George Meredith. Edited and arranged by Harry Quilter. With forty-four designs invented, drawn, and written by Laurence Housman. London: Swan, Sonnenschein & Co. 1892. 28, 36 p. il. *TCD*

Modern love: a reprint; to which is added, The sage enamoured and the honest lady; by George Meredith. London: Macmillan & Co. 1892. [viii], 108 pp. *MPL*

The nature poems of George Meredith. With 20 full-page pictures in photogravure and an etched frontispiece by William Hyde. Westminster: Archibald Constable & Co. 1898. [vii], 76 pp. il.

A limited ed. of 375 numbered copies. *TCD*

Also a limited ed. of 150 numbered copies signed by the artist.

Odes in contribution to the song of French history; by George Meredith. Westminster: Archibald Constable & Co. 1898. [viii], 94 pp. *MPL*

Poems; by George Meredith. Westminster: Archibald Constable & Co. 1898. 2 vols. il. *MPL*

Poems and lyrics of the joy of earth; by George Meredith. London: Macmillan & Co. 1883. x, 183 pp.

Cover-title is *Poems and lyrics*. *MPL*

Also [2nd ed.] 1883, 3rd ed. 1894.

Poems: The empty purse, with odes, To the comic spirit, to Youth in memory, and verses; by George Meredith. London: Macmillan & Co. 1892. [vi], 136 pp. *MPL*

A reading of earth: [poems]; by George Meredith. London: Macmillan & Co. 1888. vi, 136 pp. *MPL*

Selected poems; by George Meredith. Westminster: Archibald Constable & Co. 1897. viii, 246 pp. *MPL*

Selected poems of George Meredith. Westminster: Archibald Constable & Co. 1898. [viii], 204 pp. *OXB*

MEREDITH, Owen, pseud. *see* **BULWER-LYTTON, Edward Robert**, Lord Lytton, (Owen Meredith, pseud.)

MERIVALE, Herman Charles (1839–1906). b. Dawlish, Devon, son of Herman Merivale, Under-Secretary for India. Educated at Harrow School, and Balliol College, Oxford; BA 1861. Practised successfully as a barrister, leaving the law when his father died. He edited *The Annual Register*, 1870–80, and wrote regularly for *Pall Mall Gazette*. A playwright and novelist, he produced a succession of plays, farces and burlesques, all very popular. His health broke down, and in 1879 he published *My Experiences in a Lunatic Asylum*. He was financially ruined by a dishonest lawyer.

   Florien: a tragedy, in five acts, and other poems; by Herman Charles Merivale. London: Remington & Co. 1884. [viii], 163 pp.   *OXB*

   The white pilgrim, and other poems; by Herman Charles Merivale. London: Chapman & Hall, Ltd. 1883. xii, 255 pp.   *OXB*

MERRIN, Jack (1869–1931). b. London, son of Rev. William Merrin. Educated at King's College, London, and Christ's College, Cambridge. Worked for three years as an accountant in a Liverpool office. Ordained 1906; curate, Holy Trinity, Lee, Kent, 1895–1900, St Paul's, Cambridge, 1900–06, Stoke-next-Guildford, 1906–07; vicar, St Philip the Evangelist, Islington, 1907–12; curate, All Saints, Leyton, 1912–13, St John the Evangelist, Stratford, 1913–27; rural dean, West Ham, 1925–27; rector, Keighley, Yorkshire, 1927–31.

   Poems; by Jack Merrin. Liverpool: [Author]. 1892. 64 pp.   *OXB*

MERRYVALE, Walter

   Anita, and other poems; by Walter Merryvale. London: George Allen. 1899. viii, 155 pp.   *OXB*

METCALFE, Edward. Of Burnley, Lancashire?

   Verses; by Edward Metcalfe. London: Simpkin, Marshall, Hamilton, Kent & Co., Ltd; Burnley: Burghope & Strange. 1891. 41 pp. il.   *OXB*

METEMPSYCHOSIS: A VISION AFTER MIDNIGHT, [and other poems]. London: Longmans, Green, & Co. 1888. [vi], 79 pp.   *OXB*

MEW, Egan. Writer on china and porcelain.

   A London comedy, and other vanities: [poems]; by Egan Mew. With seven reproductions of pictures by Maurice Greiffenhagen. London: George Redway. 1897. 96 pp. il.

   Numbered copy, no mention if limited ed.   *OXB*

   Also [2nd ed.] 1899.

MEYNELL, Alice (1847–1922). b. Barnes, near London. Née Thompson, her father was a scholar, her mother a concert pianist. Most of her childhood was spent abroad, in Italy, France and Switzerland. In 1877 she married Wilfrid Meynell, author and journalist, by whom she had eight children. She wrote for various periodicals, including *The National Observer* and *Pall Mall Gazette*. Befriended and encouraged many writers, rescuing Francis Thompson from poverty. Latterly lived at Greatham, an estate in Pulborough, Sussex.

   Other poems; by Alice Meynell. [London]. 1896. 16 pp.

   Privately printed.   *OXB*

Poems; by Alice Meynell. London: Elkin Mathews & John Lane. 1893. xii, 76 pp.

A limited ed. of 550 copies. *MPL*

Also 2nd ed. 1893; [3rd ed] 1896; [4th ed.] 1896; [5th ed] 1897; [6th ed.] 1898.

MIALL, Arthur Bernard. Translator from European languages.

Nocturnes and pastorals: a book of verse; by A. Bernard Miall. London: Leonard Smithers. 1896. x, 110 pp. *OXB*

Poems; by A. Bernard Miall. London: John Lane, The Bodley Head. 1899. xvi, 175 pp. *UCD*

MICKLE, J.L. Of Edinburgh?

Poems; by J.L. Mickle. Printed Edinburgh. 1884. 126 pp. il.

For private circulation. *OXB*

MIDDLETON, Charles S. Biographer of Shelley. Lived at The Elms, Park Road, West Dulwich, London SE.

Life and immortality; by Charles S. Middleton. London: Cooper Bros. & Attwood. 1891. [ii], 48 pp. *OXB*

MIDDLETON, Eliza Maria, Lady *see* **WILLOUGHBY, Eliza Maria, Lady Middleton**

MIDDLETON, Frank Edward (1853–1909?). Educated at Shrewsbury School, and Clare College, Cambridge; BA 1876, MA 1898. Instructor, HMS *Britannia*, 1876. Ordained 1877; curate, Townstal, Dartmouth, Devon, 1876–77, St Philip's, Heigham, Norwich, 1877–78; rector, Haynford, Norfolk, 1878–87. Principal, C.M. Preparatory Institute, London, 1887–1907. Lived latterly at Blackheath Hill, London SE.

Found: or, lays of grace for pilgrims Zionward; by Frank Edward Middleton. London: James Nisbet & Co. [1883]. 80 pp. *OXB*

Herbert Pelham: or, faithful unto death: a memoir in verse; by Frank Edward Middleton. London: Jarrold & Sons. [1882]. 58 pp. *OXB*

MIDWINTER, Miles

Hours of insight: [poems]; by Miles Midwinter. London: Griffith, Farran, Okeden & Welsh. 1891. viii, 139 pp. *OXB*

MILBURN, Robert Gordon (1870–). b. Tulse Hill, Surrey, son of Robert Milburn. Educated at Tonbridge School, and Trinity College, Oxford; BA 1893, MA 1897. Ordained 1897; lecturer in philosophy, Bishop's College, Calcutta, 1901–06, and vice-principal, 1902. Lived latterly at Durris, Stubbs Wood, Chesham Bois, Buckinghamshire.

Verses; by R.G. Milburn. Oxford: B.H. Blackwell. 1898. 29 pp. *UCD*

MILDMAY, Sir Aubrey Neville St. John, (Autremonde, pseud.) (1865–1955). b. Long Marson, Yorkshire, son of Rev. Charles A. Mildmay, rector of Denton, Norfolk. Educated at Winchester College, and New College, Oxford (scholar); BA 1888, MA 1895. Trained for the ministry at Wells Theological College; curate, Witney, Oxfordshire, 1893–95, St Andrews, Fife, 1895–97, Berkeley Chapel, Mayfair, London, 1898–99. Headmaster, Vernon Church of England College, New Westminster, British Columbia, Canada, 1905–06; vicar, Penticton, 1906–07. Lecturer in classics, University of British Columbia, 1917–24. Lived latterly at Little Manor, Ringmere, Lewes, Sussex.

Poetical works of Autremonde; with, The leaven of Hamelin: a drama of 1990 [sic]. Edinburgh: St. Giles' Printing Co.; London: Elliot Stock. 1896. vi, 172 pp.   *OXB*

Vignettes; by Aubrey N. St. John Mildmay. London: Elliot Stock. [1895]. viii, 90 pp. por.

Poetry and prose.   *OXB*

MILES' BOY, pseud. Possibly Edward Jesty of Exeter, Devon.

The maid of the mountain, and other poems; by "Miles' Boy". Printed Exeter: H. Leduc. 1885. [iv], 128 pp.   *OXB*

MILLER, Charles (1812?–91). b. Thornliebank, Renfrewshire. He studied art at Glasgow University, and theology in the Hall of the United Secession Church. Ordained in 1841, becoming minister at Dunse, Berwickshire.

The three scholars, and other poems; by Charles Miller. Edinburgh: Andrew Elliot. 1882. 118 pp.   *OXB*

MILLER, Walter J. Writer on Anglican Church history.

St. Kilda: the Arcadia of the Hebrides, and psalms of life: [poems]; by Walter J. Miller. London: Elliot Stock. 1898. vi, 94 pp.   *OXB*

MILLICAN, Kenneth William, (M.K.) (1853–19). b. Leicester, son of William Millican, JP. Educated at Atherstone Grammar School, Warwickshire, and Cambridge University; BA. Trained for a medical career at St Mary's Hospital, London; MRCS, LRCP. Served as Captain, 9th Battalion, King's Royal Rifle Corps. Medical officer in Mexico and California, remaining in the United States as sub-editor of *Lancet*. He specialized in the history of medicine, medical sociology, and economics.

Passion spray; [poems]; by M.K. Printed Leicester: W.H Lead. 1889. [32] pp.   *BL*

MILLIKEN, Edwin James (1839?–97). b. Ireland. He started work as a businessman for a large engineering firm. Became a journalist in London, on staff of *Figaro*, 1870, *Punch*, 1874–97. A satirical humorist, he invented the London cockney character 'Arry', and suggested subjects for many of the weekly cartoons.

" 'Arry" ballads from Punch; by E.J. Milliken. Embellished with 105 pictures from "Mr. Punch's" gallery. London: Bradbury, Agnew, & Co. Ld. [1892]. 80 pp. il. *OXB*

Childe Chappie's pilgrimage; by E.J. Milliken. Illustrated by E.J. Wheeler. London: Bradbury, Agnew, & Co. 1883. [iv], 68 pp. il. *OXB*

How's that?: including "A century of Grace"; by Harry Furniss; Verses; by E.J. Milliken; and, Cricket sketches; by E.B.V. Christian. Bristol: J.W. Arrowsmith; London: Simpkin, Marshall, Hamilton, Kent & Co. Ltd. [1896]. 163 pp. *OXB*

MILLS, Edmund James (1840–1921). b. London, son of Charles F. Mills. Educated at Cheltenham Grammar School, and Royal School of Mines. Assistant to chemistry tutor, Glasgow University, 1861; chemistry tutor, 1862–65; for seven years in charge of Sir Charles Taylor's private laboratory; professor of technical chemistry, 1875; FRS, FCS. Lived latterly at 64 Twyford Avenue, West Acton, London W.

My only child: poems in her memory; by Edmund James Mills. Westminster: Archibald Constable. 1895. xvi, 144 pp. *OXB*

MILLS, John (1821–96). b. Ashton-under-Lyne, Lancashire, son of James Mills. Started work as a clerk in the Ashton branch of Manchester & Liverpool District Bank; appointed bank manager, Nantwich, Cheshire, 1852, and Bowdon, 1864. He devised a scheme for a new bank called the Lancashire & Yorkshire Bank, which opened in Manchester in 1872; he was general manager until 1889 then became a director. An authority on statistics, finance and banking. Involved with Professor W.B. Hodgson of Edinburgh with projects in educational reform. Lived at Northwold, Bowdon.

Vox humana: poems; by John Mills. With portraits. London: T. Fisher Unwin. 1897. xii, 95 pp. por. *MPL*

MILLS, John S. (1829–). b. Dundee, Angus. Writer, accountant, and messenger-at-arms.

Joseph o'Coble Den: a poem in six cantos; by John Mills. Dundee: Author. 1880. 90 pp. *BL*

Poems and memorial verses: or, selections from my scrapbook; by J.S. Mills. Printed Dundee: John Leng. 1880. 64 pp. *NLS*

MILLS, John Saxon. Journalist and writer on a variety of topics; on editorial staff of *Daily News*; editor of *Cape Times*. During the First World War he worked for the Ministry of Information.

Fasciculus versiculorum; by J. Saxon Mills. London: Swan Sonnenschein & Co. 1895. 80 pp. *OXB*

MILLS, John William (1846–94). Son of Rev. John Mills, rector of Orton-Waterville, Huntingdonshire. Educated at Marlborough College, and Pembroke College, Cambridge; Seatonian prizewinner, 1877. Curate, St Mary's, Bury St Edmunds, 1869–71; rector, St Lawrence's, Newland, Essex, 1872–89, St George's, Birmingham, 1889–94; Holy Trinity, Hull, Yorkshire, 1894.

After-glow: poems and sermons; by J.W. Mills. Edited by F.S. Webster. With preface by H.C.G. Moule. Birmingham: Midland Educational Co., Ltd; London: Simpkin, Marshall & Co. [1896]. xxxii, 178 pp. por., facsim.   *OXB*

MILNE, R. Schofield- *see* **SCHOFIELD-MILNE, R.**

MILNE, William
   Thoughts in rhyme and prose, relating chiefly to subjects ethical, historical, social, and philosophical; by William Milne. Edinburgh: William P. Nimmo & Co. 1880. 221 pp.   *OXB*

MILNER, Edith. Novelist, and writer on the Lumley family.
   The year's jewels: a greeting; [poems]; by Edith Milner. [York]. [1896]. [25] pp. Loose-leaf, held by ribbon. Printed on one side of leaf only.   *OXB*

MILNER, George (1829–1914). b. Manchester. Early in his career he was employed in a bookseller's shop. Taught at Bennett Street Sunday School. Edited the magazine *Odds and Ends* for over fifty years. MA, JP, and hon. Freeman of the City of Manchester. President of Manchester Literary Club from 1880 until his death.
   From dawn to dusk: a book of verses; by George Milner. Manchester: J.E. Cornish. 1896. xii, 175 p.   *JRL*

MILNES, Robert Offley Ashburton, Lord Houghton (1858–1945). Son of 1st Baron Houghton. Educated at Harrow School, and Trinity College, Cambridge. Private secretary to the Secretary for Foreign Affairs, 1883–84. Lord-in-waiting to Queen Victoria, 1886. He married the daughter of Lord Rosebery. Viceroy of Ireland, 1892–95. Earl of Crewe, 1895, marquis, 1911. Held cabinet rank, 1905–16. British ambassador in Paris, 1922–28.
   Stray verses, 1889–1890; by Robert Lord Houghton. London: John Murray. 1891. x, 115 pp.   *JRL*
   Also 2nd ed. 1893.

MINCHIN, George Minchin (18 –1914). Professor of applied mathematics, Royal Indian Engineering College, Cooper's Hill. Author of various scientific works. Lived in retirement at 149 Banbury Road, Oxford.
   Naturae veritas; by George M. Minchin. London: Macmillan & Co. 1887. 67 pp.
   Poetry and prose.   *OXB*

MISCELLANEOUS POEMS. Printed Lichfield: F.W. Meacham. 1882. iv, 112 pp.   *BL*

MISERRIMA: A NARRATIVE POEM OF THE PRESENT DAY.
London: Griffith, Farran, Okeden, & Welsh. 1890. [iv], 94 pp.   *OXB*

The MISLAID GOSPEL: A POEM, WITH NOTES AND REFER-ENCES; AND, THE WITNESSES AT JERUSALEM. London: Williams & Norgate. 1899. 47 pp. *OXB*

MITCHELL, Anthony (1868–1920). b. Aberdeen, son of John Mitchell, merchant. Educated at Aberdeen Grammar School, and Aberdeen University; MA 1890, BD 1903, DD 1912. Curate, St Mary's Cathedral, Edinburgh, 1892–93, St John's, Dumfries, 1893–95; rector, St Andrew's, Glasgow, 1895–1902; diocesan missioner of Glasgow and Galloway, 1902–04; rector, St Mark's, Portobello, 1904–05. Principal and professor of theology, Episcopal Theological College, Edinburgh, 1905–12. Bishop of Aberdeen & Orkney, 1912–17.

Tatters from a student's gown: [poems]; by Anthony Mitchell. Aberdeen: James G. Bisset. 1890. viii, 56 pp. *OXB*

MITCHELL, Thomas

Verses and sketches; by Thomas Mitchell. Edited by Charles Irvine. Printed Edinburgh: W.H. White & Co. Ltd. 1899. viii, 80 pp.

Printed for private circulation. *NLS*

MITCHELL, William. Lived at 18 Kew Terrace, Glasgow.

The crucifixion, the resurrection, the forty days and the ascension; by William Mitchell. With prefatory note by James Stalker. Glasgow: David Bryce & Son. 1892. [iv], 124 pp. *★UCD*

Also 2nd ed. 1892; 3rd ed. 1892; 4th ed. 1892.

The story of the crucifixion, the resurrection, the forty days and the ascension; by William Mitchell. Glasgow: William Collins, Sons & Co. Ltd; Glasgow: D. Bryce & Son. [1889?]. 66 pp. *★UCD*

Also Revised ed. 1890.

MITFORD, Bertram (1855–1914). Son of E.L.O. Mitford of Mitford Castle, Northumberland, and Hunmanby Hall, Yorkshire. He had a varied career, and made many sea voyages throughout the world. From 1873 he lived in South Africa, working for the Cape Civil Service. A novelist, his novels often had an African background.

Our arms in Zululand: being the three great battles of the Zulu War, in verse; together with, The death of the Prince Imperial; by Bertram Mitford. London: Griffith & Farran; New York: E.P. Dutton & Co. 1882. 78 pp. *OXB*

MOCATTA, Percy G. Song writer and muscial composer.

A legend of Florence, and other poems; by Percy G. Mocatta. London: Simpkin, Marshall & Co. Ltd. 1893. 31 pp. *OXB*

MODERN HOMER *see* **ROWBOTHAM, John Frederick**

MODERN UMAR KHAYAM, pseud.
An old philosophy in 101 quatrains; by the modern Umar Khayam. Ormskirk: T. Hutton. 1899. 20 pp.   OXB

MODYM, pseud.
Poems; by Modym. London: Wyman & Sons. 1882. 70 pp.   OXB

MOFFAT, Douglas (1844–   ). Son of Major James D. Moffat of Cawnpore, India. Educated at Christ Church, Oxford; BA 1866, MA 1869, BCL 1873. Called to the Bar, Middle Temple, 1875. He married Lilian E. Edwards of Calcutta in 1881. Lived at Harperton and Edenhall, Roxburghshire.
Crickety cricket; [poems]; by Douglas Moffat. With illustrations by the author, and frontispiece by Sir Frank Lockwood. London: Longmans, Green, & Co. 1897. 112 pp. il.   OXB
     Also 2nd ed. 1898.
Douglas; by Douglas Moffat. Aberdeen: John Avery & Co. 1884. [iv], 222 pp.   OXB

MOI-MEME, pseud. *see* **COVENTRY, Mary**, (Moi-Même, pseud.)

MOIR, Ellen Beatrice (18 –99). b. Gainsborough, Lincolnshire. She engaged in church mission work in the poor districts of Cowcaddens and Port Dundas, Glasgow. In 1896 she married Rev. F.C. Moir, rector of St Mary's, Port Glasgow. Died at Dumfries.
In memoriam Ellen Beatrice Moir. Printed Glasgow: Robert & James Maclehose, Glasgow University Press. [1899]. 71 pp. por.
     Poetry and prose.   OXB

MOLLOY, Joseph Fitzgerald, (Ernest Wilding, pseud.) (1858–1908). b. New Ross, County Wexford, son of Pierce Molloy. Educated at St Kieran's College, Kilkenny. Originally intended for the Roman Catholic priesthood, he became a novelist and writer of historical and biographical studies. He moved to London in 1878, spending winters abroad on account of poor health. Lived at 20 Norland Square, Notting Hill, London W.
Songs of passion and pain; by Ernest Wilding. London: Newman & Co. 1881. iv, 100 pp.   BL

MONCKTON-ARUNDELL, Vere, Lady Galway. Only daughter of Ellis Gosling of Busbridge Hall, Godalming, Surrey. In 1879 she married George E.M. Monckton-Arundell, 7th Viscount Galway. Lived at 1 Rutland Gardens, London SW, and Serlby Hall, Bawtry, Nottinghamshire.
The creed of love, and other poems; by Vere Viscountess Galway. Printed London: Hatchard. 1895. [vi], 72 pp.
     Privately printed.   OXB

MONEY-COUTTS, Francis Burdett (1852–1923). b. London, son of Rev. James D. Money. Educated at Eton College, and Trinity College, Cambridge; BA 1875. Student of Inner Temple, called to the Bar, 1879. He assumed the name Coutts by virtue of royal licence, 1882, granted to his mother under the will of the Duchess of St Albans. JP for Surrey. Lived at Ancote, Weybridge.

The Alhambra, and other poems; by F.B. Money-Coutts. London: John Lane, The Bodley Head. 1898. viii, 84 pp. *OXB*

Poems; by F.B. Money-Coutts. London: John Lane, The Bodley Head; New York: George H. Richmond & Co. 1896. xii, 96 pp. *OXB*

The revelation of St. Love the divine; by F.B. Money Coutts. London: John Lane, The Bodley Head. 1898. [iv], 111 pp. *OXB*

MONKHOUSE, Cosmo (1840–1901). b. London, son of a solicitor. Educated at St Paul's School. Started work for the Board of Trade, eventually becoming assistant secretary, finance department. Known principally as an art critic, he wrote several books on art and artists.

The Christ upon the hill: a ballad; by Cosmo Monkhouse. Etched by W. Strang. London: Smith, Elder & Co. 1895. [iv], 21 pp. il.

A limited ed. of 250 numbered copies, 50 of which are signed by the artist. *BL*

Corn and poppies: [poems]; by Cosmo Monkhouse. London: Elkin Mathews. 1890. xii, 162 pp.

A limited ed. of 350 copies. *MPL*

MONKMAN, Thomas Jefferson (1844–). b. Hull, Yorkshire. Educated at a private school in the town, and at Boston Spa College. He worked several years in the office of a firm of corn merchants, later holding a responsible post with Aire & Calder Navigation at Hull. Contributed to many local journals. Member of Hull Literary Club.

Lyrics: marine and rural; by Thomas Jefferson Monkman. London: Simpkin, Marshall & Co.; Hull: A. Brown & Sons. 1885. [vi], 112 pp. *OXB*

MONTAGU-DOUGLAS-SCOTT, Charles Henry

Fireside fancies, and other occasional verses; by Charles H. Montagu-Douglas-Scott. Printed London: Samuel Chick & Co. 1897. 160 pp.

Printed for private circulation. *JRL*

Odds and ends: [poems]; by Charles H. Montagu-Douglas-Scott. Second series. Printed London: S. Chick & Co. 1899. [ii], 148 pp.

Printed for private circulation. *JRL*

MONTEFIORE, Dora B. Daughter of Francis and Mary Ann Fuller of Kenley Manor, Surrey. Her father was master of Surrey Foxhounds. In 1879 she maried George B. Montefiore. Suffragist and social worker, she was a member of the Women's Social and Political Union, working closely with Elizabeth Wolstenholme-Elmy; became involved in the international movement for women's suffrage, travelling world-wide to speak for the cause. In 1906 she was sent to Holloway Gaol for demonstrating at the House of Commons.

"Singings through the dark": poems; by Dora B. Montefiore. London: Sampson Low, Marston & Co. 1898. viii, 76 pp.   *BL*

MONTGOMERY, John Wilson (1835?–1911). b. Billis, County Cavan, son of a farmer. Originally in the police force, he was appointed master of the workhouse at Bailieborough, County Cavan. Known as 'The Sweet Bard of Bailieborough'.
Fireside lyrics; by J.W. Montgomery. Printed Downpatrick: "Down Recorder" Office. 1887. viii, 85 pp.   *OXB*

MOON, Anna Maria. Née Elsdale, grand-daughter of Rev. William Leeves, composer. In 1866 she became the second wife of William Moon, inventor of an embossed type for the blind. Lived at 104 Queen's Road, Brighton, Sussex.
Stray thoughts in verse, written principally in early years; [by Anna Maria Moon]. London: S.W. Partridge. [1882]. 64 pp. il.   *MPL*

MOON, George Washington (1823–1909). b. London. Educated at a private school at Barnet. Critic, theologian, antiquarian and inventor. FRSL. Lived at 7 Prince's Terrace, Sussex Square, Brighton, Sussex, and at 16 New Burlington Street, London W.
Elijah the prophet, and other sacred poems; by George Washington Moon. 4th ed. London: Longmans, Green, & Co. 1896. xxii, 263 pp. il.   *OXB*
Elijah the prophet, and other sacred poems; by George Washington Moon. 5th ed., with an appendix of additional poems now first published. London: Longmans, Green, & Co. 1899. xxiv, 352 pp. il.   *TCD*
Poems of love and home; by George Washington Moon. London: Longmans, Green, & Co. 1899. xvi, 267 pp. por.
Poetry and prose.   *OXB*

MOON, John. Secretary of the Working Men's Christian Association for fifteen years. Lived at Maygrove Road, Kilburn Rise, London NW.
Poems: sacred and secular, on a variety of subjects, but chiefly upon lectures delivered to the Working Men's Christian Association (formerly called the 'Operatives'), at Church Street, Portman Market, and the Omega Hall, Omega Place; by John Moon. London: W. Poole [1882]. 227 pp.   *OXB*

MOORE, Mrs Bloomfield *see* **MOORE, Clara Jessup**

MOORE, Cecil (1851–85). b. Camberwell, Surrey, son of Rev. Daniel Moore. Educated at St Paul's School, and Exeter College, Oxford; BA 1874, MA 1877. Ordained 1876; curate, St Marylebone, London, 1875–77, St Mark's, St John's Wood, 1877–79, St John's, Paddington, 1879–83. Died at Tunbridge Wells, Kent.
Saint Louis, and other poems; by Cecil Moore. London: Hatchards. 1882. [10], xii, 94 pp. por.   *OXB*

MOORE, Charles Robert (1844?–). Son of John W. Moore of Hordley, Shropshire. Educated at Eton College, and Corpus Christi College, Oxford (scholar); BA 1868, MA 1870. Master at Radley College.

  The martyrdom of St. Stephen: Oxford University prize poem on a sacred subject, 1890; by Charles R. Moore. [Oxford]. [1890]. 15 pp. *OXB*

MOORE, Clara Jessup (1824–). b. Philadelphia, Pennsylvania, daughter of Augustus E. Jessup, scientist. Educated at New Haven, Connecticut. In 1842 she married Bloomfield H. Moore of Philadelphia. Her husband died in 1878, after which she became resident in England. Friend of Robert Browning.

  Gondaline's lesson; The warden's tale; Stories for children, and other poems; by Mrs Bloomfield Moore. London: C. Kegan Paul. 1881. x, 226 pp. *OXB*

  Poems; A chapter from the modern pilgrim's progress; Slander and gossip (compiled); [by Clara Jessup Moore]. 1882. 105 pp.
  Printed for private circulation. *BL*

  The warden's tale; San Moritz; The Magdalene, and other poems, new and old; by Mrs. Bloomfield Moore. London: Remington & Co. 1883. viii, 131 pp. *OXB*

MOORE, Dugald. MB.

  Nightshade and poppies: verses of a country doctor; by Dugald Moore. London: John Long. 1898. 94 pp. *OXB*

MOORE, George (1852–1933). Son of G.H. Moore, MP and County Mayo landowner. He was brought up in Ireland but educated at Oscott College, Birmingham. Novelist, playwright, and art critic, he lived in London, 1880–1901, in Dublin, 1901–11, and at 121 Ebury Street, London, 1911–33. His later career has been associated with the Celtic revival. In 1903 he renounced the Roman Catholic faith, mainly on Celtic-national grounds.

  Pagan poems; by George Moore. London: Newman & Co. 1881. iv, 164 pp. *OXB*

MOORE, Jane (1828–1916?). b. Stalybridge, Cheshire, daughter of Iorweth Davis, parson then printer of Stalybridge, who was also a town councillor. She married a Mr Moore, going with him to Bolton, Lancashire, on his appointment to a position with Tootal, Broadhurst & Lee's mills. Lived at 15 View Street, Bolton-le-Moors. In 1897 went to live in the Fylde district before returning to Stalybridge.

  Stayleybridge [sic] "in ye olden time", &c., &c.,: [poems]; by Jane Moore. Manchester: John Heywood. 1888. 32 pp. *BL*

  Wild flowers of song: a miscellaneous collection of songs and poems; by Jane Moore. Manchester: John Heywod. 1880. 128 pp. *UCD*

MOORE, John Morris- *see* **MORRIS-MOORE, John**

MOORE, Thomas Sturge (1870–1944). b. Hastings, Sussex, brother of G.E. Moore, philosopher. Educated at Dulwich College, and at art schools in London. Wood-engraver, illustrator, and art historian, he was a friend of W.B. Yeats.

The vinedresser, and other poems; by T. Sturge Moore. London: At the Sign of the Unicorn. 1899. [vii], 86 pp.   *UCD*

MOORE, William (1843–1913). b. Hordley, Shropshire, son of Rev. John W. Moore, rector. Educated at Winchester College, and New College, Oxford; BA 1866, MA 1870. Fellow of Magdalen College, 1872–79; lecturer, St John's College, 1875–77. Rector, Appleton, Berkshire, from 1878.

A harp from the willows: [poems]; by W. Moore. London: James Parker & Co. 1895. xii, 152 pp.   *UCD*

Lost chords: [poems]; by W. Moore. London: Parker & Co. 1889. iv, 171 pp.   *OXB*

Nocturnes, and other poems; by W. Moore. London: Elliot Stock. 1898. [vi], 85 pp.   *UCD*

Venta, and other poems; by [William Moore]. London: D. Nutt. 1882. [viii], 133 pp.   *UCD*

MOORHOUSE, Matthew Butterworth (1841?–   ). Son of Joshua Moorhouse of Holmfirth, Yorkshire. Educated at Queen's College, Oxford; BA 1862, MA 1864. Ordained 1864; curate, Tintwistle, Cheshire, 1863–68; perpetual curate, Hepworth, Yorkshire, 1866–71; vicar, Bushbury, Staffordshire, 1872–80, St Mary Bredin's Canterbury, 1880–88, St Luke's, South Lyncombe, Bath, from 1888.

Stories in verse, by land and sea, from legendary and other sources; by M.B. Moorhouse. Canterbury: J.A. Jennings. 1898. 284 pp.   *OXB*

MOORSOM, Robert Maude (1831?–1911). b. Cosgrove, Northamptonshire, son of Captain (later Vice-Admiral) Constantine R. Moorsom. Educated at King Edward's School, Birmingham, and Trinity College, Cambridge; BA 1854, MA 1858. Ordained 1859; curate, Poulton-le-Fylde, Lancashire, 1857–59, Barnham Broom, Norfolk, 1861; rector, Sadberge, County Durham, 1861–81. Wrote *Historical Guide to Hymns Ancient and Modern*.

The beacon-fire at Sadberge, County Durham, on jubilee night, 20 June, 1887; by Robert Maude Moorsom. London: Simpkin, Marshall, & Co.; Darlington: Bailey & Co. [1887]. 16 pp.   *OXB*

MORANT, Amy Constance. Daughter of Edwin Cracknell. In 1896 she married Robert L. Morant, a senior civil servant, knighted in 1907. Lived at 14 Thurloe Square, London SW, then at 15 Chester Terrace, Eaton Square.

Carina songs, and others; by Amy C. Morant. Westminster: Roxburghe Press. [1895]. 174 p.   *OXB*

The MORE EXCELLENT WAY: A POEM. London: Macmillan & Co. 1883. [viii], 72 pp.   *OXB*

MORELAND, Mary Norwood (1862–87). Of County Down.
Poems: by Mary Norwood Moreland. Oxford: B.H. Blackwell. 1888. [ii], 291 pp. *OXB*

MOREY, H. Served as Quartermaster Sergeant, 2nd Battalion, Royal Irish Rifles.
Rhymes from the ranks; by H. Morey. Chatham: Gale & Polden. [1888]. 98 pp. *OXB*

MORGAN, Arthur Middlemore (1831–97). b. Catherington, Hampshire, son of Francis Morgan of the Bengal Civil Service. Educated at Charterhouse, and Exeter College, Oxford; BA 1854, MA 1857. Ordained 1857; curate, Lewknor, Oxfordshire, 1856–57, Great Milton, Oxfordshire, 1858–61, Long Compton, Warwickshire, 1862–63, Swanmore, Isle of Wight, 1864–66, Newland, Worcestershire, 1868–71, Monk-Okehampton, Devon, 1871–72; rector, Huish, Devon, 1872–84; vicar, Mucking, Stanford-le-Hope, Essex, 1884–97.
Inter flumina: verses written among rivers; [by A.M. Morgan]. Oxford: Parker & Co. 1883. [viii], 114 pp. *MPL*
Also new ed. 1885.

MORGAN, Elijah. Of Clutton, Bristol.
Jubilee celebration of the Queen's reign, 1837–1887: echoes from Welsh harps: an epic poem; by Elijah Morgan. Printed Paulton: C.D. Purnell & Sons. [1887]. 32 pp. *BL*

MORGAN, John. Educated at New College, London. Of St Leonards, Sussex.
"Fairlight Glen", "Lovers' seat", and other poems; by J. Morgan. Printed Hastings: Burfield & Pennells. 1898. 51 pp. il., por. *BL*
Hastings by camera and in canto: or, pictures and poems, commemorative of the locality; by John Morgan. Printed Hastings: Burfield & Pennells. 1897. 93 pp. il
Published for the author. *OXB*

MORGAN, John (1827–1903). b. Newport, Pembrokeshire. Ordained 1851; curate, Cwmavon, Glamorganshire, 1850–52; vicar, Pontnewynydd, 1852–75; rector, Llanilid with Llanharan, from 1875. Author of *The Church in Wales*, 1884.
My Welsh home: a poem; by John Morgan. London: Elliot Stock. 1889. [iv], 95 pp. *OXB*
A trip to fairyland: or, happy wedlock, with other poetical pieces; by John Morgan. London: Elliot Stock. 1896. [vi], 95 pp. *OXB*

MORGAN, Rhys D., (Osric, pseud.) Of Cardiff.
An epic poem on Sir Nicholas Kemeys, the captor and defender of Chepstow Castle; [by Osric]. Printed Cardiff: South Wales Printing Works. 1881. [2], iv, 60 pp.
In English and Welsh. Cover-title is *The Welsh royalists*. *BL*

MORISON, Jeanie. Daughter of Rev. James Buchanan, professor of systematic theology, New College, Edinburgh, and his wife Mary Morison. She was married twice, first to Major William R. Campbell of Ballochyle, then to Hugh Miller of the Geological Survey. An occasional contributor in prose and verse to the *Sunday Magazine, Family Treasury*, etc.

Aaolus: a romance in lyrics; by Jeanie Morison. Edinburgh: William Blackwood & Sons. 1892. [viii], 108 pp. *OXB*

Doorside ditties; by Jeanie Morison. Edinbugh: William Blackwood & Sons. 1893. [vi], 80 pp. il. *OXB*

Gordon: an our-day idyll; by Jeanie Morison. London: Kegan Paul, Trench & Co. 1889. x, 127 p. *OXB*

Of "Fifine at the fair", "Christmas eve and Easter-day", and other of Mr Browning's poems; by Jeanie Morison. Edinburgh: William Blackwood & Sons. 1892. [viii], 99 pp. *OXB*

The purpose of the ages; by Jeanie Morison. With preface by A.H. Sayce. London: Macmillan & Co. 1887. xiv, 384 pp. *OXB*

Rifts in the reek; [poems]; by Jeanie Morison. Edinburgh: William Blackwod & Sons. 1898. [viii], 323 pp. il. *BL*

Sabbath songs and sonnets; and, By-way ballads; by Jeanie Morison. Edinburgh: William Blackwood & Sons. 1899. x, 157 pp. *OXB*

Saint Isadora, and other poems; by Jeanie Morison. Edinburgh: Bell & Bradfute; London: Simpkin, Marshall & Co. 1885. 82 pp. *OXB*

Selections from the poems of Jeanie Morison. Edinburgh: William Blackwood & Sons. 1890. x, 204 pp. *BL*

There as here: hints and glimpses of the unseen: [poems]; by Jeanie Morison. Edinburgh: William Blackwood & Sons. 1891. x, 100 pp. *OXB*

MORISON, Walter. DD. Presbyterian minister.

Through the postern: poems; by Walter Morison. Glasgow: James Maclehose. 1891. xii, 148 pp. *OXB*

MORITURI TE SALUTANT: METRICAL MONOLOGUES AND LEGENDS. London: George Allen. 1892. [viii], 143 pp. *OXB*

MORLEY, Charles David (1858–). b. Beverley, Yorkshire. Educated there at St Mary's School. A schoolmaster, he held appoointments at various schools in Yorkshire, Derbyshire, and Brighton, Sussex.

Aglaia unveiled: a poetical romaunt, and miscellaneous verses; by Charles D. Morley. With an original imaginative frontispiece, engraved by George Meek, and drawn by the author. London: E.W. Allen. 1883. [viii], 104 pp. il. *OXB*

The MORN THAT COMETH: OR EARTH'S RENOVATION. London: J.S. Virtue & Co., Ltd. 1882. xiv, 174 pp.
Published for the author. *OXB*

MORRAH, Herbert Arthur (1870–1939). b. Winchester, Hampshire, son of James A. Morrah, Colonel, 60th Rifles. Educated at Highgate School, and St John's College, Oxford; President of the Oxford Union, 1894. Editor of *The Literary Year Book* and other publications; an occasional contributor to magazines and reviews. Lieutenant, RNVR, Admiralty (War Staff), 1914–19.
In college groves, and other Oxford verses, chiefly reprinted from the Oxford Magazine; by H.A. Morrah. Oxford: Alden & Co. Ltd; London: Simpkin, Marshall, Hamilton, Kent & Co., Ltd. 1894. xiv, 102 pp. *OXB*

MORRIS, Alfred. Educated at St Mark's School, Holloway, London.
Passing thoughts, in verse; by Alfred Morris. London: T. Fisher Unwin. 1896. 152 pp. *OXB*

MORRIS, Charles. Captain Morris of Nice, France.
Rhymes and recitations; by Captain Morris. London: Mitchell & Hughes. 1885. iv, 36 pp. *OXB*

MORRIS, Edith
Hours of meditation: [poems]; by Edith Morris. London: Simpkin, Marshall, Hamilton, Kent & Co., Ltd; Longton: Hughes & Harber. 1890. [xiv], 129 pp. *BL*

MORRIS, Harrison Smith. Writer on Walt Whitman.
Madonna, and other poems; written by Harrison S. Morris. London: J.M. Dent & Co. 1895. 231 pp. il.
A limited ed. of 750 copies printed for America and England. *OXB*

MORRIS, Sir Lewis (1833–1907). b. Carmarthen. Educated at Sherborne School, and Jesus College, Oxford. Called to the Bar, Lincoln's Inn, 1861; practised as a conveyancer, 1861–81. He subsequently devoted himself to local work in Wales in connection with education and politics but failed as a Liberal candidate to gain a Welsh seat in Parliament. Actively supported the establishment of the University of Wales. He was knighted in 1895.
Idylls and lyrics; by Sir Lewis Morris. London: Osgood, McIlvaine & Co. 1896. vi, 152 pp. *MPL*
Also 2nd ed. 1896; 3rd ed. 1896.
The Lewis Morris birthday book: [poems]. Edited by S.S. Copeman. London: Kegan Paul, Trench & Co. 1884. [iv], 278 pp. il. *BL*
Love and sleep, and other poems; by Lewis Morris. With designs by Alice Havers and Harriett M. Bennett. London: C.W. Faulkner & Co.; New York: Cassell Publishing Co. [1893]. [46] pp. il.
Printed on card. *TCD*
Odatis: an old love-tale: a poem; by Lewis Morris. Illustrated by Alice Havers and G.P. Jacomb Hood. London: Hildesheimer & Faulkner. [1892]. [19] pp. il.
Printed on card. *TCD*
The ode of life: [poems]; by [Lewis Morris]. London: C. Kegan Paul & Co. 1880. [viii], 144 pp. *MPL*
Also 2nd ed. 1880; 3rd ed. 1880.

The poetical works of Lewis Morris. London: Kegan Paul, Trench & Co. 1882–89. 5 vols. por. *BL*

Recitation books for schools: a selecton from the poems of Sir Lewis Morris. London: Kegan Paul, Trench, Trübner & Co., Ltd. 1898. 9 vols. *BL*

Selections from the works of Sir Lewis Morris: [poems]. London: Kegan Paul, Trench, Trübner & Co., Ltd. 1897. xii, 371 pp. por. *OXB*

Songs of Britain; by Lewis Morris. London: Kegan Paul, Trench & Co. 1887. viii, 182 pp. *MPL*

    Also 2nd ed. 1887.

Songs unsung; by Lewis Morris. London: Kegan Paul, Trench & Co. 1883. viii, 208 pp. *MPL*

    Also 2nd ed. 1883; 3rd ed. 1884; 4th ed. 1884.

Songs without notes; by Lewis Morris. London: Kegan Paul, Trench, Trübner & Co., Ltd. 1894. x, 169 pp. *MPL*

Songs without notes; by Lewis Morris. 2nd ed. London: Osgood, McIlvaine & Co. 1895. x, 194 pp. *BL*

A vision of saints; [poems]; by Lewis Morris. London: Kegan Paul, Trench, Trübner & Co., Ltd. 1890. [2], vi, 304 pp. *MPL*

A vision of saints; by Lewis Morris. With twenty plates in typogravure, after works by the old masters and contemporary portraits. London: Cassell & Co., Ltd. 1892. xii, 256 pp. il., por. *BL*

The works of Lewis Morris: [poems]. London: Kegan Paul, Trench, Trübner & Co., Ltd. 1890. viii, 500 pp. por. *OXB*

The works of Sir Lewis Morris. London: Kegan Paul, Trench, Trübner & Co., Ltd. 1898. viii, 699 pp. por. *MPL*

MORRIS, William (1834–96). b. Walthamstow, London, son of a broker in the City. Educated at Marlborough College, and Exeter College, Oxford, where he became a friend of Edward Burne-Jones. On the staff of the architect G.E. Street but left to become a practising painter. A man of great energy and talent, he established the firm of Morris, Marshall, Faulkner & Co. in London, 1861–74, subsequently Morris & Co., 1874–96, to promote good design and craftsmanship. Founder, Kelmscott Press, 1890–96. Founder member of the Socialist League, and editor of its journal *Commonweal*.

Chants for socialists; by William Morris. London: Socialist League Office. 1885. 16 pp. *OXB*

Chants for socialists; by William Morris. London: 40 Berners Street. 1892. 16 pp. *BL*

The pilgrims of hope: a poem in thirteen books; by William Morris. London: "The Commonweal". 1886. [ii], 69 pp. *BL*

Poems by the way; written by William Morris. London: Reeves & Turner. 1891. [vi], 196 pp. *MPO*

    Also 2nd ed. 1892.

Poems by the way; written by William Morris. London: Reeves & Turner. 1891. [vii], 196 pp.

A limited ed. of 100 numbered copies. *BL*

Poems by the way; written by William Morris. [Hammersmith, Middlesex]: Kelmscott Press. [1891]. [iv], 197 pp.
A limited ed. of 300 copies printed in black and red. *MPL*

Poems by the way; [and], Love is enough; by William Morris. London: Longmans, Green, & Co. 1896. vi, 343 pp.
Spine-title is *The poetical works of William Morris*. *OXB*

A selection from the poems of William Morris. Edited with a memoir by Francis Hueffer. Copyright ed. Leipzig: Bernhard Tauchnitz. 1886. 320 pp. (Collection of British authors: Tauchnitz ed., vol. 2378). *OXB*

A tale of the house of the Wolfings and all the kindred of the Mark; written in prose and in verse; by William Morris. London: Reeves & Turner. 1889. [vi], 200 pp. *MPL*

MORRIS-MOORE, John. Writer on English philology.

By fits and starts: [poems]; [by] John Morris-Moore. London: Ward & Downey. 1893. 96 pp. *OXB*

MORRISON-GRANT, Lewis (1872–). b. Banffshire, son of poor parents. Educated at parish schools, then at Keith Public School.

Protomantis, and other poems; by Lewis Morrison-Grant. Paisley: Alexander Gardner. 1892. 309 pp. *OXB*

MORTERRA, Felix

The legend of Allandale, and other poems; by Felix Morterra. London: C. Kegan Paul & Co. 1880. [iv], 295 pp. *OXB*

MORTON, Mrs G.E. *see* **MORTON, Harriet**

MORTON, Harriet. Née Cave. Married G.E. Morton. Wrote Bible stories for children.

Jubilee echoes: a poem in celebration of the fifty years reign of Queen Victoria, 1837–1887; by Mrs. G.E. Morton. London: James E. Hawkins. [1889]. [32] pp. il.
Printed on card. *BL*

MOSDELL, J. Of Mortimer, near Reading, Berkshire.

The village of Mortimer, and other poems; by J. Mosdell. Reading: "Reading Observer" Steam Printing Works. 1891. xii, 189 pp. il., por. *OXB*

MOSES PEERIE, D.D., pseud. *see* **STORY, Robert Herbert**, (Moses Peerie, D.D., pseud.)

MOSSCOCKLE, Rita Frances, (Mrs Moss Cockle) (18 –1943). Daughter of Henry Sparrow of Himley, Staffordshire. In 1883 she married Charles Mosscockle, formerly solicitor and commissioner for Queensland. Lived latterly at Clewer Park, Clewer, Berkshire, and 26 Hertford Street, Mayfair, London W.

Fantasies: [poems]; by Mrs. Moss Cockle. London: Kegan Paul, Trench & Co. 1886. vi, 78 pp. *OXB*

The golden quest, and other poems; by Mrs. Moss Cockle. London: Kegan Paul, Trench, Trübner & Co., Ltd. 1890. [vi], 72 pp.   *OXB*

MOTE, Eliza. Wife of Joseph Mote, and mother of a large family. Lived at Southwood Lodge, Forest Hill, Kent.
Passing thoughts, amid life's work and life's tears: or, poems, sacred and moral; by the late Mrs. Eliza Mote. London: S.W. Partridge & Co. 1883. 61 pp.   *OXB*

MOTT, Frederick Thompson (1825–). FRGS. Lived at Birstal Hill, Leicester.
The Benscliff ballads, and other poems: a book for summer holidays; by F.T. Mott. London: Gay & Bird. 1899. xii, 118 pp.   *OXB*

MOULE, Handley Carr Glyn (1841–1920). Son of Rev. Henry Moule. Educated at Trinity College, Cambridge; BA 1864; Fellow of Trinity, 1865– 73. Principal of Ridley Hall, Cambridge, 1880–99. Norrisian professor of divinity, 1899–91. Bishop of Durham, 1902–20. An evangelical, he wrote theological and devotional works.
Christianus: a story of Antioch, and other poems; by H.C.G. Moule. Cambridge: Deighton, Bell & Co.; London: George Bell & Sons. 1883. [2], vi, 86 pp.   *OXB*
In the house of the pilgrimage: hymns and sacred songs; by H.C.G. Moule. London: Seeley & Co. Ltd. 1897. viii, 107 pp.   *OXB*

MOZLEY, John Rickards (1840–1931). Son of John Mozley of Derby. Educated at Eton College, and King's College, Cambridge; BA 1862; MA 1865. Fellow of King's, 1861–69. Assistant master at Clifton College, 1864– 65, and HM inspector of schools. Professor of pure mathematics, Owens College, Manchester, 1865–85. Lived latterly at Headingley, Leeds.
The romance of Dennell: a poem in five cantos; by John Rickards Mozley. London: Kegan Paul, Trench & Co. 1885. [viii], 283 pp.   *OXB*
A vision of England, and other poems; by John Rickards Mozley. London: Richard Bentley & Son. 1898. [x], 142 pp.   *OXB*

MUCKLEBACKET, Samuel, pseud. *see* **LUMSDEN, James**, (Samuel Mucklebackit, pseud.)

MUCKLEBACKIT, Samuel, pseud. *see* **LUMSDEN, James**, (Samuel Muclebackit, pseud.)

MUIR, Emma. Mrs Muir. Lived at 123 Ham Park Road, West Ham, Essex.
God's octave, and other poems; by Emma Muir. Printed Edinburgh: Lorimer & Gillies. [1896]. 222 pp.
Printed for private circulation.   *OXB*

MUIR, Hugh (1846–). b. Edinburgh, son of a musician and artist who deserted his family. He was brought up in Rutherglen, Lanarkshire, with his mother's people. Aged eight he was sent to work in a coal mine, but a series of accidents forced him to leave, and he eventually became a bobbin turner. With a rich tenor voice he devoted his spare time to studying music, becoming leader of Rutherglen Bank of Hope. Precentor at London Road Free Church, Glasgow, and public hall keeper, Rutherglen. Magistrate and town councillor.

Hamely echoes from an auld toun: [poems]; by Hugh Muir. Printed Glasgow: Aird & Coghill. [1899]. 219 pp. il., por. *NLS*

Reminiscences and sketches: being a topographical history of Rutherglen and suburbs; by Hugh Muir. Printe Glasgow: Bell & Bain. 1890. xvi, 256 pp. il., por.

Poetry and prose. *BL*

MUIRHEAD, James Patrick, (J.P.M.) (1813–98). Educated at Glasgow College, and Balliol College, Oxford; BA 1835, MA 1838. Admitted advocate, 1838. Published *The Life of James Watt*, 1858, and several works relating to Watt's inventions.

Folia caduca: verses to three grandchildren, 1880–1893; [by J.P.M.]. [1895]. 44 pp. *OXB*

MULCAHY, P.J. Of Salford?

Scenes in Hades; by P.J. Mulcahy. Manchester: George Woodhead & Co. 1887. 35 pp. *MPL*

MULHOLLAND, Rosa (1841–1921). b. Belfast, daughter of a doctor. Educated privately at home. A prolific writer for the popular press, and of novels with an Irish setting. In 1891 she married the historian John T. Gilbert, later knighted, and published a biography of him in 1905. Lived latterly at Villa Nova, Blackrock, County Dublin.

Vagrant verses; by Rosa Mulholland. London: Kegan Paul, Trench & Co. 1886. viii, 155 pp. *BL*

Vagrant verses; by Rosa Mulholland. London: Elkin Mathews. [1899]. viii, 155 pp. *BL*

MULVANY, Alicia A. (18 –86). b. Lough Hill, Ardara, County Donegal. She married William T. Mulvany, commissioner of public works in Ireland who was also connected with important public words in Germany. On retirement they lived at Pempelfort near Dusseldorf.

Landmarks of a long life: verses found subsequent to the writer's death; [by Alicia A. Mulvany]. Dusseldorf: C. Schaffnit. 1897. [vi], 108 pp. il.

Printed for private circulation. *BL*

Notes on the journey; by Alicia A. Mulvany. Pempelfort. [1898]. [iv], 177 pp. il., col. il., por.

Poetry and prose. *BL*

MUNBY, Arthur *see* **MUNBY, Arthur Joseph**

MUNBY, Arthur Joseph, (Jones Brown, pseud.) (1828–1910). Educated at Trinity College, Cambridge; BA 1851, MA 1856. Called to the Bar, 1855. A senior civil servant, he worked in the Ecclesiastical Commissioners' office, 1858–88. Influenced by Pre-Raphaelite morality, he taught Latin at the Working Men's College, 1860–70. He was obsessed by working women, and in 1873 he married a maidservant, Hannah, a marriage that was kept secret. Friend of R.D. Blackmore.

Ann Morgan's love: a pedestrian poem; by Arthur Munby. London: Reeves & Turner. 1896. [viii], 63 pp.   *OXB*

Dorothy: a country story, in elegiac verse; [by Arthur Joseph Munby]. With a preface. London: C. Kegan Paul & Co. 1880. xx, 86 pp.   *OXB*

Susan: a poem of degrees; by [Arthur Joseph Munby]. London: Reeves & Turner. 1893. 63 pp.   *OXB*

Vestigia restrorsum: poems; by Arthur J. Munby. London: Eden, Remington & Co. 1891. viii, 143 pp. por. (Rosslyn series).   *OXB*

Vulgar verses; by Jones Brown. London: Reeves & Turner. 1891. x, 208 pp.   *MPL*

MUNDY, James. Of Bradford, Yorkshire.

Echoes from the realm of thought: [poems]; by James Mundy. With a preface by his son. Bradford: Thornton & Pearson. 1891. 188 pp.   *★UCD*

MUNGO, David B.

Tentatives: [poems]; by David B. Mungo. Paisley: Alexander Gardner. 1898. 100 pp.   *OXB*

MUNRO, Archibald (1825–98). b. Kintyre, Argyllshire. Educated at Campbeltown Grammar School. At an early age he became head of a country school, afterwards becoming assistant teacher in a grammar school. In 1846 he was appointed to one of the higher masterships at the Normal College, Moray House, Edinburgh. Attended classes at Edinburgh University; MA 1850. He opened a private school, Clare Hall Academy, Edinburgh. President of Edinburgh Burns Club.

The casket, in rhyme: [poems]; by Archibald Munro. [2nd ed.]. Edinburgh: James Thin. 1888. [2], viii, 312 pp. il.

    1st ed. published under title *The siren casket.   BL*

The siren casket: or, the wrecker and the maid of Drum: legends of Kintyre: [poems]; by Archibald Munro. Edinburgh: James Thin. [1885]. viii, 312 pp. il.

    Spine-title is *The siren casquet.   OXB*

MUNULLOG, pseud. *see* **DERFEL, Robert Jones**, (Munullog, pseud.)

MURPHY, Joseph John (1827–94). b. Belfast, son of a merchant manufacturer. A Quaker like both his parents, he eventually became a member of the Church of Ireland. A mill owner and merchant in Belfast, he retired c. 1870. President of the Linen Hall Library. He wrote prose and verse for *The Spectator*.

Sonnets and other poems, chiefly religious; by Joseph John Murphy. London: Kegan Paul, Trench, Trübner & Co., Ltd. 1890. viii, 148 pp.   *OXB*

MURRAY, Alick (1856–   ). b. Peterwell, Aberdeenshire. He attended the village school for several years, then became an apprentice gardener at Fyvie Castle. When qualified he went to Scot's House, near Newcastle upon Tyne, subsequently obtaining positions at York, Bangor, Edinburgh, Anniston, Airthrey Castle, Dallar, and Holmdale, Leicester. Contributed verse to newspapers in various districts.

Poems; by Alick Murray. Printed Edinburgh: Bishop & Collins. 1885. iv, 140 pp.

Printed for the author.   *UCD*

MURRAY, Charlotte. Hymnwriter. Lived at St. Clare, Upper Walmer, Kent.

Earth's messages: [poems]; by Charlotte Murray. Illustrated by Fred. Hines, M. Bowley & Albert Bowers. London: Raphael Tuck & Sons. [1893]. [57] pp. il., col. il.

Printed on one side of leaf only.   *OXB*

Eon the good, and other poems; by Charlotte Murray. London: James Nisbet & Co., Ltd. 1896. viii, 125 pp. por.   *BL*

"Faith", from the epistle to the Hebrews: poems; by Charlotte Murray. Illustrated by W.J. Webb. London: Raphael Tuck & Sons. [1890]. [18] pp. il., col. il.

Printed on card.   *OXB*

Messages from the Master, and other poems; by Charlotte Murray. Stirling: Drummond's Tract Depot; London: S.W. Partridge & Co. [1880]. 158 pp.   *UCD*

More "messages": [poems]; by Charlotte Murray. Stirling, N.B.: Drummond's Tract Depot; London: S.W. Partridge & Co. [1886]. 158 pp.   *OXB*

Our homeward way: a daily text book for a month; [poems]; by Charlotte Murray. London: Ernest Nister; New York: E.P. Dutton & Co. [1893]. [32] pp. il., col. il.   *OXB*

MURRAY, Joanna Gregory (1823–83?). Née Laing. As a child she lived at the Manse of Crieff, Perthshire. Lived latterly at Dewar Place, Edinburgh.

Poems; by the late Mrs Murray (Joanna Gregory Laing). Edinburgh: J. Gardner Hitt. 1894. xiv, 226 pp.

Printed for private circulation. Cover-title is *Poems and songs*.   *BL*

MURRAY, Robert Fuller, (St. Andrews Man, pseud.) (1863–94). b. Roxbury, Massachusetts, of a Scottish father and an American mother, his father a Unitarian minister. He was brought to England in 1869, the family living successively at Kelso, York, Canterbury and Ilminster. Educated at the grammar schools at Ilminster and Crewkerne, and St Andrews University. Worked as a proof-reader for Edinburgh publishers until he became ill with tuberculosis in 1890.

Robert F. Murray: his poems. With a memoir by Andrew Lang. London: Longmans, Green, & Co. 1894. lxxii, 158 pp. *JRL*

The scarlet gown: being verses of a St. Andrews man [Robert Fuller Murray]. St. Andrews: A.M. Holden; London: Simpkin, Marshall, Hamilton & Co. 1891. viii, 124 pp. *OXB*

MUSHET, William Boyd- *see* **BOYD-MUSHET, William**

MUSINGS AND MEMORIES: [poems]. Printed Henley-on-Thames: Higgs. [1888]. viii, 90 pp. *BL*

MUTCH, Robert Sedgewick (1849–   ). b. Aberdeen. The family moved to Ellon, then to Glasgow. Educated at St Enoch's Parish School, Glasgow, then trained for teaching at the Established Church College. He became a schoolmaster at Glenapp, Ayrshire. Contributed verse to *Glasgow Weekly Herald*, and to Dumfries and Wigtownshire newspapers.

Poems and sonnets; by Robert S. Mutch. With introduction by the late John Barclay. Glasgow: Morison Bros. 1896. 136 pp. *OXB*

MY OLD PORTFOLIO: [poems]; London: Kegan Paul & Co. 1881. viii, 132 pp. *OXB*

MYERS, Ernest (1844–1921). Younger son of Rev. Frederic Myers of St. John's, Keswick, Cumberland, and brother of Frederic W.H. Myers. Educated at Cheltenham College, and Balliol College, Oxford (exhibitioner). Fellow of Wadham College; classics lecturer at Wadham and Balliol until 1871 when he went to live in London. He was called to the Bar but never practised. Published prose translations of Pindar's *Odes*, and of the last eight books of the *Iliad*.

The defence of Rome, and other poems; by Ernest Myers. London: Macmillan & Co. 1880. [vi], 134 pp. *OXB*

The judgment of Prometheus, and other poems; by Ernest Myers. London: Macmillan & Co. 1886. [viii], 126 pp. *OXB*

MYERS, Frederic William Henry (1843–1901). Son of Rev. Frederic Myers of St. John's, Keswick, Cumberland, and brother of Ernest Myers. Educated at Cheltenham College, and Trinity College, Cambridge (minor scholar); BA 1865. Fellow of Trinity, 1865; classical lecturer, 1865–69. Inspector of schools, 1872–1900. One of the founders of the Society for Psychical Research, established 1882. Died in Rome.

The renewal of youth, and other poems; by Frederic W.H. Myers. London: Macmillan & Co. 1882. xii, 232 pp. *MPL*

MYLNE, Robert Scott (1854?–   ). Son of Robert W. Scott of Westminster, London, gentleman. Educated at Oriel College, Oxford; BA 1877, BCL & MA 1880. Curate, St Peter-in-the-East, Oxford, 1878–85; chaplain, and lecturer in divinity, Pembroke College, 1885–91; chaplain, Lockerbie, Dumfriesshire, 1891–92, Bologna, Italy, 1893–94, Siena, 1895. Lived latterly at 47 Hamilton Terrace, London NW, and Great Amwell, Hertfordshire.

The deep waters of blue Galilee: a poem; by Robert Scott Mylne. London: Hatchards. 1886. 29 pp. il.   *OXB*

The **MYSTERIES OF THE ROSARY.** London: Burns & Oates; New York: Catholic Publication Society Co. 1885. [57] pp.
   Printed on one side of leaf only.   *OXB*

N

N., E.A. *see* **NEWTON, Ernest Alfred**, (E.A.N.)

N., H.M.
   The silver wedding: songs and musings. Printed London: Howard & Jones. 1888. 25 pp.   *OXB*

N., J.
   Poems; by J.N. London. 1880. 48 pp.   *BL*

N., M.L.
   Stray leaves from my notebook: prose and verse; by M.L.N. Dublin. 1881.*

N., R.T.
   Lyrical versicles; by R.T.N. Bristol: J.W. Arrowsmith; London: Simpkin, Marshall, Hamilton, Kent & Co. Ltd. [1891]. 68 pp.   *OXB*

N., W.T.
   Hymns and meditations; by W.T.N. London: Wyman & Sons. 1887. 47 pp.   *OXB*

NADEN, Constance Caroline Woodhill (1858–89). b. Edgbaston, Birmingham, daughter of Thomas Naden. Educated at Mason College, where she studied scientific subjects, winning prizes for geology. Taught at the Home for Friendless Girls in Birmingham; became president of the Ladies' Debating Society. A disciple of Robert Lewins, and a sympathizer with Herbert Spencer's philosophy, she adopted a system of 'hylo-idealism'. She wrote brilliant essays on philosophical subjects. Moved to London, living latterly at 114 Park Street, Grosvenor Square.
   The complete poetical works of Constance Naden. With an explanatory fore-word by Robert Lewins. London: Bickers & Son. 1894. xxiv, 364 pp. por.   *OXB*
   A modern apostle; The elixir of life; The story of Clarice, and other poems; by Constance C.W. Naden. London: Kegan Paul, Trench, & Co. 1887. vi, 178 pp.   *BL*

Selections from the philosophical and poetical works of Constance C.W. Naden.
Compiled by Emily and Edith Hughes. With an introduction by George M.
McCrie. London: Bickers & Son; Birmingham: Cornish Bros. 1893. xxxii,
191 pp. por. *BL*
   Songs and sonnets of springtime; by Constance C.W. Naden. London: C. Kegan
Paul & Co. 1881. xii, 172 pp. *BL*

NAEGELY, Henry, (Henry Gaelyn, pseud.) Writer on J.F. Millet.
   The mummer, and other poems; by Henry Gaelyn. London: Elliot Stock. 1895.
52 pp. *OXB*

NAISMITH, William. Philosophical writer.
   The apocalypse of man; by William Naismith. Paisley: Alexander Gardner.
1891. xii, 7–320 pp.
      Poetry and prose. *BL*
   Nature and I in talk and song: [poems]; by William Naismith. Paisley;
Alexander Gardner. 1897. 149 pp. por. *OXB*

NANTES, William Hamilton (1811?–84). b. Douglas, Isle of Man, son of
Henry Nantes, merchant of Bideford, Devon. Educated at Blundell's School,
and Trinity College, Cambridge; BA 1834, MA 1866. Ordained 1835; curate,
Powderham, Devon, 1834–35, Shipton-Gorge, Dorset, 1836–37, West &
Middle Chinnock, Somerset, 1837–41, Caundle Bishop, Dorset, 1841–44;
perpetual curate, St. Paul's, Jersey, 1844–47; vicar, East Stonehouse, Devon,
1847–73; rector, Frome-Vanchurch with Batcombe, Dorset, 1873–84. Died at
Tenby.
   Poems and hymns; by William Hamilton Nantes. Printed London: J.S. Virtue
& Co., Ltd. [1884?]. [iv], 252 pp.
      Published by his children. *BL*

NASH, Charles
   The story of the cross: a poem; by Charles Nash. London: Elliot Stock. 1887. vi,
82 pp. *OXB*

NATION, William Hamilton Codrington (1834–1914). b. Exeter, Devon,
son of William Nation, barrister. Educated at Eton College, and Oriel
College, Oxford. He went into theatre management, gave public readings,
and delivered public addresses. Manager of Sadler's Wells, Astley's, Royalty,
Holborn, Charing Cross, Terry's, Scala and Wyndham's Theatres. Lord of
the manor of Rockbeare, Devon, he gave about twenty-two acres at
Rockbeare as a public park. Lived at 2 Ryder Street, St James's, London SW.
   Prickly pear blossoms: [poems]; by W.H.C. Nation. London: Eden, Rem-
ington & Co. 1893. x, 265 pp. *OXB*
   Prickly pear blossoms: versified tales, legends, fables, oriental apologues, historiettes,
satires, descriptions of life in the streets, of animal life, and rural and marine scenery; by
W.H.C. Nation. 2nd and slightly revised ed. Illustrated. Westminster:
Roxburghe Press. [c. 1894]. 308 pp. il. *★UCD*

NATURE, DIVINITY, AND LIFE: GLEANINGS OF INNER MEAN-INGS: POETICAL SKETCHES, 1896. London: E.W. Allen. [1896]. viii, 184 pp. *OXB*

NAUGHTY JEMIMA: A DOLEFUL TALE. London: Ward, Lock, & Tyler. [1887]. 120 pp. il. *OXB*

NAUTA, pseud. Of Southampton.
"The idlers", and other poems; by Nauta. Southampton: John Adams & Sons. 1887. 38 pp. *OXB*

NAUTICUS, pseud. Of London.
Christmas eve on the moors: a ghost story; by Nauticus. London: Elliot Stock. 1882. 16 pp. *OXB*

NAYLOR, Robert Anderton. FRSL. Of Cuerden Hall, Thelwall, Cheshire.
Nugae canorae: [poems]; by R.A. Naylor. Printed London: Bowker Bros. [1888]. xx, 255 pp.
Printed for presentation only. *UCD*

NEALE, Susanna
Temperance songs; Susanna Neale. London: Bevington & Co. 1886. 16 pp. *BL*

NEEDHAM, Elizabeth Annabel (1844–). Of Kidsgrove, Cheshire. Married George C. Needham.
Leisure moments: or, breathings of a poetic spirit; [poems]; by Elizabeth A. Needham. London: James Blackwood & Co. [1889]. 172 pp. *OXB*
Poetic paraphrases; by Mrs. George C. Needham. London: James E. Hawkins; S.W. Partridge & Co. [1890]. iv, 92 pp. il. *OXB*

NEEDHAM, Frederick B. Writer of an opera.
Glenavon, and other poems; by Frederick B. Needham. London: E.W. Allen; Brighton: H. & C. Treacher; Louth: Jackson & Parker. 1882. iv, 162 pp. *UCD*

NEEDHAM, Mrs George C. *see* **NEEDHAM, Elizabeth Annabel**

NEGREPONTE, Mary P.
Io, and other verse; by Mary P. Negreponte. London: Kegan Paul, Trench, Trübner & Co., Ltd. 1891. 64 pp. *BL*

NEIL, James (18 –1915). Educated at Corpus Christi College, Cambridge. Ordained 1867; curate, St Martin's, Birmingham, 1866–69, Chesterton, Cambridge, 1869–71; incumbent of Christ Church, Jerusalem, 1871–74, Little Berwick, Shropshire, 1877–79. Lived latterly at 11 Westcliff Park Drive, Westcliff-on-Sea, Essex.
The bridal song; by James Neil. London: Lang Neil & Co. 1892. [ii], 34 pp. *OXB*
Also 2nd ed. [1892].

NEILL, Charles. b. Edinburgh. Aged thirteen he was apprenticed to the University Printing Office, Edinburgh, completing his apprenticeship at the *Edinburgh Evening Post*. As a journeyman he was employed by Messrs Paton & Ritchie. In an accident with a gun he lost his right hand and narrowly escaped death. He became a teacher, holding appointments in various towns, eventually appointed to Dornoch Parish School, Sutherland. FEIS.

Poetical musings; by Charles Neill. With a literal translation of the third and fourth books of Virgil's *Aeneid*. London: Simpkin, Marshall & Co.; Aberdeen: John Adam; Wick: William Rae; Dornoch: J. Gillespie. 1884. viii, 168 pp.   OXB

Poetical musings; by Charles Neill. 2nd ed. Aberdeen: John Avery & Co. Ltd. 1892. 2 vols in 1.   BL

NEILSON, James Macadam (1844–83). b. Campsie, Stirlingshire. He went to work at the age of seven, at twelve apprenticed at Lennox Mill as an engraver for calico printing, which became his profession. Largely self-educated, he wrote local notes for the *Stirling Observer*, and later became a district correspondent for the *Glasgow Daily Mail*. In 1875 he moved to Thornliebank, Renfrewshire.

Songs for the bairns; and, Miscellaneous poems; by the late James M. Neilson. Edited, with a biographical notice, by Wm. Freeland. Printed Glasgow: William Rankin. 1884. xvi, 184 pp.   BL

NELSON, W.J. Of Liscard, Cheshire.

Little rhymes for little people, and other verses; by W.J. Neilson. Printed Liverpool: William Spelman. 1880. 67 pp.   OXB

NESBIT, Edith (1858–1924). b. London, daughter of John C. Nesbit, agricultural chemist. Educated at a French convent, her early youth was spent at Holstead Hall, Kent. In 1880 she married the writer Hubert Bland. She began her literary career by writing verse but is best remembered by her very successful children's stories. Keenly interested in socialism, in 1883 she was one of the founders of the 'Fellowship of New Life' out of which sprang the Fabian Society. After Bland's death she married Thomas Tucker, an engineer, and retired to New Romsey.

Lays and legends; by E. Nesbit. London: Longmans, Green, & Co. 1886. viii, 197 pp.   BL

Also 2nd ed. 1887; 3rd ed. 1892.

Lays and legends (Second series); by E. Nesbit. With portrait. London: Longmans, Green, & Co. 1892. [iv], 160 pp. por.   BL

Leaves of life: [poems]; by E. Nesbit. London: Longmans, Green, & Co. 1888. x, 185 pp.   BL

Lilies round the cross: an Easter memorial; [poems]; by Edith Nesbit and Helen J. Wood. Illustrated by Fred Hines. London: Ernest Nister; New York: E.P. Dutton & Co. [1889]. [20] pp. il.   BL

The lily and the cross; by E. Nesbit. London: Griffith, Farran, Okeden & Welsh. [1887]. [16] pp. il.   BL

A pomander of verse; by E. Nesbit. London: John Lane at the Bodley Head; Chicago: A.C. McClurg & Co. 1895. x, 88 pp.
A limited ed. of 750 copies printed for England and America. *BL*
Rose leaves; by E. Nesbit. London: Ernest Nister; New York: E.P. Dutton & Co. [1895]. [16] pp. col. il. *BL*
Songs of love and empire; by E. Nesbit. Westminster: Archibald Constable & Co. 1897. xii, 168 pp. *UCD*
Songs of two seasons: [poems]; by E. Nesbit. Illustrated by J. McIntyre. London: Raphael Tuck & Sons. [1890]. [17] pp. il., col. il. *BL*
Sweet lavender; by E. Nesbit. London: Ernest Nister; New York: E.P. Dutton. [1892]. [15] pp. col. il. *BL*

NEW, Herbert (1821–93). Solicitor at Evesham, Worcestershire, 1843 to his death. He was senior partner in the firm of New, Prance, & Garrard which failed with liabilities c. £300,000 in April 1894. Registrar of Evesham County Court from 1868. Member of Evesham Town Council, an alderman, and several times mayor. Lived at Green Hill, Evesham.
Sonnets; by Herbert New. Printed Evesham: W. & H. Smith. 1885. 34 pp.
Printed for his personal friends. *OXB*

NEW HAND, pseud.
Songs of a lost world; by a new hand. London: W.H. Allen & Co. 1882. viii, 120 pp. *OXB*

NEWALL, Maria. Mrs Newall of Hare Hill, Littleborough, Lancashire.
Poems; [by Maria Newall]. Printed Manchester: G. Falkner & Sons. [1885]. [ii], 116 pp. *BL*

NEWBIGGING, Thomas (1833–). b. Glasgow. Educated at Bridgton Public School, and Guthen School, Kirkcudbrightshire. In 1844 the family moved to Lancashire, to Blackburn then to Bury. A mechanic by trade, he lived in the Rossendale area, 1851–70. Became secretary and manager of Rossendale Union Gas Co. For several years he was hon. secretary of Bacup Mechanics' Institute. In 1870 he was sent to Brazil as engineer and manager of Pernambuco Gas Works. Returned in 1875, settling in Manchester in practice as a civil and consulting engineer.
Poems and songs; by Thomas Newbigging. London: David Bogue; Bury: W.S. Barlow. 1881. viii, 252 pp. *MPL*

NEWBOLT, Sir Henry (1862–1938). b. Bilston, Staffordshire, son of a clergyman. Educated at Clifton College, and Corpus Christi College, Oxford. Called to the Bar, Lincoln's Inn, practising successfully, 1887–99. He gave up law to become a full-time writer. Novelist and popular poet, much of his time was devoted to public service. Editor of the *Monthly Review*, 1900–04. Author of the official naval history of the Great War.
Admirals all, and other verses; by Henry Newbolt. London: Elkin Mathews. 1897. 32 pp. (Shilling garland, VIII). *OXB*
Also 2nd–16th eds 1898–99.

A fair death; [ascribed to Henry Newbolt]. London: Simpkin, Marshall, & Co.; Walsall: W. Henry Robinson. [1881]. 21 pp.   OXB

The island race: [poems]; by Henry Newbolt. London: Elkin Mathews. 1898. x, 119 pp.   MPL

NEWELL, Ebenezer Josiah (1853–1916). Religious historian and hymn writer. Author of a church history of Wales.

The sorrow of Simona, and lyrical verses; by E.J. Newell. London: Kegan Paul, Trench, & Co. 1882. viii, 123 pp.   OXB

NEWELL, Temple. Irish Roman Catholic.

Episodes of joy: [poems]; by Temple Newell. London: Digby, Long & Co. 1898. 206 pp.   OXB

NEWMAN, Alfred Stilgoe (18 –96). b. Birmingham. Educated at Pembroke College, Cambridge; BA 1871, MA 1875; Seatonian prize-winner. Ordained 1873. Assistant master, King Edward VI School, Birmingham, 1872–73; second master, Lancing College, 1873–75, King's School, Peterborough, 1875–82. Curate, Emmanuel Church, Loughborough, 1882–89; rector, Tarrant Hinton, Dorset, 1889–96.

"First words and last": [poems]; by A.S. Newman. Peterborough: G.C. Caster; London: Simpkin, Marshall, & Co. [1880]. 32 pp.   OXB

NEWMAN, Henry (1838?–). Son of Edmund L. Newman of Cheltenham. Educated at Balliol College, Oxford; BA 1861, MA 1864. Curate, Eccleshall, Staffordshire, 1864, Chellaston, Derbyshire, 1864–67; perpetual curate, Stanley, Derbyshire, 1867–70, Whittingham, Gloucestershire, 1870–77, St James's, Pokesdown, Hampshire, 1877–82.

Songs of my solitude; by Henry Newman. London: Digby, Long & Co. 1895. 88 pp.   OXB

NEWSAM, William Cartwright (1861–). b. Nottingham, grandson of a Yorkshire poet (1811–44) bearing the same name. Spent most of his life in Yorkshire. A song-writer, many of his songs were set to music by leading composers, and became very popular. He contributed verse to numerous magazines.

Reveries, rhymes, and rondeaus: by William Cartwright Newsam. London: Griffith, Farran, Okeden & Welsh. 1889. 96 pp.   OXB

NEWTON, Ernest Alfred, (E.A.N.) (1868–1945). Son of Thomas B. Newton of Liverpool and Hereford. Educated at Winchester College, and King's College, Cambridge: BA 1890, MA 1894. Ordained 1893; curate, Aylesbury, 1892–94. Organizing secretary, National Society (Northern Province), 1894–96. Curate, Cookham, Berkshire, 1897–98; rector, St Paul's, Darjeeling, India, 1899–1907. On editorial staff of the *Standard* and *Daily Express*, 1907–09. Civil chaplain, Victoria, Mahe, Seychelles, 1909–14; Archdeacon of Seychelles, 1912–17.

Here and there: lyrics; by E.A.N. Liverpool: Edward Howell. 1894. xiv, 68 pp.   OXB

Sunlight and shade: lyrics; by Ernest Alfred Newton. Cambridge: J. Palmer; London: G.J. Palmer. 1890. viii, 72 pp.   *OXB*

NEWTON, Henry Chance (1854–1931). b. Kennington. Dramatic and variety critic, and playwright. Wrote for the stage from his youth. On staff of *Fun, Hood's Comic Annual*, and *Referee*; London correspondent of the New York *Dramatic Mirror*.

The penny showman, and other poems; by H. Chance Newton. London: Samuel French. [1887]. 64 pp.   *OXB*

NEWTON, Hibbert (1822–93). Educated at Trinity College, Dublin; BA 1845, BD & DD 1880. Ordained 1847; curate, Holy Trinity, Portsea, 1847–49, St Cuthbert's, York, 1852–59, St George the Martyr, Southwark, London, 1861–67; vicar, St Michael's, Southwark, 1867 to his death.

The Anglo-Fenian: God save Ireland; The two cathedrals: poems and pieces of art for the criticism of the industrial classes, with facts and figures, shewing the more dangerous conspiracy of our time; by Hibbert Newton. London: Kensit. 1890. xvi, 47 pp. facsim.   *BL*

NEWTON, Thomas, (Vagrant Viator, pseud.), (Verbos, pseud.) (Verbosper-egrinubiquitos, pseud.) A saddler of Walsall, Staffordshire. Also lived at Bayswater, London, and Windsor, Berkshire. Member of the Temple Club, London.

Dulce domum: [poems]; by a vagrant viator. London: Wyman & Sons. 1884. [iv], 88 pp. por.

Printed and published for the author.   *OXB*

Erin go bragh; by Verbosperegrinubiquitos. London: Wyman & Sons. 1885. [iv], 82 pp. por.

Printed and published for the author.   *OXB*

Gladstoniana: satirical poem; [by Verbos]. Printed [London]: Alfred Dudfield. 1886. [51] pp.

Printed on one side of leaf only.   *OXB*

Vagrant viator; by Verbosperegrinubiquitos. [Vol. I]. London: Wyman & Sons. [1882]. [iv], 98 pp.

Poetry and prose. Printed and published for the author.   *BL*

Vagrant viator; by Verbosperegrinubiquitos. [Vols II–III]. London: Wyman & Sons. [1883]. 2 vols in 1. il.

Poetry and prose. Printed and published for the author.   *BL*

NEWTON-ROBINSON, Charles, (Charles Robinson, pseud.) (1853–1913). Educated at Westminster School, and Trinity College, Cambridge. Called to the Bar, Inner Temple, 1879. Founder and chairman, Council of Land Union. A fencer, he founded the Epée Club of London, 1900; member of British épée team at Olympic Games, Athens, 1906. Live at 20 Chester Street, Belgrave Square, London SW.

The Golden Hind: a story of the invincible armada; Thessale, and other poems; by Charles Robinson. London: George Bell & Sons. 1880. viii, 123 pp.   *OXB*

Tintinnabula: new poems; by Charles Newton-Robinson. London: Kegan Paul, Trench, Trübner & Co., Ltd. 1890. [vi], 82 pp. *BL*

Ver lyrae: selected poems of Charles Newton-Robinson. With seven new lyrics. London: Lawrence & Bullen, Ltd. 1896. [vi], 135 pp. *OXB*

The viol of love: poems; by Charles Newton-Robinson. London: John Lane, Bodley Head; Boston, [Mass.]: Lamson Wolffe & Co. 1895. viii, 59 pp.

A limited ed. of 350 copies. *OXB*

NICHOL, John (1833–94). b. Montrose, Angus, son of John Pringle Nichol, professor of astronomy, Glasgow. Educated at Glasgow University, and Balliol College, Oxford. Professor of English, Glasgow University, 1862–69. With Professor Knight he founded the New Speculative Society, 1867. Literary critic, author of books on Burns, Byron and Carlyle; contributor to *Encyclopaedia Britannica*.

The death of Themistocles, and other poems; by John Nichol. Glasgow: James Maclehose. 1881. xvi, 247 pp. *MPL*

NICHOLLS, J.F.

Lays of the people; by J.F. Nicholls. London: Samuel French. [1887]. 62 pp. *OXB*

NICHOLSON, Ellen Corbet. Daughter of James Nicholson, Scottish poet. She trained for the teaching profession at Glasgow Free Normal School. As a candidate for Queen's certificate she passed highest on the list for Scotland. Appointed head teacher of a girls' school in South Shields, County Durham.

Poems; by James and Ellen C. Nicholson. London: Hamilton, Adams, & Co.; Glasgow: J. M'Geachy. 1880. 217 pp.

Not joint authorship. *UCD*

Willie Waugh, and other poems; by James & Ellen C. Nicholson. Edinburgh: J. Menzies & Co.; Glasgow: J. M'Geachy. 1884. 250 pp.

Not joint authorship. *OXB*

NICHOLSON, Isabella. Of Southport, Lancashire.

Songs of the soul; by Isabella Nicholson. London: James Nisbet & Co. [1885]. 102 pp. *OXB*

NICHOLSON, James (1822–97). b. Edinburgh. Tailor in the village of Strathavon, Lanarkshire, 1844; head of the tailoring department at Govan Workhouse, 1853–97. He wrote many temperance songs and poems. Died at Merryflats, Govan.

Poems; by James and Ellen C. Nicholson. London: Hamilton, Adams, & Co.; Glasgow: J. M'Geachy. 1880. 217 pp.

Not joint authorship. *UCD*

Wee Tibbie's garland, and other poems; by James Nicholson. Glasgow: James M'Geachy. [1880?]. 142 pp. *BL*

Wee Tibbie's garland, and other poems and readings; by James Nicholson. New & enlarged ed. Glasgow: James M'Geachy & Co. 1888. 204 pp. il.

Cover-title is *Tibbie's garland*. *UCD*

Willie Waugh, and other poems; by James & Ellen C. Nicholson. Edinburgh: J. Menzies & Co.; Glasgow: J. M'Geachy. 1884. 250 pp.
　　Not joint authorship. *OXB*

NICHOLSON, John Gambril F. Novelist and dramatist.
　　A chaplet of southernwood, from plants grown by John Gambril Nicholson: [poems]. Ashover, Derbyshire: Frank Murray. 1896. viii, 75 pp. *OXB*
　　Love in earnest: sonnets, ballades, and lyrics; by J.G.F. Nicholson. London: Elliot Stock. 1892. xii, 230 pp. *OXB*

NICKLIN, John Arnold (1871–1917). b. Llanfair, Montgomeryshire, son of Thomas Nicklin, farmer. Educated at Shrewsbury School, and St John's College, Cambridge (scholar); BA 1894. Assistant master at Liverpool College, 1896–1901. On staff of the *Daily Chronicle* and *Tribune* as reviewer and leader-writer from 1901. Lived latterly at 13 Acacia Grove, West Dulwich, London.
　　Verses; by J.A. Nicklin. London: David Nutt. 1895. 36 pp. *MPL*

NICOL, John (1894–). b. Parkhouse, near Ardrossan, Ayrshire. At eighteen he entered a clerkship at Messrs Merry & Cunningham, coal and ironmasters, at Glengarnock Ironworks, remaining with them all his working life.
　　Poems and songs; by John Nicol. Ardrossan; J.H. Mearns. 1880. viii, 200 pp. *NLS*

NICOLSON, Alexander (1827–93). b. Usabost, Isle of Skye. Educated at Edinburgh University. He became a Free Church minister for a time, then worked as a journalist before turning to law; called to the Scottish Bar, 1860. Assistant Commissioner of Scottish Education, 1865. Sheriff-substitute of Kirkcudbrightshire, 1872, of Greenock, 1885. A prolific writer, he revised the Gaelic Bible and collected Gaelic proverbs. A sub-editor of *Encyclopaedia Britannica*.
　　Verses; by Alexander Nicolson. With memoir by Walter Smith. Edinburgh: David Douglas. 1893. [vi], 127 pp. por. *UCD*

NICOLSON, Laurance James (1844–). b. Lerwick, Shetland. Son of a general merchant and shipping agent. When he was eleven his father died, and the family moved to Dalkeith, Midlothian. Apprenticed to a cabinet maker for five years until a serious illness necessitated less strenuous work. Became a clerk in the Burgh Engineer's office, Edinburgh, then in a builder's office in Dalkeith. Contributed to the Scottish press. Known as 'The Bard of Thule'.
　　Songs of Thule; by Laurance James Nicolson. Paisley: Alexander Gardner. 1894. 228 pp. por. *OXB*

NIGHTINGALE, Lady Clarence
　　The three graces, Faith, Hope, and Charity: their arrival, their reception and separate speeches to the people: [poems]; by Lady Clarence Nightingale. London: Passmore & Alabaster. 1881. 59 pp.
　　Title from cover. *OXB*

NISBET, Hume (1849–1921?). b. Stirling. Aged fifteen he emigrated to Melbourne, Australia, spending the next seven years travelling in Australia, New Zealand, and the Pacific islands; for one year he worked as an actor at the Theatre Royal, Melbourne. Returned to London in 1872 for study, then went back to Scotland; art master at the Watt College and School of Art, Edinburgh, until 1885. A prolific novelist, he illustrated some of his own books. Lived latterly at Willingdon Road, Eastbourne, Sussex.

The matador, and other recitative pieces; by Hume Nisbet. London: Hutchinson & Co. 1893. xii, 185 pp.   *OXB*

Memories of the months: [poems]; by Hume Nisbet. With illustrations by the author. London: Ward & Downey. 1889. 101 pp. il.

A limited ed. of 250 copies, in 25 of which the frontispiece has been signed by the artist.   *BL*

NO SECT ON EARTH, BUT CHRISTIANS ONLY. London: G. Morrish. [1897]. 16 pp.   *OXB*

NOBLE, James Ashcroft (1844–96). b. Liverpool, son of an employee of the Pilotage Committee. Educated at Liverpool College. Journalist and critic, he wrote for *Chamber's Journal* and other periodicals; chief reviewer for *Liverpool Albion*; edited *The Argus* Liverpool weekly paper, 1878–77; became a regular writer for *The Spectator*, 1878. He was attacked by paralysis in 1884. Moved to London, 1888; edited the weekly literary supplement of *Manchester Examiner*; part-owner of *The New Age*, started 1894. Lived latterly at 6 Patten Road, Wandsworth Common, London.

Verses of a prose-writer; by James Ashcroft Noble. Edinburgh: David Douglas. 1887. xiv, 149 pp.   *MPL*

NOBLE, Samuel (1859–). b. Arbroath, Angus. The family later moved to Aberdeen. On leaving school at fourteen he went to Dundee, where he was employed in a jute mill for two years. He served in the Royal Navy but was discharged following an accident after eight years. Returned to Dundee and started a bread shop in Ann Street. When the business failed he became keeper of the reading rooms at Killin, Perthshire, 1896.

Rhymes and recollections; by Samuel Noble. With biographical introduction by John Paul. Dundee: William Duncan. 1898. 133 pp. por.   *BL*

Also 2nd ed. 1898.

NODAL, Edith (18 –1926). Daughter of Edmund Robinson of Warrington, Lancashire. She married John Howard Nodal, journalist, who was editor of the *Manchester City News*, 1871–1904. Lived latterly at The Grange, Heaton Moor, Stockport, Cheshire.

The vision in the night, and other verses; by Edith Nodal. Manchester: Hewitson & Wright. 1898. [ii], 26 pp.

Printed for private circulation.   *MPL*

NOEL, Edward Henry (18 –84). Of Hampstead, London.
Poems; by Edward Henry Noel. London: Elliot Stock. 1884. xii, 236 pp. *UCD*

NOEL, Horace. Rev. MA.
Ballads of the English Reformation; by Horace Noel. [London]: Religious Tract Society. [1882]. 128 pp. il. *UCD*

NOEL, Hon. Roden (1834–94). Son of Lord Barham, who was made Earl of Gainsborough in 1841. Educated at Trinity College, Cambridge. Groom of the privy chamber to Queen Victoria, 1867–71. Critic and essayist on various poets from Chatterton to Whitman, and biographer of Shelley. Died at Mainz, Germany.
A little child's monument: [poems]; by the Hon. Roden Noel. London: C. Kegan Paul. 1881. xii, 147 pp. *UCD*
    Also 2nd–4th eds 1881.
A modern Faust, and other poems; by Hon. Roden Noel. London: Kegan Paul, Trench & Co. 1888. xviii, 255 pp. il. *MPL*
My sea, & other poems; by the Hon. Roden Noel. With an introduction by Stanley Addleshaw. London: Elkin Mathews; Chicago: Way & Williams. 1896. 76 pp. *UCD*
Poems of the Hon. Roden Noel. With an introduction by Robert Buchanan. London: Walter Scott, Ltd. [1892]. xxiv, 370 pp. por. (Canterbury poets). *MPL*
Poor people's Christmas: a poem; by Hon. Roden Noel. London: Elkin Mathews. 1890. 22 pp. *OXB*
Selected poems from the works of the Hon. Roden Noel. With a biographical and critical essay by Percy Addleshaw. With two portraits. London: Elkin Mathews. 1897. 198 pp. por. *MPL*
Songs of the heights and deeps; by the Hon. Roden Noel. London: Elliot Stock. 1885. viii, 214 pp. *UCD*

NOMAD, pseud. *see* **CRAFTON-SMITH, Adele**, (Nomad, pseud.)

NORRIS, William Foxley (1825?–1906). Educated at Trinity College, Oxford; BA 1848, MA 1850. Curate, Alverstoke, Hampshire, 1848–51; warden, House of Charity, Soho, London, 1851; curate, Cirencester, Gloucestershire, Newbury, Berkshire; vicar, Buckingham, 1862–79, rural dean, 1878–79; rector, Witney, Oxfordshire. from 1879.
Lays of the early English Church; by W. Foxley Norris. London: Parker & Co. 1887. xvi, 248 pp. il. *OXB*

NORROY, pseud.
The strange adventures of a carp; by "Norroy". London: Dean & Son. [1884]. 19 pp. il. *OXB*
A tale of a whale; written and illustrated by "Norroy". London: Dean & Son. [1884]. 19 pp. il. *BL*

NORTH, L. Harlingford. Essayist.
The wrong of death: a realistic poem; by L. Harlingford North. London: Digby & Long. [1892]. [iv], 80 pp.   *OXB*

NORTHALL, George F. Writer on English folk rhymes.
The "Momus" miscellanies; by George F. Northall. Printed Birmingham: Lawrence & Holland. [1890]. [xii], 136 pp. por.   *BL*

NORWOOD, J.F., (Maud Eldryth, pseud.) Of Hull, Yorkshire.
All Souls' eve; "No God", and other poems; by Maud Eldryth. London: Kegan Paul, Trench & Co. 1884. [viii], 143 pp.   *UCD*
Margaret, and other poems; by Maud Eldryth. London: Kegan Paul, Trench & Co. 1882. [vi], 142 pp.   *BL*

NOTT, John Nott Pyke- *see* **PYKE-NOTT, John Nott**

NOVUS HOMO, pseud.
Three comic poems: The ballad of the barony of Brendett; Sir Hilary's head; The monk and the devil; by Novus Homo. Oxford: J. Vincent. 1880. 24 pp.
    Title from cover.   *OXB*

NOWELL, Edward
Lyric echoes: [poems]; by Edward Nowell. London: London Literary Society. 1887. [viii], 146 pp.   *OXB*

NUGENT, Ermengarda Greville- *see* **GREVILLE-NUGENT, Ermengarda**

NUN OF KENMARE *see* **CUSACK, Mary Frances, (Sister Mary Francis Clare)**

NUTTER, Henry. Lived at Darwin House, Burnley, Lancashire.
Local rhymes; by Henry Nutter. Printed Burnley: B. Moore. 1890. 160, iii pp. por.   *MPL*

NYM, pseud. *see* **WILSON, A.J.**, (Nym, pseud.)

O

O.S.C. *see* **WALKER, William Anderson**, (O.S.C.)

OAKES, James, (Old Oak, pseud.) (1858–19   ). b. Riddings, Derbyshire, son of Charles H. Oakes. Educated at Harrow School, and Trinity College, Oxford; BA 1880, MA 1885. Colliery owner and ironmaster, Alfreton Ironworks & Riddings Collieries. JP for Derbyshire, and county councillor from 1888. A director of Messrs Moore & Robinson's Nottinghamshire Banking Co., Ltd. Lived at Riddings House, Alfreton.
Abel Acorn, farm labourer: a story of gradual development; by Old Oak. London: R. Washbourne. 1880. 79 pp. *OXB*

OATES, Charlotte (1856–1900). b. Halifax, Yorkshire, daughter of Daniel and Mary Oates. Lived at Daisy Cottage, Wyke, near Bradford. Died of cancer of the breast.
Miscellaneous poems; by Charlotte Oates. Printed Bradford: J.S. Toothill. 1898. [4], iv, 406 pp. *OXB*

OBBARD, Constance Mary. Mrs Obbard. Daughter of George H. Wright.
Burley bells; by Constance Mary Obbard. London: Kegan Paul, Trench & Co. 1885. [2], vi, 122 pp. *BL*

O'BOYLE, Thomas W. Of Westport, Kilmeena, County Mayo.
The western rover: a volume of lyrical poetry; by Thomas W. O'Boyle. Dublin: James Duffy & Sons. 1880. 82 pp. *OXB*

O'BRIEN, Charlotte Grace (1845–1909). b. Cahirmoyle, County Limerick, daughter of William Smith O'Brien, Irish nationalist and Young Ireland leader. She lived with her father in Brussels, 1854–56. As a young woman she accompanied emigrants on the 'coffin ships' to America, thereafter campaigning for improved sailing conditions. Active in Irish politics, and in the Gaelic League. A novelist and playwright, she became a Roman Catholic in 1887.
Cahirmoyle: or, the old home: [poems]; by Charlotte Grace O'Brien. [Limerick]: [Guy & Co., Ltd]. [1888]. 32 pp. *NLI*
Lyrics; by Charlotte Grace O'Brien. London: Kegan Paul, Trench & Co. 1886. x, 116 pp. *OXB*
A tale of Venice: a drama, and lyrics; by Charlotte G. O'Brien. Dublin: M.H. Gill & Son. 1880. 138 pp.
     Cover-title is *A drama and lyrics*. *NLI*

O'BRIEN, Thomas, (Clontarf, pseud.)
Songs of liberty; by Clontarf. Dublin. 1889.★

O'CONNELL, Arthur J.
Ultima Thule, and other verses; by Arthur J. O'Connell. London: Elliot Stock. 1896. vi, 70 pp. *OXB*

O'CONOR, Charles Patrick (1837–). b. County Cork, of poor parents. He went to England in his youth, writing verse for newspapers and songs for music. Appointed to a government clerkship in Canada but soon retired owing to ill-health. Known as 'The Irish Peasant Poet'. He lived at Lewisham for many years and was often thought of as a Kentish poet. Received a civil list pension of £50 a year.
Songs for soldiers; by Charles P. O'Conor. 2nd ed. London. 1884. viii, 105 pp. il. *OXB*

OCTOGENARIAN, pseud. Translator of Homer's *Odyssey*.
"Shreds and patches": or, "nostri farrago libelli": [poems]; by an octogenarian. London: Williams & Norgate; St. Leonards-on-Sea: John Stuart; Whittaker & Williams; Hastings: Yates & Son. 1884. [iv], 113 pp. *OXB*

The OCTOGENARIAN STATESMAN: [William Ewart Gladstone]. 2nd ed. (enlarged). Printed Bournemouth: Jarvis & Co. 1893. 16 pp. *BL*

O'CUIRC, Henry, pseud. *see* **QUIRK, Henry**, (Henry O'Cuirc, pseud.)

ODD FELLOW, pseud.
Odds and ends: [poems]; by an odd fellow. London: Digby, Long & Co. [1897]. 80 pp. *OXB*

ODD FELLOW, pseud. *see* **COTTON, John**, (Odd Fellow, pseud.)

ODD RHYMES: VERSES; IMITATIONS; JINGLES. London: Ideal Publishing Union, Ltd. [1899]. xxii, 64 pp. *BL*

OESTERREICHER, Jane. Baroness. Novelist and illustrator.
Light and darkness, and other poems; by Jane Oesterreicher. London: Bickers & Son. 1899. [ii], 60 pp. *BL*

OFFICER, William (1856–)
The triumph of love, and other poems; by William Officer. Peterhead: David Scott. 1896. 141 pp. il. *★UCD*

OGG, James (1849–).
Glints i' the gloamin': songs and poems; by James Ogg. Printed Aberdeen: "Free Press" Office. 1891. 208 pp. *★UCD*

OGILVIE, Will H. (1869–1963). b. Holmfield, Kelso, Roxburghshire. Educated at Fettes College, Edinburgh. Journalist and writer of sporting and hunting verse. He worked on a sheep farm in Australia, 1889–1901. Professor of agricultural journalism at Iowa State College, 1905–07. Served at the War Office during First World War. He retired to Scotland.
Fair girls and gray horses, with other verses; by Will H. Ogilvie. 1898. *★*

OGLE, Octavius (1829–94). b. Oxford, son of James Ogle, physician. Educated at Wadham College, Oxford; BA 1850, MA 1853. Fellow of Lincoln College, 1852–59. He held many positions in the University, including tutor, moderator, and public examiner. Chaplain, Warneford Asylum, from 1864. Served on Oxford City Council. Lived at 19 Park Crescent.

Idylls of Ilium, and other verses; by Octavius Ogle. Oxford: B.H. Blackwell. 1887. [iv], 103 pp. *OXB*

O'HANLON, John, (Lageniensis, pseud.) (1821–1905). b. Stradbally, Queen's County. Emigrated to Quebec, 1842. He was ordained a Roman Catholic missionary priest in Missouri. Returned to Ireland, 1853, becoming parish priest, St Mary's Irishtown, 1880–1905; canon, 1886. Writer on Irish saints and folklore, and on Irish-American history. Author of *Lives of the Irish Saints*, 10 vols. 1875–1903.

The poetical works of Lageniensis. Dublin: James Duffy & Co., Ltd. 1893. [4], viii, 328 pp. por. *MPL*

O'HARA, Cassie M. Lived near Ballymena, County Antrim. Wrote for *The Irish Monthly* and *The Catholic Fireside*.

S. Teresa of Jesus: poem in four cantos, to which was awarded the prize in the literary competition, held October, 1882, in honour of the tercentenary of the saint's death at Salamanca; by Cassie M. O'Hara. London: R. Washbourne. 1883. 31 pp. *OXB*

O'KELLY, Edmund William. Of Dublin.

Our wrongs: or, the "Merries" in Ireland: an historical poem from the Reformation to the union, A.D. 1537 to A.D. 1800; by Edmund Wm. O'Kelly. With notes. Dublin: James Duffy & Sons. [1886]. 54 pp. *TCD*

OLD, Herbert

A dream of happiness, and other poems; by Herbert Old. London: Digby, Long & Co. 1892. viii, 131 pp. *OXB*

OLD BLUE, pseud.

The tale of Eyam: or, a story of the plague in Derbyshire, and other poems; by an old blue. Derby: Richard Keene; London: Simpkin, Marshall & Co. 1888. 74 pp. il. *OXB*

OLD LADY, pseud. *see* **COOKSON, Elizabeth**, (Old Lady, pseud.)

OLD-NEW-RHYMER, pseud. *see* **PHILLIPS, Charles**, (Old-New-Rhymer, pseud.)

OLD OAK, pseud. *see* **OAKES, James**, (Old Oak, pseud.)

OLD PAST MASTER, pseud. *see* **SPARLING, Mr**, (Old Past Master, pseud.)

OLDMEADOW, Ernest James (1867–1949). b. Chester, son of George E. Oldmeadow. Educated at King's School, Chester. Edited *The Dome* 1897–1900; music critic of *The Outlook*, 1900–04; edited *The Tablet*, 1923–36. He contributed to many other periodicals. Member of Westminster City Council. Lived latterly at 20 Temple Fortune Lane, London NW.

  The little Christian year; [poems]; [by Ernest James Oldmeadow]. London: Unicorn Press. [1898]. [80] pp. (Unicorn books of verse, 2).   *OXB*

O'LEARY, Arthur. Brother of John and Ellen O'Leary of Limerick, Irish patriots and members of the Fenian Society.

  Lays of country, home and friends; by Ellen O'Leary. Dublin: Sealy, Bryers & Walker. 1890. 155 pp.

    Includes *Poems of Arthur O'Leary*.   *NLI*

    Also [Popular ed.] 1891.

O'LEARY, Ellen (1831–89). b. Tipperary, daughter of a prosperous shop-keeper, and sister of John O'Leary, prominent Fenian. She assisted James Stephens, chief organizer of Irish republicanism in directing Fenian affairs; she mortgaged her house to provide funds for Stephen's escape, 1865. Contributed verse exclusively to the *Irish People*, 1863–65. Kept house for her brother in Dublin, 1885–89. Died in Cork.

  Lays of country, home and friends; by Ellen O'Leary. Dublin: Sealy, Bryers & Walker. 1890. 155 pp.

    Includes *Poems of Arthur O'Leary*.   *NLI*

    Also [Popular ed.] 1891.

OLIVER, Edwin. Miscellaneous writer.

  Squibs: [poems]; by Edwin Oliver. London: London Literary Society. [1887]. xii, 75 pp.   *OXB*

OLIVIER, Henry Arnold (1827–   ). Son of Henry S. Olivier of Devonport, Devon. Educated at Rugby School, and Balliol College, Oxford; BA 1849, MA 1854. Curate, Worton, Wiltshire, 1849–51, St Stephen's, Brighton, 1854–57, Ryde, Isle of Wight, 1857–58, All Saints, Colchester, Essex, 1858–61; rector, Crowhurst, Sussex, 1861–64, Frensham, Surrey, 1867–70; dean and rural dean, Havant, Hampshire, 1870–74; rector, Poulshot, Wiltshire, 1874–83; chaplain, Holy Trinity, Nice, France, 1885–87, Alassio, Italy, 1888–91; vicar, Wye, Ashford, Kent, from 1892.

  Our Lord Jesus Christ "made known through the Church", from Advent to Trinity; set forth in verse by Henry Arnold Olivier. London: Henry Frowde. 1896. viii, 120 pp.

    Cover-title is *Christ made known through the Church*. Spine-title is *From Advent to Trinity*.   *OXB*

OLIVIER, Sydney Haldane, Lord Olivier, (Two Undergrads, pseud. with Hubert Craigie Campion) (1859–1943). Educated at Tonbridge School, and Corpus Christi College, Oxford. Entered the Colonial Office, 1882. A founder of the Fabian Society, its secretary, 1886–89. Colonial secretary, Jamaica, 1900–04, Governor, 1907–13; permanent secretary, Board of Agriculture, 1913–17; assistant controller of Exchequer, 1917–20; secretary for India in the first Labour cabinet, 1924. Privy councillor and Baron, 1924.
   Poems and parodies; by two undergrads. Oxford: B.H. Blackwell. 1880. 24 pp.   *OXB*

OLLERENSHAW, E.M.
   Wayside melodies; [poems]; by E.M. Ollerenshaw. Reading: J.J. Beecroft; London: Hamilton, Adams, & Co. 1887. vi, 96 pp.   *OXB*

O'MAHONY, Timothy J. (1839–   ). b. Cork. Educated there, at St Sulpice, Paris, and afterwards in Rome. Ordained priest, 1862. Professor of theology at All Hallows College, Dublin. Wrote several prose works, and contributed to many Catholic periodicals.
   Wreaths of song, from fields of philosophy; [by Timothy J. O'Mahony]. Dublin: M.H. Gill & Son. 1890. viii, 96 pp.   *BL*

ONE OF THE FOLK, pseud. *see* **WESTON, Jessie Laidlay**, (One of the Folk, pseud.)

ONE OF THOSE WHO LOVES HIS FELLOW MEN, pseud. *see* **ECKERSLEY, Edmund Ryley**, (E.R.E.), (One of Those Who Loves His Fellow Men, pseud.)

ONE WHO OUGHT TO HAVE KNOWN BETTER, pseud.
   Drivellings: [poems]; by one who ought to have known better. Birmingham: Cornish Bros. 1883. viii, 145 pp.   *BIP*

ORCHARD, Oliver
   Poems; by Oliver Orchard. London: Wilson & Macmillan. 1898. [vi], 61 pp.   *BL*

O'REILLY, John Boyle (1844–90). b. Dowth Castle, Ireland. Irish revolutionary and Fenian agent, he enlisted in the 10th Hussars to spread disaffection in Irish soldiers. Sentenced to death by court-martial but his sentence was commuted to penal servitude, 1866. He escaped from Western Australia in an American whaler, eventually reaching Boston, Massachusetts, where he settled. He took part in O'Neill's invasion of Canada, 1870, and tried to organize the escape of convicts in Australia. Edited the *Pilot*. Died in Boston.
   In Bohemia: [poems]; by John Boyle O'Reilly. Boston, [Mass.]: Pilot Publishing Co. [1886]. 97 pp.   *BL*
   Life of John Boyle O'Reilly; by James Jeffrey Roche. Together with his complete poems and speeches. Edited by Mrs. John Boyle O'Reilly. Introduction by James Cardinal Gibbons. London: T. Fisher Unwin. 1891. xx, 790 pp. il., por., facsim.

Half-title is *Life, poems and speeches of John Boyle O'Reilly*.   BL
The statutes in the block, and other poems; by John Boyle O'Reilly. Boston, [Mass.]: Roberts Bros. 1881. 110 pp.   BL
Watchwords from John Boyle O'Reilly. Edited by Katherine E. Conway. Boston, [Mass.]: Joseph George Cupples. [1891]. xliv, 60 pp. col. il.
   Poetry and prose.   NLI

ORMSBY, Arthur Sydney (1825–87). b. Seatown House, Dundalk, County Louth, son of Rev. Owen Ormsby. Articled to George Halpin, engineer, 1839–44. Resident engineer, Midland Great Western line; engineer in the United States, 1849–51; assistant colonial engineer, Melbourne, 1852, Calcutta, 1858–61. He experimented on London's water supply, and constructed water works at Hillbottom, Berkshire. Died in London.
   Heart whispers: [poems]; by A.S. Ormsby. London: James E. Hawkins. [1888]. [24] pp. il.   OXB

ORPHEUS AND EURYDICE: A POEM. London: Marshall Bros. [1882]. 28 pp.   OXB

ORR, Alexander. He contributed verse to the *Glasgow Weekly Mail*. Lived at 56 Rumford Street, Bridgeton, Glasgow.
   Laigh flichts and humorous fancies: [poems]; by Alexander Orr. Printed Glasgow. 1882. 120 pp.
   Printed for the author.   UCD

ORRED, Meta. Novelist.
   Ave (all' anima mia); by Meta Orred. London: Smith, Elder, & Co. 1880. [viii], 58 pp.   OXB
   A dream-alphabet, and other poems; by [Meta Orred]. London: Smith, Elder & Co. 1888. [vi], 114 pp.   TCD

ORROCK, Thomas. Of Edinburgh, formerly of South Queensferry, Lothian.
   Fortha's lyrics, and other poems, with a descriptive account of South Queensferry and its surroundings; by Thomas Orrock. Printed Edinburgh: Edinburgh Co-operative Printing Co., Ltd. 1880. 320 pp.
   Printed for the author.   UCD

ORWELL, pseud. *see* **SMITH, Walter Chalmers**, (Orwell, pseud.)

OSBORNE, Henry. b. Londonderry. Educated there, and at Glasgow University, graduating 1851. Presbyterian minister.
   The palace of delights, and other poems; by Henry Osborne. London: Digby, Long & Co. [1895]. [vi], 90 pp.   UCD

OSBORNE, John Allen
   The vision, and other poems; by J.A. Osborne. London: T. Fisher Unwin. 1896. 167 pp. por.   UCD

O'SHAUGHNESSY, Arthur (1844–81). b. London of Irish descent. In 1861 he went to work for the British Museum Library. In 1863 he was transferred to the Natural History Department, where he became an expert on fishes and reptiles. English correspondent of *Le Livre*. In 1873 he married the eldest daughter of the poet Westland Marston. He associated with Rossetti and the Pre-Raphaelites.

Arthur O'Shaughnessy: his life and his work, with selections from his poems; by Louise Chandler Moulton. London: Elkin Mathews & John Lane; Chicago: Stone & Kimball. 1894. 121 pp. por.   *OXB*

Songs of a worker; by Arthur O'Shaughnessy. London: Chatto & Windus. 1881. xvi, 212 pp.   *MPL*

OSMASTON, Francis *see* **OSMASTON, Francis Plumptre**

OSMASTON, Francis Plumptre (1857–   ).Son of John Osmaston (formerly Wright) of Hulland, Derbyshire. Educated at University College, Oxford; BA 1880. Barrister, Inner Temple, 1885.

Dramatic monologues; by Francis P. Osmaston. London: Kegan Paul, Trench, Trübner & Co., Ltd. 1895. [vi], 140 pp.   *OXB*

Loose blades from the one field: [poems]; by Francis Osmaston. London: Kegan Paul, Trench, Trübner & Co., Ltd. 1891. viii, 151 pp.   *OXB*

Poems; by Francis Osmaston. London: Kegan Paul, Trench, Trübner & Co. Ltd. 1897. x, 180 pp.   *OXB*

Vox amoris dei: [poems]; by Francis Osmaston. London: Swan Sonnenschein & Co. 1894. viii, 243 pp.   *OXB*

OSRIC *see* **MORGAN, Rhys D.**, (Osric)

O'SULLIVAN, Vincent (1868–19   ). b. New York, son of Eugene O'Sullivan, a merchant well-known on Wall Street. Educated at Columbia Grammar School, Oscott, in France, and at Exeter College, Oxford. A novelist, and contributor to British and American periodicals. Appointed to the commission sent to Europe by the National Catholic War Council of the United States, 1918.

The houses of sin, [and other poems]; by Vincent O'Sullivan. London: Leonard Smithers. 1897. 66 pp.

A limited ed. of 400 numbered copies.   *OXB*

Poems; by Vincent O'Sullivan. London: Elkin Mathews. 1896. viii, 68 pp.   *OXB*

OTHER DAYS: [poems]. Edinburgh: R. Grant & Son; London: Simpkin, Marshall, & Co. [1881]. viii, 76 pp.   *OXB*

OTTLEY, Ashton

A nocturnal adventure, and other verses; by Ashton Ottley. Tiverton: Gregory & Son. 1899. 119 pp.   ★*UCD*

OTTWELL, John
  Short poems; by John Otwell. London: Kegan Paul, Trench, Trübner & Co., Ltd. 1899. viii, 96 pp.   *OXB*

OUTSIDER, pseud.
  The Gladstone rule: a retrospective commentary; by an outsider. Edinburgh: William Blackwood & Sons. 1885. 72 pp.   *OXB*

OVERINGTON, Lily
  Random rhymes and Christmas chimes; by Lily Overington. London: Digby, Long & Co. [1895]. 288 pp.   *BL*

OWD WEIGHVUR, pseud. Of Greenfield, West Riding, Yorkshire.
  Warty rhymes for warty folks; by th' owd weighvur. Printed Saddleworth: Moore & Edwards. [1894]. 64 pp.   *OXB*

OWEN, Ella C.J.F.
  "Life's varied voices": poems; by Ella C.J.F. Owen. Bournemouth: F.J. Bright & Son. 1897. [vi], 50 pp.   *UCD*

OWEN, Frances Mary (1842–83). b. Glanmore, Wicklow, fourteenth and youngest child of John Synge. In 1870 she married Rev. James A. Owen, Fellow of University College, Oxford, and vice-principal at Cheltenham College. She worked among the poor at Cheltenham. Writer on Keats, George Washington, etc., and a contributor to *The Academy* and other journals. Lived at The Beeches, Suffolk Square, Cheltenham.
  Essays and poems; by Frances Mary Owen. London: John Bumpus. 1887. [viii], 252 pp.   *NLW*

OWEN, Gabrielle M.
  Poems; by Gabrielle M. Owen. London. [1888]. 40 pp.   *★NUC*

OWEN, George Vale (1869–1931). b. Birmingham, son of George Owen. Educated at the Midland Institute, and Queen's College, Birmingham. Appointed curate at Liverpool: Seaforth, 1893, Fairfield, 1895, St Matthew's, 1897; vicar, Orford, Warrington, Lancashire, 1908–22. Writer on theological subjects. Lived latterly at Farnborough, Kent.
  Leaves from the mental tree: [poems]; by Geo. V. Owen. Printed Birmingham: Tuckley & Vince. 1889. 113 pp.   *OXB*

OWEN, John (1866–96). b. Pembroke. Educated at St David's College, Lampeter, where he became lecturer on Hebrew. Ordained, 1860; curate, Alvedistone, Wiltshire, 1859–60; Bowerchalke, Wiltshire, 1860–69; appointed rector, East Anstey, Dulverton, Devon, 1869. A frequent writer for *The Academy*, and for many years a contributor to the *Edinburgh Review*.
  Verse-musings on nature, faith, and freedom; by John Owen. London: Kegan Paul, Trench & Co. 1889. x, 354 pp.   *MPL*
  Verse-musings on nature, faith, and freedom; by John Owen. Enlarged reissue. London: Swan Sonnenschein & Co. 1894. x, 374 pp.   *OXB*

OWEN, John Lorton (1845?–98). b. near Manchester. Short story writer and journalist; eight years with the *Leicester Herald*, afterwards editor of the *Saturday Herald*. Lived at Church Lane, Bowdon, Cheshire. In 1883 at Manchester Crown Court he was convicted of stealing a cheque, and sentenced to twelve months imprisonment. He went to London in 1889, and was well known as a contibutor of verse and fiction to various papers; also a novelist.

Piccadilly poems: vers de société; by J.L. Owen. Westminster: Roxburgh Press. [1897]. 170 pp. il.   *OXB*

OWNER OF THE DRUNKEN DOG, pseud. *see* **JACKSON, C.**, (C.J.), (Owner of the Drunken Dog, pseud.)

OXLEY, William Henry (1848–19). b. Redcar, Yorkshire, son of Charles C. Oxley, JP. Educated at Richmond, and St John's College, Oxford; BA 1870, MA 1874. Curate, Copredy, Oxfordshire, 1871–74, Sharow, Yorkshire, 1874–76; vicar, Grewelthorpe, Yorkshire, 1876–82; chaplain, Sorrento, Italy, 1883–85, Palermo and Marsala, Sicily, 1885–87; vicar, Petersham, Surrey, from 1891. Travelled widely in Europe and the Middle East. He owned property in Filey and Ripon, and had a house at Newton Abbot, Devon.

T' fisher folk of Filey Bay: poems chiefly in the Yorkshire dialect. London: Simpkin, Marshall & Co.; Scarborough: E.T.W. Dennis. 1888. 46 pp. il.   *★UCD*

Also 2nd ed. 1888.

Lines on the view from Petersham Hill, Richmond, Surrey; [by William Henry Oxley]. Richmond: Lewis & Hopkins. [1893]. [37] pp. il.   *OXB*

OXONIENSIS, pseud. *see* **CHILD, Gilbert William**, (Oxoniensis, pseud.)

P

P.,A.D. *see* **PHELP, A.D.**, (A.D.P.)

P., A.M.

The chord found, [and other poems]; by A.M.P. London: Marshall Bros. [1894]. 120 pp.   *OXB*

P., C.J.
   Metassai: scripts and transcripts: [poems]; by C.J.P. Glasgow. 1887. 156 pp.
      Privately printed.   *BL*

P., D.M. *see* **PANTON, David Morrieson**, (D.M.P.)

P., E. Of Ludlow, Shropshire?
   "Thine eyes shall see the King in His Beauty", and other verses; by E.P. Ludlow:
   G. Woolley. 1889. [vi], 196 pp.
      Spine-title is *Poems*.   *OXB*

P., J.W. *see* **PITCAIRN, Janet Wyld**, (J.W.P.)

P., M. *see* **M.P.**

P., M.T. *see* **PIGOTT, Montague Horatio Mostyn Turtle**, (Mostyn P.
   Pigott, pseud.), (M.T.P.)

P., V.F.C.
   Gossamer threads: a book of verses; by V.F.C.P. Warwick: Henry T. Cooke &
   Son. [189–]. 57 pp.   *★UCD*

PACKMAN, Annie. Scottish. *Songs for all seasons*; by Annie Packham,
   London: L. Lloyd. 1899. 46 pp.   *OXB*

PAGANUS, pseud. *see* **CRANMER-BYNG, Lancelot**, (Paganus, pseud.)

PAGE, R.E.
   Original verses; [by R.E. Page]. Printed Seacombe: L.J. Simpson.
   1891.   *★UCD*

PAINE, Mrs G.W. *see* **PAINE, Mary M.**

PAINE, Mary M. Daughter of C.B. Slee, head of a firm of vinegar makers of
   Horselydown. In 1863 she married George W. Paine, philanthropist, and
   chairman of three successful tea-producing companies. They had a family of
   seven sons and four daughters. Lived at Cotswold Lodge, Upper Norwood,
   London.
   A sunset idyll, and other poems; by Mrs. G.W. Paine. Edited by Edwin Oliver.
   London: Hodder Bros. 1896. [viii], 87 pp.   *OXB*

PALGRAVE, Francis Turner (1824–97). b. Great Yarmouth, Norfolk, son of Sir Francis Palgrave. Educated at Charterhouse School, and Balliol College, Oxford. Fellow of Exeter College, 1847. Vice-principal, 1850–55, of Knellar Hall, Twickenham, where he became a close friend of Tennyson. A distinguished civil servant and educationalist, he is best remembered for his anthology *The Golden Treasury*, 1861. Professor of poetry at Oxford, 1885–95.

Amenophis, and other poems, sacred and secular; by Frances T. Palgrave. London: Macmillan & Co. 1892. viii, 253 pp. *UCD*

The visions of England: [poems]; [by Francis Turner Palgrave]. Printed London: Cousins & Co. 1880–81. 2 vols.

A limited ed. of 50 copies printed for Francis T. Palgrave. *OXB*

The visions of England: [poems]; by Francis T. Palgrave. London: Macmillan & Co. 1881. xx, 353 pp. *MPO*

The visions of England: lyrics on leading men and events in English history; by Francis T. Palgrave. London: Cassell & Co., Ltd. 1889. 192 pp. (Cassell's national library, 193). *OXB*

Also re-issue 1891.

PALGRAVE, William Gifford (1826–88). Second son of Sir Francis Palgrave. Educated at Trinity College, Oxford. He joined Bombay Native Infantry, then became a Jesuit, studied in Rome, and was sent as a missionary to Syria and Arabia. Left the Jesuits in 1864 to enter the diplomatic service; British consul at Soukhoum-Kale, 1866, Trebizond, 1867, the island of St Thomas, 1873, Manila, 1876; consul-general, Bulgaria, 1878, Siam, 1880; as minister resident in Uruguay, 1887, he was reconciled to the Church.

A vision of life: semblance and reality; by William Gifford Palgrave. London: Macmillan & Co. 1891. xvi, 400 pp. *OXB*

PALMER, Charles Walter

The weed: a poem; by Charles Walter Palmer. London: C. Kegan Paul & Co. 1880. [iv], 96 pp. *OXB*

PALMER, Ellen. Novelist, and writer for children. Of Edinburgh?

The temptation of Job, and other poems; by Ellen Palmer. London: George Philip & Son; Liverpool: Philip, Son & Nephew. 1882. 124 pp. *OXB*

PALMER, Joseph William (1853–). b. Mare Street, Hackney, London. A philatelist, known as 'The Stamp King', he built up a business at 281 Strand, London, becoming the world's largest postage-stamp dealer.

A firelight fancy; by J.W. Palmer. Printed London: W. Wilfred Head & Mark. [1892]. 16 pp. *OXB*

The happy land: or, through time and space; by J.W. Palmer. London. [1886]. 16 pp. *OXB*

Shadows on the wall: a Christmas annual; by J.W. Palmer. Printed London: W. Wilfred Head & Mark. [1891]. 16 pp. *OXB*

The spirit of Christmas: or, rhyme and reason for the festive season; by J.W. Palmer. [London]. [1884]. 16 pp. *OXB*

Through fifty years: the romance of a postage stamp; by J.W. Palmer. Printed London: W. Wilfred Head & Mark. [189–]. 16 pp.   *OXB*

To dreamland and back: a Christmas fancy; by J.W. Palmer. London. [1886]. 16 pp.   *OXB*

PANTER, Charles Richard (1847?–1910). Educated at Trinity College, Dublin; BA and LL.B 1873, MA 1879, LL.D 1881. Ordained 1885; curate, Tallow, County Waterford, 1882–83, St Mary's, Newry, County Down, 1883–84, Clonmethan with Naul, County Dublin, 1884–86. At one time he was attached to St Clement Danes, London; later officiated at Pau, France.

Orpheus and Eurydice, and other poems; by Charles Richard Panter. 2nd ed. London: Simpkin, Marshall & Co.; Dublin: Sealy, Bryers & Walker. 1882. [viii], 148 pp.   *OXB*

Political cookery, including a liberal bill of fare: a satire; by Charles Richard Panter. London: Simpkin, Marshall & Co.; Dublin: Sealy, Bryers, & Walker. 1882. 47 pp.   *OXB*

PANTON, David Morrieson, (D.M.P.) (1870–19). b. Mandeville, Jamaica, son of Rev. David B. Panton, Archdeacon of Middlesex, Jamaica. Educated at Old Hall School, Shropshire, South-Eastern College, Ramsgate, and Caius College, Cambridge; BA 1892. An inspector of schools in Jamaica. University extension lecturer, 1897. Warden of the Social Settlement, Fore Street, Ipswich. Nonconformist minister, Surrey Chapel, Norwich, 1901–29. Editor of *Dawn*.

Julian the apostate, and other poems; by D.M.P. Cambridge: J. Palmer; London: G.J. Palmer. 1891. viii, 47 pp.   *OXB*

Poems by two friends: Edward Henry Blakeney and D. Morrieson Panton. Cambridge: J. Palmer; London: G. J. Palmer. 1892. viii, 44 pp.

Not joint membership.   *OXB*

PARABLE POET *see* **HAKE, Thomas Gordon**

The PARISH OF PUDDLEMUCK: [poems]. London: Simpkin, Marshall, Hamilton, Kent, & Co., Ltd; Dorchester: Henry Ling. [1890]. 23 pp.   *OXB*

PARKE, Walter, (London Hermit, pseud.). Librettist and general writer. Lived at The Hermitage, London WC.

Lays of the saintly: or, the new golden legend; by Walter Parke (The London Hermit). With twelve page illustrations and vignette by John Leitch. London: Vizetelly & Co. [1883]. x, 182 pp. il.   *OXB*

The merry muse, with graver moments: a collection of poems, humorous and serious, for reading or recitation; by Walter Parke ("The London Hermit"). London: Ward & Downey. [1890]. [viii], 128 pp. il.   *OXB*

Patter poems: humorous and serious, for readings or recitations; by Walter Parke. London: Vizetelly & Co. [1885]. viii, 120 pp. il. (John W. Leitch).   *OXB*

PARKER, Emma J.

Summer sonnets, and other verses; by Emma J. Parker. London: Grant Richards. 1898. [2], viii, 58 pp. *OXB*

PARKER, George Williams, (E.B.). Trained for the medical profession at St Thomas's Hospital, London, MRCS 1872; in Edinburgh, MRCP 1878; in London, MRCP 1883. Lived at 11 Brandenburgh Road, Chiswick, London.

The design of love; written by E.B. London: George Stoneman. [1893]. xxxii, 564 pp. il. *OXB*

PARKER, Sir Gilbert (1862–1932). b. Ontario, Canada. Educated at Trinity College, Toronto. He travelled in Canada, the South Seas, and Australia, where he joined the staff of the *Sydney Herald* in 1885. He came to England in 1889, becoming the Conservative MP for Gravesend, 1900–18. Knighted in 1902. Wrote novels, and historical works on Canada.

A lover's diary: songs in sequence; by Gilbert Parker. Cambridge: Stone & Kimball; London: Methuen & Co. 1894. 148 pp. il. (by Will. H. Low). *MPL*

PARKER, Thomas. Of Ripley, Surrey.

Revolution: a poetical and opportune exposure and forecast of things moral, social, and political, in IV parts; by T. Parker. Printed Woking: W. Moore 1891. 35 pp. *OXB*

Songs and recitations of native life and scenery, feathered song and existence; by T. Parker. [1887]. [vi], 46 pp. *OXB*

Songs and recitations of native life and scenery, feathered song and existence; by T. Parker. Printed Guildford: Biddle & Son. [1888]. [iv], 59 pp. *OXB*

PARKER, W.H.

Princess Alice, and other poems; by W.H. Parker. Basford: F.R. Webb. 1882. 32 pp.*

PARKES, Sir Henry, (Wanderer, pseud.) (1814–96). b. Stoneleigh, Warwickshire, of humble parents. Apprenticed as an ivory tuner in Birmingham before emigrating to Australia in 1839. He worked as a farm labourer then opened a shop as an ivory and bone tuner. Known as an agitator against transportation of convicts. In 1854 he was elected to the legislative council in Sydney; commissioner for emigration in England, 1861; colonial secretary, New South Wales, 1866; prime minister for several periods from 1872. Writer on Australian political history.

The beauteous terrorist, and other poems; by a wanderer. Melbourne: George Robertson & Co. 1885. iv, 91 pp.

    Spine-title is *Poems*. *BL*

Fragmentary thoughts: [poems]; by Sir Henry Parkes. Sydney: Samuel E. Lees. 1889. [2], xiv, 209 pp. *BL*

Sonnets, and other verse; by Sir Henry Parkes. London: Kegan Paul, Trench, Trübner & Co. Ltd. 1895. viii, 48 pp. *OXB*

PARKES, William Theodore (18 –1908). b. Dublin, son of Isaac Parkes, medallist. He began an artistic career as a medallist with his father, then started his own business. Pursued various forms of art, exhibiting drawings in the Royal Hibernian Academy, 1875–83; published a series of heraldic albums and sheets of arms, crests, etc. of Irish families. Also a journalist, contributing to *The Weekly Freeman, Irish Fireside*, and others, often using the pseud. Barney Brady. From 1883 he worked in London as artist, journalist, and public reciter. Lived at 27 Gower Street.

Lays of the moonlight men: tales of '98, and other Irish ballads; by William Theodore Parkes. London: Neville & Co.; Simpkin, Marshall, Hamilton, Kent & Co. [c. 1896]. [viii], 150 pp.   *UCD*

The spook ballads; by Wm. Theodore Parkes. Illustrated by the author. London: Simpkin, Marshall, Hamilton, Kent & Co. 1895. [viii], 246 pp. il. *OXB*

PARKINSON, Thomas (18 –19). Ordained 1865; curate, Bardsey Island, Wales, 1864–67, Clapham, Yorkshire, 1867–69; vicar, Clare, Suffolk, 1869–71; North Otterington, 1871–1913. Lived latterly at 2 Ure Bank Terrace, Ripon, Yorkshire. *FRHS.*

An idyl and ballads of Washburn-Dale; by Thomas Parkinson. (Reprinted, with additions, from "Lays and leaves of the forest"). Printed Folkestone: T. Kentfield. [188-]. [vi], 54 pp.   *LEP*

Lays and leaves of the forest: a collection of poems, and historical, genealogical, & biographical essays and sketches, relating chiefly to men and things connected with the Royal Forest of Knaresborough; by Thomas Parkinson. London: Kent & Co.; Harrogate: R. Ackrill. 1882. [vi], 300 pp. il. *BL*

PARR, Catherine. Mrs William Henry Kaye.

The feast of Madain, and other poems; by Catherine Parr. Norwich: A.H. Goose & Co., late Miller & Leavins. 1881. [6], vi, 184 pp. *BL*

PARR, Olive Katharine (1874–19). b. Harrow, Middlesex, daughter of Charles C. Parr, and descended from the Lancashire family of Parr, which yielded a Queen in Catherine Parr. Educated at a London convent school. Writer and social worker, she was manager of the children's branch of the Crusade of Rescue from its inauguration by Cardinal Vaughan; Catholic representative on the Hampstead Charity Organization committee.

Poems; by Olive Katharine Parr (Mary Aquinas, T.O.S.D.). With preface by H. Reginald Buckler. London: R. & T. Washbourne; New York: Benziger Bros. 1899. xvi, 61 pp. *OXB*

PARRY, William (1795–1891). Rev. Parry of Tonyrefail, Glamorgan. A Calvinistic Methodist for seventy-six years.

The old Welsh evangelist, and other poems; by William Parry. Bristol: William F. Mack. 1893. [vi], 344 pp. por. *NLW*

PARRY, William, (Gwilym Pont Taf) (1836–1903). b. Nelson, Glamorgan. Became a Baptist minister at Penarth and Ynysybwl, Glamorgan.

The victorious bard, and other poems; by William Parry (Gwilym Pont Taf). Printed Pontypridd: John W. Ford. [1894]. 212 pp. *OXB*

Welsh hillside saints; [poems]; by William Parry (Gwilym Pont Taf). Printed Manchester: J. Roberts & Sons. 1896. vi, 392 pp. *BL*

PARSLOE, Edmund, (Vox, pseud.)

Queen Victoria: a Christian historical poem; by Vox. New ed. Birmingham: "Journal" Printing Office. [1897]. 27 pp. *OXB*

PATCH, pseud. *see* **COURTENAY, L.B.**, (Patch, pseud.)

PATERSON, Jeannie Graham (1871–). b. Springburn, Glasgow. Educated at the local school. She followed the occupation of milliner. Contributed verse to local periodicals and to several religious magazines. Lived at 497 Springburn Road.

Short threads from a milliner's needle [poems]; by Jeannie Graham Paterson. Glasgow: Carter & Pratt. 1894. xvi, 240 pp. por. *BL*

PATERSON, Robert. Engraver, particularly of Scottish scenes.

Mary of Scots; Life-gold, and other poems; by R. Paterson. With illustrations by J. MacWhirter [and others], and engraved on wood by the author. Printed London: J.S. Virtue & Co., Ltd. [1895]. 226 pp. il.

Published by subscription. A limited ed. of 250 numbered copies signed by the author. *NLS*

PATMORE, Coventry (1823–96). b. Woodford, Essex, son of Peter G. Patmore, editor of the *Court Journal*. Educated privately. He considered taking holy orders but drifted into literary work. In 1846 he was appointed an assistant librarian in the British Museum, retiring in 1865. Wrote for the *Edinburgh Review, North British*, and other magazines; contributed to *The Germ*, the Pre-Raphaelite publication. Close friend of Tennyson, Ruskin, Francis Thompson, and Gerard Manley Hopkins. Lived latterly at Lymington, Hampshire.

Poems; by Coventry Patmore. 3rd collective ed. London: George Bell & Son. 1887. 2 vols.

Spine-title is *Poetical works*. *BL*

The poetry of pathos and delight, from the works of Coventry Patmore. Passages selected by Alice Meynell. With a portrait after J.S. Sargent. London: William Heinemann. 1896. xvi, 136 pp. por. *NLP*

PATMORE, Henry (1860–83). b. Finchley, London, third son of Coventry Patmore. Educated at St Cuthbert's College, Ushaw. He was always physically delicate, and disease destroyed the sight of one eye. He decided to enter law, was articled, and lodged in Hampstead. He died at the family home in Hastings on 24 February 1883.

Poems; by Henry Patmore. Printed Oxford: Henry Daniel. 1884. [6], vi, 40 pp.

    A limited ed. of 125 numbered copies.   *OXB*

PATON, Ida. Miss Paton. Lived at Home Cottage, Roseneath Street, Greenock, Renfrewshire.

    The forcing of the Khaibar Pass, with other poems; by Ida Paton. Printed Greenock: William Hutchison. 1897. [vi], 173 pp.   *OXB*

PATRICUS: HIS RELIGIOUS PROGRESS. In three parts. London: Williams & Norgate. 1892. [iv], 140 pp.   *OXB*

PATRIS, Frank

    The thane of Moen; by Frank Patris. Birmingham: Houghton & Co., Ltd; London: Simpkin, Marshall & Co. [1888]. 32 pp.   *OXB*

PATTENDEN, Frederick William Waldebrand (1857–89). Educated at Boston Grammar School, Lincolnshire, and New College, Oxford. Student at Inner Temple, called to the Bar, 1884. Worked as a tutor, then as a barrister. Died of typhoid fever.

    Verses by F.W.W. Pattenden. London: James Clarke & Co. 1891. xii, 292 pp.

    Collected and privately printed.   *OXB*

PATTENDEN, T.J. Russell

    The rolling deep, and the crested billows: a poem; by T.J. Russell Pattenden. London: S.W. Partridge & Co. [1899]. 79 pp. il.   *OXB*

PATTERSON, E. Of Cardiff.

    The mermaid, and other pieces; by E. Patterson. With an introduction by S.C.F. [Subscribers' ed.]. Printed Cardiff: Rees, Mallett & Stanbury. 1897. xvi, 132 pp.   *BL*

PATTERSON, Mary. Of Garranard, Strandtown, Belfast.

    Verses; by Robert and Mary Patterson. Printed Belfast: Alexander Mayne & Boyd. 1886. [iv], 96 pp.

    Printed for private circulation only.   *OXB*

PATTERSON, Robert. Of Garranard, Strandtown, Belfast.

    Verses; by Robert and Mary Patterson. Printed Belfast: Alexander Mayne & Boyd. 1886. [iv], 96 pp.

    Printed for private circulation only.   *OXB*

PATTIE, pseud.

    The adopted: a tale; by Pattie. Saltburn: W. Rapp & Sons. 1896. [ii], 156 pp.   *OXB*

PATTINSON, J.S. Writer on the *Rubaiyat* of Omar Khayyam.

    Far-Ben: or, poems in many models; by J.S. Pattinson. London: Swan Sonnenschein & Co., Lim. 1899. 239 pp.   *OXB*

PAUL, Charles Kegan (1828–1902). Educated at Eton College and Exeter College, Oxford; BA 1849. Curate in Oxfordshire, at Great Tew, 1851–52, at Bloxham, 1852–53. Assistant master at Eton, 1854–62. Vicar, Sturminster Marshall, Dorset, 1862–75. He resigned his Church of England living to become a publisher in London, and eventually became a Roman Catholic. Editor of *New Quarterly Magazine*.

On the way side: verses and translations; by C. Kegan Paul. London: Kegan Paul, Trench, Trübner & Co. Ltd. 1899. viii, 103 pp. *OXB*

PAUL, Sir James Balfour (1846–1931). b. Edinburgh, son of Rev. John Paul of St Cuthbert's. Educated at Edinburgh High School, and Edinburgh University. Member of the Scottish Bar, 1870. Editor of *Journal of Jurisprudence*, 1875–87. Registrar of Friendly Societies for Scotland, 1879–90; treasurer, Faculty of Advocates, 1883–1902; Lyon-King-of-Arms, 1890–1926; secretary, Order of the Thistle, 1926; president, Scottish Ecclesiastical Society, 1929–30. Writer on Scottish heraldry, art and history. Lived at 30 Heriot Row, Edinburgh.

Ballads of the bench and bar: or, the lays of the Parliament House; [by James Balfour Paul and John James Reid]. Printed Edinburgh: T. & A. Constable. 1882. 127 pp. il.

A limited ed. of 305 numbered copies, privately printed. 'All the woodcuts have been destroyed'. *UCD*

PAYNE, John (1842–1916). b. London. Educated privately. He was admitted a solicitor in 1867. Translator from the French, Italian and Arabic. Author of a biographical study of François Villon.

New poems; by John Payne. London: Newman & Co. 1880. x, 295 pp. *MPL*

PAZZO, Monaco, pseud.
Monaco Pazzo's rhymes. London: David Bogue. 1882. viii, 88 pp. *OXB*

PEACHEY, Alfred W. Of Tewkesbury, Gloucestershire.
The red rose boy; Margaret of Anjou, and other poems; by Alfred W. Peachey. Printed Gloucester: H. Osborne. 1885. [viii], 63 pp.
Cover-title is *Poems*. *BL*

PEACOCK, Florence
Poems; by Florence Peacock. Hull: William Andrews & Co., Hull Press; London: Simpkin, Marshall, Hamilton, Kent, & Co., Ltd. 1893. [viii], 82 pp. *BL*

PEARCE, Frank. Lived at 197 Lake Road, Portsmouth, Hampshire.
The entertainer: consisting of poems and songs; by Frank Pearce. Printed Southsea: J.H. Frampton. 1889. [ii], 64 pp. *OXB*

PEARCE, James. Translator from Homer's *Odyssey*.
Freya: a saga of the doom; by James Pearce. London: McCorquodale & Co., Ltd. [1885]. 32 pp. *BL*

PEARSON, Ellen Clare (1839–1914). b. Hope Park, Edinburgh, daughter of William Miller, line-engraver and Quaker. Educated at The Ladies' Institution, Park Place, Edinburgh. Member of Edinburgh Friends' Literary Society. In 1857 she left home to assist at Frenchay School, near Bristol. Visited Friends' missions in the Middle East. In 1873 she married Edward Pearson of Wilmslow, Cheshire.

A dream of a garden, and other poems; by Ellen Clare Pearson. With floral illustrations by W.F.M. Manchester: John Heywood. 1894. 63 pp. col. il.   *TCD*

PEASE, Edward Lloyd (1861–1934). Son of Henry Pease, MP for Darlington. Educated at Oliver's Mount, Scarborough, and Trinity College, Cambridge; BA 1884. A director of Pease & Partners, Ltd. In 1890 he married his cousin, Helen Blanche, daughter of Sir Joseph W. Pease. Lived at Hurworth Moor, Darlington, County Durham.

Verses; by E. Lloyd Pease. London: Hatchards. 1899. xii, 114 pp.
    Privately printed.   *UCD*

PEASE, Sir Joseph Whitwell (1828–1903). Director of several mercantile enterprises, including banking, at Darlington, County Durham. Liberal MP for South Durham, 1865–85, and Barnard Castle, 1885–1903. In 1882 he was created the first Quaker baronet. Chairman of North-Eastern Railway, 1894.

The story of a three weeks' trip to Norway in the steam yacht "Iolanthe", told to friends at home, in verse and prose; [by Sir Joseph Whitwell Pease and Sir Donald Currie]. 1890. 48, lviii pp. map.
    Verses by Pease, prose by Currie. Printed for private circulation only. Cover-title is *Three weeks' trip to Norway in the "Iolanthe"*.   *BL*

PEBBLE, Alexander. Editor of *Wild Flowers: the Leicester Magazine*.

Tama and Zulu, from "Recollections of a pebble" (a poem after the style of Don Juan), and other poems; by Alexander Pebble. London: Town & Country Publishing Co., Ltd. [c. 1880]. 79 pp.   *UCD*

PEEK, Hedley, (Frank Leyton, pseud.). Editor of *The Encyclopaedia of Sport*. Of Outwood, Surrey.

The shadows of the lake, and other poems; by F. Leyton. London: Kegan Paul, Trench, Trübner & Co., Ltd. 1890. xiv, 178 pp.   *OXB*
    Also 2nd ed. 1891.

The shadows of the lake, [and other poems]; by Frank Leyton. 3rd ed. London: Longmans, Green, & Co. 1892. vi, 143 pp.   *OXB*
    Also 4th ed. 1893.

Skeleton leaves: [poems]; by Frank Leyton. London: Kegan Paul, Trench, Trübner & Co., Ltd. 1892. [x], 147 pp.   *OXB*

Skeleton leaves, with a dedicatory poem to the late Hon. Roden Noel: [poems]; by Hedley Peek (Frank Leyton). New ed. London: Longmans, Green, & Co. 1895. 127 pp.   *OXB*

PEEL, A.W. Burke, (Two Bachelors, pseud. with Harry Debron Catling). Of Vicars Hill, London SE.

Versatile verses on the 'varsity, etc.; by two bachelors. Cambridge: J. Hall & Son. 1896. [iv], 31 pp.   *OXB*

PEERIE, Moses, pseud. *see* **STORY, Robert Herbert**, (Moses Peerie, pseud.)

PEMBER, Edward Henry (1833–1911). Educated at Harrow School, and Christ Church, Oxford; BA 1854. Called to the Bar, Lincoln's Inn, 1858; QC 1874; treasurer, 1906–07. He had a large practice at the parliamentary Bar; conducted the bill for building Manchester Ship Canal, 1885; counsel for Cecil Rhodes regarding the Jameson Raid inquiry. A prominent figure in London literary society, an accomplished musician and talker.

Adrastus of Phrygia, and other poems; with, The Hippolytus of Euripides, done into English verse; by E.H. Pember. Printed London: Chiswick Press. [vii], 219 pp.

A limited ed. of 250 numbered copies, printed for private distribution.   *OXB*

The death-song of Thamyris, and other poems; with, The Oedipus at Colonos of Sophocles, done into English verse; by E.H. Pember. Printed London: Chiswick Press. 1899. [vii], 204 pp.

A limited ed. of 250 numbered copies, printed for private distribution.   *OXB*

Debita flacco: echoes of ode and epode; by E.H. Pember. Printed London: Chiswick Press. 1891. [ix], 115 pp. il.

Poems in English and Latin. A limited ed. of 250 copies, printed for private distribution.   *OXB*

The voyage of the Phocaeans, and other poems; with, The Prometheus bound of Aeschylus, done into English verse; by E.H. Pember. Printed London: Chiswick Press. 1895. [vii], 179 pp.

A limited ed. of 250 numbered copies, printed for private distribution.   *OXB*

PEMBERTON, Harriet Louisa Childe- *see* **CHILDE-PEMBERTON, Harriet Louisa**

PENDERRICK, Maurice, pseud. *see* **BENT, Morris, (Maurice Penderrick**, pseud.)

PENGE POET *see* **GWYER, Joseph**

PENNEFATHER, Catherine (1818–93). Daughter of Rear-Admiral James W. King. In 1847 she married Rev. William Pennefather. He organized conferences at Mildmay Park, Islington, to advance missionary work. After his death in 1873 she continued this enterprise. Writer of hymns.

Songs of the pilgrim land; by C. Pennefather. Edited by E. St. B.H. London: John F. Shaw & Co. [1885]. 162 pp.   *OXB*

PENNELL, Henry (Harry) Cholmondeley- *see* **CHOLMONDELEY-PENNELL, Henry (Harry)**

PERCEVAL, C., (Kappa, pseud.)
Gathered leaves: [poems]; by Kappa. Printed London: Spottiswoode & Co.
1894. 96 pp. *★UCD*

PERCY, Henry Algernon George, Lord Percy, (Robert J. Glencairn, pseud.) (1871–1909). Eldest son of 7th Duke of Northumberland. Educated at Eton College, and Christ Church, Oxford; BA 1893; Newdigate prizewinner, 1892. Conservative MP for South Kensington, 1895–1909; parliamentary under-secretary for India, 1902–03, for foreign affairs, 1903–05. Writer on Asiatic Turkey.
Poems and songs of degrees; by Robert J. Glencairn. London: Edward Arnold. [1899]. xii, 166 pp. *OXB*

PERRING, Sir Philip (1828–1920). Son of Rev. Sir John P. Perring. Educated at Shrewsbury School, and Trinity College, Cambridge (scholar); BA 1852, MA 1855. Ordained 1854; curate in London: St James's, Westminster, 1855–60, St John's, Hackney, 1861. Succeeded his father as 4th Bart, 1866. Lived latterly at Llandovery, Exeter, Devon.
The spirit and the muse: containing original hymns and other poems, with translations from the odes of Horace; by Sir Philip Perring. 2nd ed., enlarged. London: Longmans, Green & Co. 1880. xx, 424 pp. *OXB*

PETRE, Lady Catherine (1831–82). b. Ireland, daughter of 4th Earl of Wicklow, and grand-daughter of 1st Marquess of Abercorn. In 1855 she married the Hon. Arthur C. A. Petre, son of 11th Baron Petre. Mother of Lawrence Joseph Petre, meteorologist, and of Maude D. Petre, philanthropist and 'founder' of Westminster Cathedral. A convert to Roman Catholicism, she wrote for various Catholic and other magazines.
Hymns and verses; by Lady Catherine Petre. London: Burns & Oates; New York: Catholic Publication Society Co. [1884]. viii, 182 pp. *OXB*

PETRIE, Mary Louisa Georgina *see* **CARUS-WILSON, Mary Louisa Georgina**

PETSCHLER, Alice Hadfield
The white wreath poems, and other poems; by Alice Hadfield Petschler. London: James Burns. 1896. [iv], 64 pp. *BL*

PFEIFFER, Emily (1827–90). Daughter of R. Davis, an army officer and landowner in Oxfordshire. The family lived in comparative poverty after failure of a bank. In 1853 she married J. E. Pfeiffer, a wealthy German merchant based in London. Conscious of her minimal formal education she worked hard at self-improvement, in 1884 undertaking a long journey through eastern Europe, Asia and America. Her husband died in 1889, and she never recovered from the shock. Interested in the theatre, she left a large sum to found a school of dramatic art. Lived latterly at Mayfield, West Hill, Putney, London SW.

Flowers of the night: [poems]; by Emily Pfeiffer. London: Trubner & Co. 1889. x, 138 pp. *OXB*

The rhyme of the Lady of the Rock, and how it grew; by Emily Pfeiffer. London: Kegan Paul, Trench, & Co. 1884. [vi], 184 p.
Poetry and prose. *OXB*

Sonnets; by Emily Pfeiffer. Revised and enlarged ed. London: Field & Tuer; Simpkin, Marshall & Co.; Hamilton, Adams & Co.; New York: Scribner & Welford. [1886]. vii–xviii, 115 pp. *OXB*

Sonnets and songs; by Emily Pfeiffer. New ed. London: C. Kegan Paul & Co. 1880. x, 104 pp. *OXB*

Under the aspens: lyrical and dramatical; by Emily Pfeiffer. London: Kegan Paul, Trench, & Co. 1882. x, 311 pp. il., por. *CU*

PHELP, A.D. (A.D.P.) Of Leyton, Essex.
Rambles in rhymeland: [poems]; A.D.P. Printed Leyton: Phelp Bros. 1895. [viii], 72 pp. *BL*

PHIL, pseud.
For conference and after: a plea for a rational system of national education, with a plan for solving all difficulties – religious or otherwise; by "Phil". Manchester: John Heywood. [1892?]. 32 pp. *BL*

PHILLIPS, Charles, (Old-New Rhymer, pseud.). Of 123 Brunswick Street, Hackney, London E.
Observanda variorum: an irregular poem, in several canticles; by an old-new rhymer. Canticle I. [London]: Author. [1886]. 23 pp. *OXB*

PHILLIPS, James Gordon (1852–). b. Newmill, Banffshire. Aged nine he was engaged as a 'herdsman', afterwards apprenticed to a tailor in Keith. He gained a considerable local reputation as a verse writer, contributing to the *Banffshire Journal* and the *Elgin Courier*. Interested in archaeology and natural history, he was elected secretary of Elgin & Morayshire Literary & Scientific Association. Lived at Glenlivet.
Wanderings in the highlands of Banff and Aberdeen shires; with trifles in verse; by J.G. Phillips. Printed Banff: Banffshire Journal Office. 1881. 146 pp. *EPL*

PHILLIPS, Stephen (1864–1915). b. Summertown, Oxford, son of Rev. Stephen Phillips, precentor of Peterborough Cathedral. Educated at grammar schools at Stratford and Peterborough. He studied for civil service entrance but abandoned this to go on the stage with Mr Frank Benson's company, 1885–92. Lectured on history as an army tutor, 1892–98, afterwards adopting literature as a profession. He had some success as a dramatic poet. Editor of *Poetry Review* from 1913 until his death.
Christ in Hades, and other poems; by Stephen Phillips. London: Elkin Mathews. 1897. 32 pp. (Garland of new poetry, I). *MPL*

Eremus: a poem; by Stephen Phillips. Printed Fulham: W.J. Perry [1894]. [ii], 72 pp.

  Privately printed. *OXB*

Eremus: a poem; by Stephen Phillips. London: Kegan Paul, Trench, Trübner, & Co., Ltd. 1894. [iv], 60 pp. *OXB*

Orestes, and other poems; by Stephen Phillips. Printed [London]: A.D.P. Press. 1884. [24] pp.

  Printed for private circulation. *BL*

Poems; by Stephen Phillips. London: John Lane The Bodley Head. 1898. [viii], 108 pp. *BL*

  Also 2nd–4th eds 1898.

PHILLIPS, Susan K. (1831–98?). Daughter of Rev. George K. Holdsworth, vicar of Aldborough, West Riding of Yorkshire. In 1856 she married the artist Henry Wyndham Phillips. Some of her verse was written in Yorkshire dialect. She contributed to most of the better known magazines. Lived latterly at Greenroyd, Ripon.

The last poems of Susan K. Phillips. London: Grant Richards. 1898. viii, 134 pp. *OXB*

Told in a coble, and other poems; by Susan K. Phillips. Leeds: J.S. Fletcher & Co. 1884. xvi, 148 pp. *UCD*

PHILOSOPHIA: A LYRICAL SEQUENCE. Dublin: M.H.Gill & Son. 1885. 24 pp. *OXB*

PHILPOT, William (1823–89). b. Southwold, Suffolk, son of Benjamin Philpot, Fellow of Christ's College, Cambridge. Educated at Rugby School, and Trinity College, Cambridge. Vicar of Walesby, Lincolnshire, then vicar of Bersted, Bognor, Sussex.

A scrip of salvage; from the poems of William Philpot. Edited by his son, Hamlet Philpot. London: Macmillan & Co. 1891. xii, 135 pp. *OXB*

PICKERING, Charles J.

The last David, and other poems; [by Charles J. Pickering]. London: Elliot Stock. 1883. [iv], 123 pp. *OXB*

PIDDUCK, W.G.

The legend of Bab's oak, "will o' the wisp"; [by W.G. Pidduck]. Printed Canterbury: Cross & Jackman. 1884. 28 pp. il. *OXB*

PIERCE, James (1834?–92). Son of James P. Pierce, a master at King's College School. Educated at Corpus Christi College, Cambridge; BA 1856, MA 1860. Mathematical master at Bedford Grammar School, 1866–80. Died at Teignmouth, Devon.

In cloud and sunshine: [poems]; by J. Pierce. [London]: Trübner & Co. 1890. viii, 248 pp. *OXB*

Stanzas and sonnets; by J. Pierce. London: Longmans, Green & Co. 1887. viii, 198 pp. *OXB*

PIGOTT, Montague Horatio Mostyn Turtle, (Mostyn P. Pigott), (M.T.P.) (1865–1927). b. London, son of Robert T. Pigott. Educated at Westminster School, and University College, Oxford; BA 1888, MA and BCL 1892. Barrister, Middle Temple, 1890. For many years a contributor to *The World* newspaper.

Common-room carols, and other verses, chiefly relating to Oxford; by M.T.P. Oxford: Alden & Co., Ltd; London: Simpkin, Marshall, Hamilton, Kent & Co., Ltd. 1893. viii, 122 pp. *OXB*

Songs of a session: being a lyric record of parliamentary doings during 1896; by Mostyn P. Pigott. London: A.D. Innes & Co. 1896. viii, 120 pp. *OXB*

PIGOTT, Mostyn P. *see* **PIGOTT, Montague Horatio Mostyn Turtle**, (Mostyn P. Pigott), (M.T.P.)

PIM, Mrs Edward Bedford *see* **PIM, Sophia Soltau**

PIM, Sophia Soltau (1799–1885?). Daughter of John F. Harrison, and eldest of fourteen children. The family lived on the continent. In 1825 she married Lieutenant Edward Bedford Pim, Royal Navy, who died of yellow fever in 1830 while engaged in suppression of the slave trade. She lived latterly at Leaside, Kingswood Road, Upper Norwood, London SE.

Job, and fugitive pieces; by Mrs. Edward Bedford Pim. London: Gee & Co. 1885. x, 51 pp.

Poetry and prose. *BL*

PIMLICO, Lord, pseud.

The excellent mystery: a matrimonial satire; by Lord Pimlico. London: Vizetelly & Co. 1888. 60 pp. *OXB*

PINDAR, John, pseud. *see* **LESLIE, Peter**, (John Pindar, pseud.)

PINKERTON, Percy *see* **PINKERTON, Percy Edward**

PINKERTON, Percy Edward. b. London, son of George Pinkerton. Educated in Kingston upon Thames, and in Germany. Translator of various foreign works, including operas and songs. Had a keen interest in music, philosophy, and first-class cricket. Lived at 18 St Barnabas Road, Cambridge.

Adriatica: [poems]; by Percy Pinkerton. London: Gay & Bird. 1894. viii, 104 pp. *OXB*

Galeazzo: a Venetian episode, with other poems; by Percy E. Pinkerton. Venice: F. Ongania; London: Sonnenschein & Co. 1886. 71 pp. il. *BL*

PITCAIRN, Janet Wyld, (J.W.P.) (1865–89). b. Edinburgh, daughter of A.Y. Pitcairn, and grand-daughter of Rev. Thomas Pitcairn, clerk of the General Assembly. Educated in Edinburgh. Her prose and verse was published in *Christian Week, Home Friend*, and other periodicals.

The shepherd, and other verses; by J.W.P. Edinburgh: Oliphant Anderson & Ferrier. [1889]. 102 pp. *BL*

The shepherd, and other verses; by Janet Wyld Pitcairn. New ed., revised and enlarged. Edinburgh: Oliphant, Anderson, & Ferrier. 1897. 134 pp. *BL*

PITCHFORD, John Watkins (1834?–   ). b. Hereford, son of John Pitchford, printer. Educated at Trinity College, Dublin; BA 1862, MA 1865. Ordained 1867; curate, Tattenhall, Cheshire, 1866–68, Newcastle under Lyme, Staffordshire, 1868–70, St James's, Bath, 1870–76; vicar, St Jude's, Southwark, London, from 1876.

Aelfred; by John Watkins Pitchford. London: Author. [1895]. [iv], 336 pp.   *OXB*

Bramble cloisters: [poems]; by John Watkins Pitchford. London: Elliot Stock. 1884. [iv], 121 pp.   *OXB*

Bramble cloisters; [poems]; by John Watkins Pitchford. Revised ed. London: [Author]. 1899. [iv], 80 pp.

Bound with author's *Deerleap dusk*, 1899. Spine-title is Poems.   *TCD*

Deerleap dusk: a dream of sorrow; by John Watkins Pitchford. London: [Author]. 1899. 43 pp.

Bound with author's *Bramble cloisters*, revised ed., 1899. Spine-title is *Poems*.   *TCD*

The morning song: a ninefold praise of love: [poems]; by John Watkins Pitchford. London: Elliot Stock: 1883. [vi], 373 pp.   *OXB*

PITMAN, William (1823–89). He was baptized in the Abbey Church, Bath. Died in Highgate, London.

Sacred poems; by William Pitman. 1889. 29 pp.

Cover-title is *In memoriam William Pitman*.   *TAU*

PITTITE, pseud.

Europa's moods (the gay and the warlike) and Britannia's peril, in two cantos; by a Pittite. London: Simpkin, Marshall, Hamilton, Kent & Co., Ltd. 1894. 59 pp.   *OXB*

PLANCHE, James Robinson (1796–1880). b. London, of Huguenot descent. He combined the professions of antiquary and official herald (Rouge Croix from 1854, Somerset Herald from 1866) with that of writer of burlesques and other pieces for the theatre. He was connected with several London theatres: Vauxhall Gardens, the Adelphi, the Olympic, the Lyceum, and Covent Garden.

Songs and poems, from 1819 to 1879; by J.R. Planché. London: Chatto & Windus. 1881. x, 158 pp.   *MPL*

PLARR, Victor (1863–1929). b. Strasbourg, son of Dr Gustavus Plarr. Educated at Tonbridge School, and Worcester College, Oxford; BA 1885, MA 1897. Librarian of King's College, London, 1891–97, and to the Royal College of Surgeons, 1911–22. Writer, editor, and contributor to many journals.

In the Dorian mood: [poems]; by Victor Plarr. London: John Lane, The Bodley Head; New York: George H. Richmond & Co. 1896. viii, 112 pp.   *OXB*

PLATT, Arthur. Translator from the Greek.
Marpessa: a masque, with eight odes; by Arthur Platt. Cambridge: Deighton, Bell & Co.; London: Geo. Bell & Sons. 1888. [viii], 63 pp. *OXB*

PLATT, William. Of London. Miscellaneous writer.
Do we live, do we love?; by William Platt. London: Author. 1896. xviii, 196 pp.
   Poetry and prose. *TCD*
Hope's brotherhood: a poem; by William Platt. London: "Clarion" Office; Manchester: Labour Press Society Ltd; Glasgow: "Labour Leader" Office. [c. 1896]. 32 pp. *OXB*
Women, love and life; by William Platt. London: Charles Hirsch. 1895. xii, 200 pp. il.
   Poetry and prose. *TCD*

PLEDGE, E.M. Novelist.
Loving whispers for lowly workers: [poems]; by E.M. Pledge. London: Elliot Stock. 1896. viii, 71 pp. *OXB*

PLEON, Harry. Playwright.
Recitations, rhymes and ridiculosities; by Harry Pleon. London: Howard & Co. 1893. 38 pp. *UCD*

PLUMBE, Charles. Of Sutton-in-Ashfield, Nottinghamshire.
Fugitive rhymes; by Charles Plumbe. Printed Sutton-in-Ashfield, Notts: Sherwood Press. 1884. iii pp.
   Printed by and for the author for private circulation. *UCD*

PLUMPTRE, Edward Hayes (1821–91). b. London. Educated at University College, Oxford; BA 1844, MA 1847. Fellow of Brasenose College, 1844–47. Chaplain, King's College, London, 1847–68; professor of pastoral theology, 1853–63, professor of exegesis, 1864–81. Grinfield lecturer, Oxford University, 1872–74. Dean of Wells, 1881–91. Author of theological works, verse translations of Sophocles and Aeschylus, and a biography of Bishop Ken.
Things new and old: [poems]; by E.H. Plumptre. London: Griffith & Farran. [1884]. 200 pp. *UCD*

PODD, pseud. *see* **COLE, Thomas E.**, (Podd, pseud.)

POEMS BY TWO. Dundee: D.R. Clark & Son; Greenock: M'Kelvie & Son. 1882. viii, 126 pp. *JRL*

POET OF THE MOY *see* **FLANAGAN, Edward**

A POETASTER'S HOLIDAY: [poems]. London: T. Fisher Unwin. 1890. 125 pp. *OXB*

POETICAL WILD OATS: [poems]. Illustrated by the author. London: Digby, Long & Co. [1891]. viii, 130 pp. il. *OXB*

POLITICAL EPIGRAMS, 1874–81: [poems]. London: P.S. King. 1881. 24 pp. *OXB*

POLLOCK, Sir Frederick (1845–1937). Son of Sir William F. Pollock. Educated at Eton College, and Trinity College, Cambridge. Fellow of Trinity, 1868. Called to the Bar, Lincoln's Inn, 1871; bencher, 1906. Professor of jurisprudence, University College, London, 1882–83; Corpus professor of jurisprudence, Oxford, 1883–1903. Editor of *Law Quarterly Review*, 1885–1919; editor-in-chief of *Law Reports*, 1895–1935. Wrote on many aspects of law.

Leading cases done into English, and other diversions: [poems]; by Sir Frederick Pollock. London: Macmillan & Co. 1892. x, 98 pp. *MPL*

POLLOCK, Walter Herries (1850–1926). b. London, second son of Sir William F. Pollock. Educated at Eton College, and Trinity College, Cambridge; BA 1871, MA 1875. Called to the Bar, Inner Temple, 1874. Sub-editor, *Saturday Review*, editor, 1883–94, retiring because of ill-health. Writer on French literature, of a book on Jane Austen and her contemporaries, a treatise on fencing, and several plays in collaboration with Sir Walter Besant. Organizer of the Rabelais Club.

Old and new: [poems]; by Walter Herries Pollock. London: Eden, Remington & Co. 1890. viii, 120 pp. por. (Rosslyn series). *BL*

Old and new: "Apres tant de jours": [poems]; by Walter Herries Pollock. 2nd ed. London: Eden, Remington & Co. 1890. viii, 120 pp. por. (Rosslyn series). *OXB*

Songs and rhymes: English and French; by Walter Herries Pollock. London: Remington & Co. 1882. 80 pp. *OXB*

Verses of two tongues; by Walter Herries Pollock. London: Remington & Co. 1884. 79 pp. *OXB*

POOF, pseud.

Bribery! and corruption!: the comic companion to the Corrupt Practices Act: [poems]; [by Poof]. [Illustrated by Gil]. London: Sampson Low, Marston, Searle, & Rivington. [1886]. 30 pp. il.

Title from cover. *OXB*

The fowl deceiver: a lay of the inventions exhibition; by Poor. Illustrated by Gil. London: Field & Tuer; Simpkin, Marshall & Co; Hamilton, Adams & Co. [1885]. [44] pp. il. *OXB*

POOLE, Eva L. Evered *see* **EVERED POOLE, Eva L.**

POPPLESTONE, John. Articled in London. Practised there before going to Stourmouth, Kent, where he was town clerk for forty years.

The lays of a limb of the law; by the late John Popplestone. Edited, with a memoir and postcript, by Edmund B.V. Christian. London: Reeves & Turner. 1889. xxii, 162 pp. il. *OXB*

PORRI, Louis. Lived at 4 Kent Street, Grimsby, Lincolnshire.
Poems; by Louis Porri. London: Simpkin, Marshall & Co.; Hull: "Eastern Morning News". 1882. 100 pp.   *OXB*

PORTEOUS, Provost. Of Lasswade, Midlothian.
Poems; composed by Provost Porteous, on the occasion of Her Majesty Queen Victoria's diamond jubilee, June 1897 . . . [1897]. 28 pp.   *UCD*

PORTER, George
Anachronism: an illustrated ballad; by George Porter. [London]: Remington & Co. [1881]. [ii], 159 pp. il.
        Published for the author.   *OXB*

PORTER, William (1819–   ). b. Lyme Regis, Dorset.
Poems, etc.; by W. Porter. Lyme Regis: F. Dunster. 1892. [iv], 91 pp. por.   *OXB*

PORTEUS, Thomas Cruddas (1876–1948). b. Netherton, Worcestershire, son of Rev. T. Porteus. Educated at Owens College, Manchester. Vicar, St John the Divine, Coppull, Lancashire, 1912–34. President, Lancashire Authors Association, 1938–45; president, Lancashire & Cheshire Antiquarian Society, 1940–43. Lived latterly at Summer Hill, Bolton Road, Chorley.
The rosebud recitations: new poems, histrionic, humorous, and humanitarian; by T. Cruddas Porter. Sheffield: Author. 1897. 64 pp.   *OXB*

POSTGATE, Isabella J. Novelist and general writer.
A Christmas legend, and other verses; by Isabella J. Postgate. London: Simpkin, Marshall & Co.; Birmingham: Midland Educational Co. [1889]. xii, 122 pp.   *BL*
        Also 2nd ed. 1889.
Little Saint Cyril, and other poems; by Isa. J. Postgate. With a preface by Rev. Thomas Pollock. Oxford: Mowbray & Co.; Birmingham: Midland Educational Co. [1896]. viii, 83 pp. il.   *BL*

POSTMAN BARD *see* **FAIRLEY, Cessford Ramsay Sawyers**

POSTMAN POET *see* **HYSLOP, John**

POUTE, pseud. *see* **BURGESS, Alexander**, (Poute, pseud.)

POVEY, Jane Mary, (Sister Mary Agnes). Of the Convent of Mercy, 50 Crispin Street, London E.
Thoughts in verse; by Sister Mary Agnes. London: Kegan Paul, Trench, Trübner & Co. Ltd. 1894. xii, 151 pp.   *OXB*

POWEL, Esther
The story of a life, and other poems; by Esther Powel. London: Digby, Long & Co. [1892]. [vi], 56 pp.   *OXB*
Vox humana: [poems]; by Esther Powel. London: Jarrold & Sons. 1897. 38 pp.   *OXB*

POWELL, G.A. Connected with the Government's War Refugees' Camp, Earls Court, London, during the First World War.
Aline, and other poems; by G.A. Powell. Printed London: Digby & Long. [1892]. [iv], 164 pp.
Printed for the author.   *OXB*

POWELL, George Herbert (1856–1924). Son of Rev. Thomas E. Powell of Bisham, Berkshire. Educated at Uppingham School, and King's College, Cambridge; BA 1879. Called to the Bar, Inner Temple, 1885. Worked at coaching law students. Collector of fifteenth- and sixteenth-century foreign literature. Lived at 2 Thanet Place, Temple Bar.
Occasional rhymes & reflections upon subjects social, literary, and political; by G.H. Powell. 2nd ed. revised and corrected, with notes. London: Lawrence & Bullen. 1892. x, 96 pp.   *NLS*

POWELL, Herbert. Of Winchester, Hampshire?
Lyrics of the white city: [poems]; by Herbert Powell. London: Simpkin & Co., Ltd; Winchester: Warren & Son. 1896. [x], 72 pp.   *TCD*

POWYS, John Cowper (1872–1963). b. Shirley, Derbyshire, son of Rev. Charles F. Powys. Educated at Sherborne school, and Corpus Christi College, Cambridge. After graduation he taught German at Brighton, then became a university extension lecturer; lectured in the United States, 1934–38. Writer of novels, criticism, and works on philosophy.
Odes and other poems; by John Cowper Powys. London: William Rider & Son, Ltd. 1896. [vi], 56 pp.   *OXB*
Poems; by John Cowper Powys. London: William Rider & Son, Ltd. 1899. [viii], 123 pp.   *OXB*

POWYS, Thomas Jones, pseud. *see* **JONES, Thomas**, (Thomas Jones Powys, pseud.)

PRATT, Tinsley (1871–19). b. Leicester, son of Josiah Pratt. Librarian and secretary, Portico Library, Manchester. Editor of *The Manchester Quarterly*. Assistant editor to T.C. & E.C. Jack of Edinburgh, 1911–12. Hon. secretary, Manchester Literary Club. Lived latterly at Orchard Road, Northenden.
Persephone in Hades, and other poems; by Tinsley Pratt. London: Kegan Paul, Trench, Trübner & Co. Ltd. 1899. 75 pp.   *MPO*
Wordsworth at Rydal, and other poems; by Tinsley Pratt. Manchester: John Heywood. 1897. 72 pp.   *MPL*

PRESCOTT, Thomas, (Thomas Mead, pseud.) (1819–89). b. Cambridge, son of a Methodist minister. He ran away from home to appear on the provincial stage, first appearing in London at the Victoria Theatre, 1848. Actor and comedian, a varied career included management of the Elephant & Castle Theatre. He played in Shakespearian revivals at the Lyceum until his death.
The lady of the rose, and other poems; by Thomas Mead. 1881. [ii], 241 pp. por.   *OXB*

PRESTON, Benjamin (1819–1902). b. Bradford, son of a handloom weaver. He became a wool sorter and comber, then a publican at Bingley Common in 1865. Later moved to Aldwick, then to Saltaire. Known as 'The Burns of Bradford'.
Dialect and other poems; by Ben Preston. With glossary of the local words. London: Simpkin, Marshall & Co. 1881. xiv, 263 pp. por.   *UCD*

PREVOST, Francis, pseud. *see* **BATTERSBY, Henry Francis Prevost**, (Francis Prevost, pseud.)

PRICE, Charlotte A.
Poems and lyrics for idle hours; by Charlotte A. Price. London: F.V. White & Co. 1881. viii, 244 pp.   *OXB*

PRIDEAUX, Fanny Ash (1826–94). Daughter of Richard and Mary Ball of Taunton, Somerset. In 1853 she married her second cousin, Frederick Prideaux, professor of law to the Inns of Court. She was a Quaker until she resigned to join the Church of England.
Philip Molesworth, and other poems; by Mrs. Frederick Prideaux. London: Sampson Low, Marston, Searle, & Rivington. 1886. iv, 258 pp.   *UCD*

PRIDEAUX, Mrs Frederick *see* **PRIDEAUX, Fanny Ash**

PRIME, Priestley. A Quaker. Author of *A Record of the United Brethren of Devon and Cornwall*.
Solos in verse; by Priestley Prime. London: Swan Sonnenschein & Co., Ltd. 1896. 64 pp.   *OXB*

PRIMROSE, Peter, pseud. *see* **LONGSTAFFE, John Lawrance**, (Peter Primrose, pseud.)

PRIMROSE KNIGHT, pseud.
The rime of the ancient senator: or, confessions of "an old man in a hurry": a ballad for the times, (with apologies to S.T.C.); by a primrose knight. Reading: F. Blackwell. [1889]. 16 pp.   *OXB*

PRIMROSES: AN ELEGY, IN FOUR CANTOS, WRITTEN IN MEMORY OF THE LATE EARL OF BEACONSFIELD; WITH WHICH ARE INCORPORATED 'THE SONGS OF THE PEOPLE'.
London: Griffith & Farran. 1884. [2], xii, 122 pp.   *OXB*

PRINCE, Aelian, pseud. *see* **CARR, Francis**, (Aelian Prince, pseud.)

PRIOR, John. Possibly John Prior (1861–19   ). b. Darlington, County Durham. Educated at Douai, and the English College, Rome. Vice-Rector of Bede College, and sometime Rome correspondent of *The Tablet*.

A search for fame: or, the power of example: a poem; by John Prior. Manchester: William Bremner; London: Partride & Co. [189–?]. 16 pp.   *MPL*

PROBYN, Laetitia

[Poems]; [by] Laetitia Probyn. London: Macmillan & Co. 1880. 100 pp.   *★UCD*

PROBYN, May. Daughter of Julain Probyn of Longhope, Gloucestershire. A novelist, she lived in London, becoming a friend of Katharine Tynan. She was received into the Roman Catholic Church in 1883.

A ballad of the road, and other poems; by May Probyn. London: W. Satchell & Co. 1883. viii, 130 pp.   *BL*

Pansies: a book of poems; by May Probyn. London: Elkin Mathews. 1895. [iv], 71 pp.   *OXB*

Pansies: a book of poems; by May Probyn. London: Elkin Mathews. 1895. [viii], 72 pp.

One of only three final proof copies containing the last poem 'A legend', subsequently suppressed.   *OXB*

Poems; by May Probyn. London: W. Satchell & Co. 1881. 78 pp.   *BL*

PROFESSOR OF POETRY *see* **FITZACHARY, John Christopher**

The **PROGRESS OF LOVE, PER ARDUA AD ASTRA**: [poems]. London: Digby, Long & Co. [1895]. 93 pp.   *OXB*

PROGRESSUS, pseud.

Freedom, love and brotherhood: verses; by Progressus. London: E.W. Allen. [1881]. viii, 101 pp.   *OXB*

PROTEUS, pseud. *see* **BLUNT, Wilfrid Scawen**, (Proteus, pseud.)

PROUDLOCK, Lewis. A miner of the Borders country.

The "Borderland muse": [poems]; by Lewis Proudlock. London: O'Driscoll, Lennox & Co. [1896]. [xvi], 359 pp. por.   *OXB*

PRYER, William Stephen

Rowena & Harold: a romance in rhyme of an olden time, of Hastyngs and Normanhurst; by Wm. Stephen Pryer. With illustrations & portrait of the author. London: Ward, Lock & Co.; Electric Publishing Co. [1897]. 53 pp. il.   *OXB*

Though-crystals in verse: being a selection of a few favourite odes, poems, sonnets, &c.,; by Wm. Stephen Pryer. London: Geo. Gill & Sons. [1893]. 23 pp. il. Title from cover.   *OXB*

PRYNNE, George Rundle (1818–1903). b. West Looe, Cornwall. Educated at St Catharine's College, Cambridge; BA 1840, MA 1861. Ordained 1841; vicar of St Peter's, Plymouth, from 1848 to his death. He was involved in controversy and litigation on account of his support of Dr Pusey's views on Anglican Catholicism and ritualism.

The soldier's dying visions, and other poems and hymns; by George Rundle Prynne. London: J. Masters & Co. 1881. xii, 250 pp.
Spine-title is Poems and hymns.   *OXB*

PSYCHOSIS, pseud.

Our modern philosophers, Darwin, Bain and Spencer: or, the descent of man, mind and body: a rhyme with reasons, essays, notes and quotations; by "Psychosis". London: T. Fisher Unwin. 1884. xx, 215 pp.   *OXB*

PUGHE, George Richard Gould (1831–19). b. Golfa Hall near Welshpool, Montgomeryshire, son of Rev. Richard Pughe. Educated at Oswestry, Shrewsbury School, and Trinity College, Oxford. Ordained 1859; curate, Aberhafesp, Montgomeryshire, 1857–59, St Peter's, and St John's, Blackburn, Lancashire, Holy Trinity, Darwen, Lancashire, 1860–64; vicar, Mellor, Blackburn, from 1864.

The Church in Wales: a versified review of her reverses; by G.R.G. Pughe. Blackburn: [Author]. 1894. 29 pp.   *MPL*

PUNGOLO, pseud.

The democrat's companion; by Pungolo. Leeds: J.T. Hampshire. [188–]. 108 pp.
Poetry and prose.   *LEP*

PURDIE, David Walter (1860–). b. Hutlerbury, Vale of Ettrick, Selkirkshire. Educated at the parish school, he was sent to work on a farm at the age of thirteen. He lived at Brockhill, a small croft near Ettrick Bridgend. Elected to the parish school board. Known as 'The Ettrick Bard', and self-styled 'an unlettered son of toil'.

Poems and songs; by David W. Purdie, "The Ettrick Bard". Selkirk: George Lewis & Co. 1897. [2], viii, 168 pp. por.   *OXB*

PUTMAN, Henry

His star and vesper bells: [poems]; by Henry Putman. London: H.R. Allenson. [1895]. 45 pp.   *OXB*

PYKE-NOTT, John Nott (1841–1920). Son of Rev. John Pyke. Educated at Winchester College, and Exeter College, Oxford (scholar). Lived at The Mill House, Dumbleton, Evesham, Worcestershire.

Aeonial: the flood: Gehenna: (Aurea's visions); by [John Nott Pyke-Nott]. London: Elliot Stock. 1887. [iv], 59 pp.   *OXB*

PYNE, Evelyn. A woman.

The poet in May: [poems]; by Evelyn Pyne. London: Kegan, Paul, Trench & Co. 1885. viii, 167 pp.   *OXB*

PYOTT, William (1851–   ). b. Ruthven, Forfarshire, son of a mill overseer. In his twelfth year the family moved to Blairgowrie, Perthshire, where he was sent to work in a flax mill, attending a half-time school at Craig Mill, Rattray. He worked as a cloth lapper until appointed colporteur of the district.

Poems and songs; by William Pyott. Printed Blairgowrie: Advertiser Office. [1883]. 76 pp.   *OXB*

Poems and songs; by William Pyott. New and enlarged ed. Dundee: Charles Alexander & Co. 1885. [viii], 119 pp.   *OXB*

Q

QUARTERMAN, Annie. Daughter of Matthew and Annie Steele. Mrs Quarterman of Teddington-on-Thames, Middlesex.

The "diamond": poems and sonnets; by Annie Quarterman. London: Andrews Bros. 1897. 64 pp.   *OXB*

QUASI NESSUNO, pseud.

"Agnosta", and other poems; by Quasi Nessuno. Simla: Cotton & Morris. 1894. [iv], 128 pp.   *OXB*

QUEEN'S POETESS *see* **GORDON, Ella Mary**

QUEENSBERRY, Lord *see* **DOUGLAS, John Sholto, Lord Queensberry**

QUEENSLAND POET *see* **STEPHENS, James Brunton**

QUETTEVILLE, Philip Winter De *see* **DE QUETTEVILLE, Philip Winter**

QUEX, pseud. *see* **VINSON, E.**, (Quex, pseud.)

QUILL, Albert William (1843–1908). b. County Kerry, son of Thomas Quill. Educated at Old Hall Green, Herefordshire, and Trinity College, Dublin. He was one of the few Roman Catholic scholars at Trinity before the abolition of tests. Became a barrister. Writer of several books, and contributor of verse to the *Irish Times*. Lived at Rathgar, Dublin, and Carriganas Castle, Bantry, County Cork.

Poems; by Albert W. Quill. Vol. I. Dublin: William McGee; London: Simpkin, Marshall, Hamilton, Kent & Co. 1895. 50 pp.   *BL*

QUILLER-COUCH, Sir Arthur Thomas, (Q) (1863–1944). b. Bodmin, Cornwall, son of a doctor. Educated at Newton Abbot, Clifton College, and Trinity College, Oxford. Lectured in Oxford for five years after graduation, then settled in London as a writer and journalist. He moved to Fowey, Cornwall, in 1892. Editor of *The Oxford Book of English Verse*, 1900, and *The Oxford Book of Victorian Verse*, 1912. Knighted in 1910. Appointed King Edward VII professor of English literature at Cambridge in 1912. He was elected mayor of Fowey in 1937.

Athens: a poem; by Arthur T. Quiller Couch. Bodmin: Liddell & Son. [1881]. 15 pp.
 Reprinted for private circulation. *BL*
Green bays; verses and parodies; by Q. London: Methuen & Co. 1893. xii, 91 pp. *MPL*
Poems and ballands; by Q. London: Methuen & Co. 1896. viii, 118 pp. *MPL*

QUIRK, Henry, (Henry O'Cuirc, pseud.) (1847–).b. Dublin of a Tipperary family. Educated at Clonmel, Tipperary; served for a time in the army. He became a professor of music in London. Some of his poems were set to music.

Irish songs and guard room rhymes; by Henry O'Cuirc. London; Hirst, Smyth & Son. 1881. 102 pp. *OXB*

R

R.,A.
 Faithful for ever: a poem; by A.R. London: Robert Banks. 1882. 105 pp. *★UCD*

R., A.G. *see* **RENSHAW, Alfred George**, (A.G.R.)

R., B.M.
 Sheen and shade: [poems]; by J.R. and B.M.R. 1887. 92 pp.
  Inscribed by J.R. to her children. *★UCD*

R.,C.
 Poems; by C.R. Printed London. [1892]. 31 pp.
  Printed for the author. *OXB*

R., C.C. *see* **RHYS, Charles Cureton**, (C.C.R.)

R., E.A.
 Aureliana: [poems]; by E.A.R. 1885. [vi], 123 pp.
  Printed for private circulation. *BL*

R., E.J. *see* **RENSHAW, Emily Jane**, (E.J.R.)

R., J. A woman.
The pilgrim mother, [and other poems]; by J.R. [1880]. 16 pp.   *BL*

R.J.
Sheen and shade; [poems]; by J.R. and B.M.R. 1887. 92 pp.
Inscribed by J.R. to her children.   *★UCD*

R., J. *see* **RAE, James**, (J.R.)

R., J. *see* **ROCK, James**, (J.R.)

R., M.E.
Claudia; and, The death of Ahab; by M.E.R. London: Marshall, Russell, & Co.;
Whitby: Newton & Son. 1895. [23] pp.
Printed on one side of leaf only.   *OXB*

R., M.G. *see* **REDDEN, Mary Gertrude**, (M.G.R.)

R., W. Wayside verses; by a brother and sister [Elizabeth Scott and W.R.].
Tewkesbury: W. North. [1896]. 94 pp.   *★UCD*

RABLEN, J.R.
The raft, and other poems; [by J.R. Rablen]. With an explanatory introduction.
Printed London: Chiswick Press. 1885. 146 pp.   *★UCD*

RACEHL, G.
The son of God: [poems]; by G. Racehl. London: Edward Hughes, & Co.
[1899]. 136 pp.   *OXB*

RADFORD, Dollie (1858–1920). b. Worcester, daughter of a London West
End tailor named Maitland. She married Ernest Radford, art historian and
critic. They knew Eleanor Marx, William Morris, D.H. Lawrence, G.B.
Shaw, and other leading literary figures of the day. She had three children, and
most of her married life was spent in London, in Hammersmith and at 32 Well
Walk, Hampstead.
Good night: [poems]; by Dollie Radford. With designs by Louis Davis.
London: David Nutt. 1895. [80] pp. il.
Printed on one side of leaf only.   *OXB*
A light load; [poems]; by Dollie Radford. London: Elkin Mathews. 1891. xii,
64 pp.   *OXB*
A light load: poems; by Dollie Radford. With designs by Beatrice E. Parsons.
London: Elkin Mathews. 1897. viii, 76 pp. il.   *BL*
Songs, and other verses; by Dollie Radford. London: John Lane The Bodley
Head; Philadelphia: J.B. Lippincott Co. 1895. 94 pp.   *OXB*
Songs for somebody; by Dollie Radford. Pictured by GMB [Gertrude M.
Bradley]. London: David Nutt. 1893. [67] pp. il., col. il.
Printed on one side of leaf only.   *BL*
Songs for somebody; by Dollie Radford. Pictured by G.M.B. [Gertrude M.
Bradley]. London: David Nutt. 1893. [73] pp. il., col. il.

A limited ed. of 100 numbered copies printed on Japanese vellum paper, and signed by the author and publisher. Printed on one side of leaf only. *OXB*

RADFORD, Ernest. Art historian and critic; he knew all the leading artistic and literary figures of the day. He married Dollie Maitland; most of their married life was spent in Lonon, in Hammersmith and at 32 Well Walk, Hampstead.

Chambers twain, [and other poems]; by Ernest Radford. London: Elkin Mathews. 1890. xii, 100 pp. *OXB*

Measured steps: [poems]; by Ernest Radford. London: T. Fisher Unwin. 1884. viii, 88 pp. *OXB*

Old and new: a collection of poems; by Ernest Radford. London: T. Fisher Unwin. 1895. xvi, 186 pp. por.
    A limited ed. of 500 copies. *OXB*

Translations from Heine, and other verses; by Ernest Radford. Cambridge: E. Johnson; London: William Reeves. 1882. viii, 93 pp. *UCD*

RADFORD, Sir George Heynes. b. Plymouth, Devon. Educated at Amersham College, Caversham, and University College, London. Admitted solicitor, 1872; senior partner in Messrs Radford & Frankland from 1880. JP for Surrey. Liberal MP for East Islington from 1906. Lived latterly at Chiswick House, Ditton Hill, Surbiton, Surrey.

Occasional verses; by G.H. Radford. London: J.M. Dent & Co. 1888. 40 pp. *UCD*

RAE, James, (J.R.) (1842–). b. Dennyloadhead, Stirlingshire, son of a cartwright. Educated at Allen's School, Stirling, and Bannockburn Academy. Aged sixteen he was apprenticed to a Stirling coachmaker, eventually practising his trade in Glasgow. He became manager of the coachbuilding works of Glasgow Tramway & Omnibus Co. for sixteen years, during which time he took out many patents for mechanical appliances. President of the Glasgow Bank Burns Club.

Imperial poems; by J.R. [1888]. 16 pp.
    Title from cover. *OXB*

RAE, John S. (1859–). b. Cross Gight Farm, New Deer, Aberdeenshire. When he was three the family moved to Alvah, Banffshire. Originally intended for farming, he learned drapery in Glasgow, afterwards moving to London to work in a large wholesalers.

Poems and songs; by John S. Rae. With introduction by D.H. Edwards. Edinburgh: John Menzies & Co. 1884. 240 pp. *UCD*

RAE, Thomas (1868–89). b. Galashiels, Selkirkshire. He left school aged thirteen, and was apprenticed to a draper, remaining there for two years before entering a factory. His health soon failed so that he was unable to earn a living. Wrote for the *Border Advertiser*.

Songs and verses; by Thomas Rae. With a preface by Andrew Lang. Printed Edinburgh: T. & A. Constable. 1890. xvi, 67 pp.

A limited ed. of 200 numbered copies.   *UCD*

RAE-BROWN, Campbell. Novelist, and comedy playwright.

The race with death, and other ballads and readings; by Campbell Rae-Brown. London: Ward, Lock & Co., Ltd. 1896. xii, 98 pp.   *UCD*

Rae-Brown's ballads (humorous and otherwise), for recitation and the fireside; by Campbell Rae-Brown. London: Dean & Son. [1889]. 83 pp. (Dean's books for elocutionists).

Poetry and prose.   *OXB*

Rhymes: romantic and racy, for recitation; by Campbell Rae-Brown. London: Samuel French, Ltd. [1887]. 63 pp.   *UCD*

Rhymes of the times: consisting of ballads for recitation, with prose readings "A tragedy of the turf" and "Catalina tiles"; by Campbell Rae-Brown. London: Dean & Son. [1889]. 84 pp. (Dean's books for elocutionists).   *OXB*

Ryder's last race, and other humorous recitations; by Campbell Rae-Brown. London: Dean & Son. [1889]. 79 pp. (Dean's books for elocutionists).   *OXB*

RAE-BROWN, Colin (1821–   ). b. Greenock, Renfrewshire, son of a captain in the merchant service. The family moved to Glasgow in 1831. He joined a fine art and general publishing firm, later becoming managing partner in a similar business in Greenock. In 1847 he was appointed manager of the *North British Daily Mail* in Glasgow. Friend of Thomas De Quincy, Charles Mackay, and George Cruickshank. Originated the Glasgow movement culminating in the erection of the national Wallace monument.

The dawn of love, and other poems; by Colin Rae-Brown. Complete ed. With portrait and memoir of the author [by John Muir]. Paisley: Alexander Gardner. 1892. xliv, 317 pp. por.   *MPL*

RAEBURN, Mrs

Poems: by Mrs. Raeburn. Printed Edinburgh: Morrison & Gibb. 1887. 240 pp.   *NLS*

RAFFALOVICH, Mark Andre (1864–   ). Son of Herman Raffalovich of Paris, banker. He lived in Edinburgh, a convert to Roman Catholicism. His sister married William O'Brien, MP, leader of the Independent Nationalists. A contributor to foreign periodicals.

Cyril; and, Lionel, and other poems: a volume of sentimental studies; by Mark Andre Raffalovich. London: Kegan Paul, Trench & Co. 1884. [viii], 102 pp.   *OXB*

In fancy dress: [poems]; by Mark Andre Raffalovich. London: Walter Scott. 1886. iv, 148 pp.   *OXB*

It is thyself: [poems]; by Mark Andre Raffalovich. London: Walter Scott. 1889. 147 pp.   *OXB*

The thread; and, The path; by Mark Andre Raffalovich. London: David Nutt. 1895. viii, 106 pp.   *OXB*

Tuberose and meadowsweet, [and other poems]; by Mark Andre Raffalovich. London: David Bogue. 1885. viii, 120 pp.   *UCD*

RAGG, Frederick William (1845–1929). b. Birmingham, son of Rev. Thomas Ragg of Lawley, Shropshire. Educated in Birmingham, and at Trinity College, Cambridge; BA 1874, MA 1877. Ordained 1878; curate, Nonnington, Kent, 1877–80; vicar, Masworth, Buckinghamshire, 1880–1906, retiring owing to ill-health. Lived latterly at The Manor House, Boddington, Northamptonshire.

King Alfred's dreams, and other poems; by Frederick W. Ragg. London: Rivingtons. 1899. x, 122 pp.   *OXB*

Quorsum?: a cry of human suffering: a poem; by Frederick W. Ragg. London: Rivington, Percival & Co. 1894. viii, 232 pp.   *OXB*

Sonnets, and other poems; by Frederick W. Ragg. London: Rivington, Percival & Co. 1895. 103 pp.   *OXB*

RAIKES, Henry Cecil (1838–91). Educated at Trinity College, Cambridge. Called to the Bar, Middle Temple, 1863. A Conservative, he was elected MP for Chester, 1868–80, MP for Preston, Lancashire, 1882, then MP for Cambridge University, 1882. Postmaster general, 1886–91.

A selection from the poems, translations, and occasional pieces of the late Henry Cecil Raikes. Edited by Henry St John Raikes. London: Richard Bentley & Son. 1895. viii, 132 pp.

For private circulation.   *OXB*

RAIN, AND OTHER POEMS. London: John Kensit. 1886. 92 pp.   *OXB*

RAINE, A.J.

Behind the veil: an idyl of the land of Christendom; by A.J. Raine. London: Kegan Paul, Trench, Trübner & Co. Ltd. 1896. 35 pp.   *OXB*

RALLI, Augustus (1875–1954). Son of John A. Ralli. Educated at Eton College, and Christ Church, Oxford. A literary critic, he lived latterly at 4 Royal Crescent, Bath.

The enchanted river, and other poems; by Augustus Railli. London: Digby, Long & Co. 1897. viii, 72 pp.   *OXB*

RALPH, pseud. *see* **MacGREGOR, John**, (Ralph, pseud.)

RAMSAY, Thomas (1822–   ). b. Kirkfieldbank, Lanarkshire. At the age of nine he began to learn tailoring with his father. He married Grace Cadzow of Lanark (1822–72).

Harp-tones in life's vale: being short poems, exercises in verse, and paraphrases, including a metrical version of the Book of Job and the Song of Solomon; by Thomas and Grace C. Ramsay. Edinburgh: J. Menzies & Co.; Lanark: Robert Wood; Alexander Wood. [1895]. viii, 208 pp.

Not joint authorship. Grace C. Ramsay died in 1872.   *EPL*

RAMSBOTTOM, George Frederick (1852–19). b. Bury, Lancashire, son of James Ramsbottom. Educated at St John's Schools, Bury, and London University. Curate, All Souls, Manchester, 1888–89, All Saints, Elton, Bury, 1890–91, Middleton, Lancashire, 1891–96; vicar, Middleton, 1896–98, Chapel-le-Dale, Ingleton, Yorkshire, from 1898.

Hymns and poems; by G.F. Ramsbottom. Printed London: Spottiswoode & Co. [1894]. viii, 86 pp. il. *RPL*

RAMSEY, Sherwood. Of Hull, Yorkshire.

Songs and ballads: a collection of poems; by Sherwood Ramsey. London: Simpkin, Marshall, & Co.; Hull: A. Brown & Sons. 1887. xii, 120 pp. por. *OXB*

RANKING, Boyd Montgomerie (1841–88). b. Sussex, son of Robert Ranking, surgeon. Educated at Brighton College. Called to the Bar, Inner Temple, 1866, but never practised. He was secretary to the Royal Archaeological Institute for about three years. A reviewer in the daily and weekly press, and a writer for magazines. One of the few men, not gipsies, capable of speaking Romany grammatically.

Fulgencius, with other poems, old and new; by B. Montgomerie Ranking. London: Newman & Co. 1880. xii, 407 pp. *BL*

Thorkell; by the late B. Montgomerie Ranking. London: Eden, Remington & Co. 1890. x, 288 pp. *OXB*

RATHMELL, Michael (1828–). b. Huby, Harewood, Yorkshire. He worked as a farm hand before going to Leeds at age of twenty-one, employed in a series of menial jobs. Severe illness enforced his retirement in 1884.

Spring blossoms and autumn leaves: a collection of poems; by Michael Rathmell. Printed Leeds: Fred. R. Spark. 1886. xvi, 144 pp.

Spine-title is *Poems*. *BL*

RAWCLIFFE, John (1844–19). b. Ribchester, Lancashire. Brother of Richard Rawcliffe. As a boy he worked as a bobbin winder and handloom weaver. Went to Blackburn to become a powerloom weaver. He eventually emigrated to the United States, settling in New Bedford, Massachusetts.

Pebbles fro' Ribbleside: [poems]; by Richard and John Rawcliffe. Blackburn: J. & G. Toulmin. 1891. xvi, 104 pp. por.

Not joint authorship. *OXB*

RAWCLIFFE, Richard (1839–86). b. Ribchester, Lancashire. Brother of John Rawcliffe. He worked as a calico weaver in Blackburn, returning to Ribchester in 1864 to take the post of overlooker at Ribblesdale Mill; later returned to Blackburn to work at Peel Mill, then transferred to Moorgate. Became president of the Blackburn Overlookers' Association. Member of Blackburn Literary Club. Died of tuberculosis in Melbourne, Australia, where he had gone to restore his health.

Pebbles fro' Ribbleside: [poems]; by Richard and John Rawcliffe. Blackburn: J. & G. Toulmin. 1891. xvi, 104 pp. por.
    Not joint authorship. *OXB*

RAWES, Henry Augustus (1826–85). Educated at Trinity College, Cambridge; MA 1852. He became a Roman Catholic in 1856; created DD, oblate of St Charles, by Pope Pius IX, 1875. Well known in London as a preacher and writer.
    Foregleams of the desired: sacred verses, hymns, and translations; by H.A. Rawes. 3rd ed. London: Burns & Oates. 1881. 157 pp. il. *OXB*

RAWLINSON, Sir Robert (1810–98). Civil and sanitary engineer. Employed by civil engineers, Jesse Hartley, 1831, and Robert Stephenson, 1836; chief engineer, Bridgewater Trust, 1843–47; chief engineering inspector, Local Government Board, 1849–88; head of the sanitary committee sent by the government to the Crimea, 1855. Published technical works and reports. Knighted in 1885. Lived at 11 The Boltons, London SW.
    Verses; composed and written by Sir Robert Rawlinson. London: S. Hogg. 1893. 30 pp. *OXB*

RAWNSLEY, Hardwicke Drummond (1850–1920). b. Shiplake-on-Thames, Berkshire, son of Rev. R.D.B. Rawnsley. Educated at Uppingham School, and Balliol College, Oxford; BA 1875. Ordained 1875; curate, St Barnabas's, Bristol, 1875–78; vicar, Wray, Windermere, Westmorland, 1878–83, Crosthwaite, Keswick, Cumberland, from 1883.
    Ballads of brave deeds; by H.D. Rawnsley. With a frontispiece and preface by G.F. Watts. London: J.M. Dent. 1896. x, 184 pp. il. *MPL*
    Idylls and lyrics of the Nile; by H.D. Rawnsley. London: David Nutt. 1894. xii, 148 pp. *JRL*
    Poems, ballads and bucolics; by H.D. Rawnsley. London: Macmillan & Co. 1890. xii, 246 pp. *MPL*
    Sonnets at the English lakes; by Hardwicke D. Rawnsley. London: Longmans, Green, & Co. 1881. xii, 124 pp.
        Spine-title is *Lake sonnets*. *OXB*
        Also 2nd ed. 1882
    Sonnets in Switzerland and Italy; by H.D. Rawnsley. London: J.M. Dent. 1899. xvi, 168 pp. *JRL*
    Sonnets round the coast; by H.D. Rawnsley. London: Swan Sonnenschein, Lowrey, & Co. 1887. xvi, 244 pp. *OXB*
    Valete: Tennyson and other memorial poems; by H.D. Rawnsley. Glasgow: James MacLehose & Sons. 1893. xviii, 175 pp. *OXB*

RAWSON, George (1807–89). b. Dennison Hall, Leeds, son of George Rawson. He practised as a solicitor in Leeds for many years. Married a Miss Clayton, daughter of a popular Congregational minister. Retired to Clifton, near Bristol. Writer of many hymns, including 'By Christ Redeemed'.
    Songs of spiritual thought; by George Rawson. [London]: Religious Tract Society. [1885]. 112 pp. (Companions for a quiet hour, VII). *OXB*

RAYNER, George Herbert. Lived at 11 Queen Square, Leeds.
Notes from my pipe: a book of rhyme and verse for smokers; [by] George Herbert Rayner. Leeds: Author. 1896. x, 64 pp. *LEP*

REA, Archibald Henry. Lived at 35 North Wellington Street, Dundee. Contributed verse to the local press.
The divot dyke, and other poems, including humorsome [sic] rhymes; by Archibald Henry Rea. With prefatory note by W. Mason Inglis. Printed Dundee: John Leng & Co. 1898. 118 pp. *NLS*

READ, Gideon Henry Mackenzie. Of Margate, Kent.
The Queen's jubilee, and other poems; by Gideon Henry Mackenzie Read. Printed Margate: Keble's Gazette Office. 1887. [viii], 64 pp. il., por. *BL*
Winter scenes, and other poems; by G.H.M. Read. Printed London. [1884]. x, 149 pp. il.
   Printed by subscription. Spine-title is *Poems*. *BL*

READ, T.W. Of Liverpool?
Stray quills: [poems]; by T.W. Read. Liverpool: "Journal of Commerce" Printing Works. 1897. 39 pp. il. *★UCD*

READE, Compton (1834?–). Son of Compton Reade of Bloomsbury, London, gentleman. Educated at Pembroke and Magdalen Colleges, Oxford; BA 1857, MA 1859. Ordained, 1857; curate, Burford, Oxfordshire, 1857; chaplain, Magdalen College, 1858–60; curate, Summertown, Oxford, 1861–65; chaplain, Christ Church, 1862–68; vicar, Cassington, Oxfordshire, 1868–69; rector, Elton, County Durham, 1883–84, Eldon, Hampshire, 1885–86; vicar, Bridge Solers, Herefordshire, from 1887.
Umbra coeli, [and other poems]; by Compton Reade. London: New Century Press. Ltd. 1899. 61 pp. *OXB*

READER, Emily E. Writer for children.
Echoes of thought: a medley of verse; by Emily E. Reader. London: Longmans, Green & Co. 1889. x, 146 pp. *OXB*
Voices from flower-land: original couplets: a birthday book and language of flowers; by Emily E. Reader. London: Longmans, Green, & Co. 1884. [224] pp. *OXB*
   Also 1893 ed. illustrated by Ada Brooke.

READMAN, Joseph (1860–). b. Ripon, Yorkshire. Educated at Ripon Grammar School. He wrote verse and sketches from early boyhood. In business at Stockton-on-Tees, County Durham.
Ancient Ripon and Fountains the magnificient, [and other poems]; by Joseph Readman. Hull: William Andrews & Co. 1891. [viii], 46 pp. *CU*

REASON AND FAITH: A REVERIE. London: Macmillan & Co., Ltd; New York: Macmillan & Co. 1898. viii, 98 pp. *OXB*

RED FERN, pseud. In business in Liverpool.
"Bruno", and other poems for recitation; by Red Fern. Manchester: John Heywood. 1884. 176 pp.   *OXB*

REDDEN, Mary Gertrude. (M.G.R.). An Irish Loreto nun.
Memories: [poems]; by M.G.R. Dublin: M. & S. Eaton. 1887. viii, 376 pp.   *UCD*

REEVE, Anna
Echoes of life: poems; by Anna Reeve. London: Robert Banks & Son. 1897. 194 pp.   *UCD*
Euterpe montana, and other poems; by Anna Reeve. London: S.W. Partridge & Co. 1885. [viii], 192 pp. il.   *UCD*
Lights and shadows: poems; by Anna Reeve. London: S.W. Partridge & Co. 1883. iv, 248 pp.   *BL*

REEVE, Percy. Novelist.
Love & music; [poems]; by Percy Reeve. London: David Bogue. 1883. viii, 112 pp.   *OXB*

REEVES, Boleyne, pseud. *see* **BULLEN, Peter**, (Boleyne Reeves, pseud.).

REEVES, William
The blind boy, and other poems; by William Reeves. [London]: City of London Publishing Co., Ltd. [1884]. iv, 105 pp.   *BL*

REID, Abel, pseud. *see* **LINTON, William James**, (Abel Reid, pseud.).

REID, Alan (1853–   ). b. Arbroath, Angus. Soon after his birth his parents moved to Forfar, where he was educated at the burgh school. Sent to Montrose as messenger and learner in the telegraph office, then began an apprenticeship to cabinet making in Forfar. While very young he became precentor in the parish church of Aberlemno, and subsequently in the Free Church of the same parish. Appointed leader of psalmody in the Free Church of Carnoustie. Moved to Edinburgh, where he was engaged as a teacher of singing by the School Board. Wrote and published songs and cantatas. FSA (Scotland).
Sangs o' the heatherland: Scots poems & ballads; by Alan Reid. Paisley: J. & R. Parlane; Edinburgh: John Menzies & Co.; London: Houlston & Sons. 1894. 163 pp.   *OXB*

REID, Alexander (1842–85). b. Perth. Educated at Perth Academy, and Mr Davidson's Classical Academy. In 1870 he moved to Glasgow to work for Messrs Arthur & Co., warehousemen. He contributed prose and verse to many Scottish periodicals. Lived at Maryhill, Glasgow.
Poems, lyrics and sonnets; by the late Alexander Reid. Blairgowrie: Henry Dryerre. 1886. 166 pp. por.   *NLS*

REID, John James (1842–89). b. Corfu, Greece, son of Sir James J. Reid of Dumfries. Educated at Cheltenham College, and Trinity College, Cambridge; BA 1868. Admitted advocate, 1870. Hon. secretary, East & North Scotland Liberal Association, helping to bring about his party's success at the 1880 general election. Advocate depute, 1880; Queen's advocate and lord treasurer's remembrancer for Scotland from 1881.

Ballads of the bench and bar: or, the lays of the Parliament House; [by James Balfour Paul and John James Reid]. Printed Edinburgh: T. & A. Constable. 1882. 127 pp. il.

   A limited ed. of 305 numbered copies, privately printed. 'All the woodcuts have been destroyed'.   *UCD*

REID, John Pringle (1862–   ). b. Aberlady, Haddingtonshire, son of a photographer and general merchant. He was orphaned at age of ten, and left school in his fourteenth year. For some time he worked as a gardener, then moved to Edinburgh, entering the employment of the Edinburgh & Leith Flint Glass Co.

Facts and fancies in poem and song; by John Pringle Reid. Printed Edinburgh: Turnbull & Spears. [1886]. xii, 223 pp.   *OXB*

REID, Robert, (Rob Wanlock, pseud.) (1850–1922). b. Wanlockhead, Dumfriesshire. After an elementary education he went to work in Glasgow in the counting-house of Stewart & M'Donald, manufacturers. He lived in Belfast for a short time then returned to Glasgow, entering the service of William Cross, shawl manufacturers. In 1877 he emigrated to Montreal, Canada. President, Montreal Burns Club, 1902–05.

Poems, songs, and sonnets; by Robert Reid (Rob Wanlock). Paisley: Alexander Gardner. 1894. xxiv, 264 pp. por.   *OXB*

REID, Samuel (1854–19   ). b. Aberdeen, son of the manager of the Aberdeen Copper Co. Educated at the Trades' School, and the Grammar School there. He took an art course at the Royal Scottish Academy school. In 1881 he settled in Glasgow. A talented painter, he exhibited at the Royal Academy, New Gallery, and elsewhere; gold medallist, Crystal Palace, 1899. On the artistic staff of *Good Words*, and a regular contributor to other magazines. Lived at West Grange, a mansion near Alloa, and latterly at Caversham Lodge, Chorley Wood, Hertfordshire.

Pansies and folly-bells; being the collected poems, pensive and playful, of Samuel Reid. Printed [Stirling]; Office of the Stirling Journal & Advertiser. [1892]. viii, 51 pp.

   Printed for the author.   *BL*

Pansies and folly-bells; [poems]; by Samuel Reid. London: Isbister & Co. Ltd. 1892. viii, 104 pp. por.   *OXB*

REID, William. Of London.

Romance of song: or, the muse in many moods: [poems]; by William Reid. London: David Bogue. 1884. xii, 244 pp.   *OXB*

REILLY, Robert James (1862–95?). b. Boyle, County Roscommon. Educated at the French College, Blackrock, and the Catholic University, Dublin. He trained for a medical career at St Vincent's and other Dublin hospitals; resident clinical assistant, St Vincent's; assistant surgeon, Rochford Infirmary, Essex; surgeon, African R.M.S. Co. Contributed papers to several medical journals. Lived latterly at 3 St Bruno Terrace, Rostrevor, County Down.

Songs of Arcady; by Robert James Reilly. Dublin: Sealy, Bryers & Walker. 1892. 68 pp. *TCD*

RELIGION IN EUROPE, HISTORICALLY CONSIDERED: AN ESSAY IN VERSE. London: Trübner & Co. 1883. [vi], 152 pp. *OXB*

RELIGIOUS OF THE ORDER OF ST. FRANCIS, pseud. A Franciscan nun of the Convent of the Immaculate Conception, Glasgow.

Cloister chimes: or, miscellaneous verses, including legends and stories; by a religious of the Order of St. Francis. 2nd ed. Inverness: W. Mackay; Glasgow: H. Margey; J. Lindsay. 1890. viii, 182 pp. *TCD*

RENNELL, Lord *see* **RODD, James Rennell, Lord Rennell**

RENNIE, W.S. Of Aberdeen.

Poems: democratic and local; by W.N. Cameron and W.S. Rennie. Aberdeen. 1894. 24 pp.

Not joint authorship. Title from cover. *WCM*

RENSHAW, Alfred George, (A.G.R.)

Pictures and poems; by E.J.R. and A.G.R. Lepe. 1895. [16] pp. il.

Title from cover. *BL*

Poems; by A.G.R. London: Edward Bumpus. 1888. xii, 260 pp *OXB*

Poems; by A.G.R. Printed London: Chiswick Press. 1892. viii, 104 pp. il. *OXB*

RENSHAW, Emily Jane (E.J.R.)

Pictures and poems; by E.J.R. and A.G.R. Lepe. 1895. [16] pp. il.

Title from cover. *BL*

RENTON, Gertrude, (G. Colmore, pseud.) (1860?–1926). b. England. Educated in Germany, she worked as a governess in London and Paris. She was married twice, first to Henry A. Colmore Dunn, whom she divorced, then to Henry B. Weaver. A novelist, she wrote under several pseuds.

Poems of love and life; by G. Colmore. London: Gay & Bird. 1896. viii, 104 pp. *BL*

Points of view, and other poems; by G. Colmore. London: Gay & Bird. 1898. x, 182 pp. *BL*

RENTON, William (1850–1905). b. Hull, Yorkshire, son of Rev. Andrew Renton, of Scottish descent. Educated at the Edinburgh Academy near Stuttgart, and Edinburgh University. He studied art in Paris, Rome and Florence. Oil and water-colour painter, novelist and free-thinker. Lived at Randapike, a cottage near Ambleside, Westmorland, about 1888.

Songs; by William Renton. London: T. Fisher Unwin. 1893. viii, 184 pp.　*OXB*

RENWICK, James

Poems and sonnets; by James Renwick. Paisley: Alexander Gardner. 1897. 124 pp.　*OXB*

RESKELLY, Katharine Jane (1843–93). Daughter of Robert Waylen of Devizes, Wiltshire. Married Rev. C.J. Reskelly, pastor of the Congregational Church at Littledean, Gloucestershire. Lived latterly at Newnham, Gloucestershire.

A selection from the poems of the late Mrs K.J. Reskelly. Also a biographical sketch by one of her brothers, and obituary notices by various contributors, edited by her husband. Printed Frome: Butler & Tanner. 1894. 210 pp. por.

Printed for private circulation.　*BL*

The **RETROSPECT: AN IDYL OF OTHER YEARS, IN SEVEN BOOKS.** London: John F. Shaw & Co. [1891]. 188 pp.　*OXB*

RETTIE, Thomas Leith (1854–　). b. Old Aberdeen. His father had been a farmer but was forced to find work in the town, where he supported a large family as a grazier. Educated at Woodside, aged ten he was apprenticed as a clerk. Became a cashier in a firm of flour merchants.

Plays and poems; by T. Leith Rettie. Aberdeen: John Avery & Co. 1884. [viii], 214 pp. por.　*BL*

REYNOLDS, John James (1824–88). Son of John C. Reynolds of London and Hereford. Educated in London and Hereford. Admitted solicitor, 1849; solicitor, High Court of Chancery, 1849; commissioner for oaths, 1849; high bailiff, county court, 1857–60; registrar, county court, 1860; district registrar, High Court of Justice. JP, city of Hereford, 1877; freeman, city of Hereford. Died suddenly on the Shafberg, Austria, 17 August 1888.

Occasional pieces in prose and verse, including "Five weeks from home in Switzerland and Savoy, 1856"; by the late J.J. Reynolds. Printed London: J. Martin & Son. 1891. viii, 344 pp.　*BL*

RHOADES, James (1841–1923). b. Clonmel, Tipperary, son of Rev. James P. Rhoades. Educated at Rugby School, and Trinity College, Cambridge; BA 1864, MA 1867. Won the Chancellor's medal for English verse, 1862. Assistant master, Haileybury, 1865–73, Sherborne School, 1880–93. Lived latterly at Kingsthorpe, Kelvedon, Essex.

Teresa, and other poems; by James Rhoades. London: Longmans, Green, & Co. 1893. viii, 133 pp.　*OXB*

Y RHOSIN DU, pseud.
The scent of the rose: [poems]: by Y Rhosin Du. London: Gay & Bird. 1899. x, 120 pp. *OXB*

RHYD-Y-GODOR *see* **KING, Clifford**

RHYS, Charles Cureton, (C.C.R.) (1851?–). Son of Clarence H. Rhys of Brighton, Sussex. Educated at Balliol College, Oxford. Student, Middle Temple, 1872.
Minora carmina: trivial verses; by C.C.R. London: Swan Sonnenschein, Lowey & Co. 1887. viii, 319 pp. *OXB*
"Up for the season", and other songs of society: being a second ed. of "Minora carmina"; by C.C.R. London: Swan Sonnenschein & Co. 1889. viii, 319 pp.
Spine-title is *Songs of society*. *BL*

RHYS, Ernest (1859–1946). b. London but brought up in Carmarthen and on Tyneside. He trained as a mining engineer before beginning a London career as a freelance reviewer and essayist. Edited Everyman's Library, 1906–46, in 983 vols. With W.B. Yeats he founded the Rhymers' Club at Ye Olde Cheshire Cheese, Fleet Street. Lived in Hampstead in the 1880s and in Cheyne Walk, Chelsea, 1886.
A London rose, & other rhymes; by Ernest Rhys. London; Elkin Mathews & John Lane; New York: Dodd Mead & Co. 1894. x, 100 pp.
A limited ed. of 350 copies printed for England and 150 copies for America. *NLW*
Welsh ballads, and other poems; by Ernest Rhys. London: David Nutt; Carmarthen: W. Spurrell & Son; Bangor: Jarvis & Foster. [1898]. x, 179 pp. *MPL*

RHYS, Griffith
Poems; by Griffith Rhys. London: Sampson, Low, Marston & Co. Ltd. [1896]. iv, 92 pp. *OXB*

RICARDO, pseud. *see* **McHALE, Richard**, (Ricardo, pseud.)

RICARDUS, pseud.
How can a school be conducted best?: a plea for our boys; by Ricardus. London: John Kempster & Co., Ltd. [1883]. 16 pp. *OXB*

RICE, C. Frances. Mrs Rice.
Poems, translations and hymns; by C.F. Rice. Dublin: Hodges, Figgis, & Co. 1888. viii, 96 pp. *NLW*

RICHARDSON, James Nicholson, (Two of Themselves, pseud. with Y. Richardson) (1846–1921). Son of John G. Richardson, main founder of the town of Bessbrook, County Armagh. Educated privately, and at Grove House, Tottenham. He joined the family linen business before entering Parliament in 1880 as a moderate Liberal, one of the members for County Armagh. Ill-health forced him not to seek re-election in 1885. Chairman of Bessbrook Spinning Co., he lived at Mount Caulfield, Bessbrook.

O'Neill: a tale of Mourne; by J.N. Richardson. Printed Newry: "The Reporter" Steam Printing Works. [1881?]. 32pp.   *BL*

The Quakri at Lurgan; by two of themselves. [2nd ed.]. [1889]. vi, 160 pp. por.

    Cover-title is *The Quakri at Lurgan & Grange*.   *OXB*

RICHARDSON, John Duncan (1848–   ). b. South Shields, County Durham. Moved to Hull, Yorkshire, at an early age. Wrote verse and prose for a number of London and provincial magazines and newspapers. For eight years he was editor of *The Hull and East Riding Good Templar*.

Reveries in ryhme: being a medley of musings for the million: grave, gay and grotesque; by John Duncan Richardson. Hull: Charles Henry Barnwell. 1886. 138 pp.   *★UCD*

RICHARDSON. Robert (1850–   ). by. Sydney, Australia. He graduated at Sydney University, 1870, afterwards working as a journalist in Sydney, London, and Edinburgh. Acted as correspondent to several papers and contributed to *Good Works*, *Temple Bar*, and other popular periodicals.

Willow and wattle: poems; by Robert Richardson. Edinburgh: John Grant. 1893. viii, 87 pp.   *EPL*

RICHARDSON, William. Of Ardrossan, Ayshire.

Alma mater, and other poems; by William Richardson. Glasgow: James Hadden; Ardrossan: Arthur Guthrie. 1881. 302 pp.   *MPL*

RICHARDSON, Y., (Two of Themselves, pseud. with James Nicholson Richardson). Daughter of John G. Richardson, main founder of the town of Bessbrook, County Armagh, and sister of James Nicholson Richardson.

The Quakri at Lurgan; by two of themselves. [2nd ed.]. [1899]. vi, 160 pp. por.

    Cover-title is *The Quakri at Lurgan & Grange*.   *OXB*

RICHINGS, Alfred Cornelius (1820–99). b. Mancetter, Warwickshire, son of Rev. Benjamin Richings. Educated at Christ's College, Cambridge; BA 1843; MA 1867. Ordained 1845; curate, Austrey, Warwickshire, 1844-46, Abbey Church, Bath, 1846–48, St Saviour's, Bath, 1848–50; vicar, St Matthew's, Leeds, 1850–53, Beauminster, Dorset, 1852–57; rector, Hawridge, Buckinghamshire, 1857–65; vicar, Boxmoor, Hertfordshire, 1865–99.

The Church's holy year: hymns and poems for all the Sundays and holy days of the Church; by A.C. Richings. Oxford: Parker & Co.; Boxmoor: W.H. Viney. 1885. xvi, 269 pp.   *OXB*

    Also 2nd ed. 1887; 3rd ed. 1889; 4th ed. 1891.

RICHMOND, A.W.

Verses; by A.W. Richmond. Printed Edinburgh: R. & R. Clark Ltd. 1889. 66 pp.

    Privately printed.   *★UCD*

RICHMOND, Mary E. (1853–   ). Of Edinburgh?
Roundels, sonnets, and other verses; by Mary E. Richmond. Printed Edinburgh:
R. & R. Clark. 1898. viii, 175 pp.
Privately printed. *NWL*

RICKARDS, Marcus Samuel Cam (1840–1928). b. Exeter, Devon, son of
Robert H. Rickards, gentleman, of Mount Radford. Educated at Merton
College, Oxford; BA 1875, MA 1878. Admitted solicitor, 1862; practised in
Bristol for many years. Ordained 1876; curate, Holy Trinity, Clifton,
1875–89; vicar, Twigworth, Gloucester, 1889–1913. Vice-president of the
Poetry Society. Lived latterly at The Retreat, Clevedon, Somerset.
Creation's hope; by Marcus S.C. Rickards. Clifton: J. Baker & Son. [1890]. 61
pp. *OXB*
The exiles: a romance of life; by Marcus S.C. Rickards. London: George Bell &
Sons. 1896. [iv], 142 pp. *OXB*
Lyrical studies: [poems]; by Marcus S.C. Rickards. Clifton: J. Baker & Son.
1892. 164 pp. *OXB*
Lyrics and elegiacs; by Marcus S.C. Rickards. London: George Bell & Sons.
1893. viii, 134 pp. *OXB*
Music from the maze: [poems]; by Marcus S.C. Rickards. Printed London:
Chiswick Press. 1899. x, 168pp. *OXB*
Poems of a naturalist; by Marcus S.C. Rickards. Printed London: Chiswick
Press. 1896. x, 112 pp.
Printed for the author. *OXB*
Poems of life and death; by Marcus S.C. Rickards. London: George Bell &
Sons. 1884. viii, 179 pp. *OXB*
Songs of universal life; by Marcus S.C. Rickards. Clifton: J. Baker & Son.
[1890]. 144 pp. *OXB*
Sonnets and reveries; by Marcus S.C. Rickards. Clifton: J. Baker & Son.
[1889]. viii, 178 pp. *OXB*
Also [2nd ed.] [1895].

RICKETTS, E.C., (Cornelia Wallace, pseud.)
Flowers: a fantasy; by Cornelia Wallace. London: W. Swan Sonnenschein &
Co. 1882. 44 pp. il. *OXB*
Meetings and partings, with other verses and translations; by E.C. Ricketts
('Cornelia Wallace'). London: Elliot Stock. 1896. viii, 151 pp. *OXB*
Mountain monarchs; by Cornelia Wallace. London: Swan Sonnenschein,
Lowrey & Co. 1887. 24 pp. *OXB*

RIDGWAY, E. Of Fernbrook, Penmaenmawr, Caernarvonshire.
Dorothy's troth, and other poems; by E. Ridgway. London: Richard Bentley &
Son. 1881. [viii], 104 pp. *OXB*

RIDLEY. George. Vocalist of Gateshead, County Durham.
*Lines written on the death of my brother, Herbert Ridley, surgeon, of Sir John Fife
and Partners, Newcastle-on-Tyne, England, and other verses*; [by George Ridley].
Newcastle-upon-Tyne: Tyne Printing Works Co. 1894. 48 pp. *NPL*

RIETHMULLER, Christopher James (18 –95). Novelist, dramatist, and general writer. Lived at 9 Adamson Road, Hampstead, London.
Early and late poems; by Christopher James Riethmuller. London: George Bell & Sons. 1893. viii, 132 pp.   *OXB*

RIGG, Caroline (1842–89). Daughter of John Smith, brush manufacturer of Worcester. She married Rev. James H. Rigg, Wesleyan minister, who held appointments successively in Guernsey, Brentford, Hammersmith, Stockport, Manchester and Folkestone. He was principal of the Wesleyan Normal Institution in Westminster for twenty years. She contributed short stories to *The British Workwoman*, a journal for working women, under the name Jane Elliott.
In memoriam: Caroline Rigg, born May 14th, 1824, died December 17th, 1889. Printed London: Hazell, Watson, & Viney, Ld. 1892. [viii], 111 pp.
    Her poems and a biography. Printed for private circulation.
BL

RIGG, James (1841–). b. Barrhead, Renfrewshire. Lyric poet and composer, song and hymn writer. He was conductor of Barrhead Choral Union for nine years; from 1891 choirmaster at St George's Road United Presbyterian Church, Glasgow. Lived at 18 Wilton Drive, Glasgow.
Wild flower lyrics, and other poems; by James Rigg. Paisley: Alexander Gardner. 1897. [iv], 294 pp. por.   *OXB*

THE RIME OF GLASGOW IN TWELVE CHIMES. Glasgow: William Hodge & Co. 1899. 84 pp.   *OXB*

RIX, pseud.
University rhymes, and other verses; by Rix. Glasgow: Kerr & Richardson. 1894. 106 pp.
    Published for the author.   *NLS*

ROBERTS, David Henry Bancroft (1867–92). b. Mold, Flintshire, son of Henry Roberts. Educated at Christ's Hospital, and Lincoln College, Oxford (scholar). He became a journalist.
The tombs in Westminster Abbey: Newdigate Prize poem, 1889; by David Henry Bancroft Roberts. Oxford: A. Thomas Shrimpton & Son; London: Simpkin, Marshall & Co.; Hamilton, Adams & Co. 1889. 15 pp.   *OXB*

ROBERTS, George Ashmore
Pencil rhymes and poetry; by George Ashmore Roberts. London: Digby, Long & Co. 1897. viii, 55 pp.   *OXB*

ROBERTS, Morley (1857–1942). b. London, son of an income tax inspector. Educated at Bedford Grammar School, and Owens College, Manchester. He travelled in Australia, California, and South Africa, doing casual work on farms, 1876–86. Later became a successful novelist. Friend of George Gissing.
Songs of energy; by Morley Roberts. London: Lawrence & Bullen. 1891. 98 pp.   *OXB*

ROBERTS, W. Hazlitt. Biographer of General Booth of the Salvation Army.
The pathos of poverty: [poems]; by W. Hazlitt Roberts. London: Westminster
Palace Press. [1896]. 48 pp.   *OXB*

ROBERTSON, Andrew Smith (1846–   ). b. Dunfermline, Fife, son of a
damask designer. Aged thirteen he was a pupil-teacher at St Leonard's School;
appointed teacher successively in Mid Calder, Musselburgh Grammar School,
and Patrick Academy, then tutor in the south of Scotland. In 1868 he returned
to Dunfermline and became, like his father, a damask designer. He went to
Armagh, then to Belfast, where he was employed on large and elaborate
designs for handloom. Wrote a history of the Mechanics' Library at
Dunfermline, and other prose works.
Jockie, [and other poems]: songs and ballads; by Andrew Smith Robertson.
Paisley; Alexander Gardner. 1893. 118 pp.   *OXB*

ROBERTSON, Caroline King
Spring, summer and autumn leaves, from the poetry of a life; by Caroline King
Robertson. London: T. Fisher Unwin. 1895. 151 pp.   *OXB*

ROBERTSON, Eric. MA. Vice-principal, Lahore Government College,
India; professor of literature and philosophy, University of the Punjab,
Lahore. Biographer, anthologist, and editor of the 'Great Writers' series.
The dreams of Christ, and other verses; by Eric Robertson. Lahore: Mufid-I-Am
Press. 1891. [vi], 153 pp.
    Privately printed.   *BL*

ROBERTSON, James Logie *see* **LOGIE ROBERTSON, James**

ROBERTSON, Janet Logie *see* **LOGIE ROBERTSON, Janet**

ROBERTSON, William (18 –91). Of Broughty Ferry, Forfarshire. He was
aged seventy before he began to write verse.
The echoes of the mountain muse, and legends of the past, in verse and prose; by
William Robertson. Printed Dundee: R.S. Barrie. 1893. 106 pp.   *OXB*
The mountain muse: poems and songs; by William Robertson. Printed Dundee:
John Leng. 1884. 136 pp.   *UCD*

ROBERTSON, William Bruce, (Robertson of Irvine) (1820–86). Studied at
Glasgow, and Halle, Germany; DD. Famous as a preacher, he was minister of
the Secession Church at Irvine, Ayrshire, 1843–78.
Dream of the foolish virgin, and other poems; by Robertson of Irvine. Ardrossan:
Arthur Guthrie & Sons; Edinburgh: Andrew Elliot; Glasgow: Menzies & Co.
[1898]. 152 pp. il., por.   *UCD*
Life of William B. Robertson, D.D., Irvine; by James Brown. With extracts
from his letters and poems. With two portraits. Glasgow: James Maclehose &
Sons. 1888. viii, 479 pp. por.   *BL*
    Also 2nd ed. 1889; 3rd ed. 1889.

ROBERTSON, William Davidson (1833–91). b. Dundee, Angus, son of a mill overseer. He became a clerk in a factory at Bankfoot, Auchtergaven, Perthshire; later a salesman for Auchtergaven Provision Society. Played oboe with the Dundee Philharmonic Society.

Heart echoes: [poems]; by the late William Davidson Robertson. Edited by his sister Isabella, and John Paul. Dundee: James P. Mather & Co. 1896. 81 pp. por.   *UCD*

ROBERTSON OF IRVINE *see* **ROBERTSON, William Bruce**, (Robertson of Irvine)

ROBERTSON-HICKS, Maude
Flowers from oversea [sic], and other verse; by Maude Robertson-Hicks. Rugby: George E. Over. 1893. [vi], 70 pp.
  Cover-title is *Poems*.   *OXB*

ROBINSON, Agnes Mary Frances (1857–1944). b. Leamington, Warwickshire, daughter of an architect. Educated in Brussels, in Italy, and at University College, London. She was married twice, in 1888 to James Darmester, a professor at the College de France, then in 1901 to Professor Pierre E. Duclaux, director of the Pasteur Institute. Biographer of Emily Brontë, Froissart, and Victor Hugo.

The crowned Hippolytus, translated from Euripides, with new poems; by A. Mary F. Robinson. London: C. Kegan Paul & Co. 1881. viii, 198 pp.   *UCD*

An Italian garden: a book of songs; by A. Mary F. Robinson. London: T. Fisher Unwin. 1886. viii, 104 pp.   *MPL*

Lyrics selected from the works of A. Mary F Robinson (Madame James Darmester). London: T. Fisher Unwin. 1891. viii, 140 pp. il. (Cameo series).   *MPL*

The new Arcadia, and other poems; by A. Mary F. Robinson. London: Ellis & White. 1884. [viii], 176 pp.   *MPL*

Retrospect, and other poems; by A. Mary F. Robinson (Madame James Darmester). London: T. Fisher Unwin. 1893. viii, 88 pp. il. (Cameo series).   *OXB*

Songs, ballads, and a garden play; by A. Mary F. Robinson. London: T. Fisher Unwin. 1888. 142 pp. il.   *OXB*

ROBINSON, Charles, pseud. *see* **NEWTON-ROBINSON, Charles**, (Charles Robinson, pseud.)

ROBINSON, Edith W.
The lay of Saint Tucundus: a legend of York; written by Edith W. Robinson. Illustrated by George Hodgson. London: Swan Sonnenschein, Lowrey & Co. 1887. [55] pp. il.
  Printed on one side of leaf only.   *OXB*

ROBINSON, Edward Jewitt (1821–1900). b. Camelford, Cornwall, son of Rev. Samuel Robinson, Wesleyan Methodist minister. Educated at Kingswood School, near Bristol. Wesleyan Methodist minister in Ceylon, 1846–52, then successively at Warrington, Loughborough, Hull, Leeds, Glasgow, Bolton, Bath, Hoxton, Jersey, Halifax, Swansea, Manchester, Harrogate, Cheltenham, Bedford, Runcorn, Stroud, Ambleside, Bath, and Weston-super-Mare, 1853–1900.

Passion lays: exodus of Our Lord Jesus Christ; by Edward Jewitt Robinson. London: Charles H. Kelly. 1896. 358 pp. *OXB*

ROBINSON, William. Lived in India.

From Brahm to Christ: the progress of an eastern pilgrim; by William Robinson. London: William Andrews & Co. 1898. [2], viii, 89 pp. il. (by Paul Bertram). *OXB*

ROCHDALE MAN, pseud. *see* **STANDRING, R.**, (Rochdale Man, pseud.)

ROCK, James, (J.R.)

A few poetic scraps; by J.R. Together with a (reprinted) notice of the Pre-Raphaelite "Germ", written in 1850 for a provincial journal. Printed London: Provost & Co. 1891. 67 pp.

    Cover-title is *Poetic scraps*. *OXB*

RODD, James Rennell, Lord Rennell (1858–1941). Educated at Haileybury, and Balliol College, Oxford. In 1883 he entered the diplomatic service; appointed successively to Berlin, Athens, Cairo, Rome, Stockholm; ambassador to Italy, 1908–19; British delegate to the League of Nations, 1921 and 1923. Conservative MP for Marylebone, 1928–32. Knighted, 1899. Classical and medieval scholar.

Ballads of the Fleet, and other poems; by Rennell Rodd. With a photogravure frontispiece. London: Edward Arnold. 1897. xii, 199 pp. por. *OXB*

Feda, with other poems, chiefly lyrical; by Rennell Rodd. With an etching by Harper Pennington. London: David Stott. 1886. [iv], 220 pp. il. *OXB*

Poems in many lands; by Rennell Rodd. London: David Bogue. 1883. viii, 124 pp. *OXB*

    Also 2nd ed. 1886.

Raleigh: Newdigate Prize poem, recited in the Theatre, June 9, 1880; by Rennell Rodd. Oxford: T. Shrimpton & Son; London: Simpkin, Marshall, & Co. [1880]. 18 pp. *OXB*

Rose leaf and apple leaf: [poems]; by Rennell Rodd. With an introduction by Oscar Wilde. Philadelphia: J.M. Stoddart & Co. 1882. 115 pp. il. *MPL*

Songs in the south; by Rennell Rodd. London: David Bogue. 1881. 63 pp. *OXB*

The unknown madonna, and other poems: I – Poems in many lands, Second series; II – In excelsis; III – Translations from Heine; by Rennell Rodd. With a frontispiece by W.B. Richmond. London: David Stott. 1888. [viii], 110 pp. il. *TCD*

The violet crown; and, Songs of England; by Rennell Rodd. With a frontispiece by the Marchioness of Granby. London: David Stott. 1891. viii, 158 pp. il.   *OXB*

RODD, Rennell *see* **RODD, James Rennell**, Lord Rennell

ROE, James Thorne
Poems on several of M. Gustave Doré's principal works; by Jas. Thorne Roe. London: Doré Gallery, Ltd. [1890]. 28 pp. por.   *OXB*

ROGERS, Alexander (18 –19). Educated at Haileybury. Appointed to the Indian Civil Service, 1845; served successively in Bombay, Broach, Ahmadabad, Gujarat, Surat, 1845–65; police commissioner, northern division, 1865; member of Council, Bombay, 1872; retired 1879. Translated three modern Persian plays.
Lakhmi: the Rajput's bride: a tale of Gujarat in western India; by Alexander Rogers. London: Thomas Burleigh. 1899. [viii], 160 pp.
    Spine-title is *The Rajput's bride*.   *OXB*

ROGERS, Emma
The forget-me-knot: or, the troubadour's vow, and other tales in prose and poetry; by Emma Rogers. London: Hatchards. 1883. [viii], 134 pp.
    Privately printed.   *NLI*

ROGERS, James R.
The loss of nine gallant lives, written on the capsizing of the surf boat, "Friend To All Nations", off Margate, on Thursday, December 2nd, 1897; by James R. Rogers. New ed. Printed Margate: R. Robinson & Co. [1898]. 16 pp. il., por.   *OXB*

ROMANES, George John (1848–94). b. Kingston, Canada, but brought to England at an early age. Educated at Gonville & Caius College, Cambridge (scholar); BA 1871, MA 1874. Studied physiology at University College, London, 1874–76; FRS 1879. He formed a lifelong friendship with Charles Darwin. Made investigations into the mental faculties of animals, 1881–83; professor at Edinburgh, 1886–90; Fullerian professor of physiology at the Royal Institution, 1888–91. Zoological secretary of the Linnean Society. From 1890 he lived in Oxford.
Centuria: [poems]; [by George John Romanes]. Printed London: Harrison & Sons. 1890. 108 pp.   *BL*
Poems: 1879–1889; [by George John Romanes]. Printed London: Harrison & Sons. 1889. 450 pp.
    For private circulation.   *OXB*
A selection from the poems of George John Romanes. With an introduction by T. Herbert Warren. London: Longmans, Green, & Co. 1896. xvi, 108 pp.   *OXB*

ROMNEY, E.J.
Verses; by E.J. Romney. London: Digby, Long & Co. 1895. 30 pp.   *OXB*

RONDA, pseud.
Blanche, Queen of Castile: a poem; by Ronda. London: Thomas Hookham.
1883. xvi, 275 pp.   *BL*
Also 1887 re-issue.

ROOM, Charles. Rev. Room.
Foreshadowings: a poem, in four cantos; by Charles Room. London: Elliot
Stock. 1881. [iv], 108 pp.   *OXB*

ROOM, John. Educated at St John's College, Cambridge; BA 1852. Ordained
deacon, 1852, priest 1853; curate, Keighley, Yorkshire, 1852–53. Lived at
Eastwood, Keighley.
Random rhymes; by J. Room. Keighley: T.D. Hudson. [188–   ]. 59 pp.   *LEP*

ROPER BARD *see* **WATSON, George**

ROPES, Arthur Reed, (Adrian Ross, pseud.) (1859–1933). b. London.
Educated at King's College, Cambridge; BA 1883. Fellow of King's, 1884–90.
Writer of lyrics and librettos for many musical plays including *Lilac Time* and
The Merry Widow.
Poems; by Arthur Reed Ropes. London: Macmillan & Co. 1884. xii, 96
pp.   *OXB*

ROSE, A.N. Mount, pseud. *see* **JAPP, Alexander Hay**, (A.N. Mount Rose,
pseud.)

ROSE, Henry. Of London. Writer on Ibsen and Maeterlinck.
From west to east: [poems]; by Henry Rose. London: David Stott. 1887. [viii],
196 pp.   *OXB*
Summer dreams: a vacation reminiscence: [poems]; by Henry Rose. London:
Wm. Isbister. 1883. vi, 217 pp.   *OXB*
Ten years: an old world story; by Henry Rose. London: James Nisbet & Co.
[1883]. 232 pp.   *BL*
Willow-Vale, and other poems; by Henry Rose. London: Kegan Paul, Trench,
Trübner & Co. 1898. [vi], 218 pp.   *UCD*
The works of Henry Rose, illustrated. London: Reeves & Turner. 1890. [2], iv,
390 pp. il., por.   *UCD*

**The ROSE, SHAMROCK AND THISTLE ALPHABET OF ORIGI-
NAL VERSE RETOUCHED, WITH ADDITIONS TO GREET THE
JUBILEE**. Printed Exeter: W.J. Southwood. 1887. 50 pp.   *BL*

ROSEDALE, Honyel Gough (1863–1928). b. Willenhall, Staffordshire, son of William L. Rosedale. Educated at Merchant Taylors' School, and Christ Church, Oxford; BA 1885, MA 1888. Curate in London: St Andrew's, Stockwell, 1886, Spitalfields, 1888, Holy Trinity, Canning Town, 1890; vicar, Middleton, Norfolk, 1891, St Peter's, Bayswater, 1894; resigned 1909. Rector, Copford, Colchester, Essex, from 1924. Grand chaplain of the Grand Lodge of England.

Ye book of verses; by H.G. Rosedale. Printed London: J. Tamblyn. 1896. lxii pp.   *UCD*

ROSHER, Charles. Journalist; special correspondent during the Basuto War, 1880-81, to the *Eastern Province Herald*, Port Elizabeth, South Africa; assistant editor, *African Times*, 1912–13; editor, *Egyptian Herald* in Alexandria, 1915. Literary and artistic contributor to many periodicals. FRGS.

Poems; by Charles Rosher. London: Haas & Co. [1897]. [vi], 79 pp.   *OXB*

ROSHER, Ethel Margaret

Poems; by Ethel Margaret Rosher. London: Kegan Paul, Trench, Trübner, & Co. Ltd. 1896. viii, 64 pp.

Printed for private circulation only.   *UCD*

ROSS, Adrian, pseud. *see* **ROPES, Arthur Reed**, (Adrian Ross, pseud.)

ROSS, Charles Archibald. Journalist and political writer.

A bundle of sonnets, based on the Italian model, to which is added a short account of the sonnet form gathered from various sources; by [Charles Archibald Ross]. Barnstaple: Sydney Harper & Sons. 1899. 31 pp.   *OXB*

Sonnet and song; by Charles Archibald Ross. Bournemouth: T.J. Powell. 1889. 37 pp.   *BL*

Sonnet and song; by Charles Archibald Ross. Bristol: J.W. Arrowsmith. 1894. [ii], 56 pp.   *OXB*

ROSS, James. Lived at Grove House, Belmont Road, Anfield, Liverpool.

The leper: a poem; by James Ross. Bristol: J.W. Arrowsmith; London: Simpkin, Marshall & Co. 1888. 55 pp.   *OXB*

Seymour's inheritance: a short story in blank verse; by James Ross. Bristol: J.W. Arrowsmith; London: Simpkin, Marshall & Co. 1885. 60 pp.   *OXB*

Sonnet on freedom, and twelve other poems; by James Ross. Bristol: J.W. Arrowsmith; London: Simpkin, Marshall & Co. 1886. 26 pp.   *OXB*

The wild enthusiast, and other poems; by James Ross. Bristol: J.W. Arrowsmith; London: Simpkin, Marshall & Co. 1886. 32 pp.   *OXB*

The wind, and six sonnets; by James Ross. Bristol: J.W. Arrowsmith; London: Simpkin, Marshall & Co. 1887. 24 pp.   *OXB*

ROSS, John Wilson (1818–87). b. St Vincent, Windward Islands. Educated at King's College, London. Secretary to the vendue-master of Berbice, British Guiana. Subsequently engaged in literary work in London. Playwright.

Fact and fancy: an ode for the jubilee of the Queen's reign; also, The university boat race: a song; by John Wilson Ross. London: Diprose & Bateman. 1886. 23 pp. *BL*

Gleams & glances in verse: being gleams of everything and glances at everybody; by John Wilson Ross. London: Diprose & Bateman. [1886]. 39 pp.

   Cover states *The first part: childhood*. *OXB*

ROSS, William Stewart (1844–1906). b. Kirkbean, Galloway. Teacher at the parish school, Glenesslin, Dunscore; became chief assistant master at Hutton Hall Academy. Went to Glasgow University, 1864, intent on studying for the ministry but did not complete the course. He became a full-time writer, supporting himself by writing for magazines and newspapers. Went into business as a publisher in Edinburgh, later going to London; head partner in W. Stewart & Co., educational publishers of Holborn.

Isaure, and other poems; by W. Stewart Ross. London: W. Stewart & Co.; Edinburgh: J. Menzies & Co. [1894]. 96 pp. *BL*

Lays of romance and chivalry; by W. Stewart Ross. London: W. Stewart & Co.; Edinburgh: J. Menzies & Co. [1882]. [iv], 69 pp. il. *BL*

Lays of romance and chivalry; by W. Stewart Ross. London: W. Stewart & Co.; Edinburgh: J. Menzies & Co. [1887?]. [iv], 74 pp. il.

   Different format from [1882] ed. *BL*

ROSSETTI, Christina Georgina (1830–94). b. London, daughter of Gabriele Rossetti, professor of Italian at King's College. She was educated at home, and her first verse was published when she was twelve. Her work appeared with that of her brother, Dante Gabriel Rossetti, in the Pre-Raphaelite Brotherhood's journal *The Germ* in 1850. She was one of the most spiritual of English poets, a devout high church Anglican; her life was a retiring one spent largely in caring for her mother, who lived until 1886, and in religious duties. She twice rejected proposals of marriage, breaking her engagements to the painter James Collinson and later to the translator Charles Bagot Cayley. In 1873 she contracted Graves' disease, retreating into invalidism and becoming almost a recluse.

New poems of Christina Rossetti, hitherto unpublished or uncollected. Edited by William Michael Rossetti. London: Macmillan & Co., Ltd. 1895. xxiv, 397 pp. por. *JRL*

   Also re-issue 1896.

A pageant, and other poems; by Christina G. Rossetti. London: Macmillan & Co. 1881. x, 198 pp. *MPL*

A pageant, and other poems; by Christina G. Rossetti. Boston, [Mass.]: Roberts Bros. 1881. 208 pp.

   Cover-title is *The pageant*. *BL*

Poems; by Christina G. Rossetti. New and enlarged ed. London: Macmillan & Co. 1890. xvi, 450 pp. il. *BL*

Verses; by Christina G. Rossetti. Reprinted from "Called to be saints", "Time flies", "The face of the deep". Published under the direction of the Tract Committee. London: Society for Promoting Christian Knowledge; New York: E. & J.B. Young & Co. 1893. 236 pp.   *MPL*

ROSSETTI, Dante Gabriel (1828–82). b. London, son of Gabriele Rossetti, professor of Italian at King's College. Brother of Christina Georgina Rossetti. Educated at King's College School. Studied art at F.S. Cary's Academy and at the Royal Academy. Painter as well as poet, and founder of the Pre-Raphaelite Brotherhood, with W. Holman Hunt, John E. Millais, and others. He enjoyed the patronage of John Ruskin, and knew William Morris and Burne-Jones. His wife, Elizabeth Siddal, often his model, died in 1862 after less than two years of marriage. Lived at Cheyne Walk, Chelsea, at one time sharing his house with Algernon C. Swinburne and George Meredith.

BIBLIOGRAPHY: **ROSSETTI, William Michael.** *Bibliography of the works of Dante Gabriel Rossetti.* London: Ellis. 1905.

ROSSLYN, Lord *see* **ERSKINE, Francis Robert St Clair**, Lord Erskine.

ROUS, William John (1833–1914) Son of Hon. William R. Rous of Worstead, Norfolk. Educated at Eton College, and Trinity College, Oxford. Lieutenant-Colonel, Scots Guards; served in the Crimea, thrice wounded, awarded two medals. Lived at Worstead House.
Conradin; by Lieutenant-Colonel Rous. London: Kegan Paul, Trench, & Co. 1884. vi, 63 pp.   *OXB*
Glauké; by Lieutenant-Colonel Rous. London: Franz Thimm. 1883. 56 pp.   *OXB*

ROWAN, Thomas. Of Sandyford, Ayrshire.
Poems; by Thomas Rowan. London: Frederick Shaw & Co. 1889. 160 pp.   *OXB*

ROWBOTHAM, John Frederick (1859–1925). Son of Rev. Frederick Rowbotham of St James's, Edinburgh. Educated at Edinburgh Academy, Rossall School, and Balliol College, Oxford (scholar). Studied music on the continent; author of *A History of Music*, 3 vols, 1885–87. Ordained, 1891; vicar, Ratley, 1892, rector, Huntley, 1895; chaplain, Budapest, 1896; vicar, Abbotsley, 1897, Sutton Cheney, Leicestershire, 1916. Editor and proprietor of *The Bard*, 1910. Contributed articles to the musical press. Self-styled 'The Modern Homer'.
The death of Roland: an epic poem; by John Frederick Rowbotham. London: Trübner & Co. 1887. viii, 176 pp. (Rowbotham's series of poetical romances, no. 1).   *BL*
The epic of Charlemagne: or, the death of Roland: an epic poem; by Rowbotham, the modern Homer. Southend-on-Sea: Thomas Cromwell. [1887]. viii, 176 pp. (Rowbotham's poetical romances).
Cover-title is *The death of Roland*.   *MPL*

The human epic: the twelfth epic poem of the world; by John Frederick Rowbotham. London: Belmont Publishing Co. [1890]. [iv], 213 pp.   *MPL*

The human epic; by John Frederick Rowbotham. Canto I. London: Kegan Paul, Trench, Trübner & Co., Ltd. 1890. 39 pp.   *OXB*

The human epic; by John Frederick Rowbotham. Cantos, I-V. London: Kegan Paul, Trench, Trübner & Co. (Ltd). [1891]. [vi], 96 pp.   *OXB*

ROWLEY, G.

The Tower of Babel, and other occasional pieces; by G. Rowley. 1881. 147 pp.   *★UCD*

ROWNTREE, George William (1852–1908). Educated at Rossall School, and Clare College, Cambridge; BA 1876, MA 1879. Ordained, 1877; curate in London: St Mary Magdalene's, Peckham, 1876–80, St Stephen's, Marylebone, 1880–82, St Stephen's, Paddington, 1883–86; rector, St Paul's, Aberdeen, 1886–94; vicar, Wrawby, Lincolnshire, 1894–1908.

The martyrdom of St. Stephen: the Seatonian prize poem for 1891; by George William Rowntree. Cambridge: Deighton, Bell, & Co.; London: George Bell & Sons. 1891. 16 pp.   *OXB*

Mount Zion: the Seatonian prize poem for 1895; by George William Rowntree. Cambridge: Deighton, Bell & Co.; London: George Bell & Sons. 1896. 16 pp.   *OXB*

RUGBY RHYMES, ROUGH AND READY, WITH MR JINGLE AT THE '92 INTERNATIONAL. Printed Cupar: "Fifeshire Journal". [1893]. 32 pp.   *OXB*

RULE, George. Of Gateshead, County Durham.

Northern ballads, and other poems: political, occasional, in memoriam, humorous, etc.; by George Rule. Gateshead-on-Tyne: J. Cochrane & Co.; London: "England" Publishing Co. 1884. 264 pp. por.

    Spine-title is *Poems*.   *BL*

The siege of Norham Castle; by George Rule. Gateshead-on-Tyne: John Cochrane. 1881. 35 pp. il., por.   *NPL*

RURAL PASTOR, pseud. *see* **WAKEFIELD, John**, (J.W.), (Rural Pastor, pseud.)

RURAL POSTMAN OF BIDEFORD *see* **CAPERN, Edward**

RUSHBROOKE, Alfred. Ordained 1886; missionary in Jamaica for the Colonial & Continental Society, 1882–86.

The advents: literal and spiritual: a song of adoration, a hosanna of welcome; by Alfred Rushbrooke. London: S.W. Partridge. [1894]. 30 pp.   *OXB*

RUSKIN, John (1819–1900). b. London, only son of John James Ruskin, wine-merchant. When he was four the family settled in Herne Hill. He showed early artistic talent. Educated at Rev. Dale's School, Camberwell, King's College, London, and Christ Church, Oxford; BA 1842, MA 1843. Newdigate prizewinner, 1839. In 1869 he was appointed first Slade professor of the fine arts in Oxford; in 1871 he endowed a school of drawing in the University, in the same year founding the Guild of St George. His views on art, religion and economics were often controversial, attracting criticism which affected his somewhat fragile health. He resigned the professorship in 1885, going to live at Brantwood, Lake Coniston, Lancashire. His works on art, which include *Modern Painters*, *The Seven Lamps of Architecture*, and *The Stones of Venice*, enjoyed a wide circulation.

Poems of John Ruskin. Collected and edited by James Osborne Wright. New York: John Wiley & Sons. 1882. vi, 234 pp. il.
     Spine-title is *The old water-wheel and other poems*.   *JRL*
The poems of John Ruskin. Now first collected from original manuscript and printed sources, and edited, in chronological order, with notes, biographical and critical, by W.G. Collingwood. With facsimiles of MSS. and illustrations by the author. Orpington: George Allen. 1891. 2 vols. il., facsim.
     Vol. I. Poems written in boyhood, 1826–1835. Vol. II. Poems written in youth, 1836–1845, and later poems.   *MPL*

RUSSELL, Hon. Francis Albert Rollo (1849–1914). Third son of Lord Russell. Educated at Harrow School, and Christ Church, Oxford; MA 1877. Clerk in the Foreign Office, 1872–73. Fellow of the Royal Meteorological Society. Author of works on the prevention of infectious diseases, meteorology and other scientific subjects. Lived at Steep, Petersfield, Hampshire.

Break of day, and other poems; by Rollo Russell. London: T. Fisher Unwin. 1893. 134 pp.   *OXB*
Psalms of the west: [poems]; [by Francis Albert Rollo Russell]. London: Kegan Paul, Trench & Co. 1889. [iv], 163 pp.   *MPL*
     Also 2nd ed. 1891.
Psalms of the west: [poems]; [by Francis Albert Rollo Russell]. 3rd ed. revised. London: Longmans, Green, & Co. 1897. viii, 146 pp.   *OXB*

RUSSELL, George William, (A.E.) (1867–1935). b. Lurgan, County Armagh. Educated at Rathmines School, Dublin, and the Metropolitan School of Art. He abandoned his intended career as a painter, becoming a leading figure in the Irish literary and artistic renaissance; friend of W.B. Yeats, and a founder of the Irish National Theatre Society. From 1897 he worked with the Irish Agricultural Organization Society in Dublin. In 1910 he became editor of the *Irish Statesman*. An active supporter of the Home Rule movement. Lived in Bournemouth in his last years, and died there.

The earth breath, and other poems; by A.E. New York: John Lane, Sign of The Bodley Head. [1897]. 95 pp.   *OXB*

Homeward songs by the way; [by] A.E. Dublin: Whaley. 1894. xiv, 52 pp.   *OXB*

Homeward songs by the way; [by] A.E. 2nd ed. Dublin, Whaley; London: Simpkin, Marshall & Co. 1895. [xiv], 52 pp.   *BL*

Homeward songs by the way; [by] A.E. Portland, Maine: Thomas B. Mosher. 1895. 88 pp.

A limited ed. of 925 copies.   *BL*

RUSSELL, Kate Pyer. Mrs Russell. Daughter of Rev. John Pyer.

Wayside leaves: poems various; by Kate Pyer Russell. London: John Snow & Co. 1880. [iv], 60 pp.   *BL*

RUSSELL, Matthew (1834–1912). b. Newry, County Down, brother of Lord Russell of Killowen. Educated at Castleknock College, and Maynooth. Ordained Jesuit, 1864; teacher, Crescent College, Limerick, 1864–73. He founded the *Irish Monthly*, which he edited until his death. Latterly attached to St Francis Xavier's Church, Dublin.

All day long: ejaculations & prayers in verse; by Matthew Russell. London: Catholic Truth Society. 1896. 24 pp.   *OXB*

Erin: verses Irish and Catholic; by Matthew Russell. Dublin: M.H. Gill & Son. 1881. 110 pp.   *NLI*

The harp of Jesus: a prayer-book in verse; by Matthew Russell. Dublin: M.H. Gill & Son. 1890. viii, 80 pp.   *NLI*

Idyls of Killowen: a soggarth's secular verses; by Matthew Russell. London: James Bowden. 1899. viii, 140 pp.   *CU*

Madonna: verses on Our Lady and the saints; by Matthew Russell. Dublin: M.H. Gill. 1880. 118 pp.

Bound with author's *Emmanuel*, 3rd ed. Cover-title is *Emmanuel and Madonna*. *TCD*

Also 3rd ed. 1889.

RUSSELL, Percy (1847–19). Writer and journalist. Lived at Trent House, Trent Road, Brixton. London SW.

King Alfred, and other poems; by Percy Russell. London: Wyman & Sons. 1880. viii, 175 pp.   *OXB*

RUSSELL, Rollo *see* **RUSSELL, Hon. Francis Albert Rollo**

RUSTICUS, pseud. *see* **HICKLING, George**, (Rusticus, pseud.)

RUSTON, T.E.

Drifting through dreamland: [poems]; by T.E. Ruston. London: Elliot Stock. 1895. vi, 154 pp.   *OXB*

RUTSON, Charlotte Fanny (18   -84). Miss Rutson of Newby Wiske, near Kirby Wiske, North Riding of Yorkshire. An excellent horsewoman until an injury to her knee in 1854 made her permanently lame and confined to a wheelchair.

Some verses; by Charlotte Fanny Rutson. Privately printed in memory of her, and for the use of her brothers and her friends. Printed London: G. Norman & Son. [1886]. iv, 78 pp.   *BL*

RUTTER, J.

Gordon songs and sonnets, with notes historical and biographical, written 1884–5; by J. Rutter. London: Elliot Stock. 1887. xvi, 151 pp.   *OXB*

RUTTER, Richard Ball (1826–98). b. Bristol, son of Samuel and Elizabeth Rutter, Quakers, and a nephew of the poet William Ball. When he was nineteen the family moved to Shotley Bridge, County Durham, and he was employed in a bank. In 1854 he emigrated to Australia but returned after two years to Newcastle, again engaged in a bank. Known as a reader and speaker, he contributed verse and hymns to the *British Friend* and other Quaker periodicals.

Scenes from the Pilgrim's progress: [poems]; by Richard Ball Rutter. London: Trübner & Co. 1882. [ii], 141 pp.   *OXB*

RYAN, Margaret, (Alice Esmonde, pseud.) b. Tipperary, sister of Dr John Ryan, parish priest of Ballingarry, County Tipperary, and vicar-general of Cashel diocese.

Songs of remembrance; by Margaret Ryan ("Alice Esmonde"). Dublin: M.H. Gill & Son. 1889. 136 pp.   *OXB*

RYDER, Henry Ignatius Dudley (1837–1907). Son of George Ryder. Received into the Roman Catholic Church with his parents at age of twelve. Educated at The Oratory School, Birmingham, then decided to join the congregation; sent to the English College, Rome; novice, 1856, ordained priest, 1863. Held the chair of philosophy, College of St Philip Neri. Wrote philosophical works; contributed to the *Dublin Review* and other periodicals.

Poem, original and translated; by H.I.D. Ryder. Dublin: M. H. Gill & Son. 1882. xii, 201 pp.   *OXB*

The poet's purgatory, and other poems (original and translated); by H.I.D. Ryder. Dublin: M.H. Gill. 1890. xii, 201 pp.   *OXB*

RYDER, Thomas Dudley (1825–86). b. Wells, Somerset, son of Henry Ryder, Bishop of Lichfield & Coventry. Educated at rugby School, and Oriel College, Oxford; BA 1837, MA 1840. Inspector of factories in Lancashire, 1837–49; registrar, Manchester diocese, from 1849. Barrister, Gray's Inn, 1856. Lived at Hambledon, Henley-on-Thames, Oxfordshire. Died at Sawdon Hall, Stone, Staffordshire.

Verses; by Thomas Dudley Ryder. Printed London: Harrison & Sons. 1886. [vi], 103 pp. il, por.   *OXB*

S

S.

A reminiscence, and other verses; [by S.]. [1893?]. 36 pp.   *UCD*

S. Served as a district officer in India.

C.P. [Central Provinces] pieces, and other verse; by S. Printed Allahabad: Pioneer Press. 1899. [vi], 112 pp.   *BL*

S., A.

Footsteps: [poems]; [by] A.S. London: John F. Shaw & Co. [1893]. 36 pp.   *OXB*

Idle thoughts, lovingly dedicated to the memory of one who is "with Christ, which is far better": [poems]; by A.S. London: John F. Shaw & Co. [1882]. 183 pp.   *OXB*

One year, [and other poems]; by A.S. London: John F. Shaw & Co. 1882. 64 pp.   *OXB*

S., A. *see* **SHELLSHEAR, Alicia**, (A.S.)

S., A.A. *see* **SYKES, Arthur Alkin**, (A.A.S.)

S. A-Y-D *see* **APPLEYARD, S.**, (S. A-Y-D)

S., E.D. *see* **STONE, Edward Daniel**, (E.D.S.)

S., E.L.. Lived at 53 Brook Green, London W.

A biblical zoo: a companion to homely things in holy writ; by E.L.S. London: Marshall Bros. [1899]. 15 pp.   *OXB*

S., E.S.G. *see* **SAUNDERS, Emily Susan Goulding**, (E.S.G.S.)

S., H.A.
A martyr-bishop of our day [J.C. Patteson]; by H.A.S. London: Wells Gardner, Darton, & Co. [1881]. 16 pp. il.   *OXB*

S., I. *see* **SOUTHALL, Isabel**, (I.S.)

S., J.K. *see* **STEPHEN, James Kenneth**, (J.K.S.)

S., J.M. A man who travelled alone in North America for several weeks, and was captured by Ute Indians in New Mexico.
The white Indian girl: a true romantic Indian love story; by the author J.M.S. London: Henry Sotheran & Co. 1881. 56 pp.   *OXB*

S., J.W.
Recreations: [poems]; [by] J.W.S. 1894–97. 2 vols in 1.
Printed on one side of leaf only.   *OXB*

S., L.
Edie, the little foundling, and other poems; by L.S. London: Digby, Long & Co. [1891]. 80 pp. il.   *OXB*

S., L.A.H.
Three crowns: The crown of love; The crown of suffering; and, The crown of life: being an outline of the life of Jeanne D'Albret, Queen of Navarre; by L.A.H.S. London: Chas. J. Thynne. 1894. 125 pp. por.   *UCD*

S., L.C. *see* **SMITH, Lucy Cumming**, (L.C.S.)

S., L.H.
The echo from within, [and other poems]; by L.H.S. London: James Carter. [1895]. 16 pp.
Cover-title is *Many voices*.   *OXB*

S., M. *see* **SMITH, Mary**, (M.S.)

S., M.A.
Among the rocks, and other poems; by M.A.S. London: Williams & Norgate. 1886. [viii], 112 pp.
Cover-title is *Poems*.   *OXB*

S., M.R. *see* **STEADMAN, M.R.**, (M.R.S.)

S., N.
City songs; by N.S. Dundee: William Kidd; Edinburgh: John Menzies & Co. 1893. 64 pp.   *OXB*

S., R.H.
Verses; by R.H.S. 1895. 71 p.
  Privately printed. *UCD*

S., R.P.
Fugitiva: [poems]; [by R.P.S.]. Printed Manchester: A. Ireland & Co. 1881.
104 pp.
  Printed for private circulation. Cover bears monogram R.P.S. *MPL*

S., T. An Irishman, probably of Belfast.
The spirit of sport in nature, and other poems; by T.S. London: Marcus Ward &
Co., Ltd. 1883. 156 pp. *OXB*

S., T.D. *see* **SULLIVAN, Timothy Daniel, (T.D.S.)**

S., W. *see* **SIMMS, William**, (W.S.)

SABRINA, pseud.
The lilies, and other poems; by Sabrina. London: Digby, Long & Co. [1895].
138 pp. *OXB*

SADDLEWORTHIAN, pseud. Of Saddleworth, West Riding, Yorkshire.
The hunting wars of Saddleworth: a history of local feuds; by a Saddleworthian.
Printed Oldham: Tetlow, Stubbs, & Co. [c.1890]. 54 pp.
  Reprinted from the *Oldham Standard*. *OPL*

**SAFELY LANDED: THOUGHTS ON BEREAVEMENT AND THE
OTHER LIFE**. London: James Speirs. 1896. [ii], 21 pp. *OXB*

**SAGA AND SONG: BEING A BALLAD MADE OF THE "REGINA
ELIZABETH" AND THE VALOUR OF HER BRITISH MAR-
INERS; OF SONNETS A FEW; AND OF LYRICAL VERSES A
SCANTY HANDFUL WHEREOF FEW HAVE BEEN BEFORE
PRINTED; & LASTLY A FEW ESSAYS IN ANCIENT LYRIC
METERS OF THE TROUBADOURS** . . . Printed Rugby: Rugby Press.
1895. [59] pp.
  Privately printed. *OXB*

ST. ANDREWS MAN, pseud. *see* **MURRAY, Robert Fuller**, (St. Andrews
Man, pseud.)

ST. DALMAS, H.P. Emeric De *see* **DE ST. DALMAS, H.P. Emeric**

ST. JOHN-BRENON, Edward (1847–). b. Dublin, son of Rev. William
Brenon. Educated at the High School, and Trinity College, Dublin. He
attempted to enter Parliament unsuccessfully on several occasions.
The tribune reflects, and other poems; by Edward St. John-Brenon. London:
Reeves & Turner. 1881. [viii], 136 pp. *OXB*
Two Gallian laments, and some verses; by Edward St. John-Brenon. London:
Reeves & Turner. 1884. [vi], 95 pp. *OXB*
The witch of Nemi, and other poems; by Edward St. John-Brenon. New ed.
London: Reeves & Turner. 1881. xiv, 358 pp. *OXB*

ST. LEGER, Warham (1850–94). b. Ipswich, Suffolk, son of Rev. William N. St. Leger, an Irish clergyman. Educated at the Clergy Orphan School, Canterbury, and Cambridge University; BA 1876. Contributor to *Punch* and other magazines.
   Ballads from "Punch", and other poems; by Warham St. Leger. London: David Stott. 1890. viii, 324 pp.   *OXB*

ST. MARTIN, Tristram
   The Christ in London, and other poems; by Tristram St. Martin. London: Authors' Co-operative Publishing Co., Ltd. [1890]. [iv], 162 pp.   *OXB*

SAINT SWITHAINE, Swithin, pseud. *see* **MEADOWS, Thomas**, (Swithin Saint Swithaine, pseud.)

SALISBURY CURATE, pseud. *see* **BUCHANAN, Sidney James**, (Salisbury Curate, pseud.)

SALMON, Arthur Leslie. Of Devon. Writer on the West Country.
   Haunted, and other poems; by Arthur L. Salmon. London: Spottiswoode & Co. 1894. 28 pp.   *OXB*
   Life of life, and other verse; by Arthur L. Salmon. Edinburgh: William Blackwood & Sons. 1897. x, 64 pp.   *OXB*
   Songs of a heart's surrender, and other verses; by Arthur L. Salmon. Edinburgh: William Blackwood & Sons. 1895. viii, 61 pp.   *OXB*
   West-country ballads and verses; by Arthur L. Salmon. Edinburgh: William Blackwood & Sons. 1899. viii, 82 pp.   *OXB*

SALT, Henry Stephens (1851–1939). b. India, son of Colonel Thomas H. Salt, Royal Bengal Artillery. Educated at Eton College, and King's College, Cambridge; BA 1875. Assistant master at Eton, 1875–84. Writer and social reformer. Hon. secretary, Humanitarian League, 1891–1920. Lived latterly at 15 Sandgate, Brighton, Sussex.
   The song of the respectables, and other verses; by Henry S. Salt. Manchester: Labour Press Society Ltd. 1896. 20 pp.   *WCM*

SAMUELS, Emma (1856–1904). b. Manor Cunningham, County Donegal, daughter of Rev. James W. Irvin. Educated at Alexandra College, Dublin. In 1881 she married A.W. Samuels, QC. Wrote for the *Fortnightly Review* and other periodicals.
   Shadows, & other poems; by E. Samuels. With illustrations by W. Fitzgerald. London: Longmans, Green, & Co. 1898. 40 pp. il.   *OXB*

SANDERSON, Robert (1836–). b. West Linton, Peebleshire. At age of twelve he had violin lessons from Alexander Thom, a Linton weaver. From an early age he contributed verses and sketches to provincial newspapers. A song-writer.
   Frae the Lyne valley: poems and sketches; by Robert Sanderson. Paisley: J. & R. Parlane; Edinburgh: J. Menzies & Co. 1888. [iv], 167 pp.   *UCD*

SANDS, J. Of Walls, Shetland.

King James's wedding, and other rhymes; by J. Sands. With illustrations by Charles Keene, Harry Christie, etc. Arbroath: T. Buncle. 1888. xii, 102 pp. il. *OXB*

SANDYS, Richard Hill (1801–92). b. Westminster, London, son of Hannibal Sandys. Educated at Barnstaple, Cheam, and Trinity College, Cambridge; BA 1823, MA 1826. Called to the Bar, Lincoln's Inn, 1826. Writer on legal discontent. Lived at 60 Dorset Square, London NW.

Egeus, and other poems; by Richard Hill Sandys. London: Kegan Paul, Trench, & Co. 1886. vi, 109 pp. *OXB*

SAPTE, William. Novelist, and comedy playwright.

Latterday legends: being rummy romances: [poems]; by William Sapte, Junior. London: Samuel French. [1887]. 72 pp. *OXB*

SARGANT, Alice (1858–19). b. Ireland. Writer on Shakespeare, and of plays for children. Of Quarry Hill, Reigate, Surrey.

A book of ballads; by Alice Sargant. With five etchings by William Strang. London: Elkin Mathews. 1898. 46 pp. il. *OXB*

The crystal ball: a child's book of fairy ballads; by Alice Sargant. Illustrations designed and drawn upon the wood by Mary Sargant Florence, and cut by Ida Litherland. [London]: Geo. Bell & Sons. [1895], viii, 120 pp. *OXB*

Master death: mocker and mocked; by Alice Sargant. London: J. M. Dent & Co. 1899. [ii], 32 pp. *OXB*

SARGEANT, Robert (1850–19). b. Thornton-le-Beans, near Northaller-ton, Yorkshire, son of John Sargeant of West Hartlepool. Educated at Church Square School. Head of the firm of R. Sargeant & Son, wholesale fruit merchants and importers. Mayor of West Hartlepool, 1905–06. A Wesleyan Methodist, and a Liberal in politics.

The revenge of the beasts, and other vegetarian and humanitarian verses; by Robert Sargeant. London: Nichols & Co. 1881. 35 pp. *OXB*

SARGENT, Edward George. Possibly Edward George Sargent who went into the National Provincial Bank in Dover as an apprentice in 1862. He became manager of Gillett & Co.'s Bank of Banbury, Oxfordshire. Director of Banbury Gas Light & Coke Co. Lived at Mayfield, High Town Road, Banbury.

Through cloud and sunshine, [and other poems]; by E.G. Sargent. London: Elliot Stock. 1889. [2], vi, 133 pp. *OXB*

SARJANT, L.G.

Fasti: occasional sonnets; by L.G. Sarjant. Printed Derby: Bemrose & Sons, Ltd. 1898. [56] pp. *OXB*

SATCHELL, William, (Samuel Cliall White, pseud.). Novelist.
Bedlam ballads and straitwaistcoat stories; by Saml. Cliall White. Illustrations by Allan Fen. [London: W. Satchell & Co. [1884]. 22 pp. il.
Poetry and prose.   *OXB*

SATYR, Sylvanus, pseud.
Ye palaverment of birds; by Sylvanus Satyr. London: L.N. Fowler. [1882]. 22 pp.   *BL*

SAUNDERS, Emily Susan Goulding. (E.S.G.S.). Writer on Italy.
David: a poem; by E.S.G.S. London: W.B. Whittingham & Co. 1880. 45 pp.   *BL*
Jacob: a poem; by E.S.G.S. London: Edwin Edey. 1889. 46 pp.   *BL*
The new Christian year: or, thoughts on the present lectionary: [poems]; by E.S.G.S. London: George Stoneman. 1891. xviii, 254 pp.   *OXB*

SAUNDERS, James (1842–   ). Of Wolverhampton, Staffordshire.
Raygarth's Gladys, and other poems; by James Saunders. London: Thomas Laurie. 1888. 255 pp.   *OXB*
Thorpe Thrappstone: (a Black Country idyl), and other poems; by James Saunders. London: Simpkin, Marshall, Hamilton, Kent & Co., Ltd; Birmingham: Midland Educational Co., Ltd. 1896. 70 pp.   *OXB*

SAVAGE, Walter J.
Snatches of song; by Walter J. Savage. Printed Shrewsbury: Adnitt & Naunton. 1898. 48 pp.   *OXB*

SAVAGE-ARMSTRONG, George Francis (1845–1906). b. County Dublin. Brother of the promising young poet Edmund John Armstrong (1841–65). Educated at Trinity College, Dublin, where he won several prizes for verse and prose compositions. Professor of history & English literature, Queen's College, Cork, 1870– 1905. Hon. D.Litt, Queen's University, 1891. Died at Strangford, County Down.
A garland from Greece: [poems]; by George Francis Armstrong. London: Longmans, Green, & Co. 1882. vi, 361 pp.   *OXB*
Also new ed. 1892.
Mephistopheles in broadcloth: a satire; by George Francis Armstrong. London: Longmans, Green, & Co. 1888. [iv], 100 pp.   *OXB*
Mephistopheles in broadcloth: a satire (A.D. 1888); by George Francis Savage-Armstrong. New ed. London: Longmans, Green & Co. 1892. [iv], 100 pp.   *OXB*
One in the infinite: [poems]; by George Francis Savage-Armstrong. London: Longmans, Green & Co. 1891. xii, 427 pp.   *MPL*
Poems: lyrical and dramatic; by George Francis Savage-Armstrong. 3rd ed. London: Longmans, Green & Co. 1892. viii, 340 pp.   *OXB*
Queen-Empress and Empire, 1837–1897; by George Savage-Armstrong. Belfast: Marcus Ward & Co., Ltd. 1897. 16 pp.   *OXB*

Stories of Wicklow: [poems]; by George Francis Armstrong. 1886. xii, 431 pp. *OXB*

Also new ed. 1892.

Victoria, regina et imperatrix: a jubilee song from Ireland, 1887; by George Francis Armstrong. London: Longmans, Green, & Co. 1887. 16 pp. *OXB*

SAVILE, William Hale (1859–1925). Son of Philip Y. Savile of Methley, Yorkshire. Educated at Haileybury, and Keble College, Oxford; BA 1882, MA 1885. Ordained 1883; curate, St Mary Magdalene's, Paddington, London, 1883–86, Holy Trinity, Winchester, Hampshire, 1886–88; vicar, Wykeham, Yorkshire, 1888–1903, Ormesby, Yorkshire, 1903–05, Buckingham, 1919-20; rector, St Swithin's, Winchester, 1920–25.

The fall of Carthage: a poem; by William Hale Savile. Oxford: B.H. Blackwell. 1882. 20 pp. *OXB*

The garden of the resurrection: a poem; by W.H. Savile. London: J. Masters & Co. 1886. 27 pp. *OXB*

Poems; by W.H. Savile. Oxford: B.H. Blackwell; London: Simpkin, Marshall, Hamilton, Kent & Co. 1897. viii, 61 pp. *OXB*

The preaching of S. John the Baptist: sacred poem, 1887; by William Hale Savile. Oxford: B.H. Blackwell; London: Simpkin, Marshall & Co. 1887. 24 pp. *OXB*

SAVILL, Stanley. Of Chigwell, Essex. Writer on the police service.

Songs by the way, [and other poems]; by Stanley Savill. London: Bradley, Shiner & Co. [1892]. [vi], 70 pp. *OXB*

SAYERS, Frances H., (Lady Frances H. Cecil, pseud.)

Paradise found, and other poems; by Lady Frances H. Cecil. London: James Nisbet & Co. 1882. viii, 69 pp. *OXB*

SAYLE, Charles (1864–1924). b. Cambridge, son of Robert Sayle, merchant-draper. Educated at Rugby School, and New College, Oxford; BA 1887, MA 1890. He joined the staff of Cambridge University Library in 1893; assistant librarian, 1910– 24; edited *Annals of the University Library*; published *Catalogue of Early English Printed Books*, etc. Lived latterly at 9 Brookside, Cambridge.

Bertha: a story of love: [poems]; [by Charles Sayle]. London: Kegan Paul, Trench, & Co. 1885. xvi, 60 pp. *OXB*

Erotidia: [poems]; by Charles Sayle. Rugby: George E. Over. 1889. xvi, 101 pp.

Loose-leaf insert states 'This ed. is limited to 220 copies'. *OXB*

Musa consolatrix: [poems]; [by] Charles Sayle. London: David Nutt. 1893. [x], 130 pp. *MPL*

Also a limited ed. of 20 copies on Japanese vellum.

SCARR, C.W. Of Ely, Cambridgeshire.

A fenman's fancies: a medley of verses; by C.W. Scarr. Printed Ely: Shelton & Tibbitts. 1899. 24 pp. *OXB*

SCHOFIELD-MILNE, R.

Cowboy ballads, and other ballads and poems; by R. Schofield-Milne. Manchester: John Heywood. [1891]. 108 pp. *OXB*

SCHUMANN, Hubert

Some verses; by Hubert Schumann. Printed York: H. Harrison. 1897. 68 pp. *UCD*

SCHWEITZER, Helen F.

The love-philtre, and other poems; [by] Helen F. Schweitzer. London: John Macqueen. 1897. viii, 79 pp.
A limited ed. of 250 copies. *OXB*

SCOT, A.F., pseud. *see* JAPP, Alexander Hay, (A.N. Mount Rose, pseud.), (A.F. Scot, pseud.)

SCOTT, B.H. Lived at 29 Yew Villas, Sale, Cheshire.
The censor: a satire in verse, and other poems; by B.H. Scott. Sale, Cheshire: Author. [1889?]. 33 pp. *BL*

SCOTT, Charles Henry Montagu-Douglas- *see* MONTAGU-DOUG-LAS-SCOTT, Charles Henry

SCOTT, Charles Newton. Writer on religions.
Lyrics and elegies; by Charles Newton Scott. London: Smith, Elder, & Co. 1880. viii, 74 pp. *UCD*

SCOTT, Christabel

Iona: a romance of the west; by Christabel Scott. London: Elliot Stock. 1896. [iv], 204 pp. *OXB*

SCOTT, Clement (1841–1904). b. London, son of Rev. William Scott. Junior clerk in the War Office, 1860–79. Dramatic critic for the *Sunday Times*, 1863–65, London *Figaro*, 1870, and *Daily Telegraph*, 1871–98; edited *The Theatre*, 1871–98; edited *The Theatre*, 1880–89. He was the pioneer of picturesque dramatic criticism. Adapted plays from the French for London theatres.
Lays and lyrics; by Clement Scott. London: George Routledge & Sons. 1888. 320 pp. (Routledge's pocket library). *MPL*
Lays of a Londoner; by Clement Scott. London: David Bogue. 1882. viii, 128 pp. *MPL*
Lays of a Londoner; by Clement Scott. London: Carson & Comerford. 1886. x, 93 pp. *OXB*
The new Victoria Cross: six popular pictures of England's heroes toiling day by day: [poems]; by Clement Scott. Illustrated by T.E. Ryan, (from original drawing by W.H. Pike). London: David Allen & Sons. 1894. 15 pp. il. *BL*
Poems for recitation; by Clement Scott. London: Samuel French. [1884]. 80 pp. *OXB*

SCOTT, Elizabeth
Wayside verses; by a brother and sister [Elizabeth Scott and W.R.]. Tewkesbury: W. North. [1896]. 94 pp.   *UCD*

SCOTT, George F.E.
Sursum corda: or, song and service: [poems]; by George F.E. Scott. London: Kegan Paul, Trench & Co. 1889. x, 178 pp.   *OXB*
Theodora, and other poems; by George F.E. Scott. London: Kegan Paul, Trench & Co. 1883. xii, 144 pp.   *OXB*

SCOTT, James Bedell. Educated at Trinity College, Dublin; BA 1850, MA 1858. Ordained 1852; curate, Banagher, King's County, 1851–55, Raphoe, Donegal, 1855–58, Banagher, 1858–68; rector, Banagher, from 1868.
Poems; by James Bedell Scott. Printed Belfast: Marcus Ward & Co., Ltd. 1897. 31 pp.
   Privately printed.   *NLI*

SCOTT, James Kim (1839–83). b. Urr, Kirkcudbrightshire. When he was very young his parents moved to Auchencairn on the Solway Firth. His education was limited, and at ten he was apprenticed to tailoring with his father. He studied musical composition, some of his pieces being published by E. Kohler & Son of Edinburgh. At twenty-six he was chosen conductor of psalmody in a large congregation in Edinburgh. Started a small tailoring and clothier business.
Galloway gleanings: poems and songs; by James K. Scott. Castle-Douglas: S. Gordon; Edinburgh: John Menzies & Co. 1881. [iv], 164 pp.   *OXB*

SCOTT, Rebecca. Of Castlefin, County Donegal.
Echoes from Tyrconnel: a collection of legendary and other poems; by Rebecca Scott. Londonderry: James Colhoun. 1880. 219 pp.   *OXB*

SCOTT, William Bell (1811–90). b. St Leonards, near Edinburgh, son of Robert Scott, engraver, and brother of the painter David Scott. Educated at Edinburgh High School; studied art in Edinburgh and London. In 1844 he went to Newcastle upon Tyne to establish a school of design, remaining until 1864. Exhibited at the Royal Academy and other London galleries. He was associated with the Pre-Raphaelite Brotherhood, friend of Rossetti and Swinburne. Painted the murals at Wallington House, Northumberland; examiner at the art schools, South Kensington, 1864–85. Lived at Cheyne Walk. Died at Penkill Castle, Ayrshire.
A poet's harvest home: being one hundred short poems; by William Bell Scott. London: Elliot Stock. 1882. xii, 156 pp.   *MPL*
A poet's harvest home: being one hundred short poems; by William Bell Scott. With an aftermath of twenty short poems. London: Elkin Mathews & John Lane, The Bodley Head. 1893. xii, 195 pp. il.
   A limited ed. of 300 copies.   *TCD*

SCOTT-ELLIOT, W. Theosophist. Writer on Atlantis.

The marriage of the soul, and other poems; by W. Scott-Elliot. London: Kegan Paul, Trench, Trübner & Co., Ltd. 1892. x, 55 pp.   *OXB*

SEAGER, Robert. Of Ipswich, Suffolk. Temperance reformer, and writer on the manufacture of non-alcoholic beverages.

The Victorian jubilee: an ode to Britain; by Robert Seager. With portrait of the Queen. London: National Temperance Depot. 1887. 16 pp. por.   *OXB*

SEAL, William Henry

Ione, and other poems; by W.H. Seal. London: Kegan Paul, Trench, & Co. 1883. [x], 210 pp.   *OXB*
   Also 2nd ed. 1884.

Visions of the night, in ballad and song; by William Henry Seal. London: Kegan Paul, Trench & Co. 1888. x, 124 pp.   *OXB*

SEAMAN, Sir Owen (1861–1936). Educated at Shrewsbury School, and Clare College, Cambridge. Professor of literature, Newcastle upon Tyne, 1890–1903. A gifted satirist and parodist, he joined the staff of *Punch* in 1897; assistant editor, 1902, editor, 1906–32. He was knighted in 1914.

The battle of the bays, [and other poems]; by Owen Seaman. London: John Lane, The Bodley Head. 1896. iv, 87 pp.   *BL*
   Also [2nd ed.] [1897].

Horace at Cambridge: [poems]; by Owen Seaman. London: A.D. Innes & Co. 1895. [x], 100 pp.   *OXB*

Tillers of the sand: being a fitful record of the Rosebery administration from the triumph of Ladas to the decline and fall-off: [poems]; by Owen Seaman. London: Smith, Elder, & Co. 1895. viii, 120 pp.   *MPL*

With double pipe: [poems]; by Owen Seaman. Oxford: B.H. Blackwell; Cambridge: Elijah Johnson; London: Simpkin, Marshall, & Co. 1888. [viii], 88 pp.   *OXB*

SEARELLE, Luscombe, pseud. *see* **ISRAEL, I.**, (Luscombe Searelle, pseud.)

SEATH, William. A weaver.

Rhymes and lyrics: humorous, serious, descriptive and satirical; by William Seath. (With explanatory notes). St. Helens: Westworth & Sons. 1897. 168 pp. il.   *★UCD*

SEATON, Rose. Dramatist.

Romances and poems; by Rose Seaton. London: Simpkin, Marshall, Hamilton, Kent & Co., Ltd. [1891]. [iv], 120 pp.   *BL*

SECCOMBE, Thomas Strong. Lieutenant-Colonel. Illustrated editions of many major poets.

Comic sketches from English history, for children of various ages, with descriptive rhymes; by Lieut.-Colonel T.S. Seccombe. London: W.H. Allen & Co. 1884. 56 pp. il., col. il.   *OXB*

The good old story of Cinderella, re-told in rhyme; by Lieut.-Colonel Seccombe. With seventy illustrations by the author, including twelve full-page plates printed in colours by Emrik and Binger. London: Frederick Warne & Co.; New York: A.C. Armstrong & Son. [1882]. 48 pp. il., col il.

Cover-title is *Cinderella*.   *OXB*

The story of Prince Hildebrand and the Princess Ida; by T.S. Seccombe. With 110 illustrations by the author. London: Thos. De La Rue & Co. [1880]. x, 94 pp. il.   *OXB*

SELF, William Henry. Studied for the ministry at St Bees; deacon, 1846, priest, 1847; perpetual curate, St John's Lytham, Lancashire, 1848–70.

The knight of the Wyvern, and other poems; by W.H. Self. London: P. Elliott. 1891. iv, 100 pp.   ★

SELKIRK, J.B., pseud. *see* **BROWN, James**, (J.B. Selkirk, pseud.)

SELOUS, S.

Annie's story; by S. Selous. London: Edward Jones. 1885. [iv], 104 pp.   *OXB*

SENIOR, Joseph (1819–92). A cutler and blade-forger he worked in a small smithy. Eventually he became totally blind. Lived at Crookes Road, Sheffield, Yorkshire.

Additional poems to Smithy rhymes and stithy chimes; by J. Senior. Printed Sheffield: Leader & Sons. 1884. 24 pp.   *OXB*

Smithy rhymes and stithy chimes: or, the short and simple annals of the poor, spelt by the unlettered muse of your humble bard Joseph Senior. Printed Sheffield: Leader & Sons. 1882. xvi, 88 pp.   *OXB*

SERJEANT, Farel Viret Calvin (1869–19   ). b. Seend, Wiltshire, son of Rev. James Serjeant. Educated at Repton School, and St John's College, Cambridge; BA 1890. Assistant master successively at Willington, Grantham, Beaumaris, 1891–96; master, Manchester Grammar School, 1896–1900, Nottingham High School, 1900–03, Sheffield Royal Grammar School, 1903–09, Bournemouth School, 1909–14, afterwards at Purley County Secondary School.

Angeline, and other poems; by Farel V.C. Serjeant. London: Swan Sonnenschein & Co. 1894. 63 pp.   *OXB*

SETON, Alexander T.

"The Hebridean communion": a poem, descriptive of an autumnal communion in the Island of Lewis; by Alexander T. Seton. 2nd ed. Dingwall: Lewis Munro. [1881?]. 15 pp.   *BL*

SETOUN, Gabriel, pseud. *see* **HEPBURN, Thomas Nicoll**, (Gabriel Setoun, pseud.)

SEWELL, Mary (1797–1884). b. Sutton, Suffolk, into a Quaker family, daughter of John and Ann Wright. They moved to a farm at Felsthorpe, Norfolk, in 1799. She became a governess at a school in Essex before marrying Isaac Sewell. They lived successively in Yarmouth, Stoke Newington, Brighton and Chichester. She became a member of the Church of England in 1835. Her stories and verses, expressing simple moral values, were immensely popular.

Mrs. Sewell's poems and ballads. With memoir by Miss E. Boyd-Bayly, and a special photogravure portrait of the author. London: Jarrold & Sons. [1899]. 2 vols in 1. il., por. *OXB*

Mother's last words, and other ballads; by Mrs. Sewell. London: Jarrold & Sons. [1892]. 112 pp. il., col. il. (New series of shilling books). *OXB*

Poems and ballads; by Mrs. Sewell. With a memoir by Miss E.B. Bayly. London: Jarrold & Sons. [1886]. 2 vols. *BL*

The suffering poor: A sad story; The blighted home; The midnight worker; by Mrs. Sewell. London: Jarrold & Sons. [1883]. [ii], 44 pp. *OXB*

A vision of the night; by Mrs. Sewell. London: Jarrold & Sons. [1885]. 42 pp. *OXB*

SHAIRP, John Campbell (1819–85). b. Houston House, West Lothian, son of an army officer. Educated at Edinburgh Academy, Glasgow University, and Balliol College, Oxford. Newdigate prizewinner, 1842. A master at Rugby School, 1846–56; professor of Latin, St Andrews, 1861–68; principal of the United College, St Andrews, 1868–77; professor of poetry at Oxford, 1877–87. An accomplished critic, he published works on literature, culture, philosophy and religion.

Glen Desseray, and other poems, lyrical and elegiac; by John Campbell Shairp. Edited by Francis T. Palgrave. London: Macmillan & Co. 1888. xxvi, 279 pp. *MPL*

SHARMAN, S.

Slips of the pen: [poems]; by S. Sharman. Printed Shahjahanpur: Arya Darpan Press. [1883]. [iv], 124 pp. *BL*

SHARMAN, Samuel. Of Donisthorpe, Derbyshire. Possibly Samuel Sharman, b. St Giles parish, London, son of William Sharman. Matriculated at St Catharine's College, Cambridge, 1844.

Jottings in verse: sacred and secular; by Samuel Sharman. Printed Birkenhead: Broom & Walmsley. 1889. 96 pp. *OXB*

SHARP, Isaac (1806–97). b. Brighton, Sussex, son of a businessman. Educated at a Quaker school in Essex. Part of his life was spent in Middlesbrough, where he was involved in coal-mining, iron-works, shipping, and other enterprises. He undertook extensive missionary work for the Society of Friends in Europe, America, Asia and Africa.

Saul of Tarsus, and other poems; by Isaac Sharp. London: Kegan Paul, Trench & Co. 1888. viii, 84 pp.   *OXB*

SHARP, James. A Glasgow merchant. Lived at 4 Doune Terrace, Kelvinside.
The captive king, and other poems; by James Sharp. Illustrated by Florence Holms. Paisley: Alexander Gardner. 1887. x, 272 pp. il.   *OXB*

SHARP, John (1810?–1903). Son of Rev. Samuel Sharp, vicar of Wakefield, Yorkshire. Educated at Wakefield and Leeds, and Magdalene College, Cambridge; BA 1833, MA 1836. Ordained 1834; perpetual curate, Horbury, Yorkshire, 1834–99; hon. canon of Ripon, 1885–88; hon. canon of Wakefield, 1888–1903. Leader of the Oxford Movement in the north of England.
Poems and hymns; by John Sharp. London: George Bell & Sons. 1880. xiv, 372 pp.   *OXB*

SHARP, Matilda
The journey to paradise: or, flight of the soul to its maker: a heavenly day dream: [poems]; set down by Matilda Sharp. London: Christian Life Office; E. Carlier. 1899. [viii]. 50 pp.   *BL*

SHARP, William, (Fiona Macleod, pseud.) (1855– 1905). b. Garthland Place, near Paisley, Renfrewshire, son of a merchant. Educated at Glasgow Academy, and Glasgow University. He worked in a lawyer's office, 1874–76, then went to Australia on account of his health, returning to London in 1878. Worked in a bank intermittently but had more success as a journalist and editor; edited the 'Canterbury Poets' series. Associated with the Pre-Raphaelites, he published a biography of Dante Gabriel Rossetti. He wrote novels and romances with a Celtic theme derived from the myths of early Ireland and Scotland, so becoming one of the chief representatives of the Celtic revival. The secret of his pseud. was maintained until his death.
Earth's voices; Transcripts from nature; Sospitra, and other poems; by William Sharp. London: Elliot Stock. 1884. viii, 207 pp.   *OXB*
Euphrenia: or, the test of love: a poem; by William Sharp. London: Kegan Paul, Trench & Co. 1884. [viii], 179 pp.   *OXB*
Flower o' the vine: Romantic ballads; and, Sospiri di Roma; by William Sharp. New York: Charles L. Webster & Co. 1892. 188 pp. por.   *BL*
From the hills of dream: mountain songs and island runes; by Fiona Macleod. Edinburgh: Patrick Geddes & Colleagues. [1897]. xvi, 150 pp.   *OXB*
The human inheritance; The new hope; Motherhood, [and other poems]; by William Sharp. London, Elliot Stock. 1882. viii, 184 pp.   *MPL*
Romantic ballads; and, Poems of Phantasy; by William Sharp. [London]: Walter Scott. 1888. 87 pp.
  Printed for the author.   *UCD*
  Also 2nd ed. 1889.
Sospiri di roma: [poems]; by William Sharp. Printed Rome: Societa Laziale. 1891. 115 pp.   *UCD*

SHARPE, William. b. Ireland. He trained for a medical career at Queen's University, Belfast; MD 1866, MCh 1868; Fellow of Queen's University of Ireland. Served in India as surgeon, Army Medical Depot.

The dual image: or, the renewal of the temple: a mystical poem of life; by William Sharpe. London: Hy. A. Copley. 1896. 17 pp.   *OXB*

The fall of Lucifer, and other essays and poems; by William Sharpe. London: Hy. A. Copley. 1897. [iii], 250 pp. por.   *JRL*

Humanity and the man: or, the training of the Adamite: a poem of life and evolution; by Wm. Sharpe. New ed. to which is appended Books VII and VIII of "The dual image". London: Henry A. Copley. 1898. 59, 29 pp. por.   *OXB*

SHAW, Alfred Capel (1847–19). Librarian, Central Lending Library, Birmingham Free Libraries, 1878–87, deputy chief librarian, 1887-98, chief librarian from 1898. Compiler of the *Index to the Shakespeare Memorial Library, Birmingham*, a major bibliography. Lived latterly at Claremont Road, Sparkbrook.

Two decades of song: [poems]; by A. Capel Shaw. London: Simpkin, Marshall, Hamilton, Kent & Co. Ltd; Birmingham: Cornish Bros. 1896. [viii], 112 pp.   *OXB*

The vision of Erin; by Alfred Capel Shaw. Birmingham: A.G. Beacon. 1892. [iv], 44 pp.   *OXB*

SHAW, F.J. Of Newcastle upon Tyne.

Past and future: a poem; by F.J. Shaw. Newcastle-on-Tyne: Mawson, Swan, & Morgan. 1898. 38 pp.   *NPL*

SHAW, Gertrude E.

Forget-me-nots; by Gertrude E. Shaw. London: Marcus Ward & Co. [1895]. [24] pp. col. il.   *BL*

SHAW, Thomas Angus. Admitted pensioner, Queen's College, Cambridge, 1844.

Poetical essays; by Thomas Angus Shaw. London: William Poole. 1881. [vi], 47 pp.   *OXB*

Poetical essays; by Thomas Angus Shaw. London: George Stoneman. 1888. [vi], 60 pp.   *OXB*

SHEARER, C.J. Educated at Stonyhurst College, Glasgow University, and abroad. Novelist.

In London, and other poems; by C.J. Shearer. London: Elliot Stock. 1897. viii, 198 pp.   *UCD*

SHEEHAN, Michael Francis (1865–). b. Ballyhussa, County Waterford. He contributed many poems to *Nation*, *Irish Fireside*, and other periodicals.

Smiles and sighs: a volume of poems; by Michael Francis Sheehan. With an introduction by Michael P. Hickey. Dublin: M.H. Gill & Son. 1893. 120 pp.   *OXB*

SHEILA, pseud. *see* **DOAKE, Margaret**, (Sheila, pseud.)

SHELLSHEAR, Alicia, (A.S.)

Short poems and sacred verses; by A.S. Printed London: G.E. Waters. 1892. viii, 174 pp.

Printed for private circulation only. *BL*

Short poems and sacred verses; by A.S. Second series. Printed London: G.E. Waters. 1893. 160 pp.

Printed for private circulation. *★UCD*

Short poems and sacred verses; by A.S. Third series. Printed London: G.E. Waters. 1895. 164 pp.

Printed for private circulation. *★UCD*

SHEPPARD, Henry Winter, (Martellius, pseud.) (1867–1933). Son of Major Thomas W. Sheppard, 87th Regiment. Educated at Haileybury, and Trinity College, Cambridge; BA 1890, MA 1920. A writer and scholar, specializing in biblical Hebrew.

Joy and health: [poems]; by Martellius. London: Cassell & Co., Ltd. [1892]. 56 pp. il. *OXB*

SHERARD, Robert Harborough (1861–1943). b. London, son of Rev. Bennett Sherard-Kennedy of Stapleford Hall, Melton Mowbray, Leicestershire. His mother was a grand-daughter of William Wordsworth. Educated at Queen Elizabeth College, Guernsey, and the universities of Oxford, Bonn and Paris. From 1883 he acted as special correspondent to leading English and American papers in various parts of the world. Author of novels, biographies and sociological works, in 1897 publishing *The White Slaves of England*, which revealed certain malpractices in English industry. A loyal friend of Oscar Wilde.

Whispers: being the early poems of Robert Harborough Sherard. London: Remington & Co. 1884. viii, 118 pp. *OXB*

SHERBROOKE, Lord *see* **LOWE, Robert, Lord Sherbrooke**

SHERWELL, John William. Writer on the Guild of Saddlers, a City of London Livery Co.

Poems; by John W. Sherwell. 1896. 44 pp

Printed for private circulation. *OXB*

SHORE, Arabella, (A.). Daughter of Rev. Thomas Shore, Fellow of Wadham College, Oxford. Sister of Louisa Shore. Translator from the French and Italian. Lived latterly with her sister at Orchard Poyle, near Taplow. Buckinghamshire.

Elegies and memorials; by A. and L. London: Kegan Paul, Trench, Trübner, & Co., Ltd. 1890. 63 pp.

Not joint authorship. *OXB*

Poems; by A. and L.; by Arabella and Louisa Shore. London: Grant Richards. 1897. viii, 360 pp.

Not joint authorship. *OXB*

SHORE, Louisa, (L.) (1824–95). b. Potten, Bedfordshire, daughter of Rev. Thomas Shore, Fellow of Wadham College, Oxford. Sister of Arabella Shore. After the death of her parents she found a new home in Firgrove, Sunninghill. Berkshire. A keen advocate of the advancement of women. Lived latterly with her sister at Orchard Poyle, near Taplow, Buckinghamshire. Died at Wimbledon.

Elegies and memorials; by A. and L. London: Kegan Paul, Trench, Trübner, & Co., Ltd. 1890. 63 pp.

    Not joint authorship.   *OXB*

Poems; by A. and L.; by Arabella and Louise Shore. London: Grant Richards. 1897. viii, 360 pp.

    Not joint authorship.   *OXB*

Poems; by Louisa Shore. With a memoir by her sister, Arabella Shore, and an appreciation by Frederic Harrison. London: John Lane, The Bodley Head. 1897. vi, 216 pp. por.   *OXB*

SHOREY, L., (L.S. Leytonstone, pseud.). Married woman. She lost a daughter in infancy.

The broken angel, and other poems; by L. Shorey (L.S. Leytonstone). London: George Stoneman. [1892]. 80 pp.   *OXB*

SHORT, Alfred, (One Short, pseud.)

Adventures & sketches at New Brighton, Liverpool: [poems]; by one Short. [Liverpool]. [1888]. 16 pp. il.   *BL*

SHORT, Sir Frank (1857–1945). b. Stourbridge, Worcestershire, son of J.T. Short. Educated in London. An artist, a talented master of all engraving processes, and a skilled teacher. Head of the Engraving School at the Royal College of Art; president, Royal Society of Painter Etchers, 1910–39; treasurer, Royal Academy, 1919–32.

The Boer ride; by Frank Short. London: John Long. [1898]. 31 pp.   *OXB*

SHORT, One *see* **SHORT, Alfred**, (One Short, pseud.)

SHORTER, Dora Sigerson (1866–1918). b. Dublin, daughter of Dr George Sigerson, surgeon and Gaelic scholar. Educated at home in a cultured atmosphere. Like her greatest friends, Katharine Tynan and Louise Imogen Guiney, she was a Roman Catholic. In 1896 she married the journalist and critic Clement Shorter, and settled in London. She took up sculpture, for which she had a real talent. After the Easter Rebellion of 1916 she worked on behalf of the accused and the imprisoned. She carved the memorial sculpture group of Irish patriots in Dublin Cemetery, where she herself is buried.

Ballads & poems; by Dora Sigerson (Mrs Clement Shorter). London: James Bowden. 1899. viii, 124 pp.   *OXB*

The fairy changeling, and other poems; by Dora Sigerson (Mrs Clement Shorter). London: John Lane, The Bodley Head. 1898. viii, 100 pp. il.   *NLI*

My lady's slipper, and other verses; by Dora Sigerson (Mrs Clement Shorter). New York: Dodd, Mead & Co. [1899]. viii, 157 pp.   *★NUC*

Verses; by Dora Sigerson. London: Elliot Stock. 1893. viii, 135 pp.   *MPL*

SHORTER, Thomas, (Thomas Brevior, pseud.) (1823–99). b. Clerkenwell, London. Aged eleven he became an errand boy to a book auctioneer in Fleet Street; apprenticed to a watch case finisher, 1837. Appointed secretary to the Society for Promoting Working Men's Associations, 1850; secretary of the Working Men's College, Great Ormond Street, London, 1854–67. Founded with W.M. Wilkinson *The Spiritual Magazine*, 1860; edited the *Quarterly Journal of Education*. Promoted conferences on spiritualism. He became blind many years before his death.

Echoes from bygone days: or, love lyrics and character sonnets; by Thomas Brevior. London: Allman & Son, Ltd. [1889]. vi, 73 pp.   *OXB*

Later autumn leaves: thoughts in verse, with sketches of character chiefly from our village and neighbourhood; by Thomas Brevior. London: Allman & Son, Ltd. [1896]. xviii, 130 pp. por.   *OXB*

Lyrics for heart and voice: a contribution to the hymnal of the future; by Thomas Brevior. London: F. Pitman. [1883]. [2], xiv, 425 pp.   *OXB*

Spring flowers and autumn leaves, [and other poems]; by Thomas Brevior. London: Allman & Son, Ltd. [1893]. x, 90 pp.   *BL*

SHREWSBURY, Arthur Robert (1856–1903). Rev. Shrewsbury, minister of Albion Church, Hammersmith. Lived in Chiswick, Middlesex.

The palm-branch, and other verses; by Arthur R. Shrewsbury. London: Elliot Stock. 1899. 65 pp.   *OXB*

SHREWSBURY, C.S. A married woman.

The second marriage day, and other poems; by C.S. Shrewsbury. London: London Literary Society. [1886]. viii, 311 pp.   *OXB*

SHREWSBURY, George Gravener. Educated at Merchant Taylors' School (scholar). Lived at 48 Warren Street, Fitzroy Square, London W.

Victoria regina: jubilee odes, and other poems; by Geo. Gravener Shrewsbury. London: Harrison & Sons. 1887. [17] pp.   *OXB*

Victoria regina: jubilee odes, and other poems; by Geo. Gravener Shrewsbury. [2nd ed.]. London: Harrison & Sons. 1887. [8], xii, 188 pp.
Spine-title is *Poems*.   *OXB*

SHUTTLEWORTH, Henry Cary (1850–1900). b. Cornwall, son of Rev. Edward Shuttleworth, vicar of Egloshayle. Educated at Forest School, Walthamstow, St Mary Hall, and Christ Church, Oxford. Ordained 1873; curate, St Barnabas's, Oxford, and chaplain of Christ Church, 1874–76; minor canon, St Paul's, London, 1876–84; rector, St Nicholas Cole-Abbey, London, from 1884. Professor, King's College, 1890. Founder of the Shuttleworth Club for men and women. Identified with the Christian Socialist movement. Hymn writer.

Songs; by Henry Cary Shuttleworth. London: Bowles & Cross. [1885]. 30 pp.

'Any profits will be given to the fund for the restoration of the tower of St Mary Somerset, Upper Thames Street, E.C.'   *OXB*

SIBREE, John. Educated at London University. Translator of Hegel's *Philosophy of History*. Lived at Bussage House, Stroud, Gloucestershire.

Fancy, and other rhymes; by John Sibree. London: Trübner & Co. 1880. iv, 60 pp.   *OXB*

Fancy, and other rhymes (with additions); by John Sibree. London: Trübner & Co. 1882. 88 pp.   *★UCD*

Poems, including "Fancy", "A resting-place", "To the age", and "Ellen Carew"; by John Sibree. London: Trübner & Co. 1884. [4], iv, 131 pp.   *OXB*

Poems, with two additions; and Rosalie: a tale of the Wye, in five cantos; by John Sibree. London: Kegan Paul, Trench, Trübner, & Co., Ltd. 1890. iv, 68 pp.   *OXB*

SIDNEY, Violet E.

Waima, and other verses; by Violet E. Sidney. London: Elliot Stock. 1898. viii, 88 pp.   *OXB*

SIEVWRIGHT, Colin (1819–95). b. Brechin, Angus, son of a handloom weaver. At the age of eight he worked a seventy-two-hour week for the East Mill Co. Lived at Forfar.

A garland for the ancient city: or, love songs of Brechin and its neighbourhood (with historical notes); by Colin Sievwright. 2nd ed. Brechin: D.H. Edwards. 1899. 55 pp.

Poetry and prose.   *BL*

SIGERSON, Dora *see* **SHORTER, Dora Sigerson**

SIGMA, pseud.

Swallow-flights: [poems]; by Sigma. Printed London: Henry Sotheran & Co. 1885. 165 pp.

Printed for the author.   *★NUC*

SIGNA, pseud. Of Northampton.

Poet and peasant, and other poems; by Signa. Manchester: John Heywood. 1892. 96 pp.   *OXB*

Zeppa: or, a woman's remorse, and other poems; by Signa. Northampton: H. Berrill. [1889]. 19 pp.   *OXB*

SIMMS, John R.

Notes on the way, in verse; by John R. Simms. London: Digby, Long & Co. [1897] xii, 201 pp.   *OXB*

SIMPSON, Jessie. Mrs Logie Robertson.

Blossoms: a series of child-portraits: [poems]; by Jessie Simpson. [c. 1890]. [iv], 27 pp.

Printed for private circulation.   *OXB*

SIMPSON, Samuel. Of Lancaster.

On, Christians, on! . . . , with other poems; by S. Simpson. Lancaster: E. & J.L. Milner. 1899. [vi], 333 pp. *BL*

SIMS, George Robert (1847–1922). b. London, son of George Sims. Educated at Hanwell College, and in Bonn and Paris. He began his working life in the office of a London merchant before becoming a journalist in 1874; wrote regularly for *Fun*, the *Referee*, and the *Weekly Despatch*. Published a large number of successful plays, novels, and children's stories; his study of poverty, *How the Poor Live*, appeared in the *London Daily News*. Wrote for the *Referee* under the pseud. 'Dagonet'. Lived at 12 Clarence Terrace, Regent's Park, NW.

Ballads and poems: The Dagonet ballads; The ballads of Babylon; The lifeboat, and other poems; by George R. Sims. London: Neville & Co. [1883]. 3 vols in 1. por. *MPL*

Ballads of Babylon; by George R. Sims. London: John P Fuller. 1880. viii, 156pp. *MPL*

A bunch of primroses; by Geo. R. Sims. Illustrated by J. Willis Grey. London: Raphael Tuck & Sons. [1890]. [20] pp. il., col. il.
    Printed on card. *BL*

Dagonet ditties, (from 'The Referee'); by George R. Sims. London: Chatto & Windus. 1891. viii, 152 pp. *OXB*
    Also 2nd ed. 1891.

The Dagonet reciter and reader: being readings and recitations in prose and verse, selected from his own works; by George R. Sims. London: Chatto & Windus. 1888. [viii], 136 pp. por. *OXB*

In the harbour; by George R. Sims. Illustrated by W. Langley and Percy Robertson. London: Hildesheimer & Faulkner. [1892]. [16] pp. il.
    Printed on card. *BL*

The land of gold, and other poems; by George R. Sims. London: J.P. Fuller. 1888. viii, 132 pp. *OXB*

The lifeboat, and other poems; by George R. Sims. London: J.P. Fuller. 1883. viii, 152 pp. *MPL*

Nellie's prayer; by George R. Sims. Illustrated by J. Willis Grey. London: Raphael Tuck & Sons. [1890]. [24] pp. il.
    Printed on card. *BL*

SIMS, William, (W.S.). Lived at Riversdale Cottage, Maidenhead, Berkshire, and at Devizes, Wiltshire.

A river holiday; [by W.S.]. Illustrated by Harry Furniss. London: T. Fisher Unwin. [1883]. 24 pp. il. *OXB*

"Vize" verse: a few miscellaneous trifles; by William Sims. Printed Devizes: H.F. Bull. 1884. [x], 78 pp. *OXB*

SINCLAIR, Francis, (Philip Garth, pseud.). Brought up in Glasgow and Stirling. Spent many years in New Zealand and the islands of Kauai and Nihau, returning to London in 1885.

Ballads and poems from the Pacific; by Philip Garth ("F.S.C.", "Aopouri"). London: Sampson Low, Marston, Searle & Rivington. 1885. viii, 264 pp.   *UCD*
> Also 2nd ed. 1889.

SINCLAIR, Julian

Nakiketas, and other poems; by Julian Sinclair. London: Kegan Paul, Trench & Co. 1886. [vi], 80 pp.   *OXB*

SINCLAIR, May (1863–1946). b. Rock Ferry, Cheshire, daughter of Thomas Sinclair, Liverpool shipowner. Educated at home and briefly at Cheltenham Ladies' College. The business failed, her parents separated, and she was left to support her mother by her writing. Novelist and short story writer, she also wrote on philosophical idealism, her work meeting with far greater success in America than in England. An active suffragette before the First World War, during which she served with the British Red Cross in a Field Ambulance Corps in Belgium.

Essays in verse; by May Sinclair. London: Kegan Paul, Trench, Trübner & Co., Ltd. 1891. [vi], 86 pp.   *OXB*

SINGER FROM THE SOUTH, pseud. *see* BYRNE, Edmund John, (Singer from the South, pseud.)

SKELTON, Edith

All good things come to those who wait; by Edith Skelton. London: Griffith, Farran, Okeden & Welsh. 1884. 32 pp.   *OXB*

The crucial test, and other poems; by Edith Skelton. London: Griffith, Farran, Okeden & Welsh. 1889. 128 pp.   *OXB*

"Folded wings", and other poems; by Edith Skelton. London: Griffith & Farran; Norwich: P. Soman; A.H. Goose. 1880. [iv], 64 pp.   *OXB*

SKINNER, H.J.

The lily of the Lyn, and other poems; by H.J. Skinner. London: Kegan Paul, Trench & Co. 1884. viii, 101 pp.   *OXB*

SKIPSEY, Joseph (1832–1903). b. near North Shields, Northumberland, son of a miner who was shot by a special constable during a miners' strike. From the age of seven he worked at Percy Main Collieries. Taught himself to read and write, do arithmetic, and continued to educate himself. In 1859 he was appointed storekeeper at Gateshead Iron Works, and in 1863 became sub-librarian of Newcastle upon Tyne Literary & Philosophical Society; custodian of Shakespeare's birthplace, Stratford upon Avon, 1889–91. Edited a number of vols in the 'Canterbury Poets' series.

Carols from the coal-fields, and other songs and ballads; by Joseph Skipsey. London: Walter Scott. 1886. [2], xiv, 260 pp.   *OXB*

Carols, songs, and ballads; by Joseph Skipsey. New ed. London: Walter Scott. 1888. xiv, 212 pp.   *MPL*

Songs and lyrics; by Joseph Skipsey. Collected and revised. London: Walter Scott. 1892. viii, 180 pp.   *OXB*

SKRINE, John Huntley (1848–1923). b. Warleigh, near Bath, son of Henry D. Skrine. Educated at Uppingham School (captain of school), and Corpus Christi College, Oxford (scholar); BA 1871, MA 1874. Fellow of Merton College, 1871–79. Assistant master, Uppingham School, 1873-87; warden, Trinity College, Glenalmond, Perthshire, 1888–1902. Canon, St Ninian's, Perth, 1897–1902; vicar, St Peter-in-the-East, Oxford, 1908; select preacher at Oxford, 1907–09; Brampton lecturer, 1911.

Songs of the mind, and other ballads and lyrics; by John Huntley Skrine. Westminster: Archibald Constable. 1896. xii, 144 pp. *OXB*

Under two queens: lyrics written for the tercentenary festival of the founding of Uppingham School; by John Huntley Skrine. London: Macmillan & Co. 1884. 64 pp. il. (by Charles Rossiter). *MPL*

SLADEN, Douglas Brook Wheelton (1856–1933). b. London, son of Douglas B. Sladen, solicitor. Educated at Cheltenham College, and Trinity College, Oxford; BA 1879. Went to Australia in 1879; professor of history, Sydney University, 1882–84, then returned to England before moving to New York.

Australian lyrics, &c.; by Douglas B.W. Sladen. Melbourne: George Robertson. 1883. 68 pp. *MPL*

Australian lyrics; by Douglas B.W. Sladen. 2nd ed., revised. London: Griffith, Farran, Okeden & Welsh. 1885. 99 pp. *OXB*

Frithjof and Ingebjorg, and other poems; by Douglas B.W. Sladen. London: Kegan Paul, Trench, & Co. 1882. viii, 251 pp. *OXB*

In Cornwall; and, Across the sea, with poems written in Devonshire; by Douglas B.W. Sladen. London: Griffith, Farran, Okeden & Welsh. 1884. xvi, 304 pp. *MPL*

In Cornwall: being an extract of the Cornish poems from 'In Cornwall and Across the sea'; by Douglas B.W. Sladen. With illustrations and portrait of the author, and a special introduction on Cornwall. 3rd ed. Penzance: Offices of the "West of England Magazine"; London: Elliot Stock. [1888]. 16 pp. il., por. *MPL*

Lester the loyalist: a romance of the founding of Canada; by Douglas Sladen. Tokio: Hakubunsha. 1890. 43 pp.

Printed on maple-leaf patterned rice-paper. *MPL*

A poetry of exiles, and other poems; by Douglas B.W. Sladen. Sydney: C.E. Fuller. 1883. [x], 112 pp. *MPL*

A poetry of exiles, and other poems; by Douglas B.W. Sladen. Pocket ed. London: Griffith & Farran. [1884]. [viii], 112 pp. *BL*

A poetry of exiles; by Douglas B.W. Sladen. Vol. I. 2nd ed., revised. London: Griffith, Farran, Okeden & Welsh. 1885. 100 pp. *MPL*

The queen's troth: a legend of Frithjof and Ingebjorg; by Douglas B.W. Sladen. 2nd ed. Penzance: Alverton Press; London: Elliot Stock. 1888. 22 pp. *MPL*

The Spanish Armada: a ballad of 1588; by Douglas B.W. Sladen. 2nd ed. London: Griffith, Farran, Okeden & Welsh. 1888. 24 pp. *MPL*

A summer Christmas; and, A sonnet upon the SS. "Ballaarat"; by Douglas B.W. Sladen. London: Griffith, Farran, Okeden, & Welsh. [1884]. x, 239 pp. *MPL*

SLEIGH, Herbert *see* **SLEIGH, S. Herbert**

SLEIGH, S. Herbert
The holy vision, and other poems; by Herbert Sleigh. Cambridge: Macmillan & Bowes; London: Charles Taylor. 1892. [vi], 50 pp.   *BL*
The seige of Carthage (an historical episode), and other poems; by S.H. Sleigh. London: Remington & Co. 1880. [iv], 124 pp.   *OXB*

SLIMMON, James M. Scottish.
The dead planet, and other poems; by James M. Slimmon. London: Simpkin, Marshall, Hamilton, Kent & Co. Ltd. [1898]. [xii], 219 pp.   *OXB*

SLIPPER, Robert Armine (1866–1911). Son of Rev. William A. Slipper, vicar of Tuttington, Norfolk. Educated privately, and at Magdalene College, Cambridge; BA 1888, MA 1894. Ordained 1890; curate, Tuttington, Norfolk, 1889–90, St Gregory's, Norwich, 1890–93, Kirkley, Suffolk, 1893–95, St Clement's, Norwich, 1895–99, Tivetshall, Norfolk, 1900–07, rector there from 1907 until his death.
Paulinus: or, the conversion of Northumbria: an historical poem, in six cantos; by Robert Armine Slipper. Norwich: W.A. Nudd; London: Simpkin, Marshall, Hamilton, & Co. 1892. [viii], 147 pp.   *OXB*

SLOANE, Edward A.
The golden queen: a tale of love, war, and magic; by Edward A. Sloane. London: Griffith & Farran; New York: E.P. Dutton & Co. [1882]. 206 pp.   *OXB*

SMALES, Edwin Cooke
Echoes of the city: [poems]; by Edwin C. Smales. Manchester: Joseph John Alley. 1883. viii, 100 pp.   *MPL*

SMALL, Alexander
Leisure-hour verses; by Alexander Small. Edinburgh: Andrew Elliot. 1893. 141 pp.   *OXB*

SMALL, James Grindley (1817–88). b. Edinburgh. Educated at Edinburgh High School, and Edinburgh University, where he was taught moral philosophy by Professor John Wilson. He became a Church of Scotland minister but left the ministry in 1843. Ordained Free Church minister at Bervie, near Montrose, Angus, in 1846.
The Battle of Langside, and other poems, contributed to the periodicals from 1884 to 1887; by James G. Small. Paisley: J. & R. Parlane; London: James Nisbet & Co. [1888]. 85 pp.   *BL*

SMEAL, Adam. Scottish, a member of Manchester St Andrew's Society. Lived latterly at Ravenslea, Whalley Range, Manchester.
Neddy Bruce: a story; with, Poems, English and Scotch; by Adam Smeal. Manchester: John Heywood. 1881. 175 pp.   *MPL*
Rhymes for railway reading. First series; by Adam Smeal. Manchester: Abel Heywood & Son; London: Marshall Bros. [1885?]. 104 pp.   *MPL*

SMETHAM, Henry (1854–19   ). Businessman of Strood, Kent. Secretary, Strood Institute elocution class; member of Rochester City Museum and Public Library Committees from 1888. Founded the Rochester branch of the Dickens Fellowship, 1903. Trustee of the Poor, Strood. Author of a history of Strood, and other writings on the county of Kent. Lived at 11 Alexandra Terrace, then at 78 Goddington Road, Strood.

Sketches: prose and rhyme; by Henry Smetham. London: Whiting & Co.; Strood, Kent: Sweet & Sons. 1889. viii, 188 pp.   *OXB*

SMETHAM, James (1821–89). Artist, essayist and critic, he was befriended by Rossetti, Ruskin, Ford Madox Brown, and others, all admirers of his work, but was unsuccessful as a painter. Published studies of Sir Joshua Reynolds and William Blake. Many of his paintings have been lost.

The literary works of James Smetham. Edited by William Davies. London: Macmillan & Co. 1893. viii, 288 pp.

Essays and poems.   *MPL*

SMIETON, Jane Paxton. Mrs Smieton of Dundee.

Classical tales in verse, and Sicilian idyls; by Jane Paxton Smieton. Printed Dundee: Winter, Duncan & Co. 1891. [2], vi, 80 pp.

Printed for private circulation.   *NLS*

Poems and ballads; by Jane Paxton Smieton. Printed Dundee: Winter, Duncan & Co. 1891. viii, 96 pp.

Printed for private circulation.   *NLS*

SMITH, Adele Crafton- *see* **CRAFTON-SMITH, Adele**, (Nomad, pseud.)

SMITH, Alexander Skene. Writer on financial investment.

Holiday recreations, and other poems; by Alexander Skene Smith. With a preface by Principal Cairns. London: Chapman & Hall, Ltd. 1888. xvi, 216 pp.   *OXB*

SMITH, Austin E. Of Liverpool.

The knight of Castile, and other poems; by Austin E. Smith. London: Ward, Lock, & Co. [1882]. 158 pp.   *OXB*

SMITH, Cicely Fox (18   –1954). b. Lymm, Cheshire, daughter of Richard Smith, a Manchester barrister. Educated at Manchester High School for Girls. Member of the Society for Nautical Research, she specialized in writing on ships and the sea. Member of the Lyceum Club. Lived at Court House, Overton, Hampshire, and latterly at West Halse, Bow, Devon.

The foremost trail, [and other poems]; by C. Fox Smith. London: Sampson Low, Marston & Co. 1899. viii, 88 pp.   *OXB*

"Men of men": [poems]; by C. Fox Smith. London: Sampson Low, Marston & Co. [1899?], xii, 136 pp.   *OXB*

Songs of greater Britain, and other poems; by Cicely Fox Smith. Manchester: Sherratt & Hughes. 1899. xii, 120 pp.   *MPL*

SMITH, David Coupar (1832–   ). b. Leven, Fife. Shortly after his birth the family moved to St Andrews, where he was educated at Madras College. In 1873 he became actuary of the Savings Bank of St Andrews.

St. Andrews lyrics; and, Miscellaneous poems; by D.C. Smith. Brechin; D.H. Edwards; Edinburgh: John Menzies & Co. [1885]. 235 pp.   *OXB*

SMITH, David Mitchell (1848–   ). b. Bullionfield, near Dundee, son of a farm labourer. When he was a child the family moved to Kirriemuir, where he received a fair education. First employed as a railway clerk for fourteen years, then engaged in different kinds of work before being employed by Messrs Pullar, dyers of Perth. Lived at 19 Barossa Place, Perth.

Fair city chimes: a book of verse; by David Mitchell Smith. Perth: Wood & Son. 1898. iv, 160 pp.   *BL*

SMITH, Ebenezer (1835–   ). b. High Street, Ayr. His father and grandfather were both shoemakers. Educated at a dame school, and Wallacetown Academy. He was apprenticed to shoemaking, eventually succeeding to his grandfather's business. The business failed, after which he earned his living as a journeyman in a large firm. One of his poems 'The Pharisee' entailed an action for libel in the Court of Session in 1873.

The seasons' musings: [poems]; by Ebenezer Smith. Ayr: "Ayr Observer" and "Ayrshire Argus & Express" Office. 1888. [iv], 492 pp.   *NLS*

SMITH, Edwin. Writer on chemistry, botany and zoology, and on religion.

Poems in many keys; by Edwin Smith. Southport: [Author?]. 1889. vi, 167 pp.   *UCD*

SMITH, Elizabeth (Lizzie) Horne (1876–   ). b. Hagghill, Glasgow, youngest of a family of six. Daughter of a ploughman who moved from one farm to another, she attended schools in Dumbarton, and Hamilton and Uddingston in Lanarkshire. She started work as a dairymaid at age of fifteen.

Poems of a dairymaid; by Lizzie H. Smith. Paisley: J. & R. Parlane; Edinburgh: John Menzies & Co.; London: Houlston & Sons. 1898. 131 pp. por.   *BL*

SMITH, Ernest Gilliat (1858–   ). A contributor to the *Dublin Review*, *The Tablet*, and other Catholic publications. Lived at the Poplars, Newbury, Berkshire.

Fantasies from dreamland: [poems]; by Ernest Gilliat Smith. Illustrated by Flori Van Acker. London: Elkin Mathews. 1899. 39 pp. il.   *UCD*

SMITH, Frederic

A chest of viols, and other verses; by Frederic Smith. London: Simpkin, Marshall, Hamilton, Kent & Co., Ltd; Manchester: Sherratt & Hughes. 1896. xiv, 175 pp.   *MPL*

SMITH, Mrs Frederick James *see* **SMITH, Susan Jane**

SMITH, Gregory *see* **SMITH, Isaac Gregory**

SMITH, Herbert Arthur (1852–19). b. Great Milton, Oxfordshire, son of Thomas Smith, surgeon. Educated by private tuition, and at various hospitals; MD, MRCS. Held medical and surgical appointments at Middlesex Hospital, St Marylebone Dispensary, and Ealing Cottage Hospital. A ship's doctor for a time. Specialist in mental and nervous cases, and inventor of surgical instruments. Lived at 78 Madeley Road, Ealing.

Stellar songs, and other poems, with an introductory essay on science and poetry; by Herbert A. Smith. With illustrations. London: Reeves & Turner. 1891. xii, 268 pp. por. *OXB*

SMITH, Horace (1836–1922). Son of Robert Smith, London merchant. Educated at Highgate, King's College, London, and Trinity Hall, Cambridge; BA 1860. Called to the Bar, Inner Temple, 1862; on the Midland circuit; bencher, 1886; counsel to the Mint; secretary to the Oxford Bribery Commission, 1880; recorder of Lincoln, 1881–88; metropolitan magistrate at Westminster, 1888–1917. Writer of legal texts.

Poems; by Horace Smith. London: Macmillan & Co. 1889. viii, 138 pp. *OXB*

Poems; by Horace Smith. [New ed.]. London: Macmillan & Co., Ltd. 1897. xii, 169 pp. *OXB*

SMITH, Isaac Gregory (1826–1920). b. Manchester, son of Rev. Jeremiah Smith. Educated at Rugby School, and Trinity College, Oxford (scholar); BA 1848, MA 1851. Fellow of Brasenose College, 1850-55. Rector, Tedstone Delamere, Herefordshire, 1854--72; prebendary, Hereford Cathedral, 1870; vicar, Great Malvern, Worcestershire, 1872, rural dean, Powyke, 1882. Chaplain to Bishop of St David's, 1880–1900; rector, Great Shefford, Berkshire, 1896.

Fra Angelico, and other short poems; by Gregory Smith. 2nd ed. London: Longmans, Green, & Co. 1889. viii, 141 pp. *MPL*

SMITH, James. Of 13 Commerce Street, Aberdeen.

Occasional rhymes on local subjects; by James Smith. Printed Aberdeen. 1881. 62 pp.

Printed for the author. *UCD*

SMITH, James William Gilbart- *see* **GILBART-SMITH, James William**

SMITH, Jane. Of Southampton.

Miscellaneous poems; by Jane Smith. Southampton: Author. 1891. 131 pp. *★UCD*

SMITH, Jennie M., (Daphne Hammond, pseud.). Of Bury St Edmunds, Suffolk?

Poems; by Daphne Hammond (Jennie M. Smith). Bury St. Edmund's: Bury Post & Suffolk Standard Co. (Ltd). 1888. [vi], 100 pp.   *BL*

SMITH, Lizzie H. *see* **SMITH, Elizabeth (Lizzie) Horne**

SMITH, Lucy Cumming, (L.C.S.) (18 –81). Daughter of Dr Henry Cumming of Denbigh. She married journalist William Henry Smith in 1861. Lived latterly in Brighton, Sussex.

Lines: [poems]; by L.C.S. Brighton: Bishop. 1883. [vi], 60 pp.   *UCD*

SMITH, Mary, (M.S.) (1822–89). b. Copredy, Oxfordshire, daughter of a shoemaker. A Nonconformist, she became a schoolmistress in Carlisle, Cumberland. Writer on the castles at Carlisle, Corby and Linstock.

Miscellaneous poems; by Mary Smith (M.S.). London: Bemrose & Sons; Carlisle: Wordsworth Press. 1892. viii, 295 pp.

Vol. II of *Mary Smith, schoolmistress and Nonconformist*. Vol. I is *Autobiography*.   *OXB*

SMITH, Robert

The kings of the world, and other poems; by Robert Smith. London: James Nisbet & Co. 1889. viii, 424 pp.   *OXB*

SMITH, Robert, (Myles, pseud.) (1853–). b. Kilskeery, County Tyrone. Attended the village school there, then entered a lawyer's office. After recovering from a period of bad health he became confidential clerk and manager of a Londonderry law office.

Early musings: [poems]; by Myles. Londonderry. 1884.   *

Wayside echoes and poems; by Robert Smith. Belfast: Marcus Ward & Co., Ltd. 1894. 68 pp. il.   *NLI*

SMITH, Robert Henry Soden- *see* **SODEN-SMITH, Robert Henry**

SMITH, S. Theobald. Curator of the Bridgwater Gallery.

A ramble of rhyme in the country of Cranmer and Ridley: a Kentish garland: [poems]; by S. Theobald Smith. Illustrated by Harold Oakley, from sketches by the author. London: Chapman & Hall, Ltd. 1889. 48 pp. il.   *OXB*

SMITH, Susan Jane. Married Frederick James Smith (1820–85), barrister who became Recorder of Margate, Kent. Lived at 3 Montserrat Road, Putney.

The collects of the Church of England, rendered into simple verse, for the special use of children; by Mrs. Frederick James Smith. London: J. Masters & Co. 1881. 68 pp.   *OXB*

SMITH, T. Of Fernhill.

A pathway of song: [poems]; by T. Smith. London: Elliot Stock. 1880. 45 pp. *OXB*

SMITH, Walter Chalmers (1824–1908). b. Aberdeen. Studied for the ministry at Aberdeen and Edinburgh. Preached to a Presbyterian church in London before becoming a Free Church minister in Kinross-shire; moved to Glasgow, and in 1876 to Edinburgh until his resignation in 1894. An unorthodox minister, he rose to be Moderator of the General Assembly of the Free Church of Scotland.

A heretic, and other poems; by Walter C. Smith. Glasgow: James Maclehose & Sons. 1891. viii, 247 pp. *OXB*

North country folk: poems; by Walter C. Smith. Glasgow: James Maclehose & Sons. 1883. viii, 254 pp. *MPL*

Raban: or, life-splinters, [and other poems]; by Walter C. Smith. Glasgow: James Maclehose. 1881. x, 247 pp. *MPL*

Selections from the poems of Walter C. Smith. Glasgow: James Maclehose & Sons. 1893. viii, 175 pp.

Spine-title is *Poems*. *OXB*

Thoughts and fancies for Sunday evenings: [poems]; by Walter C. Smith. Glasgow: James Maclehose. 1887. viii, 124 pp. *BL*

Also 2nd ed. 1887.

SMYTHE, Alfred (1856–). b. Dublin. FRGS. Contributor to many magazines including *Chambers's Journal*. Novelist.

Sir Dunstan's daughter, and other poems; by Alfred Smythe. London: Digby, Long & Co. [1894]. xii, 307 pp. por. *OXB*

SMYTHIES, William Gordon (1849–). Son of Rev. William Y. Smythies of Weeley, Essex. Student of Middle Temple, 1873, called to the Bar, 1875; member of the Western circuit. In 1870 he married Charlotte Mary, daughter of Rev. Thomas Keble, and niece of Rev. John Keble. Lived at 24 Brunswick Square, London WC.

Original recitations for ladies and others; by W. Gordon Smythies. London: Samuel French & Son. [1893]. [vi], 57 pp. *OXB*

SNOAD, A. Warner. Née Hull. Mrs Frank Snoad. She became an invalid. Lived at The Firs, Old Charlton.

Echoes of life: [poems]; by Mrs. Frank Snoad. Including 2nd ed. of "Clare Peyce's diary", and "As life itself". London: Chapman & Hall. 1884. xii, 339 pp. por. *OXB*

SNOAD, Mrs Frank *see* **SNOAD, A. Warner**

SO, Al-, pseud. *see* **SOMERS, Alexander**, (Al-So, pseud.)

SODEN, John Jordan (1839–1912). b. Coventry, son of Thomas Soden. Educated at King Edward's School, Birmingham, and Emmanuel College, Cambridge; BA 1854, MA 1857. Ordained, 1856; curate, Strivichall, Warwickshire, 1855–57. Second master, King Henry VIII School, Coventry, and curate, Binley, 1857–83; vicar, Little Melton, Norfolk, 1883–94; rector, Rishangles, Suffolk, 1894–1912.

Sketches in rhyme, with miscellanies, illustrated; by J.J. Soden. London: Jarrold & Sons. 1895. 60 pp. por.   *OXB*

SODEN-SMITH, Robert Henry (1822–90). Appointed keeper of the National Art Library, South Kensington Museum, in 1868. He organized the Library, compiling several catalogues to the collection.

Flower and bird posies: [poems]; by A.H. Church and R.H. Soden-Smith. Shelsey, Kew Gardens: Authors. 1890. [1]. viii, 33 pp.

Not joint authorship.   *OXB*

SOLOMONS, Rosa J. Of Dublin.

Facts and fancies: [poems]; by Rosa J. Solomons. Dublin: William M'Gee; London: Simpkin, Marshall & Co. 1883. viii, 140 pp.   *OXB*

SOMEBODY; CHIPS; AND, SOMEBODY'S LAST CARD: OR, THE OUTLINES OF A "GRAND CAREER", DEDICATED TO THE ELECTORS OF GREAT BRITAIN AND IRELAND. Manchester: John Heywood. 1885. 31 pp.   *OXB*

SOMERS, Alexander, (Al-So, pseud.) (1861–   ). b. Salford, Lancashire, of Irish parents, his father being Dr Alexander Somers, a Dublin man, a lecturer as Owens College, Manchester. Educated at Salford Grammar School, and in Belgium. Admitted solicitor, 1887; practised in Manchester.

Lays of a lazy lawyer; by Al-So. London: Leadenhall Press; Simpkin, Marshall, Hamilton, Kent & Co., Ltd; New York: Charles Scribner's Sons. 1891. 120 pp.   *OXB*

Shakespearean ballads; by Alexander Somers. Printed Manchester: George Falkner & Sons. [1890]. 79 pp. por.   *BL*

SOMERSET, Lord Henry (1849–1932). Second son of 8th Duke of Beaufort. Educated at Eton College. MP for Monmouthshire, 1871–80. Married Isabella Caroline, daughter of Lord Somers, in 1872. Controller of the Queen's household, 1874–79. Lived at Badminton House, Gloucestershire.

Songs of adieu; by Lord Henry Somerset. London: Chatto & Windus. 1889. viii, 92 pp.   *OXB*

SOMERSET, Isabella Caroline, Lady (1851–1921). Daughter of the last Earl Somers. In 1872 she married Lord Henry Somerset. She devoted her time to temperance work; president, British Women's Temperance Association, 1890–1903, and of World's Women's Christian Temperance Union, 1898–1906; founded Duxhurst farm colony for inebriate women near Reigate, Surrey, 1895.

Our village life: words and illustrations; by Lady H. Somerset. London: Sampson Low, Marston, Searle & Rivington. [1884]. [36] pp. col. il. *BL*

SOMERVILLE, George Gerald
   The retreat from Moscow, and other poems; by G.G. Somerville. London: Ideal Publishing Union, Ltd. [1899], [vi], 69 pp. *OXB*

SOMERVILLE, George Watson (1847–). b. Edinburgh. Educated at Edinburgh High School. Entered trade as a stationer in his father's business. Spent some years in Manchester, Glasgow, Sunderland, and Newcastle upon Tyne, finally settling in Carlisle, Cumberland, as a printer and lithographer. Lived in Mary Street.
   Euranthe, with other ballads & verses; by George W. Somerville. Carlisle: Author. [1888]. 251 pp. **UCD*

A SONG OF JUBILEE: V.R. I, 1837-1897. London: Elliot Stock. 1897. 32 pp. *OXB*

SONG-STRAYS: [poems]. London: T. Fisher Unwin. 1890. 267 pp. *OXB*

SONNETS. London. 1884. 36 pp. *BL*

SOUPER, William. Writer on Christian topics.
   The discipline of love: a poem; by W. Souper. London: Alexander Gardner. 1896. 97 pp. *OXB*

SOUTAR, Alexander M. (1846–). b. Muirdrum, Forfarshire, son of a farm labourer. He attended school in winter and worked on the farm in summer. At the age of fourteen he was apprenticed to a joiner. Enlisted in the army at sixteen, shortly afterwards sent to India, where he served for nine years. he returned to Scotland in 1873, obtained his discharge, and found a job as a joiner at Claverhouse Bleachfield.
   Hearth rhymes; by Alexander M. Soutar. With an introductory preface by William Rose. Dundee: A.A. Paul. 1880. 136 pp. *BL*

SOUTHALL, Isabel, (I.S.). Writer on the Prichard family of Almeley.
   Dies dominica: being hymns and metrical meditations for each Sunday in the natural year; by Margaret Evans and Isabel Southall. London: Elliot Stock. 1897. viii, 112 pp.
      Not joint authorship. *OXB*
   Rachel, and other poems; by I.S. Birmingham: Cornish Bros. 1887. 119 pp. *OXB*
   Songs of Siluria; to which is added, Fluvius lacrymarum; by M.E. and I.S. London: Elliot Stock; Birmingham: Cornish Bros. 1890. viii, 128 pp. *OXB*

SOUTHERN, Isabella J. Only daughter of Thomas P. Barkas, bookseller and alderman of Newcastle upon Tyne. Married J.P. Southern.
   Sonnets, and other poems; by Isabella J. Southern. London: Walter Scott. 1891. xii, 260 pp. *BL*

SOUTHESK, Lord *see* **CARNEGIE, James, Lord Southesk.**

SOUTHEY, Charles H. Grandson of Robert Southey, poet laureate.
  Isolda, and other poems; by Chas. H. Southey. Printed Kendall: T. Wilson.
  1897. [ii], 96 pp.   *UCD*

SOUTHWARD, Henry. Lived at Ashleigh, 35 Northen Grove, Didsbury,
Manchester.
  Mosaics: [poems]; by Henry Southward. Printed Oldham: Parker. 1894. [2],
  iv, 101 pp.   *MPL*

SPAN, Reginald Bartlet. A theosophist.
  Poems of two worlds; by Reginald B. Span. London: Digby, Long & Co. 1898.
  88 pp.   *UCD*

SPARLING, Mr, (Old Past Master, pseud.). Member of the Worshipful Co.
of Plaisterers, City of London Livery Co.
  Legends of the Worshipful Company of Plaisterers: [poems]; [by] an old past
  master. Printed London: Harrison & Sons. [1886]. 42 pp.   *UCD*

SPENCE, Peter (1806–83). b. Brechin, Forfarshire, son of a handloom
weaver. Left home at an early age for Perth, where he was apprenticed to a
grocer. He went into business with his uncle but was unsuccessful. In 1834 he
moved to London, establishing himself in a small way as a chemical
manufacturer. Moved the business to Carlisle, then to Manchester. Took out
patents for Prussian blue and other chemical compounds. One of the original
promoters of the Manchester Ship Canal enterprise. Lived at Erlington
House, Old Trafford, Manchester.
  Poems (written in early life); by Peter Spence. Printed London: Richard Clay &
  Sons. 1888. 64 pp.   *MPL*

SPENCER, John Stafford
  Sketches from nature, and other poems; by John Stafford Spencer. London:
  Pickering & Chatto. 1889. xii, 136 pp.   *OXB*

SPENCER, Richard. b. Holbeck, Leeds, Yorkshire. On leaving school he
was apprenticed to a firm of brushmakers, remaining in the job for forty-one
years. Lived at 8 Shafton Lane, Holbeck.
  Field flowers: poems; by Richard Spencer. Batley: J. Spencer Newsome; Leeds:
  C.H. Johnson. [1891]. 375 pp.
     Published for the author.   *OXB*

SPENS, Walter Cook (1842–   ). b. Glasgow, son of an actuary. After a
liberal elementary education he was apprenticed to law under the supervision
of William Burns, ardent Scottish patriot; completed his legal studies at
Edinburgh University. He became an advocate in the Supreme Court; for
several years officiated in the court at Hamilton, then appointed Sheriff-
Substitute for Lanarkshire.
  Darroll, and other poems; by Walter Cook Spens. Edinburgh: David Douglas.
  1881. x, 236 pp.   *OXB*

SPES, pseud. *see* **LUSCOMBE, Alfred**, (Spes, pseud.)

SPHYNX, pseud.
The grand old man [William Ewart Gladstone] and his clique, those asses of tartar–jingoes . . . ; by Sphynx. Printed Deptford: W. Cayzer. [1884]. 32 pp.
Title from cover. *BL*

SPRATLY, W.J. Writer on Darwinism and religion.
Religion: or, God and all things: an epic; by W.J. Spratly. Book I: Prologue. London: Digby & Long. [1889]. 66 pp. *OXB*
The rise and reign of chaos: a scientific epic: being Books II, III and IV of "Religion: or, God and all things"; by W.J. Spratly. London: Digby & Long. [1890]. 154 pp. *BL*
The spectral rock: a poem; by W.J. Spratly. London: Simpkin, Marshall & Co. 1881. 21 pp. *OXB*

SPRATT, Harmar Devereux (1821?–1906). Irish. Lived at Pencil Hill, Mallow, County Cork.
Juverna: a romance of the Geraldine, the MacCarthy More, the O'Donohue, etc., in the annals of Desmond and its chiefs in the south of Ireland; by H. Devereux Spratt. London: Digby & Long. 1888. [iv], 121 pp. *OXB*

SPROAT, George G.B. (1858–). b. Almorness Farm, Dalbeattie, Kirkcudbrightshire. Educated at the parish school there, then by Mr M'Andrew, celebrated teacher and botanist of New Galloway, with whom he boarded. In 1882 he left home to farm at High Creoch, Gatehouse. A contributor to the *Kirkcudbrightshire Advertiser* and other local papers, he was agricultural correspondent to the *Dumfries Standard*.
The rose o' Dalma Linn, and other lays o' Galloway; by George G.B. Sproat. Castle-Douglas: J.H. Maxwell. 1888. [vi], 248 pp. il. *OXB*

SPRUZEN, J.T.
The Battle of Rorke's Drift, and other poems; by J.T. Spruzen. Printed Reading: J.J. Beecroft. [1880]. 21 pp. *OXB*

SPURGEON, Thomas (1856–1917). b. London, son of Rev. C.H. Spurgeon, famous preacher. Educated at the Pastors' College, and Metropolitan Tabernacle, later studying art and wood-engraving. He became pastor of the Baptist Church, Auckland, New Zealand, 1881; Evangelist, New Zealand Baptist Union, 1889– 93; returned to London in 1893 to become minister at the Metropolitan Tabernacle, resigning through ill-health, 1908. President of Pastors' College, and of Stockwell Orphanage.
Scarlet threads; and, Bits of blue: [poems]; by Thomas Spurgeon. With preface by Mrs. C.H. Spurgeon. London: Passmore & Alabaster. 1892. 100 pp. *BL*

SPURR, Harry A. *see* **SPURR, Henry Astley**

SPURR, Henry Astley. Brother of Melancthon Burton Spurr. Writer on Alexandre Dumas.

Bachelor ballads, and other lazy lyrics; by Harry A. Spurr. Illustrated by John Hassall. London: Greening & Co., Ltd. 1899. xii, 194 pp. il.   *OXB*

If we only knew, and other poems; by Mel. B. Spurr and Hy. A. Spurr. Hull: William Andrews & Co.; London: Simpkin, Marshall, Hamilton, Kent, & Co., Ltd. 1893.[xii], 111 pp. por.

Not joint authorship.   *BL*

SPURR, Melancthon Burton. Brother of Henry Astley Spurr. Lived at 1 The Barons, Twickenham, Middlesex.

If we only knew, and other poems; by Mel. B. Spurr and Hy. A. Spurr. Hull: William Andrews & Co.; London: Simpkin, Marshall, Hamilton, Kent, & Co., Ltd. 1893. [xii], 111 pp. por.

Not joint authorship.   *BL*

Mel. B. Spurr's recitals and monologues in prose and verse. London: Samuel French, Ltd. [1899]. [ii], 64 pp.   *BL*

STABLE BOY, pseud. *see* **CHRISTIE, William**, (Stable Boy, pseud.)

STAFFORD, Jacques

Snowdon out of season: or, the misadventures of a solitary mountain climber; by Jacques Stafford. With illustrations by a native artist. London: E.W. Allen. [1887]. 47 pp. il.   *BL*

STAMP KING *see* **PALMER, Joseph William**

STANDING, Percy Cross (18 –1931). b. Rickmansworth, Hertfordshire, son of Samuel A. Standing. Educated privately. Became a journalist; assistant editor, *Labour Elector*, 1889–90, *Cricket*, 1890–91; London correspondent to *Manchester Evening News*, 1892; assistant editor, *Bangkok Times*, 1893, *Hull Daily Mail*, 1895–96, *Idler*, 1897, *Today*, 1897, *Morning Leader*, 1898, *The Lady*, 1899–1900; at Ministry of Information, 1918–19; sub-editor, *Contemporary Review*, from 1924. Lived at 3 Portland Mansions, Clapham, London SW.

Chateaux en Espagne, [and other poems]; by Percy Cross Standing. London: Digby, Long & Co. [1895], viii, 87 pp.   *OXB*

STANDRING, R., (Rochdale Man, pseud.). Lived at Healey Stones, Rochdale, Lancashire.

Healey Dell: or, the history of fairies: meetings of the Fairy Queen and Healey Dwarf in the Fairy Chapel; by R. Standring. Printed Rochdale: James Clegg. 1882. 42 pp.   *MPL*

A new pilgrim's progress: or, four pilgrims, all boys, journeying to Zion; by R. Standring. Printed Rochdale: James Clegg. 1884. 35 pp.   *RPL*

Rochdale telescope: only a penny for a view of Rochdale, and its neighbourhood too: [poems]; by a Rochdale man. [Rochdale]. [1880?]. 16 pp.   *RPL*

STANHOPE, Charles

Primrose ballads; by Charles Stanhope. London: National Liberal Printing & Publishing Association, Ltd. 1886. 16 pp. (National Liberal pamplets, 2). *★UCD*

STANILAND, William

Songs after sunset; by William Staniland. London: Elliot Stock. 1884. viii, 216 pp. *OXB*

STANLEY, Alan

Love lyrics; by Alan Stanley]. Printed Rugby: George E. Over. [c. 1890]. [35] pp. *OXB*

Love lyrics; by Alan Stanley. London: Gay & Bird. 1894. vi, 56 pp. *OXB*

STANLEY, Arthur, pseud. *see* **MEGAW, Arthur Stanley**, (Arthur Stanley, pseud.)

STANLEY, Arthur Penrhyn (1815–81). b. Alderley Rectory, Cheshire, son of the future Bishop of Norwich who was one of the Stanleys of Alderley. Educated at Rugby School, the favourite pupil of Dr Arnold, and at Balliol College, Oxford (scholar). Newdigate prizewinner, 1837. Fellow of University College, 1839–50. Ordained 1839; Canon of Canterbury, 1851. Professor of ecclesiastical history at Oxford; Canon of Christ Church, and chaplain to the Bishop of London, 1858; Dean of Westminster, 1864; chaplain to the Prince of Wales, and chaplain-in-ordinary to Queen Victoria. A popular preacher, a favourite at Court, and the most prominent figure in the Broad Church movement.

Letters and verses of Arthur Penrhyn Stanley, between the years 1829 and 1881. Edited by Rowland E. Prothero. London: John Murray. 1895. viii, 454 pp. *UCD*

STANLEY, C.K.

Forget-me-knot: poems and acting charades; by C.K. Stanley. London: Simpkin, Marshall, Hamilton, Kent & Co. Ltd. 1899. viii, 175 pp. *OXB*

STANSFIELD, Abraham, (A.S.K.) (1838–1917). b. Platt's House, Vale of Todmorden, Lancashire. Botanist and poet, he moved to Manchester in 1868, actively connecting himself with the various literary and scientific societies. For many years a contibutor to the provincial press, he edited the *Manchester Monthly*, and was founder and editor of the *Northern Gardener*. Translator of French and German poets. Lived at Kersal, Salford.

Nugae: being selections from many years' scribblings in verse; by Abm. Stansfield (A.S.K.). Printed London: Geo. Woodhead & Co. 1892. xii, 352 pp. *MPL*

STARKEY, Alfred. Educated at St. Bees. Ordained 1856; curate, St Margaret's, Lyme Regis, Dorset, St Martin's, Worcester, 1869-71; vicar, Ryton-on-Dunsmore, Coventry, Warwickshire, from 1871.

Religio clerici, and other poems; by Alfred Starkey. London: Elliot Stock. 1895. 147 pp. *OXB*

STATHAM, Francis Reginald. Minister of a Scottish Congregational Church. Composer, novelist, and general writer, he eventually settled in South Africa.
Poems and sonnets; by F. Reginald Statham. London: T. Fisher Unwin. 1895. xii, 224 pp. por. *OXB*

STEADMAN, M.R., (M.R.S.). Woman head of a school at Eastbourne, Sussex. Lived latterly at Blen-Cathra, Hindhead, Surrey.
Optimus, and other poems; by M.R.S. With a very short preface by the author. London: Swan Sonnenschein & Co., Ltd. 1897. 128 pp. por. *OXB*

STEDMAN, J.C.
Romance and reality: a poem: by J.C. Stedman. London: Skeffington & Son. 1890. viii, 432 pp. *OXB*

STEEL, Sydney
Verses for song: by Sydney Steel. Printed London: Bowers & Bowers. 1891. [ii], 51 pp. *OXB*

STEER, Samuel. Of Exeter, Devon.
The Burns centenary (July 21st, 1896): or, a trip to Caledonia: by Samuel Steer. Exeter. 1896. 15 pp. *UCD*
Wayside flowers, gathered in spare moments: [poems]: by Samuel Steer. Printed Exeter: "Daily Western Times" Office. 1880. 76 pp. *DEI*

STEGGALL, Robert (1830–90). Converted to Roman Catholicism in 1888. Died at the Croft, Southover, Lewes, Sussex. Buried at Kensal Green Cemetery.
A heart's obsession; Sonnets of the city, and other poems: by Robert Steggall. London: Elliot Stock. 1886. xii, 228 pp. *OXB*

STENBOCK, Count Stanislaus Eric (1860–95). b. Cheltenham, Gloucestershire, son of Count Eric Stenbock of Thirlestone Hall. The family originally came from Estonia. Educated privately, on the continent, and at Balliol College, Oxford, he left without taking a degree. A man of great charm, he settled in London where he was acquainted with many of the leading figures of the 1890s, including Aubrey Beardsley, Ernest Rhys, Arthur Symons, Oscar Wilde, and W.B. Yeats. Translator of Balzac's short stories. He died of alcoholism.
Love, sleep and dreams: a volume of verse: by Stanislaus Eric Stenbock. Oxford: A. Thomas Shrimpton & Son: London: Simpkin, Marshall & Co. [1881?]. [ii], 43 pp. ★
Myrtle, rue and cypress: a book of poems, songs, and sonnets: by Stanislaus Eric Stenbock. Printed London: Hatchards. 1883. 67 pp.
    Printed for the author. *OXB*
The shadow of death: a collection of poems, songs, and sonnets: by Count Stanislaus Eric Stenbock. London: Leadenhall Press, Ltd; Simpkin, Marshall, Hamilton, Kent & Co., Ltd; New York: Charles Scribner's Sons. 1893. 79 pp. *OXB*

STENHOUSE, William Macstravick. MD; a doctor who practised for a time in New Zealand, where he lost a foot in an accident. Later his spine was injured in a carriage accident, leaving him disabled. Lived at 5 Fitzroy Square, London W.

Poems, songs, and sonnets; by Wm. M. Stenhouse. Glasgow: A. Stenhouse. 1886. xvi, 248 pp. *OXB*

STEPHEN, James Kenneth, (J.K.S.) (1859–92). b. London, son of Sir James F. Stephen, judge. Educated at Eton College, and King's College, Cambridge; president, Cambridge Union, 1880. Called at the Bar, Inner Temple, 1885, but also practised journalism. He founded the weekly newspaper *The Reflector*, which failed after seventeen issues. Returned to Cambridge to set up as a tutor in 1891, acting as tutor to the Duke of Clarence. Never strong, his health failed and he died the following year.

Lapsus calami: [poems]; by J.K.S. Cambridge: Macmillan & Bowes. 1891. viii, 88 pp. *OXB*

Also re-issues in 1891 and 1892.

Lapsus calami: [poems]; by J.K.S. New ed. with considerable omissions and additions. Cambridge: Macmillan & Bowes. 1891. xii, 92 pp.

A limited large paper ed. of 150 numbered copies on hand-made paper, initialled by the author. *BL.*

Lapsus calami, and other verses; by James Kenneth Stephen. Cambridge: Macmillan & Bowes. 1896. xxii, 202 pp. por. *MPL*

Quo musa tendis: [poems]; by J.K. Stephen. Cambridge: Macmillan & Bowes. 1891. x, 84 pp. *JRL*

Also a limited ed. of 100 numbered copies printed on hand-made paper.

STEPHENS, Arthur. Bibliographer of the Bank of England.

Hope's gospel, and other poems; by Arthur Stephens. London: T. Fisher Unwin. 1886. [viii], 159 pp. *OXB*

STEPHENS, James Brunton (1835–1902). b. Borrowstounness, Linlithgowshire. Educated at Edinburgh University. A private tutor on the continent, 1854-57; schoolmaster in Greenock for six years. He emigrated to Queensland in 1866, for thirty years associated with the intellectual life of Australia; he had been tutor to a squatter's family, then held a post in the civil service. Known as 'The Queensland Poet'.

Convict once, and other poems; by J. Brunton Stephens. New ed. Melbourne: George Robertson & Co. 1888. iv, 367 pp. *NLS*

Miscellaneous poems; by J. Brunton Stephens. London: Macmillan & Co. 1880. viii, 227 pp. *MPL*

STEPHENSON, Joseph Henry (1819–   ). Son of Joseph A. Stephenson of Lympsham, Somerset. Educated at Queen's College, Oxford; BA 1841, MA 1850. Ordained, 1842; rector of Lympsham from 1844; prebendary of Wells, and rural dean, 1856; treasurer, Wells Cathedral, 1885.

Friendship, and other poems; by Joseph Henry Stephenson. London: Hamilton, Adams & Co.: Weston-super-Mare: Robbins; Lympsham: A.C. Coome. 1883. 55 pp. *TAU*

Musings & memories: a third volume of collected verses; by Joseph Henry Stephenson. London: Hamilton, Adams & Co.; Weston-super-Mare: Robbins; Lympsham: A.C. Coome. 1880. 112 pp.   *OXB*

Songs of Somerset; by Joseph Henry Stephenson. Taunton: Barnicott & Pearce. 1898. xii, 120 pp.   *UCD*

STEPHENSON, Manners
Jason of the Golden Fleece: a Cornish idyl of to-day: a three-volume novel in verse; by Manners Stephenson. London: Simpkin, Marshall, Hamilton, Kent & Co., Ltd. 1895. 131 pp   *OXB*

STERNE, Ernest Staveley
The miser: or, the ruby heart; by Ernest Staveley Sterne. London: Sterne & Co. 1890. 16 pp.   *BL*

STERRY, Joseph Ashby - *see* ASHBY-STERRY, Joseph

STEVENS, Henry (18 –87). of Bristol?
Poetry and rhymed jottings; by Henry Stevens. Printed Bristol: Lavars & Co. 1890. [iv], 43 pp.   *UCD*

STEVENS, William. Lieutenant-Colonel.
The wreck of worlds: a dream of 1845; by Lieut.-Col. W. Stevens. Windsor: Welham Clarke. 1881. 29 pp.   *MPL*

STEVENSON, A.L. Possibly Alfred Leonard Stevenson (1853?–). Son of Joseph G. Stevenson of Frant, Kent, gentleman. Educated at University College, Oxford.
Raymond: a story in verse of London and Monte Carlo; by A.L. Stevenson. London: Kegan Paul, Trench, Trübner & Co., Ltd. 1890. [viii], 121 pp.   *OXB*

Thoughts in a garden, and other poems; by A.L. Stevenson. London: Elliot Stock. 1895. x, 118 pp.   *OXB*

STEVENSON, Robert Louis (1850–94). b. Edinburgh, into a family of distinguished engineers. Educated privately, at Edinburgh Academy and Edinburgh University, he suffered chronic ill-health. He abandoned an ambition to become an engineer, turning to law; called to the Scottish Bar, 1875, but never practised. His whole life was a constant struggle against illness, most of his time being spent abroad in warmer climates. Novelist, poet, playwright, and an accomplished stylist, he is a central figure in Scottish literature. Died suddenly in Samoa of a brain haemorrhage.
Ballads; by Robert Louis Stevenson. London: Chatto & Windus. 1890. viii, 137 pp.   *MPL*

Also a large paper ed. of 100 numbered copies.

A child's garden of verses; by Robert Louis Stevenson. London: Longmans, Green, & Co. 1885. x, 101 pp.   *MPL*

Also 2nd ed. 1885.

Songs of travel, and other verses; by Robert Louis Stevenson. London: Chatto & Windus. 1896. x, 85 pp.   *MPL*

Three short poems; by Robert Louis Stevenson. London. 1898. 25 pp. facsim.

A limited ed. of 30 numbered copies printed for private distribution only.   *OXB*

Underwoods: [poems]; by Robert Louis Stevenson. London: Chatto & Windus. 1887. xviii, 139 pp.   *UCD*

Also 2nd ed. 1887.

STEVENSON, William Frederick

Qualte and Peedra, and other poems; by William Frederick Stevenson. London: Elliot Stock. [1883]. 64 pp.   *OXB*

STEWART, Alexander (1841–). b. Galston, Ayrshire. He attended Barr Street School before being apprenticed to weaving. Finding the work uncongenial he left for Ireland to work as a book-deliverer. Eventually he became involved in city mission work in Manchester, Glasgow and Birkenhead.

Bygone memories, and other poems; by Alexander Stewart. With an introductory preface by Alexander Macleod. Edinburgh: James Gemmell. 1888. xvi, 213 pp.   *OXB*

STEWART, Beatrice

Silent hours: poems; by Beatrice Stewart. First series. Eton: R. Ingalton Drake; London: Simpkin, Marshall & Co. 1894. 32 pp.   *OXB*

STEWART, Phillips

Poems; by Phillips Stewart. London: Kegan Paul, Trench & Co. 1887. [vi], 89 pp.   *OXB*

STEWART, William. Of Larkhall, Lanarkshire.

Lilts and lays frae Larkie; by William Stewart. Printed Larkhall: William Burns. 1895. viii, 238 pp.

Poetry and prose.   *OXB*

STEWART, William. Of Stirling?

Lines of Scottish lay; by William Stewart. Printed Stirling: Duncan & Jamieson. 1891. 104 pp.   *OXB*

STOCK, Elliot (1838?–1911). Bookseller and well-known publisher, particularly of poetry.

A publisher's playground: [poems]; [by Elliot Stock]. London: Kegan Paul, Trench & Co. 1888. [viii], 64 pp.   *OXB*

STOCK, Sarah Geraldina (1839–98). b. probably in Ireland. Well known as a writer on Sunday schools and foreign missions. She wrote numerous hymns, chiefly in connection with the Church Missionary Society. Died at Penmaen-mawr, Wales.

The brighter day: poems; by Sarah Geraldina Stock & E.H. Thompson. London: James E. Hawkins. [1889?]. [24] pp. il.
Some poems are joint authorship. *OXB*

Joy in sorrow: [poems]; by Sarah Geraldina Stock. 2nd ed. London: John F. Shaw & Co. [1885]. 56 pp. *OXB*
Also 3rd ed. [c. 1890].

Life abundant, and othe poems; by Sarah G. Stock. London: John F. Shaw & Co. [1892]. 245 pp. *BL*

STOCKALL. Harriett. Miss Stockall A contributor to Charles Dickens's *Household Words*.

Poems; by Harriett Stockall. Second series. London: Simpkin, Marshall, & Co. 1886. viii, 186 pp. *OXB*

STOCKDALE, Jane. Mrs Stockdale of Kendal, Westmorland

Streams from the fountain: sacred & sympathetic writings in prose & verse; by Jane Stockdale. Printed Kendal: Thompson Bros. 1886. 192 pp. *OXB*

STODDART, James Hastie (1832–88). b. Sanquhar, Dumfriesshire. Largely self-educated, at an early age he went into business in Edinburgh, Leith and Glasgow. In 1862 he was appointed sub-editor of the *Glasgow Herald*, becoming editor in 1875; the centenary of the paper was celebrated by a public banquet at St Andrew's Hall, 27 January 1882, when he was presented with his portrait.

The seven ages of prehistoric man: [poems]; by James H. Stoddart. London: Chatto & Windus. 1884. [x], 174 pp. *OXB*

STODDART, Thomas Tod (1810–80). b. Edinburgh, son of a naval officer. Educated at the Moravian Settlement near Manchester, and Edinburgh University. In 1833 he was called to the Scottish Bar but never practised. He lived at Kelso, becoming an expert and enthusiastic authority on freshwater fishing.

Angling songs; by Thomas Tod Stoddart. With a memoir by Anna M. Stoddart. Edinburgh: William Blackwood & Sons. 1889. x, 324 pp. por. *MPO*

The death-wake or lunacy: a necromaunt in three chimeras; by Thomas T. Stoddart. With an intoduction by Andrew Lang. London: John Lane; Chicago: Way & Williams. 1895. [iv], 124 pp.
A limited ed. of 500 copies printed for England and America. *OXB*

STOKES, Henry Sewell (1808–95). b. Gibraltar. A schoolfellow of Charles Dickens at Chatham, Kent. He practised as an advocate in the Stanneries Court, Cornwall. Founded the *Cornish Guardian*, 1833. Mayor of Truro, 1856; town clerk, 1859; clerk of the peace for Cornwall, 1865–95.

The chantry owl, and other verses: being a revised ed. of "Poems of Later Years"; by Henry Sewell Stokes. With additions. London: Longmans, Green, & Co. 1881. vi, 199 pp.   *UCD*

Lanhydrock: an elegy; by Henry Sewell Stokes. London: Longmans, Green & Co. 1882. 16 pp. il   *OXB*

The voyage of Arundel, and other rhymes from Cornwall; by Henry Sewell Stokes. New ed. with additions. London: Longmans, Green, & Co. 1884. viii, 225 pp. il.   *UCD*

STONE, Catherine. Of Winchfield, Hampshire.
The voice of mercy; by Catherine Stone. Guildford: Billing & Sons. 1884. iv, 77 pp.   *BL*

STONE, Edward Daniel, (E.D.S.) (1832–1916). Son of Joseph Stone, town clerk of Dorchester, Dorset. Educated at Eton College, and King's College, Cambridge; BA 1856, MA 1859. Fellow of King's, 1855–62. Ordained deacon, 1860. Assistant master at Eton, 1857–84. He kept a preparatory school at Stonehouse, Broadstairs, Kent, 1884-95. Retired to Abingdon, Berkshire, thence to his son's house at Radley College. Greek and Latin scholar.
Dorica: [poems]; by E.D.S. London: Kegan Paul, Trench & Co. 1888. viii, 173 pp.   *OXB*

STRANG, James (18 –19). b. Ayr. Educated at Dalmonach School, Dumbarton Academy, and Andersonian University, Glasgow. He had a varied journalistic and literary experience in London. On the literary and political staff of the *Glasgow Herald*. Author of numerous lyrics and librettos to cantatas, etc. which were set to music. Private secretary to Thomas Shaw, KC. Ordered to South Africa by his medical adviser, he became partner and editor of *Kroonstad Times*. In 1907 he contested Kroonstad town as an Independent in the Orange River Colony Assembly election.
Sunlight and shadow; and, Lyrics; by James Strang. London: Gay & Bird. 1898. xii, 134 pp.   *OXB*

STRANGE, T. Of Watchet, Somerset.
Collected poems & sonnets; by W.R. & T. Strange. Taunton: Edwin Goodman & Sons. 1880. 72 pp.
Not joint authorship.   *TAU*

STRANGE, W.R. Of Watchet, Somerset.
Collected poems & sonnets; by W.R. & T. Strange. Taunton: Edwin Goodman & Son. 1888. 72 pp.
Not joint authorship.   *TAU*

STRANGWAYES, Jane (1812–92). b. Bedale, Yorkshire, daughter of Edward Strangwayes, into a very old Yorkshire family. She was a staunch Conservative and supporter of the established church. In 1844 she went to live in London, where she was a constant visitor to the reading room of the British Museum. She returned to Yorkshire in 1868, and died in her eightieth year at Ainderby Steeple, near Northallerton.

Poems; by the late Jane Strangwayes. Printed London: Spottiswoode & Co. [1895]. 64 pp.
 Printed for private circulation. *MPL*

STRATTON, Joseph (1839?–19). Son of John Stratton of Clifton-Camp-ville, Staffordshire, gentleman. Educated at Worcester College, Oxford; BA 1862, MA 1867. Ordained, 1872; curate, Holy Trinity, Swansea, 1870–74, Burton-on-Trent, 1874–75; chaplain, Tonbridge Union, 1886–87; curate, Winchfield, 1887–89; master of Lucas Hospital, Wokingham, Berkshire, from 1889.
 Short sample poems; by Jos. Stratton. [Wokingham]: [Author]. [1891]. [iv], 111 pp. *BLD*

STREAMER, Col. D., pseud. *see* **GRAHAM, Harry Joscelyn Clive**, (Col. D. Streamer, pseud.)

STREATFEILD, Sophia Charlotte (1829–). Daughter of Rev. J.J. Saint, rector of Speldhurst. In 1862 she married Lieutenant Charles N. Streatfeild, Royal Navy. Hymn writer, especially for children; some of her verses were set to music as songs.
 Above these clouds: words of comfort for mourners: [poems]; by Mrs. Charles Streatfeild. London: Skeffington & Son. 1900 [i.e. 1899]. 36 pp. *CU*

STRELLEY, Webster, pseud. *see* **BATEMAN, Charles T. Tallent**, (Webster Strelley, pseud.)

STRICKLAND, Sir Walter William (1851–1938). Son of Sir Charles Strickland. Educated at Harrow School, and Trinity College, Cambridge; BA 1876. He succeeded his father at 9th Baronet in 1909. Lived abroad for many years, becoming a citizen of Czechoslovakia: ceased to use his title after 1923. Lived latterly at Sestri Levante, Liguria, Italy. Died at Buitenzorg, Java.
 Epicurean essays, in prose and verse; by W.W. Strickland. London: Robert Forder. 1898. viii, 208 pp. *OXB*
 Two mock epics: Hanuman, by Svatopluk Czech (translated from the 17th edition); and, Tantum religio: or, Sir Blasius; by W.W. Strickland. London: Robert Forder. 1894. [ii], 118 pp. *OXB*

STRONACH, George (1851–). b. Edinburgh. Educated at George Wat-son's Hospital, and Edinburgh University. Principal assistant in the Advo-cates' Library, Edinburgh, for many years. A successful song-writer, and contributor of prose and verse to leading periodicals; in 1889 he was correspondent to the largest weekly paper in Australia.
 The Gladstone A.B.C.: [poems]; [by George Stronach]. Edinburgh: William Blackwood & Sons. [1883]. [32] pp. il. *OXB*
 More gleanings from Gladstone; [by George Stronach]. Edinburgh: William Blackwood & Sons. [1881]. [22] pp. il., col. il.
  Poetry and prose. *OXB*
 New gleanings from Gladstone: [poems]; [by George Stronach]. Edinburgh: William Blackwood & Sons. [1880]. [28] pp. il. *OXB*

Our own-eries: or, the show in the meadows; [by George Stronach]. 2nd ed. Edinburgh: Robert Mitchell. [1886]. [33] pp.
Poetry and prose.   *OXB*

The people's William: [poems]; [by George Stronach]. London: W.H. Allen & Co. [1888]. [30] pp. il.   *OXB*

STUART, E.G. Mrs Stuart.
The calling of the sea, and other poems; by E.G. Stuart. London: Walter G. Wheeler; John G. Wheeler. [1891]. 64 pp.   *OXB*

STUART, Jane Isabella. Novelist.
Songs and verses; by Jane Isabella Stuart. London: Swan Sonnenschein, Lebas & Lowrey, 1886. iv, 156 pp.   *OXB*

STUBBS, Charles William (1845–1912). b. Liverpool, son of Charles Stubbs. Educated at the Royal Institution School, and Sidney Sussex College, Cambridge; BA 1868, MA 1876. Curate, St Mary's, Sheffield, 1868–71; vicar, Granborough, Buckinghamshire, 1871–84; Stokenham, Devon, 1884–88; rector, Wavertree, Liverpool, 1888-94; Dean of Ely, 1894–1906; Bishop of Truro from 1906.
Bryhtnoth's prayer, and other poems; by Charles William Stubbs. London: T. Fisher Unwin. 1899. vii, 72 pp.   *OXB*

The conscience, and other poems; by Charles William Stubbs. London: W. Swan Sonnenschein & Co. 1884. 58 pp.   *OXB*

STUCKLEY, Harry Dymond- *see* **DYMOND-STUCKLEY, Harry**

STUDDERT, Michael. Of Kilrush and Kilkee, County Clare.
A collection of humorous letters and pieces of poetry; by Michael Studdert. Dublin: Hodges, Figgis, & Co., Ltd. 1898. iv, 84 pp.
Spine-title is *Humorous letters and poetry*.   *NLI*

STUDENT, pseud.
The beauties of Festus, with descriptive index: [poems]; by a student. London: Longmans, Green & Co. 1884. viii, 88 pp.   *OXB*

STURGES, Richard Yates (1843–   ). Flautist and violinist, he studied under W. Tilly and Webbe, local teachers. Made his debut at Mr Stimpson's Monday popular concerts at Birmingham Town Hall, 1861; in 1864 he played at Mr Rea's concerts, Newcastle upon Tyne, and was for some months in the orchestra at the Theatre Royal there; he toured the provinces on several occasions. In 1884 he went to Italy to continue study of the violin.
The black philosopher: or, Scipio Africanus; by R.Y. Sturges. [Birmingham]: Birmingham Art Chambers. 1894. 16 pp.   *BL*

Song and thought: [poems]; by Richard Yates Sturges. London: George Redway. 1897. 106 pp.   *OXB*

STURGIS, Julian (1848–1904). b. Boston, Mass. Came to England with this family at the age of seven months. Educated at Eton College, and Balliol College, Oxford. Called to the Bar, Inner Temple, 1876. Novelist and playwright. Friend of George Meredith. Became a British citizen.

A book of song: [poems]; by Julian Sturgis. London: Longmans, Green, & Co. 1894. xii, 73 pp.   *UCD*

STURM UND DRANG: A VOLUME OF VERSE. London: Elliot Stock. [1882?]. viii, 128 pp.   *UCD*

SUBALTERN, pseud. *see* **IRVINE, Andrew Alexander**, (Subaltern, pseud.)

SUCCESSOR OF MAN, pseud. *see* **BENDYSHE, Thomas**, (Successor of Man, pseud.)

SUFFERER, pseud. *see* **CUST, Robert Needham**, (Lifelong Thinker and Wanderer, pseud.), (Sufferer, pseud.)

SULLIVAN, James Frank (18 –1936). Studied at South Kensington School of Art. A clever artist on the staff of *Fun* and other comic papers; also contributed to other magazines, including *Cassell's Saturday Journal* and *Strand Magazine*. Writer on the British working man and tradesman.

The great water joke; written and illustrated by J.F. Sullivan. London: Downey & Co. Ltd. 1899. 32 pp. il.   *OXB*

SULLIVAN, Timothy Daniel, (T.D.S.) (1827–1914). b. Bantry, County Cork. Politician and journalist, he wrote for the *Nation*, becoming its editor on the retirement of his brother, A.M. Sullivan. MP for Westmeath, 1880–1900. In 1886 he became Lord Mayor of Dublin, and was goaled when he defied the government over an edict. He was associated with Parnell in the Land League agitation. Lived at 90 Middle Abbey Street, Dublin.

Blanaid, and other Irish historical and legendary poems from the Gaelic; by T.D. Sullivan. Dublin: Eason & Son, Ltd. 1891. 190 pp.   *NLI*

Lays of the Land League; by T.D.S. Dublin: J.J. Lalor. [1887]. 16 pp.   *BL*

Poems; by T.D. Sullivan. Dublin: Author. [1888]. 285 pp. il., por.   *BL*
    Also re-issues called new eds.

Prison poems: or, lays of Tullamore; by T.D. Sullivan. Dublin: Nation Office. [1888]. 30 pp. il.
    Title from cover.   *TCD*

A selection from the songs and poems of T.D. Sullivan. Dublin: Sealy, Bryers & Walker; M.H. Gill & Son. 1899. viii, 210 pp.   *OXB*

A SUMMER DAY'S STROLL IN THE VALE OF CLAVERTON, NEAR BATH. Printed Bath: "Chronicle" Office. 1883. 40 pp.   *BL*

SUTHERLAND, Frank (1844–). b. Morayshire. A hairdresser, he conducted a business in Elgin. An expert angler, a musician, and a crack shot with the rifle. Wrote as 'Uncle Peter' in Scottish newspapers.

Uncle Peter's poems, entitled, Sunny memories of Morayland; by Frank Sutherland. Printed Elgin: Courant and Courier Office. [1883]. xii, 232 pp.

Spine-title is *Original poems*, cover-title is *Sunny memories of Morayland*. *BL*

SUTHERLAND, James Middleton. Writer on Wordsworth.

Douglas, and other poems; by James Middleton Sutherland. With illustrations. Douglas: Brown & Son. [1883]. xvi, 288 pp. il. *OXB*

SUTHERLAND, Jane Dunn, (Una, pseud.) (1848?–91). A teacher at Keighley Girls' Grammar School, Yorkshire, and an untiring worker for the university extension scheme. Moving to London in 1882 she took an appointment at the General Post Office, later moving to a more important post at the British Museum.

Lays of the Luri, and other rimes; by "Una". Printed Keighley: E. Craven. 1885. 36 pp. *BL*

SUTTON, Henry Septimus (1825–1901). b. Nottingham, son of a bookseller and newspaper proprietor. He was articled to a surgeon but instead turned to journalism. Editor of the *Alliance News* for more than thirty years. Author of several hymns.

Poems; by Henry Septimus Sutton. Glasgow: David M. Main. 1886. xvi, 242 pp. *MPL*

Rose's diary; by Henry S. Sutton. [Glasgow]: David Main. [1889?]. 42 pp.

A limited ed., number of copies unspecified. *BL*

Rose's diary, and other poems; by Henry Septimus Sutton. Manchester: Albert Broadbent. 1899. 41 pp.

Title from cover. *MPL*

SWAN, Robert. Rev.

The Sabbath: a poem written in early life; by Robert Swan. With biographical notes. Edinburgh: Johnstone, Hunter, & Co. 1884. 31 pp. *★UCD*

SWANN, Edward Gibbon. Miscellaneous writer.

The Koh-i-noor of the British diadem, and other fragments in verse; by Edward Gibbon Swann. Burgess Hill, Sussex: Charles N. Blanchard. 1896. [4], ii, 70 pp. *OXB*

Matters and men: a poem of fifty years ago; by Edward Gibbon Swann. 3rd ed. Burgess Hill, Sussex: Charles N. Blanchard. 1895. [8], xliv, 234 pp. por. *OXB*

SWAYNE, Margaret

A true tale of the sea, and other verses; by Margaret Swayne. With illustrations by Georgina Harston. London: Chapman & Hall. 1899. [viii], 62 pp. il. *OXB*

SWEET BARD OF BAILIEBOROUGH *see* **MONTGOMERY, John Wilson**

SWEETMAN, Elinor. Irish, a native of Queen's County. She contributed verse to *Irish Monthly* and various other journals.
Footsteps of the gods, and other poems; by Elinor Sweetman. London: George Bell & Sons. 1893. viii, 100 pp.
   A limited ed. of 300 copies.   *MPL*
Pastorals, and other poems; by Elinor Sweetman. London: J.M. Dent & Co. 1899. [vi], 92 pp.   *OXB*

SWIFT, Harold
Heart voices, in poetry and prose; by Harold Swift. London: James Speirs. 1881. viii, 200 pp.   *OXB*

SWINBORNE, Frederick Pfander (1848–19   ). b. Agra, India, son of Rev. C.G. Swinborne of Peshawar. Educated at Wurtemberg, and King's College School, London. In partnership with his brother in firm of G.P. Swinborne & Co., isinglass and gelatine manufacturers of London EC. Lived at Sunnedon, Coggeshall, Essex.
Gustavus Adolphus: an historical poem and romance of the Thirty Years' War; by Frederick Pfander Swinborne. With illustrations. London: Wyman & Sons. 1884. vi, 500 pp. il.   *BL*

SWINBURNE, Algernon Charles (1837–1909). b. Chapel Street, Belgravia, London, son of Admiral Charles H. Swinburne. He was brought up at East Dene, Bonchurch, Isle of Wight. Educated at Eton College, and Balliol College, Oxford, leaving without taking a degree. From 1860 he lived in London, a friend of Rossetti and other Pre-Raphaelites. He suffered from epilepsy and increasing deafness. In 1879 he went to live with Theodore Watts-Dunton at The Pines, Putney, remaining there for the rest of his life.
BIBLIOGRAPHY: **WISE, Thomas James.** *A Swinburne library: a catalogue of printed books, manuscripts and autograph letters by Algernon Charles Swinburne*. London: T.J. Wise. 1925.

SWINDELLS, James
The crucifixion: or, a lay for Good Friday and Easter; [by James Swindells]. Manchester: John Routledge. [1880]. 16 pp.   *MPL*

SWITHAINE, Swithin Saint, pseud. *see* **MEADOWS, Thomas**, (Swithin Saint Swithaine, pseud.)

SWORDY, Robert. Lived at Dryburn Cottage, Durham.
Fragments of verse; by Robert Swordy. Durham: Charles Thwaites. 1891. [viii], 80 pp. por.   *OXB*

SYKES, Arthur Alkin, (A.A.S.) (18 –1939). Son of Rev. Thomas B. Sykes, rector of Warbleton, Sussex. Educated at Westminster School, and Trinity College, Cambridge. Master at St John's School, Leatherhead, Surrey, 1885–87. Assistant editor of Henry Blackburn's Art Handbooks, 1891–1903; on staff of *Punch*, 1893, Reuters, 1895–96; special correspondent at Russian and Dutch coronations, and in South Africa, Palestine and elsewhere. Examiner for Civil Service Commission; statistician, Central Control Board, 1915–21. Lived at 28 Edith Road, West Kensington, London W.

A book of words, reprinted in part from Punch; [poems]; by A.A.S. With a few sketches by the author. Westminster: Archibald Constable & Co. 1895. xvi, 112 pp. il. *OXB*

SYLVANUS SATYR, pseud. *see* **SATYR, Sylvanus**, pseud.

SYLVIUS, pseud.
Gerontius: a fragment of Roman history; by Sylvius. London: Provost & Co. 1882. viii, 54 pp. *OXB*

SYMINGTON, Andrew James (1825–). b. Paisley, Renfrewshire, son of Robert B. Symington. Educated at Paisley Grammar School. He began a literary career at an early age, contributing translations of German poetry to the *Edinburgh Magazine*, *Chambers's Journal*, etc. Visited Iceland in 1859, and the United States, 1874–75. Wrote critical studies of William Cullen Bryant and of William Wordsworth. An extensive traveller, in 1863 he was elected a Fellow of the Royal Society of Antiquaries, Copenhagen. Friend of F.R. Havergal and of A.B. Grosart. Lived at Nyeholm House, Bellahouston Hill, near Glasgow.

Poems; by Andrew James Symington. Paisley: Alexander Gardner. 1885. 146 pp. *UCD*

SYMONDS, John Addington (1840–93). b. Clifton, son of a Bristol physician. Educated at Harrow School, and Balliol College, Oxford; Newdigate prizewinner. Fellow of Magdalen College, 1862. Lived in Bristol, 1868–80, but went abroad on account of poor health, finally settling at Davos Platz, Switzerland. He wrote studies of Dante, the Greek poets, Shelley, Sidney and others, and a 6 vol. work *The Renaissance in Italy*.

Anima figura: [poems]; by John Addington Symonds. London: Smith, Elder, & Co. 1882. xvi, 140 pp. *MPL*

Fragilia labilia: [poems] (written mostly between 1860 and 1862); by John Addington Symonds. 1884. 39 pp.
A limited ed. of 25 copies printed for the author's use. *BL*

Midnight at Baiae: a dream fragment of Imperial Rome; by John Addington Symonds. Printed London: "The Artist" Office. 1893. [16] pp.
A limited ed. of 100 copies. **NUC*

Miscellanies, Part I; [by John Addington Symonds]. [1885]. [283] pp.
Poetry and prose. Title from cover. Part II contains prose only. *OXB*

New and old: a volume of verse; by John Addington Symonds. London: Smith, Elder, & Co. 1880. x, 248 pp. *MPL*

Vagabunduli libellus: [poems]; by John Addington Symonds. London: Kegan Paul, Trench, & Co. 1884. xvi, 207 pp.   *MPL*

SYMONS, Arthur (1865–1945). b. Milford Haven, Pembrokeshire, son of a Methodist minister. Educated in Devon and abroad. Friend of many writers and artists in the 1890s, and a leading figure in the Decadent movement. A prolific miscellaneous writer, he wrote poetry, plays, and critical works, and translated from six languages; journalist, successively on the staff of the *Athenaeum, Saturday Review*, and the *Academy*; contributor to the *Yellow Book*, and editor of its successor *The Savoy*.

Amoris victima, [and other poems]; by Arthur Symons. London: Leonard Smithers. 1897. x, 72 pp.   *OXB*

Days and nights: [poems]; by Arthur Symons. London: Macmillan & Co. 1889. x, 202 pp.   *MPL*

Images of good and evil: [poems]; by Arthur Symons. London: William Heinemann. 1899. viii, 180 pp.   *OXB*

London nights: [poems]; by Arthur Symons. London: Leonard C. Smithers. 1895. xii, 105 pp.

A limited ed. of 550 copies, 50 copies on large paper, numbered and signed by the author, and 500 copies on small paper.   *OXB*

London nights: [poems]; by Arthur Symons. 2nd ed., revised. London: Leonard Smithers. 1897. xvi, 107 pp.

A limited ed. of 400 copies on small paper.   *OXB*

Silhouettes: [poems]; by Arthur Symons. London: Elkin Mathews & John Lane. 1892. [viii], 96 pp.   *OXB*

Silhouettes: [poems]; by Arthur Symons. 2nd ed. revised and enlarged. London: Leonard Smithers. 1896. xvi, 92 pp.

A limited ed. of 415 copies, 15 copies on large paper, and 400 copies on small paper.   *OXB*

T

T., H.G.B.

Recitations, ballads, songs (reprinted from various magazines and newspapers); by H.G.B.T. Surrey: J. Nichols; "Anerley & Penge Press". 1891. 156 pp.   *OXB*

T., M. *see* **TEESDALE, Maria**, (M.T.)

T., M.E. *see* **TOWNSEND, Mary Elizabeth**, (M.E.T.)

T., R.F. *see* **TOWNDROW, Richard Francis**, (R.F.T.)

T., S.P.
The lost umbrella: a poem in four parts, describing a private sorrow from a humorous point of view . . . ; by [S.P.T.]. Printed Oxford: Parker & Co. [1883?]. 16 pp. il.
Printed for private circulation only. *OXB*

TABLEY, Lord De *see* **WARREN, John Byrne Leicester, Lord De Tabley**

TADEMA, Laurence Alma- *see* **ALMA-TADEMA, Laurence**

TAPPER, John Wheaton Evans. Lived at Brawby, near Pickering, Yorkshire.
Songs, poems and prose; by John Wheaton Evans Tapper. Printed London: Elliot Stock. 1897. xiv, 369 pp. por.
Printed for private circulation. *UCD*

TARDREW, William H. Dramatist.
The last vestal: a poem; Human document: a tale; Fragments; by William H. Tardrew. Paris: Neal's Library; Bristol: Taylor Bros. 1890. [x], 110 pp. *OXB*

TARELLI, Charles Camp (1870–19). Contributed to the *Spectator* and other periodicals. Lived at Barton, Victoria Road, Sutton, Surrey.
Persephone, and other poems; by Charles Camp Tarelli. London: Macmillan & Co. 1898. [viii], 64 pp. *UCD*

TATE, Matthew. Of Blyth, Northumberland.
Pit life in 1893; by Matthew Tate. Printed Blyth: Alder & Co. [1894?]. 16 pp. *NPL*
Poems, songs and ballads; by Matthew Tate. Printed Blyth: Alder & Co. 1898. viii, 184 pp. por. *NPL*

TATTERSALL, J.F. Of Burnley, Lancashire.
The baptism of the Viking, and other verses; by J.F. Tattersall. London: Simpkin, Marshall, Hamilton, Kent & Co., Ltd; Burnley: Lupton Bros. [1890]. viii, 151 pp. *OXB*

TAVEY, Reginald
Shiloh, and other poems; by Reginald Tavey. London: Elliot Stock. 1895. [vi], 138 pp. *UCD*

TAYLOR, A.B. (1815?–97). A native of Scotland, he settled in Accrington, Lancashire, working as engraver to calico printers. On Sundays he preached in Baptist chapels; in 1845 he accepted the pastorate at Accrington but three years later moved to Manchester, where for thirty-eight years he was minister of the Particular Baptist Chapel, Rochdale Road. His ministrations were greatly in demand all over the county.
Occasional thoughts in verse; by the late A.B. Taylor. Together with memoir. Manchester: Brook & Chrystal; Rochdale Road Sunday School Library; London: John Gadsby. 1887. 272 pp. por. *★UCD*

TAYLOR, Arthur Mould Chapman (1864–89). b. Headington, Oxford-shire, son of John W.A. Taylor. Educated at Brasenose College, Oxford; BA 1886. Died 24 December 1889 at Marseilles, France.
Poems – written between the ages of 16 and 23 years, collected from note-books; by Arthur M.C. Taylor. Oxford. 1891. 16 pp.
Printed for private circulation.   *OXB*

TAYLOR, Frank (1844–1902). b. Bolton, Lancashire. He became head of the firm Charles Taylor & Brother, Ltd, cotton spinners. Member of Bolton School Board, 1875–76; borough magistrate, 1885; magistrate for the county of Lancaster, 1894. President of the North & East Lancashire Unitarian Mission for a number of years. Lived at Ash Lawn, Heaton, Bolton.
Musings in verse; by Frank Taylor. Printed Bolton: A. Blackshaw & Sons. 1898. x, 232 pp.
Printed for private circulation.   *BOP*

TAYLOR, Frank (1873–1913). b. London, son of Horatio Taylor. Educated at University College, London, and Lincoln College, Oxford (scholar). Histor-ian and dramatist.
Ad sodales: [poems]; by Frank Taylor. Oxford: B.H. Blackwell; London: Simpkin, Marshall, Hamilton, Kent & Co. 1895. [viii], 48 pp.
A limited ed. of 250 copies.   *OXB*
The age of Leo the tenth in Italy: the Newdigate Prize poem, 1894; by Frank Taylor. Oxford: B.H. Blackwell; London: Simpkin, Marshall, Hamilton, Kent & Co. 1894. 23 pp.   *OXB*

TAYLOR, Georgiana M. Member of the YWCA. Hymn writer.
Lays of lowly service, and other verses; by Georgiana M. Taylor. London: Morgan & Scott. [1884]. 61 pp.   *OXB*

TAYLOR, Henry (18 –1916). b. Stanford Rivers, near Ongar, Essex, son of Isaac Taylor. Educated privately and at Owens College, Manchester. Became an architect, practising with his brother in Manchester, 1861–83. FSA. Member of the Chetham Society. He retired to Tunbridge Wells, spending winters at his house in Birkdale, Southport.
Our Guild: lines written for, and respectfully dedicated to the members of the Bolton Musical Guild; by Henry Taylor. Printed Bolton: J. Scholes. 1896. 16 pp.   *BL*

TAYLOR, John William Augustus (1818–86). Son of John Taylor. Educated at Trinity College, Cambridge; BA 1840, MA 1848. Ordained 1850; curate, Framfield, Sussex, 1845–46; theological tutor, Cheltenham College, 1848–52. Head of Portswood House preparatory school, Malvern, 1853–58; head of The Rookery, Headington, Oxfordshire, 1859–83.
Poems; by J.W. Augustus Taylor. [1891]. [iii], 24 pp.
Printed for private circulation.   *OXB*

TAYLOR, Kate
Poems; by Kate Taylor. Manchester: John Heywood. 1880. xii, 188 pp.   *MPL*

TAYLOR, Kirkwood A railwayman of Derby.
"Behold the fowls of the air": thoughts in blank verse on matters social and religious; by Kirkwood Taylor. Leicester: Co-operative Printing Society Ltd; Wallasey, Cheshire: Joseph Edwards. [1899]. [iv], 118 pp.   *OXB*

TAYLOR, Margaret Scott. Novelist.
'Boys together', and other poems; by Margaret Scott Taylor. London: Kegan Paul, Trench, & Co. 1884. [2], vi, 220 pp.   *BL*

TAYLOR, Tom (1817–80). b. Bishop Wearmouth, Sunderland. County Durham. Educated at The Grange School, Glasgow University, and Trinity College, Cambridge. Fellow, 1843–44. Professor of English Language and literature, London University. Called to the Bar, Middle Temple, 1846. Secretary to the Board of Health, and the Local Government Board, 1854–71. Had a successful career as a playwright and occasional actor, producing about a hundred pieces for the stage. He also worked as a journalist, succeeding Shirley Brooks as editor of *Punch* in 1874.
Storm at midnight, and other poems; by Tom Taylor. Edited by J. Henry Burn. Printed Mintlaw, Aberdeenshire: J. Henry Burn. 1893. [25] pp.   *OXB*

TEESDALE, Maria, (M.T.) (18   –82). Mrs Teesdale of Effingham, Surrey. She had also lived in Buckinghamshire and Kent.
Poems; by M.T. Edited by her children. Printed Edinburgh: Ballantyne, Hanson & Co. 1888. 103 pp. il., por.
   For private circulation.   *BL*

TEISSIER, George Frederick De *see* **DE TEISSIER, George Frederick**

TEMPLE, Augusta
A birthday posy for young and old: verses, songs, stories, plays, etc.; by Augusta Temple. London: J. Masters & Co. 1889. [2], vi, 297 pp.   *CU*

TEMPLE, Francis
Gathered leaves: a collection in verse, with some additions in prose; by Francis Temple. Printed London. [1891]. 63 pp.
   Printed for the author.   *OXB*

TEMPLE, Rose
Parliamentary reminiscences: [poems]; by Rose Temple. Norwood: J. Platt. 1886. 70 pp.   *BL*

TEMPLE LAYTON, Bertha. Daughter of Rev. G. Phipps of Husbands Bosworth, Leicestershire. In 1877 she married Charles Temple Layton, JP. Lived at 4 Spanish Place Mansions, London W.
The way of the cross, and other verses; by B. Temple Layton. Huntingdon: Alfred Wood. [1898]. 28 pp.   *OXB*

TEMPLEMAN, Edward (1833?–). Son of John M. Templeman of Crewkerne, Somerset. Educated at Pembroke College, Oxford; BA 1856. Ordained, 1857; curate, Keystone, Huntingdonshire, 1856–58; chaplain in India, 1858–67; vicar, Higham Ferrars, Northamptonshire, 1868–85; rector, Pitchcott, Buckinghamshire, from 1885.

Poems: narrative and descriptive; by Edward Templeman. London: Elliot Stock. 1891. viii, 78 pp.   *BL*

TENNYSON, Alfred, Lord Tennyson (1809–92). b. Somersby, Lincolnshire, son of Rev. George Tennyson. Educated at Louth Grammar School, by his father at home, and at Trinity College, Cambridge; won the Chancellor's medal for poetry, 1829. He was joined at Trinity by his brothers Charles and Frederick, the three associating with the 'Apostles' group, which included Arthur Hallam, who was to be the inspiration for 'In memoriam'. The popularity of his poetry increased, and in 1850 he was appointed poet laureate in succession to Wordsworth. Lived at Farringford, Isle of Wight, 1853–68, then at Aldworth, near Haslemere, Surrey, from 1869. Created Baron Tennyson in 1884.
BIBLIOGRAPHY: **TENNYSON, Charles, & FALL, Christine.** *Alfred Tennyson: an annotated bibliography*. Athens: University of Georgia Press. 1967.

TENNYSON, Frederick (1807–98). Eldest son of Rev. George Tennyson, rector of Somersby, Lincolnshire, and brother of Alfred Tennyson. Educated at Eton College, and Trinity College, Cambridge. He travelled much on the continent, spending nearly twenty years in Florence; married the daughter of the chief magistrate at Siena. From 1859 to 1896 he lived in Jersey. At one time he followed Swedenborgianism and spiritualism.

Daphne, and other poems; by Frederick Tennyson. London: Macmillan. 1891. [iv], 522 pp.   *MPL*

The isles of Greece: Sappho and Alcaaeus; by Frederick Tennyson. London: Macmillan & Co. 1890. xvi, 444 pp.   *MPL*

Poems of the day and year; by Frederick Tennyson. London: John Lane, The Bodley Head; Chicago: Stone & Kimball. 1895. [viii], 163 pp.   *MPL*

TENNYSON, Hallam, Lord Tennyson (1852–1928). Son of Alfred, Lord Tennyson. Educated at Marlborough College, and Trinity College, Cambridge. Called to the Bar, Inner Temple. He succeeded his father to the baronage in 1892. Lived at 134 Sloane Street, London SW, and at the family homes in the Isle of Wight and Haslemere, Surrey.

Jack and the bean-stalk: English hexameters; by Hallam Tennyson. Illustrated by Randolph Caldecott. London: Macmillan & Co. 1886. 71 pp. il.   *OXB*

TERRELL, Francis A.H. Dramatist.

Lyre and star: poems; by [Francis A.H. Terrell]. London: Kegan Paul, Trench & Co. 1883. viii, 238 pp.   *MPL*

Sappho: a dream; by [Francis A.H. Terrell]. London: C. Kegan Paul & Co. 1881. [viii], 107 pp.   *OXB*

THACKWELL, Walter (1876–   ). b. Aghada, Ireland.
Thoughts in song; by Walter Thackwell. Cork: Purcell & Co.; Dublin: Eason & Sons, Ltd. 1893. 69 pp.   *OXB*

THAIN, Leslie (1853–   ). b. Devon, of Scottish descent, son of Captain J.G.H. Thain, Royal Navy. Educated at Plymouth Grammar School. Studied surgery and medicine at University Cottage Hospital, London; MRCS. He settled in the Black Mountains of Wales, at Pentillie, Longtown, Abergavenny.
Nell the kitchen angel, and other poems; by Leslie Thain. Printed Abergavenny: Thomas & Edmunds. 1885. [iv], 65 pp.   *OXB*
Poems; by Leslie Thain. Second series. Brechin: D.H. Edwards. [1890]. 38 pp.   *OXB*
Poems; by Leslie Thain. Fourth series. 3rd ed. Brechin: D.H. Edwards. [1891]. [4], viii, 138 pp.   *OXB*
Timotheus, the violin player; by Leslie Thain. 2nd ed. Printed Abergavenny: Thomas & Edmunds. [1889]. 17 pp.   *OXB*

THEAD, A.W.
The story of Jephthah, and other poems; by A.W. Thead. London: Digby, Long & Co. 1897. 125 pp.   *OXB*

THOM, James. Of Edinburgh.
The pleasure of home, and other poems; by James Thom. Edinburgh: R.W. Hunter. 1894. xii, 191 pp.   *BL*

THOM, Robert William (1816–90?). b. Annan, Dumfriesshire, son of a surgeon. He was apprenticed to a draper in Blackburn, Lancashire, returning to Scotland in 1839. Went back to Blackburn in 1847, living in Larkhill, and starting in business as a draper in Henry Street. A prominent member of Blackburn Scotsmen's Club. Eventually settled in Glasgow at 29 Govanhill Street, Govanhill.
The epochs: a poem; by Robert W. Thom. Testimonial ed. Glasgow: Author. 1884. 144 pp.   *UCD*
Poems; by Robert W. Thom. Glasgow: Author. 1880. 344 pp.   *BL*
   Also subscribers' ed. 1880.
Poems and ballads (Scotch and English); by Robert W. Thom. Glasgow: Maclaren & Sons; David Bryce & Son; Wm. Porteous & Co.; Wm. Love. 1886. 112 pp. por.   *UCD*

THOMAS, Frederick. A hatter.
Humorous and other poetic pictures: legends and stories of Devon; by Frederick Thomas. London: W. Kent & Co.; Plymouth: W. Brendon & Son; Exeter: Henry S. Eland. [1883]. viii, 296 pp.   *OXB*

THOMAS, John. Rev. Thomas, BA. Minister of Catherine Street Presbyterian Church, Liverpool.

The gateway of life, and other poems and hymns; by J. Thomas. Liverpool: Henry Young & Sons. 1899. 139 pp.   *OXB*

THOMAS, Joseph (1840–94). b. Mullion, Cornwall, son of the steward for Lord Robartes. Educated in Penzance, he became a land agent and valuer in Liskeard, then at St Michael's Mount. A preacher for the United Methodist Free Church.

Randigal rhymes; and, A glossary of Cornish words; by Joseph Thomas. Penzance: F. Rodda. 1895. xvi, 139 pp. por.   *OXB*

THOMAS, Llewelyn (1840–97). b. Caernarvon, son of Canon Thomas Thomas of Bangor. Educated at Jesus College, Oxford, becoming a Fellow in 1872 after holding teaching posts at Rossall, Llandovery and Ruthin. Vice-Principal of Jesus College, acting principal for eight years. Canon at St Asaph, 1897.

Father and son: memoirs of Thomas Thomas and of Llewelyn Thomas, with selections from the writings of the latter. Edited by Harriet Thomas. London: Henry Frowde, 1898. viii, 367 pp. por.   *OXB*

THOMAS, Richard Henry. Dr Thomas, MD. A Quaker, he wrote on the Quakers in America.

Echoes and pictures: [poems]; by Richard H. Thomas. London: James Nisbet & Co. 1895. xii, 147 pp.   *OXB*

THOMAS, Rose Haig. Mrs Thomas. Novelist, and writer on the design of stone gardens.

Pan: a collection of lyrical poems; by Rose Haig Thomas. London: Bliss, Sands & Co. 1897. viii, 95 pp.   *BL*

THOMAS, Senior

Self-triumphant: or, the lady of white towers: a tale in verse; by Senior Thomas. London: Simpkin, Marshall, Hamilton, Kent & Co., Ltd. 1890. 169 pp.   *OXB*

THOMAS, William Herbert. Of Cornwall. Writer on Mormonism, and the poets of Cornwall.

The socialist's longing, and other poems; by W. Herbert Thomas. These writings include several pieces in the Cornish dialect. Penzance: F. Rodda. 1893. [viii], 85 pp.

Cover-title is *The Christian socialist.*   *OXB*

THOMPSON, E.H.

The brighter day: poems; by Sarah Geraldine Stock & E.H. Thompson. London: James E. Hawkins. [1889?]. [24] pp. il.

Some poems are joint authorship.   *OXB*

THOMPSON, Francis (1859–1906). b. Preston, Lancashire. Educated at Ushaw College in preparation for the Roman Catholic priesthood. He studied medicine at Owens College, Manchester, for six years but failed the examinations. Made unsuccessful attempts to earn a living in London, where he lived as a tramp and became addicted to laudanum. He was rescued by Wilfred and Alice Meynell, who helped him for the rest of his life. Contributed literary criticism to *Academy* and *Athenaeum*. Died of tuberculosis.

New poems; by Francis Thompson. Westminster: Archibald Constable & Co. 1897. viii, 244 pp. *MPL*

Poems; by Francis Thompson. London: Elkin Mathews & John Lane; Boston, [Mass.]: Copeland & Day. 1893. x, 83 pp. il.

A limited ed. of 500 copies. *OXB*

Also 2nd – 5th eds 1894–95.

Sister-songs: an offering to two sisters; by Francis Thompson. John Lane at The Bodley Head; Boston, [Mass.]: Copeland & Day. 1895. [viii], 65 pp. il. *MPL*

THOMPSON, Hugh. Of Rothesay, Bute.

Poems and essays; by Hugh Thompson. Printed Rothesay: For subscribers. 1885. viii, 112 pp. *OXB*

THOMPSON, Sir Peile (1844–). Son of Sir Matthew Thompson. Educated at Rugby School, and Trinity College, Cambridge; BA 1867, MA 1877. Ordained, 1880; curate, Monken Hadley, Middlesex, 1877–81, Christ Church, Marylebone, London, 1881–85. Lived at Park Gate, Guiseley, Leeds.

[*Epigrammata*]; [by Peile Thompson]. Printed Leeds: J. Strafford. [189-]. 106 pp. *LEP*

THOMPSON, Rachel. Miss Thompson of Malmesbury, Wiltshire. Youngest of a large family.

In honour to a triune God: original poems; written by Rachel Thompson. Printed Malmesbury: N. Riddick. 1890. 69 pp. *OXB*

THOMPSON, Samuel Ashton *see* **YATES, Samuel Ashton Thompson**

THOMPSON, Silvanus Phillips (1851–1916). Educated at London University. Professor of physics, University College, Bristol; principal and professor of applied physics and electrical engineering, City & Guilds Technical College, Finsbury, 1885–1916. He published works on electricity and magnetism.

Monodies: [poems]; [by William Charles Braithwaite and Silvanus Phillips Thompson]. Printed Chiswick: Chiswick Press. 1892. 24 pp.

A limited ed. of 100 numbered copies, privately printed for the Westminster Portfolio Society. Not joint authorship. *OXB*

THOMPSON, Williams Mort, (Landlubber, pseud.). Fourth president of the Sette of Odd Volumes. A Freemason, he lived at 16 Carlyle Square, London SW.

A president's persiflage; spoken by his oddship Brother W.M. Thompson . . . at the Freemasons' Tavern, Great Queen Street . . . December 7th, 1883. London: C.W.H. Wyman. 1883. 16 pp. *OXB*

Sea-doggerel: a souvenir of a trip to Boulogne on board "La Marguerite" on September 13th, 1894; read at Limmer's Hotel on November 2nd; by a landlubber (W. Mort Thompson). Printed London: Bedford Press. 1894. 16 pp. *OXB*

THOMPSON, George William (1845–19). b. Aberdeen, son of George Thompson. Educated at Aberdeen Grammar School, and Aberdeen University. Entered banking in 1864, joining staff of the Alliance Bank; worked for the Oriental Bank Corporation of China and Japan, 1864–83; founded the first European bank in Persia, 1888; founded the African Banking Corporation, 1891, of which he was chief manager then a director. Lived latterly at Mayfield, Southcliff, Essex.

Verses from Japan; [by George William Thompson]. London: Wyman & Sons. 1884. 38 pp. *OXB*

THOMSON, J.E., (Violet Flint, pseud.) Medical student. Lived at Torrington Mansions, London.

A golfing idyll: or, the skipper's round with the deil on the links of St. Andrews; [by Violet Flint]. 2nd ed. St. Andrews: W.C. Henderson & Son; Edinburgh: John Menzies & Co.; London: Simpkin, Marshall, Kent & Co. Ltd. 1893. viii, 36 pp. *OXB*

Also 3rd ed. 1897.

THOMSON, James, (B.V.) (1834–82). b. Port Glasgow, son of James Thomson, an officer in the merchant service. In 1842 the family moved to London, where both his parents died. Brought up in an orphanage, he trained for army teaching at the Royal Military Asylum, Chelsea. Served in Cork, Plymouth, Aldershot and Dublin, from 1851. Increasing alcoholism led to his dismissal from the army in 1862. Subsequently he became a clerk in London, visited Colorado as a mining agent, and for a short time in 1873 was a war correspondent in Spain. Friend of Charles Bradlaugh and other notable secularists.

The city of dreadful night, and other poems; by James Thomson ("B.V."). London: Reeves & Turner. 1880. [viii], 184 pp. *BL*

The city of dreadful night, and other poems; by James Thomson ("B.V."). 2nd ed. London: Reeves & Turner; Bertram Dobell. 1888. [viii], 184 pp. *OXB*

The city of dreadful night, and other poems: being a selection from the poetical works of James Thomson, ("B.V."). London: Bertram Dobell. 1899. xx, 256 pp. *JRL*

Poems, essays and fragments; by James Thomson ("B.V."). Edited, with preface, by John M. Robertson. With portrait. London: A. & H. Bradlaugh Bonner; Reeves & Turner. 1892. xvi, 267 pp. por. *MPL*

The poetical works of James Thomson ('Bysshe Vanolis'). Edited by Bertram Dobell with a memoir of the author. London: Reeves & Turner; Bertram Dobell. 1895. 2vols. por.   *MPL*

Shelley: a poem; with other writings relating to Shelley; by the late James Thomson (B.V.). To which is added an essay on the poems of William Blake by the same author. Printed Chiswick: Charles Whittingham & Co. at the Chiswick Press. 1884. xii, 128 pp.

Printed for private circulation only, and limited to 190 copies, 160 copies of which are printed on toned paper, and 30 copies on Whatman's hand-made paper. Each copy is numbered and signed by the editor B.D.   *OXB*

Vane's story: Weddah and Om-El-Bonain, and other poems; by James Thomson. London: Reeves & Turner. 1881. viii, 184 pp.   *MPL*

A voice from the Nile, and other poems; by the late James Thomson ("B.V."). With a memoir of the author by Bertram Dobell. London: Reeves & Turner. 1884. xlxii, 263 pp. por.   *MPL*

THOMSON, John. Scottish.
Golfing and other poems and songs; by John Thomson. Glasgow: William Hodge & Co. 1893. x, 84 pp. por.   *OXB*

THOMSON, John Ebenezer Honeyman (1841–). b. Glasgow. He suffered ill-health until the family moved to Dennyloanhead, Stirlingshire. Educated at Glasgow and Edinburgh Universities; MA, BD. Minister in the United Presbyterian Church.
The upland tarn: a village idyll; [by John Ebenezer Honeyman Thomson]. Edinburgh: David Douglas. 1881. [iv], 167 pp.   *OXB*

THOMSON, Robert. Educated at Pembroke College, Cambridge; BA 1856, MA 1881. Ordained 1858; curate in Lincolnshire: Ulceby with Croxton & Kirmington, 1857–58, Metheringham, 1858–61, North Kelsey, 1861–64; vicar, Skipsea, Hull, Yorkshire, 1864. Lived latterly at 3 Elmford Terrace, Morley, Leeds.
A dream of paradise: a poem; by Robert Thomson. London: Elliot Stock. 1898. [ii], 96 pp.   *OXB*
The heavenly bridegroom: a poem; by Robert Thomson. London: Eliot Stock. 1899. [viii], 94 pp.   *OXB*

THOMSON, William (1860–83). b. Glasgow. The family moved to the village of Bellshill when he was nine, but he afterwards returned to Glasgow to learn tailoring, entering his father's business while still a boy. He contributed numerous pieces to newspapers and literary periodicals. Suffered serious illness from 1882.
Leddy May, and other poems; by William Thomson. Glasgow: T.W. Farrell. 1883. xii, 193 pp.   *EPL*
Leddy May, and other poems; by William Thomson. 2nd ed. Glasgow: T.W. Farrell; M'Laren & Son. 1883. 207 pp.   *EPL*

THORNELY, James Lamport (18 –1900). Son of James Thornely, Liverpool solicitor and president of Liverpool Law Society. Admitted solicitor, 1889; member of the firm Thornely & Cameron of Liverpool until his death. Author of *Monumental Brasses of Lancashire & Cheshire*, 1893.
Moments apart: being a miscellany of verse; by James L. Thornely. Printed Edinburgh: Robb & Co. 1894. 83 pp.
　　Privately printed. A limited small paper ed. of 200 numbered copies. *OXB*
　　Also a limited large paper ed. of 50 numbered copies signed by the author, 1894.

THORNHILL, Bensley. Writer of comic opera.
Gorse bloom, and other poems, for reading and recitation; by Bensley Thornhill. London: London Literary Society. [1886]. [iv], 90 pp.　*OXB*

THORNTON, Cyrus
Voices of the street; [poems]; by Cyrus Thornton. London: Elliot Stock. 1887. 48 pp.　*OXB*

THORNTON, Fairelie. Writer on Christian topics.
Work for Jesus: poems; by Fairelie Thornton. London: S.W. Partridge & Co. [1884]. 112 pp.　*OXB*

THORNTON, H.G. Blake
The luck of the longest day, and other recitations, ballads and songs; by H.G. Blake Thornton. Surrey: J. Nichols, Anerley & Penge Press. 1892. 112 pp.　*OXB*

THORNTON, Leslie Melville (1858?–19). Son of Reginald Thornton of Clapham, Middlesex. Educated at Marlborough College, and University College, Oxford (scholar); BA 1880, MA 1883. Appointed to the Indian Civil Service; served in the North West Provinces and Oudh in senior posts; district and sessions judge, 1902; retired 1906.
Occasional pieces; [poems]; by Leslie Melville Thornton. Calcutta: W. Newman & Co. 1881. [viii], 54 pp.　*BL*

THORPE, Elphinstone
Lyrics from lazyland; by Elphinstone Thorpe. London: H.J. Glaisher. 1899. viii, 84 pp.　*OXB*

THORPE, Thomas (1829–). b. Milton, Dunbartonshire, son of a block-printer. In 1834 the family settled in Strathblane, Stirlingshire, where he attended the village school and continued his education at evening classes. He was apprenticed to block-printing but eventually worked as a warehouseman. In 1862 he settled in Busby, Renfrewshire, employed by Messrs Inglis & Wakefield.
Poems by the wood, field, and fireside; by Thomas Thorpe. Edinburgh: John Menzies & Co. 1883. 254 pp.
　　Poetry and prose.　*BL*

THRELFALL, Evelyn, Lady. Daughter of John F. Baird. In 1891 she married Sir Richard Threlfall, physicist and chemical engineer. Lived at Oakhurst, Church Road, Edgbaston, Birmingham.
Starlight songs; by Evelyn Threlfall. London: Kegan Paul, Trench, Trübner, & Co. Ltd. 1895. 99 pp. *OXB*

THRING, Edward (1821–87). Educated at Eton College, and King's College, Cambridge; Porson prizeman, and Fellow of King's, 1844. Appointed headmaster of Uppingham School, 1853, advancing the school to a foremost position. Founder of the Headmasters' Conference, 1869. Established the first public school mission to the London poor. Writer on education, and of several books of English grammar.
Borth lyrics; by Edward Thring. With illustrations by C. Rossiter. Engraved by Dalziel Brothers. Uppingham: John Hawthorn. 1881. 32 pp. il. *OXB*
Poems and translations; by Edward Thring. London: T. Fisher Unwin. 1887. 150 pp. *OXB*
Uppingham School songs; and, Borth lyrics; by Edward Thring. London: T. Fisher Unwin. 1887. 81 pp. *OXB*

THROUGH DARK TO LIGHT: OR, A DAY AT THE SEA: [poems]. London: Remington & Co. 1882. [viii], 154 pp. *OXB*

THURSTAN, Frederick William, (Count Ernest, pseud.) (1853–19). b. Colombo, Ceylon, son of Rev. Joseph Thurstan. Educated at Guernsey College, and Christ's College, Cambridge; BA 1876, MA 1879; winner of Chancellor's English medal, 1874. Assistant master, King's College, Farnborough, 1876. Conducted an army and civil service preparatory establishment in London, 1876–79. Managing director of the Dilettante Club, 1880. Assistant master, Kingsley College, Devon, 1881–85; taught at Oxford Military College, 1886, Aldershot Army College, 1887, La Martinière College, Lucknow, India, 1888–94; private tutor, 1894–1901. Lived latterly at Old Windsor, Berkshire.
Reveries, fantasias and songs: poems; by Count Ernest. London: Ward, Lock & Co. Ltd. [1898]. 32 pp. *OXB*

THWAITES, Clara. A contributor to many periodicals.
A peal of bells: poems; by Clara Thwaites. Illustrated by C.G. Noakes. [London?]: Hildesheimer. 1888. ★
Songs for labour and leisure; by Clara Thwaites. London: James Nisbet & Co. 1885. viii, 152 pp. *BL*

TIBBETTS, J.F. Of Brackley, Northamptonshire.
Ambition: a poem; by J.F. Tibbetts. 2nd ed. Oxford: Alden & Co. Ltd. 1893. 26 pp. *OXB*

TIFFANY, Thomas. Of Yorkshire.

My own reciter, consisting of new sentimental, patriotic, comic, temperance, and Yorkshire dialect recitations; by Thomas Tiffany. London: Milner & Co., Ltd. [1897]. 288 pp.

Published by request. ★*UCD*

TILBURY, Caroline

Candlewicks: a year of thoughts and fancies: [poems]; by Caroline Tilbury. London: Elliot Stock. 1897. [viii], 97 pp. *BL*

TINDALL, Alfred Frederick. Lived at 30 Wyndham Street, Bryanston Square, London W.

Mystical lays; Soul reveries, and other poems; by A.F. Tindall. London: Author. 1888. [ii], 44 pp. *OXB*

Ode on the marriage of H.R.H. the Duke of York and H.S.H. the Princess May of Teck, and other poems; by A.F. Tindall. London: E.W. Allen. 1893. 3 vols in 1. *OXB*

TISSINGTON, Richard

Bob-o-link ballads; by Richard Tissington. London: Banks & Ashwell. [1881]. [viii], 174 pp. *BL*

TO CHARLES ERNEST GREEN, ESQ. ON HIS GIVING UP THE ESSEX HOUNDS, APRIL, 1893. Printed London: Smith & Ebbs. [1893]. [ii], 18 pp. *OXB*

TODD, Adam Brown (1822–1915). b. Craighall Farmhouse, Mauchline, Ayrshire. His father was a friend of Robert Burns. Author and journalist, he began writing for the *Kilmarnock Journal*. His diamond jubilee as a journalist was celebrated in 1904, when he received a £40 annuity from the government. Lived at Breeezyhill Cottage, Cumnock, Ayrshire.

The circling year, and other poems; by A.B. Todd. London: Elliot Stock. 1880. x, 136 pp. *OXB*

TODD, Henry. Possibly Henry Todd (1865–1918). For many years headmaster of St John's School, Baxenden, Lancashire.

North country ballads; by Henry Todd. London: Horace Cox. 1895. 41 pp. ★*UCD*

TODHUNTER, John (1839–1916). b. Dublin, Educated at Trinity College, Dublin, where he studied medicine, also in Paris and Vienna; MD 1866. Practised in Dublin before moving to London in 1874. Professor of English literature at Alexandra College, Dublin, 1870–74. He abandoned medicine for literature, his plays having some success in their day. Member of the Rhymers' Club, and friend of the Yeats family. Died in Chiswick.

The banshee, and other poems; by John Todhunter. London: Kegan Paul, Trench & Co. 1888. x, 148 pp. *OXB*

Forest songs, and other poems; by John Todhunter. London: Kegan Paul, Trench & Co. 1881. x, 104 pp. *OXB*

Three Irish bardic tales: being metrical versions of the three tales known as the three sorrows of story-telling; by John Todhunter. London: J.M. Dent & Co. 1896. viii, 161 pp. *OXB*

TOLLEMACHE, Beatrix Lucia (1840–1926). b. London, daughter of Lord Egerton of Tatton. In 1870 she married Hon. Lionel Arthur Tollemache, second son of Lord Tollemache of Helmingham. Lived at Haslemere, Surrey, and at 40 Wilton Crescent, London SW.

Engelberg, and other verses; by Beatrix L. Tollemache. London: Percival & Co. 1890. x, 129 pp. il. *MPL*

Engelberg, and other verses; by Beatrix L. Tollemache (Hon. Mrs Lionel Tollemache). 2nd ed. London: Rivingtons. 1898. xii, 105 pp. il. *OXB*

Safe studies; by the Hon. Mr. and Mrs. Lionel A. Tollemache. London: William Rice. 1891. xvi, iii–vii, 429 pp.

Miscellaneous prose, but contains poems by B.L.T. (Beatrix Lucia Tollemache). *JRL*

TOM, Squire, Jun.

A good little book for the grown-up boys and girls: all the poetry and the pictures; by Squire Tom, Jun. London: Digby, London & Co. [1892]. 30 pp. il. *OXB*

TOMKINS, Mrs Daniel

Twilight verses; by Mrs. Daniel Tomkins. London: Jarrold & Sons. [1886]. 199 pp. *OXB*

TOMKINS, Henry George (1827–1907?). Son of Charles Tomkins. Educated at Trinity College, Cambridge. Ordained. 1858; curate, Kegworth, Leicestershire, 1857–58, St Michael's, Derby, 1858–59, West Coker, Somerset, 1860–63, St Marychurch, Devon, 1863–64, Woodbury-Salterton, Devon, 1864–66; rector, St Paul's, Exeter, 1866–68; vicar, Branscombe, 1868–72. Served on various Church Commissions. Lived latterly at Park Lodge, Weston-super-Mare, Somerset.

Poems, chiefly sacred; by Henry George Tomkins. London: Parker & Co. 1891. viii, 120 pp. *UCD*

TOMKINS, Zitella E. Of Swansea, Glamorgan.

Sister Lucetta, and other poems; by Zitella E. Tomkins. London: Kegan Paul, Trench & Co. 1887. viii, 114 pp. *BL*

TOMLIN, Edward Locke (1855–19). b. Great Cumberland Place, London, son of Sackett Tomlin. Educated at Harrow School, and University College, Oxford; BA & MA 1881. Student of Inner Temple, 1876. Liveryman of the Goldsmiths' Co. JP and deputy lieutenant of Kent; high sheriff of Kent, 1902. Lived at Angley Park, Cranbrook.

Gleanings: [poems]; by Edward Locke Tomlin. London: Longmans, Green, & Co. 1891. x, 115 pp. *OXB*

Rhymelets: by Edward Locke Tomlin, London: Longmans, Green, & Co. 1891. viii, 92 pp. *OXB*

TOMLINSON, Charles (1808–97). b. London. Scientific writer. He kept a day school with his brother at Salisbury, Wiltshire. Attended science lectures at University College, London. Lecturer on experimental science, King's College School, London. Made important discoveries concerning surface tension of liquids. FCS, 1867, FRS, 1872. Dante lecturer, University College, London, 1878–80.

Sonnets; by Charles Tomlinson. London: James Cornish & Sons. 1881. viii, 184 pp. *OXB*

TOMLINSON, William Robert (1811?–99). Son of Nicholas Tomlinson, Captain, later Admiral, Royal Navy. Educated at the Royal Naval College, Portsmouth, and St John's College, Cambridge; BA 1833, MA 1836. Ordained, 1837; curate, Hove, Sussex, 1835–37; vicar, Whiteparish, Wiltshire, 1837–78, and rector, Sherfield-English, Hampshire, 1837–92. Lived latterly at Briarswood, Rodwell, Weymouth.

Metastasis; by Wm. R. Tomlinson. London: George Redway. 1896. 84 pp. *OXB*

TOMLINSON, William Weaver (1858–1916). b. Driffield, Yorkshire. Brought up in Beverley, where he was educated by Mr Dyson. In 1872 the family moved to Newcastle-upon-Tyne, where he attended the Royal Grammar School. Worked in the accountant's office of the North Eastern Railway Co. Author of a guide to Newcastle and one to Northumberland. Lectured to Newcastle Literary & Philosophical Society on the poets of Newcastle. Translated the work of several French poets. Lived at Whitley Bay.

First-fruits: [poems]; by William Weaver Tomlinson. Printed Newcastle-upon-Tyne: M. & M.W. Lambert. 1881. viii, 112 pp. *NPL*

TOMSON, Graham Rosamund, pseud. *see* **MARRIOTT WATSON, Rosamund**, (Graham Rosamund Tomson, pseud.)

TOURTEL, Herbert Bird (1874–). Son of Peter Tourtel of St Peter Port, Guernsey. Educated at Elizabeth College, and Trinity College, Cambridge.

The coming of Ragnarok, and other poems; by Herbert Bird Tourtel. Guernsey: Frederick Blondel Guerin; London: Simpkin, Marshall, Hamilton, Kent, & Co., Ltd. 1895. [viii], 63 pp. *GPR*

TOWERS, Walter (1841–). b. Carronshore, Stirlingshire. He worked as a pattern-maker at Falkirk Foundry. He went into business on his own account for several years but it was a failure. From 1885 he was engaged as foreman pattern-maker at the Bonnybridge Foundry. Wrote songs and operettas. Lived at 175 Paisley Road West, Glasgow.

Poems, songs, and ballads; by Walter Towers. Glasgow: A. Bryson & Co. 1885. 205 pp. *BL*

TOWNDROW, Richard Francis, (R.F.T.). Of Great Malvern, Worcestershire.

A garden, and other poems; by Richard Francis Towndrow. London: T. Fisher Unwin. 1892. 93 pp. *OXB*

A life; Love, and other poems; by R.F.T. London: Kegan Paul, Trench & Co. 1889. xii, 152 pp. *OXB*

Sonnets of love, life and death; by R.F.T. Guildford: A.C. Curtis. 1896. [15] pp. For private circulation only. Printed on one side of leaf only. *OXB*

TOWNSEND, David (1807–). Of Kettering, Northamptonshire. He sang his own songs with his own violin accompaniment on the streets of Kettering.

Heroes of Kettering, and other records: [poems]; by David Townsend. [Kettering]. 1892. 32 pp. *OXB*

Jubilee melodies; by David Townsend. Printed Kettering: W.E. & J. Goss. 1887. 16 pp. *OXB*

TOWNSEND, Mary Elizabeth, (M.E.T.). Mrs Townsend.

Original poems and translations; by M.E.T. Printed Edinburgh: Turnbull & Spears. [1887]. 84 pp. Printed for private circulation only. *OXB*

So tired, and other verses; by M.E. Townsend (M.E.T.). London: Rivingtons. 1882. 48 pp. *OXB*

So tired, and other verses; by M.E. Townsend. New and enlarged ed. London: Longmans, Green, & Co. 1894. viii, 52 pp. *OXB*

TOWNSEND-FARQUHAR, Sir Robert (1841–). Son of Sir Walter M. Townsend-Farquhar. Educated at the Military Academy, Woolwich; lieutenant, Royal Artillery, 1859, retired 1866. He succeeded his brother to the baronetcy in 1877. Lived at The Wray, Grasmere, Westmorland.

A shilling for my thoughts: [poems]; by Sir R.T. Farquhar. Ambleside: G. Middleton, 1890. vi, 85 pp. *OXB*

TOWY, Joannes *see* **JONES, John**, (Joannes Towy)

TOYNBEE, William (1849–19). Son of Joseph Toynbee, London surgeon. Educated at Harrow School. Student, Inner Temple, called to the Bar, 1881; equity draftsman and conveyancer. Director, Land & House Property Corporation Ltd from 1904, and of Neuchatel Asphalt Co. Ltd from 1906. Member of St James, Oriental, and Burlington Fine Arts Clubs. Lived latterly at 30 South Eaton Place, London SW.

Lays of common life; by William Toynbee. London: Remington & Co. 1890. [viii], 123 pp. *OXB*

An oaten flute, and other versicles; by William Toynbee. Printed London: Chiswick Press. 1897. [viii], 64 pp. *OXB*

An oaten flute, and other versicles; by William Toynbee. London: H.J. Glaisher. 1899. viii, 64 pp. *OXB*

Song-words; by William Toynbee. London: Simpkin, Marshall & Co.; R. & A. Spalding. [1888]. 57 pp. *OXB*

TRAILL, Henry Duff (1842–1900). Educated at Merchant Taylors School, and St John's College, Oxford; BA 1865, BCL 1868, DCL 1873. Called to the Bar, Inner Temple, 1869. On staff of *Pall Mall Gazette*, 1873–80, and *St James's Gazette*, 1880–82; chief political leader-writer, *Daily Telegraph*, 1882–97; editor, *Observer*, 1889–91; first editor of *Literature*, 1897–1900.

Recaptured rhymes: being a batch of political and other fugitives, arrested and brought to book; by H.D. Traill. Edinburgh: William Blackwood & Sons. 1882. viii, 162 pp. *OXB*

Saturday songs; by H.D. Traill. London: W.H. Allen & Co. 1890. viii, 124 pp. *OXB*

TRASK, Harold Ernest. Educated at Lincoln College, Oxford; BA 1901, MA 1902. Curate, St John's, Hackney, London, 1902. Lived at Courtfield, Norton-sub-Hamdon, Somerset.

The awakening: a prose allegory; Verses, chiefly lyrical; A dream legend; by Harold Ernest Trask. Printed Yeovil: E. Whitby & Son. [1894]. 53 pp. *TAU*

TRAVERS, Eva L. *see* **EVERED POOLE, Eva L**.

TREGELLES, Jane M. An invalid, she lived at Harewood House, Darlington, County Durham.

Childhood's memories, and other poems; by Jane M. Tregelles. Darlington: A.E. Tregelles. 1890. 88 pp. *BL*

TRENCH, Frederic Herbert (1865–1923). b. Ireland, nephew of the Archbishop of Dublin. Educated at Keble College, Oxford. Employed by the Board of Education, 1891–1909. Artistic director, Haymarket Theatre, London, 1909–11. From 1911 he lived abroad, mainly in Italy. Died at Boulogne, France.

Savonarola; by Frederic Herbert Trench. Printed Oxford: Alden & Co. [1886?]. [iv], 16 pp. *BL*

TREVALDWYN, Benn Wilkes Jones. Ordained priest, 1857; curate, Launceston, Cornwall, 1855–58, Rugby, Warwickshire, 1859, Sibson, Leicestershire, 1859–67; rector, Nether-Whitacre, Coleshill, Warwickshire, from 1867.

Songs and rhymes and simple verses; by B.W.J. Trevaldwyn. London: Elliot Stock. 1896. x, 102 pp. *OXB*

TREVELYAN, Robert Calverley (1872–1951). Son of Sir George Otto Trevelyan, historian, and brother of George Macaulay Trevelyan. Educated at Harrow School, and Trinity College, Cambridge. Prose and essay writer, he made many translations from Greek authors.

Mallow and asphodel: [poems]; by R.C Trevelyan. London: Macmillan & Co., Ltd. 1898. [vi], 55 pp. *OXB*

TREVOR, George Herbert (1840–19). Son of Rev. George Trevor. Educated at Marlborough College. Entered the Royal Artillery, 1858, and the Indian Staff Corps, 1862. He held various appointments, 1867–95, retiring as agent to the Governor-General of Rajputana, and chief commissioner of Ajmir. CSI, 1891.

Rhymes of Rajputana; by G.H. Trevor. London: Macmillan & Co. 1894. xiv, 237 pp.   *OXB*

TREWEEK, C.A.

Poems; by C.A. Treweek. [London]: [London Literary Society]. [1885]. [viii], 175 pp.   *OXB*

TRIST, John Fincher. Major Trist of Tristford, Devon. JP for Cornwall and Devon; deputy lieutenant for Cornwall.

A loyal ode to commemorate the events that occurred at Harberton on Her Majesty's jubilee day, the 21st of June, for the (by command) 20th June, 1887, [and other poems]; composed by Major Trist. Printed Totnes: Mortimer Bros. 1887. 72 pp. por.

Cover-title is *Harberton jubilee reminiscences*.   *BL*

TROTT, J.C.

A collection of poems and songs: descriptive, sentimental & humorous; by J.C. Trott. Halifax: "Guardian" Printing Works. 1895. [4], viii, 196 pp.   *BL*

TRUE BRITON, pseud. Of London.

Ben-Dizzy the bold!: a retrospect, in verse, dedicated to the electors of England; by a true Briton. Newington Butts: B. Buckmaster. [1880]. 16 pp.   *OXB*

Conservative election songs (to well-known tunes): by true Briton. London: Provost & Co. [1880]. 24 pp.   *OXB*

The TRUE HISTORY AND THE INTERESTING LEGEND OF THE WILLOW-PATTERN PLATE, DONE INTO RHYME. Hanley: Allbut & Daniel. 1882. 36 pp. col. il.   *OXB*

TRUE THOMAS YE RHYMER, pseud. Of Rotherham, Yorkshire.

Lays of the Corporation: or, Christmas carols for the Borough of Rotherham; by true Thomas ye rhymer. Printed Rotherham: Albert Crookes. [1880?]. 57 pp.   *★UCD*

TRUMAN, Joseph (1842–19). b. Nottingham, son of Joseph Truman. Educated locally. In 1873 he started business in the lace trade at Carver's Factory; built the Junction Mills at Ilkeston, Derbyshire, 1885; perfected and patented a new machine for producing lace curtains; the firm was also engaged in wood-carving by machine.

Afterthoughts: [poems]; by Joseph Truman. Printed London: Strangeways & Sons. 1888. 40 pp.

Printed for private circulation.   *★UCD*

Afterthoughts: [poems]; by Joseph Truman. London: Macmillan & Co. 1889. viii, 66 pp.   *CU*

TUCK-IT-IN-WELL, pseud. A woman.

A small book of original poems; by Tuck-it-in-well. Printed Oxford: Parker & Co. 1887. 35 pp. *OXB*

TUCKER, Barton Shepherd (1850–91). Son of Rev. John K. Tucker, rector of Pettaugh, Suffolk. Educated at Clifton College, and Corpus Christi College, Cambridge; BA 1877. Ordained 1879; curate, Welborne, Norfolk, 1878–79, St John the Evangelist, Clifton, Bristol, 1879–82, All Saints, Brighton, 1882-83, St John the Evangelist, Edinburgh, 1883–84; chaplain, Royal Navy, serving on several ships, 1884–91.

Framlingham Castle: or, visions of the past, in prose and verse; by B.S. Tucker. Ipswich: Pawsey & Hayes. [c. 1889]. 47 pp. *★UCD*

TUNG CHIA, pseud.

Lays of Cathay and others: a collection of original poems; by "Tung Chia". Illustrations by H.H. Shanghai: Kelly & Walsh, Ltd. 1890. [vi], 85 pp. il. *OXB*

TUNSTALL, Henry Edmund. Lived at Oak Cottage, Stubshaw Cross, Ashton-in-Makerfield, Lancashire.

The apostle of the gentiles, and other poems; [by Henry Edmund Tunstall]. Printed Ince, Wigan: Albert E. Murray. [1898]. 72 pp. por. *OXB*

TUPPER, Margaret Elenora (1840–94). b. Albury, Surrey, youngest daughter of Martin F. Tupper. A prolific writer of verse and prose, she contributed to local papers. She had a genuine talent for painting, and taught at regular classes. Lived with her father at 13 Cintra Road, Upper Norwood, London, until his death in 1889.

Little loving-heart's poem book; by Margaret Elenora Tupper. With forty illustrations. London: Griffith & Farran; New York: E.P. Dutton & Co. 1882. xii, 164 pp. il. *BL*

The scent of heather, and other writings in prose and poetry; by Margaret Elenora Tupper. London: Leadenhall Press Ltd; Simpkin, Marshall, Hamilton, Kent & Co., Ltd; New York: Charles Scribner's Sons. 1895. 215 pp. *OXB*

TUPPER, Martin Farquhar (1810–89). b. Marylebone, London, son of an eminent surgeon. Educated at Charterhouse, and Christ Church, Oxford. Prevented by a stammer from taking holy orders, he was nevertheless called to the Bar, Lincoln's Inn, in 1835 but did not practise. His volume of poems *Proverbial Philosophy* sold a million copies in America alone; he occasionally gave readings from his work to audiences in England and Scotland. An ingenious inventor and novelist. FRS, DCL. Lived at Albury House, near Guildford, Surrey.

Jubilate!: an offering for 1887; from Martin F. Tupper. London: Sampson Low, Marston, Searle, & Rivington. [1887]. 40 pp. *OXB*

A selection from the works of Martin Farquhar Tupper. London: Ward, Lock, & Co. [1886]. [2], viii, 239 pp. (Moxon's miniature poets).

Spine-title is *Poems*. *OXB*

TURBERVILLE, William

Life's quest, [and other poems]; by William Turberville. London: Kegan Paul, Trench, Trübner & Co. Ltd. 1896. 186 pp. *OXB*

The triumph of love: poems; by William Turberville. London: Kegan Paul, Trench, Trübner & Co. Ltd. 1894. viii, 224 pp. *OXB*

TURNER, George Gladstone

Errata: [poems]; by G. Gladstone Turner. London: Longmans, Green, & Co. 1886. vi, 90 pp. *OXB*

Hypermnestra: a Graeco-Egyptian myth; by George Gladstone Turner. London: Longmans, Green, & Co. 1881. [vi], 91 pp. *OXB*

Somnia; [poems]; by G. Gladstone Turner. London: Longmans, Green, & Co. 1887. vi, 94 pp. *OXB*

TURNER, Harold Pilkington (1870–1950). b. Rochdale, Lancashire. Educated at The Leys School, Cambridge, and Owens College, Manchester; LL.B, BA. Chairman of Owens College Union, 1895–96. Practised as a barrister for a time then became a university administrator; secretary to the Senate, Manchester University, 1912–33; one of the secretaries of the University Settlement, Ancoats. Chairman, north-west district of the Workers' Educational Association. Lived latterly at Alderley Edge, Cheshire.

Harp tones and lute notes: poems; by Harold Pilkington Turner. Manchester: J. Brook & Co.; London: Simpkin, Marshall & Co. 1892. 64 pp. *OXB*

Lotos and Asphodel: [poems]; by H. Pilkington Turner. Manchester: J.E. Cornish. 1890. 47 pp.

Printed for private circulation. *MPL*

TURNER, Mary. Née Burrows. Of Tunbridge Wells, Kent.

Sketches of our village, and other rhymes of early and later years; by Mary Turner. Printed Tunbridge Wells: Lewis Hepworth. 1883. x, 127 pp. *BL*

TURNER, Maud E. Kirby- *see* KIRBY-TURNER, Maud E.

TUTTIETT, Mary Gleed, (Maxwell Gray, pseud.) (1847–1923). b. Newport, Isle of Wight, daughter of Frank B. Tuttiett, surgeon. A popular novelist, she published short stories, sketches and essays in various magazines. She was keenly interested in women's rights. At one time lived at 2 Mount Ararat Road, Richmond, Surrey, but latterly settled in Ealing, where she died.

The forest chapel, and other poems; by Maxwell Gray. London: William Heinemann. 1889. viii, 128 pp. *OXB*

Lays of the dragon slayer; by Maxwell Gray. London: Bliss, Sands & Foster. 1894. [iv], 192 pp. *OXB*

Westminster chimes, and other poems; by Maxwell Gray. London: Kegan Paul, Trench, Trübner & Co., Ltd. 1890. xii, 203 pp. *OXB*

TWEDDELL, George Markham (1823–). b. Garden House, Stokesley, Cleveland, Yorkshire. His life was spent at Stokesley apart from a period as master of Bury Industrial and Ragged Schools. Lived at Rose Cottage, Stokesley.

    A hundred Masonic sonnets, illustrative of the principles of the craft, for Freemasons and non-Masons; by George Markham Tweddell. Stokesley, Yorkshire: Author. 1887. viii, 104 pp.   *OXB*

TWISADAY, Florence Mary
    "Only one life", and other poems; by Forence Mary Twisaday. Printed London: Burt & Sons. 1899. 28 pp.   *BL*

TWO BACHELORS, pseud. *see* **CATLING, Harry Debron**, with **PEEL, A.W. Burke**, (Two Bachelors, pseud.)

TWO BROTHERS, pseud.
    Poems of life; by two brothers. Oxford: B.H. Blackwell; London: Methuen & Co. 1891. [viii], 158 pp.   *OXB*

The TWO COLTS. Printed Minehead: Dunn. [1886]. 29 pp. (Legends of the west, no. 1).
    Printed in aid of the Cutcombe Lending Library.   *OXB*

TWO OF THEMSELVES, pseud. *see* **RICHARDSON, James Nicholson**, with **RICHARDSON, Y.**, (Two of Themselves, pseud.)

TWO TRAMPS, pseud. *see* **JONES, James**, with **HODGSON, S.M.**, (Two Tramps, pseud.)

TWO UNDERGRADS, pseud. *see* **CAMPION, Hubert Craigie**, with **OLIVIER, Sydney Haldane**, (Two Undergrads, pseud.)

A TWO YEARS' CHRONICLE: [poems]. London: Hutchinson & Co. 1893. [2], iv, 105 pp.   *OXB*

TYERMAN, Nelson Rich
    A child-fantasy, and other poems; by Nelson Rich Tyerman. London: Elliot Stock. [1885]. viii, 119 pp.   *OXB*

TYLOR, Louis. Dramatist.
    Chess: a Christmas masque: [poems]; by Louis Tylor. London: T. Fisher Unwin. 1888. 112 pp.   *JRL*

TYNAN, Katharine (1861–1931). b. Clondalkin, County Dublin, daughter of a farmer. A Roman Catholic, she was educated at Siena Convent, Drogheda, and began writing at the age of seventeen. In 1883 she married Henry A. Hinkson, a lawyer. They first made their home in London but later moved to County Mayo when he was appointed a resident magistrate. A prolific writer, she was a leading member of the Irish literary revival, and a friend of Yeats, Parnell, the Meynells and the Rossettis. Hinkson died in 1919, and his widow spent the rest of her life in London. Died at Wimbledon.

Ballads and lyrics; by Katharine Tynan. London: Kegan Paul, Trench, Trübner & Co., Ltd. 1891. xiv, 153 pp. *MPL*

Cuckoo songs; by Katharine Tynan Hinkson. London: Elkin Mathews & John Lane; Boston, [Mass.]: Copeland & Day. 1894. x, 108 pp.
A limited ed. of 500 copies printed for England. *OXB*

Louise de la Valliére, and other poems; by Katharine Tynan. London: Kegan Paul, Trench & Co. 1885. viii, 103 pp. *OXB*

A lover's breast-knot: [poems]; by Katharine Tynan (Mrs Hinkson). London: Elkin Mathews. 1896. [x], 51 pp.
A limited ed. of 500 copies. *MPL*

Shamrocks: [poems]; by Katharine Tynan. London: Kegan Paul, Trench & Co. 1887. viii, 198 pp. *OXB*

The wind in the trees: a book of country verses; by Katharine Tynan (Mrs Hinkson). London: Grant Richards. 1898. x, 106 pp. *MPL*

TYNDALL, M.C.
Rhymes, real and romantic; [by] M.C. Tyndall. Bristol: J.W. Arrowsmith; London: Simpkin, Marshall, Hamilton, Kent & Co. Ltd. [1890]. vii, 131 pp. *OXB*

TYRER, Alfred J. Of Wolverhampton, Staffordshire.
Songs & poems; by Alfred J. Tyrer. London: Simpkin, Marshall, Hamilton, Kent & Co. Ltd.; Wolverhampton: W. Charles Lister. [1896]. 94 pp. *OXB*

TYRER, Cuthbert Evans (1851–1902). Son of Evan Tyrer of Southport, Lancashire. Went to Oxford University as a non-collegiate student; BA 1878. Adopted a financial career, starting as a clerk in the Manchester & Salford Bank. His health was never robust, and he resigned from the bank, devoting himself to study and travel abroad. For many years a member of Manchester Literary Club. Died at Rimini, Italy.
Fifty sonnets; by C.E. Tyrer. London: Kegan Paul, Trench & Co. 1888. viii, 51 pp. *MPL*

TYRWHITT, Richard St. John (1827–95). b. London, son of Robert P. Tyrwhitt, barrister. Educated at Christ Church, Oxford; BA 1849, MA 1852. Tutor at Christ Church, 1852–56; rhetoric reader, 1856. Ordained, 1851; vicar, St Mary Magdalen's, Oxford, 1858–72. A skilled water colourist, he exhibited at the Royal Academy. Writer on Christian art.

Battle and after, concerning Sergeant Thomas Atkins, Grenadier Guards, with other verses; by R. St. John Tyrwhitt. London: Macmillan & Co. 1889. xiv, 95 pp.   *OXB*

Free field: lyrics, chiefly descriptive; by R. St. John Tyrwhitt. London: Macmillan & Co. 1888. viii, 114 pp.   *OXB*

TYTLER, Christina Catherine Fraser- *see* **FRASER-TYTLER, Christina Catherine**

U

U., U.
The shadow o'er the earth, & c.: [poems]; by U. U. London: G. Morrish. [1882]. 20 pp.   *OXB*

UNA, pseud. *see* **SUTHERLAND, Jane Dunn**, (Una, pseud.)

UNCLE PETER *see* **SUTHERLAND, Frank**

UNDER THE UMBRELLA: OR, THE GRAND OLD MAN'S [i.e. William Ewart Gladstone's] GARLAND OF ELECTION LYRICS. Edinburgh: E. & G. Goldsmid. 1885. 16 pp.   *OXB*

UNDERDOWN, Emily, (Norley Chester, pseud.). Contributed verse to literary magazines.
Dante vignettes: [poems]; by Norley Chester. London: Elliot Stock. 1895. [61] pp.
    Printed on one side of leaf only.   *OXB*
Songs and sonnets; by Norley Chester. London: Elliot Stock. 1899. viii, 134 pp.   *MPL*

UNPOPULAR PREACHER, pseud.
Mob rule: a satire for the times; by an unpopular preacher. London: William Ridgway. 1888. 16 pp.   *OXB*

The UNUTTERABLES: OR, PSEUDO-MARTYRDOM: A MARVELLOUS MODERN LEGEND. London: Platt & Burdett. 1883. 29 pp.   *OXB*

UPH, T.

Crumbs of verse; by T. Uph. London: James Nisbet & Co. [1884]. 98 pp. *UCD*

UPWARD, Allen (1863–1926). b. Worcester, son of Monmouthshire banker and landowner. Educated at the Royal University of Ireland. For a time was prominent in Irish national affairs. A barrister, he practised in South Wales. He made an unsuccessful bid for a parliamentary seat in 1895. Volunteered to fight in the Greco-Turkish War, 1897. The author of numerous novels.

A day's tragedy: a novel in rhyme; by Allen Upward. Illustrated. London: Chapman & Hall. 1897. 254 pp. il. *OXB*

Songs in Ziklag; by Allen Upward. London: Swan Sonnenschein, Lowrey & Co. 1888. [vi], 170 pp. *OXB*

URQUHART, Sir James (1864–1930). b. Dundee, son of William Urquhart, solicitor. Educated at Dundee High School, Palmer's School, Essex, and Edinburgh University; DL. Apprenticed to a firm of writers to the signet in Edinburgh, qualifying as a solicitor. Clerk, Dundee Educational Trust. Received hon. LL.D from St Andrew University. Of 148 Nethergate, Dundee.

Mary, and other poems; by James Urquhart. Printed Dundee: John Leng & Co. 1883. 200 pp. *BL*

USHER, John (1809–96). Son of John Usher, laird of Toftfield. The property was sold to the Abbotsford estate, and the family moved to Weirbank, near Montrose, Forfarshire. Educated at Melrose Academy, and Edinburgh University. In 1824 the family moved to East Lothian, and in 1835 he began the tenancy of Stodrig, a farm on the Duke of Roxburgh's estate, Kelso. Secretary to the Border Union Agricultural Society, he was a contributor to agricultural and sporting journals.

Poems and songs; by John Usher. Kelso: J. & J.H. Rutherfurd. 1894. viii, 118 pp. por. *OXB*

V

V., B. *see* **THOMSON, James**, (B.V.)

V., E.R.

With Him for ever, and other poems; by E.R.V. 2nd ed. London: James Nisbet & Co. 1890. xii, 209 pp. *OXB*

V., K.E.
The circle of saints: hymns and verses for the holy-days of the English calendar; by K.E.V. With a preface by T.B. Dover. London: Swan Sonnenschein, Lowrey & Co. 1886. viii, 264 pp.   *OXB*
The circle of seasons: hymns and verses for the seasons of the Church; by K.E.V. With an introduction by T.B. Dover. London: Elliot Stock. 1889. [vi], 178 pp.   *OXB*

VAE VICTIS, pseud.
The age of lead: a twenty years' retrospect, in three fyttes; by Vae Victis. 2nd ed. Edinburgh: David Douglas. 1885. [iv], 93 pp.   *OXB*

VAGRANT, pseud.
Companion pictures: or, the political see-saw; [by Vagrant]. London: David Bogue. 1883. [31] pp. il. (by the author).
    Printed on one side of leaf only.   *OXB*

VAGRANT VIATOR, pseud. *see* **NEWTON, Thomas**, (Vagrant Viator, pseud.)

VAGRANT, Noel
Darkness and light: a poem; by Noel Vandal. London: Swan Sonnenschein, Lowrey & Co. 1888. 31 pp.   *OXB*

VANGUARD, pseud. *see* **WOOD, Thomas Winter**, (Vanguard, pseud.)

VAN STRAALAN, Robert, (Lucretius Keen, pseud.)
Romance and rhyme; by Lucretius Keen. Printed Stoke Newington: Thompson. [1897]. 46 pp. il.
    Title from cover.   *BL*

The VEIL THAT NO ONE LIFTS: [poems]. London: T. Fisher Unwin. 1892. 61 pp.   *OXB*

VEITCH, John (1829–94). b. Peebles, son of a soldier. Educated locally, and at Edinburgh University, where he studied theology. Acted as assistant to Sir William Hamilton, then to Professor Fraser, 1855–60. Professor of logic, metaphysics and rhetoric at St Andrews University, 1860–64; professor of logic, Glasgow University, 1864–94. A prolific and accomplished writer.
Merlin, and other poems; by John Veitch. Edinburgh: William Blackwood & Sons. 1889. vi, 192 pp.   *OXB*

VEITCH, Russell
Willow leaves: a wreath of memories: [poems]; written by Russell Veitch. London: Unicorn Press. 1898. 59 pp. (Unicorn books of verse, 3).   *OXB*

VELEY, Margaret (1843–87). b. Braintree, Essex, daughter of Augustus C. Veley of Swiss descent, who practised as a solicitor in the town. Educated at home by governesses but spent one term at Queen's College, Tufnell Park, becoming a good French scholar. Her stories and verse were published in *Blackwood's Magazine* and other journals. She moved to London in 1880, living at 45 Matheson Road, Kensington. Family bereavements greatly affected her later writing.

A marriage of shadows, and other poems; by Margaret Veley. With biographical preface by Leslie Stephen. London: Smith, Elder, & Co. 1888. xxvi, 149 pp.
    Cover-title is *Poems*. *MPL*

VERBOS, pseud. *see* **NEWTON, Thomas**, (Verbos, pseud.)

VERBOSPEREGRINUBIQUITOS, pseud. *see* **NEWTON, Thomas**, (Verbosperegrinubiquitos, pseud.)

VERE, Aubrey De *see* **DE VERE, Aubrey**

VEREY, Joseph
    Poems, grave and gay; by Joseph Verey. London: Tinsley Bros. 1880 [iv], 152 pp. *OXB*

VERNEY-CAVE, Alfred, Lord Braye (1849–1928). b. Mayfair, London, son of Henrietta, Baroness Braye, and Edgell Wyatt-Edgell of Milton Place, Surrey. Educated at Eton College, and Christ Church, Oxford. He succeeded his mother to the title in 1879, assuming the surnames Verney-Cave by royal licence. A convert to Roman Catholicism, he took a deep interest in Catholic affairs. Served as Lieutenant-Colonel, 3rd Batallion, Leicestershire Regiment, 1897–1904; served in Boer War.

Poems; by Alfred, Lord Braye. Edited, with a preface on the latest school of English poetry by F.A. Paley. London: George Bell & Sons. 1881. xxxii, 184 pp. *OXB*

Poems: a selection from the works of Lord Braye. New ed. with an advertisement. London: Robert Washbourne. [1888?]. 184 pp. *OXB*

VERSES. Printed London: J.A. Squire. [189–]. 58 pp. ★*UCD*

VIALLS, Mary Alice. Daughter of Frederick J. Vialls, a master at Merchant Taylors' School. As 'Alicia' in *The Daily News* she conducted the women's columns and other departments for several years; contributed to many other periodicals. Published translations from Dante, Heine, Victor Hugo, and François Coppée. Lived at Parliament Hill Mansions, Highgate Road, London NW.

Music fancies, and other verses; by Mary Alice Vialls. Westminster: Archibald Constable & Co. 1899. viii, 128 pp. *BL*

VICTORY, Louis, H. Irish journalist, and author of several books; a frequent contributor to *Weekly Irish Times*. He went to live in New Zealand.
Collected verses; by Louis H. Victory. Dublin: Vincent O'Brien. 1893. 64 pp.   *OXB*
Poems; by Louis H. Victory. London: Elliot Stock. 1895. viii, 70 pp.   *OXB*

VIKING, Erl, pseud.
Songs of the cascades; by Erl Viking. London: Horace Cox. 1894. xiv, 192 pp.   *BL*

VILES, Arthur Ernest
Drops in life's ocean: original verses; by Arthur Ernest Viles. London: Houlston & Sons. 1888. 64 pp. por.   *OXB*

VILLAGE PEASANT, pseud.
Poetry, the press and the pulpit; by a village peasant. London: Digby, Long & Co. [1894]. [iv], 66 pp.   *OXB*

VINCENT, Claud. Educated at Yeovil, Somerset, in union with the College of Perceptors, at Harlow, Essex, and at Swindon High School. Entered Warminster Theological College.
First poems; by Claud Vincent. London: T. Mills & Co.; Bideford: Thomas Tedrake. 1882. 52 pp.   *OXB*

VINCENT, George. Lived at 31 East Street, Taunton, Somerset.
The Messiah: a poem; by George Vincent. Taunton: Author. 1890. 2 vols.   *TAU*
Songs of a patriot; by George Vincent. Taunton: Author. 1897. [iv], 192 pp.   *TAU*

VINSON, Edward, (Quex, pseud.) (1860–19   ). b. Bexley, Kent, son of William Vinson, JP. Educated at Ramsgate. Owned land and farms in Kent and elsewhere. Member of Bexley Local Board, 1887–98. Treasurer of Dartford Liberal Association, 1903–09.
My friend: a sonnet-sequence; by Quex. London: T. Fisher Unwin. 1894. [102] pp.   *OXB*

VIOLET, pseud. *see* **GORDON, Mrs D.H.**, (Violet, pseud.)

VOX, pseud. *see* **PARSLOE, Edmund**, (Vox, pseud.)

VULCAN, Lionel, pseud. *see* **EMSLEY, William**, (Lionel Vulcan, pseud.)

VYNE, Elvin

Gather'd fragments: poems; by Elwin Vyne. Printed London: Dryden Press. 1891. [iv], 48 pp. *BL*

Gather'd fragments: poems; by Elwin Vyne. New ed. with additions. London: Bertram Dobell. 1897. viii, 143 pp. *OXB*

Leila: or, the signet ring: a poem; by Elwin Vyne. London: J. & E. Bumpus. 1899. 16 pp. *OXB*

VYSE, Maud. Short story writer.

The poetic year, and other poems; by Maud Vyse. London: H.R. Allenson. 1896. viii, 68 pp. *BL*

W., A. A woman, probably connected with Cambridge University.

The king of the silver city, and other poems; by A.W. London: Women's Printing Society Ltd. [1882]. [viii], 88 pp. *UCD*

W., A. *see* **WHITCOMBE, A.**, (A.W.)

W., A.G. Of Malvern, Worcestershire.

Trifles in verse; [by] A.G.W. Malvern: [Author?]. 1889. [35] pp.
Privately printed. Author's MS. note in OXB copy states 'Six copies only of this edition have been printed. This is no. 4'. *OXB*

W., C.E. *see* **WOODS, Charlotte Elizabeth**, (C.E.W.)

W., E. *see* **WEATHERHEAD, Emma**, (E.W.)

W., C.R.W.

Tel-El-Kebir: poem, etc.; by C.R.W.W. London: Religious Book Society. 1883. 64 pp. *UCD*

W., E.A. *see* **WALKER, Eliza Ann**, (E.A.W.)

W., E.D. *see* **WEST, Elizabeth Dickinson**, (E.D.W.)

W., E.L. *see* **WILBY, E.L.**, (E.L.W.)

W., F. *see* **WILSON, Francis**, (F.W.)

W., F. *see* **WOODHOUSE, F.**, (F.W.)

W., F.H.
Passing thoughts for passing hours: [poems]; by F.H.W. London: [London Literary Society]. [1885]. [vi], 79 pp.   *OXB*

W., G.
A case of olden time discipline: [poems]; [by G.W.]. Printed [Aberdeen]: Aberdeen Journal Office. [1899]. 21 pp.
    For private circulation only.   *OXB*

W., H.
Lyrical and other verse; by H.W. London: Upfield Green & Co. 1899. [iv], [79] pp.
    Printed on one side of leaf only.   *OXB*

W., J. *see* **WAKEFIELD, John**, (J.W.), (Rural Pastor, pseud.)

W., J.F.T.
This is the tree that Ben raised: a political satire (illustrated); dedicated (without permission) to "The G.O.M."; by J.F.T.W. London: Simpkin, Marshall & Co.; Chelmsford: "Essex Weekly News" Office. [1883]. [32] pp. il.   *OXB*

W., J.R.
A book of verse; by J.R.W. London: Kegan Paul, Trench & Co. 1888. vi, 92 pp.   *OXB*

W., L. Of St Dominic's Convent, Stone, Staffordshire.
Poems from the secret doctrine, also some tussocks and twitterings; by L.W. Printed Rome: Forzani & Co. [1897]. 79 pp.   *BL*
Songs in the night; [by L.W.]. London: G. Morrish. [1886]. 16 pp.
    Title from cover.   *OXB*
Songs in the night, and other poems; by [L.W.]. 2nd ed. London: Burns & Oates, Ltd; New York: Catholic Publication Society Co. 1887. x, 211 pp.   *OXB*
"Sweet spices": poems; by L.W. London: The Depot. [1889]. 31 pp.
    Title from cover.   *OXB*

W., M. *see* **WYKEHAM, Marie**, (M.W.)

W., M.E.
A few stray thoughts: [poems]; by M.E.W. London: William Poole. [1881]. 23 pp.   *OXB*

W., M.H.

Protestant rhymes: or, gleanings from English history, in verse, with an appendix; by M.H.W. Oxford: J. Pembrey. 1883. 40 pp. *OXB*

Rhymes for youthful historians, designed to assist the memory in retaining the principal events in the history of England, and the most important dates in ancient history; [by M.H.W.]. New ed., brought down to the present time, with additional notes, and thirty-seven portraits of sovereigns. London: Allman & Son. [c. 1890]. viii, 72 pp. il. *OXB*

W., N.

An altered part, [and other poems]; [by N.W.]. London: Digby, Long & Co. [1891]. 63 pp. *OXB*

W., R.S. *see* **WATSON, Robert Spence**, (R.S.W.)

W., T.A., (Bible Student, pseud.)

"From faith to faith": meditations in sonnet verse on the scripture biographies of Abraham, Isaac, and Jacob; by a Bible student [T.A.W.]. Oxford: Parker & Co. 1882. 48 pp.

Cover-title is *Sonnets on the scripture biographies of Abraham Issac and Jacob*. *BL*

W., W. *see* **WHITE, Walter**, (W.W.)

W., W. *see* **WHITTINGHAM, William**, (W.W.)

WADDIE, Charles (1836–   ). b. Edinburgh, of Forfarshire parents. Educated at private school. Author of several successful plays.

The pessimist, and other poems; by Charles Waddie. Edinburgh: Waddie & Co. Ltd. 1896. 51 pp. *UCD*

Raymond and Laura: tragedy; The heir of Linn: tragi-comedy, and other poems; by Charles Waddie. Edinburgh: Waddie & Co. Ltd. 1898. [ii], 190 pp.

Spine-title is *Dramas*. *OXB*

Scotia's darling seat: a home rule sermon, and other poems; by Charles Waddie. Edinburgh: Waddie & Co. 1890. 44 pp. *OXB*

WADDIE, James Sinclair. Of Edinburgh.

The ballad of fair Margaret, and other poems; by James Sinclair Waddie. Edinburgh: Waddie & Co. Ltd. 1899. [iv], 41 pp.

Cover-title is *Fair Margaret*. *UCD*

WADDIE, John. Dramatist.

Divine philosophy: a poem; by John Waddie. London: Kegan Paul, Trench & Co. 1889. vi, 192 pp. *MPL*

WADDINGTON, Samuel (1844–   ). Son of Thomas Waddington of Boston Spa, Yorkshire. Educated at St Peter's School, York, St John's School, Huntingdon, and Brasenose College, Oxford; BA 1865. Originally intending to enter the Church, he was employed at the Board of Trade. Biographer of Arthur Hugh Clough; compiler of several verse anthologies. Lived at 47 Connaught Street, Hyde Park, London W.

Poems; by Samuel Waddington. London: George Bell & Sons. 1896. xii, 124 pp.   OXB

Sonnets, and other verse; by Samuel Waddington. London: George Bell & Sons. 1884. x, 104 pp.   OXB

WADHAM, James. Lived at 4 Heckmondwike Road, Dewsbury, Yorkshire.

Prophetic times fulfilled and prophetic time of the end: [poems]; written by James Wadham. Dewsbury: Author. 1891. 15 pp.   OXB

WAGSTAFF, E.H.

A dream of creation, and other poems and ballads; by E.H. and J.M. Wagstaff. London: Hazell, Watson, & Viney, Ltd. 1899. 112 pp.   OXB

WAGSTAFF, Jeanie Marion

A dream of creation, and other poems and ballads; by E.H. and J.M. Wagstaff. London: Hazell, Watson & Viney, Ltd. 1899. 112 pp.   OXB

WAITE, Arthur Edward (1857–1942). Brought up in Kent. Writer on Freemasonry, magic and mysticism. Lived latterly at 156 High Street, Ramsgate, Kent.

Israfel: Letters; Visions; and, Poems; by Arthur Edward Waite. London: E.W. Allen. 1886. 114 pp.   OXB

WAITHMAN, Helen Maud

Charybdis, and other poems; by H.M. Waithman. London: Eden, Remington & Co. 1891. x, 176 pp.   OXB

Year in year out: a book of the months. Illustrated by Walter Paget. Verses by Helen M. Waithman. London: Ernest Nister; New York: E.P. Dutton & Co. [1890]. [36] pp. il., col. il.   BL

WAKEFIELD, John, (J.W.), (Rural Pastor, pseud.) (1798–1888). b. Uttoxeter, Staffordshire, son of Thomas Wakefield. Educated at St Edmund Hall, Oxford; BA 1824, MA 1828. Ordained 1824; curate, Belper, Derbyshire, 1824–26, St Werburgh's, Derby, 1826–30, Darley Abbey, 1830–37, All Saints, Derby, 1837–39; vicar, Preenchurch, Shropshire, 1852–75; rector, Hughley, Shropshire, 1851–88.

Hymns and spiritual songs: recreations in age and seclusion of a rural pastor (J.W.). Printed Much Wenlock: W. Lawley. [1888]. 2 vols in 1.   BL

WAKEFIELD, Bishop of *see* **HOW, William Walsham**

WALDEMAR OF CAPE TOWN, AND OTHER YARNS OF FACT AND FANCY: [poems]. Liverpool: Lee & Nightingale. 1896. 102 pp. *MPL*

WALFORD, Edward (1823–97). Educated at Balliol College, Oxford (scholar); MA 1847. Ordained 1846. He became a Roman Catholic in 1853 but returned to the Church of England in 1860. A journalist in London, 1858–69. Re-admitted as a minister in 1871. Edited numerous biographical, genealogical and topographical works. Lived latterly at Ventnor, Isle of Wight.
Patient Griselda, and other poems; by Edward Walford. London: Chatto & Windus; Ventnor: Knight's Library. 1894. viii, 178 pp. por. *OXB*

WALKER, Bettina (18 –93). b. Dublin. Although not originally intended for the musical profession, she studied the piano chiefly under Adolphe Henselt, settling in London c. 1890 as an exponent of his teaching method. Died at Fulham.
Songs and sonnets; by Bettina Walker. London: Richard Bentley & Son. 1893. viii, 100 pp. por. *TCD*

WALKER, Eliza Ann, (E.A.W.). Miscellaneous writer.
Hymns and thoughts in verse; by E.A.W. Series I and II. London: William Hunt & Co. 1887. xvi, 168 pp. *OXB*

WALKER, James. Of Newsome Cross, Huddersfield, Yorkshire.
The eternal, and other poems; by James Walker. London: Swan Sonnenschein & Co. 1895. 72 pp. *OXB*

WALKER, James. Of Gaberston, Alloa, Clackmannanshire, and of Carnock, Fife.
Description of a jaunt to Auld Reekie, and other Scotch poems; by James Walker. Printed Glasgow: Bell & Bain. 1882. viii, 296 pp. por.
     Spine-title is *Scotch poems*. *NLS*
The king's realm, and other poems; by James Walker. London: Bemrose & Sons; Carlisle: G. & T. Coward. 1881. viii, 139 pp. *OXB*

WALKER, John (1861–1932). b. Wythburn, Thirlmere, Cumberland. Educated in the village school at St John's-in-the-Vale. He went to work at an early age, moving to Bury, Lancashire, where he held an appointment in a large woollen manufacturing company. A frequent contributor to newspapers and magazines.
Hubert and Emmeline: poems on nature, and other poems; by John Walker. Edinburgh: William Paterson. [1887]. 64 pp. *OXB*

WALKER, Josiah (1805–82). b. Perth, son of Josias Walker, professor humanity, Glasgow University. Educated at Glasgow Grammar School, Glasgow College, and Trinity Hall, Cambridge. Ordained 1837; curate, Folkesworth, Huntingdonshire, vicar, Stetchworth, Cambridgeshire, then vicar, Wood Ditton. He left the Church of England priesthood after receipt of a legacy, moving to London to live the life of a scholar. In 1860 his health began to fail, and he retired to Edinburgh.

Memorial of a country vicar: being selections from the unpublished MSS. of the late J. Walker. Edited by his daughter, Mrs. A. Rogerson. With memoir by E.K. Bennet. [1883]. xi, 112 pp.

Poetry and prose. Printed for private circulation.   *BL*

WALKER, Mary Jane. Daughter of John Deck of Bury St Edmunds, Suffolk, and sister of James G. Deck, hymn writer. In 1848 she married Dr Walker, sometime rector of Cheltenham. She wrote hymns, some of which appeared in leaflet form.

Thomas Drowry, the blind boy of Gloucester, martyr, in 1556; by M.J. Walker. 2nd ed. London: W. Kent & Co.; Cheltenham: W.T. Hardy. 1886. 23 pp.   *OXB*

WALKER, Thomas Andrew (1823–1905). Son of Robert S. Walker of Middlesex. Educated at St John's College, Oxford; BA 1845, MA 1851. Ordained 1847; curate, Chadlington, Oxfordshire, 1846–51, Pitsford, Northamptonshire, 1851–54, Bournemouth, 1854–55; domestic chaplain to Lord De Tabley, Cheshire, 1855–65; curate, Kilham, Yorkshire, 1870–75, Barkingside, Essex, 1875–79, then vicar, 1879–85. Lived latterly at South Park, Ilford, Essex.

The two standards: a meditation in verse, in three parts; by T.A. Walker. London: Skeffington & Son. 1890. 32 pp.   *OXB*

WALKER, William Anderson, (O.S.C.) (1860?–1950). Son of General George Walker of Bath. Educated at Bath College, and King's College, Cambridge; BA 1883. Assistant master, Hurstleigh School, Tunbridge Wells, 1884, Crawley Grange, 1885–86, Bath College, 1888–93; headmaster, Garfield House School, Devon, 1893–1904, Upcott House, Devon, 1905–14, Hamilton House, Bath, 1914–18. Lived latterly at 7 Lansdowne Place, Clifton.

Chimes of song; [poems]; by O.S.C. Bath: Charles Hallett. 1889. [ii], 93 pp.   *BL*

WALLACE, Alexander

The pyramids: a prize poem; by Alexander Wallace. Glasgow: David Robertson; Edinburgh: Oliver & Boyd; Paisley: Murray & Stewart. 1891. 56 pp.   *★UCD*

WALLACE, Cornelia, pseud. *see* **RICKETTS, E.C.**, (Cornelia Wallace, pseud.)

WALLACE, Edgar (1875–1932). b. Greenwich, London, brought up by foster-parents. He left school aged twelve, taking a succession of jobs until he joined the army at eighteen; served as a private soldier in the Royal West Kent Regiment, and in the Royal Army Medical Corps in South Africa. There he contributed to local journals and, on his discharge in 1899, became a correspondent with Reuters, and later with the *Daily Mail*. A prolific writer and best-selling novelist, especially of detective stories.

The mission that failed: a tale of the raid, & other poems; by Edgar Wallace. Cape Town: Cape Times Ltd. [1898]. 52 pp. por. *OXB*

WALLACE, Gerald

A ballad of charity, and other poems; by Gerald Wallace. Edinburgh: David Douglas. 1898. xii, 202 pp. *OXB*

WALLER, Bryan Charles (1853–19). b. Thornton, Lonsdale, Yorkshire, son of Nicholas Waller and nephew of Bryan Waller Procter. Educated at Richmond School, Yorkshire, and Edinburgh University; MD. Lecturer on pathology at the School of Medicine, Edinburgh; later in practice as a consultant. Author of medical papers. Lived at Masongill House, Kirkby Lonsdale.

Perseus with the Hesperides; by Bryan Charles Waller. London: George Bell & Sons. 1893. [iv], 327 pp. *MPL*

WALLER, John Rowell (1854–). b. Cragg Head, a remote place on the Durham moors. Apprenticed to a joiner at Houghton-le-Spring, he began to write for publication at age of sixteen. He regularly contributed to the *Yorkshire Chronicle*, during the day working at his trade at Upsall Castle near Thirsk. In 1876 he moved to Bishop Auckland; in 1881 was in business as an ironmonger at Houghton-le-Spring; later worked for an engineering firm in Sunderland. Lived at Wallsend-on-Tyne, Northumberland.

Rambles and musings: [poems]; by John Rowell Waller. Darlington: William Dresser. 1886. viii, 136 pp. il. *LEP*

Wayside flowers: being, The Battle of Otterburn, and other poems; by John Rowell Waller. Printed Bedlington: George Richardson. 1881. xii, 128 pp. *NPL*

Woodland and shingle: poems and songs; by John Rowell Waller. Darlington: William Dresser. 1883. viii, 128 pp. por. *OXB*

WALPOLE, Maud *see* **HOLLAND, Maud**

WALPOLE, Spencer Horatio (1806–98). Educated at Eton College, and Trinity College, Cambridge; BA 1828. Called to the Bar, Lincoln's Inn, 1831; QC 1846; practised in Rolls Court until 1852. Conservative MP for Midhurst, Sussex, 1846–56, and for Cambridge University, 1856–82; Home Secretary, 1852, 1858–59, 1866; forced to resign because of his mismanagement of meetings in Hyde Park, May 1867.

The saviour of mankind: a poem; by Spencer Horatio Walpole. Printed London: Spottiswoode & Co. 1891. 32 pp.

Printed for private circulation. *BL*

WALTERS, Edmond (1848–   ). Son of Thomas D. Walters of Swanswick, near Bath. Educated at Magdalen College, Oxford; BA 1871, MA 1874. Student, Lincoln's Inn, 1869. Ordained 1873; curate, Somerleyton, Suffolk, 1873–76; rector, March Baldon, Oxfordshire, 1876–85; vicar, Langford, 1885–92. Lived latterly at San Luis Rey, California.

Martin Luther: a poem; by Edmond Walters. London: Alexander & Shepheard. 1884. iv, 187 pp.   *OXB*

The Pearl of Anjou, and other poems; by Edmond Walters. London: Alexander & Shepheard. 1884. iv, 187 pp.   *OXB*

WALTERS, John Cuming, (Cap and Bells, pseud.) (18   –1933). b. Birmingham, son of John Walters of Swansea. Educated at King Edward's School, Birmingham. Journalist and miscellaneous writer, he was sub-editor, *Birmingham Daily Gazette*, and for ten years assistant editor and leader-writer; editor, *Manchester City News* for twenty-five years. President, Manchester Literary Club; president, Dickens Fellowship, 1910–11. Lived latterly at Sledmere, Egerton Road, Chorlton-cum-Hardy, Manchester.

In folly land, and other jingles; by Cap and Bells. London: William Andrews & Co. 1897. viii, 103 pp.   *MPL*

WALTERS, Sophia Lydia

Lostara: a poem; by Sophia Lydia Walters. London: Elliot Stock. 1890. [viii], 167 pp.   *BL*

WALTON, Elisha. Commercial traveller.

Ballads and miscellaneous verses; by Elisha Walton. Author's ed. Hanley: Allbut & Daniel. 1898. [x], 134 pp. por.   *BL*

WALTON, Ellis, pseud. *see* **COTTON, Mrs F. Percy**, (Ellis Walton, pseud.)

WALTON, Horace. Of Ventnor, Isle of Wight?

Echoes from youthland: [poems]; by Horace Walton. London: Marshall, Russell & Co., Ltd; Ventnor: W.J. Knight. [1896]. viii, 83 pp.   *OXB*

WANDERER, pseud.

All the earth round: a nautical poem, in six cantos; by a wanderer. London: Elliot Stock. 1892. x, 270 pp.   *OXB*

WANDERER, pseud. *see* **PARKES, Sir Henry**, (Wanderer, pseud.)

WANLOCK, Rob, pseud. *see* **REID, Robert**, (Rob Wanlock, pseud.)

WARBURTON, Rowland Eyes Egerton- *see* **EGERTON-WARBUR-TON, Rowland Eyes**

WARD, Bernard Rowland, (Kentish Rag, pseud.) (1863-19   ). b. Winchester, son of Bernard E. Ward. Educated at Winchester College, and Balliol College, Oxford. Entered the Royal Engineers as lieutenant, 1882; captain in the military works department, India, stationed at Ootacamund in 1893; instructor, Royal Military Academy, Woolwich, 1900–03; district officer, harbour defences, Halifax, Nova Scotia; colonel, 1909.

Regimental rhymes, and other verses; by Kentish rag. London: Gale & Polden, Ltd. [1893]. [xii], 75 pp.   *UCD*

Regimental rhymes, and other verses; by Kentish rag. Calcutta: Thacker, Spink & Co. 1893. [xii], 75 pp.   *BL*

WARD, Frederick William Orde, (Frederick Harald Williams, pseud.) (1843–1922). b. Blendworth, Hampshire, son of Edward L. Ward. Educated at Tonbridge School, and Wadham College, Oxford; BA 1865. Vicar, Pishill, 1883–88; rector, Nuffield, Oxfordshire, 1888–97. Travelled widely in Australia and South Africa. Lived latterly at 4 Milnthorpe Road, Meads, Eastbourne, Sussex.

Confessions of a poet: [poems]; by F. Harald Williams. London: Hutchinson & Co. 1894. xvi, 492 pp. por.   *OXB*

English roses: [poems]; by F. Harald Williams. London: Simpkin, Marshall, Hamilton, Kent & Co., Ltd. 1899. 598 pp. por   *UCD*

Matin bells; and, Scarlet and gold: [poems]; by F. Harald Williams. 2nd ed. Westminster: Roxburghe Press. 1897. 550 pp. por.   *OXB*

'Twixt kiss and lip: or, under the sword: [poems]; by [Frederick William Orde Ward]. 3rd ed. London: Gardner & Co. 1890. [10], xiv, 826 pp. por.   *OXB*

Women must weep, [and other poems]; by F. Harald Williams. London: Swan Sonnenschein, Lowrey & Co. 1888. viii, 196 pp.   *OXB*

Also 3rd ed. 1888

WARD, James (1851–1927). b. Nottingham, son of James Ward. Educated at Cleveland House Academy, Nottingham. Book collector and bibliophile, an elected member of the Bibliographical Society, 1898. He published works on parish registers and local MSS. Personal member of the Baptist Union of Great Britain & Ireland. Freeman of Nottingham, 1888.

Poems & elegies; by James Ward. Printed London: Alabaster, Passmore & Sons. 1883. [iv], 108 pp. por.

Printed for the author.   *BL*

WARDE, Walter Eldred. Writer on human anatomy, and on the militia. Of Bath, Somerset.

Lines grave and gay: [poems]; by W. Eldred Warde. London: Field & Tuer; Simpkin, Marshall & Co.; Hamilton, Adams & Co.; New York: Scribner & Welford. [1885]. [viii], 95 pp.   *OXB*

WARDEN, Francis Heywood (1850?–84). b. and brought up in England. Of independent means, he spent his early manhood in Mexico and North America, later on the continent of Europe. He died in his thirty-fourth year.
   The poems of Francis Heywood Warden. With a notice by Dr Vanroth. Edinburgh: William Blackwood & Sons. 1885. vi, 155 pp.   OXB

WARDROP, Alexander (1850–   ). b. Whitburn, Linlithgowshire, son of a weaver. He became a tailor by trade, working in his own business at West Calder, Midlothian. Went to America to make a new start but returned home after a few months, settling in Coatbridge, Lanarkshire.
   Johnnie Mathison's courtship and marriage; with, Poems and songs; by Alex Wardrop. Printed Coatbridge: Alex. Pettigrew. 1881. 135 pp.   OXB
   Mid-Cauther Fair: a dramatic pastoral, with other poems, songs, and prose sketches; by Alexander Wardrop. Glasgow: Aird & Coghill. [1887]. 279 pp.   BL

WARING, Anna Laetitia (1823–1910). b. Neath, Glamorgan, daughter of Elijah and Deborah Waring, both Quakers. A hymn writer, she resigned membership of the Society of Friends to join the Church of England.
   Hymns and meditations; by A.L. Waring. London: Society for Promoting Christian Knowledge; New York: E. & J.B. Young & Co. [c. 1880]. viii, 200 pp.   BL
   Also many re-issues called new eds to 1896.

WARKWORTH, Lord *see* **LOVAINE, Henry Algernon George, Lord Warkworth**

WARLEIGH, Henry Smith (18 –92). Educated at St. Bees. Chaplain, Parkhurst Prison, Isle of Wight, 1846–61; rector, St Andrew's with St Michael & St Nicholas, Hertford, 1861–67, Ashchurch, Gloucestershire, 1867–79; vicar, Castleton, Derbyshire, from 1879. Lived latterly at Heene, Worthing, Sussex.
   The ages: past, present, and future: a story of marvels in blank verse; by Henry Smith Warleigh. London: Simpkin, Marshall, & Co.; Worthing: Kirshaw. 1889. xx, 329 pp.   OXB

WARLOW, James. Irish novelist
   Faith: its pleasure, trials and victories, and other poems; by James Warlow. London: Longmans, Green, & Co. 1882. [iv], 188 pp. por.   OXB

WARREN, Herbert *see* **WARREN, Sir Thomas Herbert**

WARREN, John Leicester, Lord De Tabley (1835–95). b. Tabley House, Cheshire. Brought up in Italy and Germany. Educated at Eton College, and Christ Church, Oxford. Attached to the British Embassy at Constantinople, 1859–60. Called to the Bar, Lincoln's Inn, 1860, but never practised. Stood as Liberal candidate for Mid-Cheshire in 1868 but was unsuccessful. Served as an officer in the Cheshire Yeomanry. From 1871 he lived in London as a literary recluse in the society of just a few friends. An enthusiastic expert on botany, book-plates, and Greek coins.

Poems dramatic and lyrical; by John Leicester Warren, Lord De Tabley. With illustrations by C.S. Ricketts. London: Elkin Mathews & John Lane at the Sign of The Bodley Head; New York: Macmillan & Co. 1893. xiv, 213 pp. il.

A limited ed. of 600 copies, printed March 1893. *MPL*

Also reprint, April 1893, not a limited ed.

Poems dramatic and lyrical; by Lord De Tabley. Second series. London: John Lane at the Sign of The Bodley Head; New York: Macmillan & Co. 1895. viii, 160 pp.

A limited ed. of 550 copies printed for England. *MPL*

Poems dramatic and lyrical; by John Leicester Warren, Lord De Tabley. With illustrations by C.S. Ricketts. [3rd ed.]. London: John Lane, Bodley Head; New York: Macmillan & Co. 1896. xii, 213 pp. il. *OXB*

WARREN, Herbert *see* **WARREN, Sir Thomas Herbert**

WARREN, Samuel Hazzledine (1873–1958). b. Loughton, Essex. Lived on the edge of Epping Forest during the greater part of his life. Amateur geologist and prehistorian who won an international reputation. His fine collection of fossils is in the British Museum. He held several high offices in learned societies, and received medals from the Geological Society and the Geologists' Association.

Britain to arms!: verses on the Transvaal War, November, 1899; by S. Hazzledine Warren. London: Eden Fisher & Co. 1899. 15 pp. *OXB*

WARREN, Sir Thomas Herbert (1853–1930). b. Bristol, son of A.W. Warren, JP. Educated at Clifton College, and Balliol College, Oxford. Fellow and tutor, Magdalen College, 1877–85. Vice-Chancellor of Oxford University, 1906–10; professor of poetry, 1911–16. Education expert, he contributed to the *Quarterly, Monthly Review, Spectator*, etc.

By Severn sea, & other poems; by Herbert Warren. Printed Oxford: H. Daniel. 1897. [viii], 72 pp.

A limited ed. of 130 numbered copies. *OXB*

By Severn sea, and other poems; by T. Herbert Warren. London: John Murray. 1898. xii, 80 pp. *MPL*

THE WATCH-SONG OF HEABANE THE WITNESS: A POEM BASED ON THE TRADITIONS OF THE EARLY HISTORY OF THE WORLD. London: John Murray. 1897. viii, 164 pp. *OXB*

WATERFALL, Henry. Of Sheffield, Yorkshire.

Rivelin rhymes; by Henry Waterfall. Printed Sheffield: J. Robertshaw. 1880. xiv, 129 pp. il., facsim. *UCD*

WATERHOUSE, Elizabeth (1835–1918). Daughter of John Hodgkin, barrister. In 1860 she married Alfred Waterhouse, eminent architect. They lived in Yattendon Court, Berkshire, the house which he had built. Lady of the manor of Yattendon, patroness of the living, and owner of most of the land in the parish, she promoted Village Industries, producing copper and brass repoussé work done by the villagers.

Verses; by Elizabeth Waterhouse. Newbury: Thomas Hawkins. 1897. [viii], 56 pp.   *UCD*

WATSON, Aaron (1850–1907). b. Fritchley, Derbyshire. Aged twenty-three he became a journalist, training in the provinces. He started the *Newcastle Critic*, which failed, then joined the *Newcastle Weekly Chronicle* as assistant editor until 1880, when he pursued a literary career in London as a freelance reporter. Eventually he returned north to edit the *Shields Gazette*, working among the shipping, mining and manufacturing industries of the Tyne. Lived at Whitley-by-the-Sea.

More waifs and strays: [poems]; by Aaron Watson. Printed Newcastle-on-Tyne: R. Ward & Sons. 1898. [iv], 46 pp.   *UCD*

Waifs and strays: [poems]; by Aaron Watson. Shields. 1886.   *★NUC*

WATSON, David. Minister of St Clement's, Glasgow. Writer on the work of the Church of Scotland.

Discipleship, and other poems; by David Watson. Paisley: Alexander Gardner. 1886. 91 pp.   *OXB*

WATSON, Edmund Henry Lacon (1865–1948). Son of Rev. Henry L. Watson of Sharnford, Leicestershire. Educated at Winchester College, and Caius College, Cambridge; BA 1887, MA 1894. Admitted to Inner Temple, 1886. Assistant master, Park House School, Reading, 1888–90, Blair Lodge School, Scotland, 1890–94. He turned to journalism, a contributor to *Punch* for many years. Employed in postal censorship, 1914–17. Reuters special correspondent on the Italian and French fronts, 1917–19. Lived at Pembroke Road, Kensington, London W.

Verses, suggested and original; by E.H. Lacon Watson. London: A.D. Innes & Co. 1896. viii, 152 pp.   *OXB*

WATSON, Edward John (1846–1929). Son of Dr John Watson of London. Educated at Merchant Taylors' School, and Christ's College, Cambridge (scholar). Called to the Bar, Lincoln's Inn, 1871. Ordained 1874; curate, Frome, Somerset, 1872–75, Christ Church, St Leonards-on-Sea, Sussex. Received into the Roman Catholic Church by Cardinal Newman, 1876. Assistant master, St Edmund's College, Ware, then at Oscott College. Ordained priest, 1879; after curacies in London he returned to St Edmund's, Ware, as parish priest; chaplain, St Charles's, Brentwood, Essex, 1902–13. One of the founders of Westminster Cathedral. Lived latterly at Chelmsford.

Living faith: an ode for St. Edmund's day, 1893, at St. Edmund's College, (Old Hall); by Edward J. Watson. London: Burns & Oates, Ltd. [1893]. [19] pp.   *OXB*

WATSON, George (1846–). Rope-spinner of Dundee. Known as "The Roper Bard".

Love's task: poems and songs; by George Watson, 'The Roper Bard'. Second series. Dundee: James Moffat. 1899. 288 pp. por.   *UCD*

WATSON, Richard (1833–1918). b. Middleton-in-Teesdale, County Durham, son of a miner. At the age of six he was sent to the school run by his father's employers. Aged ten he went to work in the mine of the London Lead Co. After his father died he helped support his mother, two brothers, and six sisters.

Poetical works of Richard Watson. With a brief sketch of the author. Printed Darlington: William Dresser. 1884. xii, 136 pp.
    Cover-title is *Poems & songs of Teesdale*.   *OXB*

WATSON, Robert Spence, (R.S.W.) (1837–1911). Son of Joseph Watson of Gateshead, County Durham. Educated at the Friends' School, York, and St Andrews University. He qualified as a solicitor. President, National Liberal Association, 1890–1902. Secretary, Newcastle-on-Tyne Literary & Philosophical Society, 1862–93. President of the Peace Society.

Wayside gleanings: [poems]; by R.S.W. Printed Newcastle-on-Tyne: J. Forster. 1880. [iv], 124 pp.
    Printed for private circulation.   *NPL*

WATSON, Robert Williams Seton (1879–1951). Son of William L. Watson of Ayton. Educated at Winchester College, and New College, Oxford, also studied in Berlin, Paris and Vienna. Expert on central European and Balkan history and politics. Founder and joint-editor of *New Europe*, 1916–20; joint-editor of *Slavonic Review*; hon. secretary, Serbian Relief Fund, 1914–21. Masaryk professor of Central European history, King's College, London, 1922; the first professor of Czechoslovak studies, Oxford University, 1945–49.

Scotland for ever!, and other poems; by R.W. Seton Watson. Edinburgh: David Douglas. 1898. [x], 63 pp.
    Spine-title is *Poems*.   *OXB*

WATSON, Rosamund Marriott *see* **MARRIOTT WATSON, Rosamund**, (Graham Rosamund Tomson, pseud.)

WATSON, Sir William (1858–1935). b. Burley-in-Wharfedale, Yorkshire, son of a farmer who became a merchant in Liverpool. Brought up in Liverpool, educated at a school in Southport. His poetry soon became popular and was admired by Gladstone. He was constantly inspired by current events, and deplored the weakening of the British Empire. Visited America several times on lecture tours. He was considered for the poet laureateship in 1913. Knighted 1917.

The collected poems of William Watson. London: John Lane. 1898. xiv, 305 pp.   *MPL*

The collected poems of William Watson. London: John Lane. 1899. [2] xvi, 305 pp. por.

A limited large paper ed. of 120 copies, of which 90 are for sale in England and America.   *BL*

Also 3rd ed. and [4th ed.] 1899.

The eloping angel: a caprice; by William Watson, London: Elkin Mathews & John Lane. 1893. [vi], 31 pp.   *MPL*

Epigrams of art, life, and nature: [poems]; by William Watson. Liverpool: Gilbert G. Walmsley. 1884. [iv], [100], 8 pp.   *JRL*

The father of the forest, and other poems; by William Watson. With portrait after a photograph by Frederick Hollyer. London: John Lane; Chicago: Stone & Kimball. 1895. viii, 72 pp. por.   *MPL*

Also 2nd ed. 1895; also a limited ed. of 75 copies, 1895.

The hope of the world, and other poems; by William Watson. London: John Lane The Bodley Head. 1898. [viii], 83 pp.   *MPL*

Also a limited large paper ed. of 125 copies, of which 75 are for sale, 1898; [2nd ed.] 1898; [3rd ed.] 1898.

Lachrymae musarum (October 6th, 1892); by William Watson. Printed London. 1892. 18 pp. il.

A limited ed. of 100 copies printed for private distribution.   *JRL*

Lachrymae musarum, and other poems; by William Watson. London: Macmillan & Co. 1892. viii, 78 pp.   *JRL*

Odes, and other poems; by William Watson. London: John Lane; New York: Macmillan & Co. 1894. xii, 112 pp.   *MPL*

Also 2nd ed. 1894, 3rd & 4th eds 1895.

Poems; by William Watson. London: Macmillan & Co. 1892. x, 148 pp.   *MPL*

The poems of William Watson. New ed. rearranged by the author, with additions. New York: Macmillan. 1893. viii, 238 pp. por.   *★NUC*

The prince's quest, and other poems; by William Watson. London: C. Kegan Paul & Co. 1880. [viii], 152 pp.   *OXB*

The prince's quest, and other poems; by William Watson. London: Elkin Mathews & John Lane. 1892. [xii], 152 pp.

A limited ed. of 265 copies.   *JRL*

The prince's quest, and other poems; by William Watson. London: Elkin Mathews. 1893. [viii], 147 pp.   *MPL*

The prince's quest, and other poems; by William Watson. [3rd ed.]. London: John Lane. 1896. [viii], 146 pp.   *NLP*

The purple east: a series of sonnets on England's desertion of America; by William Watson. With a frontispiece by G. F. Watts. London: John Lane. 1896. 48 pp. il.   *JRL*

Also [2nd ed.] & [3rd ed.] 1896; and a limited large paper ed. of 75 copies 1896.

Shelley's centenary (August 4th, 1892); by William Watson. Printed London 1892. 18 pp. por.

A limited ed. of 25 copies printed for private distribution.   *JRL*

Wordsworth's grave, and other poems; by William Watson. London: T. Fisher Unwin. 1890. 76 pp. il. (Cameo series, 3).   *MPL*

Also 2nd ed. 1891.

The year of shame: [poems]; by William Watson. With an introduction by the Bishop of Hereford. London: John Lane, The Bodley Head. 1897. 75 pp. il. *MPL*

Also [2nd ed.] 1897; also a limited large paper ed. of 75 copies printed for sale in England and America, 1897.

WATSON, William Henry. Writer on the great cities of the western world. Lived in Rome.

The angelic pilgrim: an epical history of the Chaldee Empire; by William Henry Watson. London: George Redway. 1882. viii, 284 pp. *OXB*

WATT, James (1871–   ). b. Edinburgh, son of James Watt. Educated at Dumfries Academy, Edinburgh University, and Balliol College, Oxford (scholar).

The siege of Caerlaverock Castle; by James Watt. Dumfries: J. Anderson & Son; Edinburgh: John Menzies & Co. 1898. 20 pp. *OXB*

WATT, James E. (1839–   ). b. Montrose, Angus, son of a salmon fisher. The family moved several times to find work. Aged nine he was sent to Craigo Bleachfield, Forfarshire, where he worked eleven hours a day. After a spell as a farm lad he was apprenticed to a brass-finisher in Montrose; the work damaged his health so he became a weaver of floor-cloth in a flax-spinning mill.

Poetical sketches of Scottish life and character; by James E. Watt. Printed Dundee: John Leng & Co. 1880. 168 pp. *OXB*

WATT, Walter (1826–   ). b. Edinburgh. He received very little schooling, and aged seven began to serve an apprenticeship in the tobacco trade. Learned the elements of education at evening school. In his spare time he constructed violins, self-taught. Lived latterly at 84 Main Street, Pollockshaws, near Glasgow.

Sketches in prose and poetry; by Walter Watt. Printed Glasgow: Donald Mackay & Co. 1881. xx, 135 pp.

Published by the author. *NLS*

WATTS, John George. Educated at a charity school. He first went to work in a furrier's warehouse, then became a porter at Billingsgate Fish Market, eventually opening his own business there. Lived at 16 York Terrace, Albany Road, and latterly at 8 Brunswick Square, Camberwell, London SE.

A lay of a cannibal island, and other poems, gay and grave; by John George Watts. London: Judd & Co. Ltd. 1887. xii, 118 pp. *OXB*

WATTS, R. D. Of Longton, Staffordshire.

Five pounds reward, and other poems; by R.D. Watts. London: Simpkin, Marshall, Hamilton, Kent & Co., Ltd; Hanley: Allbut & Daniel. 1891. viii, 138 pp. *OXB*

WATTS, Thomas (1845–87) b. Wexford, son of a non-commissioned officer in the Royal Marine Artillery. Apprenticed to tailoring, on becoming a journeyman he visited most of the principal towns in the United Kingdom. Lived at Broomhouse Cottage, Dunse, Berwickshire.

Woodland echoes: [poems]; by Thomas Watts. Kelso: J. & J.H. Rutherford. 1880. x, 191 pp.   *OXB*

WATTS-DUNTON, Theodore (1836–1914). b. St Ives, Cambridgeshire, son of a solicitor. Educated at a local school and at home. He settled in London in 1874, becoming a prominent figure in poetry circles; a leading critic on the *Athenaeum* and the *Examiner*; contributed a treatise on poetry to *Encyclopaedia Britannica*; became an expert on gypsy lore. On intimate terms with Rossetti and his circle. He organized the life and affairs of Swinburne, who lived with him from 1879. Lived in Great James Street, Bloomsbury, 1872–73, and at The Pines, Putney, 1879–1914.

The coming of love, and other poems; by Theodore Watts-Dunton. London: John Lane The Bodley Head. 1898. xiv, 268 pp.   *MPL*

Also 2nd–6th eds 1898–99.

Jubilee greeting at Spithead to the men of greater Britain; by Theodore Watts-Dunton. London: John Lane. 1897. [viii], 32 pp.   *OXB*

WATTS-JONES, Hannah, (British Matron, pseud.). Welsh. Travelled in Italy, Canada, and the United States.

Jackanory: [poems]; by a British Matron. Printed Bolton: Tillotson & Son. [1897?]. 47 pp.   *BL*

WAUGH, Arthur (1866–1943). b. Midsommer Norton, Somerset, son of Dr Alexander Waugh. Educated at Sherborne School, and New College, Oxford; BA 1889. Literary critic and publisher; managing director and publisher, Chapman & Hall Ltd, 1902–30; chairman of the board, 1926.

Gordon in Africa: Newdigate Prize poem, 1888; by Arthur Waugh. Oxford: A. Thomas Shrimpton & Son; London: Simpkin, Marshall, & Co.; Hamilton, Adams, & Co. 1888. 20 pp.   *OXB*

Legends of the wheel: [poems]; by Arthur Waugh. Bristol: J.W. Arrowsmith; London: Simpkin, Marshall, Hamilton, Kent & Co. Ltd. [1898]. 144 pp.   *OXB*

WAUGH, Edwin (1817–90). b. Rochdale, Lancashire, son of a shoemaker. Educated at various local schools, he was apprenticed to a local printer and bookseller; worked as a journeyman in London and elsewhere. In 1874 he left the trade to become assistant secretary to the Lancashire Public Schools Association. One of the most active members of Manchester Literary Club. Contributed to the *Manchester Examiner*. Lived at Kersal Moor, and latterly at New Brighton, Cheshire, in failing health. Granted a civil list pension, 1881.

Factory folk during the cotton famine; by Edwin Waugh. Manchester: John Heywood. 1881. [x], 246 pp. il. (Waugh's complete works, vol. II).

Poetry and prose.   *BL*

Poems and songs; by Edwin Waugh. Manchester: John Heywood. 1883. [2], vi, 243 pp. il. (Waugh's complete works, vol. X).   *MPL*

Poems and songs; by Edwin Waugh. Second series. Liverpool: Gilbert G. Walmsley; Oldham: W.E. Clegg. 1889. viii, 234 pp. il.   *HPL*

Poems and songs; by Edwin Waugh. Edited by George Milner, with a preface and an introductory essay on the dialect of Lancashire considered as a vehicle for poetry. Manchester: John Heywood. [1893] xxxii, 302 pp. il., facsim.   *MPL*

WEALL, Stanley (1862–   ). b. Brixton, Surrey, son of William Weall. Educated at St John's College, Oxford (scholar); BA 1883, MA 1889. Called to the Bar, Inner Temple, 1884.

Babylon bound: a morality, and other poems; by Stanley Weall. London: Elliot Stock. 1886. [xii], 119 pp.   *OXB*

WEATHERHEAD, Emma, (E.W.). Of Hazelwood, Derbyshire?

Leaves from Hazelwood: [poems]; by E.W. Printed London. 1894. [ii], 52 pp. Printed for private circulation.   *BL*

WEATHERLY, Frederic Edward (1848–1929). b. Portishead, Somerset, son of Frederick Weatherly. Educated at Brasenose College, Oxford (scholar). Called to the Bar, Inner Temple, 1887. Published many books for children, and numerous well-known songs, including 'Danny Boy' and 'Roses of Picardy'. Lived latterly at Bathwick Lodge, Bath.

Dresden china, and other songs; by F.E. Weatherly. London: Diprose & Bateman. 1880. [iv], 128 pp.   *OXB*

The good shepherd, [and other poems]; by Fred. E. Weatherly. Illustrated by Alice Reeve. London: Hildesheimer & Faulkner; New York: Geo. C. Whitney. [1888]. [16] pp. il.

Printed on card.   *OXB*

Over the hills away!: poems; by Frederic E. Weatherly. Illustrations by Harriett M. Bennett. London: Hildesheimer & Faulkner; New York: Geo. C. Whitney. [1892]. [56] pp. il., col. il.

Printed on card.   *OXB*

The seven ages of woman: a dramatic and musical sketch, [and other poems]; by Frederic E. Weatherly. Specially composed for and recited by Mrs. Albert Barker. London: Simpkin, Marshall, Hamilton, Kent & Co. Ltd. [1892]. 24 pp.   *OXB*

Songs and echoes; by Frederic E. Weatherly. Illustrated by Emily Barnard. London: Raphael Tuck & Sons. [1893]. [48] pp. il., col. il.

Printed on card.   *OXB*

The star of Bethlehem, [and other poems]; by Frederic E. Weatherly. Illustrated by M. Ellen Edwards. Vignettes by John C. Staples. London: Hildesheimer & Faulkner; New York: Geo. C. Whitney. [1888]. 48 pp. il.   *OXB*

There's many a slip twixt cup and lip, and other proverbs in verse; by Fred. E. Weatherly. With illustrations by W.J. Hodgson. [London]: Hildesheimer & Faulkner. [1885]. 22 pp. il., col. il.   *OXB*

WEBB, Frederick George. Writer on elocution. Lived in Edmonton, Middlesex.

The dash for the colours, and other ballads and sketches for the home and platform; by Frederick George Webb. London: Ward, Lock & Bowden, Ltd. 1895. [viii], 152 pp.

Cover-title is *72 original recitations.   OXB*

WEBB, Godfrey (1833?–   ). Son of Robert S. Webb of Milford, Surrey. Educated at Radley School, and Brasenose College, Oxford; BA 1854.

Random rhymes &c.; by Godfrey Webb. Printed London: F. Chifferiel & Co. 1882. [vi], 68 pp.

Printed for private circulation.   *UCD*

WEBB, William Trego (1847–1934). b. Ipswich, Suffolk, son of Rev. James Webb, Baptist minister. Educated in Ipswich, and at Caius College, Cambridge; BA 1870, MA 1874. Assistant master, La Martiniere College, Calcutta, 1870–75; entered the Indian Educational Service, Bengal, 1875; professor of English literature, Dacca College, 1875–78, Presidency College, Calcutta, 1878–92.

Four children in prose and verse; by W. Trego Webb. London: Macmillan & Co., Ltd. 1896. 63 pp.   *UCD*

Indian lyrics: [poems]; by W. Trego Webb. Calcutta: Thacker, Spink & Co. 1884. xvi, 234 pp.   *UCD*

WEBBER, James B. A working man of Melrose, Roxburghshire, later living at 226 Morrison Street, Edinburgh.

Rambles around the Eildons: [poems]; by James B. Webber. Hawick: Dalgleish & Craw. 1883. viii, 167 pp.   *UCD*

Rambles round the Eildons: [poems]; by James B. Webber. 2nd ed. Printed Hawick: Craw & Edgar. 1895. viii, 186 pp.   *UCD*

WEBSTER, Alphonsus W. Writer on the workhouse Sunday schools.

Fragments of coloured glass: poems and ballads: historical, religious, Australian and miscellaneous; by Alphonsus W. Webster. London: Digby, Long & Co. [1894]. xii, 274 pp.   *OXB*

WEBSTER, Augusta (1837–94). b. Poole, Dorset, daughter of Vice-Admiral George Davies, who held various Coast Guard commands. The family lived for six years in Banff Castle, and she attended school in Banff. In Paris and Geneva she learned French, later studying Greek, Italian and Spanish. In 1863 she married Thomas Webster, law lecturer and Fellow of Trinity College; he later practised as a solicitor in London. Dramatist, essayist and novelist, she was twice elected to the London School Board, representing Chelsea. Some of her essays were reprinted by the Women's Suffrage Society.

A book of rhyme; by Augusta Webster. London: Macmillan & Co. 1881. viii, 146 pp.   *BL*

Mother & daughter: an uncompleted sonnet-sequence; by the late Augusta Webster, to which are added seven (her only other) sonnets. With an introductory note by William Michael Rossetti. London: Macmillan & Co. 1895. 51 pp.   *MPL*

Selections from the verse of Augusta Webster. London: Macmillan & Co. 1893. viii, 212 pp.   *BL*

WEDGE, F.L.W. Of Coventry, Warwickshire?
Chips, sporting and otherwise, in verse and prose; by F.L.W. Wedge. Coventry: W.W. Curtis; London: Hamilton, Adams & Co. [1886]. viii, 196 pp. il.   *BL*

WEEDS FROM A WILD GARDEN: [poems]. London: Elliott Stock. 1891. iv, 127 pp.   *OXB*

WEEKES, Charles (1867–19). Irish. Educated at Trinity College, Dublin, but did not graduate. Associated with Yeats and George William Russell (AE). Close friend and correspondent of Russell, he published Russell's *Homeward Songs by the Way*, 1894, under the name Whaley. Latterly lived in London.
Reflections and refractions: [poems]; [by] Charles Weekes. London: T. Fisher Unwin. 1893. viii, 114 pp.   *OXB*

WELLS, Andrew. Emigrated to Neutral Bay, Sydney, Australia.
Poems; by Andrew Wells. Glasgow: William Hodge & Co. 1899. x, 264 pp.   *OXB*
The riddle of life: a poem; by Andrew Wells. Sydney: Turner & Henderson. 1892. 64 pp.   *BL*

WELLS, Edward Toovey
Bruce's heart, and other poems; by Edward Toovey Wells. London: Digby Long & Co. [1894]. 41 pp.   *OXB*

WELLS, George. Novelist, and writer on Temple Bar, London.
Golden wishes: a book for the autographs of friends and a record of their birthdays; with a thought for each day of the year: [poems]; by George Wells. London: Frederick Warne & Co. 1885. [100] pp. il.
    Interleaved.   *BL*

WELLWOOD, Arthur
Snatches of world-song: [poems]; by Arthur Wellwood. Glasgow: Aird & Coghill; Edinburgh: John Menzies & Co. 1891. 96 pp.   *NLW*

WELLWOOD, J.P. Scottish.
Lays of the Scotch worthies, and other poems; by J.P. Wellwood. Paisley: Alexander Gardner. 1881. [viii], 295 pp.   *OXB*

WELSH, S.E.
Poems and rhymes; by S.E. Welsh. Collected after the writer's death. Printed Uxbridge: Hutchings. 1889. 124 pp.
    Printed for private circulation only.   ★*UCD*

WEMYSS, Rosslyn Erskine, Lord Wester Wemyss (1864–1933). Had a distinguished naval career. Entered the Royal Navy, 1877; served in royal yacht *Osborne*, 1887–89, commander, 1898; 2nd in command *Ophir*, 1901; captain, *Osborne*, 1903–05; commanded *Balmoral Castle*, 1910; rear-admiral, 1911; commanded 12th Cruiser squadron 1914–15; involved in the Dardanelles campaign, 1915; vice-admiral 1916; commander-in-chief, East Indies & Egypt station, 1916–17; deputy sea lord then first sea lord, 1917; admiral of the fleet, 1919. Created baron 1919.

The maid of Norway and other poems; by R. Erskine Wemyss. Printed [London]: Messrs. Hatchard. 1893. [iv], 108 pp.

Privately printed for the author.   *NLS*

WENTWORTH, Philip, pseud. *see* **BALL, Peter**, (Philip Wentworth, pseud.)

WERNER, Alice (1859–1935). English philologist, educated at Cambridge University. She lived in Africa, 1893–96, 1911–13. Professor of Swahili and Bantu, London University, from 1921. Author of books on race, mythology, African languages, also of poems and stories.

A time and times: ballads and lyrics of east and west; by A. Werner. London: T. Fisher Unwin. 1886. viii, 158 pp.   *OXB*

WESLEY, Samuel J. Wesleyan minister. Served as a missionary in Madras, India.

Life and death, viewed from a Christian standpoint: reflections in original verse on Philippians i, 21; by Samuel J. Wesley. Bangalore, Mysore Province: Isaac & Co. [1889]. [iv], 73 pp.   *OXB*

WEST, Elizabeth Dickinson, (E.D.W.). Daughter of Dean West of Dublin. Married Edward Dowden, professor of English literature, Trinity College, Dublin.

Verses; by E.D.W. Dublin: E. Ponsonby. 1883. iv, 47 pp.   *BL*

WEST, York

Edward III, Part I, Mortimer (not for public representation), and other poems, ballads, &c.; by York West. London: Alexander & Shepheard. 1885. iv, 115 pp.   *OXB*

WESTBROOK, Mary Ann. Of Sandown, Isle of Wight.

Songs of the isle, seaside musings, etc., etc.: [poems]; by Mary Ann Westbrook. Sandown: Taylor & Mearman. [1880?]. [vi], 44 pp.   *BL*

WESTCOMBE, Anna Louisa (1821–96). b. Alcester, Warwickshire, youngest child of Samuel and Elizabeth Westcombe, who were Quakers. Educated in Worcester, she became a teacher at her sister's school in the town. Manager of a Dorcas Society which provided clothes for the poor; a regular visitor at Worcester Infirmary.

Leaves from the banks of Severn: [poems]; by A.L. Westcombe. London: S.W. Partridge & Co. [1880]. [vi], 148 pp. il.   *OXB*

WESTER WEMYSS, Lord *see* **WEMYSS, Rosslyn Erskine**, Lord Wester Wemyss.

WESTON, Jessie Laidley, (One of the Folk, pseud.) (18 –19). Writer on Arthurian romances and legends, she contributed to *Athenaeum, Folk Lore*, and other periodicals. Member of the Lyceum Club. Lived in Paris.
  Lohengrin fifty years after; by one of the folk. London: David Nutt. 1895. 25 pp. *OXB*
  The rose-tree of Hildesheim, and other poems; by Jessie L. Weston. London: David Nutt. 1896. [vi], 73 pp. *OXB*

WESTWOOD, Thomas (1814–88). Son of Thomas Westwood of Enfield, Middlesex. As a boy he visited the house of Charles Lamb, who fostered his literary tastes. He went to Belgium, becoming secretary and director of the Tournai–Jourbise Railway, 1844. Collected a valuable library of books on angling, which he sold on leaving England; published writings on the bibliography of angling. Died in Brussels.
  Gathered in the gloaming: poems of early and later years; by T. Westwood. Printed London: Chiswick Press. 1885. xii, 348 pp. *MPL*
  In memoriam, Izaak Walton, obiit 15th December, 1683: twelve sonnets and an epilogue; by T. Westwood. [London]: William Satchell. [1884]. [35] pp.
    Printed on one side of leaf only. *MPL*

WHALLEY, H.J.
  Awaking in paradise: a meditation; by H.J. Whalley. London: J Masters & Co. 1893. 15 pp. *OXB*

WHAT OF "FANCY FAIRS?". London: Elliot Stock. [1884]. 15 pp. *OXB*

WHEELER, Frederick
  The Victory, and other poems; by Frederick Wheeler. London: London Literary Society. 1887. [vi], 111 pp. *OXB*

WHIGHAM, William (18 –19). Educated at Trinity College, Dublin; BA 1884, MA 1894. Curate, Donaghendry, County Tyrone, 1881–82, Castleconnor, County Sligo, 1883–84, Lisnaskea, County Fermanagh, 1884–86, Carlingford, County Louth, 1887, Clogher, County Tyrone, 1889–90, Holy Trinity, Blackburn, Lancashire, 1898–99, All Saints, Stibbard, Norfolk, 1899–1900, Newton Poppleford, Devon, 1900–02, St Leonard's, Cleator, 1902–04.
  Poems and hymns; by W. Whigham. Printed Castle Cary: J.H. Roberts. 1896. [22] pp.
    Title from cover. *TAU*

WHISTLER, pseud.
  Memoir of and by "The Whistler". Arbroath: T. Buncle. 1889. [ii], 24 pp. il.
    Poetry and prose. *OXB*

WHITBY, Charles Joseph (1864–19   ). b. Yeovil, Somerset, son of Joseph Whitby. Educated at Oakham School, Emmanuel College, Cambridge, and Guy's Hospital; BA & MB 1888, MD 1892. He held medical appointments successively in Liverpool, Matlock, Limpley Stoke, and Clifton; in general medical practice in Bath from 1903. Contributed to medical and other journals. Lived at 2 The Paragon, Bath.

The love-song of Barbara; by Charles Joseph Whitby. London: Elliot Stock. 1890. vi, 92 pp.   *OXB*

WHITCOMBE, A., (A.W.). Of Cheltenham, Gloucestershire.

Poems; by A.W. Cheltenham. 1887. [79] pp.

Privately printed pieces bound together with a special title-page.   *★NUC*

WHITE, Ida L. Married George White, founder, editor and proprietor of the *Ballymena Observer*. Lived at The Tryst, Lyle Hill.

The three banquets, and prison poems; by Ida White. London: Swan, Sonnenschein, & Co. 1890. [6], x, 198 pp.   *OXB*

WHITE, John Davis (1820?–93). Founder, editor and printer of *The Cashel Gazette*. An enthusiastic antiquary, he took a keen interest in local affairs, Synodsman and diocesan librarian of Cashel. Of St Dominic's Abbey, Cashel.

Rhymes; by John Davis White. Printed Cashel: At the author's press. 1885. [viii], 128 pp.

A limited ed. of 50 copies.   *TCD*

WHITE, Samuel Cliall pseud. *see* **SATCHELL, William**, (Samuel Cliall White, pseud.)

WHITE, Walter, (W.W.) (1811–93). b. Reading, Berkshire, son of John White, upholsterer. He followed his father's trade at Reading, 1825–34 and 1839–42; cabinet-maker in New York, 1834–39; clerk to Joseph Mainzer in London, 1842–44; attendant in library of The Royal Society, then librarian, 1861–84. He contributed many articles to *Chambers's Journal*. Lived at 18 Grove Road, Brixton, London.

The prisoner and his dream: a ballad; [by W.W.]. London: Jarrold & Sons. [1885?]. 32 pp.   *BL*

WHITE, William H. Lived at 12 Dalry Road, Edinburgh.

Tales in verse; by William H. White. Printed Edinburgh: W.H. White. 1882. 36 pp.   *UCD*

WHITEHEAD, Anthony (1804–96?). Of Reagill, Westmorland.

Legends of Westmorland, and other poems, with notes; by Anthony Whitehead. Printed Penrith: R. Scott. 1896. 76 pp.   *BL*

WHITEHOUSE, A.W. Of Wednesbury, Staffordshire.

Poems, grave and gay; by A.W. Whitehouse. Printed Wednesbury: Thomas Southern & Son. 1885. viii, 160 pp.   *UCD*

WHITLEY, William, (Ethywil Milliwa, pseud.). Of Woodstock, Oxfordshire.
A few thoughts in rhyme, dedicated to various characters; by Ethywil Milliwa. [Woodstock]: [Author]. 1887. 33 pp. *OXB*

WHITTAKER, Joseph. Of Wolverhampton, Staffordshire.
In divers tones: poems; by Joseph Whittaker. Wolverhampton: Whitehead Bros; London: Clarion Newspaper Co., Ltd. 1895. 118 pp. *OXB*
Poems; by Joseph Whittaker. Wolverhampton: Arthur Whitehead. 1892. 96 pp. *OXB*

WHITTEN, Henry. Of Wetheral, Carlisle, Cumberland.
The burning of Moscow: a poem; by Henry Whitten. Printed Gloucester: John Bellows. 1883. 24 pp. *BL*

WHITTINGHAM, William, (W.W.). Printer of Surbiton, Surrey.
The south of England: or, a tour into some parts of Devon and Cornwall, in which the Lands End and the Lizard were visited as well as other places . . . extracted from a diary that was kept at the time, and at length rendered into verse; by W.W. Surbiton: Author. 1884. xii, 359 pp.
Printed by the author. Cover-title is *Devon and Cornwall*. *BL*

WHITWORTH, Laura A. (1851–). b. Manchester, daughter of Rev. Richard Dudding. Her first fifteen years were spent at Bennington Rectory, near Boston, Lincolnshire, where her father was curate. Educated at St Mary's Hall, Brighton. In 1875 she married Edwin Whitworth, inventor and engineer. They lived successively in Manchester, Ripon, Sleaford and Nottingham.
Glimpses "beyond the veil": poems spiritual, and songs earthly; by Laura A. Whitworth. London: W.H. Beer & Co. 1884. 95 pp. *OXB*

WIGLESWORTH, Esther. Of Torquay, Devon. She was engaged in Church penitentiary work.
Songs of perseverance: a manual of devotional verse; by Esther Wiglesworth. With a preface by John Ellerton. London: James Nisbet & Co. 1885. 94 pp. *OXB*

WIGRAM, William Knox (1825–85). Son of Octavius Wigram of Dulwich, Surrey. Educated at Trinity College, Cambridge; BA 1847, MA 1850. Called to the Bar, Lincoln's Inn, 1852. A successful barrister, he was the author of legal texts. A governor of Christ's Hospital. Lived at The Chestnuts, Twickenham, Middlesex.
Twelve wonderful tales: [poems]; by W. Knox Wigram. New and revised ed. London: Richard Bentley & Son. 1883. viii, 229 pp. *OXB*

WIGSTON, William Francis C. Served in the 60th Rifles. Dramatist, and writer on Shakespeare and Francis Bacon.
Poems; by W.F.C. Wigston. Printed London: S. & J. Brawn. 1885. v, 81 pp.
Privately printed. *OXB*

WILBRAHAM, Frances M. Miscellaneous writer, and translator from the German.

Hal, the barge boy: a sketch from life; by Frances M. Wilbraham. London: Society for Promoting Christian Knowledge. [1883]. 74 pp. il.   *OXB*

WILBY, E.L., (E.L.W.). Of Leicester.

Meditations on nature's teaching, and other poems; by E.L.W. Printed Leicester: Geo. Gibbons & Co. [1896]. 66 pp.

Cover-title is *Nature's teaching*.   *OXB*

One head, one book; [by E.L.W.]. London: A.L. MacDermott. [1897]. [ii], 20 pp.   *BL*

WILDE, Oscar, (C.3.3. pseud.) (1854–1900). b. Dublin, son of Sir William Wilde, eminent surgeon and antiquary. Educated at Portora Royal School, Trinity College, Dublin, and Magdalen College, Oxford; Newdigate prize-winner, 1878. At Oxford he cultivated an aesthetic pose for which he quickly became famous. Travelled in Italy and Greece before settling in London, 1878. Novelist, dramatist, short story writer; his comedies were highly successful, His career was abruptly terminated when he was prosecuted for homosexual practices and sentenced to two years in Reading Gaol, 1895–97. After release he lived in Paris, where he died.

The ballad of Reading Gaol; by C.3.3. London: Leonard Smithers. 1898. [69] pp.

A limited ed. of 800 copies printed on hand-made paper, and 30 copies on Japanese vellum. Printed on one side of leaf only.   *OXB*

Also [2nd]–7th eds, 1898–99.

The ballad of Reading Gaol; by C.3.3. New York: Benj. R. Tucker. 1899. [ii], 44 pp.   *WCM*

Poems; by Oscar Wilde. London: David Bogue. 1881. x, 237 pp.   *MPL*

The sphinx; by Oscar Wilde. With decorations by Charles Ricketts. London: Elkin Mathews & John Lane. 1894. [35] pp. il.

A limited ed. of 200 copies for England.   *OXB*

WILDING, Ernest, pseud. *see* **MOLLOY, Joseph Fitzgerald**, (Ernest Wilding, pseud.)

WILKINS, Adela

Verses for song; by Adela Wilkins. London: Remington & Co. 1890. iv, 31 pp.   *OXB*

WILKINS, William (1852–1915). b. Castle of Zanto, Ionian Islands, son of an army surgeon. His family gave the name Wilkinstown to a village in County Wexford and one in County Westmeath. Educated at Dundalk Grammar School, and Trinity College, Dublin; BA 1878, MA 1880. He was appointed headmaster of Dublin High School, 1879.

Songs of study; by William Wilkins. London: C. Kegan Paul & Co. 1881. xii, 217 pp.   *OXB*

WILKINSON, J.H. Rev. Wilkinson of Falmouth, Cornwall.
"Bible echoes", (in verse); with an essay on 'The ministry of the poets'; by J.H. Wilkinson. [2nd ed.]. Printed Falmouth: Fred H. Earle. 1889. 100 pp.   *NLW*

WILKINSON, Thomas Carlos. Son of Thomas Foreman Wilkinson. Translator from the German. Of South Bank, Ispwich, Suffolk.
The conquest; [by Thomas Foreman Wilkinson]; and other poems by Thomas Carlos Wilkinson. London: William Hunt & Co. 1881. [viii], 184 pp.   *OXB*
The conquest; [by Thomas Foreman Wilkinson]; and other poems by Thomas Carlos Wilkinson. London: Simpkin, Marshall & Co.; Ipswich: Pawsey & Hayes. 1882. [viii], 184 pp.   *OXB*

WILKINSON, Thomas Foreman. Father of Thomas Carlos Wilkinson.
The Conquest; [by Thomas Foreman Wilkinson]; and other poems by Thomas Carlos Wilkinson. London: William Hunt & Co. 1881. [viii], 184 pp.   *OXB*
The conquest; [by Thomas Foreman Wilkinson]; and other poems by Thomas Carlos Wilkinson. London: Simpkin, Marshall & Co.; Ispwich: Pawsey & Hayes. 1882. [viii], 184 pp.   *OXB*

WILLETT, George. Of Waterlooville, Hampshire.
Common things treated in an uncommon way; [by George Willett]. Printed Portsmouth: G. Chamberlain's Steam-Printing Works. 1889. [ii], 101 pp.
   Poetry and prose.   *OXB*

WILLETT, Henry. Assembled a collection of pottery and porcelain which he lent to Brighton and other museums. Lived at Arnold House, Brighton, Sussex.
Quaint conceits for fruit-trenchers, after ye olde manere: [poems]; [by Henry Willett]. Brighton: Author. 1885. [31] pp.
   Privately printed. Printed on one side of leaf only.   *OXB*

WILLIAM O' YE WEST, pseud. *see* **FORSYTH, William**, (William o' Ye West, pseud.)

WILLIAMS, Antonia
The sword and the everlasting image, to those who work: [poems]; [by Antonia Williams]. Manchester: Labour Press Society Ltd. [1895?]. 64 pp.   *WCM*

WILLIAMS, Edward (1830?–1905). b. Dudley, Worcestershire. As a young man he went to Australia to search for gold. Connected with Aston, Birmingham, for forty years. Liberal Unionist member of Warwickshire County Council. Lived at Dundonald House, Aston.
De Buckley: or, incidents of Australian life; by Edward Williams. Printed Birmingham: Heathcote. 1887. [4], iii, 102 pp.   *OXB*
The Merlin: tales in verse, about the land and the sea; by Edward Williams. Printed Birmingham: Heathcote. 1888. [iv], 113 pp. il.   *OXB*

WILLIAMS, Frederick Harald, pseud. *see* **WARD, Frederick William Orde**, (Frederick Harald Williams, pseud.)

WILLIAMS, J.W. Lived at 119, Leathwaite Road, Clapham Junction, London SW.

Jubilee on the brain: topical, typical & satirical; by J.W. Williams. Printed London: R.B. Hayward. [1887]. 32 pp.   *BL*

Poems; by J.W. Williams. London: Elliot Stock. 1880. [iv], 64 pp.   *OXB*

WILLIAMS, James, (Briefless Barrister, pseud.) (1851–1911). Son of James Williams of Fir Grove, Lancashire, gentleman. Educated at Liverpool College, and Lincoln College, Oxford. Fellow of Lincoln; All Souls reader in Roman Law. Called to the Bar, Lincoln's Inn, 1875. JP for Flintshire; High Sheriff, 1906–07. Lived at 113 Durham Road, East Finchley, Middlesex, and latterly at Oakenholt Hall, Flintshire. Hon. LL.D, Yale.

Briefless ballads and legal lyrics; by a briefless barrister. London: Stevens & Sons. 1881. 52 pp.   *OXB*

Briefless ballads and legal lyrics; by James Williams. Second series. London: Adam & Charles Black. 1895. 96 pp.   *OXB*

Ethandune, and other poems; by James Williams. London: Adam & Charles Black. 1892. vi, 119 pp.   *UCD*

A lawyer's leisure: [poems]; by James Williams. London: Kegan Paul, Trench & Co. 1887. viii, 128 pp.   *OXB*

Simple stories of London: verses suitable for recitation; by James Williams. Edinburgh: Adam & Charles Black. 1890. [viii], 59 pp.   *OXB*

A story of three years, and other poems; by J. Williams. London: Kegan Paul, Trench & Co. 1883. 101 pp.   *UCD*

Ventures in verse; by James Williams. London: Methuen & Co. 1898. viii, 124 pp.   *OXB*

WILLIAMS, Leonard (1871–   ). b. Swansea, Glamorgan, son of Leonard D. Williams of Bridgend. Educated at Clifton College, and Balliol College, Oxford. Correspondent for *The Times* in Madrid. Published illustrated books on Spain, including the arts and crafts of the country.

Ballads and songs of Spain; by Leonard Williams. London: Digby, Long & Co. [1896]. [vi], 96 pp.   *OXB*

WILLIAMS, Pownall Toker (1850–1911). Son of Joshua Williams, barrister of Finchley, Middlesex. Educated at Eton College, and Balliol College, Oxford; BA 1871, MA 1875. Landscape artist.

Pictoris otia: poems; by Pownall Toker Williams. Printed London: Woodfall & Kinder. 1889. 77 pp.

Printed for the author.   *NLW*

WILLIAMS, Thomas Cyprian (1854–1932). Son of Joshua Williams, barrister. Educated at Eton College, and Trinity College, Cambridge. Called to the Bar, Lincoln's Inn, 1877. Professor of law, University College, London. Writer on the law of land purchase.

Lyrics of Lincoln's Inn, with notes for the benefit of the unlearned; by T. Cyprian Williams. London: Sweet & Maxwell, Ltd. 1896. 60 pp.   *OXB*

WILLIAMS, William Phillpotts. Master and huntsman of Netton Harriers, Wiltshire. Lived at Llangarran, Salisbury.

Plain poems; by W. Phillpotts Williams. Salisbury: Brown & Co.; London: Simpkin, Marshall, Hamilton, Kent & Co., Ltd. 1896. viii, 143 pp.   *OXB*

Poems in pink; by W. Phillpotts Williams. Salisbury: Brown & Co.; London: Simpkin, Marshall, Hamilton, Kent & Co. 1894. viii, 79 pp.   *OXB*

   Also 2nd ed. 1895.

Rhymes in red; by W. Phillpotts Williams. With 31 illustrations by Cuthbert Bradley. Salisbury: Brown & Co.; London: Simpkin, Marshall, Hamilton, Kent & Co. Ltd. 1899. xii, 108 pp. il.   *OXB*

WILLIAMSON, David R. (1855–   ). b. Kirkmaiden, Wigtonshire, son of the minister. Educated at the parish school, then studied divinity at Edinburgh University. He became assistant minister at Dryfesdale, Dumfriesshire, then in 1888 succeeded his father as minister of his native parish. Contributed verse to national and local periodicals. His songs were published in London with great success.

Poems of nature and life; by David R. Williamson. Edinburgh: William Blackwood & Sons. 1888. x, 112 pp.   *MPL*

WILLIAMSON, Effie (1815–82). b. Selkirk, daughter of Robert Milne, a ploughman. After a short educaation she worked at a loom in a mill, then spent several years in service before her marriage. Most of her life was spent in Galashiels, apart from a few years in Ireland. She won several small literary prizes for her verse and prose.

The tangled web: poems and hymns; by Effie Williamson. Edinburgh: Robert Williamson. Galashiels: David Craighead. 1883. viii, 160 pp.   *BL*

WILLIAMSON, Joshua Redfearn, (J. Redfearn Aden, pseud.)

The ballad of a jester, and other poems; by J.R. Williamson. Darwen: J.J. Riley; Manchester: John Heywood. [1891]. [iv], 150 pp. il.   *MPL*

WILLIS, Edward Cooper (1831–1912). b. London, son of Dr Thomas Willis of Leamington, Warwickshire. Educated at Ludlow and Tonbridge Schools, Brighton Proprietary College, and Caius College, Cambridge; MB 1858. Studied at King's College Hospital; MRCS 1852. Practised medicine in Kensington for a time. Called to the Bar, Inner Temple, 1865; on the South-Eastern circuit; QC 1882. Lived at Shooter's Hill Road, Blackheath, London SE.

Tales and legends in verse; by E. Cooper Willis. London: Kegan Paul, Trench & Co. 1888. [vi], 159 pp.   *OXB*

WILLMORE, Edward. Novelist, and general writer.

The soul's departure, and other poems; by Edward Willmore. London: T. Fisher Unwin. 1898. 96 pp. il. (Cameo series).   *OXB*

WILLOUGHBY, Eliza Maria, Lady Middleton. Daughter of Sir A.P. Gordon Cumming. In 1869 she married Digby W.B. Willoughby, who succeeded his father as 9th Baron Middleton in 1877. Lived at Wollaton House, Nottinghamshire, and Settrington House, Birdsall, Yorkshire.

The story of Alastair Bhan Comyn: or, the tragedy of Dunphail: a tale of romance; by the Lady Middleton. Edinburgh: William Blackwood & Sons. 1889. xiv, 276 pp.

Cover-title is *Alastair Bhan Comyn*.   *OXB*

WILLOX, David. A Freemason.

Poems and sketches; by David Willox. Glasgow: Alex. Malcolm & Co. 1898. 319 pp. por.   *OXB*

WILLS, Samuel b. Devon. Schoolmaster of Kingsbridge House, Brace-bridge, Lincoln, later teaching in Brixham, Devon. Founder of the Railway Servants' Orphanage, Derby.

Musings in moorland and marsh: [poems]; by Samuel Wills. Printed Lincoln: Akrill, Ruddock & Keyworth. 1895. [xvi], 446 pp. por.   *OXB*

Also 2nd–4th eds 1895.

WILLS, Samuel Richard. Educated at Trinity College, Dublin; BA 1854, MA 1858. Curate, Birr, King's County, 1855–67; vicar, Kilfenaghty, 1867–72; rector, Rathkeale, 1872, canon of Limerick, and chaplain to Rathkeale Workhouse, County Limerick.

Kilkee: a poem; by S.R. Wills. Limerick: G. M'Kern & Sons; Dublin: William McGee; London: Simpkin, Marshall & Co. 1889. [94] pp. il.   *BL*

Wellington: a day dream of the past; by S.R. Wills. Dublin: George Herbert. 1885. 29 pp.   *OXB*

WILLS, William Gorman (1828–91). b. Dublin, son of Rev. James Wills. Educated at Waterford Grammar School, and Trinity College, Dublin, but left without taking a degree. He studied art at the Royal Irish Academy, had some success as a portrait painter, but is best known as a dramatist to the Lyceum Theatre, where he wrote very successful plays with Sir Henry Irving in leading roles; his popular play *Olivia* featured Ellen Terry in one of her greatest triumphs. He died in Guy's Hospital, London.

Melchior; by W.G. Wills. Printed London: Hutchings & Crowsley, Ltd. 1884. [vi], 196 pp.

For private circulation.   *BL*

Melchior; by W.G. Wills. London: Macmillan & Co. 1885. [vi], 345 pp.   *OXB*

WILMOT, Herbert Charles

"English bards and their reviewer": a satire; by Herbert Charles Wilmot. 2nd ed. Printed Singapore: "Singapore and Straits Printing Office". 1894. [23] pp.

Printed on one side of leaf only.   *BL*

WILSON, A.J., (Faed, pseud.), (Nym, Pseud.). Writer on bicycling and motor cycling.

Duffersville: its cycling chronicles, and other sketches; by "Faed" and "Nym". Dublin: "Irish Cyclist & Athlete"; London: Iliffe & Son; Shrewsbury: F.W. Jervis. 1889. viii, 98 pp.
   Poetry and prose. *OXB*

Riding rhymes: or, every bicycle club its own music hall; and, Faed's comic almanac for 1880; by "Faed". Illustrated. London: Etherington & Co. [1881]. 57 pp. il. *BL*

WILSON, Alexander Stephen. b. Rayne, Aberdeenshire, son of a tenant farmer. Educated at the parish and other schools. Aged fifteen he was apprenticed to a firm of land surveyors; worked in railway engineering in various parts of the country. He assisted Charles Darwin in some experiments. Writer on physics.

The lyric of a hopeless love; by A. Stephen Wilson. London: Walter Scott. 1888. [iv], 408 pp. *OXB*

Songs and poems; by A. Stephen Wilson. Edinburgh: David Douglas. 1884. xii, 336 pp. *OXB*

WILSON, Claude (1860–1937). b. Liverpool, son of Charles Wilson. Educated at private schools in England and Germany, at Owens College, Manchester, Edinburgh and London Universities, and in Vienna; MB, MD, FRCP. Practised medicine in Tunbridge Wells, Kent, from 1887; published numerous papers in *Lancet*; held appointments on several medical bodies.

Sonnets to the Queen, and other poems; by Claude Wilson. London: Remington & Co. 1880. [vi], 193 pp. *OXB*

WILSON, Crawford (1825–90?). b. Mallow, County Cork. Writer of some successful novels and plays, he contributed poems to many English periodicals. A well-known member of the Savage Club and the Whitefriars Club, London.

Pastorals and poems; by Crawford Wilson. London: Kegan Paul, Trench & Co. 1889. viii, 388 pp. *OXB*

WILSON, Daniel (1801–81). b. Pineberry Hill, Halifax, Yorkshire, one of nine children. He was taught to read and write by his father at home. A member of the General Baptist Church at Queenshead, then transferred to Halifax; became a cottage preacher, then a local preacher. He was employed as a periodical bookseller, working all over the West Riding. Eventually owned a retail shop in Halifax.

Justice and mercy: a sacred poem; by Daniel Wilson. With portrait and life of the author. Halifax: John Wilson & Co. 1883. xvi, 103 pp. por. *LEP*

WILSON, David (1864–1933). Son of David Wilson of Glasgow. Educated at Hutcheson's Grammar School, and Glasgow University. Called to the Bar,

1890; worked in the Indian Civil Service, 1883–1912, in Burma, 1886–1911. Writer on Thomas Carlyle. Lived latterly at 16 Beresford Terrace, Ayr.

After-dinner ditties; by David Wilson. Glasgow: Maclaren & Sons. 1891. 64 pp.   *BL*

WILSON, Francis, (F.W.) (1846–19). b. Armitage, Staffordshire, son of Rev. Francis Wilson. Educated at Uppingham School, and Emmanuel College, Cambridge. Took holy orders; assistant master and chaplain, Cheam School, 1868–85; headmaster, Woking School, 1885–94. Lived latterly at The Grange, Woking, Surrey.

Things which must shortly come to pass: Revelation I, 1 in verse; with explanatory notes; by F.W. London: Office of "My Little Friend". [1880]. 31 pp.   *OXB*
Where shall I worship when I am saved?, in verse; by F.W. [London]: London Gospel Tract Depot. [1880]. 20 pp.   *OXB*

WILSON, George Henry (1848–19). b. Brampton, Norfolk, son of Edmund Wilson. Educated at public schools. In 1873 he started business as a mungo and shoddy manufacturer in Ossett, Yorkshire. President of Ossett Liberal Association; alderman of Ossett Borough, mayor, 1894–95. Sometime president of the Chamber of Commerce. Lived at Heath House, Ossett.

Miscellaneous poems; by G.H. Wilson. Ossett: S. Cockburn & Son. 1896. viii, 107 pp.   *LEP*

WILSON, James H. (1853–). b. Newcastle upon Tyne, son of William and Sarah Wilson, Quakers. Left school aged sixteen and entered his father's office. Spent some years in London and elsewhere, travelling for a London firm in Northumberland and the Border towns.

Zalmoxis, and other poems; by James H. Wilson. London: Elliot Stock. 1892. viii, 216 pp.   *OXB*

WILSON, James Spotswood
The devil's trade; by James Spotswood Wilson. Manchester: John Heywood. 1884. 31 pp.
   Poetry and prose.   *MPL*

WILSON, John Of Pontefract, Yorkshire.
Poems; by John Wilson. London: R. Washbourne. 1889. 80 pp.   *OXB*
Pomfret cakes: poems; by John Wilson. London: R. Washbourne. 1886. vi, 73 pp.   *OXB*

WILSON, Lisa (18 –193). An invalid as a girl, she was an aspiring young writer who turned to Christina Rossetti for advice, becoming a firm friend. Their letters were destroyed. She was one of the few attending Rossetti's funeral.

Verses; by Lisa Wilson (Christina Grey). London: Bliss, Sands & Co. 1896. 112 pp.   *BL*

WILSON, Lister. Of Alford, Lincolnshire.
Ocean echoes from the Lincolnshire coast, for old and young: [poems]; by Lister Wilson. London: Digby & Long. 1888. 66 pp. *OXB*

WILSON, Mary Louisa Georgina Carus – *see* **CARUS-WILSON, Mary Louisa Georgina**

WILSON, Robert. Writer on the life and times of Queen Victoria.
Laurel leaves: [poems]; by Robert Wilson. Westminster: Archibald Constable & Co. 1899. 141 pp. *OXB*

WILSON, T. Alderson
Perseus, and other essays in verse; by T. Alderson Wilson. London: Ranken & Co. 1882. iv, 80 pp. *OXB*

WILSON, William (1830–). b. Burntisland, Fife, son of a sailor. He received a limited education, then became an apprentice blacksmith in Edinburgh for seven years. The next seven years were spent as leading engine-smith for the London & North Western Railway Co. in Buckinghamshire; moved to a similar post in Brighton before returning to Edinburgh in 1863 as foreman engine-smith. A powerful worker for reform of the burgh franchise.
Echoes of the anvil: songs and poems; by William Wilson. With portrait, and illustrations by Thomas Wilson. Edinburgh: John Menzies & Co. 1885. 244 pp. il., por. *OXB*
    Also 2nd ed. 1886.

WILTON, Richard (1827–1903). b. Doncaster, Yorkshire. Educated at Doncaster Grammar School, and St Catharine's College, Cambridge; BA 1851, MA 1861. Ordained 1852; curate, Broseley, Shropshire, 1851–54; perpetual curate, St Thomas's, York, and chaplain to the York Union; vicar, Kirkby-Wharfe, 1857–66; rector, Londesborough, East Riding; domestic chaplain to Lord Londesborough. Contributed much prose and verse to magazines.
Benedicite, and other poems; by Richard Wilton. London: Wells Gardner, Darton, & Co. [1889]. xvi, 158 pp. *UCD*
Sungleams: rondeaux and sonnets; by Richard Wilton. London: "Home Words" Publishing Office. [1882]. 118 pp. il. *UCD*

WINDT, Henry De *see* **DE WINDT, Henry**, (H. De W.)

WINGATE, David (1828–92). b. Cowglen, near Glasgow, son of a collier who was killed in a pit explosion. Attended the parish school until the age of nine, when he was sent to work down the mine. He published two vols of verse in the 1860s, the proceeds enabling him to attend Glasgow School of Mines; became a colliery manager, devoting his spare time to study and writing. He was married twice, his second wife being a descendant of Robert Burns.
Poems and songs; by David Wingate. Glasgow: Kerr & Richardson. 1883. [viii], 128 pp. por. *BL*

Select poems and songs; by David Wingate. Glasgow: Kerr & Richardson. 1890. viii, 192 pp. por. *BL*

WINN, Henry. Of Fulletby, Lincolnshire.
Winceby fight, and sketches of the Civil War in Lincolnshire; by Henry Winn. Printed Horncastle: Watson Joll. 1885. 24 pp. *BL*

WINNINGTON-INGRAM, Arthur Henry. Educated at Christ Church, Oxford; BA 1841, MA 1847. Ordained, 1841; curate, Worcester, diocesan inspector of schools; rector, Harvington, Evesham, 1845–87; rural dean, Pershore, 1853; hon. canon of Worcester from 1854.
The brides of Dinan: a tale of the barons' war, in six cantos; by Arthur H. Winnington Ingram. London: George Bell & Sons. 1888. 191 pp. *★UCD*

WINSCOMBE, Cave *see* **WINSCOMBE, John Cave** (Cave Winscombe, pseud.)

WINSCOMBE, John Cave, (Cave Winscombe, pseud.)
"Resurgam", and lyrics; by Cave Winscombe. London: "Home Words" Publishing Office. [1899]. 32 pp. *OXB*
Westminster: past and present: [poems]; by J. Cave Winscombe. London: W.H. Allen. 1887. 64 pp. *OXB*

WINSER, Lilian
Lays and legends of the Weald of Kent; by Lilian Winser. With illustrations by Margaret Winser. London: Elkin Mathews. 1897. [viii], 80 pp.
A limited ed. of 500 copies. *MPL*

WINTER, William Harris. Educated at Trinity College, Dublin, a pupil of Edward Dowden. Ordained 1884; curate, Lavey and Larah, County Cavan, 1882–86; incumbent of Taughnagh, Ballymote, from 1886.
Rienzi, and other poems; by William H. Winter. Dublin: William McGee; London: Simpkin, Marshall, & Co. 1884. [iv], 56 pp. *NLI*

WISE, Thomas James (1859–1937). Clerk and later partner in a London oil firm. He collected a library of works of English poets which formed the Ashley Library, eventually sold to the British Museum. Occupied in publishing bibliographies of major poets, 1893–1931. After his death many of the pamphlets in his collection were found to have been forged.
Verses; by Thomas J. Wise. Printed London: Fullford. 1882. [vi], 29 pp.
Printed for private circulation only. Note in author's hand states 'Of this book 35 copies only were printed. Not for sale'. *BL*
Verses; by Thomas J. Wise. Printed London: Fullford. 1882. [vi], 27 pp.
A limited ed. of 4 copies printed on vellum. *OXB*
Verses; by Thomas J. Wise. Printed London: Fullford. 1883. [vi], 27 pp.
Printed for private circulation only. Note in author's hand states 'Not for sale. A limited ed. of 6 numbered copies printed on rough white paper'. *BL*

WITCOMB, Charles. Writer on the structure of English verse.
Poems; by C. Witcomb. Worthing: Walter Paine. 1891. 111 pp. *★UCD*

WITHERS, Percy (1867–1947). b. Sale, Cheshire, son of John Withers. Educated at Manchester Grammar School, and Owens College, Manchester; MB, BS, MRCS, LRCP. House surgeon, Manchester Royal Infirmary. Lecturer in English literature, Oxford University extension. An executive of the National Trust for thirty-two years. Lived latterly at Epwell Mill, Banbury, Oxfordshire.

Poems; by Percy Withers. Manchester: Geo. Falkner & Sons. 1894. [2], vi, 40 pp. *MPL*

WOLFE, Thomas. Of Brinklow, near Coventry, Warwickshire. Self-styled 'Minstrel, harmonist and poet'.

Lovely spiritual songs of heaven: "Hark! the bells of the beautiful land", &c.; by Thomas Wolfe. Printed Rugby: A. Frost & Sons. [1894]. 15 pp. *OXB*

WOLFSOHN, Edward W.

Varieties in verse: national, social, in memoriam, with letters and notes relating to the incidents treated; by Edward W. Wolfsohn. Bedford: Arthur Ransom; London: Hamilton, Adams, & Co. [1885]. [iv], 80 pp. *OXB*

WOLLASTON, John Thomas Burton. Graduated from Lichfield Theological College, 1868; ordained 1870; curate, Hednesford, Staffordshire, 1870–73; chaplain, Montgomery County Prison, and Forden Union, 1874–81, Shropshire & Montgomeryshire County Asylum, from 1881.

A sinful woman; by J.T. Burton Wollaston. London: James Blackwood & Co. [1881]. 130 pp. il. *OXB*

WOLSTENHOLME-ELMY, Elizabeth, (Ellis Ethelmer, pseud.) (1834–1918). Daughter of a Methodist minister from Eccles, Lancashire, she was orphaned as a child. Educated at the Moravian School, Fulneck, Yorkshire. An ardent feminist, she founded the Manchester Schoolmistresses' Association in 1865; hon. secretary, Manchester Women's Suffrage Society, 1865; hon. secretary, Married Women's Property Committee, 1867–82; formed the Women's Emancipation Union, 1891; founder member, Women's Franchise League, 1899; member of the Women's Social and Political Union.

Woman free; by Ellis Ethelmer. Congleton: Women's Emancipation Union. 1893. [vi], 238 pp.

Poetry and prose. *OXB*

The WONDERFUL STORY OF WISDOM, LOVE AND GRACE DIVINE. [With] fifteen illustrations. London: Elliot Stock. [1892]. 60 pp. il. *OXB*

WOOD, Alfred Hope. Lived at The Hollies, Hastings, Sussex.

Shiloh: a few meditations on the person, work, offices, characters and names of the Lord Jesus Christ, as revealed in the scriptures of divine truth: [poems]; by Alfred H. Wood. Oxford: J.C. Pembrey; London: W. Wileman. 1888. viii, 76 pp. *OXB*

WOOD, Andrew (1834–1917). b. India, son of Andrew Wood. Educated at Blackheath, and Trinity College, Cambridge; BA 1855, MA 1858. Assistant master, Blackheath Proprietory School, 1855 and 1858–62. Ordained 1857; curate, Droxford, Hampshire, 1856–58, Ruddington, Nottinghamshire, 1862–66; vicar, Skillington, Lincolnshire, 1866–82; rector, Great Ponton, 1882–1917; prebendary of Lincoln, 1910–17.

Bethel: being thoughts on Genesis xxviii. 12 and Hosea xii. 4; by Andrew Wood. Printed London: Eyre & Spottiswoode. [1885?]. 16 pp. *BL*

WOOD, Edmund

Poems; by Edmund Wood. London: Kegan Paul, Trench & Co. 1887. viii, 168 pp. *OXB*

WOOD, Helen J. Writer for children.

Lilies round the cross: an Easter memorial: [poems]; by Edith Nesbit and Helen J. Wood. Illustrated by Fred Hines. London: Ernest Nister; New York: E.P. Dutton & Co. [1889]. [20] pp. il. *BL*

WOOD, Hickory *see* **WOOD, Jay Hickory**

WOOD, Jay Hickory (18 –1913). b. Manchester of Scottish parents, and educated there. An apprentice at a home-trade warehouse in the city; later became an insurance secretary. Wrote pantomimes, songs, musical pieces, and a biography of Dan Leno. Lived latterly at Chellow Dene, Purley, Surrey.

Hickory Wood's soliloquies; including, Wild West dramatics: the sequel to, The cricket club of Red Nose Flat. London: Samuel French, Ltd; New York: Samuel French. [1899]. 48 pp.
  Poetry and prose. *OXB*
Recitations: comic and otherwise; by Jay Hickory Wood. London: James Bowdon. 1898. [iv], 116 pp.
  Poetry and prose. *OXB*

WOOD, John William. Worked for H.M. Customs Service, Dovercourt.

Tales and sketches in prose and verse; by J.W. Wood. London: Simpkin, Marshall & Co.; Harwich: E.H. Wood. 1880. [viii], 131 pp. *OXB*
Tales and sketches in prose and verse; by J.W. Wood. London: Elliot Stock. 1888. xii, 177 pp. *OXB*

WOOD, John Wilson (1834–85). b. Cupar-Fife, son of a baker. Aged twelve he was apprenticed to his father, following the trade for four years. Entered a solicitor's office and began to study law. Went to America, staying two years before returning to Cupar-Fife, where he became a grocer and spirit merchant. Served as a town councillor. Lived at 70 Bonnygate.

The gipsy heir, and other poems; by John W. Wood. Printed Cupar-Fife: A. Westwood & Son. 1883. [ii], 152 pp. *BL*

WOOD, Martin Harvey, (Bath Idler, pseud.). Of Bath, Somerset.

Idle hours: [poems]; by a Bath idler. Printed Bath: Bath & Cheltenham Gazette Printing Works. [1881]. xii, 106 pp. *TAU*

WOOD, Sam. Of Barnsley, Yorkshire?
Random rhymes; by Sam Wood. Barnsley: W.R. Massie. 1896. [viii], 60 pp. *BL*

WOOD, Thomas Winter (Vanguard, pseud.). Novelist.
The collected poems of Thomas Winter Wood (Vanguard). London: Simpkin, Marshall, Hamilton, Kent, & Co,; Plymouth: W.F. Westcott. 1893. [4], viii, 336 pp. por.
Spine-title is Poems. *OXB*

WOODALL, S.S.
Ondar the just, [and other poems]; by S.S. Woodall. London: James Nisbet & Co. 1890. viii, 128 pp. *OXB*

WOODBURN, R.H.
The palace of health: a poem; by R.H. Woodburn. Paisley: Alexander Gardner. 1891. 61 pp. *OXB*

WOODHOUSE, Arthur
Poem[s]; by Arthur Woodhouse. London: London Literary Society. [1884]. 64 pp. *OXB*

WOODHOUSE, F., (F.W.)
Poems, fugitive pieces and hymns; by F.W. Printed London: G. Norman & Son. 1884. [ii], 126 pp. *OXB*

WOODHOUSE, Samuel (1810–). b. Flamborough, Yorkshire. He received a liberal education, and in early manhood conducted a school. Surveyor of taxes, 1842–52, afterwards becoming the agent for several large estates in the East Riding. He was elected to Hull Town Council in 1865, becoming an alderman in 1874. FRHS.
The queen of the Humber: or, legends historical, traditional, and imaginary, relating to Kingston-upon-Hull: a poem in ten cantos; by Samuel Woodhouse. London: Henry S. Philips & Co.; Hull: M.C. Peck & Son. 1884. [viii], 224 pp. *UCD*

WOODLAND, O.M. Lived at The Rise, Sunningdale, Berkshire.
Little Dot's song: a tale, and various poems; by O.M. Woodland. Sunningdale: S.W. Longhurst. 1895. 24 pp. *BL*

WOODROW, Thomas John
Reeds shaken with the wind: [poems]; by T.J. Woodrow. London: Woodrow & Co., Ltd. [1893]. 60 pp. *UCD*

WOODRUFF, Cumberland Henry (1847–). Son of Rev. John Woodruff, vicar of Upchurch, Kent. Educated at Winchester College, and Merton College, Oxford; BA 1870, MA 1875. Called to the Bar, Lincoln's Inn, 1875. Appointed keeper of Chancery Masters documents, 1885.

The children's year: verses for the Sundays and holy days throughout the year; by C.H. Woodruff. With an introduction by the Lord Bishop of Southwell. London: Longmans, Green, & Co. 1891. xvi, 214 pp.   *OXB*

WOODS, Charlotte Elizabeth, (C.E.W.)

Gatherings; by C.E.W. London: Leadenhall Press; Simpkin, Marshall, Hamilton, Kent & Co., Ltd; New York: Scribner & Welford. [1890]. iv, 239 pp.

    Poetry and prose.   *CU*

"Have ye read it? Look sharp!"; by Mrs R.W. Woods. London: Leadenhall Press, Ltd; Simpkin, Marshall, Hamilton, Kent & Co., Ltd; New York: Charles Scribner's Sons. 1894. 235 pp.

    Poetry and prose. Published for the authoress.   *BL*

WOODS, Margaret Louisa (1856–1945). b. Rugby, Warwickshire, daughter of Rev. George G. Bradley, Dean of Westminster. Educated at home and at Miss Gawthrop's School, Leamington. In 1879 she married Rev. H.G. Woods, president of Trinity College, Oxford, 1887–97. Lived at Plas Meini, Festiniog, North Wales, and latterly at Vine Cottage, Thursley, Godalming, Surrey.

Aëromancy, and other poems; by Margaret L. Woods. London: Elkin Mathews. 1896. 40 pp. (Shilling garland, IV).   *OXB*

    Also published in the Garland of New Poetry series, 1896.

Lyrics; by Margaret L. Woods. Printed Oxford: H. Daniel, Fellow of Worcester College. 1888. [x], 64 pp.

    A limited ed. of 125 numbered copies.   *BL*

Lyrics & ballads; by Margaret L. Woods. London: Richard Bentley & Son. 1889. viii, 100 pp.   *BL*

Songs; by Margaret L. Woods. Oxford: Daniel. 1896. 30 pp.

    A limited ed. of 200 numbered copies.   *OXB*

WOODWARD, George Ratcliffe (1848–1934). b. Birkenhead, Cheshire, son of George R. Woodward. Educated at Elstree and Harrow Schools, and Caius College, Cambridge (scholar); BA 1872, MA 1876. Ordained 1875; curate, St Barnabas's, Pimlico, London, 1874–82; vicar, Great & Little Walsingham, Norfolk, 1882–88; rector, Chelmondiston, Suffolk, 1888–94; preacher, London diocese, 1899–1903; curate, St Mark's, Marylebone Road, 1903–06. An authority on the history of church music. Lived latterly at 24 Alderney Street, London SW.

Legends of the saints: [poems]; by G.R. Woodward. London: Kegan Paul, Trench, Trübner & Co. Ltd. 1898. viii, 104 pp.   *OXB*

WOOLLAM, Wilfred *see* **WOOLLAM, Wilfred Beet**

WOOLLAM, Wilfred Beet (1856–). Son of Thomas Woollam of Sheffield, Yorkshire. Educated at Wesley College, Sheffield, and Peterhouse, Cambridge; BA 1883, MA 1890, LL.M 1898.

Child Illa, and other poems; by Wilfred Woollam. Sheffield: J. Arthur Bain; London: Simpkin, Marshall, Hamilton, Kent & Co., Ltd. 1898. viii, 343 pp. *UCD*

Gleanings: [poems]; by Wilfred B. Woollam. Cambridge: E.M. Jones. 1881. [iv], 75 pp. *OXB*

WOOLNER, Thomas (1825–92). b. Hadleigh. Pupil of William Behnes, sculptor; studied at the Royal Academy from 1842. Made the acquaintance of Rossetti, and became one of the original Pre-Raphaelite Brethren, 1847; contributed poems to *The Germ*. He went out to the Australian goldfields; practised painting in Melbourne and Sydney before returning to England in 1854. A long series of works in sculpture included statues and portrait-busts of the most eminent men of the day. Royal Academician, 1874.

Poems: Nelly Dale; Children; by Thomas Woolner. London: George Bell & Sons. 1887. 32 pp. *OXB*

Pygmalion; by Thomas Woolner. London: Macmillan & Co. 1881. [viii], 208 pp. *MPL*

Silenus; by Thomas Woolner. London: Macmillan & Co. 1884. [viii], 136 pp. *MPL*

Tiresias; by Thomas Woolner. London: George Bell & Sons. 1886. [viii], 141 pp. *OXB*

WORDSWORTH, Elizabeth (1840–1932). b. Harrow, Middlesex, where her father, Christopher Wordsworth, was headmaster of Harrow School. Grandniece of William Wordsworth. Educated at home. In 1878 she was appointed the first principal of Lady Margaret Hall, the Oxford women's college. She made the college her life's work. In 1886 she founded another women's college, St Hugh's Hall. DBE, hon. MA & DCL.

In doors and out: poems; by E. Wordsworth. London: Hatchards. 1881. x, 131 pp. *BL*

St. Christopher, and other poems; by Elizabeth Wordsworth. London: Longmans, Green, & Co. 1890. viii, 286 pp. *BL*

WORDSWORTH, W. Served in India; CIE.

Gleanings of verse; by W. Wordsworth. Printed London: Bickers & Son. 1899. x, 114 pp.

Printed for private circulation only. *BL*

WORKING MAN, pseud.

The two benchers: or, prosperity versus poverty, and other poems; by a working man. London: E.W. Allen & Co. 1888. 103 pp. *OXB*

WOTT, Sir Scalter, pseud.

The art of Midlothian: or, the lay of the lost minstrel; by Sir Scalter Wott. London: Diprose & Bateman. [c. 1885]. [ii], 27 pp.   *OXB*

WRATISLAW, Theodore (1871–1933). Dramatist, and writer on Swinburne.

Caprices: poems; by Theodore Wratislaw. London: Gay & Bird. 1893. [ix], 49 pp.

A limited ed. of 100 numbered copies. Two poems were suppressed in all but two copies; OXB copy is one of the two copies retaining the leaf, pp. 31 and 32, bearing the poems 'To a Sicilian Boy' and 'L'éternal Féminin'.   *OXB*

Love's memorial: [poems]; [by Theodore Wratislaw]. Printed Rugby: Geo. E. Over. 1892. [viii], 64 pp.

A limited ed. of 35 numbered copies signed by the publisher.   *BL*

Orchids: poems; by Theodore Wratislaw. London: Leonard Smithers. 1896. viii, 56 pp.

A limited ed. of 250 copies on small paper, and 10 copies on Japanese vellum.   *OXB*

Some verses; by [Theodore Wratislaw]. Printed [Rugby]: Rugby Press. 1892. [vi], 21 pp.   *OXB*

WRAY, Samuel (1826–85). b. Sancton, Yorkshire. A Methodist, he began to preach at the age of eighteen; became a Wesleyan minister on circuit, 1853–84, at Bedford, Wisbech, Penzance, Windsor, Midsomer Norton, Bodmin, Bradford, Grimsby, Hitchin, Pontefract, Mansfield, Ryde, Sheffield, Rochdale and Bradford.

The innocents: a poem, in three books; by Samuel Wray. London: Hodder & Stoughton. 1880. xx, 320 pp.   *OXB*

WRAY, William. Lived at Bethany Terrace, Grovehill Lane, Beverley, Yorkshire.

George and Clara: or, true unto death: a poetical tale; by William Wray. With a preface by the Rev. Canon Wilton. Beverley: Author; Hull: Charles Henry Barnwell. 1891. [viii], 152 pp.   *OXB*

A WREATH OF MAY: LINES ON THE BETROTHAL OF THEIR ROYAL HIGHNESSES THE DUKE OF YORK AND THE PRINCESS VICTORIA MARY OF TECK. London: George Bell & Sons. 1893. 16 pp.   *OXB*

WRIGGLESWORTH, John (1856–1903). b. Castleford, Yorkshire. He started work aged nine as a wedger to a crate maker at Aire & Calder Glass Bottle Works; at sixteen he became a pony driver in a coal mine. Contributed poems to local papers and temperance magazines. Lived at The Crescent, Greetland, Halifax.

Grass from a Yorkshire village: [poems]; by John Wrigglesworth. Westminster: Roxburghe Press. [1897]. 150 pp.   *OXB*

WRIGHT, George Robert (1819?–1900). Archaeologist, folklorist and writer. An original member of the British Archaeological Association, 1843, he contributed regularly to its *Journal*. FSA, 1857. Founder and organizing secretary of the Junior Athenaeum Club. Died at Kew, Surrey.

Local lays and legends, fantastic and imaginary; by George R. Wright. London: J.W. Jarvis & Son. 1885. xii, 112 pp.   *OXB*

WRIGHT, Gertrude. Lived at The Cottage, Moneymore, Ireland.

Voices from Erenagh: [poems]; by Gertrude Wright. Belfast: University Book-Publishing House. 1886. 224 pp.   *NLW*

WRIGHT, M. Of Birmingham?

Poems; by M. Wright. Printed Birmingham: J.S. Wilson. [1882]. 59 pp.   *★UCD*

WRIGHT, Marian Saunders

Paraphrases on sermons preached by Professor Elmslie, D.D.: [poems]; by Marian Saunders Wright. London: Elliot Stock. 1891. [vi], 45 pp.   *OXB*

WRIGHT, Thomas (1859–1936). b. Olney, Buckinghamshire. Headmaster of Cowper School, Olney. Writer on Olney and neighbourhood, and biographer of Daniel Defoe and William Cowper.

The acid sisters, and other poems; by Thomas Wright. Olney: Author. 1897. x, 152 pp.   *OXB*

WRIGHT, Thomas Henry (1854–   ). b. Cork. His mother was of German extraction. Educated at Quaker schools in Cork and Waterford. He left the Society of Friends in early life to become a Roman Catholic. Represented in several anthologies of Irish poetry. Lived latterly in Dublin.

Eddies: [poems]; by T.H. Wright. [London: Simpkin, Marshall & Co., Ltd; Dublin: Eason & Sons, Ltd]. [1896]. [ix], 68 pp.   *OXB*

WRIGHT, William, (Bill O' Th' Hoylus End, psued.). (1836–   ). b. near Howarth, Yorkshire, son of a musician. Educated at Keighley National School. Left school to learn warp-dressing. Joined a group of strolling players; later enlisted in the West Yorkshire Rifles; after leaving the army he returned to the trade of warp-dressing at Keighley.

Revised edition of poems; by Bill o' th' Hoylus End. Keighley: John Overend. 1891. 160 pp. por.

Spine-title is *Poems*.   *OXB*

WYATVILLE, George

Victoria: regina et imperatrix, and other poems; by George Wyatville. Birmingham: Cornish Bros. 1897. iv, 124 pp.   *OXB*

WYKEHAM, Marie (M.W.) (1858–84). Of Kherwarra, Rajputana, India.

In memoriam M.W. 1886. 55 pp. por.

Privately printed.   *OXB*

WYLIE, L. Of Belfast?

Gems of love and truth, in poem and prose; by L. Wylie. Printed Belfast: "Belfast News-Letter" Office. 1897. xvi, 229 pp.   *NLI*

WYNNE, Frances (1866–93). b. Colton, a village in Ireland. She married Henry Wynne, her cousin. Her husband took holy orders and was appointed to a curacy at Stepney Green in the East End of London. She died giving birth to their son.

Whisper!, [and other poems]; by Frances Wynne. London: Kegan Paul, Trench, Trübner & Co., Ltd. 1890. 62 pp.   *CU*

Whisper!, [and other poems]; by Frances Wynne. London: Elkin Mathews and John Lane at the sign of The Bodley Head. 1893. 62 pp. por.   *★UCD*

WYNNE, Shirley, pseud. A woman from Hull, Yorkshire. She contributed verse to magazines.

Argentine, and other poems; by Shirley Wynne. London: Elliot Stock. 1880.   ★

Y

Y., A.S.A.

Lord Randolph: a poem, in four cantos; [by A.S.A.Y.]. Portsmouth: Henry Lewis; London: Hamilton, Adams & Co. [1889]. 300 pp.   *OXB*

Y., M. *see* **YOUNG, M.**, (M.Y.).

Y., M.A.F.

Measured language: [poems]; by M.A.F.Y. [1880?]. vi, 58 pp. Printed for private circulation.   *BL*

Y., W.S. *see* **YOUNG, William Siddons**, (W.S.Y.)

YATES, Samuel Ashton Thompson (1843?–1903). Son of Samuel H. Thompson of Thingwell Hall, Liverpool. Educated at Harrow School, and Jesus College, Cambridge; BA 1868, MA 1872. Ordained 1869; curate, Scarborough, Yorkshire, 1868–71; Lytham, Lancashire, 1871–75. Assumed the additional name of Yates. Lived at 43 Phillimore Gardens, London.

Thoughts by the way: [poems]; by S.A. Thompson Yates. London: Hatchards. 1886. 16 pp.   *OXB*

Thoughts by the way: Sicily: [poems]; by S.A. Thompson Yates. Printed London: Strangeways & Sons. 1891. 36 pp.

   Printed for private circulation. *OXB*

Thoughts by the way: Spain: [poems]; by S.A. Thompson Yates. London: Hatchards. 1888. 22 pp. *OXB*

YEATS, William Butler (1865–1939). b. Sandymount, Dublin, son of the artist John Butler Yeats and brother of the artist Jack Butler Yeats. He lived in London, 1874–83; educated at Godolphin School, Hammersmith, and Erasmus Smith School, Dublin; studied art in Dublin, 1883–86, but left art school to concentrate on poetry. He lived mainly in London but spent part of each year in Ireland. Friend of William Morris and W.E. Henley, he was a founder member of the Rhymers' Club, and a member of the *Yellow Book* group. Concerned with Irish nationalism, from 1899 he became involved in revival of the Irish theatre, co-founder with Lady Gregory and Edward Martyn of the Abbey Theatre, Dublin; its director from 1904 until his death.

   The Countess Kathleen, and various legends and lyrics; by W.B. Yeats. London: T. Fisher Unwin. 1892. 143 pp. il. (by J.T. Nettleship). (Cameo series). *NLI*

   Poems; by W.B. Yeats. London: T. Fisher Unwin. 1895. xii, 286 pp. *BL*

   Poems; by W.B. Yeats. [New ed.]. London: T. Fisher Unwin. 1899. xii, 298 pp. por. *MPL*

   The wanderings of Oisin, and other poems; by W.B. Yeats. London: Kegan Paul, Trench & Co. 1889. vi, 156 pp. *MPL*

   The wanderings of Oisin: dramatic sketches, ballads & lyrics; by W.B. Yeats. London: T. Fisher Unwin. 1892. vi, 156 pp. il. *BL*

   The wind among the reeds: [poems]; by W.B. Yeats. London: Elkin Mathews, 1899. viii, 108 pp. *BL*

YELD, Charles (1841–1905). Son of William Yeld, railway Post Office clerk of Carlisle, Cumberland. Educated at Carlisle Grammar School, Rugby School, and St John's College, Cambridge; BA 1865, MA 1869. Ordained 1867; curate, St Peter-at-Arches, Lincoln, and assistant master, Lincoln Grammar School, 1865–68; in Nottingham, 1868–91; assistant master, Nottingham High School, 1868–72; curate St Matthew's, 1868–74; vicar, St John the Baptist's, 1874–83; headmaster, University School, 1883–91; vicar, Exton, Rutland, 1891–94, Grassendale, Lancashire, 1894–1905.

   The Yeld re-union: Ben Rhydding, August 20th–25th, 1888; [by Charles Yeld]. Printed Nottingham: James Bell. 1888. [ii], 102 pp.

   For private circulation. *OXB*

YELDHAM, Walter, (Aliph Cheem, pseud.) (1837–1916). Son of Stephen Yeldham, London surgeon. Educated at King's College School, and Caius College, Cambridge; LL.B 1860. Admitted Inner Temple, 1857, but not called to the Bar. Entered the army in 18th Hussars; lieutenant 1862, captain 1868; adjutant to Lord Roberts in the march from Kabul to Kandahar; retired 1877.

Lays of the sea-side: a rhythmical rendering of seaside stories and incidents; by Aliph Cheem. Printed London: Army & Navy Co-operative Society, Ltd. 1887. 232 pp. *OXB*

YELLOWLEES, Julia Kerr (18 –88). Lived in the Border Country. Her family moved to London for six years when she was twelve, afterwards to Newcastle upon Tyne, then to Edinburgh. A Sunday school teacher at the United Presbyterian Church, Edinburgh. Died after a long illness.
Poems; by Julia Kerr Yellowlees. Printed Edinburgh: Robert R. Sutherland. 1889. xii, 133 pp. *NLS*

YEOMAN, William Joseph. Novelist and dramatist.
Fugitive fancies: poems; by William Joseph Yeoman. London: Digby, Long & Co. [1895]. viii, 87 pp. *MPL*

YOLANDE, pseud.
*The Church's seasons, and other verses*l; by Yolande. London: Longmans, Green, & Co. 1891. viii, 124 pp. *OXB*

YONGE, Charlotte Mary (1823–1901). b. Otterbourne, near Winchester, only daughter of a Hampshire squire and magistrate. She was largely educated by her father, and became a Sunday school teacher at age of seven. From 1853 she was influenced by John Keble, vicar of the neighbouring parish of Hursley, who urged her to propagate his religious views in fiction. Editor of the *Monthly Packet*; published over one hundred and fifty books, the proceeds devoted to church and missionary projects.
Verses on the gospels, for Sundays and holydays; by Charlotte M. Yonge. London: Walter Smith. 1880. [iv], 139 pp. *OXB*

YOUART THE MAN! [William Ewart Gladstone]: **A LEGEND OF IDHAR**. London: Wyman & Sons. [1884]. 24 pp. *BL*

YOUNG, Amy Cripps. Of Wolverhampton, Staffordshire?
Thoughts and dreamings; by Amy Cripps Young. London: Simpkin, Marshall, Hamilton, Kent & Co.; Wolverhampton: Alfred Hinde. [1896]. 152 pp.
Poetry and prose. *CU*

YOUNG, David (1852–   ). b. Smediton Farm, Carmyllie, Angus. He trained for journalism but eventually settled down on the family farm to assist his aged parents. Contributed articles on agricultural subjects to *The Scotsman* and other journals.
Unbeaten tracks: [poems]; by David Young. 2nd ed. London: Newman & Co. 1882. 103 pp. *UCD*

YOUNG, George John. Of Tettenhall College, Tettenhall, Wolverhampton, Staffordshire.

The vision, and other poems; by the late George John Young. Printed Edinburgh: R. & R. Clark. 1890. [viii], 52 pp.

Printed for private circulation. Cover-title is *Poems*. *OXB*

YOUNG, Jane, pseud. *see* **ABERCROMBIE, Beatrice**, (Jane Young, pseud.)

YOUNG, John (1825–91). b. Campsie, Stirlingshire, son of a farm labourer. The family moved to Glasgow, where he became a working carter until an accident left him with a permanently maimed hand. He was forced to enter a poorhouse, staying for six years until proceeds of his book *Lays from the Poorhouse*, 1860, enabled him to leave. Lived latterly at 3 Swan Street, Port Dundas, Glasgow. Almost blind in his later years.

Selections from my first volume, Lays from the Poorhouse (published November, 1860), with an appendix containing several hitherto unpublished poems; by John Young. Glasgow: George Gallie. 1881. [iv], 172 pp. *UCD*

YOUNG, Margaret, (M.Y.). (1817–94). Daughter of a Glasgow merchant who died in 1849. The family then moved to The Hermitage, Broughty Ferry, Forfarshire. Educated at home, she became interested in church work, and taught at a free school for mill girls. Contributed verse to several local journals.

Echoes of the time: [poems]; by M.Y. Broughty Ferry: David Thompson. 1883. 247 pp. *★UCD*

YOUNG, Robert. A working man, he lived at Silverwells Place, Bothwell, Lanarkshire.

Love at the plough, and other poems; by Robert Young. Biggar: John H. Wilson. [c. 1888]. 256 pp. *NLS*

YOUNG, Thomas (1806–86). b. Dundee, Angus, son of a corn-merchant. Worked in a solicitor's office for five years then moved to Edinburgh; appointed to the Sasines department of the Register House, a post he held for thirty-four years. Retired to Tayport, Fife.

Poems and songs; by Thomas Young. Printed Edinburgh: Bishop & Collins. 1885. 96 pp. *NLS*

YOUNG, William Siddons, (W.S.Y.). Writer of Latin verse.

Senilia (1891–1894): [poems]; [by] W.S.Y. 2nd ed. London: Marcus Ward & Co., Ltd. 1895. [iv], 29 pp. por.

Privately printed. In Italian, English and Latin. *BL*

YOUNGMAN, Thomas George. Of Bury St Edmunds, Suffolk?

Poems; by the late Thomas George Youngman. London: Kegan Paul, Trench & Co. 1884. viii, 188 pp. *OXB*

YOUNGS, Ella Sharpe. Miss Youngs. A dramatist, she lived at Sidney House, Sinclair Road, Kensington, London W.

The apotheosis of Antinoüs, and other poems; by Ella Sharpe Youngs. London: Kegan Paul, Trench & Co. 1887. viii, 214 pp. por.   *OXB*

A heart's life; Sarpedon, and other poems; by Ella Sharpe Youngs. London: Kegan Paul, Trench & Co. 1884. viii, 166 pp.   *OXB*

Paphus, and other poems; by Ella Sharpe Youngs. London: Kegan Paul, Trench & Co. 1882. viii, 158 pp.   *OXB*

YOUTH AND OLD AGE, AND OTHER POEMS. London: Simpkin, Marshall, & Co. 1883. 231 pp.   *OXB*

YOUTH AND OLD AGE, AND OTHER POEMS. Printed [London]: London Literary Society. 1887. [iv], 262 pp.
    Printed for the author.   *OXB*

YULE, John T. (1848–   ). b. Milnathort, Kinross-shire. At the age of twelve he went to learn the shoemaking trade, working in Dollar, Clackmannan-shire, and the village of Scotland-Well. He was appointed letter-carrier at Alva, c. 1873, shoemaking in his spare time.

Mable Lee: a sketch; by John T. Yule. Selkirk: George Lewis. 1885. 24 pp.   *NLS*

Z

ZARAC, pseud.

An Indian night, and other poems; by Zarac. Edinburgh: R.W. Hunter. [1899]. 38 pp.   *OXB*

ZENO, pseud.

A plea for God, and aspirations for man: [poems]; by Zeno. London: Kegan Paul, Trench, Trübner & Co., Ltd. 1896. viii, 156 pp.   *OXB*

ZETA, pseud.

Lyrics and ballads; by Zeta. London: Provost & Co. [1881]. [2], iv, 110 pp.   *OXB*

ZETO, pseud.

Vashti: a tragedy, and other poems; by Zeto. London: Kegan Paul, Trench, Trübner & Co. Ltd. 1897. viii, 256 pp.   *OXB*

TITLE INDEX

For filing purposes the definite or indefinite article at the beginning of a title is ignored.

NOTES

NOTES

NOTES

NOTES

NOTES

NOTES

NOTES

NOTES